PRENTICE HALL

Realidades 1

Peggy Palo Boyles
Oklahoma City, OK

Victoria M. Contreras
Edinburg, TX

Bárbara González Pino
San Antonio, TX

Myriam Met
Rockville, MD

Richard S. Sayers
Longmont, CO

Carol Eubanks Wargin
Glen Ellyn, IL

Boston, Massachusetts
Upper Saddle River, New Jersey

Front and back covers: Dancers from the state of Jalisco, Mexico

ISBN 0-13-116300-0

6 7 8 9 10 08 07 06

Realidades authors

Peggy Palo Boyles

During her foreign language career of over thirty years, Peggy Palo Boyles has taught elementary, secondary, and university students in both private and public schools. She currently serves as the Foreign Language/ESL Curriculum Coordinator for the Putnam City Schools in Oklahoma City, OK. She was a member of the ACTFL Performance Guidelines for K–12 Learners task force and served as a Senior Editor for the project. Ms. Boyles is currently President of the National Association of District Supervisors of Foreign Language (NADSFL). She frequently conducts foreign language workshops for state and national organizations, public school districts, and private schools throughout the country.

Victoria M. Contreras

Victoria M. Contreras started her foreign language-teaching career at the secondary level, and has taught at U.T.-Pan American in Edinburg, Texas for more than thirty years. Since completing her Ph.D. in 1989, she has been active in state and national organizations such as TFLA, the American Association of Teachers of Spanish and Portuguese (AATSP), and the American Council on the Teaching of Foreign Languages (ACTFL). She was a member of the Languages Other Than English (LOTE) Writing Team for the Texas Essential Knowledge and Skills (TEKS), and also chaired the Teacher Education Committee that wrote the document for the preparation of pre-service teachers. She has done extensive research on teaching about Spanish for Native Speakers. She is co-author of a textbook for native speakers and has also written a training module on teaching Spanish to the native speaker. She conducts workshops for public school districts locally and throughout the state of Texas.

Bárbara González Pino

Bárbara González Pino is Associate Professor at the University of Texas at San Antonio where she teaches foreign language methods and Spanish at all levels. She coordinated the lower-division Spanish program there for 20 years. She is a former high school and adult education Spanish teacher. Dr. González Pino has served as president of the Texas Foreign Language Association, president of the Texas Association of College and University Language Supervisors, executive council member of the American Council on the Teaching of Foreign Languages, and as Chief Rater of the Texas Oral Proficiency Test of Spanish. She was founding head of the Southwest Conference on Language Teaching. Dr. González Pino is known for her work on proficiency and prochievement testing of languages and the teaching of Spanish to heritage speakers.

Myriam Met

For most of her professional life, Myriam (Mimi) Met has worked in the public schools, starting as a high school teacher in New York City. Other positions include supervisor of language programs in the Cincinnati Public Schools, K–12, and Coordinator of Foreign Languages, K–12, for Montgomery County Public Schools, MD. She is currently deputy director of the National Foreign Language Center, where she is responsible for K–12 language education policy analysis. Dr. Met has served on the Advisory Board for the National Standards in Foreign Language Learning, the task force that developed national standards in Spanish, and co-chaired the Pacesetter Spanish task force for the College Board.

Richard S. Sayers

Rich Sayers has been an educator in world languages for 25 years. He taught Spanish at Niwot High School in Longmont, CO, for 18 years, where he also served as department chair, Teacher on Special Assignment coordinating the district foreign language department, and board member of the Colorado Congress of Foreign Language Teachers. In 1991, Mr. Sayers was selected as one of the Disney Company's Foreign Language Teacher Honorees for the American Teacher Awards. He presently serves as a board member of the Southwest Conference on Language Teaching. Mr. Sayers is Senior National Consultant for Pearson Prentice Hall.

Carol Eubanks Wargin

Carol Eubanks Wargin has taught Spanish for 20 years at Glen Crest Middle School, Glen Ellyn, IL, and has also served as Foreign Languages department chair. In 1997, Ms. Wargin's presentation "From Text to Test: How to Land Where You Planned" was honored as the best presentation at the Illinois Conference on the Teaching of Foreign Languages (ICTFL) and at the Central States Conference on the Teaching of Foreign Languages (CSC). She was twice named Outstanding Young Educator by the Jaycees.

Contributing Writers

Eduardo Aparicio
Chicago, IL

Daniel J. Bender
New Trier High School
Winnetka, IL

Marie Deer
Bloomington, IN

Leslie M. Grahn
Howard County Public Schools
Ellicott City, MD

Thomasina Hannum
Albuquerque, NM

Nancy S. Hernández
World Languages Supervisor
Simsbury (CT) Public Schools

Patricia J. Kule
Fountain Valley School
of Colorado
Colorado Springs, CO

Jacqueline Hall Minet
Upper Montclair, NJ

Alex Paredes
Simi Valley, CA

Martha Singer Semmer
Breckenridge, CO

Dee Dee Drisdale Stafford
Putnam City Schools
Oklahoma City, OK

Christine S. Wells
Cheyenne Mountain
Junior High School
Colorado Springs, CO

Michael Werner
University of Chicago
Chicago, IL

National Consultants

Yvonne Cádiz
Tampa, FL

María R. Hubbard
Braintree, MA

Jan Polumbus
Tulsa, OK

Patrick T. Raven
Milwaukee, WI

Joseph Wieczorek
Baltimore, MD

Texas Advisory Board

Maria M. Barrera
Spanish Teacher
W. B. Ray High School
Corpus Christi Independent School District
Corpus Christi, Texas

Mary E. Galvan
Spanish Teacher
Lanier Middle School
Houston Independent School District, Central Area
Houston, Texas

Benjamin F. Griffith
Spanish Teacher
M.B. Lamar High School
Houston Independent School District
Houston, Texas

Annette Lowry
Supervisor of Foreign Language (retired)
Fort Worth Independent School District
Fort Worth, Texas

Marian Newland
Spanish Teacher (retired)
R. L. Paschal High School
Fort Worth Independent School District
Fort Worth, Texas

Clemencia Pinto-Almond
Spanish Teacher
Law Enforcement and Criminal Justice High School
Houston Independent School District
Houston, Texas

Cherryl Pritts
Spanish Teacher
Randolph Field High School
Randolph Field Independent School District
Universal City, Texas

Susan Stanford
Spanish Teacher
Ronald Reagan High School
North East Independent School District North East
San Antonio, Texas

Roy "Gene" Stewart
Spanish Teacher
Smithson Valley High School
Comal Independent School District
San Antonio, Texas

M. Teresa Tattersall
Spanish Teacher
Communications Arts High School
Northside Independent School District
San Antonio, Texas

Tabla de materias

Para empezar

For: Online Table of Contents
Visit: www.phschool.com
Web Code: jck-0001

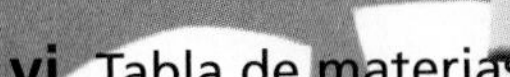

Mis amigos y yo

Capítulo 1A
¿Qué te gusta hacer?

Objectives

- Talk about activities you like and don't like to do
- Ask others what they like to do
- Understand cultural perspectives on favorite activities

Video Highlights

- **A primera vista:** *¿Qué te gusta hacer?*
- **GramActiva Videos:** infinitives; making negative statements

Capítulo 1B
Y tú, ¿cómo eres?

Objectives

- Talk about personality traits
- Ask and tell what people are like
- Use adjectives to describe people
- Understand cultural perspectives on friendship

Video Highlights

- **A primera vista:** *Amigos por Internet*
- **GramActiva Videos:** adjectives; definite and indefinite articles; word order: placement of adjectives

Tema 2 La escuela

Capítulo 2A
Tu día en la escuela

Objectives
- **Talk about school schedules and subjects**
- **Discuss what students do during the day**
- **Ask and tell who is doing an action**
- **Compare your school with that of a student in a Spanish-speaking country**

Video Highlights
- **A primera vista:** *El primer día de clases*
- **GramActiva Videos:** subject pronouns; present tense of *-ar* verbs

Capítulo 2B
Tu sala de clases

Objectives
- **Describe a classroom**
- **Indicate where things are located**
- **Talk about more than one object or person**
- **Understand cultural perspectives on school**

Video Highlights
- **A primera vista:** *Un ratón en la clase*
- **GramActiva Videos:** the verb *estar;* plurals of nouns and articles

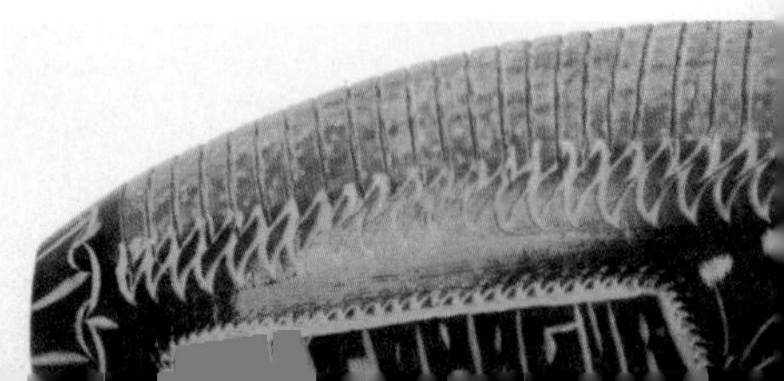

Tema 3

La comida

Capítulo 3A
¿Desayuno o almuerzo?

Objectives
- Talk about foods and beverages for breakfast and lunch
- Talk about likes and dislikes
- Express how often something is done
- Understand cultural perspectives on meals

Video Highlights
- **A primera vista:** *El desayuno*
- **GramActiva Videos:** present tense of *-er* and *-ir* verbs; *me gustan, me encantan*

Capítulo 3B
Para mantener la salud

Objectives
- Talk about foods and beverages for dinner
- Describe what people or things are like
- Discuss food, health, and exercise choices
- Understand cultural perspectives on diet and health

Video Highlights
- **A primera vista:** *Para mantener la salud*
- **GramActiva Videos:** the plurals of adjectives; the verb *ser*

Tema 4 Los pasatiempos

Fiesta en familia

Capítulo 5A
Una fiesta de cumpleaños

Objectives

- **Describe families**
- **Talk about celebrations and parties**
- **Ask and tell ages**
- **Express possession**
- **Understand cultural perspectives on family and celebrations**

Video Highlights

- **A primera vista:** *¡Feliz cumpleaños!*
- **GramActiva Videos:** the verb *tener;* possessive adjectives
- **Videomisterio: *¿Eres tú, María?,*** Episodio 1

Capítulo 5B
¡Vamos a un restaurante!

Objectives

- **Talk about family celebrations**
- **Describe family members and friends**
- **Ask politely to have something brought to you**
- **Order a meal in a restaurant**
- **Understand cultural perspectives on family celebrations**

Video Highlights

- **A primera vista:** *En el restaurante Casa Río*
- **GramActiva Videos:** the verb *venir;* the verbs *ser* and *estar*
- **Videomisterio: *¿Eres tú, María?,*** Episodio 2

Tema 6
La casa

Capítulo 6A
En mi dormitorio

Objectives
- **Talk about your bedroom**
- **Describe bedroom items and electronic equipment**
- **Make comparisons**
- **Understand cultural perspectives on homes**

Video Highlights
- **A primera vista:** *El cuarto de Ignacio*
- **GramActiva Videos:** making comparisons; the superlative; stem-changing verbs: *poder* and *dormir*
- **Videomisterio:** ***¿Eres tú, María?,*** Episodio 3

Capítulo 6B
¿Cómo es tu casa?

Objectives
- **Identify rooms in a house**
- **Name household chores**
- **Tell where you live**
- **Understand cultural perspectives on different types of housing**

Video Highlights
- **A primera vista:** *Los quehaceres de Elena*
- **GramActiva Videos:** affirmative *tú* commands; the present progressive tense
- **Videomisterio:** ***¿Eres tú, María?,*** Episodio 4

Tema 7

De compras

Capítulo 7A
¿Cuánto cuesta?

Objectives
- **Talk about clothes, shopping, and prices**
- **Describe your plans**
- **Talk about what you want and what you prefer**
- **Point out specific items**
- **Understand cultural perspectives on shopping**

Video Highlights
- **A primera vista:** *Una noche especial*
- **GramActiva Videos:** stem-changing verbs: *pensar, querer,* and *preferir;* demonstrative adjectives
- **Videomisterio:** ***¿Eres tú, María?,*** Episodio 5

Capítulo 7B
¡Qué regalo!

Objectives
- **Talk about buying gifts**
- **Tell what happened in the past**
- **Use direct object pronouns**
- **Understand cultural perspectives on gift-giving**

Video Highlights
- **A primera vista:** *Un regalo especial*
- **GramActiva Videos:** the preterite of *-ar* verbs; verbs ending in *-car* and *-gar;* direct object pronouns
- **Videomisterio:** ***¿Eres tú, María?,*** Episodio 6

Tema 8

Experiencias

Capítulo 8A
De vacaciones

Objectives

- Talk about things to do on vacation
- Describe places to visit while on vacation
- Talk about events in the past
- Understand cultural perspectives on travel and vacations

Video Highlights

- **A primera vista:** *¿Qué te pasó?*
- **GramActiva Videos:** the preterite of *-er* and *-ir* verbs; the preterite of *ir;* the personal *a*
- **Videomisterio:** ***¿Eres tú, María?,*** Episodio 7

Capítulo 8B
Ayudando en la comunidad

Objectives

- Discuss volunteer work and ways to protect the environment
- Talk about what people say
- Talk about what people did for others
- Understand cultural perspectives on volunteer work

Video Highlights

- **A primera vista:** *Cómo ayudamos a los demás*
- **GramActiva Videos:** the present tense of *decir;* indirect object pronouns; the preterite of *hacer* and *dar*
- **Videomisterio:** ***¿Eres tú, María?,*** Episodio 8

Tema 9 Medios de comunicación

Capítulo 9A
El cine y la televisión

Objectives

- **Describe movies and television programs**
- **Express opinions about media entertainment**
- **Talk about things you have done recently**
- **Understand cultural perspectives on common gestures**

Video Highlights

- **A primera vista:** *¿Qué dan en la tele?*
- **GramActiva Videos:** *acabar de* + infinitive; *gustar* and similar verbs
- **Videomisterio: *¿Eres tú, María?,*** Episodio 9

Apéndices

Capítulo 9B
La tecnología

Objectives

- **Talk about computers and the Internet**
- **Learn to ask for something and to tell what something is used for**
- **Talk about knowing people or knowing how to do things**
- **Understand cultural perspectives on using technology**

Video Highlights

- **A primera vista:** *¿Cómo se comunica?*
- **GramActiva Videos:** the present tense of *pedir* and *servir; saber* and *conocer*
- **Videomisterio: *¿Eres tú, María?,*** Episodio 10

México

México

Capital: México, D.F.

Population: 106.2 million

Area: 761,606 sq mi / 1,972,550 sq km

Languages: Spanish (official), Nahuatl, various Mayan and other indigenous languages

Religions: Roman Catholic, Protestant

Government: federal republic

Currency: *peso mexicano*

Exports: manufactured products, oil and oil products, silver, coffee, cotton

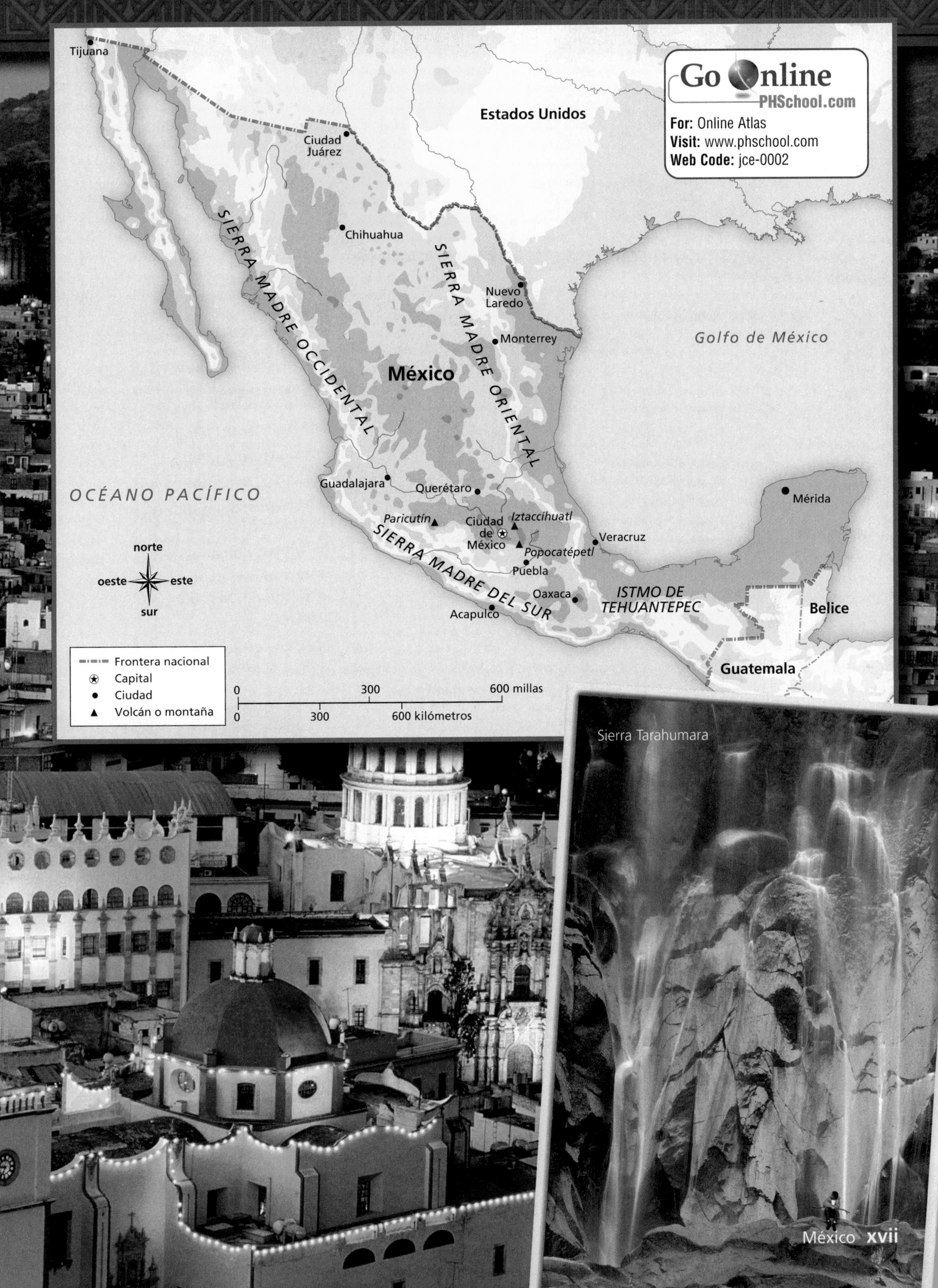
Go Online
PHSchool.com
For: Online Atlas
Visit: www.phschool.com
Web Code: jce-0002
Tijuana
Estados Unidos
Ciudad Juárez
Chihuahua
SIERRA MADRE OCCIDENTAL
SIERRA MADRE ORIENTAL
Nuevo Laredo
Monterrey
Golfo de México
México
OCÉANO PACÍFICO
Guadalajara
Querétaro
Mérida
Paricutín
Ciudad de México
Iztaccíhuatl
Popocatépetl
Veracruz
Puebla
SIERRA MADRE DEL SUR
Oaxaca
ISTMO DE TEHUANTEPEC
Acapulco
Belice
Guatemala
norte
oeste
este
sur
Frontera nacional
Capital
Ciudad
Volcán o montaña
0
300
600 millas
0
300
600 kilómetros
Sierra Tarahumara

América Central

Guatemala

Capital: Guatemala

Population: 14.7 million

Area: 42,043 sq mi / 108,890 sq km

Languages: Spanish (official), Quiche, Cakchiquel, Kekchi, Mam, Garifuna, Xinca, and other indigenous languages

Religions: Roman Catholic, Protestant, traditional Mayan beliefs

Government: constitutional democratic republic

Currency: *quetzal*, U.S. dollar *(dólar)*

Exports: fuels, machinery and transport equipment, construction materials, grain

Honduras

Capital: Tegucigalpa

Population: 7 million

Area: 43,278 sq mi / 112,090 sq km

Languages: Spanish (official), indigenous languages

Religions: Roman Catholic, Protestant

Government: democratic constitutional republic

Currency: *lempira*

Exports: coffee, bananas, shrimp, lobster, meat, zinc, wood

El Salvador

Capital: San Salvador

Population: 6.7 million

Area: 8,124 sq mi / 21,040 sq km

Languages: Spanish (official), Nahua

Religions: Roman Catholic, Protestant

Government: republic

Currency: U.S. dollar *(dólar)*

Exports: offshore assembly parts, equipment, coffee, sugar, shrimp, textiles, chemicals, electricity

Canal de Panamá

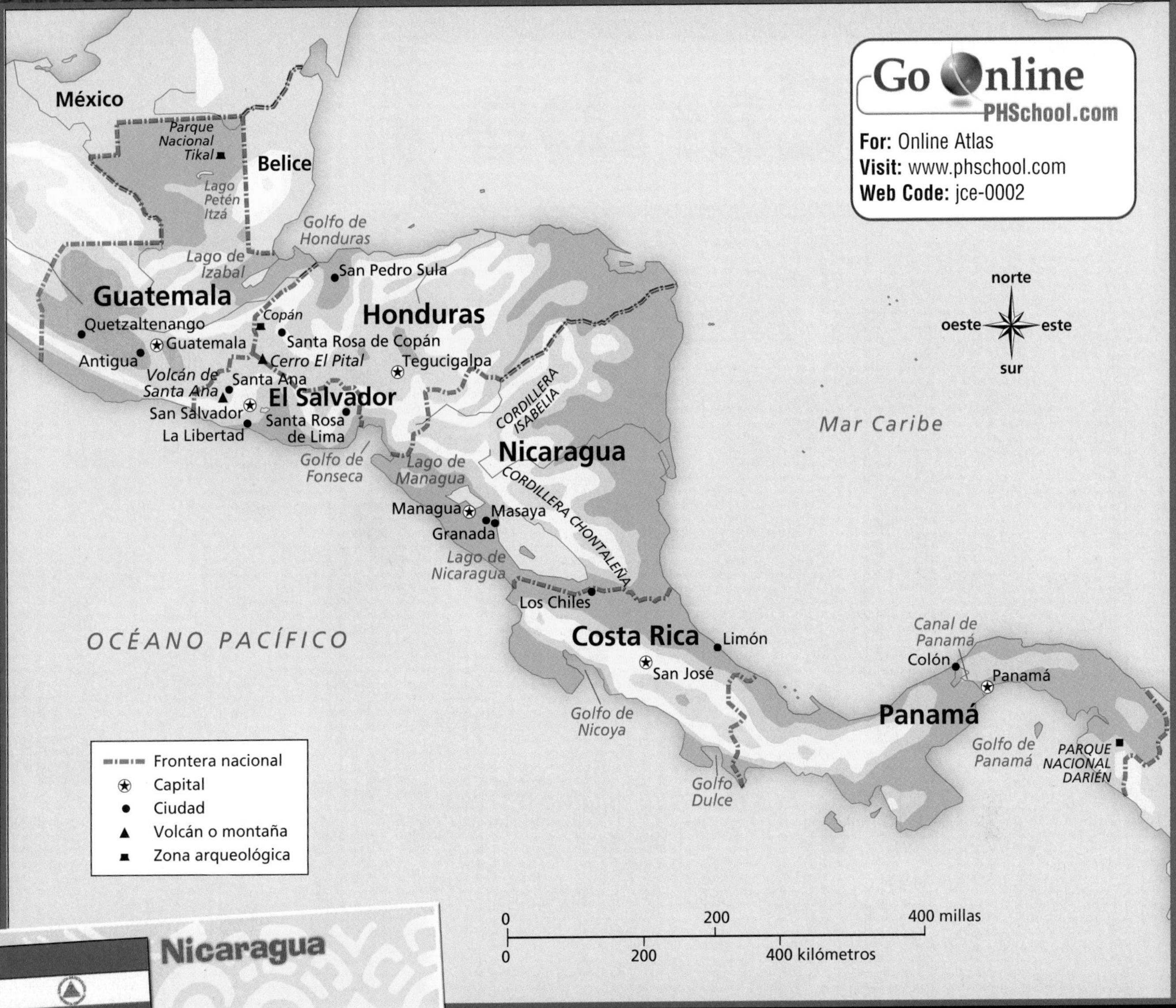

Go Online
PHSchool.com
For: Online Atlas
Visit: www.phschool.com
Web Code: jce-0002

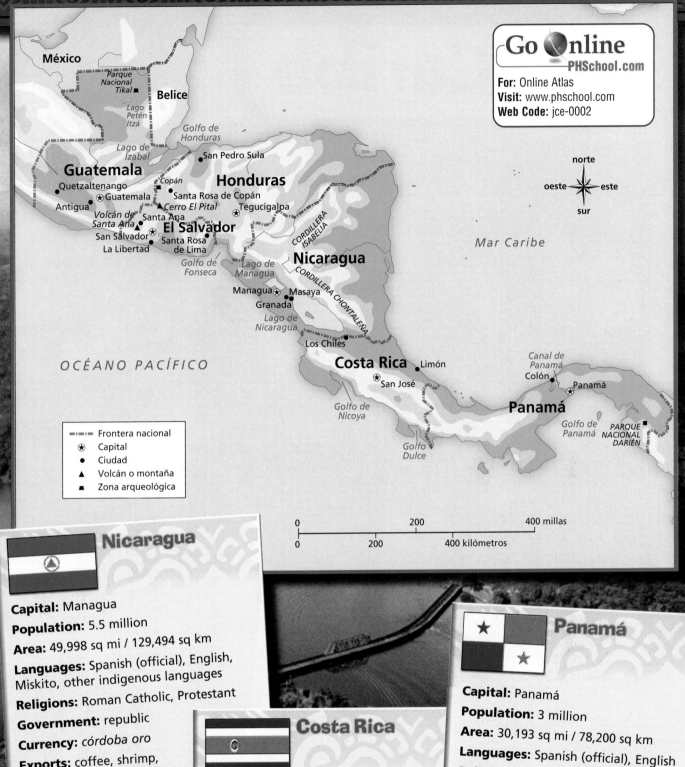

Frontera nacional
Capital
Ciudad
Volcán o montaña
Zona arqueológica

0 200 400 millas
0 200 400 kilómetros

Nicaragua

Capital: Managua
Population: 5.5 million
Area: 49,998 sq mi / 129,494 sq km
Languages: Spanish (official), English, Miskito, other indigenous languages
Religions: Roman Catholic, Protestant
Government: republic
Currency: *córdoba oro*
Exports: coffee, shrimp, lobster, cotton, tobacco, meat, sugar, bananas, gold

Costa Rica

Capital: San José
Population: 4 million
Area: 19,730 sq mi / 51,100 sq km
Languages: Spanish (official), English
Religions: Roman Catholic, Protestant
Government: democratic republic
Currency: *colón de Costa Rica*
Exports: coffee, bananas, sugar, textiles, electronic components

Panamá

Capital: Panamá
Population: 3 million
Area: 30,193 sq mi / 78,200 sq km
Languages: Spanish (official), English
Religions: Roman Catholic, Protestant
Government: constitutional democracy
Currency: *balboa,* U.S. dollar *(dólar)*
Exports: bananas, sugar, shrimp, coffee

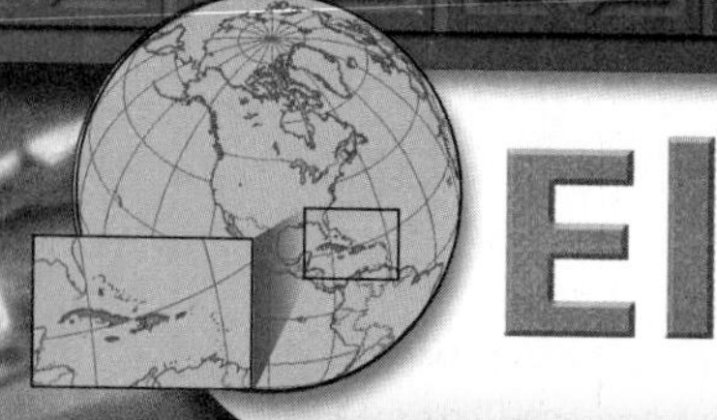

El Caribe

El Morro, San Juan, Puerto Rico

El arrecife de coral, República Dominicana

República Dominicana

Capital: Santo Domingo
Population: 9 million
Area: 18,815 sq mi / 48,730 sq km
Languages: Spanish (official)
Religions: Roman Catholic, Protestant
Government: representative democracy
Currency: *peso dominicano*
Exports: ferronickel, sugar, gold, silver, cocoa, tobacco, meat

Cuba

Capital: La Habana
Population: 11.3 million
Area: 42,803 sq mi / 110,860 sq km
Languages: Spanish (official)
Religions: Roman Catholic, Protestant, and other religions
Government: Communist state
Currency: *peso cubano*
Exports: sugar, nickel, tobacco, shellfish, medical products, citrus, coffee

Puerto Rico

Capital: San Juan
Population: 3.9 million
Area: 3,515 sq mi / 9,104 sq km
Languages: Spanish and English (both official)
Religions: Roman Catholic, Protestant
Government: commonwealth of the United States
Currency: U.S. dollar
Exports: manufactured goods, oil and oil products, silver, coffee, cotton

América del Sur
(Parte norte)

Colombia

Capital: Bogotá

Population: 43 million

Area: 439,736 sq mi / 1,138,910 sq km

Languages: Spanish (official)

Religion: Roman Catholic

Government: republic

Currency: *peso colombiano*

Exports: textiles, oil and oil products, coffee, gold, emeralds, bananas, tobacco, cotton, wood, hydroelectricity

Ecuador

Capital: Quito

Population: 13.4 million

Area: 109,483 sq mi / 283,560 sq km

Languages: Spanish (official), Quechua, and other indigenous languages

Religion: Roman Catholic

Government: republic

Currency: U.S. dollar *(dólar)*

Exports: oil, textiles, bananas, shrimp, cocoa, sugar, meat

Perú

Capital: Lima

Population: 27.9 million

Area: 496,226 sq mi / 1,285,220 sq km

Languages: Spanish (official), Quechua (official), Aymara, and other indigenous languages

Religion: Roman Catholic and other religions

Government: constitutional republic

Currency: *nuevo sol*

Exports: gold, zinc, copper, fish and fish products, textiles

Las ruinas de Machu Picchu, Perú

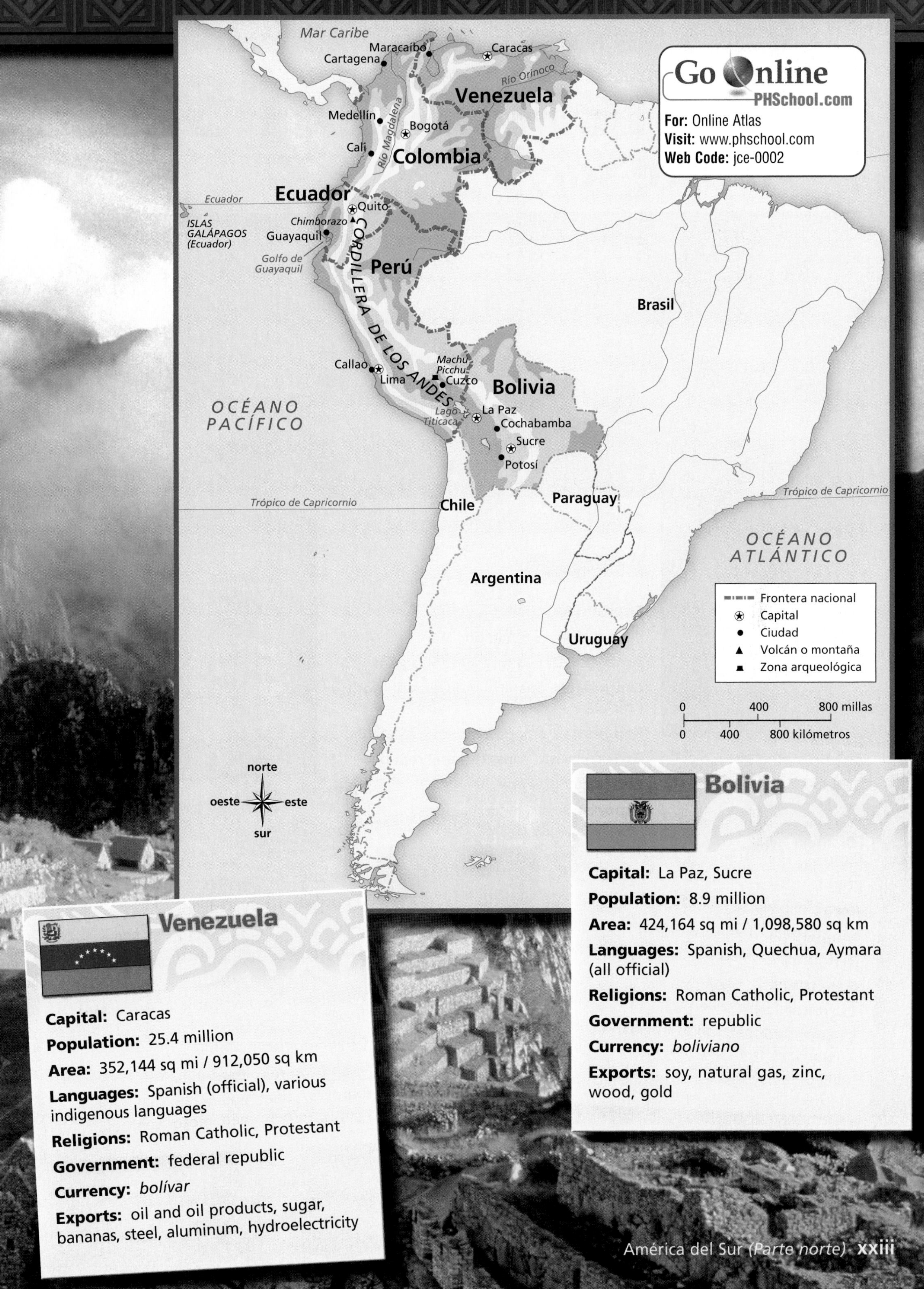

Venezuela

Capital: Caracas

Population: 25.4 million

Area: 352,144 sq mi / 912,050 sq km

Languages: Spanish (official), various indigenous languages

Religions: Roman Catholic, Protestant

Government: federal republic

Currency: *bolívar*

Exports: oil and oil products, sugar, bananas, steel, aluminum, hydroelectricity

Bolivia

Capital: La Paz, Sucre

Population: 8.9 million

Area: 424,164 sq mi / 1,098,580 sq km

Languages: Spanish, Quechua, Aymara (all official)

Religions: Roman Catholic, Protestant

Government: republic

Currency: *boliviano*

Exports: soy, natural gas, zinc, wood, gold

América del Sur
(Parte sur)

Monte Fitz Roy, Patagonia, Argentina

Paraguay

Capital: Asunción
Population: 6.3 million
Area: 157,047 sq mi / 406,750 sq km
Languages: Spanish and Guaraní (both official)
Religions: Roman Catholic, Protestant
Government: constitutional republic
Currency: *guaraní*
Exports: sugar, meat, tapioca, hydroelectricity

Chile

Capital: Santiago
Population: 16 million
Area: 292,260 sq mi / 756,950 sq km
Languages: Spanish (official)
Religions: Roman Catholic, Protestant
Government: republic
Currency: *peso chileno*
Exports: copper, fish, transport equipment, fruit, paper and pulp, chemicals, hydroelectricity

Argentina

Capital: Buenos Aires
Population: 39.5 million
Area: 1,068,302 sq mi / 2,766,890 sq km
Languages: Spanish (official), English, French, Italian, German
Religions: Roman Catholic, Protestant, Jewish
Government: republic
Currency: *peso argentino*
Exports: meat, edible oils, fuels and energy, cereals, feed, motor vehicles

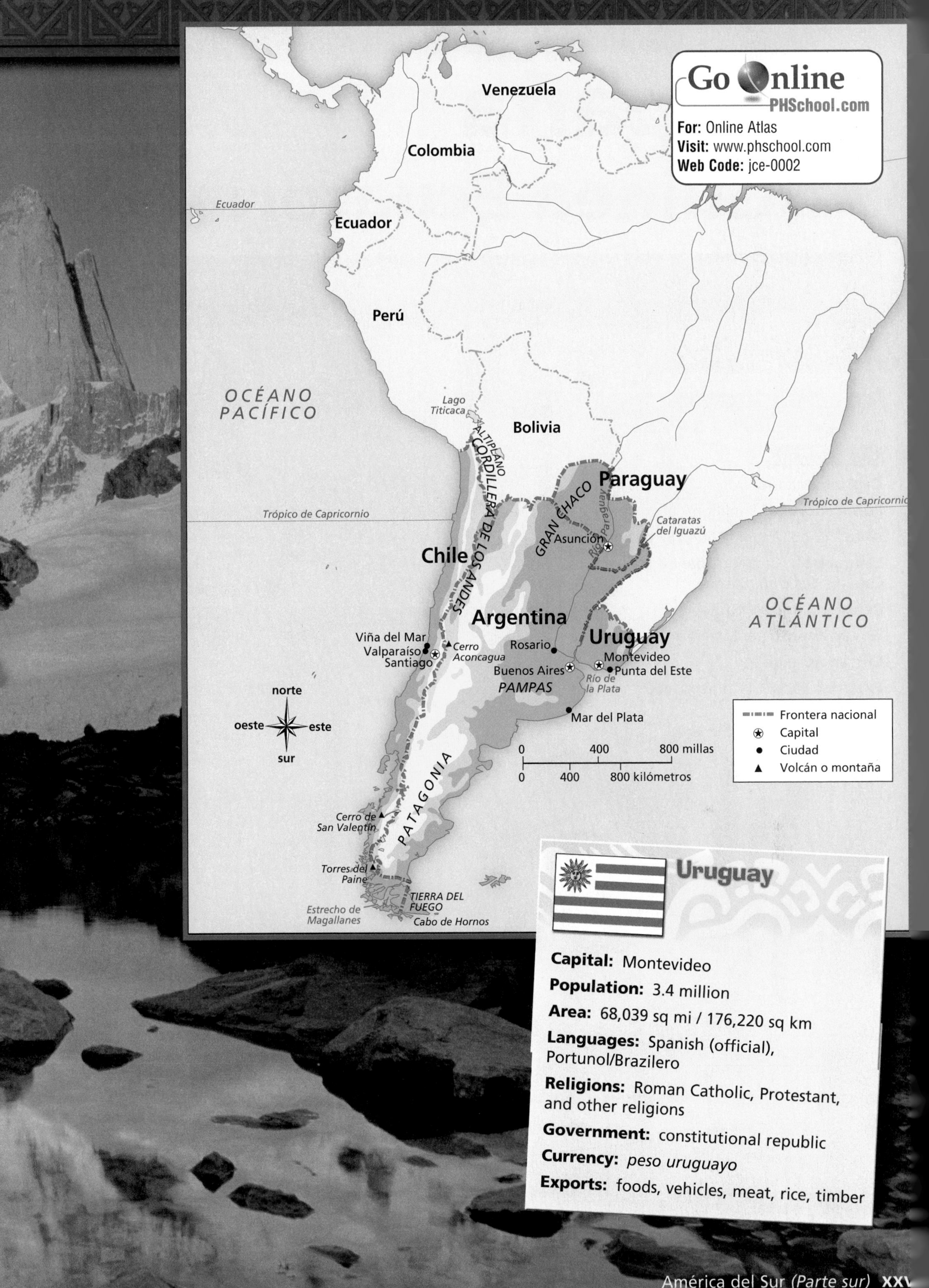

Uruguay

Capital: Montevideo

Population: 3.4 million

Area: 68,039 sq mi / 176,220 sq km

Languages: Spanish (official), Portunol/Brazilero

Religions: Roman Catholic, Protestant, and other religions

Government: constitutional republic

Currency: *peso uruguayo*

Exports: foods, vehicles, meat, rice, timber

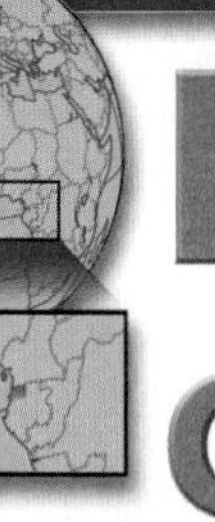

España
Guinea Ecuatorial

España

Capital: Madrid

Population: 40.3 million

Area: 194,897 sq mi / 504,782 sq km

Languages: Castilian Spanish (official), Catalan, Galician, Basque

Religion: Roman Catholic

Government: parliamentary monarchy

Currency: *euro*

Exports: food, machinery, motor vehicles

El Alcázar de Segovia, Segovia, España

Go Online
PHSchool.com
For: Online Atlas
Visit: www.phschool.com
Web Code: jce-0002
norte
oeste
este
sur
Golfo de Vizcaya
Francia
Santiago de Compostela
Galicia
Asturias
Cantabria
Bilbao
País Vasco
Pamplona
Navarra
PIRINEOS
La Rioja
Río Ebro
Castilla-León
Valladolid
OCÉANO ATLÁNTICO
Zaragoza
Aragón
Cataluña
Barcelona
España
Madrid
Portugal
Mar Mediterráneo
Menorca
Mallorca
Castilla-La Mancha
Extremadura
Valencia
Valencia
Mérida
Ibiza
ISLAS BALEARES
SIERRA MORENA
Alicante
Córdoba
Murcia
Río Guadalquivir
Sevilla
Andalucía
Granada
Málaga
Estrecho de Gibraltar
Frontera nacional
Capital
Ciudad
0 100 200 millas
0 100 200 kilómetros
ISLAS CANARIAS
La Palma
Lanzarote
Fuerte-ventura
Tenerife
La Gomera
El Hierro
Gran Canaria
OCÉANO ATLÁNTICO
0 50 millas
0 50 kilómetros
Malabo
Isla Bioko
0 25 50 millas
0 25 50 kilómetros
norte
oeste
este
sur
Golfo de Guinea
Camerún
Guinea Ecuatorial
Ebebiyin
OCÉANO ATLÁNTICO
Mbini
PARQUE NACIONAL MONTE ALEN
Gabón
Frontera nacional
Capital
Ciudad
Guinea Ecuatorial
Capital: Bata
Population: 535,881
Area: 10,831 sq mi / 28,051 sq km
Languages: Spanish and French (both official), Fang, Bubi, Ibo, pidgin English
Religions: Roman Catholic, traditional African religions, and other religions
Government: republic
Currency: franco CFA
Exports: oil, timber, cocoa, coffee

Playa, Guinea Ecuatorial

Estados Unidos

Estados Unidos

Capital: Washington, D.C.

Population: 296 million

Area: 3,717,813 sq mi / 9,631,418 sq km

Languages: English, Spanish, other Indo-European languages, Asian and Pacific Islander languages, other languages

Religions: Protestant, Roman Catholic, Jewish, Muslim, and other religions

Government: federal republic

Currency: U.S. dollar

Exports: motor vehicles, aerospace equipment, telecommunications, electronics, consumer goods, chemicals, food, wheat, corn

Las grandes llanuras

Una clase en Austin, Texas

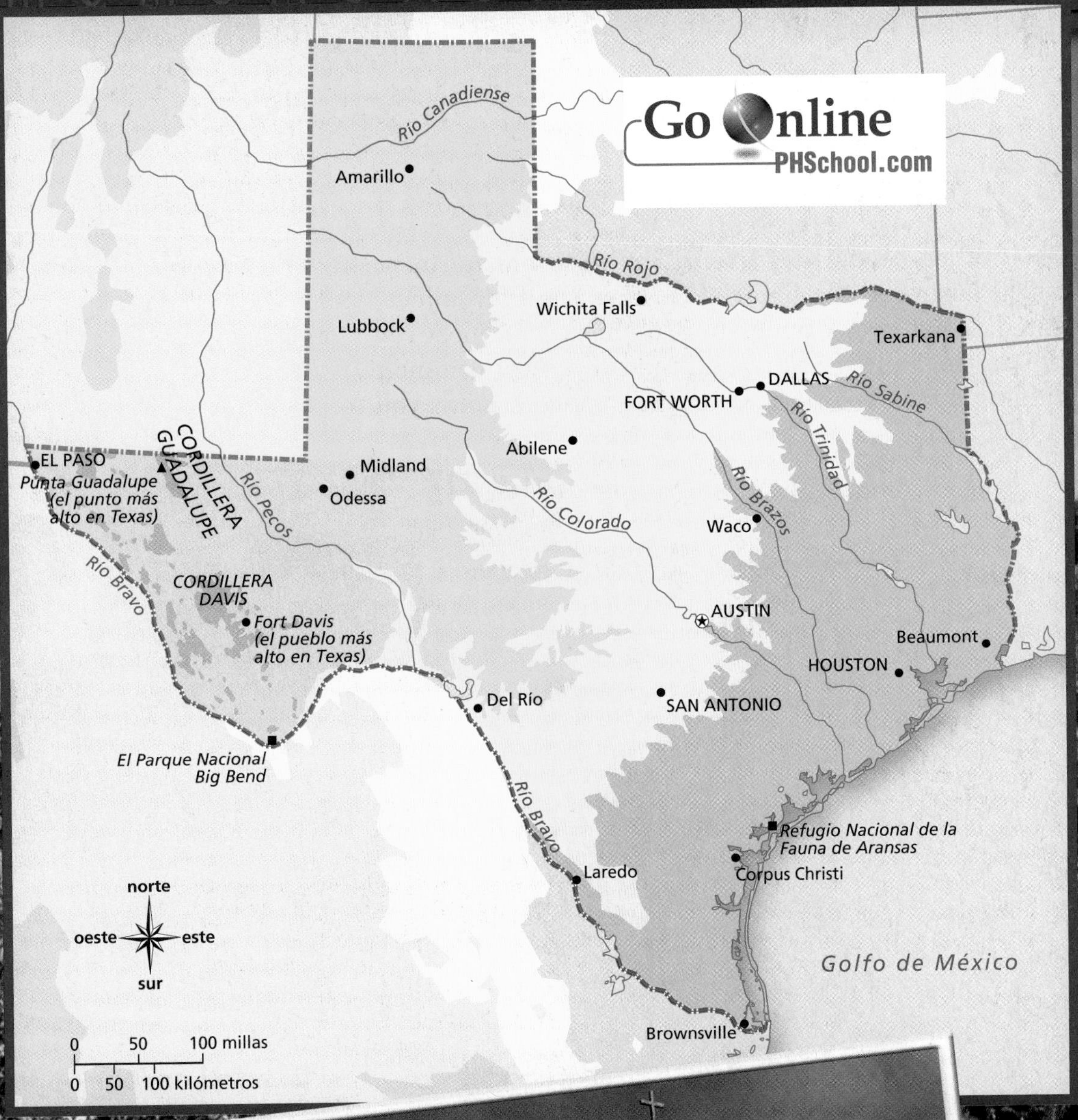

Go Online
PHSchool.com

Río Canadiense
Amarillo
Río Rojo
Wichita Falls
Lubbock
Texarkana
DALLAS
FORT WORTH
Río Sabine
Río Trinidad
Abilene
EL PASO
CORDILLERA GUADALUPE
Punta Guadalupe (el punto más alto en Texas)
Río Pecos
Midland
Odessa
Río Brazos
Río Colorado
Waco
Río Bravo
CORDILLERA DAVIS
Fort Davis (el pueblo más alto en Texas)
AUSTIN
Beaumont
HOUSTON
Del Río
SAN ANTONIO
El Parque Nacional Big Bend
Refugio Nacional de la Fauna de Aransas
Corpus Christi
Laredo
norte
oeste
este
sur
Golfo de México
Brownsville
0 50 100 millas
0 50 100 kilómetros

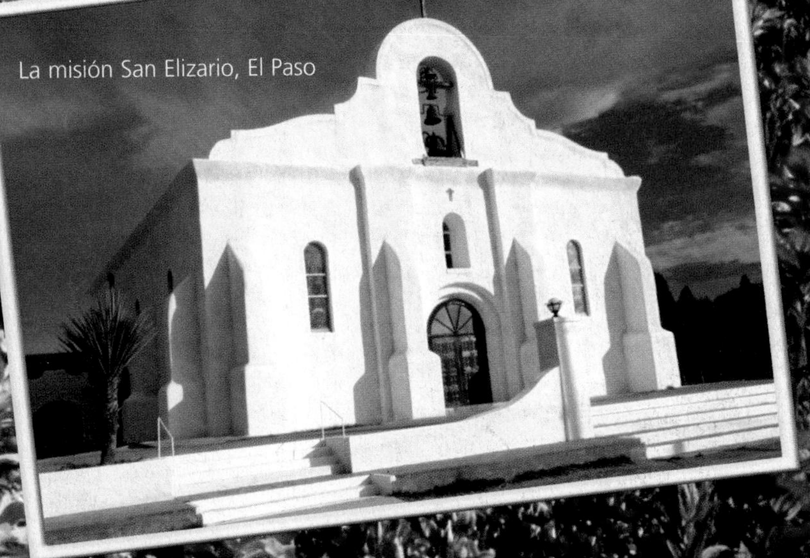
La misión San Elizario, El Paso

Why Study Spanish?

Over 340 million people who live in Spain, 18 Latin American countries, Puerto Rico, Equatorial Guinea, the Philippines, and the United States speak Spanish. It is the second most common language in the United States and the third most commonly spoken language in the world. Studying Spanish helps you to:

Understand culture The Spanish-speaking world is rich in music, food, art, literature, history, and everyday traditions. Learning about culture helps you understand other people's perspectives, patterns of behavior, and contributions to the world at large. ▶

▲ Expand career opportunities Your career options expand as businesses in the twenty-first century look for employees who can communicate in Spanish.

Enjoy your Spanish experiences Climb the Incan ruins of Machu Picchu. Volunteer to build a school in Mexico. Enjoy a meal at a Mexican restaurant. Speaking Spanish enriches your experience whether at home or in another country. ▶

Improve your language skills Studying Spanish improves your first-language skills: vocabulary, grammar, reading, and writing. Research shows your test scores may improve!

Study Tips

For: More tips for studying Spanish
Visit: www.phschool.com
Web Code: jce-0003

Take risks, relax, and be patient. The goal of studying Spanish is to communicate! So don't wait until you get it perfect. Just start talking, and you'll get better and better! You'll make some mistakes, but the longer you practice, the more improvement you'll see.

Here are some easy tips to help you learn Spanish!

Use what you already know. You already know lots of Spanish words such as *rodeo, hasta la vista, tacos, armadillo, sombrero, piñata, mesa,* and *tango*. Use your knowledge of English to help you figure out new words such as *comunicación, delicioso, limón,* and *oficina*. You'll find Spanish is easier if you use what you already know.

You don't need to understand everything. As you hear or read Spanish, you'll come across words or expressions you don't know. Try to figure out what the meaning might be. Above all, don't stop! Keep on listening or reading. You'll be surprised how much you can understand without knowing every word.

Look for Strategy and ¿Recuerdas? boxes. Throughout **Realidades**, you'll see boxes that provide strategies or remind you of something you've already learned. The information in the boxes will help you learn.

Make flashcards. One way to learn a new word is to make a flashcard. Create a picture of the word on an index card. On the back, write the word in Spanish. Then use the card to study: look at the picture and say the word or look at the picture and write the word.

Have fun! You'll find lots of activities that allow you to work with other students, play games, act out skits, explore the Internet, create projects, and use technology. Try out all of the activities and you'll have fun.

Strategy

Using graphic organizers
Drawing diagrams can help you understand how things are related.

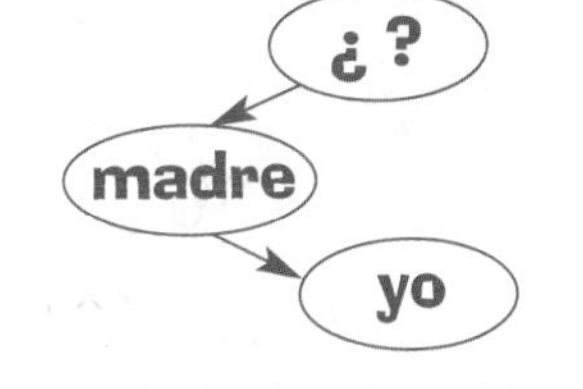

¿Recuerdas?

In Capítulo 2B you learned that *de* shows possession and is the equivalent of *-'s* and *-s'*:
- el regalo **de** Esteban

You also learned *mi(s)* and *tu(s)*.

Texas Essential Knowledge and Skills

The state of Texas has developed a framework for learning Spanish that focuses on five goals that develop communication and cross-cultural understanding. These goals are: Communication, Cultures, Connections, Comparisons, and Communities. **Realidades 1** is organized around these goals and provides a wide variety of activities that will enable you to achieve these standards.

Use your Spanish to understand a mystery video filmed in Spain.

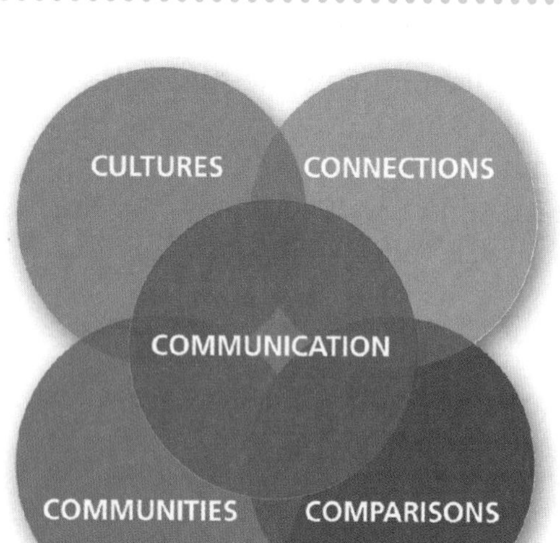

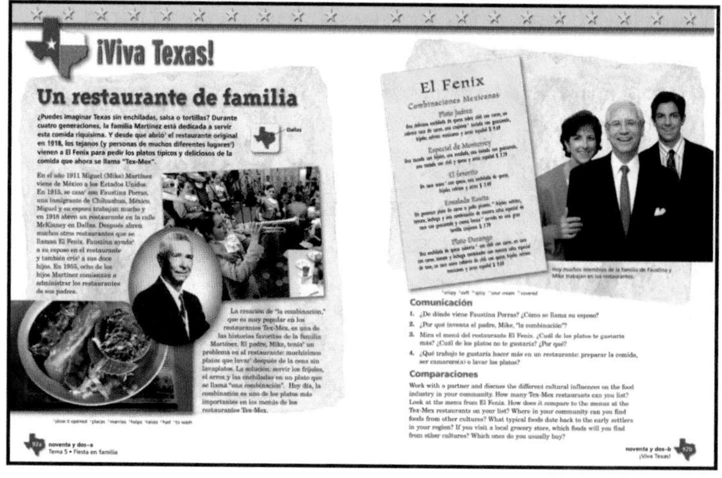

¡Viva Texas!

Un restaurante de familia

¿Puedes imaginar Texas sin enchiladas, salsa o tortillas? Durante cuatro generaciones, la familia Martínez está dedicada a servir esta comida riquísima. Y desde que abrió[1] el restaurante original en 1918, los tejanos (y personas de muchos diferentes lugares[2]) vienen a El Fenix para pedir los platos típicos y deliciosos de la comida que ahora se llama "Tex-Mex".

Dallas

En el año 1911 Miguel (Mike) Martínez viene de México a los Estados Unidos. En 1915, se casa[3] con Faustina Porras, una inmigrante de Chihuahua, México. Miguel y su esposa trabajan mucho y en 1918 abren un restaurante en la calle McKinney en Dallas. Después abren muchos otros restaurantes que se llaman El Fenix. Faustina ayuda[4] a su esposo en el restaurante y también cría[5] a sus doce hijos. En 1955, ocho de los hijos Martínez comienzan a administrar los restaurantes de sus padres.

La creación de "la combinación," que es muy popular en los restaurantes Tex-Mex, es una de las historias favoritas de la familia Martínez. El padre, Mike, tenía[6] un problema en el restaurante: muchísimos platos que lavar[7] después de la cena sin lavaplatos. La solución: servir los frijoles, el arroz y las enchiladas en un plato que se llama "una combinación". Hoy día, la combinación es uno de los platos más importantes en los menús de los restaurantes Tex-Mex.

[1]since it opened [2]places [3]marries [4]helps [5]raises [6]had [7]to wash

El Fenix
Combinaciones Mexicanas
Plato Juárez
Especial de Monterrey
El favorito
Plato Durango

Hoy muchos miembros de la familia de Faustina y Mike trabajan en los restaurantes.

crispy soft spicy sour cream covered

Comunicación

1. ¿De dónde viene Faustina Porras? ¿Cómo se llama su esposo?
2. ¿Por qué inventa el padre, Mike, "la combinación"?
3. Mira el menú del restaurante El Fenix. ¿Cuál de los platos te gustaría más? ¿Cuál de los platos no te gustaría? ¿Por qué?
4. ¿Qué trabajo te gustaría hacer más en un restaurante: preparar la comida, ser camarero(a) o lavar los platos?

Comparaciones

Work with a partner and discuss the different cultural influences on the food industry in your community. How many Tex-Mex restaurants can you list? Look at the menu from El Fenix. How does it compare to the menus at the Tex-Mex restaurants on your list? Where in your community can you find foods from other cultures? What typical foods date back to the early settlers in your region? If you visit a local grocery store, which foods will you find from other cultures? Which ones do you usually buy?

92a noventa y dos-a
Tema 5 • Fiesta en familia

noventa y dos-b 92b
¡Viva Texas!

Read about Hispanic cultural traditions and heritage in Texas.

Communication

The goal of learning Spanish is to communicate with people who speak Spanish, either by speaking and listening or by reading and writing. As you study the language, you'll use your Spanish in a variety of ways. You may listen to a radio broadcast, watch a television show, have a conversation with a friend, read an advertisement, or write an e-mail to a pen pal who speaks Spanish.

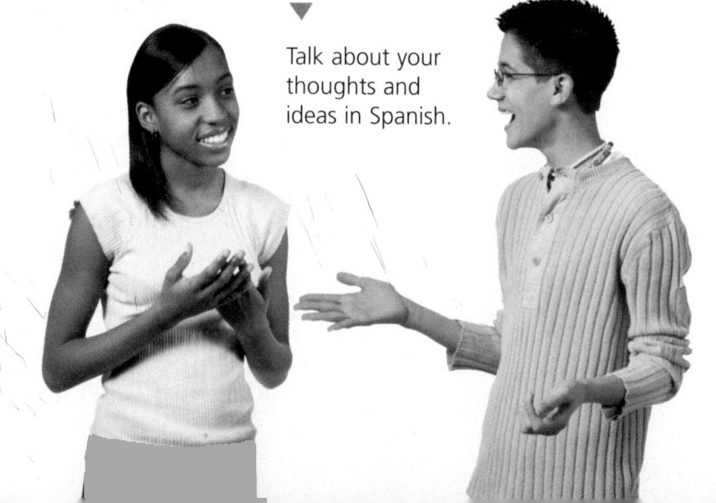

Talk about your thoughts and ideas in Spanish.

Culture

You'll learn about, experience, and understand the diverse cultures of the Spanish-speaking world.

Tema 5 • Fiesta en familia

Capítulo 5B

¡Vamos a un restaurante!

Chapter Objectives

- Talk about family celebrations
- Describe family members and friends
- Ask politely to have something brought to you
- Order a meal in a restaurant
- Understand cultural perspectives on family celebrations

Video Highlights

A primera vista: *En el restaurante Casa Río*
GramActiva Videos: the verb *venir;* the verbs *ser* and *estar*
Videomisterio: *¿Eres tú, María?*, Episodio 2

Country Connection

As you learn about family celebrations, describing family members, and restaurants, you will make connections to these countries and places:

Go Online PHSchool.com
For: Online Atlas
Visit: www.phschool.com
Web Code: jce-0002

Fondo cultural

Extended families tend to be close-knit in Spanish-speaking cultures. Parents, children, grandparents, aunts, uncles, and cousins get together often for meals or just to spend time together, and not just on special occasions. In fact, it is not uncommon for three generations to live under one roof or in the same neighborhood.

- How does the idea of extended families in Spanish-speaking cultures compare with what happens with you and your friends?

Orgullo de familia (1997), Simón Silva

doscientos cuarenta y siete 247
Capítulo 5B

▶ Learn about cultural practices and make comparisons to your own experiences.

Connections

Reinforce and expand your knowledge of other subject areas using Spanish.

▼ Practice your math skills—*en español.*

ARROZ CON LECHE

Para 8

300 gramos de arroz
un poco de vainilla

3 litros de leche
canela[1]

400 gramos de azúcar

Pon el arroz en remojo[2] con la leche una hora y media. Luego cocina a fuego lento[3] una hora más o menos. Añade[4] el azúcar y la vainilla y cocina unos 5 minutos más. Pon el arroz en el refrigerador y esparce[5] un poco de canela encima.

[1]cinnamon [2]soak [3]cook slowly [4]Add [5]sprinkle [6]measure

Conexiones Las matemáticas

1 kilo (k) = 2,2 libras *(pounds)*
1 gramo (g) = 0,035 onzas *(ounces)*
1 litro (l) = 1,057 cuartos *(quarts)*

Multiplica los kilos, gramos o litros por su medida[6] correspondiente en el sistema que usas.

Calcula las onzas o los cuartos que hay en 300 gramos de arroz, tres litros de leche y 400 gramos de azucar.

- ¿Cuántas libras hay en dos kilos de arroz?

¿Recuerdas?

You know that *de* shows possession or relationship and is the equivalent of *-'s* and *-s':*

- el regalo **de** Ana
- los primos **de** mis amigos

▲ Study tips help you compare languages.

Comparisons

You'll learn about languages and cultures by comparing your language and culture to those of people who speak Spanish.

Communities

Participate in opportunities to use Spanish outside the classroom. Discover ways to use Spanish in your community and in your career choices.

▶ Explore how to use Spanish in your community.

There may be community service organizations in your neighborhood where knowing Spanish is helpful. These organizations include medical clinics, food kitchens, senior centers, career counseling and job training, and after-school programs. Volunteering your skills for these agencies is the first step to finding out if you would be interested in pursuing work in the nonprofit sector.

- Check with local agencies to find out which ones offer services in Spanish (or in other languages). Develop a class list of volunteer opportunities in your community in which you could use your Spanish skills.

Texas Essential Knowledge and Skills for Languages Other Than English

Here is a detailed description of what will be expected of you in order to meet the requirements of the Texas Essential Knowledge and Skills.

Level I - Novice Progress Checkpoint

Knowledge and skills

(1) Communication. The student communicates in a language other than English using the skills of listening, speaking, reading, and writing.

The student is expected to:

(A) engage in oral and written exchanges of learned materials to socialize and to provide and obtain information;

(B) demonstrate an understanding of simple, clearly spoken, and written language such as simple stories, high-frequency commands, and brief instructions when dealing with familiar topics; and

(C) present information using familiar words, phrases, and sentences to listeners and readers.

(2) Cultures. The student gains knowledge and understanding of other cultures.

The student is expected to:

(A) demonstrate an understanding of the practices (what people do) and how they are related to the perspectives (how people perceive things) of the culture being studied; and

(B) demonstrate an understanding of the products (what people create) and how they are related to the perspectives (how people perceive things) of the culture being studied.

(3) Connections. The student uses the language to make connections with other subject areas and to acquire information.

The student is expected to:

(A) use resources (that may include technology) in the language and cultures being studied to gain access to information; and

(B) use the language to obtain, reinforce, or expand knowledge of other subject areas.

(4) Comparisons. The student develops insight into the nature of language and culture by comparing the student's own language and culture to another.

The student is expected to:

(A) demonstrate an understanding of the nature of language through comparisons of the student's own language and the language studied;

(B) demonstrate an understanding of the concept of culture through comparisons of the student's own culture and the culture studied; and

(C) demonstrate an understanding of the influence of one language and culture on another.

(5) Communities. The student participates in communities at home and around the world by using languages other than English.

The student is expected to:

(A) use the language both within and beyond the school setting through activities such as participating in cultural events and using technology to communicate; and

(B) show evidence of becoming a lifelong learner by using the language for personal enrichment and career development.

Listen to Spanish: Audio Files

For: Audio files
Visit: www.phschool.com
Web Codes: see below

As you learn Spanish, it's very helpful to practice your listening skills as much as you can. To help you do that, you can go to www.PHSchool.com and download audio files that you can listen to on your own player or computer. Just enter the appropriate Web Code from this list for the section of the chapter that you're working on, and you'll see a menu that lists all the available files. Download the ones you want. The more you listen, the faster you'll learn!

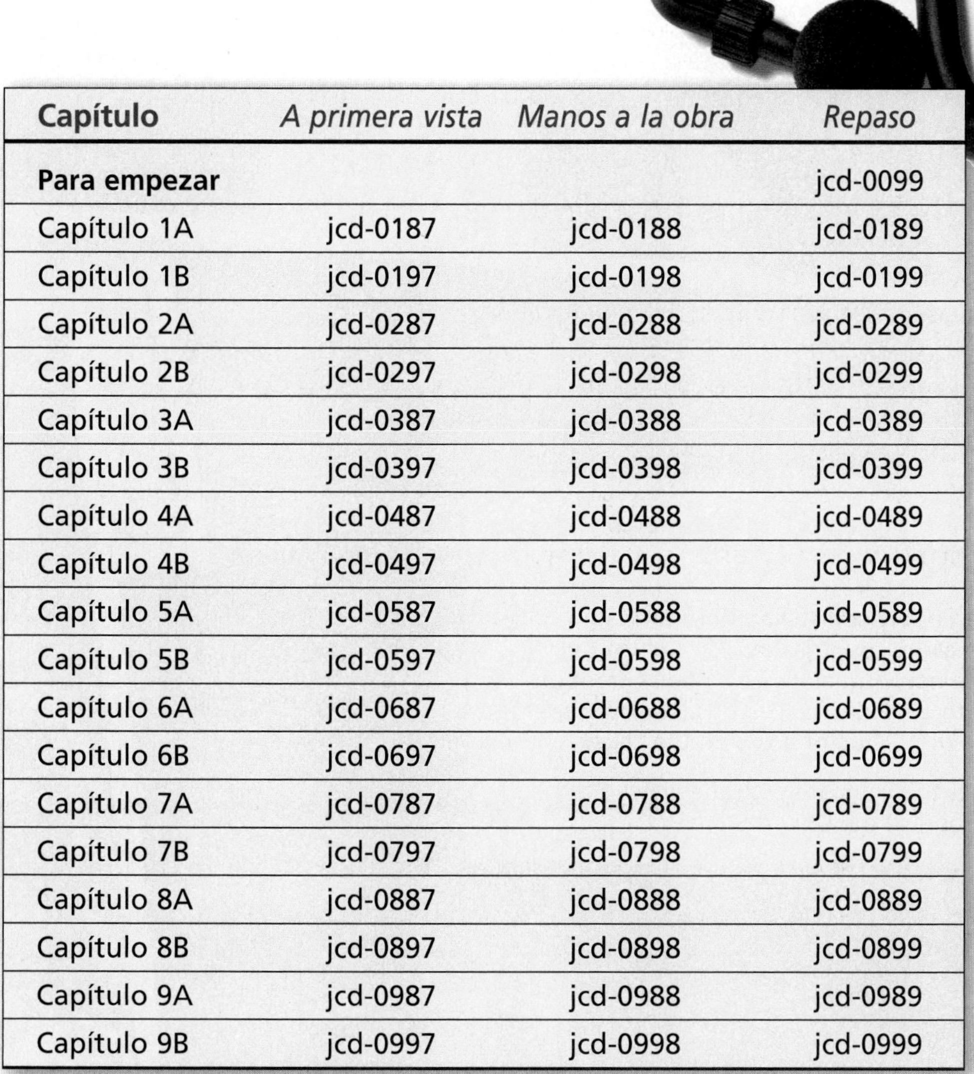

Capítulo	*A primera vista*	*Manos a la obra*	*Repaso*
Para empezar			jcd-0099
Capítulo 1A	jcd-0187	jcd-0188	jcd-0189
Capítulo 1B	jcd-0197	jcd-0198	jcd-0199
Capítulo 2A	jcd-0287	jcd-0288	jcd-0289
Capítulo 2B	jcd-0297	jcd-0298	jcd-0299
Capítulo 3A	jcd-0387	jcd-0388	jcd-0389
Capítulo 3B	jcd-0397	jcd-0398	jcd-0399
Capítulo 4A	jcd-0487	jcd-0488	jcd-0489
Capítulo 4B	jcd-0497	jcd-0498	jcd-0499
Capítulo 5A	jcd-0587	jcd-0588	jcd-0589
Capítulo 5B	jcd-0597	jcd-0598	jcd-0599
Capítulo 6A	jcd-0687	jcd-0688	jcd-0689
Capítulo 6B	jcd-0697	jcd-0698	jcd-0699
Capítulo 7A	jcd-0787	jcd-0788	jcd-0789
Capítulo 7B	jcd-0797	jcd-0798	jcd-0799
Capítulo 8A	jcd-0887	jcd-0888	jcd-0889
Capítulo 8B	jcd-0897	jcd-0898	jcd-0899
Capítulo 9A	jcd-0987	jcd-0988	jcd-0989
Capítulo 9B	jcd-0997	jcd-0998	jcd-0999

Fondo cultural

Social relations are somewhat more formal in Spanish-speaking countries than in the United States, since new acquaintances usually greet one another with a handshake. Friends, however, greet each other with a hug or a kiss on the cheek.

- How does this compare with the way you greet people in the United States?

Para empezar

Objectives

1 En la escuela

- Greet people at different times of the day
- Introduce yourself to others
- Respond to classroom directions
- Begin using numbers
- Tell time
- Identify parts of the body

2 En la clase

- Talk about things in the classroom
- Ask questions about new words and phrases
- Use the Spanish alphabet to spell words
- Talk about things related to the calendar
- Learn about the Aztec calendar

3 El tiempo

- Describe weather conditions
- Identify the seasons
- Compare weather in the northern and southern hemispheres

1 En la escuela

¡Hola! ¿Cómo te llamas?

Objectives

- Greet people at different times of the day
- Introduce yourself to others
- Respond to classroom directions
- Begin using numbers
- Tell time
- Identify parts of the body

—**¡Buenos días, señor!**
—¡Buenos días! **¿Cómo te llamas?**
—**Me llamo** Felipe.

—**¡Buenas noches!** ¿Cómo te llamas?
—**¡Hola!** Me llamo Graciela. **¿Y tú?**
—Me llamo Lorenzo.
—Mucho gusto.
—**Igualmente.**

—**¡Buenas tardes, señora!**
—¡Buenas tardes! ¿Cómo te llamas?
—Me llamo Beatriz.
—**Mucho gusto.**
—**Encantada.**

Nota

A woman or girl says *encantada.*
A man or boy says *encantado.*

Exploración del lenguaje

Señor, señora, señorita

The words *señor, señora,* and *señorita* mean "sir," "madam," and "miss" when used alone. When they are used with people's last names they mean "Mr.," "Mrs.," and "Miss," and are abbreviated *Sr., Sra.,* and *Srta.* Note that the abbreviations are capitalized.

In Spanish you should address adults as *señor, señora,* or *señorita,* or use the titles *Sr., Sra.,* and *Srta.* with their last names.

Actividad 1 Escuchar

Buenos días

Listen as people greet each other. Then point to the clock that indicates the time of day when the greetings are probably taking place.

a.

b.

c.

Actividad 2 Hablar

¿Cómo te llamas?

Your teacher will divide the class in half. Students in one half of the class will introduce themselves and shake hands, and students in the other half will say they are pleased to meet the others. Move quickly from person to person until time is called. Then switch roles.

Modelo

A —*¡Hola! ¿Cómo te llamas?*
B —*Me llamo David. ¿Y tú?*
A —*Me llamo Antonio. Mucho gusto.*
o: *Encantado.*
B —*Igualmente.*

> **¿Recuerdas?**
> If you are a girl, you say *encantada*.

Actividad 3 Hablar

¡Hola!

Work with a partner. Choose a clock from Actividad 1 and greet each other appropriately for the time of day. Then find out your partner's name. Follow the model. Change partners and repeat.

Modelo

A —*Buenas tardes.*
B —*Buenas tardes. ¿Cómo te llamas?*
A —*Me llamo Paco. ¿Y tú?*
B —*Me llamo Lourdes. Mucho gusto.*
A —*Encantado.*

Más práctica

Practice Workbook P-1

For: List of Spanish names
Visit: www.phschool.com
Web Code: jcd-0001

Los nombres

Chicas

Alicia
Ana
Beatriz
Carmen
Cristina
Dolores (Lola)
Elena
Gloria
Inés
Isabel (Isa)
Juana
Luisa
Luz María (Luzma)
Margarita
María
María Eugenia (Maru)
Marta
Teresa (Tere)

Chicos

Alejandro
Antonio (Toño)
Carlos (Chacho, Cacho)
Diego
Eduardo (Edu)
Federico (Kiko)
Francisco (Paco)
Guillermo (Guille)
Jorge
José (Pepe)
Juan
Manuel (Manolo)
Miguel
Pablo
Pedro
Ricardo
Roberto
Tomás

¡Hola! ¿Cómo estás?

—Buenos días, Adela.
¿Cómo estás?

—**Bien, gracias,** Sr. Ruiz.
¿Y usted?

—Bien, gracias.

—Buenas tardes, Sr. Ruiz.
¿Cómo está Ud.?

—**Muy** bien, gracias. ¿Y tú?

—Bien, gracias.

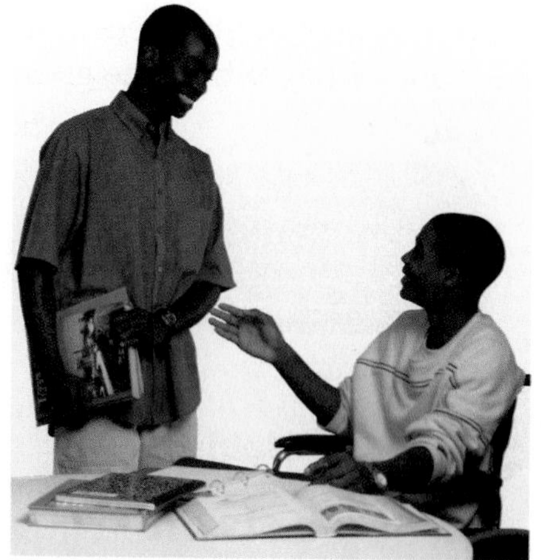

—Buenas noches, Miguel.
¿Qué tal?

—**Regular.** ¿Y tú, Carlos?
¿Qué pasa?

—**Nada.**

—**¡Adiós, Srta.** Moreno!
¡Hasta luego!

—**¡Hasta mañana!**

—¡Hasta luego, Juan!

—**¡Nos vemos!**

¿Recuerdas?

Señor, señora, and *señorita* are abbreviated to ***Sr., Sra.,*** and ***Srta.*** before a person's last name.

Exploración del lenguaje

Tú vs. *usted*

For most Spanish speakers there are two ways to say "you": *tú* and *usted*. Use *tú* when speaking to friends, family, people your own age, children, and pets. *Usted* is formal. Use it to show respect and when talking to people you don't know well, older people, and people in positions of authority. In writing, *usted* is almost always abbreviated *Ud.*, with a capital *U*.

Would you say *tú* or *Ud.* when talking to the following people?

- your brother
- your teacher
- your best friend
- your friend's mother
- your cat
- your principal
- a new acquaintance who is your age

Escuchar

¿Hola o adiós?

Make a chart on your paper with two columns. Label one *Greeting*, the other *Leaving*. Number your paper from 1–8. As you hear each greeting or leave-taking, place a check mark in the appropriate column next to the number.

Greeting	Leaving
1.	
2.	
3.	

Hablar

¡Hola! ¿Qué tal?

Work with a partner. Greet each other and ask how your partner is. Say good-bye. Then change partners and repeat.

Modelo

A —*Hola, Luisa. ¿Qué tal?*
B —*Bien, Lupe. ¿Y tú?*
A —*Regular. ¡Hasta luego!*
B —*¡Adiós!*

Leer

Mucho gusto

Read the conversation and then reply *sí* or *no* to the statements.

Profesor: Buenos días. Me llamo José Guzmán. ¿Y tú?

Estudiante: Me llamo María Hernández. Mucho gusto.

Profesor: Igualmente. ¿Cómo estás, María?

Estudiante: Bien, gracias. ¿Y Ud.?

Profesor: Muy bien, gracias. Hasta luego.

Estudiante: Adiós, señor.

1. The people knew each other.
2. The teacher is a man.
3. We know the last names of both people.
4. The student talks to the teacher in a formal tone.
5. Neither person is feeling well today.

Más práctica
Practice Workbook P-2

¡Atención, por favor!

—¡Silencio, **por favor!** Abran el libro en la página 10.

—¡Atención! Cierren el libro.

—Repitan, por favor: Buenos días.

—Buenos días.

—Levántense, por favor.

—Siéntense, por favor.

—Saquen una hoja de papel. Escriban los números.

—Entreguen sus hojas de papel.

Escuchar

¡Siéntense!

You will hear some classroom commands. Listen carefully and act them out.

Más práctica
Practice Workbook P-3

Los números

cero

uno

dos

tres

cuatro

cinco

seis

siete

ocho

nueve

10	diez	21	veintiuno, . . .
11	once	30	treinta
12	doce	31	treinta y uno, . . .
13	trece	40	cuarenta
14	catorce	50	cincuenta
15	quince	60	sesenta
16	dieciséis	70	setenta
17	diecisiete	80	ochenta
18	dieciocho	90	noventa
19	diecinueve	100	cien
20	veinte		

Actividad 8 **Hablar**

Los números

Supply the missing number. Then read the sequence in Spanish.

1. 1, ___, 3
2. 6, ___, 8
3. 7, ___, 9
4. 10, ___, 12
5. 14, ___, 16
6. 17, ___, 19
7. 23, ___, 25
8. 29, ___, 31

Actividad 9 **Pensar/Hablar**

Más números

With a partner, provide the missing numbers in each sequence. Then say the number sequence aloud in Spanish.

1. 1, 2, 3, . . . 10
2. 2, 4, 6, . . . 20
3. 1, 3, 5, . . . 19
4. 5, 10, 15, . . . 60
5. 3, 6, 9, . . . 39
6. 10, 20, 30, . . . 100

Go Online PHSchool.com
For: More practice: *los números*
Visit: www.phschool.com
Web Code: jcd-0002

Actividad 10 **Hablar/Escuchar/Escribir**

Números y más números

Tell your partner these numbers in Spanish. He or she will write them using numerals, not words. Then check your partner's work.

1. the phone numbers used to dial for information and emergencies
2. the bar code number on the back of your Spanish book
3. your house or apartment number
4. number of minutes it takes you to get from your home to school
5. number of months until your next birthday

Azulejos *(tiles)* de cerámica

¿Qué hora es?

In Spanish, to ask what time it is, you say *¿Qué hora es?* Here are some answers:

Es la una.

Son las dos.

Son las tres y cinco.

Son las cuatro y diez.

Son las cinco y cuarto.

Son las seis y media.

Son las siete menos veinte.

Son las ocho cincuenta y dos.

Actividad 11 **Hablar**

¿Qué hora es?

Work with a partner to ask and answer questions about the time. Use these clocks.

Modelo

A —*¿Qué hora es?*
B —*Son las diez.*

1. 

2. 

3. 

4. 2:20
5. 

6. 

Actividad 12 **Escuchar**

La hora

Write the numbers 1–8 on a sheet of paper. Write the times you hear with numerals—1:00, 2:15, and so on.

Más práctica
Practice Workbook P-4

La persistencia de la memoria / The Persistence of Memory (1931), Salvador Dalí

Oil on canvas, 9 1/2 x 13 in. (24.1 x 33 cm). Given anonymously. © 2004 Salvador Dalí, Gala-Salvador Dalí Foundation/Artists Rights Society (ARS), New York.† A.K.

El cuerpo

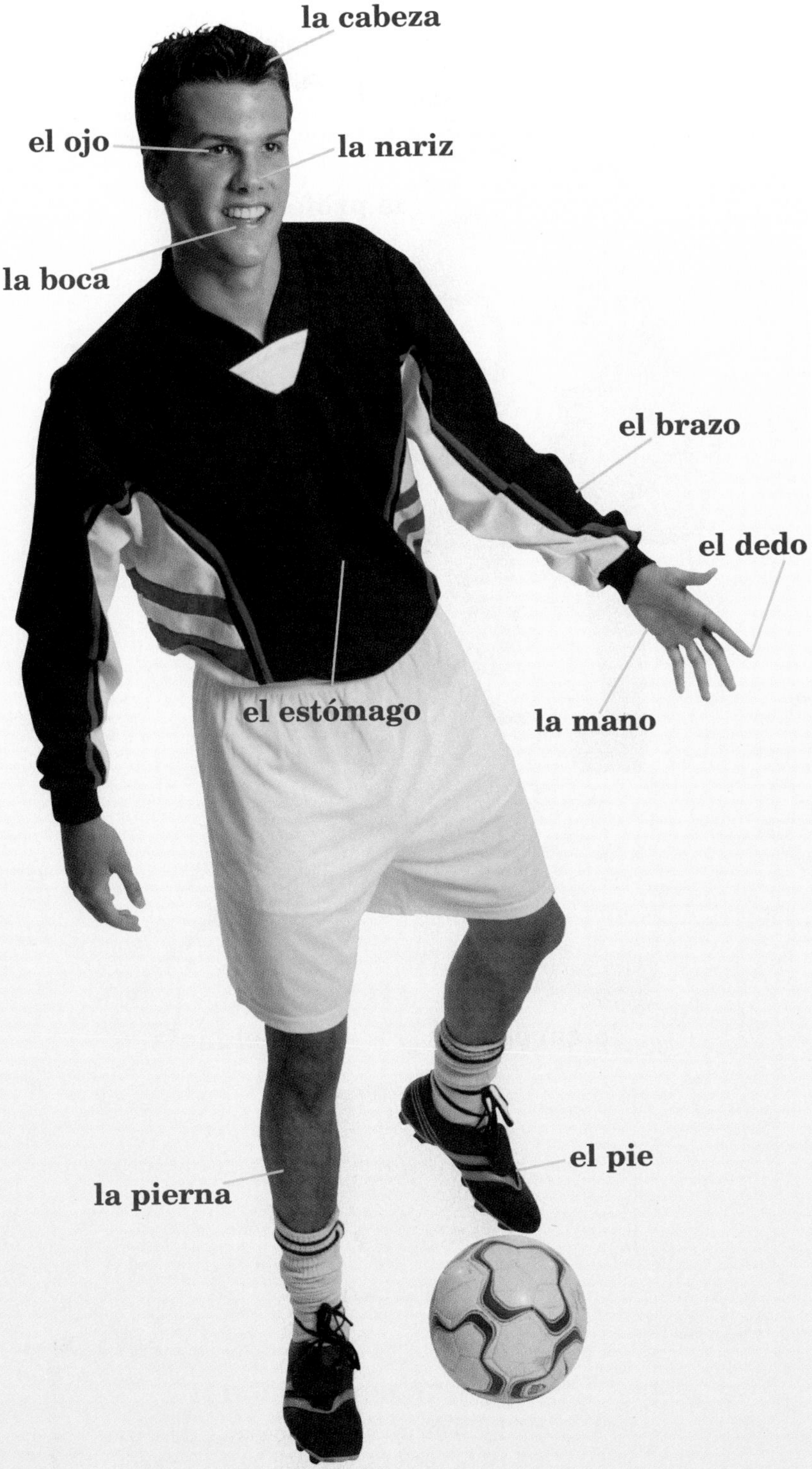

la cabeza
el ojo
la nariz
la boca
el brazo
el dedo
el estómago
la mano
la pierna
el pie

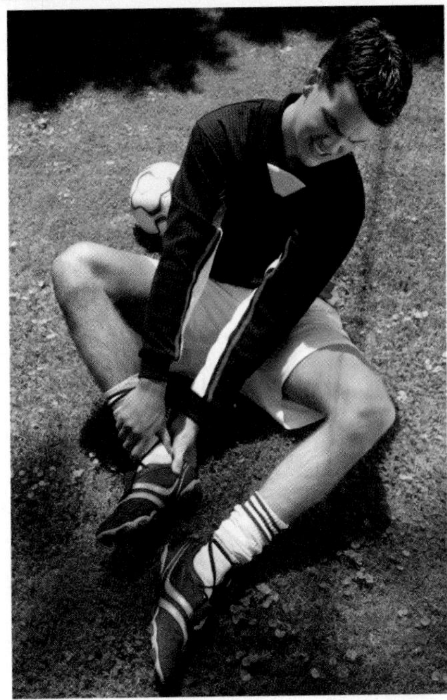

“¡Ay! Me duele el pie.”

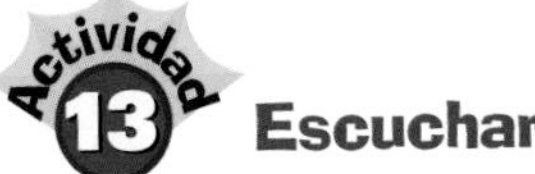

Actividad 13 **Escuchar**

Señalen

You will hear some commands. Listen carefully and act out the commands. When you hear the word *señalen,* you should point to that part of the body.

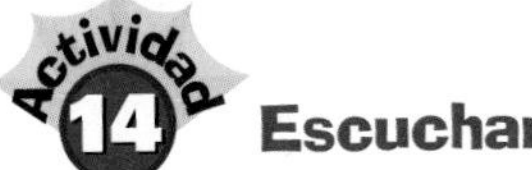

Actividad 14 **Escuchar**

Juego

Play the game *Simón dice . . .* (Simon Says). Listen and follow the leader's directions. Remember that if the leader does not say *"Simón dice,"* you should not do the action.

Más práctica
Practice Workbook P-5

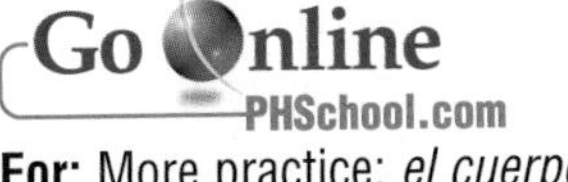

Go Online PHSchool.com
For: More practice: *el cuerpo*
Visit: www.phschool.com
Web Code: jcd-0003

2 En la clase

La sala de clases

Objectives

- Talk about things in the classroom
- Ask questions about new words and phrases
- Use the Spanish alphabet to spell words
- Talk about things related to the calendar
- Learn about the Aztec calendar

el estudiante **el profesor**

—¿Qué quiere decir *lápiz?*

—Quiere decir *pencil.*

la estudiante **la profesora**

—¿Cómo se dice *book* en español?

—Se dice *libro.*

el pupitre

el bolígrafo

la carpeta

el lápiz

el cuaderno

la hoja de papel

el libro

Escuchar

El libro, el lápiz, . . .

You will hear the names of classroom objects. After you hear each word, hold up the object if you have it on your desk or point to it if it is somewhere in the classroom.

También se dice . . .

In many Spanish-speaking countries or regions, you will hear different words for the same thing. Words like these are highlighted in the *También se dice* . . . sections.

For example, in Spain a classroom is ***el aula,*** while in Mexico, it is ***el salón de clases.***

Actividad 2 Hablar

¿Cómo se dice . . . ?

Talk with a partner about items and people in your classroom.

Modelo

A —*¿Cómo se dice* book *en español?*
B —*Se dice* libro.

1. 
2. 
3. 
4. 
5. 

Modelo

mano

A —*¿Qué quiere decir* mano?
B —*Quiere decir* hand.

6. cuaderno
7. hoja de papel
8. cabeza
9. carpeta
10. brazo

Gramática

Nouns

Nouns refer to people, animals, places, things, and ideas. In Spanish, nouns have gender. They are either masculine or feminine.

Most nouns that end in *-o* are masculine. Most nouns that end in *-a* are feminine.

Masculine	Feminine
el libro	la carpeta
el bolígrafo	la hoja de papel

The definite articles *el* and *la* also point out if a word is masculine or feminine. They both mean "the."

Spanish nouns that end in *-e* or a consonant must be learned as masculine or feminine. You should practice them with their definite articles, *el* or *la*.

Masculine	Feminine
el profesor	la noche
el lápiz	la conversación

Actividad 3 Gramática Pensar/Escribir

¿Masculino o femenino?

Look at these words and decide whether each one is masculine or feminine. Rewrite each word and add the appropriate definite article *(el* or *la)*.

1. pierna
2. nariz
3. cuaderno
4. hora
5. pupitre
6. pie
7. profesora
8. estudiante

Más práctica

Practice Workbook P-6

For: More practice: *en la clase*
Visit: www.phschool.com
Web Code: jcd-0004

El alfabeto

a	be	ce	de	e	efe
ge	hache	i	jota	ka	ele
eme	ene	eñe	o	pe	cu
ere	erre	ese	te	u	ve *or* uve
doble ve *or* doble u	equis	i griega *or* ye	zeta		

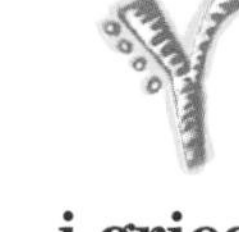

—**¿Cómo se escribe** *libro*?

—**Se escribe** ele-i-be-ere-o.

Actividad 4 **Escuchar/Escribir**

Escucha y escribe

On a sheet of paper, write the numbers 1–8. You will hear several words you know spelled aloud. Listen carefully and write the letters as you hear them.

Actividad 5 **Hablar/Escribir**

Pregunta y contesta

Work with a partner. Use the pictures to ask and answer according to the model. As Student B spells the words, Student A should write them out. When you are finished, check your spelling by looking at p. 10.

Modelo

A —*¿Cómo se escribe* lápiz?
B —*Se escribe ele-a acento-pe-i-zeta.*

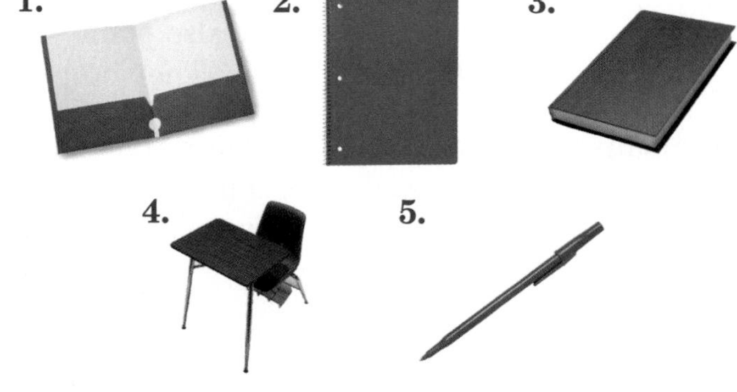

  Hablar

¿Cómo te llamas?

Work with a partner. Follow the model to find out each other's names and how they are spelled. Then change partners and repeat.

Modelo

A —*¿Cómo te llamas?*
B —*Me llamo María.*
A —*¿Cómo se escribe María?*
B —*Se escribe eme-a-ere-i acento-a.*

Strategy

Sustaining a conversation
If you need your partner to spell a word again, say *Repite, por favor.*

Exploración del lenguaje

Punctuation and accent marks

You have probably noticed that in Spanish, questions begin with an upside-down question mark (*¿*) and exclamations with an upside-down exclamation point (*¡*). This lets you know at the beginning of a sentence what kind of sentence you are reading.

You have probably also noticed the accent mark *(el acento)* on words like *días* and *estás.* When you write in Spanish, you must include these accents and punctuation marks.

Try it out! Rewrite these sentences and insert the correct punctuation and accents.

Como estas Que tal Hasta luego Y tu

Fondo cultural

The Maya were among the early civilizations in the Western Hemisphere to develop a form of writing with symbols, known as hieroglyphics *(los jeroglíficos).* Each symbol, or glyph, represents a word or an idea.

- With what other hieroglyphic writing are you familiar?

Jeroglíficos mayas

 Escribir/Hablar/Escuchar

Juego

1. Play this game in pairs. Each player makes a list of five Spanish words that you have learned. Don't let your partner see your words.
2. Spell your first word aloud in Spanish. Don't forget any accent marks. Your partner will write the word as you spell it. Then your partner will spell a word for you to write. Take turns until you have spelled all the words on your lists.
3. Check each other's papers. The winner is the player with the most words spelled correctly.

El calendario y la fecha

AGOSTO — el mes						
lunes	martes	miércoles	jueves	viernes	sábado	domingo
				1	2	3
4	5	6	7	8	9	10
11	12	13	14	15	16	17
18	19	20	21	22	23	24
25	26	27	28	29	30	31

el día

la semana

Los meses del año

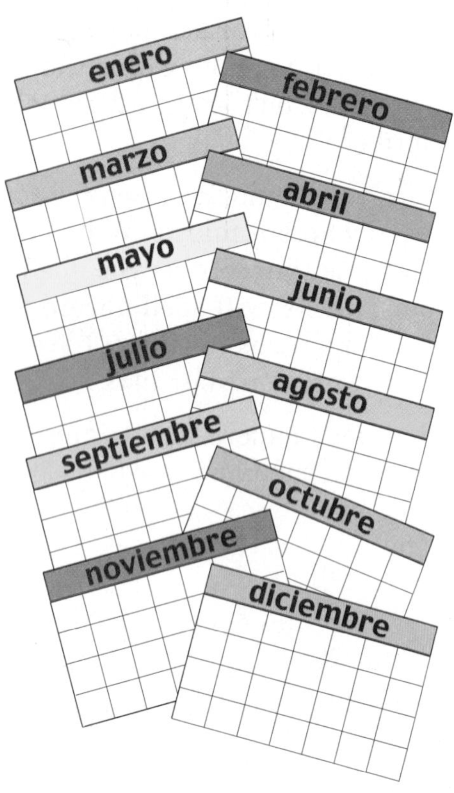

—**¿Qué día es hoy?**

—**Hoy** es lunes. **Mañana** es martes.

—**¿Cuántos** días **hay en** el mes de agosto?

—Hay treinta y un días.

> **Nota**
>
> Notice that the days of the week and the months of the year are not capitalized in Spanish, except at the beginning of sentences.
>
> The first day of the week in a Spanish-language calendar is *lunes.*

—**¿Cuál es la fecha?**
—**Es el** 22 **de** agosto.

—¿Cuál es la fecha?
—Es **el primero** de agosto.

Nota

To say the first day of the month, use *el primero.* For the other days, use the numbers *dos, tres,* and so on.

Hablar

Hoy y mañana

Ask and answer according to the model.

Modelo

lunes
A —*¿Qué día es hoy?*
B —*Hoy es lunes. Mañana es martes.*

1. martes
2. sábado
3. jueves
4. miércoles
5. viernes
6. domingo

El Cinco de Mayo es un día festivo en México.

Leer/Escribir

Días de fiesta

Read the following sentences and rewrite them, making the necessary corrections.

1. El Día de San Patricio es el 14 de enero.
2. El Día de San Valentín es en junio.
3. Januká es en febrero.
4. La Navidad *(Christmas)* es el 25 de noviembre.
5. El Día de la Independencia de los Estados Unidos *(United States)* es el 4 de junio.
6. El Año Nuevo *(New Year's Day)* es en diciembre.
7. Hoy es el 3 de agosto.

Escribir

El calendario

julio						
lunes	martes	miércoles	jueves	viernes	sábado	domingo
	1	2	3	4	5	6
hoy — 7	8	9	10	11	12	13
14	15	16	17	18	19	20
21	22	23	24	25	26	27
28	29	30	31			

Answer the questions based on the calendar page above.

1. ¿Cuál es la fecha hoy?
2. ¿Qué día de la semana es?
3. ¿Qué día es mañana?
4. ¿Cuál es la fecha mañana?
5. ¿Cuántos días hay en este *(this)* mes?
6. ¿Cuántos días hay en una semana?

Fondo cultural

Los sanfermines, or the "Running of the Bulls," is a popular two-week festival in Pamplona, Spain, named for the town's patron saint, San Fermín, who is commemorated on July 7 each year. The celebration includes daily bullfights, but before they begin the real fun starts! As the bulls are released from their pens and run through the streets, many people run ahead or alongside them to the bullring.

- What festivals are you familiar with in which animals play a role?

Más práctica

Practice Workbook P-7, P-8

Go Online PHSchool.com

For: More practice: *el calendario*
Visit: www.phschool.com
Web Code: jcd-0005

Leer

The Aztec calendar

The Aztecs were a nomadic tribe that finally settled in the valley of central Mexico in 1325. They established their capital, Tenochtitlán, on a swampy lake and built a mighty empire that dominated most of Mexico. The Aztec empire flourished until 1521, when it was defeated by the Spaniards, led by Hernán Cortés.

Conexiones | La historia

One of the most famous symbols of Mexico is the monolith, or huge stone, carved by the Aztecs in 1479. Known today as the Aztec calendar or the Sun Stone, the carving weighs almost 24 tons and is approximately 12 feet in diameter. The Aztecs dedicated it to the sun, represented by the face in the center. The calendar represents a 260-day year.

Pensar

Here are several glyphs representing days found on the Sun Stone. Match the glyph with the Spanish word. What do you think each of the glyphs represents? Why do you think the Aztecs included those symbols on their calendar?

1. 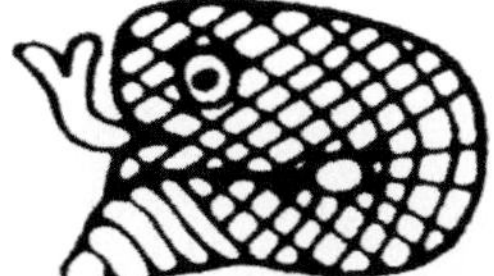
2. 
3. 
4. 
5. 
6. 

a. Jaguar
b. Perro
c. Movimiento
d. Serpiente
e. Cráneo
f. Agua

3 El tiempo

¿Qué tiempo hace?

Objectives

- Describe weather conditions
- Identify the seasons
- Compare weather in the northern and southern hemispheres

Hace sol.

Hace calor.

Hace frío.

Hace viento.

Llueve.

Nieva.

Las estaciones

la primavera

el verano

el otoño

el invierno

Escuchar

El tiempo

You will hear six descriptions of different weather conditions. Write the numbers 1–6 on a sheet of paper. Then, next to each number, write the letter of the photo for which the weather is being described.

a. 

b. 

c. 

d. 

Hablar

¿Qué tiempo hace?

Work with a partner. Ask and answer the questions based on the city and weather information for each item.

Modelo

Miami / julio / 

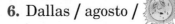

A —*¿Qué tiempo hace en Miami en julio?*
B —*Hace sol.*

1. Denver / enero /
2. Chicago / octubre /
3. San Francisco / noviembre /
4. Washington, D.C. / junio / 
5. Minneapolis / diciembre /
6. Dallas / agosto / 

Hablar/Escribir

Las estaciones

Answer the questions based on where you live.

1. ¿Qué tiempo hace en la primavera? ¿En el otoño? ¿En el verano? ¿En el invierno?
2. ¿En qué estación hace frío? ¿Calor? ¿Sol? ¿Viento?
3. ¿En qué estación llueve?
4. ¿En qué estación nieva?

Más práctica

Practice Workbook P-9

Leer/Pensar/Escribir/Hablar

Read about the seasons in the northern and southern hemispheres and then answer the questions.

Conexiones La geografía

Did you know that the seasons for the northern and southern hemispheres are reversed? When it's winter in the northern hemisphere, it's summer in the southern hemisphere and vice versa. So if you want to ski all year round, go from the slopes of the Rockies in Colorado in December to those of the Andes in Bariloche, Argentina in July. Or for a December getaway to a warmer climate, go to one of the coastal resorts at Viña del Mar, Chile.

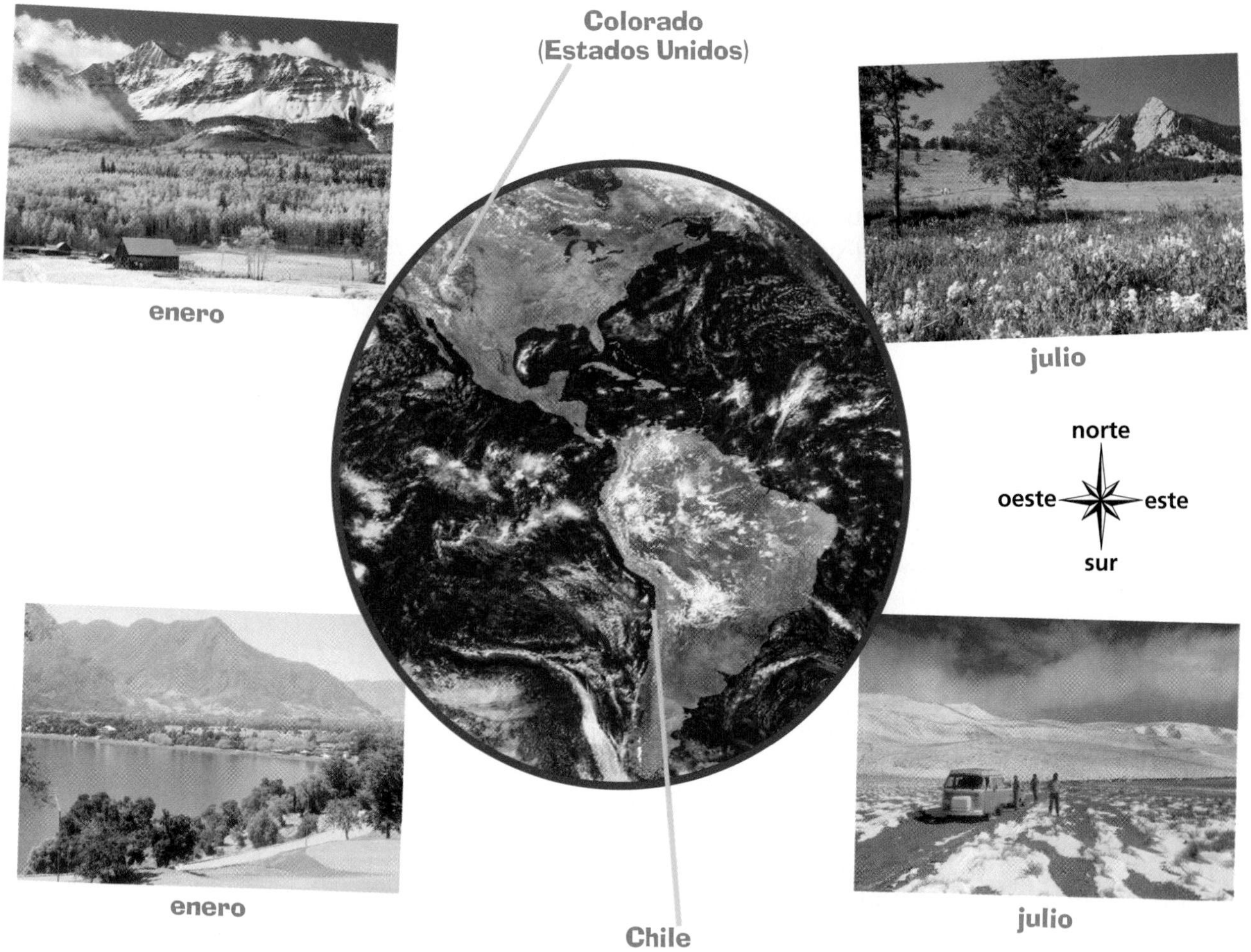

Colorado (Estados Unidos)

enero

julio

norte
oeste
este
sur

enero

Chile

julio

1. En febrero, ¿qué tiempo hace en Chile?
2. En junio, ¿qué tiempo hace en Colorado?
3. En tu comunidad, ¿qué tiempo hace en diciembre? ¿Y en agosto?

Ciudad	diciembre	julio
Chicago	36°F / 2°C	75°F / 24°C
Los Ángeles	67°F / 19°C	88°F / 31°C
Miami	76°F / 24°C	97°F / 36°C
Nueva York	41°F / 5°C	74°F / 23°C
Seattle	41°F / 5°C	66°F / 19°C
St. Louis	36°F / 2°C	81°F / 27°C
Asunción, Paraguay	85°F / 29°C	75°F / 24°C
Bogotá, Colombia	66°F / 19°C	64°F / 17°C
Buenos Aires, Argentina	78°F / 26°C	50°F / 10°C
Caracas, Venezuela	80°F / 27°C	80°F / 27°C
Ciudad de México, México	70°F / 21°C	74°F / 23°C
Guatemala, Guatemala	72°F / 22°C	74°F / 23°C
La Habana, Cuba	76°F / 24°C	82°F / 28°C
La Paz, Bolivia	58°F / 15°C	55°F / 13°C
Lima, Perú	76°F / 24°C	67°F / 19°C
Quito, Ecuador	65°F / 18°C	67°F / 19°C
San José, Costa Rica	78°F / 26°C	78°F / 26°C
San Juan, Puerto Rico	74°F / 23°C	80°F / 27°C
Santiago, Chile	82°F / 28°C	50°F / 10°C
Tegucigalpa, Honduras	70°F / 21°C	81°F / 27°C

Hablar/Escribir

¿Hace calor o hace frío?

Work with a partner. Discuss the weather in six different places on the chart.

Modelo

A —*¿Qué tiempo hace en Chicago en diciembre?*
B —*Hace frío.*

Nota

In most parts of the world, people express temperatures in Celsius. A simple way to convert from Celsius to Fahrenheit is to multiply the temperature by $\frac{9}{5}$, then add 32.

30°C = <u>?</u> F

$30 \times \frac{9}{5} = 54 + 32$

30°C = 86°F

Hablar

¿Y qué tiempo hace en . . . ?

Work with a partner. Ask about the temperature in six different places on the chart.

Modelo

A —*¿Cuál es la temperatura en Quito en diciembre?*
B —*Sesenta y cinco grados.*
o: *Dieciocho grados.*

Para decir más . . .

la temperatura temperature
grados degrees

For: More practice: *el tiempo*
Visit: www.phschool.com
Web Code: jcd-0006

Chapter Review

Repaso del capítulo

To prepare for the test, check to see if you . . .
- recognize the vocabulary
- can perform the tasks on p. 23

Vocabulario

En la escuela

to greet someone

Buenos días.	Good morning.
Buenas noches.	Good evening.
Buenas tardes.	Good afternoon.
¡Hola!	Hello!
¿Cómo te llamas?	What is your name?
Me llamo . . .	My name is . . .
Encantado, -a.	Delighted.
Igualmente.	Likewise.
Mucho gusto.	Pleased to meet you.
señor, Sr.	sir, Mr.
señora, Sra.	madam, Mrs.
señorita, Srta.	miss, Miss

to ask and tell how someone is

¿Cómo está Ud.? *(formal)*	How are you?
¿Cómo estás? *(familiar)*	How are you?
¿Qué pasa?	What's happening?
¿Qué tal?	How are you?
¿Y tú? / ¿Y usted (Ud.)?	And you?
(muy) bien	(very) well
nada	nothing
regular	okay, so-so
gracias	thank you

to say good-bye

¡Adiós!	Good-bye!
Hasta luego.	See you later.
Hasta mañana.	See you tomorrow.
¡Nos vemos!	See you!

to tell time

¿Qué hora es?	What time is it?
Es la una.	It's one o'clock.
Son las . . . y / menos . . .	It's . . . *(time)*.
y cuarto / menos cuarto	quarter past / quarter to
y media	thirty, half-past

to count up to 100 (Turn to p. 7.)

to talk about the body (Turn to p. 9.)

En la clase

to talk about the classroom

el bolígrafo	pen
la carpeta	folder
el cuaderno	notebook
el estudiante, la estudiante	student
la hoja de papel	sheet of paper
el lápiz	pencil
el libro	book
el profesor, la profesora	teacher
el pupitre	(student) desk
la sala de clases	classroom

to say the date

el año	year
el día	day
el mes	month
la semana	week
¿Qué día es hoy?	What day is today?
¿Cuál es la fecha?	What is the date?
Es el *(number)* de *(month)*.	It's the . . . of . . .
Es el primero de *(month)*.	It's the first of . . .
hoy	today
mañana	tomorrow

to say the days of the week and the months of the year (Turn to p. 14.)

other useful words

¿cuántos, -as?	how many?
en	in
hay	there is / there are
por favor	please

to ask for help

¿Cómo se dice . . . ?	How do you say . . . ?
Se dice . . .	You say . . .
¿Cómo se escribe . . . ?	How is . . . spelled?
Se escribe . . .	It's spelled . . .
¿Qué quiere decir . . . ?	What does . . . mean?
Quiere decir . . .	It means . . .

Más práctica

Practice Workbook Puzzle P-10

Practice Workbook Organizer P-11

For: Test preparation
Visit: www.phschool.com
Web Code: jcd-0007

El tiempo

to talk about the weather

¿Qué tiempo hace?	What's the weather like?
Hace calor.	It's hot.
Hace frío.	It's cold.
Hace sol.	It's sunny.
Hace viento.	It's windy.
Llueve.	It's raining.
Nieva.	It's snowing.

to talk about the seasons

la estación	season
el invierno	winter
el otoño	fall, autumn
la primavera	spring
el verano	summer

Preparación para el examen

1 Escuchar On the exam you will be asked to listen to and understand people as they greet each other and introduce themselves. To practice, listen to some students greet people in the school halls. Answer these questions about each greeting: Is it morning or afternoon? Was the greeting directed to an adult? How did that person respond?

To review, see pp. 2–5 and Actividades 1, 4.

2 Escuchar You will be asked to listen to and understand someone announcing the current date and time. To practice, listen to the message and answer the questions: What is the time of day? What is the date?

To review, see pp. 7–8 and Actividad 12; pp. 14–16 and Actividad 10.

3 Leer You will be asked to read and understand a description of the weather for a given day. To practice, read the weather forecast below. Answer the questions: What is the date? What are the high and low temperatures? What is the weather like?

El dos de septiembre
Hoy en San Antonio hace sol. La temperatura máxima es 75 grados y la mínima es 54. No llueve.

To review, see pp. 18–21 and Actividades 2–6.

4 Leer You will be asked to read a list of school supplies and identify them. To practice, copy the school supply list below onto a sheet of paper. Please note: *un, una* mean "a" or "an." Then look to see whether you have any of the items on your desk right now. Make a check mark next to each item you have.

un cuaderno	un lápiz	una hoja de papel
un bolígrafo	una carpeta	un libro

To review, see p. 10.

¡Viva Texas!

El tiempo en Texas

¿Qué tiempo hace en Texas? Depende de[1] la región. El tiempo es diferente en diferentes regiones. En el invierno, hace buen tiempo en Corpus Christi mientras[2] hace frío en Amarillo. En el verano, llueve en Orange mientras hace sol en Laredo.

[1] That depends on [2] while

Precipitación anual en Texas

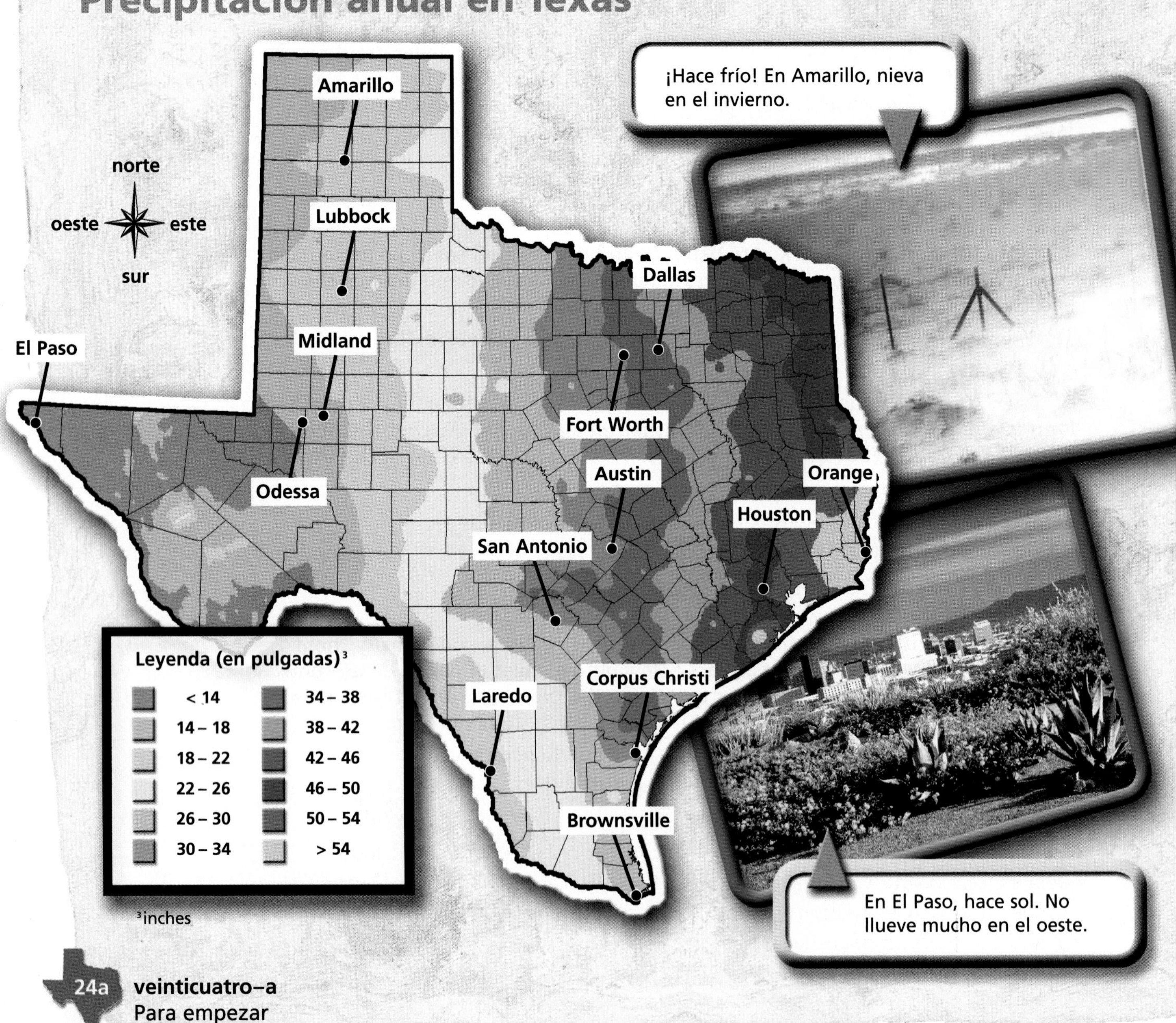

[3] inches

En el centro de Texas, hace buen tiempo en la primavera.
Es el primero de agosto. Hace calor en Brownsville.
Hace viento y llueve en Corpus Christi.

ciudad	julio		diciembre	
	temperatura	precipitación*	temperatura	precipitación*
El Paso	83°F / 28°C	1.49	45°F / 7°C	.77
Amarillo	78°F / 26°C	2.68	37°F / 3°C	.61
Brownsville	84°F / 29°C	1.77	61°F / 16°C	1.11
Austin	84°F / 29°C	1.97	52°F / 11°C	2.44
Houston	85°F / 29°C	4.36	56°F / 13°C	3.78
Orange	82°F / 28°C	5.34	52°F / 11°C	5.22

* en pulgadas

Comunicación

1. ¿Cuál es la temperatura en Brownsville en julio?
2. ¿Llueve mucho *(a lot)* en Orange en julio?
3. ¿Hace calor en Amarillo en diciembre?
4. ¿Qué tiempo hace en El Paso en julio?
5. ¿Cuál es la temperatura en Houston en diciembre?

Para decir más . . .

grados degrees

Comparaciones

Working with a partner, compare the weather in different parts of Texas with the weather in Spanish-speaking countries. Using the chart on this page and the one on p. 21, find some similarities and differences among the climates in different places. Were you surprised, for example, that the summer and winter temperatures for Santiago, Chile and Orange, Texas are similar? Did anything else surprise you?

Tema 1 • Mis amigos y yo

Fondo cultural

Pablo Picasso (1881–1973), one of the best-known Spanish artists of the twentieth century, had a long, productive career creating art in a wide range of styles and forms. He showed remarkable artistic talent as a child and had his first exhibition when he was 13 years old. *Three Musicians* is an example of Picasso's cubist painting style.

- Study this painting and list some characteristics that show why this style is known as "cubism."

Musiciens aux masques / Three Musicians (1921), Pablo Picasso

Capítulo 1A

¿Qué te gusta hacer?

Chapter Objectives

- **Talk about activities you like and don't like to do**
- **Ask others what they like to do**
- **Understand cultural perspectives on favorite activities**

Video Highlights

A primera vista: *¿Qué te gusta hacer?*
GramActiva Videos: infinitives; making negative statements

Country Connection

As you learn to talk about what you and your friends like to do, you will make connections to these countries and places:

For: Online Atlas
Visit: www.phschool.com
Web Code: jce-0002

Concierto de Carlos Santana

A primera vista

Vocabulario y gramática en contexto

Objectives

Read, listen to, and understand information about

- **activities people like and don't like to do**

bailar

escuchar música

practicar deportes

nadar

correr

esquiar

—¡**Me gusta mucho** bailar!

—**A mí también. Y también me gusta** escuchar música.

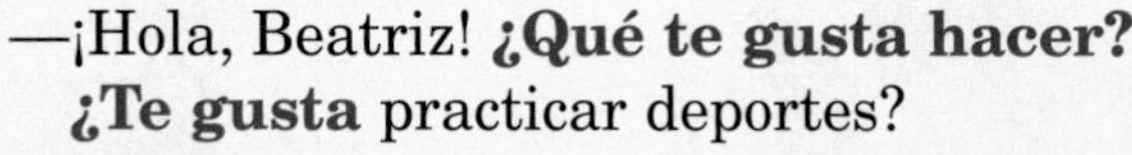

—¡Hola, Beatriz! **¿Qué te gusta hacer?** **¿Te gusta** practicar deportes?

—**¡Sí!** Me gusta mucho practicar deportes. Me gusta correr, nadar y esquiar. **¿Y a ti?** ¿Qué te gusta hacer?

escribir cuentos

montar en monopatín

ver la tele

usar la computadora

dibujar

cantar

montar en bicicleta

jugar videojuegos

—A mí me gusta mucho escribir cuentos y dibujar. **¡No me gusta nada** cantar!

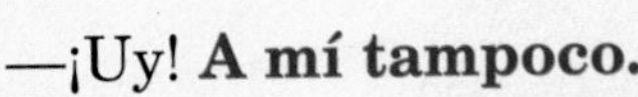

—¡Uy! **A mí tampoco.**

—**¿Qué te gusta más,** ver la tele **o** montar en bicicleta?

—**Pues, no me gusta ni** ver la tele **ni** montar en bicicleta. Me gusta usar la computadora y jugar videojuegos. Y a ti, ¿qué te gusta más?

Escuchar

¿Te gusta o no te gusta?

You will hear Rosa say what she likes to do and doesn't like to do. Give a "thumbs-up" sign when you hear her say something she likes to do and a "thumbs-down" sign when she says something she doesn't like to do.

Más práctica

Practice Workbook 1A-1, 1A-2

Escuchar

Me gusta . . .

Listen to what some people like to do. Point to the picture of the activity each describes.

For: Vocabulary practice
Visit: www.phschool.com
Web Code: jcd-0101

¿Qué te gusta hacer?

You're going to meet eight students from around the Spanish-speaking world and find out what they like and don't like to do. You'll be able to figure out where they live by looking at the globes on the page.

Strategy

Using visuals
Look at the pictures with each postcard to help you understand the meaning of the new words.

- Can you predict what each student likes to do?

"Y yo me llamo Ana. A mí me gusta **hablar por teléfono.**"

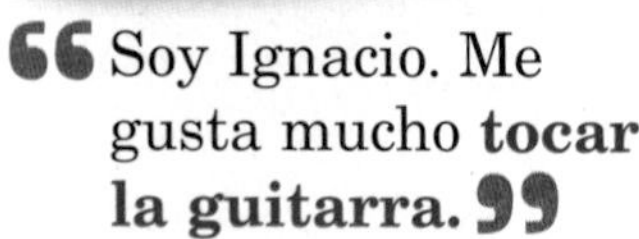

"Soy Ignacio. Me gusta mucho **tocar la guitarra.**"

"¡Hola! Me llamo Claudia y me gusta usar la computadora y **pasar tiempo con mis amigos.**"

"Yo soy Teresa. También me gusta usar la computadora, pero **me gusta más** jugar videojuegos."

“Yo soy Esteban. A mí me gusta **patinar.**”

“¡Hola, amigos! Me llamo Angélica y me gusta mucho montar en bicicleta.”

“¿Qué tal, amigos? Soy Gloria. A mí me gusta **ir a la escuela,** y también me gusta **trabajar.**”

“Me llamo Raúl. Me gusta ir a la escuela . . . más o menos . . ., pero me gusta más **leer revistas.**”

Actividad 3 **Leer**

¿Comprendes?

On a sheet of paper, write the numbers 1–6. Read the following statements by the characters in the *Videohistoria* and write *C (cierto)* if the statement is true, or *F (falso)* if it is false.

1. **Angélica:** No me gusta montar en bicicleta.
2. **Raúl:** Me gusta mucho leer revistas.
3. **Esteban:** Me gusta patinar.
4. **Claudia:** Me gusta pasar tiempo con mis amigos.
5. **Teresa:** No me gusta usar la computadora.
6. **Gloria:** Me gusta trabajar.

Más práctica

Practice Workbook 1A-3, 1A-4

Actividad 4 **Escribir/Hablar**

Y tú, ¿qué dices?

Write your answers to these questions.

1. ¿Qué te gusta más, leer revistas o montar en monopatín?
2. ¿Qué te gusta más, jugar videojuegos o bailar?
3. ¿Qué te gusta hacer en junio? ¿Y en diciembre?

For: Vocabulary practice
Visit: www.phschool.com
Web Code: jcd-0102

Manos a la obra

Vocabulario y gramática en uso

Objectives

- Talk about activities
- Say what you like and don't like to do
- Ask others what they like to do
- Learn about infinitives and negative statements

Escribir

¿Te gusta o no te gusta?

Complete the following sentences with one of the activities shown, or with any of the other activities shown on pp. 26–29.

1. Me gusta ___.
2. No me gusta ___.
3. Me gusta mucho ___.
4. No me gusta nada ___.
5. Me gusta ___.
6. No me gusta ni ___ ni ___.

Modelo

Me gusta practicar deportes.

¡Respuesta personal!

Escribir

Me gusta o no me gusta

Find four activities on pp. 26–29 that you like to do and four that you don't like to do. Copy this chart on your paper and write the activities in the corresponding columns.

Modelo

Me gusta	No me gusta
correr	cantar

Hablar

¡A mí también!

Using the information from Actividad 6, tell your partner three activities that you like to do. Your partner will agree or disagree with you. Follow the model. Then switch roles and repeat the activity.

Modelo

A —*Me gusta correr.*
B —*¡A mí también!*
o: *¡A mí no me gusta!*

Actividad 8 **Hablar**

¿Qué te gusta hacer?

Ask your partner whether he or she likes doing the activities below. Your partner will answer using one of the two responses shown. Then switch roles and answer your partner's questions.

Modelo

A —*¿Te gusta montar en monopatín?*
B —*Sí, me gusta mucho.*
o: *No, no me gusta nada.*

Estudiante A
¿Te gusta . . . ?

Estudiante B

¡Respuesta personal!

En el verano, me gusta pasar tiempo con mis amigos en la Plaza Mayor de Madrid, España.

Fondo cultural

Outdoor cafés are popular gathering places throughout the Spanish-speaking world. Friends go there to enjoy a snack or light meal, catch up with one another, or just watch people go by.

- Where do you go to spend time with friends or to meet new ones? How does your experience compare with that of the Spanish teens shown here at a café in Madrid's Plaza Mayor?

También se dice . . .

No me gusta nada = No me gusta para nada *(muchos países)*

Gramática

Infinitives

Verbs are words that are most often used to name actions. Verbs in English have different forms depending on who is doing the action or when the action is occurring:

I **walk**, she **walks**, we walk**ed**, etc.

The most basic form of a verb is called the infinitive. In English, you can spot infinitives because they usually have the word "to" in front of them:

to swim, **to** read, **to** write

Infinitives in Spanish, though, don't have a separate word like "to" in front of them. Spanish infinitives are only one word, and always end in *-ar, -er,* or *-ir:*

nad**ar**, le**er**, escrib**ir**

GramActiva VIDEO

To learn more about infinitives, watch the **GramActiva** video.

Actividad 9 Gramática **Escribir**

¿Cuál es?

On a sheet of paper, make a chart with three columns for the headings *-ar, -er,* and *-ir.* Then look at these pictures of activities. Write the infinitive for each activity under the corresponding head. Save your chart to use in Actividad 11.

Modelo

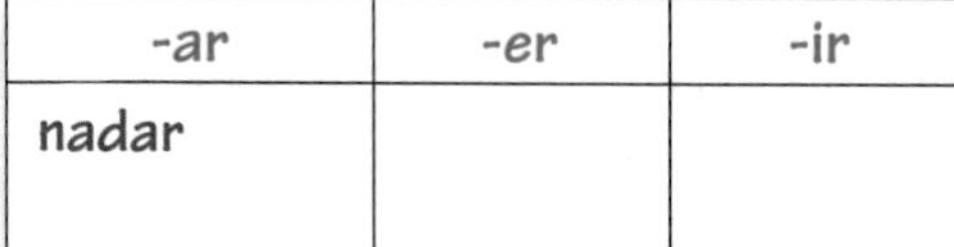

-ar	-er	-ir
nadar		

Actividad 10 Gramática **Escuchar/GramActiva**

Tres papeles

Tear a sheet of paper into three equal parts. Write *-ar* on one piece, *-er* on another piece, and *-ir* on the third piece. You will hear several infinitives. Listen carefully to the endings. Hold up the paper with the ending that you hear.

Gramática **Escribir**

El verbo es . . .

Here are some verbs in English. Look them up in the English-Spanish glossary at the back of the book and write down the Spanish infinitives on the chart you made in Actividad 9.

to walk   to live   to eat   to study   to have

It's easy to talk about the things you like to do once you know the infinitive, because you just add the infinitive to *Me gusta.* Try writing this sentence in Spanish: *I like to sleep.*

Strategy

Using a dictionary or glossary
When you need to look up a verb, always look under the infinitive form.

Escribir/Hablar

Encuesta: ¿Qué te gusta hacer?

1. Ask four classmates to tell you two things they like to do *(¿Qué te gusta hacer?)* and two things they don't like to do *(¿Qué no te gusta hacer?)*. Record their names and responses on a chart like this one.
2. Work in groups of four. Add up the results of your interviews to see which activities are the most popular and which ones are the least popular.
3. Share your results with the class.
   1. Las actividades más *(most)* populares:
   2. Las actividades menos *(least)* populares:

Modelo

	Me gusta	No me gusta
Beto	nadar ir a la escuela	patinar usar la computadora

Actividad	Me gusta	No me gusta
tocar la guitarra	III	I
cantar	I	III
trabajar	II	II

Escuchar/Escribir

Escucha y escribe

Write the numbers 1–7 on a sheet of paper. You will hear Raúl say seven things that he likes to do. Write them down as he says them. Spelling counts!

¿Recuerdas?

Remember to include any accent marks when you spell a word.

Más práctica
Practice Workbook 1A-5

For: Practice with infinitives
Visit: www.phschool.com
Web Code: jcd-0103

Exploración del lenguaje

Cognates

Words that look alike and have similar meanings in English and Spanish are called **cognates** *(cognados)*. Here are examples from this chapter:

Spanish	English
popular	popular
usar	to use
guitarra	guitar
computadora	computer

Try it out! Look at pp. 26–29 and make a list of seven cognates from the vocabulary on those pages.

Strategy

Recognizing cognates
Becoming skilled at recognizing cognates will help you understand what you read and will increase your vocabulary.

Fondo cultural

Jaime Antonio González Colson (1901–1975) was an artist from the Dominican Republic. His works usually focused on the people and culture of his homeland.

The *merengue*, the dance shown in this painting, originated in the Dominican Republic in the nineteenth century. One of the instruments used to accompany it is the *güiro* (shown at the top right), made from a gourd and played by scraping it with a forked stick.

- What instruments set the rhythms in the music that you listen to?

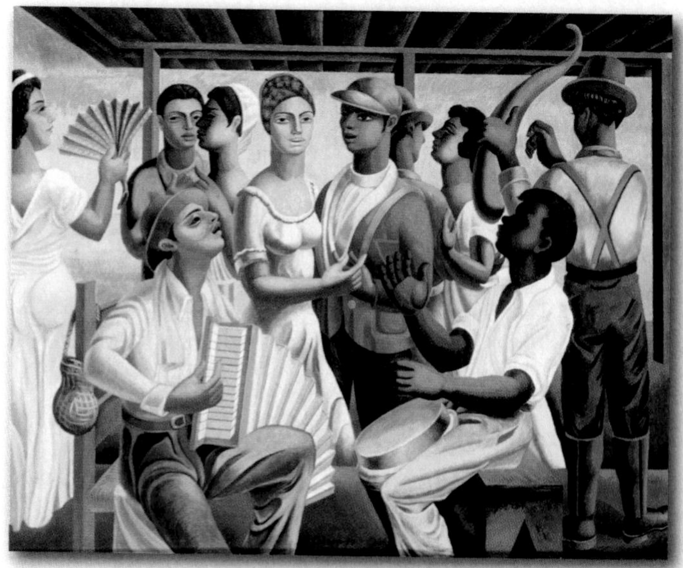

Merengue (1937), Jaime Antonio González Colson
Courtesy of Museo Bellapart, Dominican Republic.

Las maracas, el güiro, la cabassa y las claves son instrumentos típicos de la música del Caribe.

Leer/Escuchar/Escribir

El baile y la música del mundo hispano

Each country in the Spanish-speaking world has distinct musical styles and traditions. Many of the unique rhythms and dances of Spanish-speaking countries are now popular in the United States. This music features instruments such as guitars, violins, accordions, and various types of percussion such as *güiros,* sticks, cymbals, cow bells, and drums. As you read the captions, see how many words you can understand due to their similarity to English words. After you read, your teacher will play examples of each type of music. Listen for the different instruments used.

Conexiones La música

El flamenco es un baile típico de España. El instrumento más importante en el flamenco es la guitarra.

En Argentina, el tango es muy popular. Es un baile romántico.

En la República Dominicana, el baile tradicional es el merengue. El merengue tiene muchos ritmos africanos.

En Puerto Rico, la salsa es el baile preferido. El ritmo de la salsa es popular en la música de los Estados Unidos también.

La cumbia es el baile más famoso de Colombia.

- Reread each of the captions and make a list of seven cognates.
- Make a list of instruments you heard in the different songs. You might need to listen to the music again.

Gramática

Negatives

To make a sentence negative in Spanish, you usually put *no* in front of the verb or expression. In English you usually use the word "not."

No me gusta cantar.	*I do **not** like to sing.*

To answer a question negatively in Spanish you often use *no* twice. The first *no* answers the question. The second *no* says, "I do *not . . . (don't)*." This is similar to the way you answer a question in English.

¿Te gusta escribir cuentos?	*Do you like to write stories?*
No, no me gusta.	***No, I don't.***

In Spanish, you might use one or more negatives after answering *"no."*

¿Te gusta cantar?	*Do you like to sing?*
No, no me gusta **nada.**	***No, I don't** like it **at all.***

If you want to say that you do not like either of two choices, use *ni . . . ni:*

No me gusta **ni** nadar **ni** dibujar.	***I don't** like **either** swimming **or** drawing.*
	*I like **neither** swimming **nor** drawing.*

¿Recuerdas?

Did you remember that *nada* has another meaning?

- ¿Qué pasa? **Nada.**

In this case, *nada* means "nothing."

GramActiva VIDEO

To learn more about negatives, watch the **GramActiva** video.

Gramática **Leer/Escribir**

Una persona muy negativa

Fill in the blanks in the dialogue with one of these expressions: *no, nada, tampoco, ni . . . ni.*

Tomás es un nuevo estudiante en la clase y es una persona muy negativa.

Ana: Hola, Tomás. ¿Te gusta escuchar música?
Tomás: No, **1.** me gusta.
Ana: Pues, ¿qué te gusta más, jugar videojuegos o usar la computadora?
Tomás: No me gusta **2.** jugar videojuegos **3.** usar la computadora.
Ana: ¿Te gusta practicar deportes?
Tomás: No, no me gusta **4.** practicar deportes.
Ana: Pues, Tomás, no me gusta pasar tiempo con personas negativas.
Tomás: ¡A mí **5.** !

Gramática

Hablar

¡No, no me gusta!

Today you feel as negative as Tomás. With a partner, respond to each question saying that you don't like to do any of these activities.

Modelo

A —*¿Te gusta ver la tele?*
B —*No, no me gusta ver la tele.*

Estudiante A

1. 
2. 
3. 
4. 
5. 
6. 

No, no me gusta . . .

Gramática

Hablar

¿Qué te gusta más?

Find out what your partner likes more. Then switch roles.

Modelo

A —*¿Qué te gusta más, nadar o esquiar?*
B —*Pues, me gusta más nadar.*
o: *Pues, no me gusta ni nadar ni esquiar.*

1.  
2.  
3.  
4.  

For: Practice with negatives
Visit: www.phschool.com
Web Code: jcd-0104

Más práctica

Practice Workbook 1A-6

Gramática

Expressing agreement or disagreement

To agree with what a person likes, you use *"a mí también."* It's like saying "me too" in English.

Me gusta pasar tiempo con amigos.	*I like to spend time with friends.*
A mí también.	***Me too.***

If someone tells you that he or she dislikes something, you can agree by saying *"a mí tampoco."* It's like saying "me neither" or "neither do I" in English.

No me gusta nada cantar.	*I don't like to sing at all.*
A mí tampoco.	***Me neither.***

Escribir/Hablar

¿También o tampoco?

Write a list of three things that you like to do and three things that you don't like to do. Tell your partner the activities on your list. Your partner will agree or disagree based upon his or her personal preferences. Follow the model.

Modelo

A —*Me gusta mucho bailar.*
B —*A mí también.*
o:
A —*No me gusta nada cantar.*
B —*A mí tampoco.*
o: *Pues, a mí me gusta cantar.*

Leer/Escribir

Opiniones

Read the opinions of two students on snowboarding. Then answer the questions.

1. Who thinks that snowboarding is "neither a fad nor a sport"? What does he or she consider it to be?
2. What does the other person consider snowboarding to be? What else does this person say about snowboarding?
3. ¿A ti te gusta el *snowboard?* En tu opinión, ¿es un deporte o una moda?

EL "SNOWBOARD" ¿DEPORTE O MODA?

Ni lo uno ni lo otro
"El snowboard no es ni moda[1] ni deporte. Lo practico como hobby."
Rafael

¿Moda?
"El snowboard es un deporte de invierno como el esquí. A mí me gusta mucho y lo practico mucho. ¡No es una simple moda, es todo un deporte! Y es buen ejercicio."[2]
Alicia

[1] fad [2] good exercise

Go Online PHSchool.com
For: Practice with agreement or disagreement
Visit: www.phschool.com
Web Code: jcd-0105

Más práctica
Practice Workbook 1A-7

Pronunciación

The vowels *a, e,* and *i*

The vowel sounds in Spanish are different from those in English. In Spanish, each vowel has just one sound. Spanish vowels are also quicker and shorter than those in English.

The letter *a* is similar to the sound in the English word *pop.* Listen to and say these words:

andar	cantar	trabajar
hablar	nadar	pasar

The letter *e* is similar to the sound in the English word *met.* Listen to and say these words:

tele   me   es   Elena   deportes

The letter *i* is similar to the sound in the English word *see.* As you have already seen, the letter *y* sometimes has the same sound as *i.* Listen to and say these words:

sí   escribir   patinar   lápiz   ti   mí

Try it out! Listen to and say this rhyme:

A E I El perro canta para ti.
A E I El tigre baila para mí.

Try it again, substituting *el gato* for *el perro* and *la cebra* for *el tigre.*

El español en la comunidad

Hispanics in the United States make up approximately 13 percent of the total population and are the fastest-growing minority group. By the year 2050, the Hispanic population is expected to be almost 25 percent of the total United States population. Because of this, many Spanish-language media sources—magazines, newspapers, television, radio, and Internet—are available throughout the country.

- Make a list of Spanish-language media sources in your community. Try to find local, regional, national, or even international sources. If possible, bring in examples. How much can you understand?

These sources will help you improve your Spanish, and you'll learn about Spanish-speaking cultures as well.

¡Adelante!

Objectives

- Read about favorite activities of some teenagers
- Understand cultural perspectives regarding dancing
- Give an oral presentation about your activities
- Learn facts about Spain

Lectura

¿Qué te gusta hacer?

Here are some notes that four students have written to a popular teen magazine. All four are looking for e-pals. As you read their notes, think about how their likes and interests compare to yours.

Strategy

Using cognates
Use what you already know about cognates to figure out what new words mean.

Puerto Rico
Marisol, 14 años

"¿Te gusta practicar deportes y escuchar música? ¡A mí me gusta mucho! También me gusta jugar al básquetbol. ¡Hasta luego!"

Colombia
Daniel, 13 años

"Me gusta mucho ver la tele y escuchar música clásica. También me gusta tocar el piano y pasar tiempo con amigos en un café o en una fiesta. ¿Y a ti?"

España

Silvia, 17 años

"Me gusta leer revistas, bailar y cantar. Soy fanática de la música alternativa. También me gusta hablar por teléfono con amigos. ¿Y a ti? ¿Qué te gusta hacer?"

Guinea Ecuatorial

Pablo, 15 años

"Me gusta mucho jugar al vóleibol y al tenis. Me gusta escribir cuentos y también me gusta organizar fiestas con amigos. No me gusta ni jugar videojuegos ni ver la tele. ¡Hasta pronto!"

¿Comprendes?

1. Draw a bar graph. Indicate on the graph how many of the four young people like each of these types of activities: *televisión, música, deportes, pasar tiempo con amigos.* Which are the most popular?
2. Of the four students, with whom do you have the most in common?
3. Write a personal message similar to those in the magazine. Use one of them as a model.

For: Internet link activity
Visit: www.phschool.com
Web Code: jcd-0106

La cultura en vivo

¿Te gusta bailar?

Thanks to the worldwide popularity of Latin music, Latin dances have captured the attention of people of all ages. As a result, people all around the United States are learning dances such as the merengue, tango, and salsa. Here is a dance you can learn. It is called the mambo, and it originated in Cuba in the 1940s.

Bailando el mambo

El mambo

Directions

Beat 1 (of the music): Step forward with the left foot and slightly raise the right foot in a rocking motion.

Beat 2: Step back down on the right foot.

Beat 3: Place the left foot next to the right foot.

Beat 4: Hold both feet in place with the left and right feet next to each other.

Repeat the same motion, now moving backwards.

Beat 5: Step backward with the right foot and slightly raise the left foot in a rocking motion.

Beat 6: Step back down on the left foot.

Beat 7: Place the right foot next to the left foot.

Beat 8: Hold both feet in place with the left and right feet next to each other.

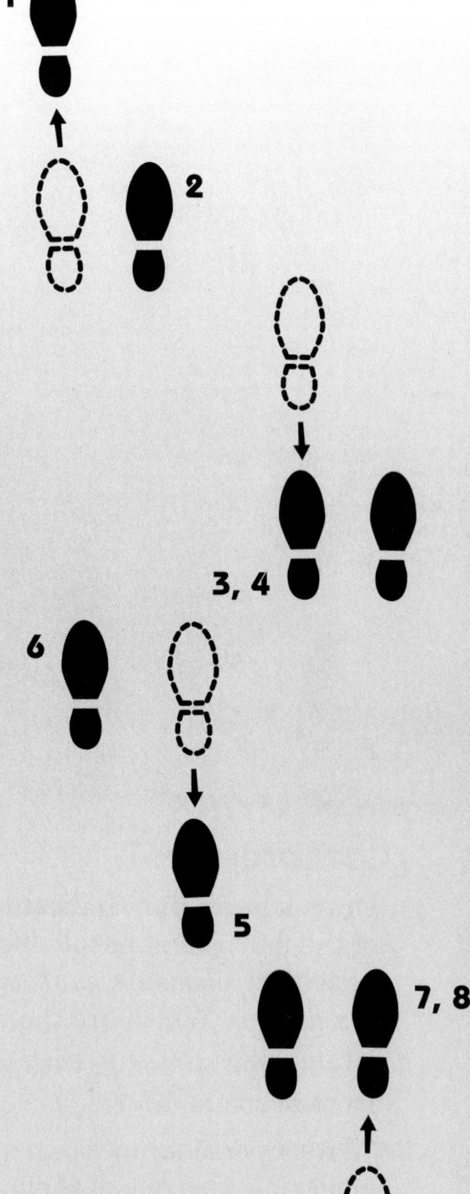

These steps are repeated throughout the music. If partners dance together, then the male should start with his left foot going forward and the female should start with her right foot going backward.

Think about it! How is doing the mambo with a partner different from dances you might do? What dances do you know from the United States that are danced with a partner?

Presentación oral

A mí me gusta mucho . . .

Task

You are a new student at school and have been asked to tell the class a little bit about your likes and dislikes.

1 Prepare Copy this diagram on a sheet of paper. Write a list of at least five activities that you can include in the three different ovals.

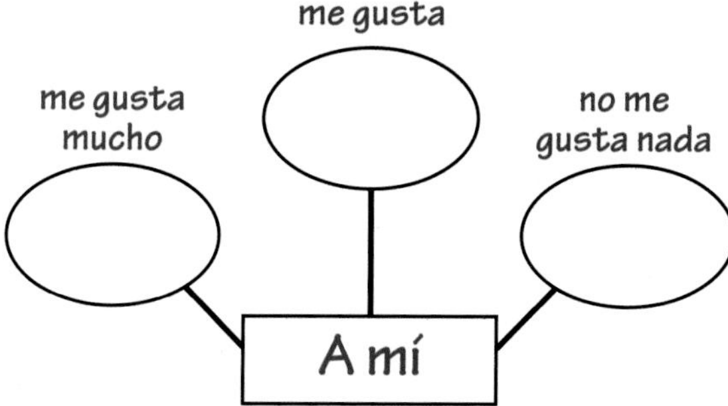

Using your list, create a poster or other visual aid to illustrate the three categories and at least five activities. To illustrate the activities, you can make drawings, cut pictures out of magazines, or show photos of yourself doing the activity. Make sure that each activity is easy to identify. You will use this visual as part of your presentation.

Strategy

Creating visuals
Making a diagram can help you organize a presentation.

2 Practice Go through your presentation with a few class members. You can use your notes the first time or two, but then practice using only the visuals.

Modelo

Me gusta mucho . . .
Me gusta . . .
No me gusta nada . . .

3 Present Talk about yourself using the visual you have created. Remember to look at the Evaluation list below so you know what you need to emphasize in your presentation. Be sure to begin the presentation with your name. During the presentation, try to:

- use complete sentences
- speak clearly
- use the visuals to keep yourself focused

4 Evaluation Your teacher may give you a rubric explaining how your presentation will be graded. You might be graded on:

- how much information you communicate
- how easy it is to understand you
- how clearly and neatly your visuals match what you are saying

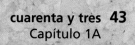

El mundo hispano

España

The Spanish empire once included parts of Italy and the Netherlands, much of the Americas and the Caribbean, the Philippines, and colonies in Africa. Today, Spain is a country of rich regional and cultural traditions with a population of more than 40 million people.

Spain was one of the most important provinces of the ancient Roman empire. The Spanish language is very closely related to Latin, the language of that empire. Roman engineering also left its mark on the Spanish landscape, and some Roman bridges are still in use after almost 2,000 years! This photo shows the Roman aqueduct in Segovia, which was constructed entirely without mortar or clamps.

¿Sabes que . . . ?

Spain has five official languages: Spanish, Catalan, Basque, Galician, and Valencian. Originally the language of Castile in central Spain, Spanish is the primary national language and is also spoken in most of Spain's former empire in North, Central, and South America.

Para pensar

Spain has been influenced by many civilizations, including those of the ancient Greeks, Romans, and Moors. What civilizations have most affected the language, culture, and customs of the United States?

For: Online Atlas
Visit: www.phschool.com
Web Code: jce-0002

Originally a royal retreat, the Parque del Buen Retiro is now a favorite place for the traditional Sunday-afternoon *paseo* (stroll). Throngs of people come to enjoy the Retiro's lakes, gardens, and museums, or simply to spend time with friends or family. What are your favorite places to go walking with friends? Why? ▼

▲ Arabic-speaking Moors from North Africa ruled much of Spain for nearly 800 years. Córdoba in southern Spain became one of the most important cities in Islam, and its mosque, the Mezquita, was one of the largest in the world. The Alhambra in Granada (shown above) is a strongly fortified and beautiful complex of palaces and gardens. It was also the last stronghold of the Moors in Spain, falling to Spain's Catholic monarchs in 1492.

The Bilbao Guggenheim Museum opened in October 1997 and houses a collection of modern and contemporary art. The building's titanium-paneled curves and concrete blocks imitate the harbor of Bilbao, a principal seaport and former shipbuilding center in the heart of the Basque country in the north.

Repaso del capítulo

Vocabulario y gramática

Chapter Review

To prepare for the test, check to see if you . . .
- **know the new vocabulary and grammar**
- **can perform the tasks on p. 47**

to talk about activities

bailar	to dance
cantar	to sing
correr	to run
dibujar	to draw
escribir cuentos	to write stories
escuchar música	to listen to music
esquiar	to ski
hablar por teléfono	to talk on the phone
ir a la escuela	to go to school
jugar videojuegos	to play video games
leer revistas	to read magazines
montar en bicicleta	to ride a bicycle
montar en monopatín	to skateboard
nadar	to swim
pasar tiempo con amigos	to spend time with friends
patinar	to skate
practicar deportes	to play sports
tocar la guitarra	to play the guitar
trabajar	to work
usar la computadora	to use the computer
ver la tele	to watch television

to say what you like to do

(A mí) me gusta ___.	I like to ___.
(A mí) me gusta más ___.	I like to ___ better. (I prefer to ___.)
(A mí) me gusta mucho ___.	I like to ___ a lot.
A mí también.	I do too.

to say what you don't like to do

(A mí) no me gusta ___.	I don't like to ___.
(A mí) no me gusta nada ___.	I don't like to ___ at all.
A mí tampoco.	I don't (like to) either.

For *Vocabulario adicional,* see pp. 472–473.

to ask others what they like to do

¿Qué te gusta hacer?	What do you like to do?
¿Qué te gusta más?	What do you like (prefer) better?
¿Te gusta ___?	Do you like to ___?
¿Y a ti?	And you?

other useful words and expressions

ni . . . ni	neither . . . nor, not . . . or
o	or
pues . . .	well . . .
sí	yes
también	also, too
y	and

Más práctica

Practice Workbook Puzzle 1A-8
Practice Workbook Organizer 1A-9

For: Test preparation
Visit: www.phschool.com
Web Code: jcd-0107

Preparación para el examen

On the exam you will be asked to . . .	Here are practice tasks similar to those you will find on the exam . . .	If you need review . . .
 **1 Escuchar** Listen to and understand a description of what someone likes to do	Listen to a voice mail from a student looking for a "match-up" to the homecoming dance. a) What are two things this person likes doing? b) What is one thing this person dislikes doing?	**pp. 26–29** *A primera vista* **p. 27** Actividades 1–2 **p. 33** Actividad 13
 **2 Hablar** Talk about yourself and what you like and don't like to do and ask the same of others	You agreed to host a student from the Dominican Republic for a week. What can you tell him or her about yourself in a taped message? Include a brief description of what you like to do. How would you ask the student to tell you something about himself or herself?	**p. 30** Actividad 7 **p. 31** Actividad 8 **p. 33** Actividad 12 **p. 37** Actividades 16–17 **p. 43** *Presentación oral*
 **3 Leer** Read and understand someone's description of himself or herself	Read this pen pal e-mail from a Spanish-language magazine. What types of things does the person like to do? Does this person have anything in common with you? What is it? ¡Hola! A mí me gusta mucho usar la computadora y tocar la guitarra. No me gusta ni ir a la escuela ni leer. En el verano me gusta nadar y en el invierno me gusta esquiar. ¿Y a ti? ¿Qué te gusta hacer?	**pp. 26–29** *A primera vista* **p. 29** Actividad 3 **p. 36** Actividad 15 **p. 38** Actividad 19 **pp. 40–41** *Lectura,* no. 3
4 Escribir Write about yourself with a description of things you like and don't like to do	A school in the Dominican Republic wants to exchange e-mails with your school. Tell your e-pal your name and what you like to do and don't like to do.	**p. 30** Actividades 5–6 **p. 33** Actividad 12 **p. 38** Actividad 18 **p. 41** *¿Comprendes?*
 **5 Pensar** Demonstrate an understanding of cultural differences regarding dancing	How would you describe the Latin dances that have become popular in the United States? With what countries do you associate each dance? With what type of music or rhythms do you associate each dance?	**p. 34** *Fondo cultural* **p. 35** Actividad 14 **p. 42** *La cultura en vivo*

Fondo cultural

Frida Kahlo (1907–1954) is one of the best- known Mexican painters. In spite of a childhood illness, a crippling traffic accident, and many hospital stays throughout her life, Kahlo was a successful painter and led a very active social life. She used her artwork as an outlet for her physical and emotional suffering.

- Frida Kahlo painted over fifty self-portraits. What is she saying about herself through this painting?

Autorretrato con mono (1938), Frida Kahlo

Capítulo 1B

Y tú, ¿cómo eres?

Chapter Objectives

- Talk about personality traits
- Ask and tell what people are like
- Use adjectives to describe people
- Understand cultural perspectives on friendship

Video Highlights

A primera vista: ***Amigos por Internet***

GramActiva Videos: adjectives; definite and indefinite articles; word order: placement of adjectives

Country Connection

As you learn how to describe yourself and your friends, you will make connections to these countries and places:

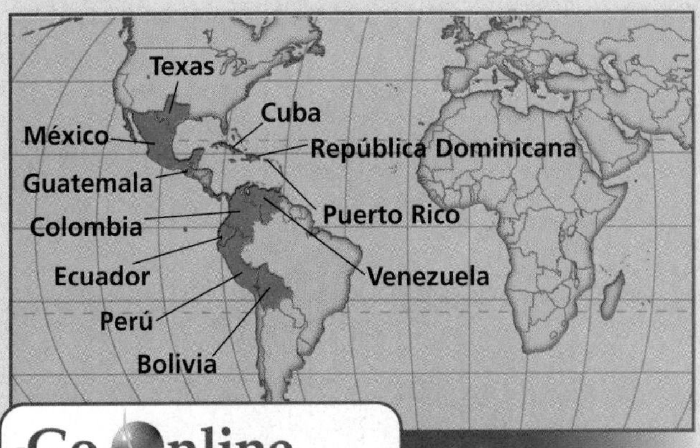

Go Online PHSchool.com

For: Online Atlas
Visit: www.phschool.com
Web Code: jce-0002

Un grupo de amigos, Mercedes, Texas

A primera vista

Vocabulario y gramática en contexto

Objectives

Read, listen to, and understand information about
- **personality traits**

"¿El chico? **Es mi amigo. ¿Cómo se llama?** Se llama Marcos. **¿Cómo es?** Pues . . .

la chica

. . . él es **deportista. Le gusta** mucho practicar deportes.

Pero a veces es **impaciente . . .**

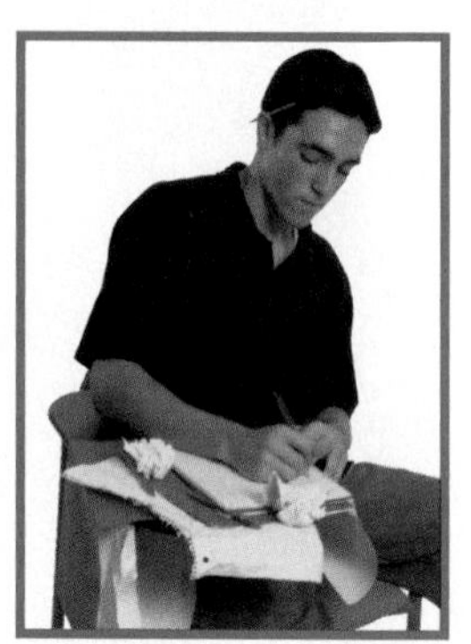

. . . también es **un** chico **desordenado.**"

"Mi amiga Sarita es **una buena** amiga. **Ella** no es **muy** deportista . . .

el chico

. . . pero es una chica **artística . . .**

. . . y muy **ordenada.**

Es una chica muy **inteligente.**"

Más vocabulario

atrevido, -a	daring
paciente	patient
reservado, -a	shy
simpático, -a	nice, friendly
talentoso, -a	talented

"Hola, me llamo Luz. ¿Yo? ¿Cómo **soy**? Pues . . .

. . . soy **estudiosa** . . .

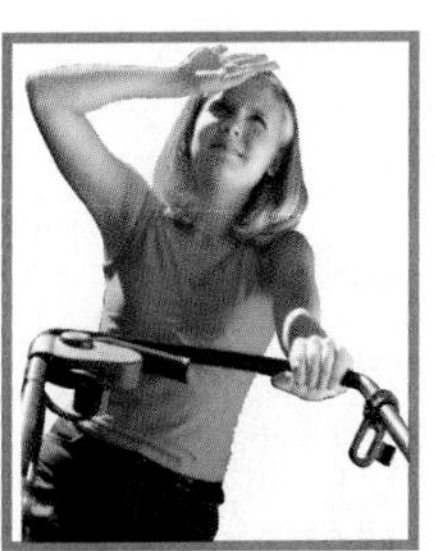

. . . y **trabajadora** . . .

. . . y también **graciosa** . . .

. . . pero **según mi familia** ¡a veces soy **perezosa**! Y tú, **¿cómo eres?**"

Actividad 1 **Escuchar**

¿Marcos o Sarita?

Look at the pictures of Marcos and Sarita. Listen to the descriptions. If a word describes Marcos, point to his picture. If a word describes Sarita, point to her picture.

Actividad 2 **Escuchar**

¿Cierto o falso?

You will hear some statements about Luz. Give a "thumbs-up" sign if the statement is true, or a "thumbs-down" sign if it is false.

Más práctica

Practice Workbook 1B-1, 1B-2

For: Vocabulary practice
Visit: www.phschool.com
Web Code: jcd-0111

Videohistoria

Amigos por Internet

See what happens when *Chica sociable* sends an e-mail message to Esteban.

Strategy

Using cognates
You will see some unfamiliar words in this story. Many of these are cognates. Use their similarity to English words to determine their meaning.

- What does *sociable* mean?
- What does *ideal* mean?

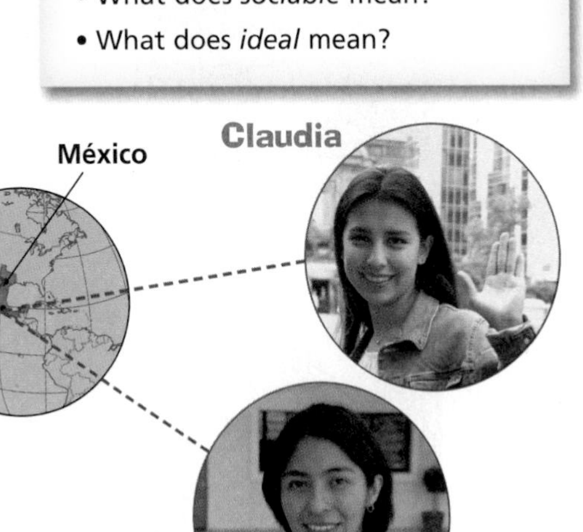

1 **Pedro:** Esteban, escucha: "Hola, ¿cómo eres? ¿Qué te gusta hacer? Me gusta mucho hablar con mis amigos. Me llamo *Chica **sociable.*** Escríbeme."

Esteban: ¡Ja! *Chica sociable.* A responder. Escribe, Pedro. . . .

5 **Teresa:** "Soy muy desordenada. Me gusta hablar por teléfono. Y no me gusta ir a la escuela. Escríbeme. *Chica sociable.*"

6 **Claudia:** Un momento . . . uno más de mí. Escribe. . . "Yo soy *Chica misteriosa.* Soy amiga de *Chica sociable.* Soy muy simpática."

7 **Claudia:** "Y me gusta ir a la escuela. Soy estudiosa y trabajadora. Yo no soy tu chica ideal. *Chica misteriosa.*"

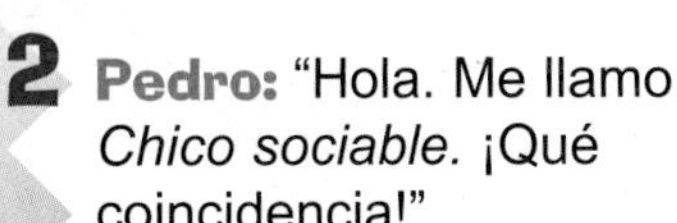

2 **Pedro:** "Hola. Me llamo *Chico sociable.* ¡Qué coincidencia!"

3 **Pedro:** "Me gusta pasar tiempo con mis amigos. **No soy** muy **serio.** Según mis amigos, soy gracioso."

4 **Claudia:** ¡*Chica sociable*! ¡Ja!

Teresa: Yo soy *Chica sociable.*

Claudia: ¡No! ¿Tú **eres** *Chica sociable*? ¡¿Mi buena amiga . . . ?!

8 **Esteban:** Pues, Pedro. ¿*Chica sociable* o *Chica misteriosa?*

Pedro: *Chica misteriosa.* Me gusta la escuela y a ella le gusta la escuela también.

Esteban: Perfecto. A mí me gusta más *Chica sociable.*

Actividad 3 **Escribir/Hablar**

¿Comprendes?

Read each of the sentences below and indicate which character is being described: *Chica sociable* or *Chica misteriosa.*

1. Me gusta hablar por teléfono.
2. Me gusta ir a la escuela.
3. Soy simpática.
4. No soy muy ordenada.
5. Soy trabajadora.

Más práctica

Practice Workbook 1B-3, 1B-4

For: Vocabulary practice
Visit: www.phschool.com
Web Code: jcd-0112

Actividad 4 **Escribir/Hablar**

Y tú, ¿qué dices?

1. Find five cognates in the *Videohistoria* and write what you think they mean in English.
2. Write an activity that goes with each of these characteristics.
   sociable estudioso trabajador
3. ¿Qué te gusta más, usar la computadora o hablar por teléfono?

Manos a la obra

Vocabulario y gramática en uso

Objectives

- Talk about what people are like
- Ask people to talk about themselves and others
- Describe your own personality traits

Escribir

¿Cómo es el chico o la chica?

Choose the correct word to describe each of the people in the pictures.

Modelo

El chico es *(impaciente / estudioso).*

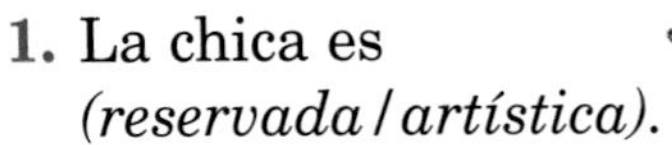

1. La chica es *(reservada / artística).*
2. La chica es *(graciosa / perezosa).*
3. El chico es *(reservado / deportista).*

4. El chico es *(desordenado / atrevido).*

5. La chica es *(artística / atrevida).*

6. El chico es *(estudioso / desordenado).*

Escribir

Mi amigo José

Maritza is talking about her friend José. Read the sentences, then choose the appropriate word to fill in each blank.

Modelo

No es un chico impaciente. Es muy paciente.

trabajador	deportista	bueno
paciente	estudioso	sociable
gracioso	desordenado	

1. Le gusta mucho practicar deportes. Es ___.
2. A veces no es serio. Es un chico ___.
3. Le gusta pasar tiempo con amigos. Es muy ___.
4. No es un chico ordenado. Es ___.
5. Le gusta ir a la escuela. Es ___.
6. No es perezoso. Es un chico muy ___.
7. Es simpático. Es un amigo muy ___.

Gramática

Adjectives

Words that describe people and things are called adjectives *(adjetivos)*.

- In Spanish, most adjectives have both masculine and feminine forms. The masculine form usually ends in the letter *-o* and the feminine form usually ends in the letter *-a*.
- Masculine adjectives are used to describe masculine nouns.

Marcos es ordenado y simpático.	*Marcos is organized and nice.*

- Feminine adjectives are used to describe feminine nouns.

Marta es ordenada y simpática.	*Marta is organized and nice.*

- Adjectives that end in *-e* describe both masculine and feminine nouns.

Anita es inteligente.	*Anita is smart.*
Pedro es inteligente también.	*Pedro is also smart.*

Masculine	Feminine
ordenado	ordenada
trabajador	trabajadora
paciente	paciente
deportista	deportista

- Adjectives whose masculine form ends in *-dor* have a feminine form that ends in *-dora*.

Juan es trabajador.	*Juan is hardworking.*
Luz es trabajadora.	*Luz is hardworking.*

- Some adjectives that end in *-a*, such as *deportista*, describe both masculine and feminine nouns. You will need to learn which adjectives follow this pattern.

Tomás es deportista.	*Tomás is sports-minded.*
Marta es deportista también.	*Marta is also sports-minded.*

GramActiva VIDEO

Want more help with adjectives? Watch the **GramActiva** video.

Gramática **Escribir**

Roberto y Yolanda

Copy the Venn diagram on a sheet of paper. Which words from the list below could only describe Roberto? Write them in the oval below his name. Which words could only describe Yolanda? Write them in the oval below her name. Which words could describe either Roberto or Yolanda? Write them in the overlapping area.

artístico	atrevida	deportista	estudiosa
graciosa	impaciente	simpático	inteligente
ordenada	paciente	perezosa	reservado
serio	sociable	talentosa	trabajador

Modelo

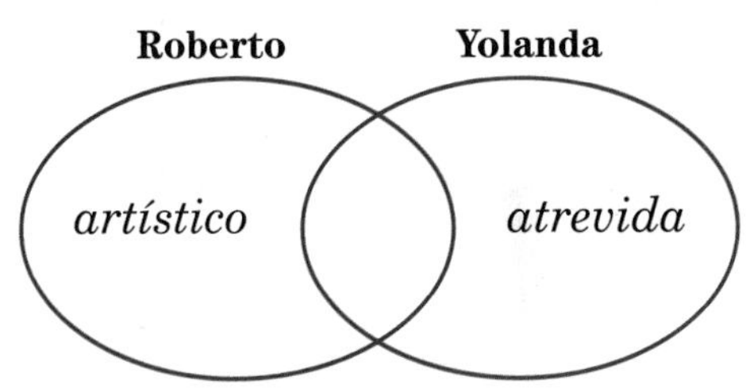

Actividad 8 Gramática  Hablar

¿Cómo es Paloma?

Work with a partner to ask and answer questions about the people shown below.

Modelo

Paloma
A —*¿Cómo es Paloma?*
B —*Paloma es trabajadora.*

1. Elena 

2. Marisol 

3. Felipe 

4. Juan 

5. Lola 

6. Gloria 

Actividad 9 Gramática  Hablar

Juego

Choose an adjective and act it out for a small group or the class. The other students take turns asking you questions. The first to ask a question with the correct adjective (in the correct form) gets to do the next charade.

Modelo

A —*¿Eres ordenada?*
B —*Sí, soy ordenada.*
o: *No, no soy ordenada.*

Actividad 10 Gramática Escribir

Yo soy . . .

Make a chart like the one on the right. Write at least two adjectives in each column to say what you are like and are not like. Include *muy* and *a veces* when they are appropriate. Save your work to use in later activities.

Modelo

Soy	No soy
estudiosa	perezosa
muy trabajadora	impaciente
deportista	

Actividad 11 Gramática **Hablar/Escribir**

¿Eres estudioso(a)?

Use your chart from Actividad 10. Talk with your partner about your personality traits. Take notes on what your partner tells you. Make another two-column chart, but with the headings *Es* and *No es*. Fill it in with information about your partner. You will use this chart in the next activity.

Modelo

A —*¿Cómo eres?*
B —*Soy estudiosa y muy trabajadora. También soy deportista. ¿Y tú?*
A —*Soy artístico. Según mis amigos, soy talentoso. No soy perezoso.*

Actividad 12 Gramática **Escribir/Hablar**

Mi amigo(a)

Use the information from the previous activity to write a short description of yourself and your partner. Read your description to a small group or the class.

Modelo

Me llamo Luisa. Soy estudiosa y trabajadora. Y soy deportista. Mi amiga se llama Susana. Ella es simpática. También es deportista y trabajadora.

Exploración del lenguaje

Cognates that begin with *es* + consonant

Many words in Spanish that begin with *es* + consonant are easy to understand because they have the same meaning as English words. Knowing this pattern helps you recognize the meaning of new Spanish words and learn them quickly.

Try it out! Look at these words, then cover up the *e* at the beginning. Name the English words that come from the same root word.

estudiante	**es**tudioso	**es**cuela	**es**tómago
esquiar	**es**pecial	**es**tricto	**es**cena

Es muy deportista. Le encanta esquiar.

Hablar

¿Qué te gusta hacer?

Trabaja con otro(a) estudiante. Pregunta y contesta según el modelo.

Modelo

A —*¿Te gusta correr?*
B —*Sí, soy deportista.*
o: *No, no soy deportista.*
o: *Sí, pero no soy muy deportista.*

Estudiante A

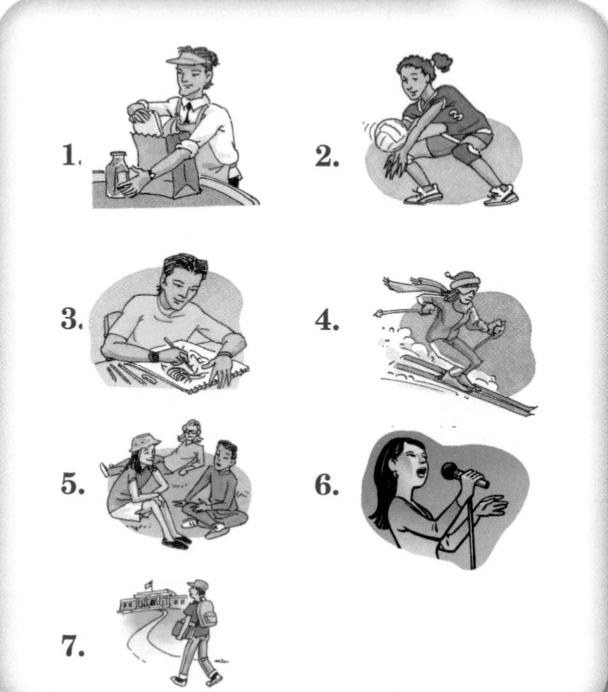

Estudiante B

Fondo cultural

Simón Bolívar (1783–1830) liberated the territory that is now Venezuela, Colombia, Ecuador, Peru, and Bolivia from Spanish rule. A daring military commander and statesman, Bolívar is revered in South America as *el Libertador* (the Liberator).

- Name three leaders who had a similar influence on events of their time.

Simón Bolívar (siglo xix), Anónimo
Chromolitho. Private Collection / Archives Charmet / Bridgeman Art Library.

Más práctica

Practice Workbook 1B-5

For: Practice with adjective agreement
Visit: www.phschool.com
Web Code: jcd-0114

Leer/Escribir

El poema "Soy Elena"

The following poem is called a *diamante.* Can you guess why? After you've read the poem, answer the questions.

Conexiones | **La literatura**

Soy Elena
En general, soy
reservada y ordenada.
A veces, soy atrevida,
graciosa o impaciente.
No soy ni deportista
ni artística.
¡Yo soy yo!

1. Which activity would you invite Elena to do based on what she has told you about herself?

   dibujar   montar en monopatín   escuchar música

2. Rewrite the poem replacing *Soy Elena* with *Soy Tomás.*

Escribir

Y tú, ¿qué dices?

Write *un poema diamante* about yourself. Choose adjectives that best describe you. Look back at Actividad 10 for some ideas. Substitute your adjectives in the poem above. Be sure to write the poem in the form of a diamond. You might want to use calligraphy or an appropriate font on the computer and add pictures to illustrate your work.

Gramática

Definite and indefinite articles

El and *la* are called definite articles and are the equivalent of "the" in English. *El* is used with masculine nouns; *la* is used with feminine nouns. You've already seen words with definite articles:

el libro *the book* la carpeta *the folder*

Un and *una* are called indefinite articles and are the equivalent of "a" and "an" in English. *Un* is used with masculine nouns; *una* is used with feminine nouns:

un libro *a book* **una** carpeta *a folder*

el	the
la	the

un	a, an
una	a, an

Strategy

Learning by repetition
When you learn a new noun, say it aloud, along with its definite article, as often as you get a chance. Eventually, you will find that words just "sound right" with the correct definite article and you will know whether nouns are masculine or feminine.

GramActiva VIDEO

Want more help with definite and indefinite articles? Watch the **GramActiva** video.

Actividad 16 Gramática **Escuchar/GramActiva**

¿El o la?

Write the word *el* in large letters on a sheet of paper or an index card. Write *la* in large letters on another sheet. You will hear eight words you already know. When you hear a masculine word, hold up the paper with *el*. When you hear a feminine word, hold up the paper with the word *la* on it.

El Mercado, San Antonio, Texas

Hablar

¿Qué es?

Tell your partner the names of the things pictured below.

Modelo

A —*¿Qué es?*
B —*Es un brazo.*

1. 
2. 
3. 
4. 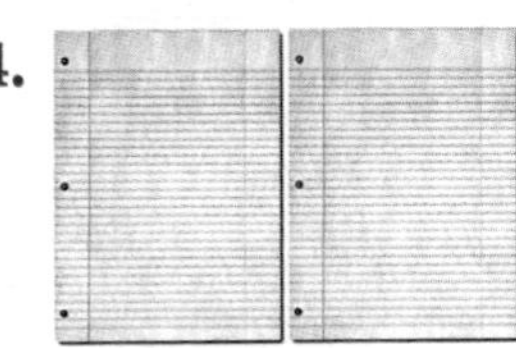
5. 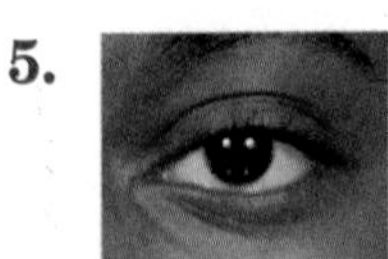
6. 
7. 
8. 

Actividad 18 Gramática **Escribir**

La escuela de Diego

Diego is talking about people at his school. Read the sentences and complete each one with *un* or *una*.

1. La Sra. Secada es ___ profesora simpática.
2. Alicia es ___ estudiante trabajadora.
3. Juan Carlos es ___ chico perezoso.
4. Germán es ___ chico sociable.
5. El Sr. Guzmán es ___ profesor gracioso.
6. Adriana es ___ chica muy seria.
7. La Srta. Cifuentes es ___ profesora paciente.
8. Arturo es ___ estudiante talentoso.

Más práctica
Practice Workbook 1B-6

For: Practice with articles
Visit: www.phschool.com
Web Code: jcd-0113

Pronunciación

The vowels *o* and *u*

In Spanish, the pronunciation of the letter *o* is similar to the vowel sound in the English word "boat" but is always cut very short. Say these words, concentrating on making a short *o* sound.

bolígrafo	gracioso	cómo
teléfono	tampoco	otoño

In Spanish, the pronunciation of the letter *u* is similar to the vowel sound in the English word "zoo." Say these words.

mucho	lunes	usted
octubre	estudioso	según

¡Ojo! Careful! Sometimes the words we mispronounce most are the ones that remind us of English words.

Try it out! Pronounce these words, concentrating on the Spanish vowel sounds:

agosto	regular	tropical	música
gusto	universidad	Uruguay	Cuba

El mundo

Gramática

Word order: Placement of adjectives

In Spanish, adjectives usually come after the noun they describe. Notice how *artística* follows *chica* in the Spanish sentence.

Margarita es **una chica artística.** *Margarita is an artistic girl.*

Did you notice that in the English sentence the adjective comes before the noun?

Here's a simple pattern you can follow when writing a sentence in Spanish.

Subject	Verb	Indefinite Article + Noun	Adjective
Margarita	es	una chica	muy artística.
Pablo	es	un estudiante	inteligente.
La Sra. Ortiz	es	una profesora	muy buena.

¿Recuerdas?

To make a sentence negative you place the word *no* before the verb.

- Eduardo **no es** un chico serio.
- **No** me **gusta** jugar videojuegos.

Gramática **Escribir**

Frases desordenadas

Rewrite these scrambled words to create a sentence. Follow the "building-blocks" pattern above and be sure to add a period at the end of each sentence.

Modelo

perezoso Antonio es chico un
Antonio es un chico perezoso.

1. artística es una chica Marina
2. es un Tito perezoso chico
3. deportista chica una es Paquita
4. Marcos chico un es reservado no
5. chico no Rafael es estudioso un
6. no una Teresa chica es inteligente

Gramática **Escuchar/Escribir**

Escucha y escribe

You will hear a description of Arturo, Marta, and Belinda. Write what you hear.

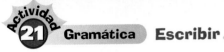

Gramática **Escribir**

¿Cómo es . . . ?

You are sitting in your school cafeteria with a new exchange student from Costa Rica. Describe the other students based on their activities.

Modelo

Emilia es una chica talentosa.

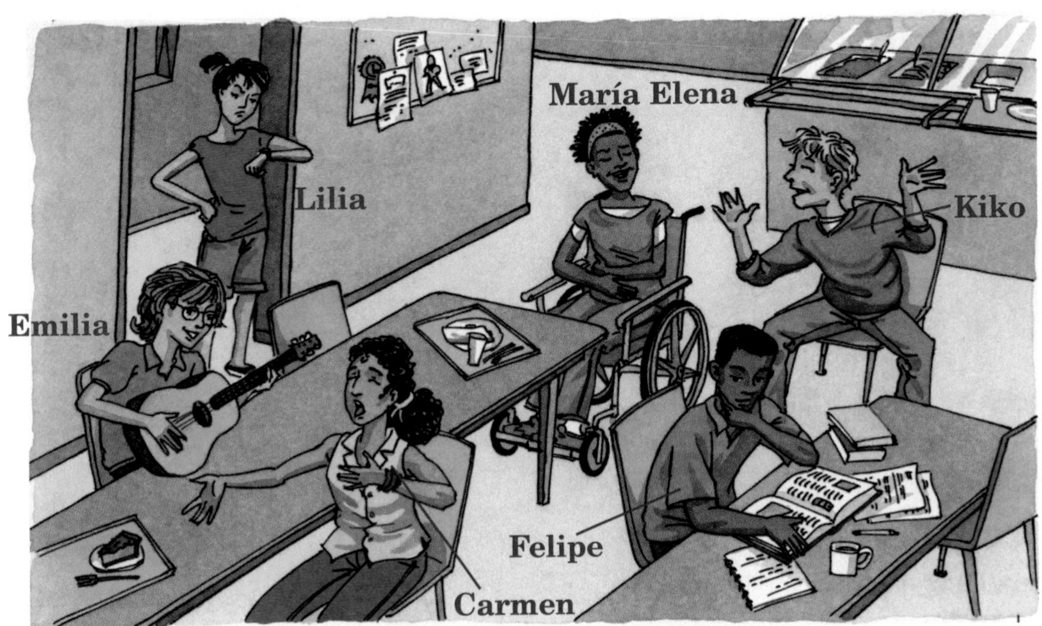

Escribir/Hablar

Y tú, ¿qué dices?

1. Según tu familia, ¿cómo eres?
2. Según tu mejor *(best)* amigo(a), ¿cómo eres?
3. Y tú, ¿cómo eres?

Paciente, inteligente, trabajador, ordenado . . . These four qualities will make you a good candidate for any job. And if you add *bilingüe* to the list, your job qualifications will be enhanced.

Make a list of careers in which your knowledge of Spanish would be an asset. Which of these careers are of interest to you?

Más práctica

Practice Workbook 1B-7

For: Practice with placement of adjectives
Visit: www.phschool.com
Web Code: jcd-0115

¡Adelante!

Objectives

- Read and understand an article about personality traits
- Understand cultural perspectives on friendship
- Write a letter to a pen pal
- Learn facts about the Caribbean

Lectura

Un *self-quiz*

¿Hay una relación entre los colores y la personalidad? Según un *self-quiz* de la revista *Amigos,* tus colores favoritos revelan perfectamente cómo eres.

Strategy

Using visual clues to get meaning

You have not yet learned the Spanish words for colors, but see if you can figure out what they are from the visual clues in the article.

¿Cómo eres tú? ¡Los colores revelan tu personalidad!

¿Eres una chica? ¿Te gusta el rojo? ¿Eres un chico? ¿Te gusta el rojo?	Eres muy apasionada. Eres atrevido.
¿Eres una chica? ¿Te gusta el verde? ¿Eres un chico? ¿Te gusta el verde?	Eres una chica natural. Eres muy generoso.
¿Eres una chica? ¿Te gusta el azul? ¿Eres un chico? ¿Te gusta el azul?	Eres muy talentosa. Eres un chico sociable.
¿Eres una chica? ¿Te gusta el anaranjado? ¿Eres un chico? ¿Te gusta el anaranjado?	Eres una chica artística. Eres gracioso.
¿Eres una chica? ¿Te gusta el violeta? ¿Eres un chico? ¿Te gusta el violeta?	Eres una chica muy independiente. Eres un chico romántico.
¿Eres una chica? ¿Te gusta el amarillo? ¿Eres un chico? ¿Te gusta el amarillo?	Eres una chica muy trabajadora. Eres muy serio.

¿Comprendes?

1. You probably were able to understand most of the words in the quiz. Write the English meaning for these Spanish cognates from the reading:

- revelan
- natural
- independiente
- generoso
- apasionada
- romántico

2. According to the "self-quiz," what should be the favorite colors of these teenagers?

   a. A Beto le gusta estar con amigos.

   b. A Margarita le gusta dibujar.

   c. A Lorenzo le gusta el trabajo voluntario.

   d. A Lupe le gusta estudiar. Es muy seria.

   e. A Isabel le gusta estar con amigos, pero también le gusta estar sola *(alone)*.

3. Which of the colors in this reading best matches your personality? Why?

Modelo

Amarillo: *Soy una chica trabajadora. Me gusta ir a la escuela.*

Fondo cultural

Huipil is the word for the colorful, hand-woven blouse worn by female descendants of the Maya. The color, design, and style of weaving are unique to each *huipil* and identify the background and specific village of the weaver. Hundreds of designs and styles of weaving have been identified in the Mayan regions, which are located principally in Guatemala and parts of Mexico.

- What do you wear that might represent your personality or likes and dislikes?

Una niña con huipil

For: Internet link activity
Visit: www.phschool.com
Web Code: jcd-0116

Perspectivas del mundo hispano

¿Qué es un amigo?

Marcos, a Costa Rican student on an exchange program in the United States writes:

"When I arrived in the United States, I was amazed at all the friends my host brother and sister had. They knew a lot of people. These friends came to the house frequently, and we went out in groups. People were very open when meeting me. We'd spend some time together and get to know each other in a short amount of time. And once you got to know them, you ended up talking about everything!"

Brianna, a United States student on an exchange program in Colombia writes:

"After I spent my year in Colombia, I learned that the concept of friendship is a little different than in the United States. My host brother and sisters spent a lot of time with their family. They knew people at school and from after-school activities, but they had just a few close friends and we'd do things with them. It was definitely a smaller group than I was used to. It seems that it took longer to become close friends with people too."

Dos amigas estudiando en Cozumel, México

In Spanish, two expressions are used frequently to describe friendly relationships: *un amigo,* which means "friend," and *un conocido,* which means "acquaintance." You already know the word *amigo. Conocido* comes from the verb *conocer,* which means "to meet." Each expression implies a different type of relationship.

Check it out! In many Spanish-speaking countries you'll find lots of expressions for someone who is your friend: *hermano, cuate (México), amigote (España),* and *compinche (Uruguay, Argentina, España).* Make a list of the expressions for "a friend" that are popular in your community. How would you explain them to someone from a Spanish-speaking country?

Amigos en una fiesta en España

Think about it! Compare how the United States perspective on friendship is different from that of a Spanish-speaking country. Use the terms *amigo* and *conocido* as you make the comparison.

Presentación escrita

Amigo por correspondencia

Task
Write an e-mail in which you introduce yourself to a prospective pen pal.

1. **Prewrite** Think about information you want to give. Answer these questions to help you organize your e-mail message.
   - ¿Cómo te llamas?
   - ¿Cómo eres?
   - ¿Qué te gusta hacer?
   - ¿Qué no te gusta hacer?

2. **Draft** Write a first draft of your e-mail message using the answers to the questions above. Begin by introducing yourself: *¡Hola! Me llamo . . . .* When you are finished, end with *Escríbeme pronto.* ("Write to me soon.")

   ¡Hola! Me llamo Pati. Soy atrevida y muy deportista. Me gusta mucho nadar y correr, pero me gusta más esquiar. ¡No me gusta nada jugar videojuegos! Escríbeme pronto.

3. **Revise** Review the first draft of your e-mail and share it with a partner. Here are some things to look for:
   - Is it well organized?
   - Does it include all the information from the Prewrite questions?
   - Is the spelling accurate? Did you use the correct form of the adjectives to describe yourself?
   - Did you include the opening and the closing?

   Decide whether or not you want to use your partner's suggestions. Rewrite your draft.

4. **Publish** Type up your e-mail. You might want to send it to a pen pal in another class or school, send it to your teacher, or print it and give it to someone else in the class to answer.

5. **Evaluation** Your teacher may give you a rubric for grading your e-mail. You probably will be graded on:
   - completion of task
   - following the writing process by turning in the Prewrite and first draft
   - using adjectives correctly

Strategy

Using the writing process
To create your best work, follow each step in the writing process.

El mundo hispano

El Caribe

A chain of islands extending from the Bahamas in the north to Trinidad in the south, the Caribbean or West Indies is a region of extraordinary cultural and linguistic diversity. The Spanish-speaking countries are Cuba, Puerto Rico, and the Dominican Republic, which occupies the eastern portion of the island of Hispaniola.

Christopher Columbus first landed on the island of Hispaniola in 1492. He returned the following year with 1,000 colonists and founded Isabela, the first European colony in America, on the northern coast of Hispaniola.

¿Sabes que . . . ?

Most Cubans are descendants of people who originally came to the island from Spain and Africa. Although almost all Cubans speak Spanish as their first language, some also speak Lucumi, which is closely related to West African languages. Many people in other parts of the Caribbean speak creole languages, which combine elements of African and European tongues.

Para pensar

African traditions have inspired reggae, calypso, salsa, merengue, and many other musical styles in the Caribbean. What are some of the musical styles from the United States that have been influenced by African traditions?

For: Online Atlas
Visit: www.phschool.com
Web Code: jce-0002

The Universidad Autónoma de Santo Domingo, located in the capital of the Dominican Republic, Santo Domingo, is the oldest university in the Americas. It was founded in 1538—almost 100 years before Harvard—and continues to be one of the most important in the Caribbean.

Opened in 1963, the Arecibo Observatory in Puerto Rico has the largest single-dish radio telescope in the world. Some 200 scientists from around the world conduct research at Arecibo every year. In the early 1990s astronomers at Arecibo discovered the first planets outside our solar system.

The Caribbean is famous for its diverse musical styles that fuse African and European influences. Some groups even combine salsa, rumba, cha-cha-cha, and other Caribbean musical styles with jazz, hip-hop, and rock and roll.

Chapter Review

Repaso del capítulo

Vocabulario y gramática

To prepare for the test, check to see if you . . .
- know the new vocabulary and grammar
- can answer the questions on p. 71

to talk about what you and others are like

artístico, -a	artistic
atrevido, -a	daring
bueno, -a	good
deportista	sports-minded
desordenado, -a	messy
estudioso, -a	studious
gracioso, -a	funny
impaciente	impatient
inteligente	intelligent
ordenado, -a	neat
paciente	patient
perezoso, -a	lazy
reservado, -a	reserved, shy
serio, -a	serious
simpático, -a	nice, friendly
sociable	sociable
talentoso, -a	talented
trabajador, -ora	hardworking

to ask people about themselves or others

¿Cómo eres?	What are you like?
¿Cómo es?	What is he / she like?
¿Cómo se llama?	What's his / her name?
¿Eres . . . ?	Are you . . . ?

to talk about what someone likes or doesn't like

le gusta . . .	he / she likes . . .
no le gusta . . .	he / she doesn't like . . .

to describe someone

soy	I am
no soy	I am not
es	he / she is

to tell whom you are talking about

el amigo	male friend
la amiga	female friend
el chico	boy
la chica	girl
la familia	family
yo	I
él	he
ella	she

other useful words

a veces	sometimes
muy	very
pero	but
según	according to
según mi familia	according to my family

adjectives

Masculine	Feminine
ordenado	ordenada
trabajador	trabajadora
paciente	paciente
deportista	deportista

definite articles

el	the
la	the

indefinite articles

un	a, an
una	a, an

For *Vocabulario adicional,* see pp. 472–473.

Más práctica

Practice Workbook Puzzle 1B-8

Practice Workbook Organizer 1B-9

For: Test preparation
Visit: www.phschool.com
Web Code: jcd-0117

Preparación para el examen

On the exam you will be asked to . . .	Here are practice tasks similar to those you will find on the exam . . .	If you need review . . .
 **1 Escuchar** Listen to and understand a description of a friend	Listen as a character in a Spanish soap opera describes his ex-girlfriend. What does he think her good qualities are? What does he think her shortcomings are? Can you understand why he broke up with her?	**pp. 50–53** *A primera vista* **p. 57** Actividades 11–12 **p. 62** Actividad 20
 **2 Hablar** Talk about yourself in terms of how you see yourself	While you're talking to your Spanish teacher, you realize that she doesn't know the "real you." Tell her some things about yourself that would help her understand you.	**pp. 50–53** *A primera vista* **p. 56** Actividad 9 **p. 57** Actividad 11 **p. 58** Actividad 13 **p. 63** Actividad 22
 **3 Leer** Read and understand a description of someone	In a popular Spanish magazine, you see an interview with the actor who plays the part of a teenager, Carlos, in a TV show you have been watching. See if you can understand what he is saying about the character he plays: ¡No me gusta nada el chico! Él es muy inteligente, pero le gusta hablar y hablar de NADA. Es ridículo. Es muy impaciente y perezoso. Él no es ni simpático ni gracioso. Yo soy un actor . . . ¡no soy como Carlos!	**pp. 50–53** *A primera vista* **p. 59** Actividad 14 **pp. 64–65** *Lectura*
 **4 Escribir** Write a short paragraph describing yourself	The first issue of your school's online newspaper is called "Getting to Know You." Submit a brief profile of yourself. Mention what your family thinks of you and list some things you like to do. For example: Yo soy una chica deportista y muy sociable. Según mi familia, soy graciosa. Me gusta patinar y hablar por teléfono.	**pp. 56–57** Actividades 10–12 **p. 59** Actividad 15 **p. 63** Actividad 22 **p. 67** *Presentación escrita*
 **5 Pensar** Demonstrate an understanding of cultural perspectives on friendship	Explain the differences between the terms *amigo* and *conocido* in Spanish-speaking cultures. How does this compare to words that we use in the United States?	**p. 66** *Perspectivas del mundo hispano*

¡Viva Texas!

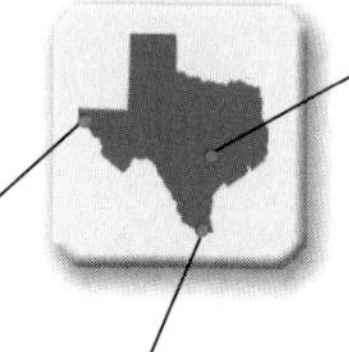

Según mis amigos. . .

¿Cómo eres según tus profesores y según tus amigos? A veces una persona es diferente cuando no está[1] en la escuela. Lee[2] unas descripciones de estos[3] estudiantes tejanos.

[1] isn't [2] Read [3] these

El Gladys Porter Zoo, Brownsville

"Soy Miguel. En la sala de clases, soy estudioso y trabajador, pero según mis amigos soy artístico y un poco perezoso. No me gusta nada trabajar los fines de semana. Me gusta más dibujar. Me gusta dibujar los animales en el Gladys Porter Zoo, en Brownsville."

"Me llamo Enrique. Según mi profesor, soy paciente y reservado. Me gusta mucho leer libros y escribir cuentos. Según mis amigos, no soy ni paciente ni reservado. Soy atrevido y sociable. Me gusta mucho hablar por teléfono con mis amigos. En el verano me gusta ir al Northeast YMCA Skatepark en El Paso."

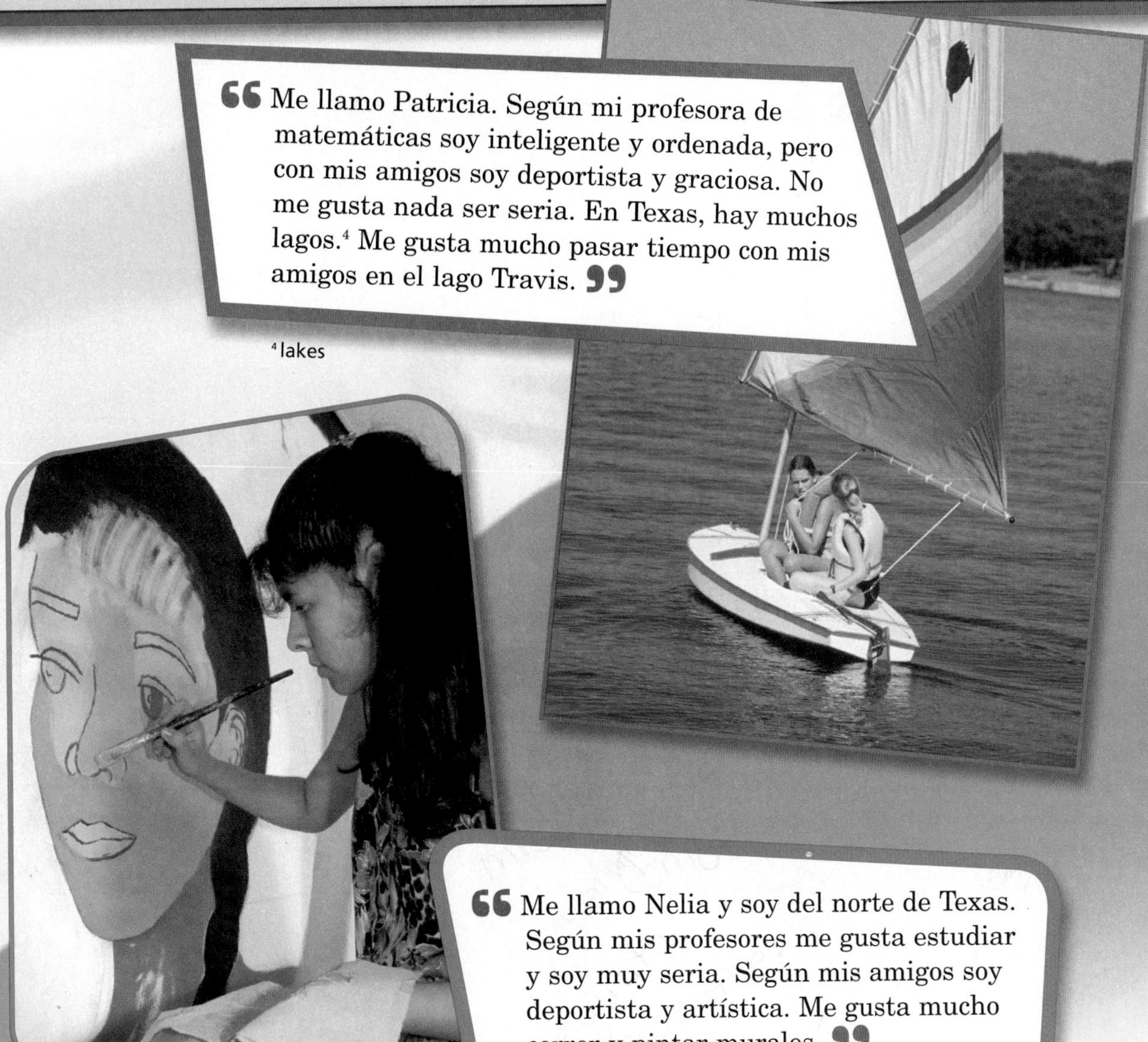

“Me llamo Patricia. Según mi profesora de matemáticas soy inteligente y ordenada, pero con mis amigos soy deportista y graciosa. No me gusta nada ser seria. En Texas, hay muchos lagos.[4] Me gusta mucho pasar tiempo con mis amigos en el lago Travis.”

[4] lakes

“Me llamo Nelia y soy del norte de Texas. Según mis profesores me gusta estudiar y soy muy seria. Según mis amigos soy deportista y artística. Me gusta mucho correr y pintar murales.”

¿Comprendes?

Based on the readings, write *según los profesores* for each statement that is a description according to teachers, or *según los amigos* if it is a description according to friends.

1. A Nelia le gusta mucho practicar deportes.
2. A Miguel le gusta estudiar y trabajar.
3. A Patricia le gusta ir a la escuela. No es una chica desordenada.
4. Miguel no es muy trabajador, pero es muy talentoso.
5. A Enrique le gusta hablar con amigos. Es muy sociable.

Comunicación

Write a description of yourself according to your teachers and another according to your friends. Then interview three classmates by asking them these questions:

1. Según tus profesores, ¿cómo eres?
2. Según tus amigos, ¿cómo eres?

Fondo cultural

Colombian artist Fernando Botero (1932–) is among the best known and most respected Latin American artists. His works have been exhibited around the world in prestigious museums, galleries, and open-air places. Botero's style is unique and recognizable. Pedrito Botero, shown in the painting, was the artist's son. He died in a car accident when he was four years old.

- Based upon the painting, how could you describe Botero's style?

Pedrito (1997), Fernando Botero

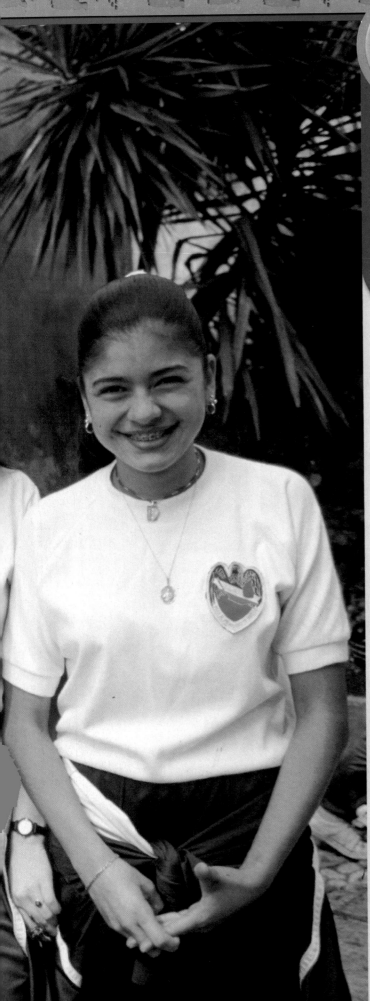

Tu día en la escuela

Chapter Objectives

- Talk about school schedules and subjects
- Discuss what students do during the day
- Ask and tell who is doing an action
- Compare your school with that of a student in a Spanish-speaking country

Video Highlights

A primera vista: ***El primer día de clases***

GramActiva Videos: subject pronouns; present tense of *-ar* verbs

Country Connection

As you learn about the school day in Spanish-speaking countries, you will make connections to these countries and places:

For: Online Atlas
Visit: www.phschool.com
Web Code: jce-0002

A primera vista

Vocabulario y gramática en contexto

Objectives

Read, listen to, and understand information about
- **the school day**

El horario de Alicia

“Me gusta mucho mi **horario. En la primera hora, tengo la clase de** tecnología . . . ¡es mi clase **favorita!** Es **interesante** y **práctica.** Pero a veces es **difícil.**”

primera hora		**tecnología**
segunda hora		**arte**
tercera hora		**ciencias sociales**
cuarta hora		**ciencias naturales**
quinta hora		**el almuerzo**
sexta hora		**español**
séptima hora		**matemáticas**
octava hora		**inglés**
novena hora		**educación física**

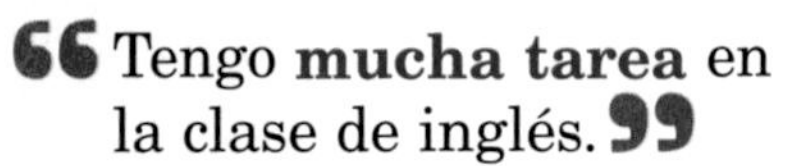

“Tengo **mucha tarea** en la clase de inglés.”

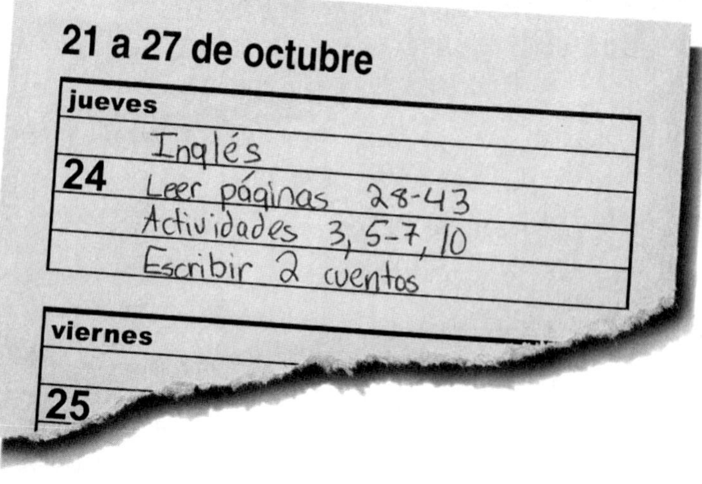

21 a 27 de octubre
jueves
24
Inglés
Leer páginas 28-43
Actividades 3, 5-7, 10
Escribir 2 cuentos
viernes
25

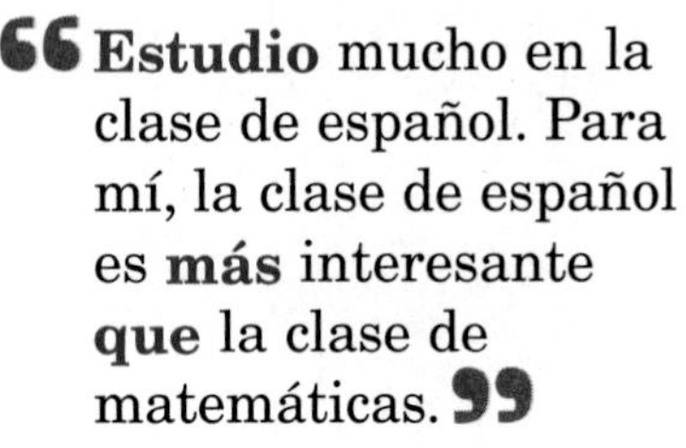

“**Estudio** mucho en la clase de español. Para mí, la clase de español es **más** interesante **que** la clase de matemáticas.”

“**Para** la clase de matemáticas **necesito una calculadora** y **una carpeta de argollas.**”

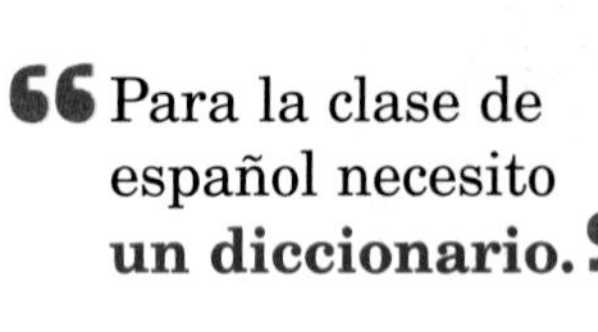

“Para la clase de español necesito **un diccionario.**”

Más vocabulario

décimo, -a — tenth

Escuchar

¿Sí o no?

You will hear Alicia make several statements about her school day and schedule. Give a “thumbs-up” sign if what she says is true or a “thumbs-down” sign if what she says is false.

Escuchar

El horario de Alicia

Listen to Alicia as she describes her class schedule. Touch the picture of each class as you hear it.

Más práctica

Practice Workbook 2A-1, 2A-2

For: Vocabulary practice
Visit: www.phschool.com
Web Code: jcd-0201

Videohistoria

El primer día de clases

Es el primer día de clases en la Escuela Bilingüe en la Ciudad de México.

Strategy

Using context clues
You can often guess the meaning of new words by reading the words around them and understanding what the rest of the sentence or paragraph is about.

- Based on the words around it, what does *enseña* mean in Panel 2?

1 **Claudia:** Teresa, ¿qué clase **tienes** en la primera hora?

Teresa: Tengo la clase de inglés.

5 **Teresa:** **Necesitas hablar** con el señor Treviño, en la oficina.

Claudia: Buena idea.

6 **Claudia:** Buenos días, señor Treviño. Necesito hablar con Ud. Tengo la clase de matemáticas . . .

Sr. Treviño: Sí, sí, Claudia, pero ahora no es posible. Mañana.

7 **Srta. Santoro:** Buenos días, estudiantes. Las matemáticas son muy interesantes y prácticas, ¿verdad?

Estudiantes: Sí, profesora.

Srta. Santoro: Y es muy importante **estudiar** y trabajar mucho . . .

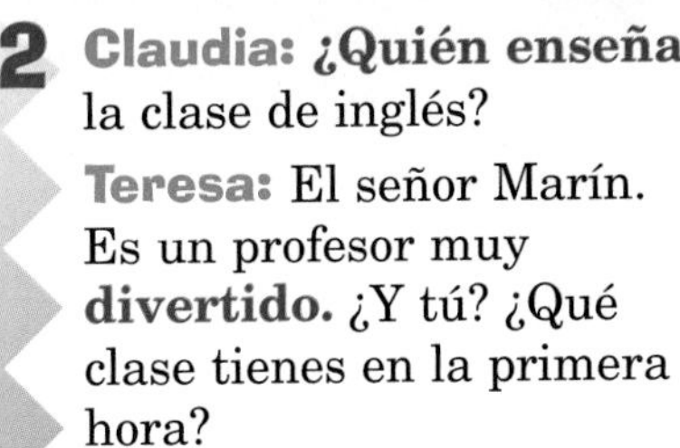

2 **Claudia: ¿Quién enseña** la clase de inglés?

Teresa: El señor Marín. Es un profesor muy **divertido.** ¿Y tú? ¿Qué clase tienes en la primera hora?

3 **Claudia:** Tengo la clase de matemáticas. Me gusta mucho. Para mí es muy **fácil.** Y, ¿qué tienes en la segunda hora?

Teresa: La clase de educación física.

4 **Teresa:** Y en la segunda hora, ¿qué clase tienes, Claudia?

Claudia: A ver . . . En la segunda hora, tengo la clase de matemáticas. ¡Y también tengo la clase de matemáticas en la tercera, en la cuarta, en la quinta y en la sexta hora!

8 **Srta. Santoro:** ¿Claudia?

Claudia: ¡Tengo seis clases de matemáticas hoy!

Srta. Santoro: ¡Seis! Es **aburrido,** ¿no? . . .

Leer/Escribir

¿Comprendes?

Read each sentence. Write *sí* if it is correct or *no* if it is incorrect.

1. Es el primer día de clases.
2. A Teresa le gusta la clase de inglés.
3. Para Claudia, la clase de matemáticas es difícil.
4. Claudia tiene la clase de educación física en la segunda hora.
5. Según la profesora, la clase de matemáticas es muy práctica.
6. En la sexta hora la clase de matemáticas es interesante.

Más práctica

Practice Workbook 2A-3, 2A-4

For: Vocabulary practice
Visit: www.phschool.com
Web Code: jcd-0202

Manos a la obra

Vocabulario y gramática en uso

Objectives

- Discuss the school day
- Ask and tell about likes and dislikes
- Learn to use subject pronouns
- Learn to use verbs that end in *-ar*

Leer/Escribir

Un horario

Read the list of classes offered at a high school in Querétaro, Mexico. This school has a special focus on the arts. Answer the questions about the schedule.

CENTRO DE EDUCACIÓN ARTÍSTICA 

"IGNACIO MARIANO DE LAS CASAS"

PRIMER SEMESTRE	
Español	5 h semanales
Matemáticas	5 h semanales
Historia universal	3 h semanales
Educación cívica y ética	3 h semanales
Biología	3 h semanales
Introducción a la física	3 h semanales
Inglés	3 h semanales
Danza	3 h semanales
Teatro	3 h semanales
Artes plásticas	3 h semanales
Música	3 h semanales
	Total 37 h semanales

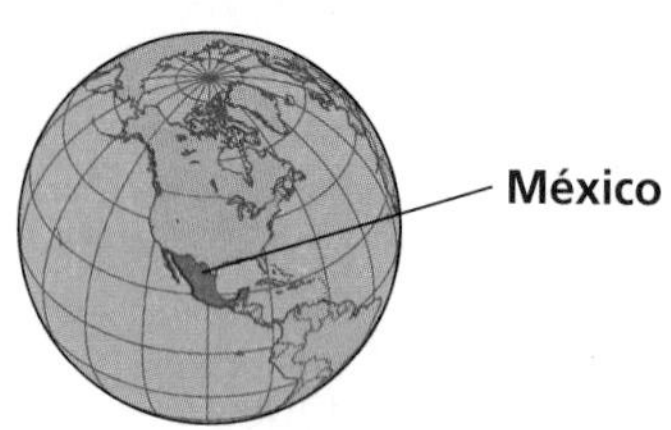

1. ¿Cuántas clases hay cada *(each)* semana?
2. ¿Cuántas horas de inglés hay?
3. ¿Cuántas clases de ciencias sociales hay?
4. ¿Cuántas clases de ciencias naturales hay?
5. Escribe los nombres de las diferentes clases de arte.

Escribir

Mi horario

Write out your class schedule. Copy the chart and provide the information for each class.

Modelo

Hora	Clase	Profesor(a)
la primera hora	la clase de inglés	la Sra. Sánchez

¿Recuerdas?

Use *señor, señora,* and *señorita* when talking **to** adults. Use *el* in front of *señor* and *la* in front of *señora* or *señorita* when talking **about** adults.

Hablar

Mucha tarea

With a partner, ask and tell if you have a lot of homework in each class.

Modelo

A —*¿Tienes mucha tarea en la clase de matemáticas?*
B —*Sí, tengo mucha tarea.*
o: *No, no tengo mucha tarea.*
o: *No estudio matemáticas.*

Estudiante A

Estudiante B

¡Respuesta personal!

Escribir

Me gusta más . . .

Write sentences stating which of the two classes you like better and why. Use the list of adjectives to help with your response. Save your paper for Actividad 8.

aburrida	divertida	interesante
difícil	fácil	práctica

Modelo

inglés/español
Me gusta más la clase de español. Es divertida.
o: *Me gusta más la clase de español. No es aburrida.*
o: *No me gusta ni la clase de español ni la clase de inglés.*

1. inglés / español
2. arte / educación física
3. inglés / matemáticas
4. ciencias sociales / ciencias naturales
5. tecnología / música
6. matemáticas / ciencias sociales

Hablar

¿Qué te gusta más?

With a partner, ask and tell which classes from Actividad 7 you like best and why.

Modelo

A —*¿Te gusta más la clase de inglés o la clase de español?*
B —*A ver . . . Para mí, la clase de español es más divertida que la clase de inglés.*

Escribir/Hablar

Y tú, ¿qué dices?

1. ¿Qué clase te gusta más?
2. ¿Cómo es la clase?
3. ¿En qué hora tienes la clase?
4. ¿Quién enseña la clase?
5. ¿Tienes mucha tarea en la clase?

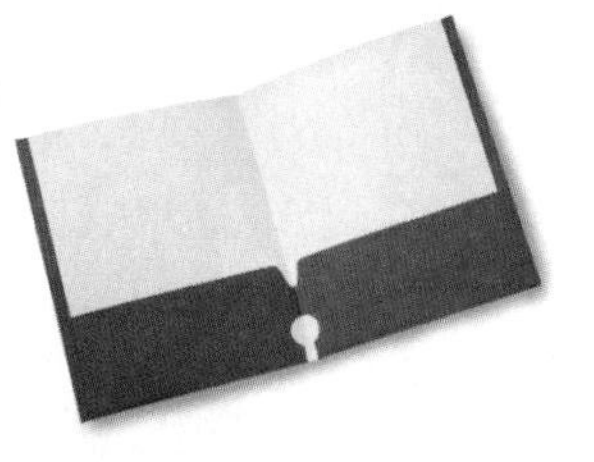

Fondo cultural

Studying English While you're in Spanish class at your school, large numbers of Spanish-speaking students are studying to learn the most popular foreign language worldwide: English. Many children begin to study English in grade school and continue through high school. They often attend special language school for additional English classes. When visiting a Spanish-speaking country, you might easily find someone who is eager to practice his or her English skills with you in exchange for helping you improve your Spanish.

- Why do you think English is so popular in other countries? Are you studying Spanish for similar reasons?

Estudiantes mexicanos en una clase de inglés

Exploración del lenguaje

Connections between Latin, English, and Spanish

Many words in English and Spanish are based on Latin. Seeing the relationship between these words will help expand your English or Spanish vocabulary. Look at the list of Latin root forms for the numbers 1 to 10.

Try it out! For each Roman numeral listed, choose one of the root forms (if more than one is listed) and write down a Spanish or English word you know that is based on that root.

Try it out! The Roman year used to begin with the month of March. Knowing that, can you explain why *septiembre, octubre, noviembre,* and *diciembre* use the Latin root forms for seven, eight, nine, and ten?

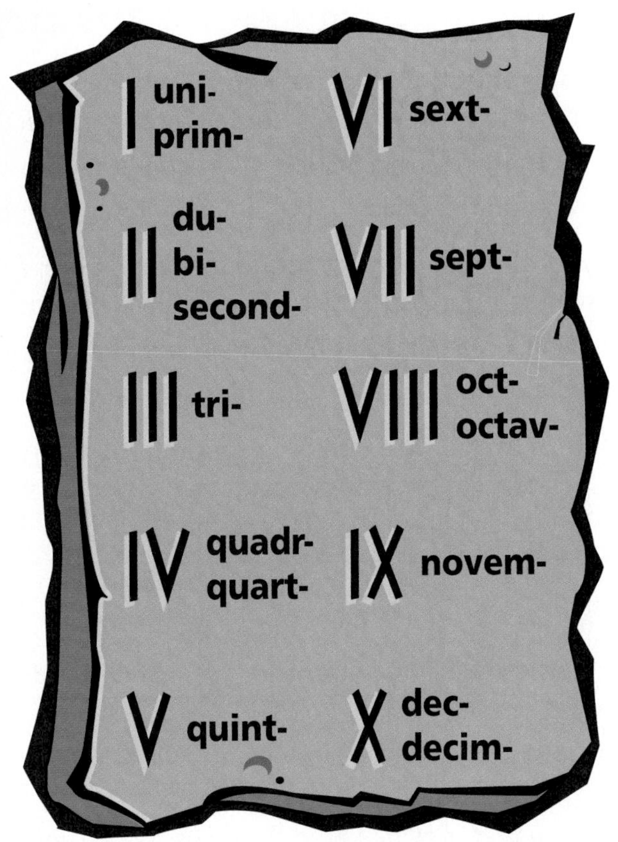

Fondo cultural

Many Spanish words are derived from Latin because Spain was once part of the Roman Empire. Rome occupied most of Spain from about 209 B.C. to 586 A.D. During that time, massive public structures, including aqueducts and theaters, were built. Some of these, such as the aqueduct that towers over the modern city of Segovia, are still standing. The Latin name for Spain was *Hispania.*

- Can you see the similarity between *Hispania* and the country's name in Spanish, *España?*

El acueducto de Segovia

Gramática

Subject pronouns

The subject of a sentence tells who is doing the action. You often use people's names as the subject:

Gregorio escucha música.	***Gregory*** *listens to music.*
Ana canta y baila.	***Ana*** *sings and dances.*

You also use subject pronouns *(I, you, he, she, we, they)* to tell who is doing an action. The subject pronouns replace people's names:

Él escucha música.	***He*** *listens to music.*
Ella canta y baila.	***She*** *sings and dances.*

Here are all the subject pronouns in Spanish:

yo	I	nosotros nosotras	we *(masc., masc./fem.)* we *(fem.)*
tú	you *(familiar)*	vosotros vosotras	you *(masc., masc./fem.)* you *(fem.)*
usted (Ud.)	you *(formal)*	ustedes (Uds.)	you *(formal)*
él ella	he she	ellos ellas	they *(masc., masc./fem.)* they *(fem.)*

Tú, usted, ustedes, and *vosotros(as)* all mean "you."

- Use *tú* with family, friends, people your age or younger, and anyone you call by his or her first name.
- Use *usted* with adults you address with a title, such as *señor, señora, profesor(a),* etc. *Usted* is usually written as *Ud.*
- In Latin America, use *ustedes* when speaking to two or more people, regardless of age. *Ustedes* is usually written as *Uds.*
- In Spain, use *vosotros(as)* when speaking to two or more people you call *tú* individually: *tú* + *tú* = *vosotros(as).* Use *ustedes* when talking to two or more people you call *usted* individually.

If a group is made up of males only or of both males and females together, use the masculine forms: *nosotr**os**, vosotr**os**, ell**os**.*

If a group is all females, use the feminine forms: *nosotr**as**, vosotr**as**, ell**as**.*

You can combine a subject pronoun and a name to form a subject.

Alejandro y yo = **nosotros**	Pepe y tú = **ustedes**
Carlos y ella = **ellos**	Lola y ella = **ellas**

GramActiva VIDEO

Want more help with subject pronouns? Watch the **GramActiva** video.

Actividad 10 Gramática **Escuchar/Hablar/GramActiva**

¡Señala!

Your teacher will name several subject pronouns. Point to people in the classroom who represent the pronoun you hear. After you have practiced with your teacher, practice with a partner.

Actividad 11 Gramática **Escribir**

¿Es ella?

What subject pronouns would you use to talk about these people?

Modelo

Gloria
Ella.

1. Carlos
2. Felipe y yo
3. María y Sarita
4. Pablo, Tomás y Anita
5. el señor Treviño
6. tú y Esteban

Actividad 12 Gramática **Hablar**

¿Tú, Ud. o Uds.?

Tell whether you would use *tú, Ud.,* or *Uds.* with these people.

1. 

2. 

3. 

4. 

5.

6. 

7. 

8. 

Más práctica

Practice Workbook 2A-5

Go Online PHSchool.com

For: Practice with subject pronouns
Visit: www.phschool.com
Web Code: jcd-0203

Gramática

Present tense of *-ar* verbs

You already know that the infinitive forms of Spanish verbs always end in *-ar*, *-er*, or *-ir*.

The largest group of verbs end in *-ar*. *Hablar* is one of these *-ar* verbs.

You will want to use verbs in ways other than in the infinitive form. To do this, you will drop the *-ar* ending and make changes.

To create the forms of most *-ar* verbs, you first drop the *-ar* from the infinitive, leaving the stem:

hablar → habl-

Then you add the verb endings *-o, -as, -a, -amos, -áis,* or *-an* to the stem.

Here are the forms of *hablar:*

(yo)	habl**o**	(nosotros) (nosotras)	habl**amos**
(tú)	habl**as**	(vosotros) (vosotras)	habl**áis**
Ud. (él) (ella)	habl**a**	Uds. (ellos) (ellas)	habl**an**

In Spanish, the present tense form of a verb can be translated into English in two ways:

Hablo español. — *I speak* Spanish.
I am speaking Spanish.

¿Recuerdas?

You already know many *-ar* verbs, such as *cantar* and *bailar.*

The verb endings always indicate who is doing the action. In this case, they tell *who* is speaking. Because of this, you can often use the verb without a subject:

Hablo inglés. ¿**Hablas** español?

Subject pronouns are often used for emphasis or clarification.

Ella habla inglés pero **él** habla español.

GramActiva VIDEO

Want more help with verbs that end in *-ar?* Watch the **GramActiva** video.

Gramática **Escuchar/Pensar/GramActiva**

¿Una mano o dos?

You will hear eight *-ar* verbs. If the ending tells you one person is performing the action, raise one hand. If the ending tells you more than one person is doing something, raise both hands.

Strategy

Listening for information
Always listen carefully for the endings on verbs to know who is doing the action.

Gramática **Escribir/Hablar**

¿Qué estudian?

Look at the pictures and tell what these people are studying.

Modelo

Tomás
Tomás estudia música.

1. Laura

2. Josefina, Elena y yo

3. tú

4. Catalina y José

5. Joaquín y tú

6. yo

Gramática  **Escuchar/Hablar/GramActiva**

Juego

1. Work with a partner and tear a sheet of paper into eight pieces of equal size. Write a different subject pronoun on each piece *(yo, tú, él, ella, Ud., nosotros, ellas, Uds.)*. Place the subject pronouns face down in a pile.
2. Your teacher will say an infinitive. One partner will select the top piece of paper from the pile, read the subject pronoun, and say the correct verb form. A correct answer earns one point. Place the "used" subject pronouns in a separate pile. Take turns selecting from the pile and answering.
3. When your teacher calls time, shuffle the pieces of paper with subject pronouns and place them in a new pile face down. When the next verb is read aloud, continue play. The partner with the most correct answers is the winner.

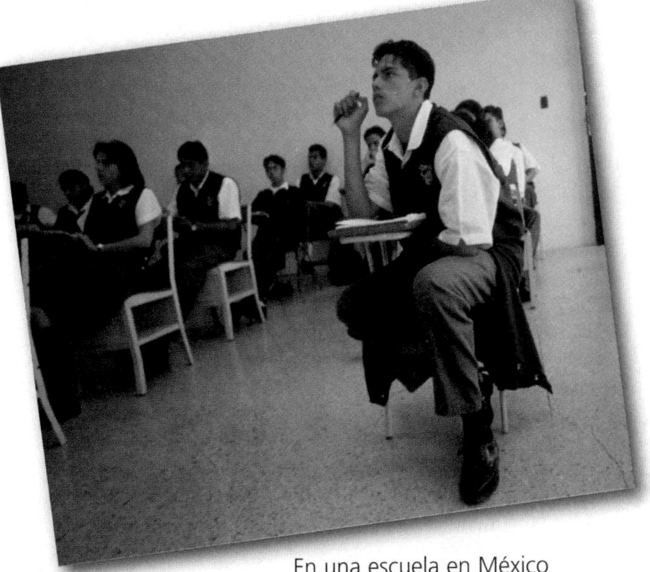

En una escuela en México

Más práctica

Practice Workbook 2A-6, 2A-7

For: Practice with *-ar* verbs
Visit: www.phschool.com
Web Code: jcd-0204

Escribir

En la escuela

Use the verbs in the list to complete the sentences about what different activities take place during school.

Modelo

Yo estudio mucho en la clase de español.

necesitar	hablar	dibujar
usar	practicar	enseñar
patinar	bailar	

1. Lupe y Guillermo ___ mucho en la clase de arte.
2. Tú ___ la computadora en la clase de tecnología.
3. Yo ___ una calculadora y una carpeta para la clase de matemáticas.
4. Tomás y yo ___ deportes en la clase de educación física.
5. ¿Quién ___ la clase de ciencias naturales?
6. Marta ___ mucho en la clase de español.

Escuchar/Escribir

Escucha y escribe

Listen to a student describe this picture of himself and other students during their *recreo.* Write what you hear.

El recreo

Fondo cultural

El recreo In Spanish-speaking countries, students usually have *el recreo* (recess or break) in the school *patio.* Students take time to relax and spend time with friends, eat a snack, or participate in activities such as a quick game of basketball, soccer, or volleyball.

- How is this similar to your school? How is it different?

Escribir/Hablar

Actividades y más actividades

1. Work with a partner. Copy the Venn diagram on a sheet of paper. Label the oval on the left *Yo.* Label the oval on the right with the name of your partner. Label the overlapping area *Nosotros* or *Nosotras.*

Modelo

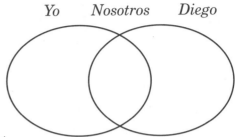

Yo *Nosotros* *Diego*

2. From the list below, choose five activities you do a lot. Write your activities in the oval labeled *Yo.* Be sure to conjugate the verb in the *yo* form.

montar en bicicleta	pasar tiempo con amigos	trabajar
hablar por teléfono	practicar deportes	cantar
escuchar música	hablar español	bailar
dibujar	nadar	
estudiar	usar la computadora	

3. Interview your partner. Ask questions to find out the five activities your partner wrote in his or her diagram. When you find out an activity, write it in the right oval of your diagram. Be sure to conjugate the verb in the *él / ella* form. Save your diagram for Actividad 19.

Modelo

A —*¿Dibujas mucho?*
B —*A ver . . . No, no dibujo mucho.*
A —*Pues, ¿trabajas mucho?*
B —*Sí, trabajo mucho.*

¿Recuerdas?

When you answer in the negative, you often use *no* twice. The first *no* answers the question. The second *no* goes before the verb and means "not."

Escribir

Nosotros(as) . . .

Compare the two sides of your diagram. Write the activities you and your partner both do in the center. Be sure to use the *nosotros(as)* form. Then use your completed diagram from Actividad 18 to write about what you and/or your partner do. Write at least five complete sentences.

Modelo

Diego y yo trabajamos.
Yo dibujo.

  Escribir/Hablar

Y tú, ¿qué dices?

1. En tu escuela, ¿quién enseña la clase de arte? ¿Quién enseña la clase de educación física?
2. En tu escuela, ¿quién canta muy bien *(well)*? ¿Quién dibuja muy bien?
3. ¿Escuchan tus amigos(as) mucha música? ¿Bailan bien tú y tus amigos(as)?
4. ¿Qué estudias en la primera hora?
5. ¿Qué clase tienes en la tercera hora?

Una estudiante en la clase de español

 Leer/Pensar

Los números maya

Long before the Spaniards set foot in the Americas, many different civilizations already existed here. One of these, the Maya, lived in southern Mexico and Central America, where their decendants still make their home. One of the accomplishments of the ancient Maya was the development of a system of mathematics.

Conexiones | Las matemáticas

The Maya used three symbols to write numbers: a dot •, a bar —, and a drawing of a shell. The dot equals 1, the bar equals 5, and the shell equals 0. Mayan numbers were written from bottom to top, not from left to right. Look at the Mayan numbers below.

0 1 2 3 4

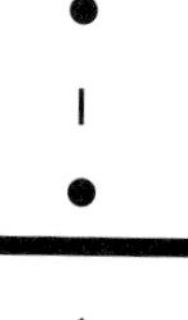 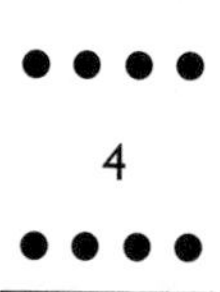

5 6 7 8 9

What would these Mayan numbers be in our numbering system?

1.  2.  3.

Now write these numbers in the Mayan system.

4. 13 5. 16 6. 19

Are you familiar with any other numbering systems that remind you of the Mayan system?

Pronunciación

The letter *c*

In Spanish the pronunciation of the letter *c* depends on the letter that follows it.

When the letter *c* comes before *a, o, u,* or another consonant, it is pronounced like the *c* in "cat." Listen to and say these words:

computadora	**ca**ntar	es**cu**ela
tampo**co**	**có**mo	to**ca**r
correr	practi**ca**r	**Ca**rlos

When the letter *c* comes before *e* or *i,* most Spanish speakers pronounce it like the *s* in "Sally." Listen to and say these words:

ve**ce**s	so**ci**able	gra**ci**oso	gra**ci**as
ha**ce**r	on**ce**	do**ce**	tre**ce**

Try it out! Listen to this rhyme. Listen particularly for the sound of the letter *c.* Then repeat the rhyme.

0 + 4 = 4

4 + 0 = 4

Cero más cuatro,
o cuatro más cero,
siempre° son cuatro. *always*
¿No es verdadero°? *true*

Say the rhyme again, first replacing *cuatro* with *doce,* then replacing *cuatro* with *trece.* Then say the rhyme quickly several times.

El español en la comunidad

Do you know about opportunities to learn Spanish in your community outside of your school? Do some research using the Internet, college brochures, and the Yellow Pages about Spanish classes or private lessons offered in your community. Make a list of your findings. Why do you think people in your community want to study Spanish?

Hay clases de español en las universidades de Texas.

¡Adelante!

Lectura

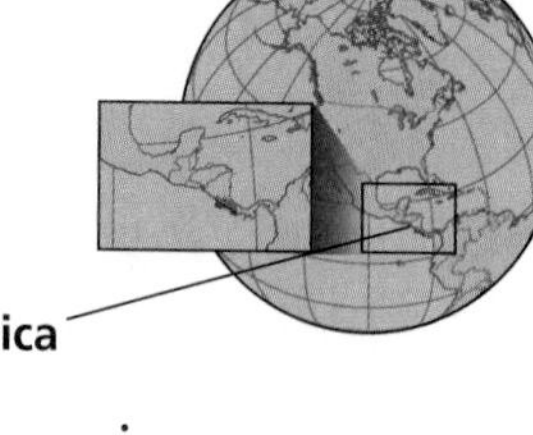

Consider what an immersion experience in Spanish would be like for you as you read this brochure from a Spanish language school in Costa Rica.

Objectives

- Read a brochure about a school in Costa Rica
- Learn soccer fan chants
- Talk about some of your classes
- Learn facts about Mexico

Strategy

Using photos
Look at the photos to help you understand the contents of a brochure or advertisement.

La Escuela Español Vivo

¡Una experiencia fabulosa en Costa Rica!
¡Estudia español con nosotros en la Escuela Español Vivo!

Es verano, el mes de junio. Eres estudiante en Santa Ana, un pueblo en las montañas de Costa Rica.

¿Y cómo es una clase? Hay cinco estudiantes en tu clase. Uds. escuchan, hablan y practican el español todo el día. También usan la computadora.

En la escuela hay estudiantes de muchos países: Estados Unidos, Inglaterra, Francia, Brasil, Canadá, Japón, India, Sudáfrica y otros. ¡Todos estudian español!

Los sábados y los domingos hay actividades muy interesantes: visitar un volcán o un parque nacional, nadar en el océano Pacífico . . . ¡y más!

sábados/domingos
- visitar un volcán
- visitar un parque nacional
- nadar en el océano Pacífico

El horario de clases en la escuela es:

hora	lunes a viernes
08:00–10:30	Clases de español
10:30–11:00	Recreo
11:00–13:00	Clases de español
13:00–14:00	Almuerzo
14:00–15:30	Conversaciones
15:30–16:30	Clase de música y baile

¿Por qué la Escuela Español Vivo?

- **La naturaleza de Costa Rica en el pueblo de Santa Ana**
- **Amigos de muchos países**
- **Mucha práctica y conversación en español**
- **Clases de música y baile**
- **Excursiones los sábados y domingos**

¿Comprendes?

1. When does the program take place?
2. Describe what a class is like.
3. What activities are offered on the weekends?
4. How many hours are spent on learning and using Spanish each week?
5. Would you like to study Spanish in Costa Rica? Why or why not?

For: Internet link activity
Visit: www.phschool.com
Web Code: jcd-0205

La hora in Spanish-speaking countries is usually shown using the 24-hour clock on official schedules and timetables. Times in the morning are shown as 00:00 (midnight) through 11:59 (11:59 A.M.), 1:00 P.M. is shown as 13:00, 2:00 P.M. is 14:00, and so on.

- Look at the times in the *horario* from the train station. At what time does the train from Alicante arrive?

Próximas LLegadas
Regionales y L. Recorrido
H.Prev. Procedencia Vía
13:46 TOLEDO
13:49 CARTAGENA
14:15 SANTANDER 5
15:20 ALICANTE 5
15:30 BARCELONA 5
15:46 TOLEDO 4

En una estación de trenes de Madrid

La cultura en vivo

Aficionados al fútbol

El fútbol (soccer) is the favorite sport in most Spanish-speaking countries. In fact, it is the most popular sport in the entire world. It has grown in popularity in the United States over the past years. As with other sports you are familiar with, *fútbol* has loyal fans, cheers, team songs, and sometimes cheerleaders. If you attended a game in Venezuela at the Escuela Secundaria Bolívar you might hear the following chant:

Jugando al fútbol en la Ciudad Universitaria, Madrid, España

Chiquitibúm a la bim bom bam
A la bío
A la bao
A la bim bom bam
¡Bolívar! ¡Bolívar!
¡Ra, ra, ra!

Except for the school name, the words of this chant do not have any meaning.

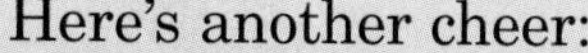

Here's another cheer:

¡Se ve! ¡Se siente!	**You see it, you feel it!**
¡Bolívar está presente!	**Bolívar is here!**
¡Que sí, que no!	**Oh, yes, oh, no!**
¡Bolívar ya ganó!	**Bolívar has already won!**
¡A la bío, a la bao!	**¡A la bío! ¡A la bao!**
¡El otro está cansao!	**The other team is tired!**

Try it out! In groups of five, select one of the chants and use it for a model to create a chant for one of your school teams. Present it to the class.

Think about it! How are these cheers and fan enthusiasm similar to or different from the cheers at your school?

Aficionados al fútbol

Presentación oral

Mis clases

Task

Imagine that a student from Costa Rica has just arrived at your school. Tell the student about some of your classes.

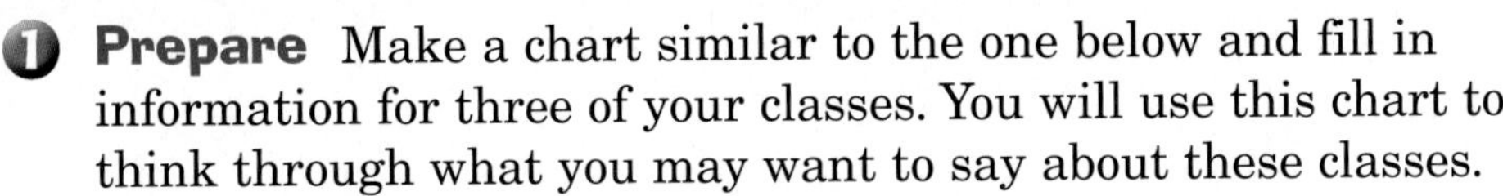

1 Prepare Make a chart similar to the one below and fill in information for three of your classes. You will use this chart to think through what you may want to say about these classes.

Hora	Clase	Comentarios	Profesor(a)
primera	la clase de español	me gusta hablar español	la Sra. Salinas
cuarta	la clase de arte	difícil	el Sr. Highsmith
octava	la clase de ciencias naturales	divertida	la Srta. Huerta

Strategy

Using graphic organizers
Simple charts can help you organize your thoughts for a presentation.

2 Practice Go through your presentation several times. You can use your notes in practice, but your teacher may not want you to use them when you present. Try to:

- mention the information about your classes and your teachers
- use complete sentences
- speak clearly

Modelo

En la primera hora tengo la clase de español. Me gusta hablar español. La clase es muy divertida. La Sra. Salinas es la profesora.

3 Present Describe the three classes you selected.

4 Evaluation Your teacher may give you a rubric for how your presentation will be graded. You probably will be graded on:

- how complete your preparation is
- how much information you communicate
- how easy it is to understand you

El mundo hispano

México

With a population of more than 100 million people, Mexico is the most populous Spanish-speaking country. It has been shaped by ancient indigenous civilizations, European colonialism, and immigration, as well as by its proximity to the United States.

The Mayan city of Tulum, situated on a cliff overlooking the Caribbean, was a major port from about 1200 until the Spaniards arrived in the early 1500s. The Mayan civilization dates from 750 B.C., and includes ancient cities throughout southern Mexico, including the Yucatan Peninsula, and parts of Central America. Today many people in these areas speak one of approximately 30 languages and dialects that developed from ancient Maya.

¿Sabes que . . . ?

The butterfly reserve at El Rosario, Michoacán, lies in the mountains not far from Mexico City. From November through February every year, millions of monarch butterflies migrate to this area from the north, covering the branches of the area's tall pine trees.

Para pensar

These two pages show a brief overview of Mexico. If you were asked to create a similar overview of the United States, what would you highlight? Select five photographs and write a brief caption for each one. Share your results with a small group or the whole class.

For: Online Atlas
Visit: www.phschool.com
Web Code: jce-0002

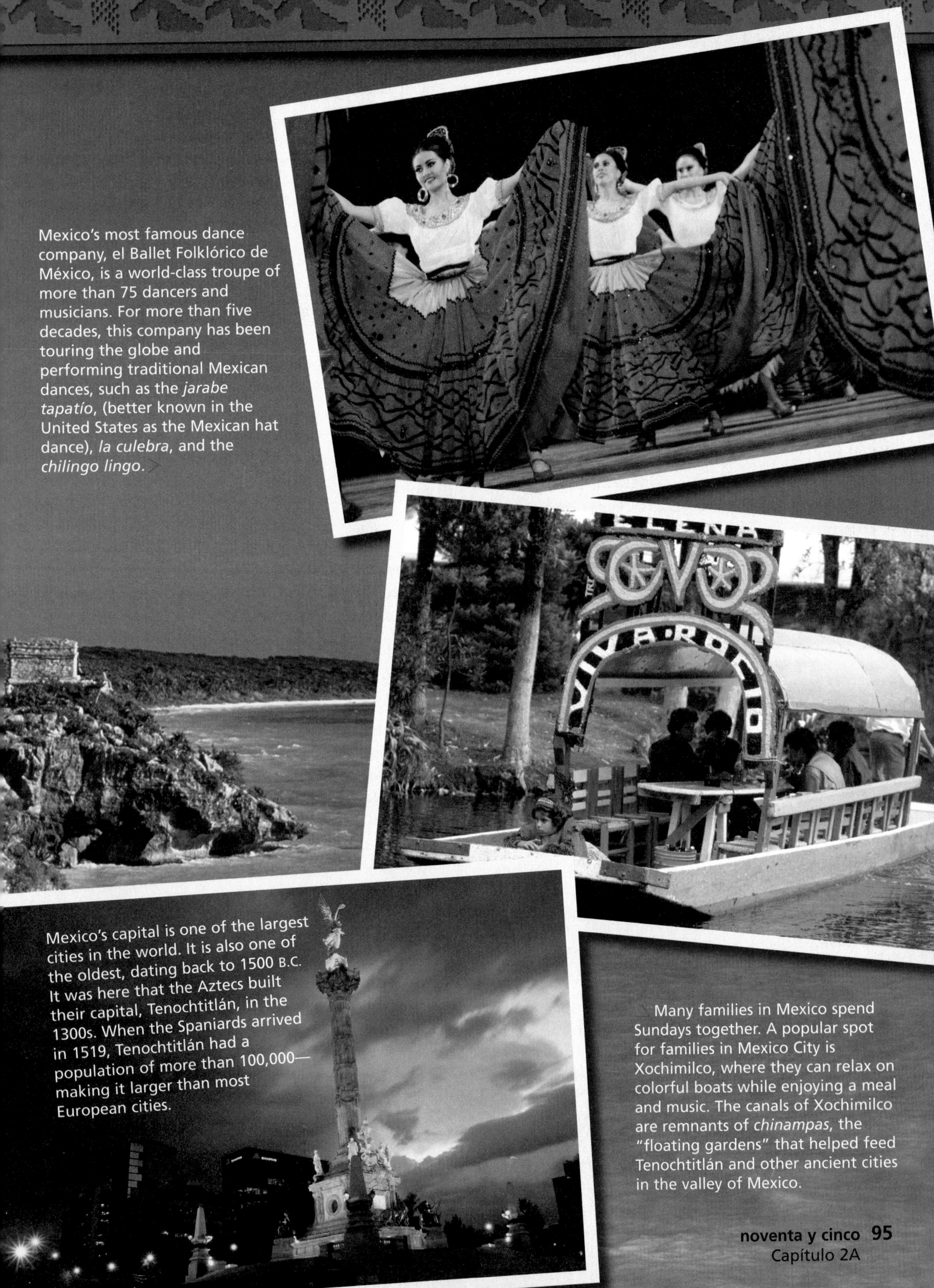

Mexico's most famous dance company, el Ballet Folklórico de México, is a world-class troupe of more than 75 dancers and musicians. For more than five decades, this company has been touring the globe and performing traditional Mexican dances, such as the *jarabe tapatío*, (better known in the United States as the Mexican hat dance), *la culebra*, and the *chilingo lingo*.

Mexico's capital is one of the largest cities in the world. It is also one of the oldest, dating back to 1500 B.C. It was here that the Aztecs built their capital, Tenochtitlán, in the 1300s. When the Spaniards arrived in 1519, Tenochtitlán had a population of more than 100,000—making it larger than most European cities.

Many families in Mexico spend Sundays together. A popular spot for families in Mexico City is Xochimilco, where they can relax on colorful boats while enjoying a meal and music. The canals of Xochimilco are remnants of *chinampas*, the "floating gardens" that helped feed Tenochtitlán and other ancient cities in the valley of Mexico.

Repaso del capítulo

Chapter Review

Vocabulario y gramática

To prepare for the test, check to see if you . . .
- know the new vocabulary and grammar
- can perform the tasks on p. 97

to talk about your school day

el almuerzo	lunch
la clase	class
la clase de . . .	. . . class
arte	art
español	Spanish
ciencias naturales	science
ciencias sociales	social studies
educación física	physical education
inglés	English
matemáticas	mathematics
tecnología	technology/computers
el horario	schedule
en la . . . hora	in the . . . hour (class period)
la tarea	homework

to describe school activities

enseñar	to teach
estudiar	to study
hablar	to talk

to talk about the order of things

primero[*], **-a**	first
segundo, -a	second
tercero[*], **-a**	third
cuarto, -a	fourth
quinto, -a	fifth
sexto, -a	sixth
séptimo, -a	seventh
octavo, -a	eighth
noveno, -a	ninth
décimo, -a	tenth

[*]Changes to *primer, tercer* before a masculine singular noun.

For *Vocabulario adicional,* see pp. 472–473.

to talk about things you need for school

la calculadora	calculator
la carpeta de argollas	three-ring binder
el diccionario	dictionary
necesito	I need
necesitas	you need

to describe your classes

aburrido, -a	boring
difícil	difficult
divertido, -a	amusing, fun
fácil	easy
favorito, -a	favorite
interesante	interesting
práctico, -a	practical
más . . . que	more . . . than

other useful words

a ver . . .	Let's see
¿Quién?	Who?
para	for
mucho	a lot
(yo) tengo	I have
(tú) tienes	you have

subject pronouns

yo	I	**nosotros** **nosotras**	we *(masc., masc./fem.)* we *(fem.)*
tú **usted (Ud.)**	you *(fam.)* you *(form.)*	**vosotros** **vosotras** **ustedes (Uds.)**	you *(masc., masc./fem.)* you *(fem.)* you *(form.)*
él **ella**	he she	**ellos** **ellas**	they *(masc., masc./fem.)* they *(fem.)*

hablar *to talk*

hablo	**hablamos**
hablas	**habláis**
habla	**hablan**

Más práctica

Practice Workbook Puzzle 2A-8
Practice Workbook Organizer 2A-9

Go Online PHSchool.com
For: Test preparation
Visit: www.phschool.com
Web Code: jcd-0206

Preparación para el examen

	On the exam you will be asked to . . .	Here are practice tasks similar to those you will find on the exam . . .	If you need review . . .
	**1 Escuchar** Listen and understand as people talk about their new schedules and what they think of their classes	Listen to two students who have just attended some of the classes on their new schedules. a) Which class does each one like? Why? b) Which class does each one dislike? Why?	**pp. 74–77** *A primera vista* **p. 75** Actividades 1–2 **p. 79** Actividad 7 **p. 80** Actividades 8–9
	**2 Hablar** Talk about activities you and your friends have in common	To get to know you, your homeroom advisor asks you to talk or write about what you and your friends have in common, such as school subjects that you all study and music or activities that you all like. For example, *cantamos.* You might also tell how you and your friends are different. For example, *Yo toco la guitarra y ellos practican deportes.*	**p. 80** Actividad 8 **p. 86** Actividad 16 **p. 87** Actividades 18–19 **p. 93** *Presentación oral*
	**3 Leer** Read and understand someone's e-mail description of his or her classes	Read this e-mail that your friend received from his e-pal. What does the e-pal study in school? What does he think of his classes? Do you agree or disagree? Why? ¿Cómo son mis clases? A ver . . . Yo tengo ocho clases. Estudio ciencias naturales, inglés, español, educación física, geografía, matemáticas, tecnología y ciencias sociales. ¡Me gusta más la clase de inglés! Necesito hablar inglés aquí en Ecuador, pero es MUY difícil. Mi clase de geografía es muy aburrida y mi clase de educación física es muy divertida. Y, ¿cómo son tus clases?	**pp. 74–77** *A primera vista* **p. 78** Actividad 4 **p. 90–91** *Lectura*
	**4 Escribir** Write your schedule including hour, class, and teacher's name, and give opinions about the classes	Write a note to a counselor listing reasons why you want to drop two of the classes on your schedule. What might be some reasons for wanting to change classes? You might say that your first hour class is boring and that your second hour class is difficult for you.	**p. 78** Actividad 5 **p. 79** Actividades 6–7 **p. 93** *Presentación oral*
	5 Pensar Demonstrate an understanding of cultural practices concerning sports	Think about the sports at your school that attract the most fans to their games or competitions. Are these the same sports that are most popular in Spanish-speaking countries? How do spectators show their enthusiasm? How is this similar to or different from the United States?	**p. 92** *La cultura en vivo*

Fondo cultural

Sor Juana Inés de la Cruz (1648–1695), born near Mexico City, was one of the greatest intellectuals of her time. She wrote poetry, essays, music, and plays. Sor Juana also defended a woman's right to an education at a time when few women had access to it. She entered a convent at the age of 19 and over the years built a library of several thousand books. Sor Juana's living quarters in the convent became a meeting place for other writers and intellectuals, who were drawn to her because of her intelligence and knowledge.

- How are various aspects of Sor Juana's life represented in this painting? If you were to pose for a portrait, what objects would you include that represent you and your interests?

Sor Juana Inés de la Cruz, arte mexicano del siglo xvii
Institut Amatller d'Art Hispànic-Arxiu Mas.

Capítulo 2B

Tu sala de clases

Chapter Objectives

- Describe a classroom
- Indicate where things are located
- Talk about more than one object or person
- Understand cultural perspectives on school

Video Highlights

A primera vista: ***Un ratón en la clase***

GramActiva Videos: **the verb *estar;* plurals of nouns and articles**

Country Connection

As you learn how to describe your classroom, you will make connections to these countries and places:

For: Online Atlas
Visit: www.phschool.com
Web Code: jce-0002

udiantes mexicanos

A primera vista

Vocabulario y gramática en contexto

Objectives

Read, listen to, and understand information about
- the classroom
- where objects are located

“¡Hola! Me llamo Enrique. **Aquí está mi** sala de clases. Son las nueve y **los** estudiantes **están en** la clase de español. **Hay** muchos estudiantes en mi clase. ¿Cuántos estudiantes hay en **tu** clase?”

—Elena, ¿es tu disquete?

—No, es el disquete **de** David.

El cuaderno está **debajo de la** calculadora.
La calculadora está **encima del** cuaderno.
Los bolígrafos están **al lado del** diccionario.
La bandera está **detrás de la** computadora.
La silla está **delante de la** mesa.

Actividad 1 Escuchar

¿Qué hay en la sala de clases?

Look at Enrique's classroom. You will be asked if certain things are there. If you see the item mentioned, raise your hand and give a "thumbs-up" sign. If you don't see it, give a "thumbs-down" sign.

Actividad 2 Escuchar

En la sala de clases

Look at the picture of Enrique's classroom again. Listen to where various items are located. If the description is correct, raise one hand, but if the description is not correct, raise both hands.

Más práctica

Practice Workbook 2B-1, 2B-2

For: Vocabulary practice
Visit: www.phschool.com
Web Code: jcd-0211

Videohistoria

Un ratón en la clase

¿Qué pasa en la clase de ciencias sociales? Lee la historia.

Strategy

Predicting the outcome
Look at the pictures before you read to help you predict what will happen.

- Will Manolo get away with his prank?

1 **Claudia:** **¿Qué es esto?**

Teresa: Es mi hámster. Es para la clase de ciencias naturales.

Claudia: ¿Cómo se llama?

Teresa: Paquito.

5 **Claudia:** ¡Está **allí,** delante de la mesa!

Teresa: ¡Ay, mi Paquito!

Manolo: Pues, ahora está detrás de la computadora, encima de los disquetes.

Teresa: ¡Manolo! Es el ratón de la computadora. No es mi Paquito.

6 *El director de la escuela, el Sr. Treviño, entra en la clase.*

Carlos: ¡Ay! ¡Aquí está! Está en mi **mochila.**

Sr. Treviño: ¡Silencio, por favor!

7 **Sr. Treviño:** Teresa, hablamos en mi oficina.

Teresa: Sí, señor.

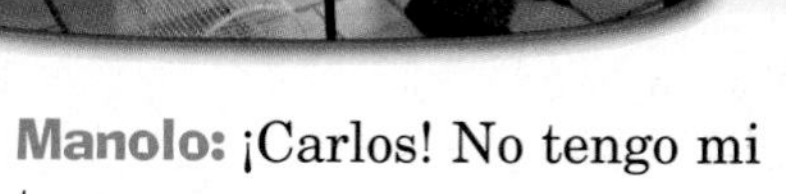

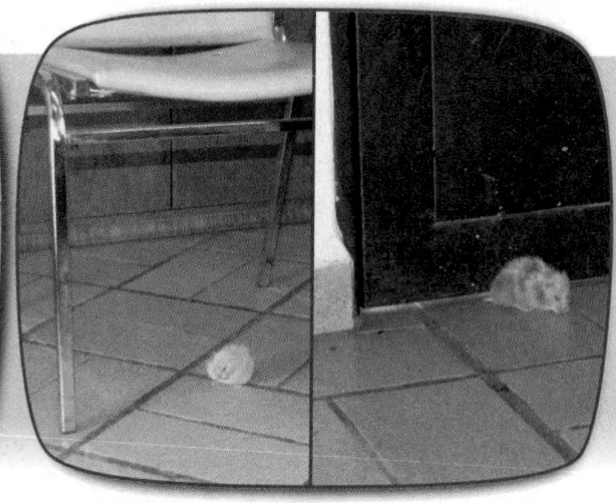

2 **Manolo:** ¡Carlos! No tengo mi tarea.

Carlos: ¿Qué?

Manolo: Tengo una idea . . .

3 **Carlos:** ¡Un ratón! Profesora, ¡hay un ratón debajo del escritorio!

Profesora: ¿Un ratón en la clase de ciencias sociales? **¿Dónde** está? ¿Dónde?

4 **Estudiante:** Ahora está debajo de la silla.

Manolo: Y ahora está al lado de la puerta. **Es un** ratón muy impaciente.

Teresa: ¡No es un ratón! Es mi hámster, y se llama Paquito.

8 **Profesora:** Y ahora, Manolo, ¿tu tarea?

Manolo: Pues, profesora . . .

Leer

¿Comprendes?

Answer *cierto* or *falso* to the following statements.

1. El hámster es para la clase de inglés.
2. Manolo no tiene la tarea.
3. Paquito está al lado de la puerta.
4. Paquito está encima de los disquetes.
5. Paquito está detrás de la mochila.
6. El director está muy serio.

Más práctica

Practice Workbook 2B-3, 2B-4

For: Vocabulary practice
Visit: www.phschool.com
Web Code: jcd-0212

Manos a la obra

Vocabulario y gramática en uso

Objectives

- Communicate about a classroom
- Ask and tell how someone feels
- Talk about where someone or something is located
- Learn to use the verb *estar*, the plurals of nouns, and the plurals of articles

Escribir

¿Qué hay?

Write the names of the things you see.

Modelo

Hay una bandera.

1. 
2. 
3. 
4. 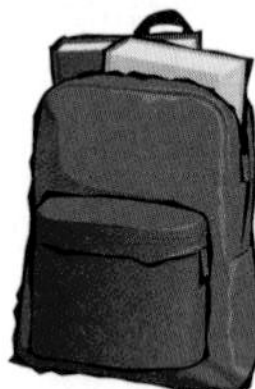
5. 

6. 
7. 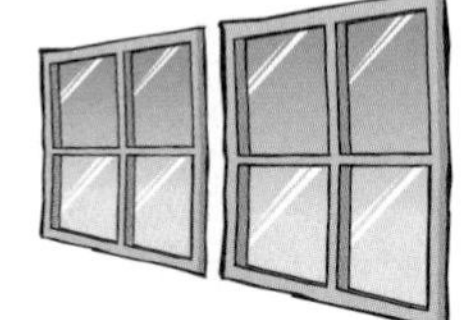
8. 

Pensar/Escribir

¿Es lógico o no?

Write the word that doesn't belong in each group. Then supply a word that logically belongs.

Modelo

el disquete el teclado la pantalla la ventana
La ventana—¡No! La computadora—¡Sí!

1. una mesa una silla una mochila un escritorio
2. la sala de clases al lado de detrás de encima de
3. un diccionario una calculadora un reloj una computadora
4. leer estudiar escribir bailar
5. está habla necesitan trabaja
6. el profesor la chica el estudiante el señor

Haciendo la tarea

  **Hablar**

¿Dónde está?

Take turns with a partner to ask and tell where various items in Beto's bedroom are located.

Modelo

A —*¿Dónde está el escritorio?*
B —*Está debajo de la ventana.*

> **Nota**
>
> When the preposition *de* is followed by the masculine definite article *el*, the contraction *del* must be used.
>
> - La papelera está al lado del escritorio.

Estudiante A

¿Dónde está . . . ?

Estudiante B

al lado de
delante de
debajo de
detrás de
encima de

   **Hablar/Escuchar**

Juego

1. Work with a partner. Your partner will face away from you and have a blank piece of paper and a pen or a pencil.
2. Choose four classroom items and arrange them on your desk, putting objects on top of others, next to each other, and so forth.
3. Your partner will ask you questions about what is on your desk and how the items are positioned. Based on your answers, he or she will try to draw the arrangement on your desk.
4. When your teacher calls time, see how closely the picture matches the actual arrangement. Then switch roles.

Modelo

A —*¿Tienes un disquete?*
B —*No, no tengo un disquete.*
A —*¿Tienes una calculadora?*
B —*Sí, tengo una calculadora.*
A —*¿Dónde está?*
B —*Está encima de la carpeta.*

> **Para decir más . . .**
>
> **a la izquierda de** to the left of
> **a la derecha de** to the right of

Exploración del lenguaje

Language through gestures

In Spanish, just as in English, nonverbal body language in the form of gestures, or *gestos,* is very important to communication.

You saw the expression *¡Ojo!* in the video *Un ratón en la clase*. The word literally means "eye," but it is used to mean "be careful" or "pay attention." It is usually accompanied by a gesture, and often people use the *¡Ojo!* gesture without saying the word.

Estudiantes mexicanas

Fondo cultural

School uniforms Many schools in Spanish-speaking countries require their students to wear uniforms. Often students wear a full uniform, like the ones you see in the photo. Sometimes the uniform consists of something more like a smock that is worn over a student's regular clothes and helps protect them from becoming dirty or torn during the school day.

- How are these uniforms similar to or different from those worn by high school students in the United States?

Escribir/Hablar

Y tú, ¿qué dices?

Describe your classroom.

1. ¿Dónde está la puerta?
2. ¿Qué está al lado de la puerta?
3. ¿Hay ventanas en la clase? ¿Cuántas?
4. ¿Hay un reloj en la clase? ¿Dónde está?
5. ¿Cuántos escritorios y sillas hay?
6. ¿Qué más *(What else)* hay?

Gramática

The verb *estar*

The *-ar* verbs you have used until now are called **regular verbs** because they follow a regular pattern. Verbs that do not follow a regular pattern are called **irregular verbs.**

Estar is irregular because the *yo* form doesn't follow a regular pattern and because the forms *estás, está,* and *están* require accent marks.

Use *estar* to tell how someone feels or where someone or something is located.

(yo)	**estoy**	(nosotros) (nosotras)	**estamos**
(tú)	**estás**	(vosotros) (vosotras)	**estáis**
Ud. (él) (ella)	**está**	Uds. (ellos) (ellas)	**están**

¿Recuerdas?

You have used the verb *estar* to ask how someone is.

- ¿Cómo **estás?**
- ¿Cómo **está** Ud.?

GramActiva VIDEO

Want more practice with the verb *estar*? Watch the **GramActiva** video.

Actividad 9 **Gramática** **Escribir**

¡Hola! ¿Cómo estás?

Write the correct forms of *estar* on a separate sheet of paper.

Marcos: ¡Buenos días! ¿Cómo __1.__ Uds.?

Paula y Roberta: ¡Hola, Marcos! Nosotras __2.__ bien, gracias. ¿Y tú?

Marcos: __3.__ muy bien. ¿Dónde __4.__ Pedro y Juana?

Roberta: Pedro __5.__ en la sala de clases. Juana __6.__ en la oficina.

Actividad 10 **Gramática**   **Hablar**

¿En qué clase están?

Take turns with a partner to give the correct forms of *estar* as you tell what class each person is in.

ella

Modelo

Ella está en la clase de tecnología.

1. yo

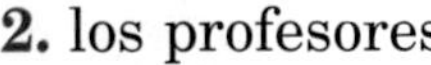

2. los profesores

3. la profesora

4. nosotros

5. ella

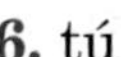

6. tú

Gramática **Escuchar**

¿Cierto o falso?

Write the numbers 1–6 on a sheet of paper. Listen to the statements about Javier's Spanish club photo and write *cierto* or *falso* based on the information provided as you view the photograph from *your* perspective.

Gramática  **Hablar**

¿Y dónde están todos?

Work with a partner. Using the club picture above, find out where the various students are located from *Javier's* perspective. Follow the model.

Modelo

A —*¿Y dónde está Lucita?*
B —*Lucita está encima del escritorio.*

1. Julián y Mateo
2. Rosa
3. Sara
4. yo
5. el Sr. Salas
6. Lucita y José
7. Benito
8. Sara y yo

En la clase de ciencias naturales

Escribir/Hablar

Juego

Work with a partner. Write down the name of someone in the classroom. Your partner can ask only *sí / no* questions to find out the name. When your partner has guessed the mystery student's identity, change roles.

Modelo

A —*¿Es una estudiante?*
B —*Sí.*
A —*¿Está al lado de Tomás?*
B —*No.*
A —*¿Está detrás de mí?*
B —*Sí.*
A —*¿Es Patricia?*
B —*Sí.*

Para decir más . . .

detrás de mí	behind me
detrás de ti	behind you

Leer/Pensar

Conexiones | Las matemáticas

Los precios de mochilas en el mundo hispano

Most countries have their own currencies. In Mexico, people pay for their purchases in *pesos,* in Peru they use *nuevos soles,* and so on. The value of each currency can go up or down daily in relation to other countries' currencies. For example, a dollar might be worth 10 Mexican *pesos* one day and 9.5 *pesos* the following day. Read the prices for *una mochila* in six different countries.

1. How much does a typical *mochila* cost in your community?
2. Convert the prices for *una mochila* into dollars. You can find a currency converter on the Internet.
3. How do these prices compare to those in your community? Why might the same item have different values in different countries?

Más práctica
Practice Workbook 2B-5

For: Practice with *estar*
Visit: www.phschool.com
Web Code: jcd-0214

Gramática

The plurals of nouns and articles

To make nouns plural you usually add *-s* to words ending in a vowel and *-es* to words ending in a consonant.

silla → sillas   teclado → teclados   cartel → carteles

Singular nouns that end in *z* change the *z* to *c* in the plural.

el lápiz → los lápices

The plural definite articles are *los* and *las*. Like *el* and *la*, they both mean "the."

las sillas → *the chairs*

The plural indefinite articles are *unos* and *unas*. They both mean "some" or "a few."

unos carteles → *some posters*

Singular	Plural
el reloj la ventana	los relojes las ventanas
un disquete una mesa	unos disquetes unas mesas

¿Recuerdas?

You have used definite and indefinite articles in the singular:

- **el, la** = the
- **un, una** = a, an

GramActiva VIDEO

Want more help with plurals? Watch the **GramActiva** video.

Actividad 15 Gramática Escribir

Palabras plurales

Write the plural forms of the articles and nouns below.

1. el cuaderno
2. la bandera
3. la papelera
4. el profesor
5. una clase
6. una mochila
7. un escritorio
8. un pupitre

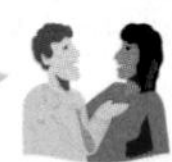

Actividad 16 Hablar/Leer

¡A estudiar!

Marta and Berta are getting ready for school. Read the dialogue with a partner and fill in the blanks with the correct definite articles.

Marta: ¿Dónde están __1.__ lápices?

Berta: Aquí están, en __2.__ mochila.

Marta: ¿Y tienes __3.__ bolígrafos y __4.__ libros?

Berta: No. Están allí, encima de __5.__ mesa, debajo de __6.__ ventanas.

Marta: Ah, sí. ¿Y __7.__ cuadernos y __8.__ carpetas? ¿Dónde están?

Berta: Están encima de __9.__ mesa, detrás de __10.__ computadoras.

Gramática **Escuchar/Hablar**

Más palabras plurales

You will hear eight words. Say the plural form of each word as you hear it.

Modelo

You will hear: *el libro*
You will say: *los libros*

Hablar

Es el cuaderno de . . .

Work in groups of four. Each of you should choose a classroom object you have brought to class. Show your group what you have chosen. Your teacher will collect all the items, then place them in view in different parts of the classroom. Ask your group where your object is. Take turns until all members of your group have asked their question.

Modelo

A —*¿Dónde está mi calculadora?*
B —*Tu calculadora está debajo de la silla de Margarita.*

Nota

In Spanish, you express possession by using *de* and the name of the owner of the item.

- el escritorio **de** la profesora
  the teacher's desk

El español en el mundo del trabajo

School districts in the United States have many positions in which employees need to speak Spanish. For example, school counselors work with new students and parents from Spanish-speaking countries. Counselors help them set up schedules, talk about school policies, and answer questions. Both the parents and the new students feel much more comfortable when the counselor can communicate with them in Spanish.

- Does your district need employees who speak Spanish? In what other jobs within a school system would speaking Spanish be helpful?

Hablar/Escribir

Una clase de inglés

Look at this picture of a high school English class in Spain.

1. Study the photograph and make a list in Spanish of items you can name.
2. Write two questions about the photograph, then ask your partner the questions. Use the models below.

Modelo

A —*¿Cuántos estudiantes hay en la clase?*
B —*Hay diez estudiantes.*
A —*¿Hay banderas en la clase?*
B —*No, no hay banderas.*

¿Qué es esto?	¿Quién está . . . ?
¿Cuántos(as) . . . hay?	¿Hay . . . ?
¿Dónde está(n) . . . ?	¿Qué hay?

Escribir

Y tú, ¿qué dices?

Look around your classroom and write five sentences about it.

Modelo

En mi clase de español hay 33 estudiantes. Hay 35 pupitres y un escritorio. El escritorio está delante de los pupitres. La computadora está encima del escritorio. No hay bandera en mi clase.

Más práctica

Practice Workbook 2B-6, 2B-7

For: Practice with plurals
Visit: www.phschool.com
Web Code: jcd-0213

Pronunciación

The letter *g*

In Spanish, the letter *g* sounds like *g* in "go" when it is followed by *a*, *o*, or *u*, although it often has a slightly softer sound than in English. Listen to and say the following words and sentences:

Gustavo	domin**go**	ten**go**
a**go**sto	pre**gu**nta	lue**go**
ami**go**	ar**go**llas	**ga**to

In Spanish, the letter *g* sounds like the letter *h* in "hot" when it is followed by *e* or *i*. Listen to and say the following words. Some of these words you have not yet heard or seen. Can you guess the meanings of the cognates?

inteli**ge**nte	**ge**neroso	**ge**neral
gimnasio	tecnolo**gí**a	biolo**gí**a

Try it out! See if you can guess how to pronounce the following Spanish first names. Keep in mind the pronunciation rules for the *g* sound.

Gabriela	Ángela	Gerardo
Gilberto	Gustavo	Rodrigo
Olga	Rogelio	Gregorio

Fondo cultural

School gyms are rare in Spanish-speaking countries. Students usually have physical education classes in the school's *patio*. High school students usually have P.E. one or two times a week, sometimes before or after regular school hours. School sports teams are also less common than in the United States.

- What are some reasons that schools in Spanish-speaking countries might place less emphasis on physical education, sports, and gymnasiums?

En la clase de educación física

¡Adelante!

Objectives

- Read about an important program of the United Nations
- Learn about cultural differences in schools
- Write a note describing your classroom
- Learn facts about Central America

Lectura

Strategy

Predicting outcomes
Think about what you would consider to be basic rights for children around the world. Jot down four of them on a piece of paper. As you read the article, see if your ideas are included.

El UNICEF y una convención para los niños[1]

¿Sabes que es un privilegio estar en una escuela, tener una mochila con libros, unos lápices, una calculadora, unas hojas de papel y un profesor bueno? En ciertas[2] naciones, ir a la escuela es difícil o no es posible.

El UNICEF es la organización internacional de las Naciones Unidas que trabaja para los niños. UNICEF es una sigla[3] inglesa que significa "Fondo Internacional de Emergencia de las Naciones Unidas para los Niños." Tiene siete oficinas regionales en diversas naciones y un Centro de Investigaciones en Italia.

El 20 de noviembre de 1989, la Organización de las Naciones Unidas escribió[4] "una convención para los niños" en inglés, árabe, chino, ruso y francés.

[1]children [2]certain
[3]acronym [4]wrote

Esta convención dice que[5] los niños de todas[6] las naciones necesitan:

- **dignidad**
- **una casa**
- **protección**
- **una buena dieta**
- **la práctica de deportes**
- **atención especial para los niños con problemas físicos**
- **amor y la comprensión de la familia**
- **expresar sus opiniones**
- **una comunidad sin[7] violencia**
- **ir a la escuela para ser inteligentes y sociables**

[5]says that [6]all [7]without

¿Comprendes?

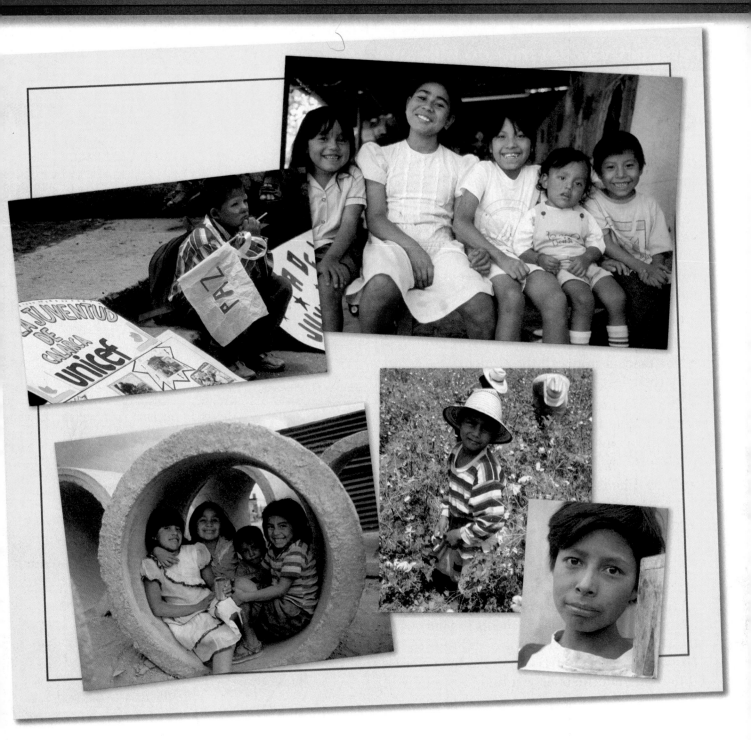

1. Para los estudiantes de todas las naciones es fácil estar en una escuela y tener una mochila. ¿Cierto o falso?
2. ¿Cuántas oficinas regionales tiene UNICEF?
3. ¿Qué significa la sigla UNICEF?
4. ¿Dónde está el Centro de Investigaciones?
5. La convención es para los niños de todas las naciones. ¿Cierto o falso?
6. Según la convención para los niños, ¿cuáles *(what)* son cuatro cosas que necesitan los niños?

For: Internet link activity
Visit: www.phschool.com
Web Code: jcd-0215

Perspectivas del mundo hispano

¿Cómo es la escuela?

Did you know that students in many Spanish-speaking countries spend more time in school than you do? The graph to the right shows the length of the school year in various countries.

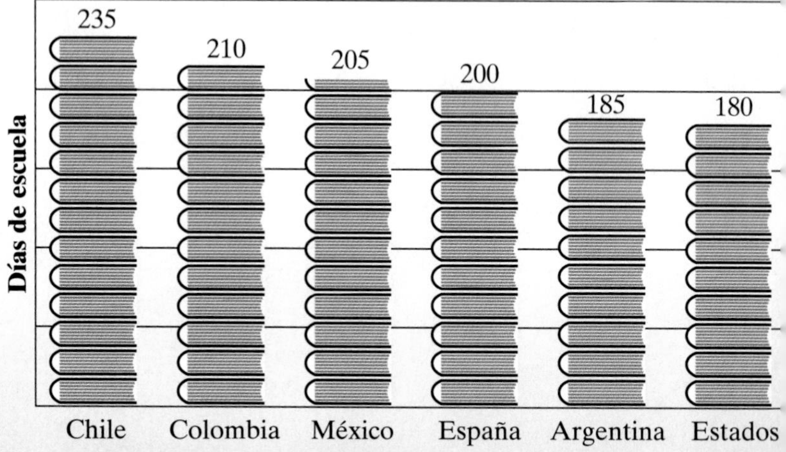

Here are some other facts you may not know:

- In many schools, when a teacher enters the classroom, the students stand.
- The teacher may call the students by their last name.
- The students, on the other hand, are more likely to address their teacher simply as *maestro(a), profesor(a),* or just *profe,* without a last name.
- Class time is generally spent with the teacher lecturing rather than with class discussion.
- Many public and private schools require uniforms.

Check it out! How are other schools in your area similar to or different from yours? How are they similar to or different from those in Spanish-speaking countries? Make a list of schools in your area and describe these similarities and differences. Are some schools more formal? Do students take classes that are different from the ones you take?

Think about it! Based on the information above, what might you assume are the attitudes toward school in Spanish-speaking cultures? How are these the same as or different from attitudes in your community? List five suggestions that might help an exchange student from Mexico City adjust to your school.

Presentación escrita

Tu sala de clases

Task

Your pen pal from Mexico is coming to visit your school next semester and would like to know what to expect. Write her a note describing your Spanish classroom.

Strategy

Creating visuals
Creating a sketch or a drawing can help you remember the things you want to write about in a description.

1. **Prewrite** Draw a simple sketch of your classroom, showing the classroom items you intend to describe in your note. Label the items.

2. **Draft** Write the first draft of your note. Your sketch will help you remember which items you want to describe and where they are located. Use the model to help you organize your writing.

   Modelo

   En mi sala de clases hay cuatro ventanas. Mi pupitre está delante del escritorio de la profesora. La bandera está al lado de la puerta. Las computadoras están encima de la mesa.

3. **Revise** Read through your paragraph and check for correct spelling as well as for the criteria under Evaluation.

   Share your work with a partner. Your partner should check the following:

   - Is your paragraph easy to understand?
   - Is there other information you could add?
   - Are there any errors?

   Rewrite your paragraph making any necessary changes.

4. **Publish** Make a final copy of your note. You may exhibit it in the classroom or add it to your portfolio.

5. **Evaluation** Your teacher may give you a rubric for how your paragraph will be graded. You probably will be graded on:

   - use of vocabulary
   - correct use of the verb *estar*
   - amount of information provided

El mundo hispano

América Central

Central America is made up of seven countries: Belize, Guatemala, El Salvador, Honduras, Nicaragua, Costa Rica, and Panama. Spanish is the official language in all of these countries except Belize, which was colonized by the British.

Costa Rica has set aside large tracts of land for conservation, helping to preserve fragile ecosystems. The oldest park in Costa Rica, Santa Rosa, protects endangered sea turtle nesting sites and the last dry tropical forest in Central America.

¿Sabes que . . . ?

Carlos I of Spain first proposed a canal across the Isthmus of Panama in 1524. In the 1880s, French efforts to build a canal across the isthmus were hindered in large part by diseases. When Panama won its independence from Colombia in 1903, it signed a treaty with the United States granting it rights to the Canal Zone. The United States completed the canal in 1914, and it was turned over to Panama in 1999.

Para pensar

In the early nineteenth century some people imagined that the United States would extend south to Panama. How do you think the United States would be different today if their predictions had come true? How do you think Mexico and Central America would be different?

For: Online Atlas
Visit: www.phschool.com

Founded by the Spanish in 1524, the Nicaraguan city of Granada became an important trading center. The town enjoys easy access to the Caribbean, yet is located less than 100 miles from the Pacific. In the nineteenth and twentieth centuries Nicaragua was proposed as an alternate site for a canal linking the Atlantic and Pacific oceans.

Guatemala has a large indigenous population, many descended from the Maya. These women are wearing the traditional hand-woven *huipil*, which is a very "communicative" part of their clothing. The *huipil* identifies the wearer's village, her marital status, her religious beliefs, wealth, and personality. A well-woven *huipil* may last between 20 to 30 years.

From the 1500s to the end of the 1700s, the coasts of Spanish America were plagued by pirates. Panamanian ports were perfect targets, since the silver and gold mined in Peru were loaded on Panama's Pacific coast and carried overland to the Atlantic, where they were put on ships bound for Spain. Fuerte San Lorenzo, on Panama's Atlantic coast, was part of a network of forts that were meant to protect ships and their precious cargo.

Repaso del capítulo

Vocabulario y gramática

Chapter Review

To prepare for the test, check to see if you . . .
- know the new vocabulary and grammar
- can perform the tasks on p. 121

to talk about classroom items

la bandera	flag
el cartel	poster
la computadora	computer
el disquete	diskette
la mochila	bookbag, backpack
la pantalla	(computer) screen
la papelera	wastepaper basket
el ratón	(computer) mouse
el reloj	clock
el sacapuntas	pencil sharpener
el teclado	(computer) keyboard

to talk about classroom furniture

el escritorio	desk
la mesa	table
la silla	chair

to talk about parts of a classroom

la puerta	door
la ventana	window

to indicate location

al lado de la/del	next to, beside
allí	there
aquí	here
debajo de la/del	underneath
delante de la/del	in front of
detrás de la/del	behind
¿Dónde?	Where?
en	in, on
encima de la/del	on top of

to indicate possession

de	of
mi	my
tu	your

to identify (description, quantity)

Es un(a) . . .	It's a . . .
Hay	There is, There are
¿Qué es esto?	What is this?

estar *to be*

estoy	estamos
estás	estáis
está	están

to identify gender and quantity of nouns

los, las	the
unos, unas	some

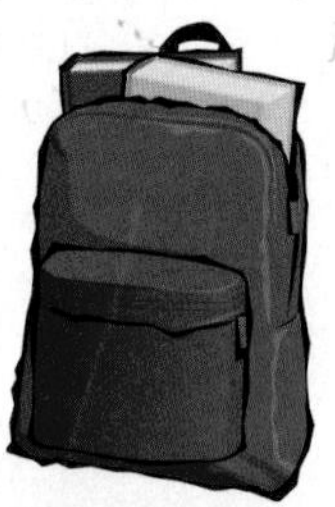

For *Vocabulario adicional,* see pp. 472–473.

Más práctica

Practice Workbook Puzzle 2B-8

Practice Workbook Organizer 2B-9

For: Test preparation
Visit: www.phschool.com
Web Code: jcd-0216

Preparación para el examen

On the exam you will be asked to . . .	Here are practice tasks similar to those you will find on the exam . . .	If you need review . . .
 **1 Escuchar** Listen to identify classrooms and locations	Listen as a student frantically asks some of his friends where he left his homework. Can you identify all of the classrooms and places they suggest that he look?	**pp. 100–103** *A primera vista* **p. 105** Actividades 6–7 **p. 111** Actividad 18
 **2 Hablar/Escribir** Talk or write about where someone is located by describing where that person is in relation to objects in the classroom	You are trying to find out the name of someone in your class. You ask the person next to you, but he doesn't understand whom you are talking about. Give at least three statements that would help him identify the person. You might include where he or she is in relation to the teacher's desk, the window, someone else's desk, and so on.	**pp. 100–103** *A primera vista* **p. 105** Actividades 6–7 **p. 108** Actividades 11–12 **p. 109** Actividad 13 **p. 111** Actividad 18
 **3 Leer** Read and understand a letter that contains questions and concerns about school issues	The school counselor has asked you to help him read a note written by a new Spanish-speaking student at school. After reading it, tell the counselor what the problem is and the kinds of questions the student asks. Necesito una clase para la primera hora. ¿Cómo es la clase de tecnología, fácil o difícil? ¿Qué necesito para la clase? ¿Cuántos estudiantes hay en la clase? ¿Hay mucha tarea?	**pp. 100–103** *A primera vista* **p. 112** Actividad 19 **p. 114** *Lectura*
4 Escribir Write an email to a friend about one of her classes	You have just moved to a new town and are sending an e-mail to a friend from your old school. You have lots of questions about her classes. Write at least three questions about one of her classes: whether she likes it, how many students are in it, where her desk is in the room, what else is in the room, etc.	**pp. 100–103** *A primera vista* **p. 112** Actividad 19
 **5 Pensar** Demonstrate an understanding of cultural differences in schools	Think about how students and teachers interact within a typical classroom in a Spanish-speaking country. What are at least four things you might find different from most schools in the United States?	**p. 106** *Fondo cultural* **p. 113** *Fondo cultural* **p. 116** *Perspectivas del mundo hispano*

¡Viva Texas!

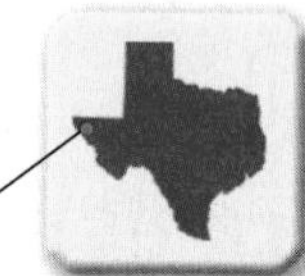

Clases en inglés y español

The Ysleta Independent School District has a goal: All of their students will be fluent in at least two languages by the time they graduate high school. They plan to achieve this goal through their dual language program. In many schools, students are just starting to learn Spanish by the time they get to middle or high school, but these days some students in Texas are starting much earlier. At the Alicia Chacón Elementary School, first grade students who come from English-speaking families, as well as those who come from Spanish-speaking families, get the opportunity to learn math, science, social studies, and other core courses in two languages. At Del Valle High School, students are taking all of their subjects in both Spanish and English, and some are learning a third language. Read about the Ysleta dual-language program and how the students who participate are on the fast track to becoming bilingual.

Los estudiantes en la escuela primaria Alicia Chacón empiezan a tomar[1] clases en dos idiomas[2] en el primer grado. Los profesores enseñan las clases en inglés o en español.

Todos los estudiantes del primer y segundo grado aprenden[3] a leer y a escribir en dos idiomas. En el quinto grado 45% de sus clases son en español, 45% en inglés y 10% en otro idioma. En el octavo grado casi[4] todos los estudiantes son bilingües en inglés y español.

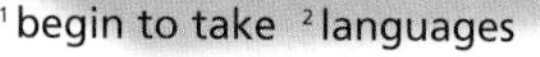

[1] begin to take [2] languages

[3] learn [4] almost

En la escuela preparatoria Del Valle hay la oportunidad de estudiar álgebra, geografía, pre-cálculo, física y otros cursos típicos en inglés y español. Usan el sistema del horario "block" para completar el trabajo de un año en un semestre. Aquí ves el horario de un estudiante en su primer y segundo año de la escuela preparatoria.

Horario de clases

Primer semestre del primer año

Hora	Clase
8:45–10:20	Salud[5]
10:25–11:55	Biología (dos idiomas)
11:55–12:35	Almuerzo
12:35 - 2:05	Inglés 1
2:10 - 3:45	Discurso[6]

Segundo semestre del primer año

Hora	Clase
8:45–10:20	Educación física: fútbol
10:25–11:55	Geografía (dos idiomas)
11:55–12:35	Almuerzo
12:35 - 2:05	Arte
2:10 - 3:45	Debate

Primer semestre del segundo año

Hora	Clase
8:45–10:20	Educación física: natación[7]
10:25–11:55	Historia (dos idiomas)
11:55–12:35	Almuerzo
12:35 - 2:05	Alemán[8] II
2:10 - 3:45	Inglés II

Segundo semestre del segundo año

Hora	Clase
8:45–10:20	Educación física: natación
10:25–11:55	Álgebra II (dos idiomas)
11:55–12:35	Almuerzo
12:35 - 2:05	Tecnología (dos idiomas)
2:10 - 3:45	Física y química integradas (dos idiomas)

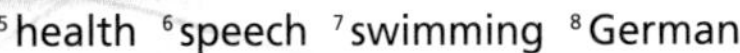
5 health 6 speech 7 swimming 8 German

Comunicación

1. When do students begin studying in the dual-language program?
2. What percentage of your day is spent using Spanish? How does this compare with language use in the fifth grade at Alicia Chacón Elementary School?
3. What kinds of classes can a dual-language student at Del Valle High School take? In your opinion, what are the advantages and disadvantages of taking these types of courses in another language?

Conexiones

Read the class schedules from Del Valle High School. Then work with a partner to answer these questions.

1. ¿Cuántas horas de clase hay en un día en la escuela secundaria Del Valle?
2. ¿Para qué clases necesitas una calculadora?
3. Es el segundo semestre del primer año y es la una de la tarde. ¿En qué clase estás?
4. ¿Qué clase del primer semestre del segundo año te gusta más? ¿Qué clase del primer semestre del segundo año no te gusta nada?

Fondo cultural

Bartolomé Murillo (1617–1682) was the first Spanish painter to become famous throughout Europe. Several of his early paintings featured children from his native Sevilla. Murillo used color, light, and a natural portrayal of his subjects to create memorable masterpieces.

- Study the painting and come up with three adjectives that describe it. Would you say the impression Murillo gives of the boys is positive or negative? Why?

Niños comiendo fruta (ca. 1650), Bartolomé Murillo

Capítulo 3A

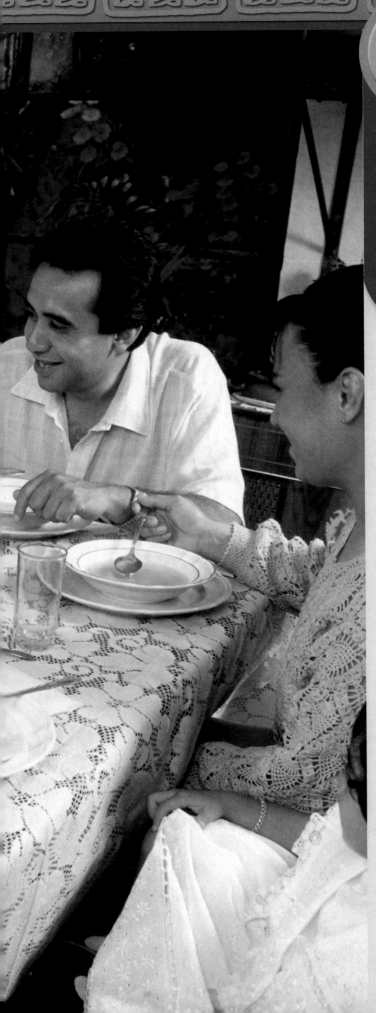

¿Desayuno o almuerzo?

Chapter Objectives

- Talk about foods and beverages for breakfast and lunch
- Talk about likes and dislikes
- Express how often something is done
- Understand cultural perspectives on meals

Video Highlights

A primera vista: *El desayuno*

GramActiva Videos: present tense of *-er* and *-ir* verbs; *me gustan, me encantan*

Country Connection

As you learn about foods and meals, you will make connections to these countries and places:

Go Online PHSchool.com

For: Online Atlas
Visit: www.phschool.com
Web Code: jce-0002

A primera vista

Vocabulario y gramática en contexto

Objectives

Read, listen to, and understand information about
- foods and beverages for breakfast and lunch

El Supermercado de la Plaza
¡Abierto las 24 horas!
¡Ofertas de hoy!
¡Toda la comida que necesitas!
$2.29
las salchichas
$2.45
el tocino
$2.35
el jamón
el cereal
$3.59
SALVADO CON PASAS
$3.25
el queso
$.79
el yogur de fresa
$1.29
los huevos
los plátanos
$.69
$1.80
el jugo de manzana
$2.50
el jugo de naranja
$1.39
la limonada
la leche
$1.75
$2.40
el té
$1.89
el pan
$2.29
las galletas
el agua*
$1.09

*Note that *agua* is a feminine noun. However, you use the masculine article *el* to make it easier to say.

"**El desayuno** es mi **comida** favorita. **En el desayuno,** yo **como** cereal **con** leche, tocino y **pan tostado. Todos los días bebo** jugo de naranja. **Nunca** bebo té **sin** leche. Y tú, ¿qué **comes** en el desayuno?"

"Me encanta el Restaurante de la Plaza. La comida es muy buena. **En el almuerzo,** como una ensalada de frutas o un sándwich de jamón y queso. **Siempre** bebo agua. Es importante **beber** mucha agua, **¿verdad?"**

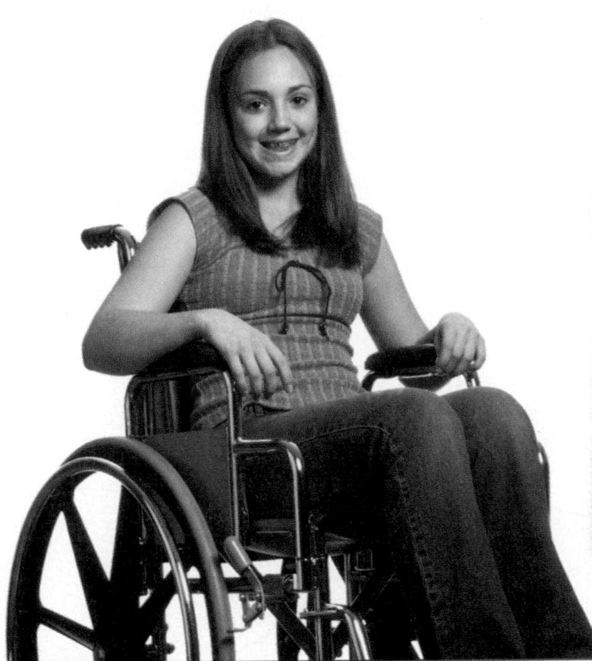

El Restaurante de la Plaza
¡Para un almuerzo rápido!
$3.25
la ensalada de frutas
$3.50
el sándwich de jamón y queso
$1.75
la pizza
$3.75
la hamburguesa
$1.00
el café
$1.50
el perrito caliente
$1.00
los refrescos
$1.25
las papas fritas
$1.35
los jugos
$1.80
la sopa de verduras
$1.00
el té helado

Escuchar

¿Beber o comer?

Listen to the names of ten foods and beverages. If an item is a food, pantomime eating. If it's a beverage, pantomime drinking.

Escuchar

¿El desayuno o el almuerzo?

Listen as different people tell what they are eating. Hold up one hand if the meal is *el desayuno* and hold up both hands if it is *el almuerzo.*

Más práctica

Practice Workbook 3A-1, 3A-2

For: Vocabulary practice
Visit: www.phschool.com
Web Code: jcd-0301

Videohistoria

El desayuno

Tomás es de los Estados Unidos. Está en Costa Rica para estudiar. ¿Qué come el primer día? Lee la historia.

Strategy

Using prior experience
Think about breakfast. Do you like a big breakfast? A small one? No breakfast at all? Look at the pictures and see if you can figure out how Tomás feels about breakfast.

1 **Mamá:** A ver . . . tocino, salchichas, huevos . . .

Papá: ¡Uy! Es mucha comida. No **comprendo.** Tú nunca comes el desayuno.

Mamá: No es mi desayuno. Es para Tomás, **por supuesto.** Los americanos comen mucho en el desayuno.

5 **Tomás:** **Comparto** los huevos, el tocino y las salchichas.

Raúl: **¿Compartes** tu desayuno? Muchas gracias, Tomás.

6 **Raúl:** ¿Y qué **bebes?**

Tomás: Jugo de naranja, por favor.

Raúl: Te gusta la leche, ¿no?

Tomás: **Más o menos.**

7 **Raúl:** Papá, ¿unos huevos?

Papá: No, gracias. ¡La comida es para Uds.!

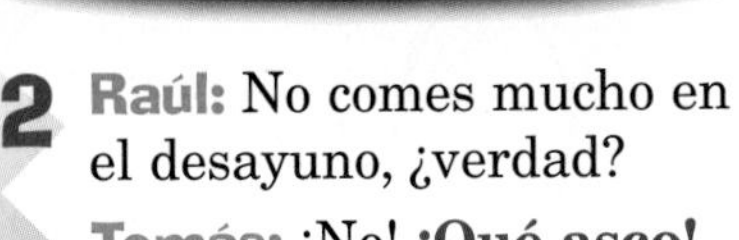

2 **Raúl:** No comes mucho en el desayuno, ¿verdad?

Tomás: ¡No! **¡Qué asco!**

3 **Tomás:** No me gusta nada el desayuno. A veces bebo jugo de naranja y como pan tostado.

Raúl: Yo tampoco como mucho.

4 **Mamá:** Buenos días, Tomás. Aquí tienes tu desayuno. Huevos, tocino, salchichas, pan tostado, cereal con leche . . .

Tomás: Gracias. Es un desayuno muy bueno. **Me encantan** los huevos y el tocino.

8 **Mamá:** **¿Cuál** es tu almuerzo favorito, Tomás?

Tomás: Me gustan las hamburguesas, la pizza, **la ensalada . . .**

Mamá: Bueno . . . ¡pizza, hamburguesas y ensalada para el almuerzo!

Escribir

¿Comprendes?

Lee las frases. Escribe los números del 1 al 6 en una hoja de papel y escribe *C (cierto)* si la frase es correcta y *F (falso)* si es incorrecta.

1. Tomás está en Costa Rica.
2. La mamá de Rául siempre come mucho en el desayuno.
3. A Tomás le gusta comer mucho en el desayuno.
4. Hoy Tomás no come mucho en el desayuno.
5. Tomás comparte el desayuno con Raúl.
6. A Tomás le gustan las hamburguesas y la pizza.

Más práctica

Practice Workbook 3A-3, 3A-4

For: Vocabulary practice
Visit: www.phschool.com
Web Code: jcd-0302

Manos a la obra

Vocabulario y gramática en uso

Objectives

- Talk about foods and beverages for breakfast and lunch
- Ask and tell what people eat and drink for breakfast and lunch
- Express likes and dislikes
- Learn to use the present tense of *-er* and *-ir* verbs and *me gustan / me encantan*

Pensar/Escribir

¿El desayuno o el almuerzo?

Think about what people usually eat for breakfast and lunch. Copy the Venn diagram on a sheet of paper. Which foods pictured below would usually be eaten for breakfast, and which for lunch? Write the Spanish words in the appropriate oval for *el desayuno* or *el almuerzo.* Which items could be eaten for either breakfast or lunch? Write them in the overlapping area.

Modelo

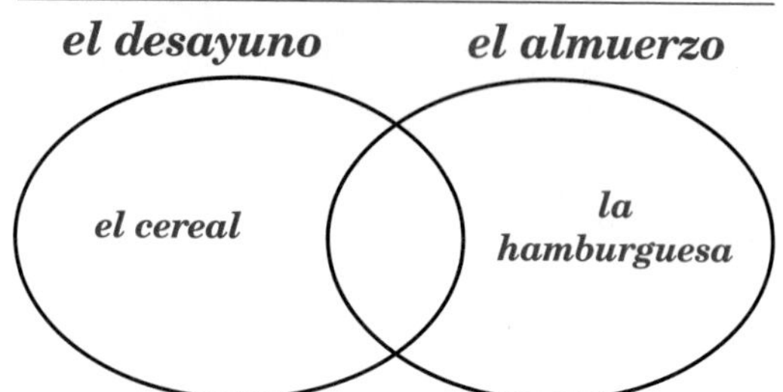

Escuchar/Escribir

¿Dónde están?

Vas a escuchar ocho descripciones sobre el dibujo de esta página. Escribe los números del 1 al 8 en una hoja de papel y escribe *C* si la descripción es cierta y *F* si es falsa.

Actividad 6 **Escribir**

¿Qué bebes?

1. On a sheet of paper, make three columns with these headings: *Todos los días, A veces, Nunca.* Write the names of these beverages under the appropriate heading based on how often you drink them.

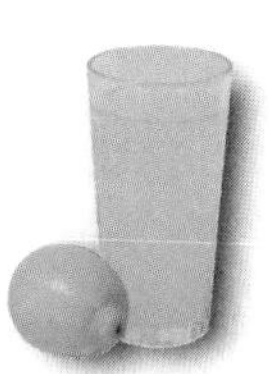

2. Write complete sentences telling how often you drink these beverages.

Modelo

Bebo limonada todos los días.
Bebo leche a veces.
Nunca bebo café.

También se dice . . .

beber = tomar *(México)*
el jugo = el zumo *(España)*
la naranja = la china *(Puerto Rico)*
las papas = las patatas *(España)*
el plátano = la banana, el guineo *(Puerto Rico)*
el sándwich = el bocadillo *(España)*, la torta *(México)*

Actividad 7 **Hablar**

¿Qué comes?

Trabaja con otro(a) estudiante y habla de lo que comes.

Modelo

A —*¿Comes cereal?*
B —*Sí, como cereal todos los días.*
o: *No, nunca como cereal.*

Estudiante A

Estudiante B

Sí, todos los días.
Sí, a veces.
Sí, siempre.
No, nunca.
No, ¡qué asco!

Hablar

Mis comidas favoritas

Trabaja con otro(a) estudiante y habla de las comidas que te gustan y que no te gustan.

Modelo

A —*Te gustan los plátanos, ¿verdad?*
B —*Sí, ¡por supuesto! Me encantan.*

Estudiante A

Estudiante B

Sí, ¡por supuesto! Me encantan.
Sí, más o menos.
No, no me gustan.
No, ¡qué asco!

Exploración del lenguaje

Using a noun to modify another noun

In English, one noun is often used to describe another noun: *vegetable soup, strawberry yogurt.* Notice that the noun that is being described comes second.

In Spanish, however, the noun that is being described comes first and is followed by *de* + the describing noun: *la sopa* ***de*** *verduras, el yogur* ***de*** *fresa.* Notice that you don't use a definite article in front of the second noun.

The form of the noun following *de* does not change even when the first noun becomes plural.

el sándwich de **jamón**
los sándwiches de **jamón**

Try it out! Name five examples of foods or beverages from this chapter that follow this pattern.

Now that you know the pattern, say what these foods and beverages are called in Spanish:

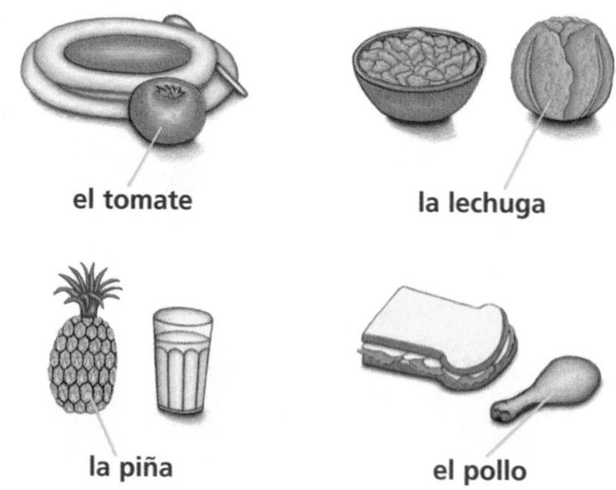

Leer

El intercambio entre dos mundos

Conexiones | La historia

Think about how your meals would be different without corn, beans, squash, tomatoes, limes, avocados, chiles, peanuts, cashews, turkey, pineapples, yams, potatoes, vanilla, and chocolate. What do these foods have in common? They all had their origin in the Americas and were unknown in Europe until Columbus brought them there from his voyages in the fifteenth century. Today these foods are found in dishes in many countries.

The product exchange benefited both sides of the Atlantic Ocean. The Europeans brought to the Americas a wide range of foods including chicken, pork, beef, milk, cheese, sugar, grapes, and grains such as wheat and barley.

Leer/Escribir

Las enchiladas

Read the list of ingredients for a traditional Mexican dish of *enchiladas*. Based upon the information you just read and saw on the map, write which ingredients had their origins in the Americas and which came from Europe.

Enchiladas de pollo[1] con salsa de tomate

Ingredientes:

12 tortillas de maíz[2]
1 taza[3] de pollo
1 taza de queso fresco[4]
6 tomates grandes[5]
2 cebollas[6] no muy grandes
crema
aceite[7] de maíz

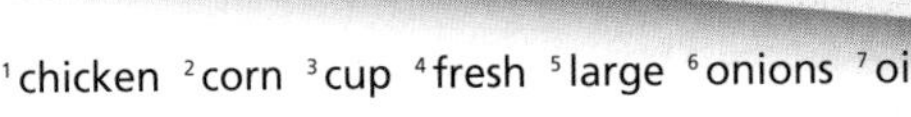

[1]chicken [2]corn [3]cup [4]fresh [5]large [6]onions [7]oil

Escribir/Hablar

Y tú, ¿qué dices?

1. ¿Cuál es tu comida favorita, el desayuno o el almuerzo?
2. ¿Cuál es tu almuerzo favorito? ¿Y tu desayuno favorito?
3. ¿Qué frutas te gustan más?

Gramática

Present tense of *-er* and *-ir* verbs

To create the present-tense forms of *-er* and *-ir* verbs, drop the endings from the infinitives, then add the verb endings *-o, -es, -e, -emos* / *-imos, -éis* / *-ís,* or *-en* to the stem.

Here are the present-tense forms of *-er* and *-ir* verbs using *comer* and *compartir:*

(yo)	com**o**	(nosotros) (nosotras)	com**emos**
(tú)	com**es**	(vosotros) (vosotras)	com**éis**
Ud. (él) (ella)	com**e**	Uds. (ellos) (ellas)	com**en**

(yo)	compart**o**	(nosotros) (nosotras)	compart**imos**
(tú)	compart**es**	(vosotros) (vosotras)	compart**ís**
Ud. (él) (ella)	compart**e**	Uds. (ellos) (ellas)	compart**en**

- Regular *-er* verbs that you know are *beber, comer, comprender, correr,* and *leer.*
- Regular *-ir* verbs that you know are *compartir* and *escribir.*
- You also know the verb *ver*. It is regular except in the *yo* form, which is *veo.*

¿Recuerdas?

The pattern of present-tense *-ar* verbs is:

toco	tocamos
tocas	tocáis
toca	tocan

GramActiva VIDEO

Want more practice with *-er* and *-ir* verbs? Watch the **GramActiva** video.

Gramática Escribir

¿Quiénes comparten el almuerzo?

On a sheet of paper, write complete sentences saying what each person is sharing and with whom. Follow the model.

Modelo

Elena / una manzana / Raúl
Elena comparte una manzana con Raúl.

1. Tomás / una pizza / María
2. tú / unos sándwiches / Ramón
3. nosotros / unas papas fritas / los estudiantes
4. Uds. / unas galletas / el profesor
5. ellas / unos perritos calientes / nosotros
6. tú y yo / unos plátanos / Luis y Roberta
7. yo / ¿-? / mi amigo

Una familia almorzando

Hablar

¿Qué beben y qué comen?

Work with a partner. Use the verbs *comer* and *beber* to ask questions. Then answer them according to the model.

Juan / desayuno

Modelo

A —*¿Qué come Juan en el desayuno?*
B —*Juan come pan tostado.*

Miguel y Carlos / almuerzo

Modelo

A —*¿Qué beben Miguel y Carlos en el almuerzo?*
B —*Miguel y Carlos beben limonada.*

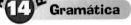

1. Raúl y Gloria / desayuno 
2. tú / almuerzo 
3. Graciela y Carlos / desayuno 

4. Carolina / almuerzo 
5. tu familia y tú / desayuno 
6. tú / almuerzo **¡Respuesta personal!**

Actividad 14 Gramática **Leer/Escribir**

Una tarjeta postal

Lee la tarjeta postal *(post card)* de una amiga de Venezuela. En una hoja de papel, escribe la forma correcta del verbo apropiado que está entre paréntesis.

Querida Amalia,

Elena y yo estamos en Caracas. Nosotras __1.__ *(comprender / correr)* todos los días y __2.__ *(comer / ver)* muy bien.

Los estudiantes aquí __3.__ *(comer / leer)* mucha pizza y __4.__ *(ver / beber)* mucho café. Ellos __5.__ *(leer / beber)* muchos libros y __6.__ *(escribir / ver)* mucho también para las clases. Las clases son difíciles pero me encantan.

En la clase de español nosotros __7.__ *(correr / leer)* revistas y cuentos en español. Elena __8.__ *(comprender / beber)* muy bien pero para mí es un poco difícil.

Tengo que estudiar. ¡Hasta luego!
Tu amiga,
Carolina

Más práctica
Practice Workbook 3A-5

For: Practice with *-er* and *-ir* verbs
Visit: www.phschool.com
Web Code: jcd-0303

Escribir/Hablar

Los sábados y la comida

What do you and your classmates eat and drink for breakfast and lunch on Saturdays? Make a chart like the one below on a sheet of paper and complete each box with information about yourself. Then survey two classmates to find out what their habits are. Record the information in the chart.

	¿Qué comes?	¿Qué bebes?
el desayuno	yo: huevos, pan tostado, tocino Sandra: cereal, plátanos, pan tostado	
el almuerzo		

Para decir más . . .

la crema de cacahuates	peanut butter
el pan dulce	breakfast pastry
el panqueque	pancake
el pollo	chicken

Modelo

Los sábados, ¿qué comes en el desayuno? ¿Qué bebes?
¿Qué comes en el almuerzo? ¿Qué bebes?

Actividad 16

Escribir/Hablar

Los hábitos de la clase

Use your completed chart from Actividad 15 to write summary statements based on your survey. Be prepared to read your sentences to the class.

Modelo

Sandra y yo comemos huevos y cereal en el desayuno.
Gregorio no bebe jugo de naranja en el desayuno y le gusta mucho la leche.
Sofía come cereal y bebe leche en el desayuno.

Fondo cultural

El desayuno From the popular *churros* and hot chocolate in Spain to the *pan dulce* served in many countries, a wide variety of foods can be found on the breakfast table in the Spanish-speaking world. Most often, people prefer a light breakfast of bread or a roll, coffee or tea, and possibly juice. Items such as cereal, eggs, ham, or sausage are less common.

- In Spain you can ask for a *desayuno americano*. What do you think you would be served?

¿Qué comen en el desayuno?

Gramática

Me gustan, me encantan

Use *me gusta* and *me encanta* to talk about a singular noun.

Me gusta **el té** pero me encanta **el té helado.**

Use *me gustan* and *me encantan* to talk about plural nouns.

Me encantan **las fresas** pero no me gustan mucho **los plátanos.**

When you use *me gusta(n)* and *me encanta(n)* to talk about a noun, include *el, la, los,* or *las.*

Me encanta **el** jugo de naranja pero no me gusta **la** leche.

¿Qué te gustan más, **las** hamburguesas o **los** perritos calientes?

GramActiva VIDEO

Want more help with *me gustan / me encantan?* Watch the **GramActiva** video.

Gramática **Escuchar/GramActiva**

¿Gusta o gustan?

1. Tear a sheet of paper in thirds. On the first piece, write *No.* On the second piece write *me gusta.* On the third piece, write *n.*
2. You will hear eight food items. Indicate whether you like each item by holding up one, two, or all three pieces of paper. Remember to use *me gustan* when the item you hear is plural!

Gramática **Escribir**

¿Qué te gusta?

Indicate how much you *do* or *do not* like the foods pictured below.

Modelo

Me gustan las manzanas.
o: *No me gustan nada las manzanas.*
o: *Me encantan las manzanas.*

1. 

2. 

3. 

4. 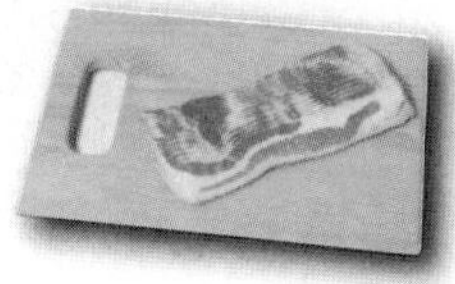

5. 

6. 

   **Escribir/Hablar**

¿Qué te gusta más?

1. A popular magazine has provided this survey to see how much you and a friend have in common. On a sheet of paper, write the numbers 1–7 and then write your preferences.
2. Take turns asking your partner about the survey items. Keep track of your similarities and differences. See how the magazine rates you.

Modelo

¿La comida mexicana o la comida italiana?

A —*¿Qué te gusta más, la comida mexicana o la comida italiana?*
B —*Me gusta más la comida italiana.*
o: *No me gusta ni la comida mexicana ni la comida italiana.*
A —*A mí también.*
o: *A mí me gusta la comida mexicana.*
o: *A mí tampoco.*

¿Qué te gusta más?

¿Tu amigo(a) y tú son muy similares o muy diferentes? Completa este *quiz* y compara tus respuestas con las de un(a) amigo(a).

1	la comida mexicana	*o*	la comida italiana
2	el desayuno	*o*	el almuerzo
3	el cereal con fruta	*o*	el cereal sin fruta
4	las revistas	*o*	los libros
5	la música rock	*o*	la música rap
6	los amigos graciosos	*o*	los amigos serios
7	las hamburguesas con queso	*o*	las hamburguesas sin queso

Respuestas similares:

7–6 ¡Uds. son gemelos![1]
5–4 Tienen mucho en común, ¿verdad?
3–2 ¡Un poco similares / un poco diferentes!
1–0 ¿Los opuestos[2] se atraen?[3] ¡Por supuesto!

[1] twins [2] opposites [3] attract

Pronunciación

The letters *h* and *j*

In Spanish, the letter *h* is never pronounced. Listen to and say these words:

hora	hablar	hasta	hola
hoy	hace	hacer	hotel

The letter *j* is pronounced like the letter *h* in "hat" but with more of a breathy sound. It is made far back in the mouth—almost in the throat. Listen to and say these words:

trabajar	dibujar	jugar	videojuegos
hoja	jueves	junio	julio

Try it out! Find and say five examples of foods or beverages from this chapter that have *h* or *j* in their spelling.

Try it out! Say this *trabalenguas* three times as fast as you can:

Debajo del puente de Guadalajara había un conejo debajo del agua.

Leer/Escribir/Hablar

¿Qué comida hay en el Ciberc@fé @rrob@?

Lee el menú y contesta las preguntas.

Menú del Ciberc@fé @rrob@

Desayunos

No. 1	Huevos: *(jamón, tocino, chorizo[1])*	$18.00
	Con cóctel de fruta	$20.00
No. 2	Sincronizadas: *(tortilla de harina,[2] queso amarillo, jamón)*	$22.00
	Con cóctel de fruta	$24.00
No. 3	Cuernitos: *(jamón, queso, tomate y lechuga)*	$20.00
	Con cóctel de fruta	$22.00
No. 4	Chilaquiles: *verdes o rojos*	$14.00
	Con cóctel de fruta	$16.00
No. 5	Omelet: *(con pollo, jamón, tomate, cebolla, champiñones[3] o queso)*	$18.00
No. 6	Crepas *(champiñones, jamón, pollo)*	$12.50

Refrescos $5.00 Café $4.00 Jugos $7.50 Té o té helado $4.00

Tel.: 212 03 95

16 de septiembre #65
Col. Centro

[1] spicy sausage [2] flour [3] mushrooms

Strategy

Skimming
Look quickly through the menu. What meal is it for? Find three dishes you recognize and two that are new to you.

Crepas de cuitlacoche

Chilaquiles

¿Comprendes?

1. Comes el desayuno No. 1 con un jugo de naranja. ¿Cuál es el precio *(price)* del desayuno?
2. Comes un omelet con un café. ¿Cuál es el precio?
3. No te gustan nada los huevos. ¿Qué comes del menú?
4. No te gusta ni el café ni el té helado. ¿Qué bebes?

El español en la comunidad

Foods from different Spanish-speaking countries have become very popular in the United States. Visit a local grocery store and make a list of different types of foods that come from Spanish-speaking countries. Which of these foods have you tried?

Más práctica
Practice Workbook 3A-6, 3A-7

For: Practice with *me gusta(n) / me encanta(n)*
Visit: www.phschool.com
Web Code: jcd-0304

¡Adelante!

Lectura

Objectives

- Read about fruits that are native to the Americas
- Learn about a snack in Spanish-speaking countries, *churros y chocolate*
- Maintain a conversation about what you like, including your food preferences
- Learn facts about the northern part of South America

Frutas y verduras de las Américas

Hay muchas frutas y verduras que son originalmente de las Américas que hoy se comen en todos los países. Las verduras más populares son la papa, el maíz, los frijoles y muchas variedades de chiles. También hay una gran variedad de frutas como la papaya, la piña y el aguacate. Estas frutas y verduras son muy nutritivas, se pueden preparar fácilmente y son muy sabrosas. La papaya y la piña son frutas que se comen en el desayuno o de postre. ¿Cuáles de estas frutas comes?

Strategy

Making guesses
When you find an unknown word, try to guess the meaning. Is it a cognate? What might it mean within the context of the reading and other words around it? Keep reading and the meaning may become clear.

la papaya

Es una fruta con mucha agua. Es perfecta para el verano. Tiene más vitamina C que la naranja.

el aguacate

La pulpa del aguacate es una fuente de energía, proteínas, vitaminas y minerales. Tiene vitaminas A y B.

el mango

Aunque[1] el mango es originalmente de Asia, se cultiva en las regiones tropicales de muchos países de las Américas. Tiene calcio y vitaminas A y C como la naranja.

[1]Although

Licuado de plátano

El licuado es una bebida muy popular en los países tropicales. ¡Es delicioso y muy nutritivo!

Ingredientes:
- –1 plátano
- –2 vasos de leche
- –1 cucharadita de azúcar
- –hielo

Preparación:
1. Cortar el plátano.
2. Colocar los ingredientes en la licuadora.
3. Licuar por unos 5 ó 10 segundos.

¿Comprendes?

1. ¿Qué vitaminas tienen las frutas en la página anterior?
2. De las frutas y verduras en el artículo, ¿cuáles *(which ones)* te gustan? ¿Cuáles no te gustan?
3. ¿Qué otras frutas te gustan? ¿Comes estas frutas en el desayuno o en el almuerzo?
4. ¿Qué fruta no es originalmente de las Américas?

For: Internet link activity
Visit: www.phschool.com
Web Code: jcd-0305

Fondo cultural

Frutas y verduras During winter, the United States imports a wide range of fruits from Chile such as cherries, peaches, and grapes. When you purchase grapes from a supermarket in January, look to see if they have a label that says *Producto de Chile* or *Importado de Chile*.

- What are some other fruits and vegetables in your local market that are products of other countries?

La cultura en vivo

Churros y chocolate

In many Spanish-speaking countries, a popular snack is the combination of *churros y chocolate.* Churros are long, slender doughnut-like pastries fried in hot oil. Small restaurants called *churrerías* specialize in churros and cups of delicious hot chocolate You can also find churros being sold in stands on the street.

Chocolate y churros

Try it out! Here's the recipe to try. Churros are high in fat and calories, so you won't want to sample too many of them!

Churros

1 cup water	$\frac{1}{2}$ cup unsalted butter *(= 1 stick)*
$\frac{1}{4}$ teaspoon salt	1 cup all-purpose flour
4 large eggs	oil for deep frying
1 cup sugar	

In a heavy saucepan, bring water, butter, and salt to a full boil. Remove from heat. Add the flour all at once, stirring briskly. Stir until the mixture pulls away from the side of the pan and forms a ball. Put the mixture in a bowl. With an electric mixer on medium speed, add one egg at a time. After adding the last egg, beat the mixture for one more minute.

With adult supervision, heat 2–3 inches of oil to 375° F in a deep, heavy pan. Fit a pastry bag or cookie press with a $\frac{1}{2}$–inch star tip. Pipe out 6 inch-long tubes of dough into the oil. ***Be extremely cautious adding dough to the oil, because the oil may spatter and burn you!*** Fry, turning a few times, for 3–5 minutes or until golden brown. Place the sugar on a plate. Drain the churros well on paper towels and then roll them in the sugar.

Chocolate caliente

To make hot chocolate in Mexico, cacao beans are ground to a powder. Cinnamon, powdered almonds, and sugar are then added, and hot milk is poured in. The mixture is whipped with a wooden whisk called *un molinillo* or *un batidor.* You can find Mexican-style chocolate for making *chocolate caliente* in many supermarkets.

Un molinillo

Think about it! What kinds of food and drink do you and your friends like? Is chocolate among the popular choices? Can you think of combinations of food and drink that are popular with many people in the United States? Are these combinations popular elsewhere?

Presentación oral

¿Y qué te gusta comer?

Task
An exchange student from the United States is going to Uruguay. You and a partner will role-play a telephone conversation in which you each take one of the roles and gather information about the other person.

1. **Prepare** You will role-play this conversation with a partner. Be sure to prepare for both roles. Here's how to prepare:

   Host student: Make a list of at least four questions that you might ask the exchange student. Find out what he or she likes to study, his or her favorite activities, and what he or she likes to eat and drink for breakfast and lunch.

   Exchange student: Jot down some possible answers to questions that the host student might ask and be prepared to provide information about yourself.

2. **Practice** Work in groups of four in which there are two exchange students and two host students. Work together to practice different questions and different responses. Here's how you might start your phone conversation:

   HOST STUDENT: ¡Hola, Pablo! Soy Rosa.
   EXCHANGE STUDENT: ¡Hola, Rosa! ¿Cómo estás?
   HOST STUDENT: Bien, gracias. Pues Pablo, ¿te gusta . . . ?

   Continue the conversation using your notes. You can use your notes in practice, but not during the role-play.

3. **Present** You will be paired with another student, and your teacher will tell you which role to play. The host student begins the conversation. Listen to your partner's questions and responses and keep the conversation going.

4. **Evaluation** Your teacher may give you a rubric for how the presentation will be graded. You probably will be graded on:
   - completion of task
   - how well you were understood
   - your ability to keep the conversation going

Strategy

Making lists
Making lists of questions can help you in conversations where you need to find out specific information.

El mundo hispano

América del Sur

Parte norte

Venezuela, Colombia, Ecuador, Peru, and Bolivia form a region of contrasts, with mountains and lowlands, rain forests and deserts, immense wealth and extreme poverty, remote villages and modern cities. A rugged geography, ancient indigenous civilizations, and abundant natural resources have made this one of the most culturally diverse regions in the world.

Constructed more than 500 years ago, the terraced fields in the highlands of Bolivia were a sophisticated system for conserving soil and water, and some remain in use today. In the 1980s archaeologists reconstructing ancient agricultural systems on the shore of Lake Titicaca (at 12,500 feet the highest navigable body of water in the world) found that these ancient systems worked better in this difficult environment than many modern agricultural techniques.

¿Sabes que . . . ?

The term *America* first appeared on a German map in 1507. The Americas are named for the Italian navigator Amerigo Vespucci, who produced the first European charts of mainland South America in 1497.

Para pensar

The countries of northern South America are lands of varied geography. Think about the North American continent. It is also a land of geographical contrasts. In what ways are both regions rich in natural resources, environmentally protected areas, and ancient civilizations?

For: Online Atlas
Visit: www.phschool.com
Web Code: jce-0002

"Rediscovered" in 1911, the mountaintop city of Machu Picchu in Peru was part of the Incan empire, which in the sixteenth century extended from present-day Ecuador to Chile. Machu Picchu's buildings were made of huge, precisely carved stone blocks that were hauled into place without wheels or heavy draft animals.

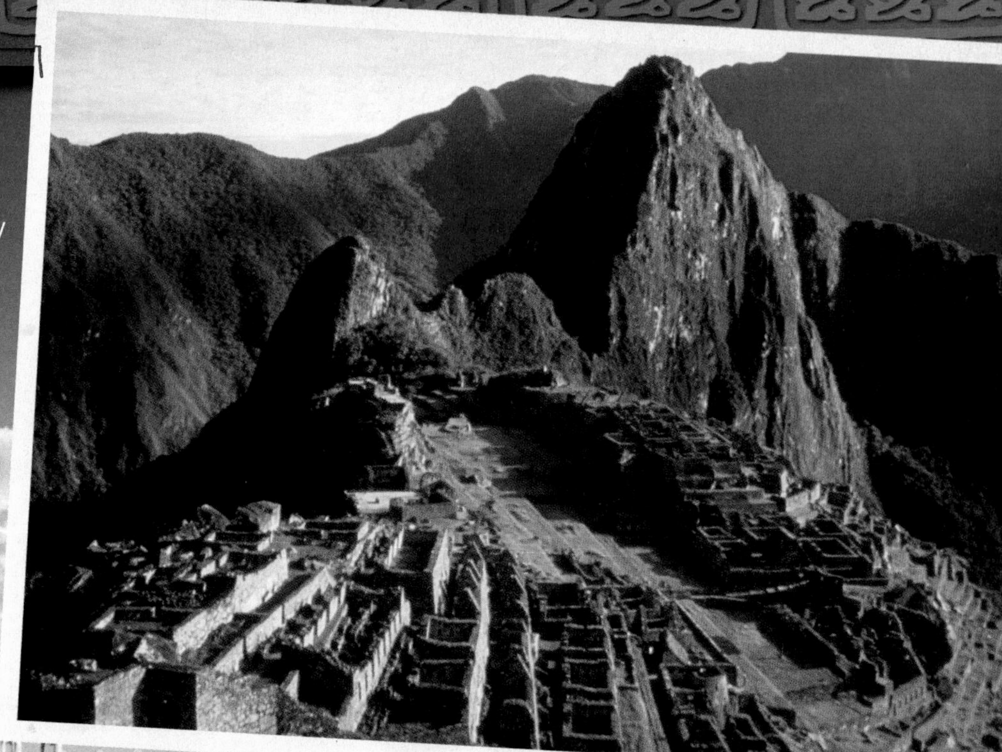

Venezuela is one of the most important sources of oil consumed in the United States. Other important Latin American oil producers include Mexico, Colombia, Ecuador, and Peru, with new deposits being found every year. Latin America and Canada account for approximately 48 percent of oil imports to the United States. In contrast, the Middle East accounts for approximately 30 percent.

The Galápagos Islands, also called *las islas encantadas* (the enchanted islands), lie 600 miles off the coast of Ecuador. It is believed that the Incas may have traveled to the islands in large ocean-going rafts. In 1835, the naturalist Charles Darwin spent weeks here studying the islands' unique animal life. *Galápagos* are giant tortoises that are native to these islands, which are now a national park and wildlife sanctuary.

Repaso del capítulo

Chapter Review

Vocabulario y gramática

To prepare for the test, check to see if you . . .

- know the new vocabulary and grammar
- can perform the tasks on p. 145

to talk about breakfast

en el desayuno	for breakfast
el cereal	cereal
el desayuno	breakfast
los huevos	eggs
el pan	bread
el pan tostado	toast
el plátano	banana
la salchicha	sausage
el tocino	bacon
el yogur	yogurt

to talk about lunch

en el almuerzo	for lunch
la ensalada	salad
la ensalada de frutas	fruit salad
las fresas	strawberries
la galleta	cookie
la hamburguesa	hamburger
el jamón	ham
la manzana	apple
la naranja	orange
las papas fritas	French fries
el perrito caliente	hot dog
la pizza	pizza
el queso	cheese
el sándwich de jamón y queso	ham and cheese sandwich
la sopa de verduras	vegetable soup

to talk about beverages

el agua *f.*	water
el café	coffee
el jugo de manzana	apple juice
el jugo de naranja	orange juice
la leche	milk
la limonada	lemonade
el refresco	soft drink
el té	tea
el té helado	iced tea

to talk about eating and drinking

beber	to drink
comer	to eat
la comida	food, meal
compartir	to share

to indicate how often

nunca	never
siempre	always
todos los días	every day

to say that you like / love something

Me / te encanta(n) ___.	I / you love (___).
Me / te gusta(n) ___.	I / you like (___).

other useful words

comprender	to understand
con	with
¿Cuál?	Which? What?
más o menos	more or less
por supuesto	of course
¡Qué asco!	How awful!
sin	without
¿Verdad?	Right?

present tense of *-er* verbs

como	comemos
comes	coméis
come	comen

present tense of *-ir* verbs

comparto	compartimos
compartes	compartís
comparte	comparten

For *Vocabulario adicional,* see pp. 472–473.

Más práctica

Practice Workbook Puzzle 3A-8

Practice Workbook Organizer 3A-9

For: Test preparation
Visit: www.phschool.com
Web Code: jcd-0306

Preparación para el examen

On the exam you will be asked to . . .	Here are practice tasks similar to those you will find on the exam . . .	If you need review . . .
 **1 Escuchar** Listen and understand as people describe what they eat and drink for lunch	Listen as three students describe what they typically eat and drink for lunch. Which is most like the kind of lunch you eat? Did they mention anything you could not buy in your school cafeteria?	**pp. 124–127** *A primera vista* **p. 125** Actividades 1–2 **p. 128** Actividad 5
 **2 Hablar** Tell someone what you typically eat for breakfast and ask the same of others	Your Spanish club is meeting for breakfast before school next week. Find out what other people in your class typically eat for breakfast. After you tell at least two people what you eat for breakfast, ask what they like to eat. Does everyone eat the same kind of breakfast or do you all like to eat different things?	**p. 129** Actividad 7 **p. 130** Actividad 8 **p. 131** Actividad 11 **p. 133** Actividad 13 **p. 134** Actividades 15–16 **p. 141** *Presentación oral*
3 Leer Read and understand words that are typically found on menus	You are trying to help a child order from the lunch menu below, but he is very difficult to please. He doesn't like anything white. And he refuses to eat anything that grows on trees. Which items from the menu do you think he would refuse to eat or drink? ALMUERZO hamburguesa — plátanos pizza — manzana ensalada — leche	**pp. 124–127** *A primera vista* **p. 131** Actividad 10 **p. 137** Actividad 20 **pp. 138–139** *Lectura*
 **4 Escribir** Write a list of foods that you like and others that you dislike	Your Spanish club is sponsoring a "Super Spanish Saturday." Your teacher wants to know what foods the class likes and dislikes so that the club can buy what most people like. Write the headings *Me gusta(n)* and *No me gusta(n)* in two columns. List at least four items that you like to eat and drink for breakfast and four items for lunch. Then list what you don't like to eat and drink for these same meals.	**p. 128** Actividad 4 **p. 129** Actividad 6 **p. 131** Actividad 11 **p. 134** Actividad 16 **p. 135** Actividad 18 **p. 137** Actividad 20
 **5 Pensar** Demonstrate an understanding of cultural differences regarding snacks	Think about popular food combinations in the United States, such as a cup of coffee and a doughnut. What is a similar combination that is popular in many Spanish-speaking countries, and where are you able to buy it?	**p. 140** *La cultura en vivo*

Fondo cultural

Diego Rivera (1886–1957) This detail of a mural entitled *La Gran Tenochtitlán* by Mexican artist Diego Rivera is located in the Palacio Nacional in Mexico City. It shows *el tianguis,* the bustling marketplace at Tenochtitlán, capital of the Aztec Empire. In the foreground there are many kinds of merchandise being traded, including corn and different varieties of beans. This mural is one of many by Rivera that focus on pre-Columbian life and civilizations.

- What impression do you think Rivera is giving about life in the pre-Columbian civilizations?

Detalle de *La Gran Tenochtitlán* (1945), Diego Rivera

Capítulo 3B

Para mantener la salud

Chapter Objectives

- Talk about foods and beverages for dinner
- Describe what people or things are like
- Discuss food, health, and exercise choices
- Understand cultural perspectives on diet and health

Video Highlights

A primera vista: *Para mantener la salud*

GramActiva Videos: the plurals of adjectives; the verb *ser*

Country Connection

As you learn about foods and health, you will make connections to these countries and places:

Go Online
PHSchool.com
For: Online Atlas
Visit: www.phschool.com
Web Code: jce-0002

…cado al aire
… en España

A primera vista

Vocabulario y gramática en contexto

Objectives

Read, listen to, and understand information about:

- **food groups and foods on the Food Guide Pyramid**
- **activities to maintain good health**
- **ways to describe food**

La pirámide nutritiva es la forma más práctica de indicar la comida que **debes** comer **cada día. Para mantener la salud,** es importante comer de **todos** los grupos.

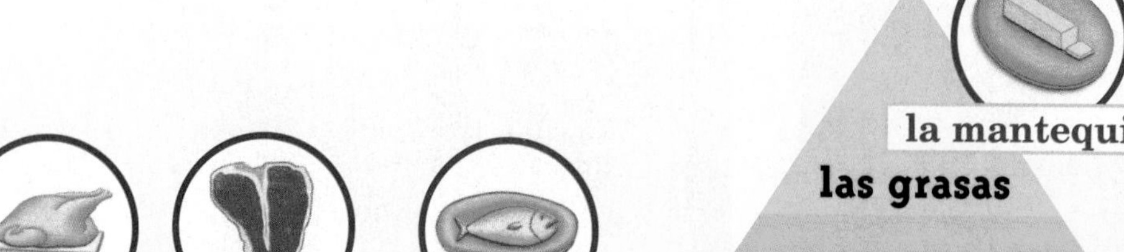

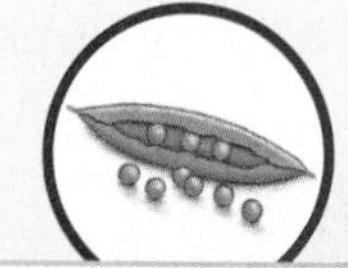

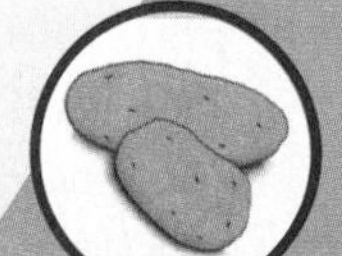

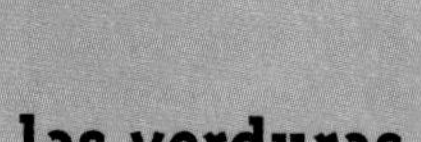

“¡Me encantan las verduras! Como **muchas** ensaladas con lechuga y tomates.”

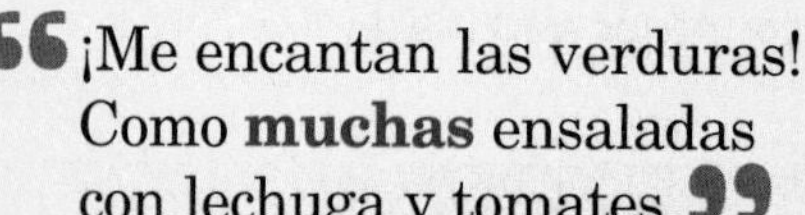

“También me gustan las zanahorias y las judías verdes.”

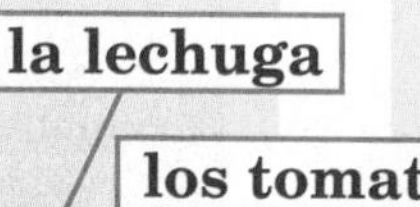

“¡Mi amiga Claudia no come comida buena **para la salud!** Come **muchos** pasteles y helado. **Son horribles.**”

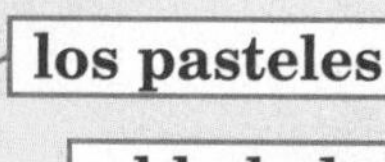

caminar

levantar pesas

—¿Qué **haces** para mantener la salud?

—Pues, cada día **hago ejercicio.** Camino, monto en bicicleta y practico deportes.

—¡Uf! **Tengo hambre. ¿Por qué** no comemos **algo** en el restaurante "A tu salud"? Los sándwiches son muy **sabrosos.**

—¡Por supuesto!

Escuchar

¿Qué debes comer?

Your teacher is giving a lecture on foods that you should eat from the Food Guide Pyramid. Touch each item as it is mentioned. Listen carefully for the names of the foods.

Más práctica
Practice Workbook 3B-1, 3B-2

Escuchar

Para mantener la salud

Listen to students talk about things they do. Give a "thumbs-up" sign if they are describing things that are healthy and a "thumbs-down" sign if the things are unhealthy.

For: Vocabulary practice
Visit: www.phschool.com
Web Code: jcd-0311

Videohistoria

Para mantener la salud

¿Qué hacen Raúl, Tomás y Gloria para mantener la salud? Lee la historia.

Strategy

Using visuals to make predictions
Before you read the story, use the pictures to predict what will happen. This will help you understand the story better as you read.

- How did your predictions compare with what you read?

1 **Tomás:** **Tengo sed . . .**
Raúl: ¿Qué **prefieres?** ¿Te gusta el café? El café de Costa Rica es muy bueno.
Tomás: ¡Pero el café es **malo** para la salud! **Prefiero una bebida** como . . . un jugo de fruta.

5 **Tomás:** ¡Me gusta hacer algo cada día! Hago ejercicio, levanto pesas o camino todos los días.

6 **Tomás:** Tengo hambre.
Raúl: ¿Por qué no comemos en la soda?*

7 **Tomás:** La comida aquí es muy buena. Ahora no tengo hambre. ¿Y tú?
Raúl: **¡Creo que no!**
Gloria: Pues, **creo que** debemos ir a casa.

* *La soda* is the word for a casual restaurant in Costa Rica.

2 **Raúl:** ¡Ah! **Estoy de acuerdo,** un refresco.

Tomás: Raúl, ¿por qué hablas de *refrescos?* A mí me gustan los jugos de fruta.

Gloria: Porque, Tomás, ¡un *refresco* en Costa Rica *es* un jugo de fruta!

3 **Raúl:** Dos refrescos de mango con leche.

Gloria: Y un refresco de mango con agua, por favor.

4 **Tomás:** ¡Es *muuuy* sabroso!

Gloria y Raúl: Sí, sí . . . ¡y todos los refrescos aquí son buenos para la salud!

Gloria: Tomás, ¿qué haces para mantener la salud?

8 **Mamá:** ¡A comer **la cena!**

Los jóvenes: *¡Uf!*

Actividad 3 **Escribir/Hablar**

¿Comprendes?

1. ¿Por qué no bebe café Tomás?
2. En Costa Rica, ¿qué es *un refresco?*
3. ¿Los refrescos en Costa Rica son buenos o malos para la salud?
4. Según Tomás, ¿cómo es la comida en la soda?
5. En casa, ¿qué está en la mesa?

Más práctica

Practice Workbook 3B-3, 3B-4

Go Online PHSchool.com

For: Vocabulary practice
Visit: www.phschool.com
Web Code: jcd-0312

Manos a la obra

Vocabulario y gramática en uso

Objectives

- Talk about dinner foods
- Express food preferences
- Describe people and foods
- Talk about healthy and unhealthy lifestyles
- Learn to use the plurals of adjectives and the verb *ser*

Leer/Escribir

¡Claro que no!

For each group of words, choose the word or expression that doesn't belong and write it down on a sheet of paper. Then think of one more word or expression that does fit with the group and write it down beside the first word you wrote.

Modelo

la cebolla   la lechuga   la uva
la uva   . . .   *la zanahoria*

1.	el pollo	el pescado	el arroz
2.	las zanahorias	los pasteles	las judías verdes
3.	caminar	correr	ver la televisión
4.	malo	horrible	sabroso
5.	comer mucho	levantar pesas	hacer ejercicio
6.	los tomates	el pan	los espaguetis
7.	cada día	un día	todos los días
8.	el bistec	las papas	el pollo
9.	la mantequilla	el helado	el pescado

Pensar/Escribir

¿En el refrigerador o no?

Escribe dos listas. En la primera lista escribe las comidas y bebidas que deben estar en el refrigerador. En la segunda lista escribe las comidas y bebidas que no necesitan estar en el refrigerador.

Fondo cultural

El mate is the national beverage of Argentina, Paraguay, and Uruguay. This herbal tea is shared among family and friends. It is served hot in a hollow gourd, also called *un mate,* with a straw called *una bombilla.*

- What national beverage does the United States have that compares to *mate?*

Hablar

¿Qué prefieres?

Ask your partner which of two foods he or she prefers. Your partner will answer and ask you which one you prefer.

Modelo

A —*¿Qué prefieres, carne o pescado?*
B —*Prefiero carne. Y tú, ¿qué prefieres?*
o: *No como ni carne ni pescado. Y tú, ¿qué prefieres?*
A —*Prefiero pescado.*

Estudiante A

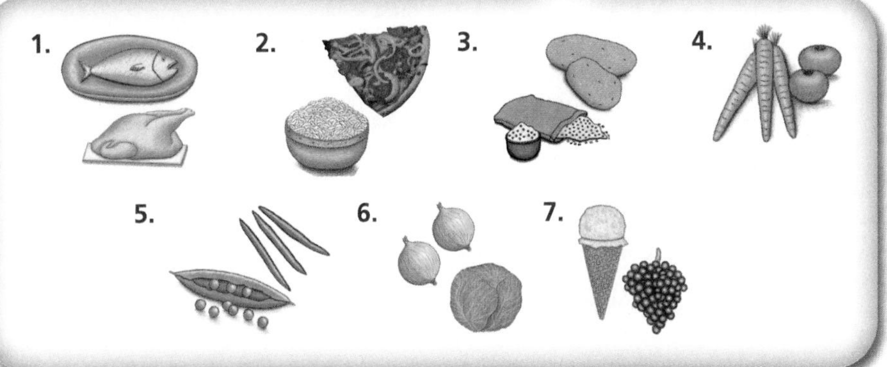

Estudiante B

¡Respuesta personal!

Hablar/Pensar

¿Sí o no?

Habla de lo que debes comer y beber para mantener la salud.

Modelo

A —*¿Debo beber leche cada día para mantener la salud?*
B —*Creo que sí.*
o: *Creo que no.*

Estudiante A

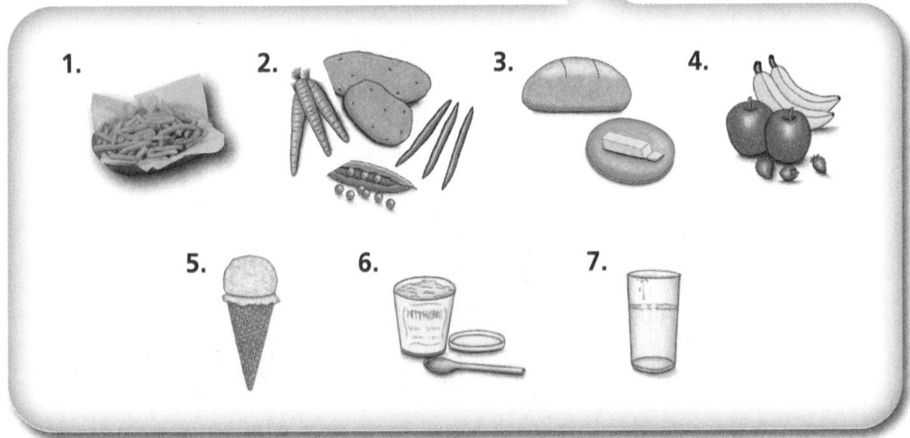

Estudiante B

Creo que . . .

Hablar

¿Hay algo para comer?

Habla de lo que debes comer y beber a las horas indicadas.

Modelo

A —*Son las ocho de la mañana y tengo hambre y sed. ¿Qué debo comer y beber?*
B —*Debes comer cereal y pan tostado, y debes beber jugo de manzana.*

Para decir más . . .

de la mañana	in the morning
de la tarde	in the afternoon
de la noche	in the evening

Estudiante A

1. 
2.
3.
4. 
5. 
6.

Estudiante B

¡Respuesta personal!

Leer/Escribir

Los buenos consejos

Da consejos *(Give advice)* sobre lo que es bueno o malo para la salud. Copia y completa las frases. Necesitas tus frases para la Actividad 10.

1. Para mantener la salud, debes ____ todos los días.
2. Necesitas beber ____ cada día.
3. Debes comer ____ en la cena.
4. ____ es malo para la salud.
5. El jugo de zanahoria es ____.
6. Debes comer ____ todos los días.
7. Nunca debes comer ____.

Hablar

¿Estás de acuerdo?

Lee tus consejos de la Actividad 9 a otro(a) estudiante. ¿Está de acuerdo con tus consejos?

Modelo

A —*Para mantener la salud, debes practicar deportes todos los días.*
B —*Estoy de acuerdo.*
o: *No estoy de acuerdo.*

También se dice . . .

los guisantes = los chícharos *(México)*, las arvejas *(Argentina)*
el tomate = el jitomate *(México)*

Actividad 11 Leer/Escribir/Hablar

¿Qué haces . . .?

Take this test on healthy activities to see how you rate.

1. Write your answers in complete sentences on a sheet of paper.
2. Ask a partner each question. Tally your partner's *sí* and *no* answers.
3. Write three recommendations so your partner can have a healthier lifestyle.

Modelo

Debes caminar o correr todos los días.

¿Qué haces para mantener la salud?

Contesta las preguntas según las actividades que haces cada día. Cada "sí" = 1 punto.

- ❑ **1.** ¿Haces ejercicio?
- ❑ **2.** ¿Practicas deportes?
- ❑ **3.** ¿Comes verduras?
- ❑ **4.** ¿Comes frutas?
- ❑ **5.** ¿Caminas o corres?
- ❑ **6.** ¿Comes un buen desayuno?
- ❑ **7.** ¿Comes comida que es buena para la salud?
- ❑ **8.** ¿Bebes cinco vasos* de agua?
- ❑ **9.** ¿Pasas tiempo con amigos?
- ❑ **10.** ¿Ves tres horas o menos de televisión?

9–10 puntos *¡Felicidades! ¡Haces mucho para mantener la salud!*

6–8 puntos *Bueno, pero debes hacer más para mantener la salud.*

0–5 puntos *¡Ay, ay, ay! Necesitas hacer algo para mantener la salud.*

*glasses

Pronunciación

The letters *l* and *ll*

In Spanish, the letter *l* is pronounced much like the letter *l* in the English word "leaf." Listen to and say these words:

lechuga	lunes	pasteles	helado
almuerzo	sol	abril	difícil

For most Spanish speakers, the letter combination *ll* is similar to the sound of the letter *y* in "yes." Listen to and say these words:

llamo	silla	allí	llueve
cebolla	pollo	ella	mantequilla

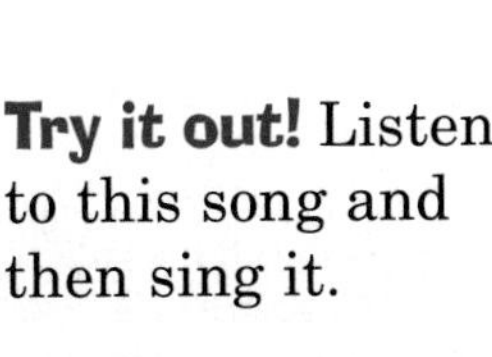

Try it out! Listen to this song and then sing it.

Canta el gallo, canta el gallo
con el kiri, kiri, kiri, kiri, kiri;
La gallina, la gallina
con el cara, cara, cara, cara, cara;
Los polluelos, los polluelos
con el pío, pío, pío, pío, pío, pío, pí.

Gramática

The plurals of adjectives

Just as adjectives agree with a noun depending on whether it's masculine or feminine, they also agree according to whether the noun is singular or plural. To make adjectives plural, just add an *-s* after the vowel at the end of the adjective. If the adjective ends in a consonant, add *-es*.

La hamburguesa es sabrosa. **Las** hamburguesa**s** son sabrosa**s**.

El pastel es muy popular. **Los** pastel**es** son muy popular**es**.

When an adjective describes a group including both masculine and feminine nouns, use the masculine plural form.

La lechuga, **las** zanahoria**s** y **los** tomate**s** son buen**os** para la salud.

Don't forget that the singular form of *mucho* means "much" or "a lot of," but that the plural form, *muchos(as),* means "many."

No como mucha carne, pero como much**as** verdur**as**.

¿Recuerdas?

Adjectives agree in gender with the masculine or feminine nouns they describe:

- **El bistec** es sabros**o**.
- **La ensalada** es sabros**a**.

GramActiva VIDEO

Want more help with the the plurals of adjectives? Watch the **GramActiva** video.

Gramática  **Pensar/Leer/GramActiva**

¿Sabroso o sabrosa?

Your teacher will give you a GramActiva worksheet. Tear or cut apart the different adjective stems and endings that are printed on the sheet. Then your teacher will show you pictures of several foods. Show how you feel about each food item by holding up the appropriate adjective stem and the appropriate ending.

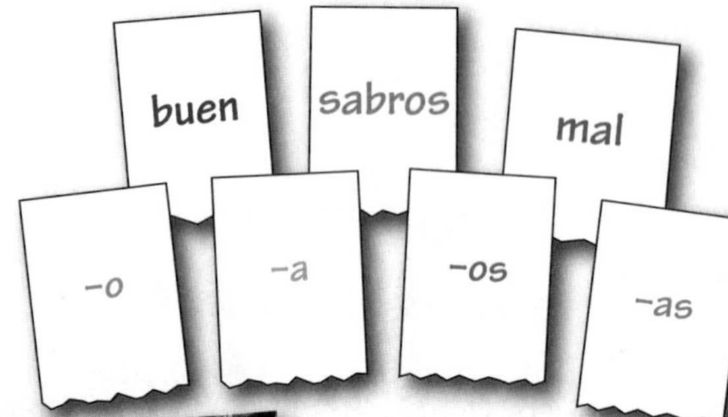

Fondo cultural

La Tomatina How would you like to attend a festival where a gigantic food fight with tomatoes is the highlight of the day? That's what happens at the annual *Fiesta de la Tomatina* in Buñol, Spain. After the town council distributes more than 130 tons of ripe tomatoes to participants, the two-hour long tomato-throwing festival begins.

- Describe any food festivals unique to your community or your state. How do they compare to *La Tomatina?*

La Tomatina en Buñol, España

Gramática  Escribir/Hablar

¿Cómo son?

1. For each of these adjectives, name two famous people, cartoon characters, or people in your school whom the adjective fits. Then write a sentence that describes both of them.

Modelo

A —*Creo que Cameron Diaz y Antonio Banderas son talentosos.*

1. artístico, -a	**3.** atrevido, -a	**5.** serio, -a	**7.** divertido, -a
2. deportista	**4.** gracioso, -a	**6.** talentoso, -a	**8.** trabajador, -a

2. Now read your sentences to a partner. Does your partner agree? Who fits the adjectives in your partner's opinion?

Modelo

B —*Estoy de acuerdo. Julia Roberts y Tom Cruise son talentosos también.*

o: *Sí, pero Julia Roberts y Tom Cruise son más talentosos que Cameron Diaz y Antonio Banderas.*

Más práctica

Practice Workbook 3B-5

For: Practice with plural of adjectives
Visit: www.phschool.com
Web Code: jcd-0313

  Escribir/Hablar

¿Qué prefieres?

Your class will be divided into groups of five to see what your favorite foods and beverages are.

Conexiones | Las matemáticas

1. Ask your group members what their favorites are from each of the following groups: *frutas, verduras, carnes,* and *bebidas.* Write the answers on a sheet of paper.

Modelo

A —*¿Qué verduras prefieres?*

B —*Prefiero zanahorias.*

2. Tally the results to see which foods and beverages are the most popular in each group. Indicate these favorites on a bar graph as shown. As a group, write four sentences that summarize your results. Compare your group's preferences to those of the other groups.

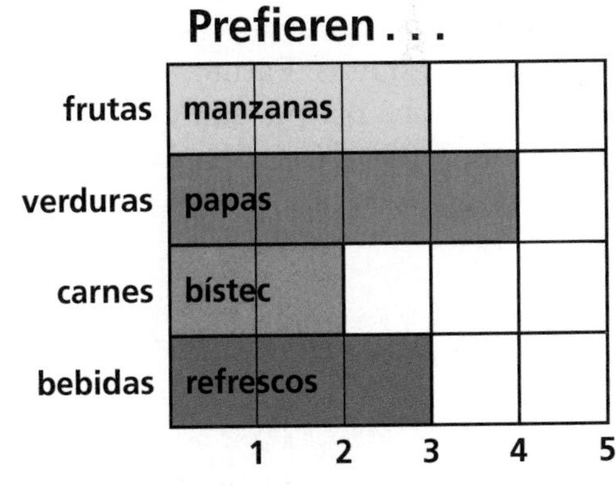

Modelo

Del grupo de las verduras, cuatro estudiantes prefieren papas.

Gramática

The verb *ser*

Ser, which means "to be," is an irregular verb. Use *ser* to describe what a person or thing is like. Here are the present-tense forms:

(yo)	soy	(nosotros) (nosotras)	somos
(tú)	eres	(vosotros) (vosotras)	sois
Ud. (él) (ella)	es	Uds. (ellos) (ellas)	son

¿Recuerdas?

In previous chapters, you learned how to talk about what a person is like.

—Tú **eres** muy deportista, ¿no?

—Sí, **soy** deportista.

—Mi amigo Pablo **es** deportista también.

GramActiva VIDEO

Want more help with the verb *ser?* Watch the **GramActiva** video.

Actividad 15 **Gramática** **Leer/Escribir**

Línea romántica

Rafa has to tell his father why the cell phone bill was so high. Complete his explanations by using the correct form of the verb *ser*.

¡Ay, Papá, tú __1.__ muy estricto! ¡Yo __2.__ un chico *muuuy* sociable! Hablo con mis amigas porque todas __3.__ muy simpáticas. Hablo con Lidia porque nosotros __4.__ muy deportistas. Mis conversaciones con ella siempre __5.__ muy interesantes. Fátima __6.__ muy estudiosa. Hablamos mucho porque ella y yo __7.__ inteligentes y hablamos de las clases. Y hablo con Lorena porque __8.__ muy graciosa y nosotros __9.__ muy buenos amigos.

Actividad 16 **Escuchar/Escribir**

Escucha y escribe

You will hear comments from five customers about the food being sold in a market. On a sheet of paper, write the numbers 1–5. As you listen, write the comments next to the numbers.

Hablar/Escribir

En tu escuela

Describe the people and places in your school.

Modelo

el / la profesor(a) de tu clase de español
La profesora de mi clase de español es muy simpática.

1. tu clase de español
2. las chicas en tu clase de español
3. los chicos en tu clase de español
4. el / la director(a) de tu escuela
5. la comida de la cafetería
6. tú y tus amigos

Gramática

Hablar

¿Sabroso o malo?

En tu opinión, ¿cómo son las comidas y las bebidas? Habla con un(a) compañero(a). Usa los verbos *comer* o *beber.*

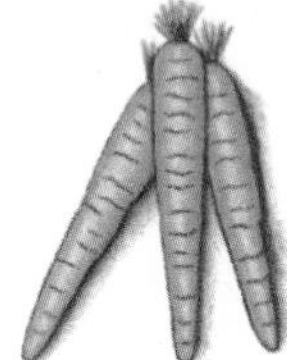

Modelo

A —*¿Comes zanahorias en la cena?*
B —*No, no como zanahorias en la cena porque son horribles.*
o: *Sí, como zanahorias en la cena porque son buenas para la salud.*

Estudiante A

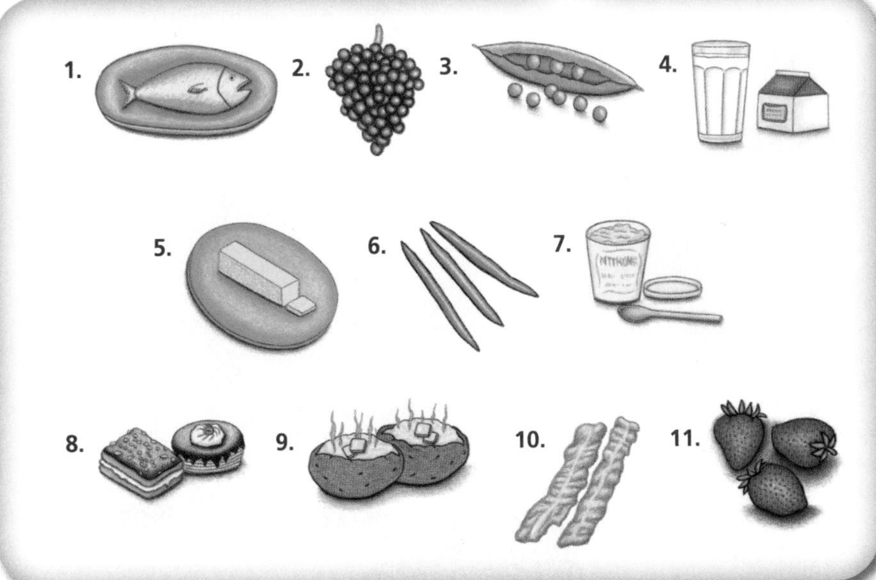

Estudiante B

(muy) sabroso
bueno para la salud
malo para la salud
horrible
¡Respuesta personal!

Más práctica

Practice Workbook 3B-6, 3B-7

For: Practice with *ser*
Visit: www.phschool.com
Web Code: jcd-0314

Fondo cultural

Los mercados, or open-air markets, are common throughout Latin America. Many towns have a central market, held on a given day of the week, where people come from all around to buy and sell food, as well as flowers, crafts, and clothing.

- How does this market compare with the ways in which fruits and vegetables are bought and sold in your community?

Un mercado guatemalteco

Exploración del lenguaje

Where did it come from?

The names of many foods in Spanish come from Latin as well as from other languages as diverse as Arabic, Italian, Greek, Turkish, and English. While it's clear that the word *espaguetis* comes from the Italian word *spaghetti,* it's not obvious that the word *zanahoria* comes from the Arabic word *safunariya.*

Try it out! Read the Spanish words in the first column and match them up to their counterparts in their language of origin.

agua	*piscatu* (latín)
arroz	*aqua* (latín)
pan	*beefsteak* (inglés)
bistec	*panis* (latín)
salchichas	*pullu* (latín)
pescado	*kahvé* (turco)
café	*salciccia* (italiano)
pollo	*óryza* (griego)

El español en el mundo del trabajo

Rick Bayless's career as a world-class Mexican chef began at the age of 14, when he visited Mexico and decided to study Spanish. Since 1978, Rick has opened gourmet Mexican restaurants, created and starred in cooking shows, written cookbooks, and won many awards.

- How would Rick's Spanish skills be helpful in his career?

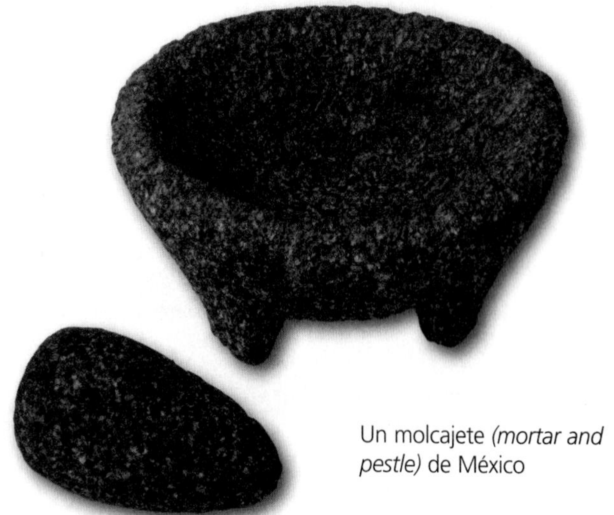

Un molcajete *(mortar and pestle)* de México

Leer/Escribir

Una pizza para la buena salud

Lee este anuncio *(ad)* de una pizzería y contesta las preguntas.

Strategy

Using cognates
Be sure to look for cognates to help you read this ad.

Pizzería Lilia
¡Pizzas saludables!

A veces la pizza tiene muchas calorías y grasas que no son buenas para la salud.

La Pizzería Lilia tiene una variedad de pizzas con ingredientes que son buenos y saludables.

- Menos queso
- Usamos ingredientes nutritivos
  - Más verduras (tienen pocas calorías y son muy nutritivas)
- Evita[1] la combinación de carnes
  - Las carnes tienen mucho sodio y grasas
  - El pollo o el jamón es mejor[2] que las salchichas

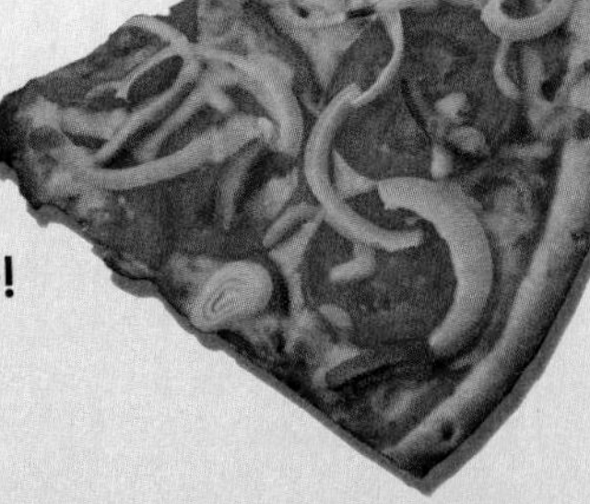

¡Llámanos!
¡Estamos aquí para servirte!
372 42 89
Calle Independencia 28

[1]Avoid [2]better

1. Find and list three cognates in this ad.
2. Write three recommendations in Spanish for a healthier pizza.

Escribir/Hablar

Y tú, ¿qué dices?

1. Describe tu pizza favorita.
2. ¿Crees que la pizza es buena o mala para la salud? ¿Por qué?
3. ¿Qué verduras prefieres? ¿Qué verduras no te gustan?
4. ¿Qué ejercicio haces con los brazos? ¿Qué ejercicio haces con las piernas?

En un café en Murcia, España

¡Adelante!

Objectives

- Read about a sports diet and learn some facts about an athlete
- Understand cultural perspectives on health care
- Make a poster about good health habits
- Learn facts about the southern part of South America

Lectura

La comida de los atletas

Lee este artículo *(article)* de una revista deportiva. ¿Qué comen y qué beben los atletas profesionales para mantener la salud y estar en buena forma?

Strategy

Skimming

List three things that you would expect to find in an article about athletes' eating habits. Skim the article to find the information.

¿Qué come un jugador de fútbol?

Los jugadores[1] de fútbol comen comidas equilibradas con muchos carbohidratos, minerales y vitaminas. Ellos consumen cerca de 5.000 calorías en total todos los días.

17% Proteínas

13% Grasas

70% Carbohidratos

Para el desayuno el día de un partido,[2] un jugador típico come mucho pan con mantequilla y jalea,[3] yogur y té.

Para el almuerzo antes del[4] partido, come pan, pasta, pollo sin grasa, verduras, frutas y una ensalada.

Para la cena después del[5] partido, el atleta come papas, carne sin grasa y más verduras y frutas.

También es muy importante beber muchos líquidos. La noche antes del partido, el jugador bebe un litro de jugo de naranja y durante el partido bebe hasta[6] dos litros de agua y bebidas deportivas.

[1] players [2] game [3] jam [4] before the [5] after the [6] up to

Nombre: Edwin Tenorio
Fecha de nacimiento: 16/6/76
Lugar de nacimiento: Esmeraldas
País de nacimiento: Ecuador
Nacionalidad: ecuatoriano
Equipo: Barcelona
Función: Ofensa
Edwin Tenorio es jugador del Barcelona, un equipo[7] de fútbol profesional en Ecuador.
[7]team

¿Comprendes?

1. ¿Qué debe comer Edwin Tenorio antes de un partido de fútbol?
2. ¿Qué debe beber?
3. ¿Qué comida no debe comer Edwin?
4. ¿Es tu dieta diferente de la dieta de un jugador de fútbol profesional? ¿Cómo?
5. ¿Cuál es la fecha de nacimiento *(birth date)* de Edwin? Escribe tu fecha de nacimiento cómo lo hacen en los países hispanohablantes.

Go Online
PHSchool.com

For: Internet link activity
Visit: www.phschool.com
Web Code: jcd-0315

Fondo cultural

¡Goooooooooooool! Scoring the winning *gol* in soccer is the most exciting moment of the game. *El fútbol* is the most popular sport in the world, and it has many *fanáticos* (fans) in every Spanish-speaking country. Every four years, teams throughout the world compete regionally in order to become one of the 32 teams to advance to the World Cup *(la Copa Mundial)* competition. Many Spanish-speaking countries compete in what has become the most widely watched sporting event in the world. Since the competition began in 1930, two Spanish-speaking countries have won the World Cup competition: Uruguay in 1930 and 1950 and Argentina in 1978 and 1986.

- How does the enthusiasm for soccer in the United States compare with the rest of the world's view of this sport? Why do you think this is so?

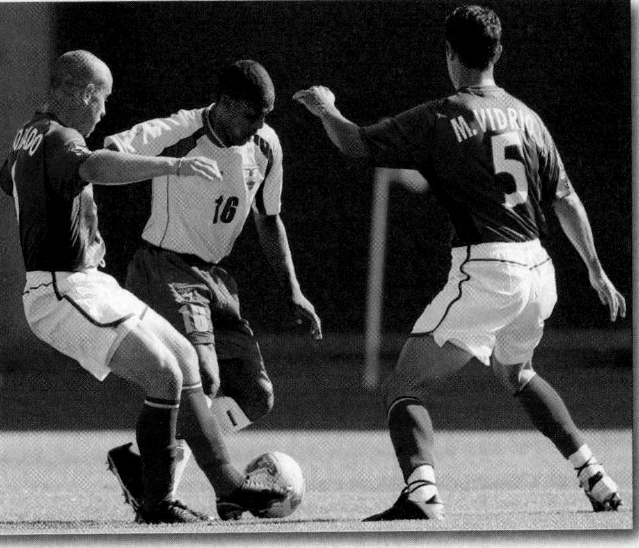

Jugadores de fútbol

El mundo hispano

América del Sur

Parte sur

A large proportion of the people of Argentina, Uruguay, and Chile live in cities. As in the United States, these cities have been shaped by mass immigration from southern and eastern Europe during the nineteenth and twentieth centuries. Many more Paraguayans, in contrast, live in the countryside.

In the early 1900s, the area of *las cataratas de Iguazú* was made an Argentine national park. Three countries—Brazil, Argentina, and Paraguay—meet at these spectacular falls, which are four times the width of Niagara Falls and 50 percent higher. Hundreds of species of insects, birds, and mammals are found in the area, and at least 500 species of butterflies. As many as 15,000 tourists a day visit the falls, a worrisome number for environmental groups, who continue to lobby against nearby hotel construction projects.

¿Sabes que . . . ?

At 22,840 feet (7,021 meters), Argentina's Cerro Aconcagua is the highest point in the Western Hemisphere, but it is considered a relatively easy climb. Chile's Torres del Paine, consisting of three granite towers, are nearly 6,000 feet lower, but their sheer cliffs, high winds, and extreme cold make them some of the most challenging climbs in the world. Both mountains are part of the Andes, a range that extends from Colombia to the southern tip of South America.

Para pensar

Think about what it would be like to be an immigrant arriving in one of the countries of southern South America. Would you prefer the city life of Buenos Aires, Argentina, Montevideo, Uruguay, or Santiago, Chile? Or would the countryside of Paraguay be more appealing? Why?

For: Online Atlas
Visit: www.phschool.com
Web Code: jce-0002

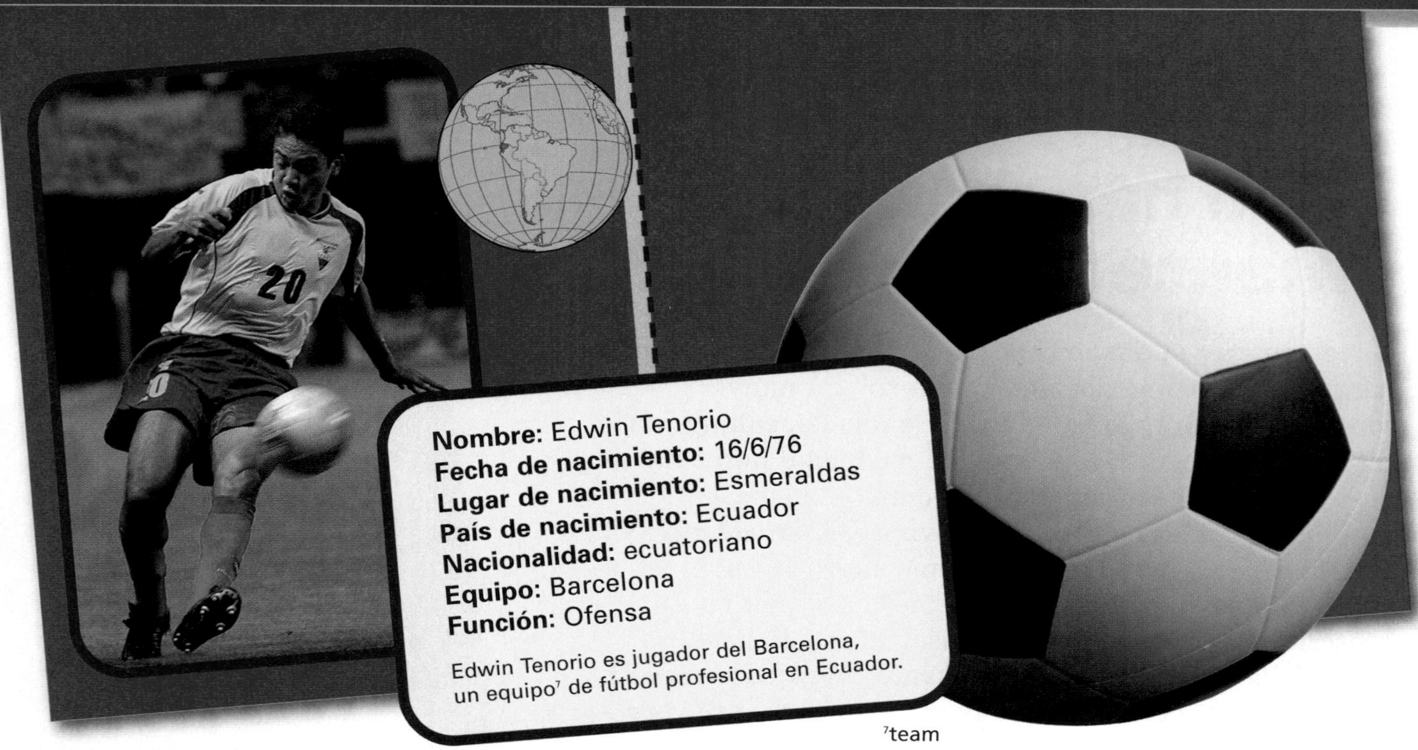

Nombre: Edwin Tenorio
Fecha de nacimiento: 16/6/76
Lugar de nacimiento: Esmeraldas
País de nacimiento: Ecuador
Nacionalidad: ecuatoriano
Equipo: Barcelona
Función: Ofensa
Edwin Tenorio es jugador del Barcelona, un equipo[7] de fútbol profesional en Ecuador.

[7]team

¿Comprendes?

1. ¿Qué debe comer Edwin Tenorio antes de un partido de fútbol?
2. ¿Qué debe beber?
3. ¿Qué comida no debe comer Edwin?
4. ¿Es tu dieta diferente de la dieta de un jugador de fútbol profesional? ¿Cómo?
5. ¿Cuál es la fecha de nacimiento *(birth date)* de Edwin? Escribe tu fecha de nacimiento cómo lo hacen en los países hispanohablantes.

Go Online PHSchool.com
For: Internet link activity
Visit: www.phschool.com
Web Code: jcd-0315

Fondo cultural

¡Gooooooooooooool! Scoring the winning *gol* in soccer is the most exciting moment of the game. *El fútbol* is the most popular sport in the world, and it has many *fanáticos* (fans) in every Spanish-speaking country. Every four years, teams throughout the world compete regionally in order to become one of the 32 teams to advance to the World Cup *(la Copa Mundial)* competition. Many Spanish-speaking countries compete in what has become the most widely watched sporting event in the world. Since the competition began in 1930, two Spanish-speaking countries have won the World Cup competition: Uruguay in 1930 and 1950 and Argentina in 1978 and 1986.

- How does the enthusiasm for soccer in the United States compare with the rest of the world's view of this sport? Why do you think this is so?

Jugadores de fútbol

Perspectivas del mundo hispano

¿Qué haces para mantener la salud?

Have you ever eaten chicken soup when you have a cold? How about putting aloe on a sunburn? In many countries, including those in the Spanish-speaking world, traditional remedies consisting of medicinal herbs have been used for centuries to treat common medical problems. In Mexico, a mint known as *yerbabuena* may be made into tea and given to someone with a stomachache. Remedies such as these may not be prescribed by licensed physicians, but people have confidence in them because they have been passed down through the generations. Many of those herbs are very safe, though some may have harmful side effects.

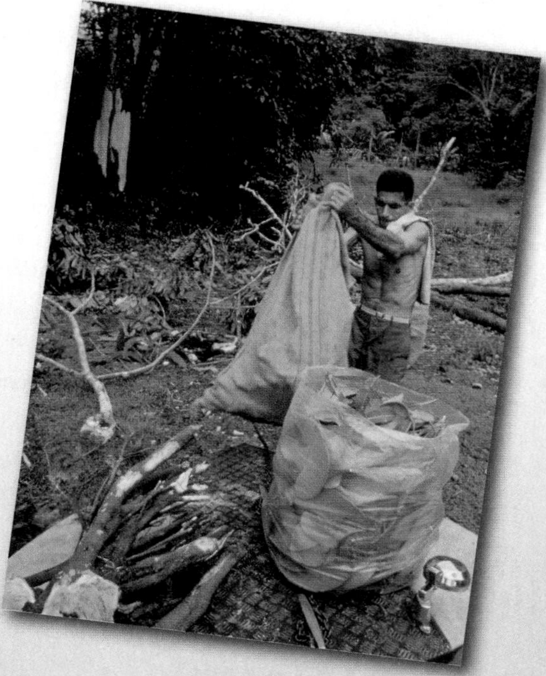

En la selva de Amazonas, Perú

Researchers are studying traditional herbal remedies to find modern-day medical solutions. In the Amazon rainforest in South America, an amazing abundance of plant life may hold the key to treating a wide variety of common ailments and diseases. Drug companies are looking for cures found in these plants and herbs that could be reproduced in today's modern drugs.

Increasingly, medicinal herbs are accepted not only as the basis for pharmaceutical drugs, but also for their own inherent healing qualities. In many countries, including the United States, herbal remedies are sometimes used in combination with conventional health care.

En un mercado en la Ciudad de México

Check it out! What alternatives to conventional medical care are available in your community? Make a list of all the health care services you can think of that are not provided by traditional physicians. Are there health stores that sell herbal medicines? What types of herbal medicines are being sold and what remedies are attributed to these medicines?

Think about it! In many Spanish-speaking cultures, herbal remedies have been accepted for centuries. Do you think that medicinal herbs can provide relief and cures? Why or why not?

Presentación escrita

Para mantener la salud

Task

You are doing some research for your health class on good eating and exercise habits. Make a poster in Spanish with five suggestions for better health.

1. **Prewrite** Talk to classmates, teachers, the school nurse, and your parents about good eating and exercise habits, especially for teens. Then list their ideas under the following headings to help you organize your information:
   - *Debes comer . . .*
   - *No debes comer mucho(a) . . .*
   - *Debes beber . . .*
   - *No debes beber mucho(a) . . .*
   - *Debes . . . para mantener la salud.*

2. **Draft** Write the first draft. Decide how to present the information in a logical way. Think about using visuals for clarity. Sketch them on your draft. Give the poster a title.

3. **Revise** Share your draft with a partner. Your partner should check the following:
   - Have you communicated the five suggestions well?
   - Do the visuals help convey meaning and make the poster attractive?
   - Are the vocabulary and grammar correct?

   Decide whether to use your partner's suggestions, and then rewrite your poster.

4. **Publish** Make a final copy, adding attractive illustrations or designs and making necessary changes. You might want to:
   - post it in the nurse's office, at a local community center, or in your classroom
   - include it in your portfolio

5. **Evaluation** Your teacher may give you a rubric for how your poster will be graded. You probably will be graded on:
   - completion of task
   - accuracy of vocabulary and grammar
   - effective use of visuals

Strategy

Gathering information
Use information from a variety of sources to help you create a more complete presentation on a topic.

El mundo hispano

América del Sur

Parte sur

A large proportion of the people of Argentina, Uruguay, and Chile live in cities. As in the United States, these cities have been shaped by mass immigration from southern and eastern Europe during the nineteenth and twentieth centuries. Many more Paraguayans, in contrast, live in the countryside.

In the early 1900s, the area of *las cataratas de Iguazú* was made an Argentine national park. Three countries—Brazil, Argentina, and Paraguay—meet at these spectacular falls, which are four times the width of Niagara Falls and 50 percent higher. Hundreds of species of insects, birds, and mammals are found in the area, and at least 500 species of butterflies. As many as 15,000 tourists a day visit the falls, a worrisome number for environmental groups, who continue to lobby against nearby hotel construction projects.

¿Sabes que . . . ?

At 22,840 feet (7,021 meters), Argentina's Cerro Aconcagua is the highest point in the Western Hemisphere, but it is considered a relatively easy climb. Chile's Torres del Paine, consisting of three granite towers, are nearly 6,000 feet lower, but their sheer cliffs, high winds, and extreme cold make them some of the most challenging climbs in the world. Both mountains are part of the Andes, a range that extends from Colombia to the southern tip of South America.

Para pensar

Think about what it would be like to be an immigrant arriving in one of the countries of southern South America. Would you prefer the city life of Buenos Aires, Argentina, Montevideo, Uruguay, or Santiago, Chile? Or would the countryside of Paraguay be more appealing? Why?

For: Online Atlas
Visit: www.phschool.com
Web Code: jce-0002

The Spanish were able to topple large, centralized empires such as those of the Aztecs and Incas quickly, but they were never able to conquer the smaller indigenous groups in the more remote regions. Chile's Pehuenche suffered defeats in the nineteenth century, but they still struggle to maintain their lands and culture.

Spain introduced horses, cows, sheep, and pigs to the Americas in the sixteenth century, transforming the ecology, culture, and economy of the region. In the nineteenth century, the growth of cities, the expansion of railways, and improvements in shipping created a worldwide market for South American meat and hides—and helped spur the development of the cowboy culture throughout the Americas. As on ranches in the western United States and northern Mexico, the main house of an Argentine or Uruguayan *estancia* served as a residence, office, and military stronghold.

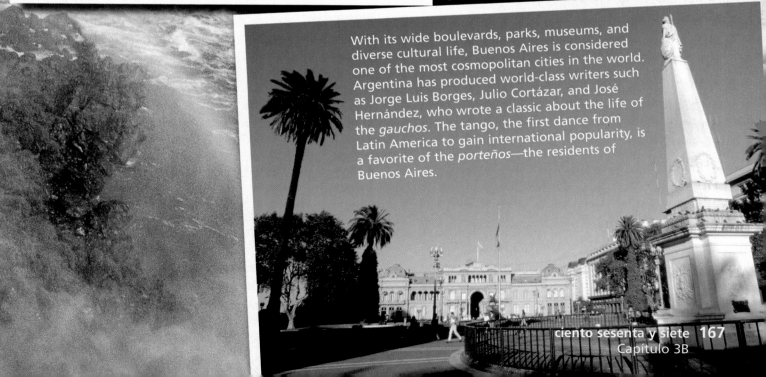

With its wide boulevards, parks, museums, and diverse cultural life, Buenos Aires is considered one of the most cosmopolitan cities in the world. Argentina has produced world-class writers such as Jorge Luis Borges, Julio Cortázar, and José Hernández, who wrote a classic about the life of the *gauchos*. The tango, the first dance from Latin America to gain international popularity, is a favorite of the *porteños*—the residents of Buenos Aires.

Repaso del capítulo

Chapter Review

To prepare for the test, check to see if you . . .

- know the new vocabulary and grammar
- can perform the tasks on p. 169

Vocabulario y gramática

to talk about food and beverages

la cena	dinner
el bistec	beefsteak
la carne	meat
el pescado	fish
el pollo	chicken
la cebolla	onion
los guisantes	peas
las judías verdes	green beans
la lechuga	lettuce
las papas	potatoes
los tomates	tomatoes
las uvas	grapes
las zanahorias	carrots
el arroz	rice
los cereales	grains
los espaguetis	spaghetti
las grasas	fats
la mantequilla	butter
el helado	ice cream
los pasteles	pastries
las bebidas	beverages

to talk about being hungry and thirsty

Tengo hambre.	I'm hungry.
Tengo sed.	I'm thirsty.

to discuss health

caminar	to walk
hacer ejercicio	to exercise
(yo) hago	I do
(tú) haces	you do
levantar pesas	to lift weights
para la salud	for one's health
para mantener la salud	to maintain one's health

For *Vocabulario adicional,* see pp. 472–473.

to indicate a preference

(yo) prefiero	I prefer
(tú) prefieres	you prefer
deber	should, must

to indicate agreement or disagreement

creer	to think
Creo que . . .	I think . . .
Creo que sí / no.	I (don't) think so.
(No) estoy de acuerdo.	I (don't) agree.

to ask a question or give an answer

¿Por qué?	Why?
porque	because

to express quantity

algo	something
muchos, -as	many
todos, -as	all

to describe something

horrible	horrible
malo, -a	bad
sabroso, -a	tasty, flavorful

other useful words

cada día	every day

plurals of adjectives

Masculine	Feminine
Singular / Plural	Singular / Plural
sabroso / sabrosos	sabrosa / sabrosas
popular / populares	popular / populares

ser *to be*

soy	**somos**
eres	**sois**
es	**son**

Más práctica

Practice Workbook Puzzle 3B-8
Practice Workbook Organizer 3B-9

Go Online PHSchool.com
For: Test preparation
Visit: www.phschool.com
Web Code: jcd-0316

Preparación para el examen

On the exam you will be asked to . . .	Here are practice tasks similar to those you will find on the exam . . .	If you need review . . .
 1 **Escuchar** Listen and understand as people describe a healthy or unhealthy lifestyle	Listen as two people are interviewed about their habits. See if you can tell which one is an Olympic skier and which one is a drummer. Be prepared to explain your "educated guesses."	**pp. 148–151** *A primera vista* **p. 149** Actividad 2
 2 **Hablar** Express your opinion about food preferences	During a telephone survey, you are asked some questions in Spanish about your food preferences. Say whether you think each food choice is good or bad for your health.	**p. 153** Actividades 6–7 **p. 154** Actividades 8, 10 **p. 157** Actividad 14 **p. 159** Actividad 18
3 **Leer** Read and compare what people do and eat in order to determine whether they lead a healthy or unhealthy lifestyle	Read the online conversation that you have just joined in a chat room. Decide whether each person has a healthy or unhealthy lifestyle, based on what they tell each other. Chato: ¿Qué hago yo? Cuando hace buen tiempo, corro por treinta minutos. Cuando llueve, levanto pesas. Chispa: No me gusta hacer ejercicio. Prefiero comer papas fritas. Son muy sabrosas. Andrés: ¿Papas fritas? Son horribles para la salud. Para mantener la salud, nunca debes comer papas fritas.	**pp. 148–151** *A primera vista* **p. 154** Actividad 9 **p. 155** Actividad 11 **p. 161** Actividad 19 **pp. 162–163** *Lectura*
 4 **Escribir** Write a list of things a person should do to maintain a healthy lifestyle	Many people think that teens don't know anything about a healthy lifestyle. You and your friends are compiling a top-ten list of ways to improve teens' health. Write at least three suggestions for the list.	**p. 154** Actividad 9 **p. 155** Actividad 11 **p. 161** Actividad 19 **p. 165** *Presentación escrita*
 5 **Pensar** Demonstrate an understanding of cultural perspectives regarding health care	Give an example of an herbal remedy that is accepted in a Spanish-speaking country as a remedy for a common ailment. Compare this with a similar herbal/natural remedy believed by many in the United States to be a cure for a common ailment.	**p. 164** *Perspectivas del mundo hispano*

¡Sabrosa y buena para la salud!

La comida Tex-Mex refleja la tradición de la comida de los mexicanos de Coahuila, Nuevo León y Tamaulipas mezclada[1] con los sabrosos ingredientes de la comida de los vaqueros[2] del sur de Texas. Las tortillas de harina,[3] el bistec, los frijoles refritos y el queso del norte de México son deliciosos pero, ¿son buenos para la salud? Todo depende de los ingredientes.

[1] mixed [2] cowboys [3] flour

El maíz

Los frijoles

Las tortillas de maíz

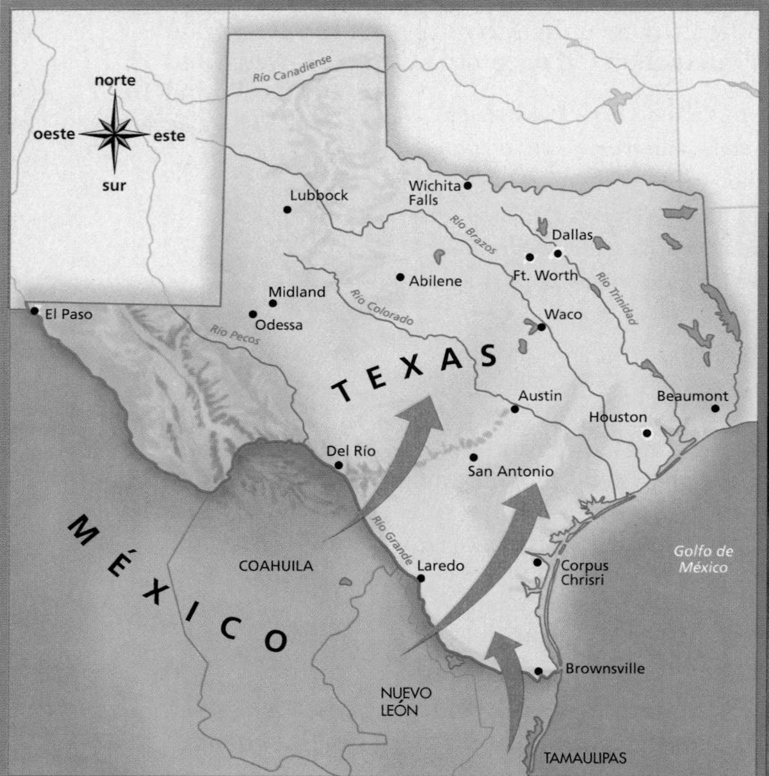

Desde los años 1600 hasta los 1800 muchos mexicanos inmigran del norte de México al sur y centro del área que hoy llamamos Texas.

El nopal, planta oficial del estado de Texas

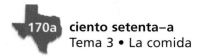

El pescado

Los chiles

Los tacos de pescado con nopales

Ingredientes:
1 cucharada[5] de aceite de oliva
1 jalapeño
1 diente de ajo[6]
1/2 cucharadita[7] de orégano
1/2 taza[8] de cilantro
1 lima
2 tomates
20 onzas de pescado
10 onzas de nopales
6 tortillas de maíz

[5] tablespoon [6] garlic [7] teaspoon [8] cup

Los tacos de pescado tienen menos grasa que los tacos de bistec y queso. Los nopales con el pescado es un plato sabroso.

Migas con frijoles negros[9]

Ingredientes:
4 huevos grandes
2 cucharadas de salsa picante
2 cucharaditas de cilantro
1 cucharada de aceite de oliva
2 tortillas de maíz en pedacitos[10]
1/4 taza de cebolla amarilla[11]
1/2 taza de aguacate
1 jalapeño
1 tomate
3/4 taza de frijoles negros
2/3 taza de queso (grasa reducida)

[9] black [10] little pieces [11] yellow

Las migas son el desayuno favorito de muchos tejanos. Son deliciosas y no son malas para la salud.

¿Comprendes?

Read the statements below and indicate if they are *cierto* or *falso* based upon the reading. Rewrite any false statements.

1. La comida Tex-Mex es una combinación de la comida de Santa Fé, Nuevo México y Texas.
2. Tamaulipas está al oeste de Nuevo León.
3. El nopal es un tipo de carne.
4. Hay carne en las migas con frijoles negros.
5. En la comida Tex-Mex, hay varios tipos de tortillas.

Conexiones

Write two to three sentences describing a typical dish served at your favorite Tex-Mex restaurant or other restaurant. Then use the Food Guide Pyramid at the beginning of Capítulo 3B to tell where each ingredient belongs. Is the dish you describe healthful? Why or why not?

Los tacos

Fondo cultural

El quitasol is a work by Spanish painter Francisco de Goya (1746–1828). He made this painting in 1777 as a design to be used in the manufacture of a royal tapestry. At that time Goya was already famous for the elegance of his artwork and his ability to capture ordinary events in realistic detail. The brilliant colors of this painting suggest a happy moment of relaxation for two young people.

- Why do people who live in the city go out to the country to relax?

El quitasol (1777), Francisco de Goya

Oil on canvas, 104 x 152 cm. Museo Nacional del Prado, Madrid, Spain. Photo credit: Scala / Art Resource, NY.

¿Adónde vas?

Chapter Objectives

- Talk about locations in your community
- Discuss leisure activities
- Talk about where you go and with whom
- Learn how to ask questions
- Understand cultural perspectives on leisure activities

Video Highlights

A primera vista: ***Un chico reservado***

GramActiva Videos: **the verb *ir;* asking questions**

Country Connection

As you learn about leisure activities, you will make connections to these countries and places:

Go Online PHSchool.com
For: Online Atlas
Visit: www.phschool.com
Web Code: jce-0002

El Parque del Buen Retiro, Madrid, España

A primera vista

Vocabulario y gramática en contexto

Objectives

Read, listen to, and understand information about

- places to go to when you're not in school

el gimnasio

el parque

el centro comercial

ir de compras

el trabajo

la lección de piano

el cine

ver una película

la biblioteca

la piscina

—En tu **tiempo libre después de** las clases, ¿qué haces?

—**Voy al** gimnasio **para** levantar pesas y al parque para correr. ¿Y tú?

—Hoy voy **a** mi trabajo. No voy a mi lección de piano.

—**¿Con quién** vas al centro comercial?

—Voy con Guillermo, y **después vamos** al cine. ¿Y tú?

—Voy a la biblioteca para estudiar. Después voy al **Café** del Mundo con Lucila.

la playa

el restaurante

el campo

las montañas

—¿Qué haces **los** domingos?

—Voy **con mis amigos** a la playa. Allí comemos el almuerzo. Hay un restaurante muy bueno. ¿Y tú?

—**Generalmente** voy al campo o a las montañas.

Más vocabulario

la iglesia	church
la mezquita	mosque
la sinagoga	synagogue
el templo	temple; Protestant church

Actividad 1 Escuchar

¿Estás de acuerdo?

You will hear Elena describe where she does seven activities. If a statement is logical, give a "thumbs-up" sign. If it is not logical, make a "thumbs-down" sign.

Actividad 2 Escuchar

¡Muchas actividades!

Listen to Antonio describe his weekly list of after-school activities. As he names his activities, touch the corresponding picture(s).

Más práctica
Practice Workbook 4A-1, 4A-2

For: Vocabulary practice
Visit: www.phschool.com
Web Code: jcd-0401

Videohistoria

Un chico reservado

¿Qué pasa cuando Ignacio, Elena y Ana hablan con el estudiante nuevo *(new)*? Lee la historia.

Strategy

Scanning
Use the visuals to predict what different activities Ana, Elena, Ignacio, and Javier are talking about. Then look in the dialogues to find the corresponding word or phrase that describes each activity.

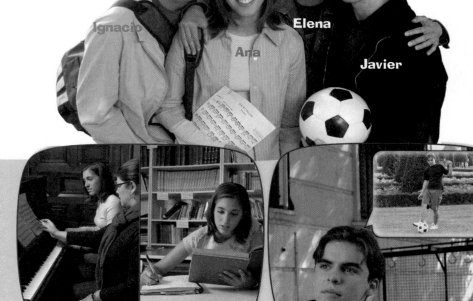

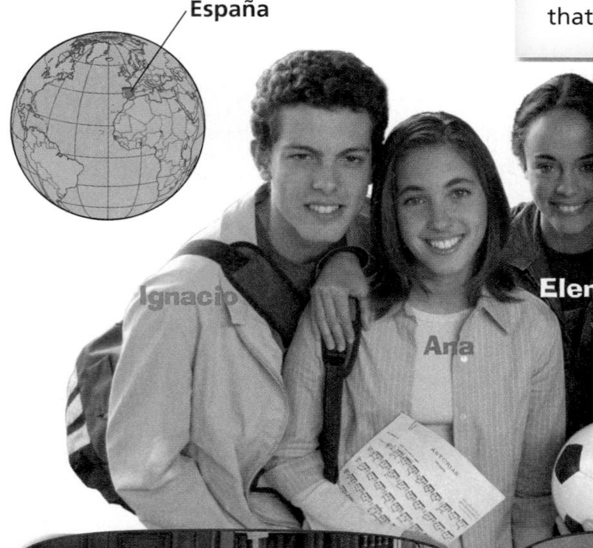

1 **Ignacio:** Mira, el estudiante nuevo es un poco reservado, ¿verdad?

Elena: Ah, sí . . . Está allí **solo.** ¿Por qué no hablamos con él?

Ignacio: Sí, ¡vamos!

5 **Ana:** Los lunes voy a mi lección de piano y los martes, miércoles y jueves voy a la biblioteca para estudiar. Y Javier, ¿qué haces **los fines de semana?**

6 **Javier:** ¿Los fines de semana? **Me quedo en casa.** No tengo muchos amigos aquí.

Ignacio: ¿Qué te gusta hacer?

Javier: ¡Me gusta el fútbol!

7 **Ana:** **¡No me digas!** Pues, nosotros vamos al parque para practicar fútbol.

Javier: **¿Cuándo?**

Ana: El sábado.

Javier: Está bien.

2 **Elena:** Hola. Me llamo Elena. Él es Ignacio, y ella es Ana.

Javier: Mucho gusto. Me llamo Javier.

Elena: Encantada . . . **¿De dónde eres?**

Javier: Soy **de** Salamanca.

3 **Ana:** Pues, Javier, ¿vas después de las clases **con tus amigos?**

Javier: No, voy **a casa.**

4 **Javier:** **¿Adónde** vais* vosotros después de las clases?

Elena: Los lunes, miércoles y viernes voy a mi trabajo en el centro comercial.

Ignacio: Generalmente voy al gimnasio. Me gusta levantar pesas.

8 **Elena:** Pero Ana, ¿fútbol?

Ana: ¿Por qué no? ¡No tiene muchos amigos y le gusta el fútbol!

Leer/Escribir/Hablar

¿Comprendes?

En una hoja de papel completa las frases según la *Videohistoria.*

1. Javier es de . . .
2. Después de las clases Javier va . . .
3. Después de las clases Ignacio va al . . .
4. El jueves Ana va a la . . .
5. A Javier le gusta practicar . . .
6. Todos van al parque el . . .

Más práctica

Practice Workbook 4A-3, 4A-4

For: Vocabulary practice
Visit: www.phschool.com
Web Code: jcd-0402

*Remember that in Spain, the *vosotros(as)* form of verbs is used when speaking to a group of people you would address individually with *tú.*

Manos a la obra

Vocabulario y gramática en uso

Objectives

- Communicate about leisure activities
- Tell where you go and with whom
- Learn to use the verb *ir* and how to ask questions

Escribir/Hablar

¿Qué haces en . . . ?

Completa las frases lógicamente.

1. Hago ejercicio en . . .
2. Nado en . . .
3. Veo películas en . . .
4. Leo libros y revistas en . . .
5. Voy de compras en . . .
6. Esquío en . . .
7. Como el desayuno en . . .

Escribir

¿Vas mucho a . . . ?

On a sheet of paper, copy the diagram below and write the names of the places you go under the appropriate expression of frequency.

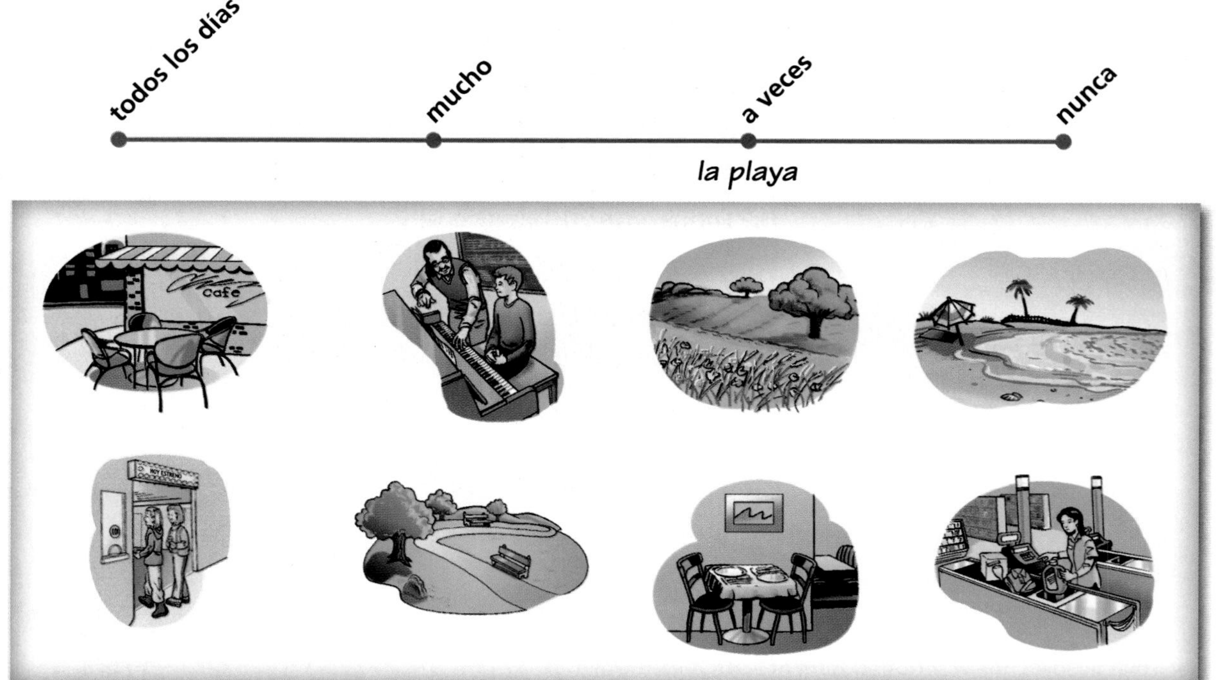

  **Hablar**

¡No me digas!

Work with a partner. Using what you wrote for Actividad 5, take turns saying where you go and how often. React to your partner's statements. Follow the model.

Modelo

A —*Voy a la playa a veces.*
B —*¡No me digas! Yo voy a la playa a veces también.*
o: *¡No me digas! Yo nunca voy a la playa.*
o: *Pues, yo voy a la playa todos los días.*

Nota

When ***a*** is used before ***el,*** the two words form the contraction ***al*** *(to the):*

a + el = al

- Voy **al** centro comercial a veces, pero voy **a la** piscina mucho.

También se dice . . .

la piscina = la alberca *(México);* la pileta *(América del Sur)*

el restaurante = el restaurán *(América del Sur)*

 **Escuchar/Escribir**

Escucha y escribe

Look at the painting of Plaza Morazán in Tegucigalpa, Honduras. On a sheet of paper, write the numbers 1–6. You will hear six statements about the painting. Write what you hear.

Fondo cultural

Strolling through the main square *(la plaza)* of most towns and cities in Spanish-speaking countries is a popular activity for young and old alike. Plaza Morazán is the main square in the capital city of Honduras, Tegucigalpa. The square is named after Francisco Morazán (1792–1842), a Honduran general and head of state.

- What social gathering place in your community is similar to *la plaza?*

Plaza Morazán en Tegucigalpa (1969), José Antonio Velásquez

Exploración del lenguaje

Origins of the Spanish days of the week

The word *sábado,* like many Spanish words, is based on Latin. The Spanish days of the week come from the Latin names for the gods, planets, sun, and moon, all of which were important in Roman daily life.

Try it out! Match the Spanish days of the week with their Latin origins.

1. lunes	**a.** *dies Mercurii:* named after Mercury, the god of commerce and travelers
2. martes	**b.** *dies Veneris:* named after Venus, the goddess of beauty and love
3. miércoles	**c.** *dies lunae:* the day dedicated to the moon *(luna)*
4. jueves	**d.** *dies solis:* named after the sun *(sol),* but later changed to *dies Dominicus,* which means "the Lord's day"
5. viernes	**e.** *dies Martis:* dedicated to Mars, the god of war
6. sábado	**f.** *dies Saturni:* named after Saturn; also called *dies Sabbati,* based on the Hebrew word *shabbath,* or "day of rest"
7. domingo	**g.** *dies Jovis:* named after Jove, or Jupiter, the ruler of the gods

- Since you know *día* means "day" in Spanish, what is the word for "day" in Latin?

Hablar

¿Adónde vas?

Habla con otro(a) estudiante sobre los lugares *(about the places)* adónde vas y cuándo vas allí.

Modelo

los lunes

A —*¿Adónde vas los lunes?*

B —*Generalmente voy a mi lección de piano.*

o: *Generalmente me quedo en casa.*

Nota

To say that something usually happens on a certain day every week, use ***los*** with the day of the week:

- Generalmente ellos van al campo **los viernes** o **los sábados.**

Estudiante A

1. los miércoles
2. los viernes
3. los sábados
4. los domingos
5. los fines de semana
6. después de las clases

Estudiante B

¡Respuesta personal!

   **Hablar/Pensar/Escribir**

Cuando no estamos en la escuela . . .

¿Cómo pasan el tiempo tus compañeros de clase cuando no están en la escuela? Sigue *(follow)* los pasos.

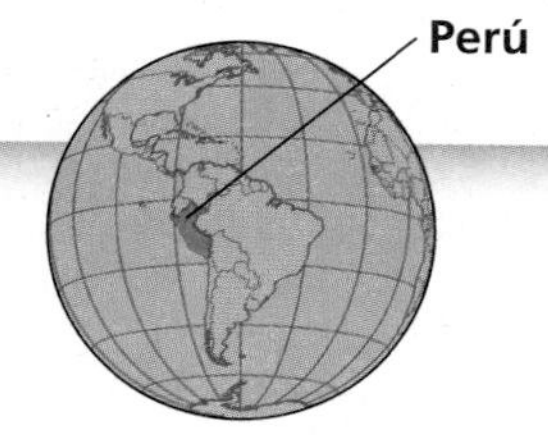

Conexiones | Las matemáticas

Muchos jóvenes pasan el día en la playa en Perú.

1. Working in groups of four, take turns asking each person how often he or she does the activities listed below. Answer using *mucho*, *a veces*, or *nunca*. Keep a group tally of the responses.

ver películas	usar la computadora	ir a un trabajo
correr	ir de compras	ir a la biblioteca

Modelo

A —*¿Con qué frecuencia* (How often) *usas la computadora?*
B —*Uso la computadora mucho.*

2. Get together with another group of four and combine the results of your tally sheets. Prepare summary statements to report to the class.
3. Report your summary statements to the class and make a class total. Convert each total to a percentage.
4. Create a bar graph for each activity that shows the class's frequency of participation.

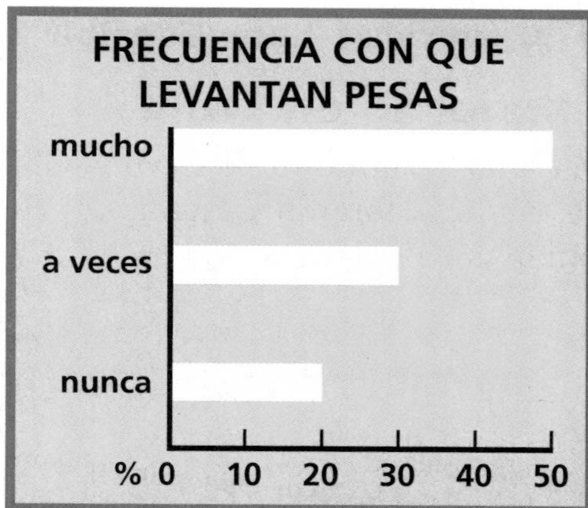

 **Escribir/Hablar**

Y tú, ¿qué dices?

1. ¿Dónde ves más películas, en casa o en el cine?
2. Cuando vas de compras, ¿adónde vas?
3. ¿Adónde vas los fines de semana?
¿Vas solo(a) o con tus amigos?

Gramática

The verb *ir*

To say where someone is going, use the verb *ir*. Here are its present-tense forms:

(yo)	**voy**	(nosotros) (nosotras)	**vamos**
(tú)	**vas**	(vosotros) (vosotras)	**vais**
Ud. (él) (ella)	**va**	Uds. (ellos) (ellas)	**van**

The verb *ir* is almost always followed by *a*. To ask where someone is going, use *¿Adónde?*

¿Adónde vas? **Where** are you going **(to)**?

- You will often hear people say *¡Vamos!* This means, "Let's go!"

¿Recuerdas?

You have used the infinitive *ir* to talk about going to school.

- Me gusta **ir** a la escuela.

GramActiva VIDEO

Want more help with the verb *ir*? Watch the **GramActiva** video.

Actividad 11 Gramática **Leer/Escribir**

Un invierno en Chile

María, una estudiante de Corpus Christi, Texas, pasa un año en Santiago, Chile, con una familia chilena. Lee la carta *(letter)* y escribe las formas apropiadas del verbo *ir*.

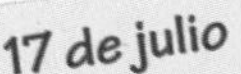

17 de julio

Querida Sonia,

¿Cómo estás? Yo, bien. Generalmente paso tiempo en casa los fines de semana, pero a veces yo __1.__ a Portillo con la familia para esquiar. Hace mucho frío allí y por eso mi "mamá" chilena no __2.__ siempre con nosotros. En Portillo hay una escuela para los esquiadores y muchos chicos simpáticos __3.__ a las lecciones. También hay un cibercafé con computadoras. Muchas personas __4.__ allí para pasar tiempo con los amigos. Nosotros __5.__ el domingo. Y tú, ¿__6.__ a la playa todos los días con tus amigos?

Hasta luego,

María

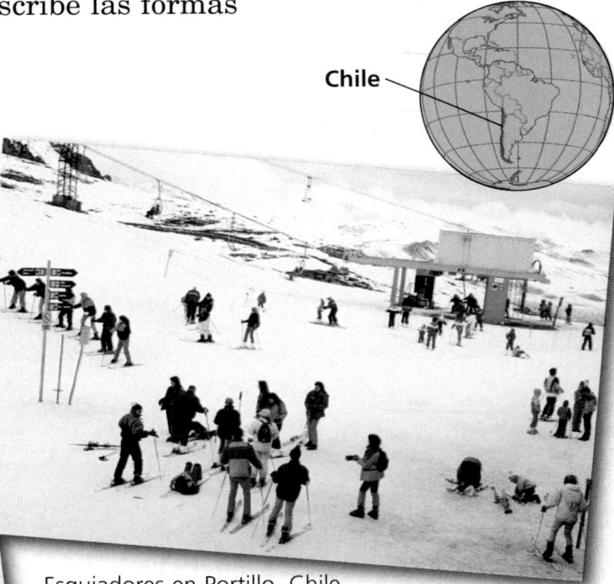

Esquiadores en Portillo, Chile

 Gramática Leer/Hablar

La carta

Lee la carta de María en la Actividad 11 y contesta las preguntas.

1. ¿Quién no va a veces con la familia a Portillo?
2. ¿Por qué a María le gusta ir a las lecciones de esquí?
3. ¿Adónde van para usar las computadoras?
4. ¿Cuándo van al cibercafé?
5. ¿Adónde van muchas personas para pasar tiempo con los amigos?

 Gramática Leer/Hablar/Escribir

¿Adónde van todos?

1 Where you go often depends on what you like to do. Read these sentences and then tell where the people go to do the activity.

Modelo

Te gusta esquiar. ¿Adónde vas?
Voy a las montañas para esquiar.

1. Te gusta levantar pesas.
2. Tú y tu amigo corren mucho.
3. Tus amigos y tú ven muchas películas.
4. A tu amigo le gusta comer bistec.
5. Tus amigas nadan muy bien.
6. Tus amigos hacen ejercicio todos los días.

2 Now write four sentences about yourself and your friends, saying where you go and for what purpose.

Modelo

Vamos a . . . para . . .

Estudiantes en el gimnasio

Fondo cultural

Sports clubs and gyms are very popular in Spanish-speaking countries. Since there are few school-based sports teams, many young people join private gyms for individual exercise or play for privately sponsored teams in order to compete in their favorite sports.

- What do you think students would do if your school did not offer opportunities for playing and competing in sports?

Actividad 14 Gramática

Escribir/Hablar

Juego

Play this game in teams of two.

1. With a partner, write five sentences saying what the two of you like to do in your free time and when. Also write sentences saying where you go for these activities.

   Modelo

   Nosotros corremos después de las clases. (Vamos al gimnasio.)

2. Read one of your statements about activities to another team of classmates, but don't read the part that tells where you go. Then have one person try to guess where you go to do this activity. If the student answers correctly, his or her team wins a point. The team that earns the most points wins.

   Modelo

   A —*Nosotros corremos después de las clases.*
   B —*Uds. van al gimnasio, ¿verdad?*
   A —*Sí, vamos al gimnasio para correr.*
   o: *No, no vamos al gimnasio para correr. Vamos al parque.*

El español en la comunidad

In many businesses and neighborhoods in the United States, you can hear Spanish being spoken. For example, the Pilsen neighborhood in Chicago, Illinois, is home to one of the nation's largest Mexican communities. The colorful murals, thriving businesses, and popular restaurants give Pilsen its own character.

- Are there areas near you where you can see expressions of community for Spanish speakers? What are they?

En la comunidad de Pilsen en Chicago

Pronunciación

Stress and accents

How can you tell which syllable to stress, or emphasize, when you see words written in Spanish? Here are some general rules.

1. When words end in a vowel, *n*, or *s*, place the stress on the **next-to-last syllable.** Copy each of these words and draw a line under the next-to-last syllable. Then listen to and say these words, making sure you stress the underlined syllable:

centro	pasteles	piscina
computadora	trabajo	parque
mantequilla	escriben	generalmente

2. When words end in a consonant (except *n* or *s*), place the stress on the **last syllable.** Listen to and say these words, making sure you stress the last syllable:

señor	nariz	escribir
profesor	reloj	arroz
español	trabajador	comer

3. When a word has a written accent, place the stress on the **accented syllable.** One reason for written accents is to indicate exceptions to the first two rules. Listen to and say these words. Be sure to emphasize the accented syllable.

café	número	teléfono
difícil	película	lápiz
fácil	plátano	artístico

Try it out! Listen to the first verse of the song "La Bamba" and say each word with the stress on the correct syllable. Then listen to the recording again and see if you can sing along with the first verse.

Para bailar la bamba, para bailar la bamba
se necesita una poca de gracia,
una poca de gracia y otra cosita
y arriba y arriba,
y arriba y arriba y arriba iré,
yo no soy marinero, yo no soy marinero,
por ti seré, por ti seré, por ti seré.

Más práctica
Practice Workbook 4A-5

For: Practice with *ir*
Visit: www.phschool.com
Web Code: jcd-0403

Gramática

Asking questions

You use interrogative words *(who, what, where,* and so on) to ask questions.

¿Qué?	*What?*	**¿Adónde?**	*(To) Where?*
¿Cómo?	*How?, What?*	**¿De dónde?**	*From where?*
¿Quién?	*Who?*	**¿Cuál?**	*Which?, What?*
¿Con quién?	*With whom?*	**¿Por qué?**	*Why?*
¿Dónde?	*Where?*	**¿Cuándo?**	*When?*
¿Cuántos, -as?	*How many?*		

In Spanish, when you ask a question with an interrogative word you put the verb before the subject.

¿Qué **come Elena** en el restaurante? — *What **does Elena eat** at the restaurant?*
¿Adónde **van Uds.** después de las clases? — *Where **do you go** after classes?*
¿Por qué **va Ignacio** a la playa todos los días? — *Why **does Ignacio go** to the beach every day?*

You have already used several interrogative words. Notice that all interrogative words have a written accent mark.

For simple questions that can be answered by *sí* or *no,* you can indicate with your voice that you're asking a question:

¿Ana va a la biblioteca?

OR: **¿Va Ana** a la biblioteca?

OR: Ana va a la biblioteca, **¿verdad?**

GramActiva VIDEO

Use the **GramActiva** video to help you learn more about asking questions.

Gramática **Pensar/Escribir**

Preguntas revueltas

Your new pen pal from Bolivia has sent you an e-mail, but all his questions are scrambled. Unscramble them and write them in the correct order. Then answer his questions.

1. ¿ / eres / de dónde / tú / ?
2. ¿ / Uds. / adónde / van / los fines de semana / ?
3. ¿ / al centro comercial / cuándo / van / Uds. / ?
4. ¿ / clases / tienes / cuántas / ?
5. ¿ / tú / qué / después de las clases / haces / ?
6. ¿ / vas / tú / con quién / al centro comercial / ?

Gramática **Leer/Pensar/Escribir**

¿Cómo es el cine?

Lee este anuncio del cine.

CINE PARQUE ARAUCO

Excelente calidad de proyección	Diariamente funciones continuadas desde el mediodía
Estacionamientos iluminados, gratis	Funciones de trasnoche los miércoles, viernes y sábados
Para su comodidad, aire acondicionado	Palomitas recién preparadas
Las únicas butacas reclinables de la ciudad	Servicio amable y eficiente
Excelentes instalaciones para discapacitados	Precios especiales para grupos y arriendos de salas de cine

SITUADO DELANTE DEL CENTRO COMERCIAL GIGANTE

Según el anuncio del Cine Parque Arauco, escribe la palabra apropiada para cada pregunta.

1. ¿____ es la calidad de la proyección en el cine? *Excelente.*
2. ¿____ comen muchas personas allí? *Palomitas.*
3. ¿____ es el nombre del cine? *Cine Parque Arauco.*
4. ¿____ van las personas a ver películas muy tarde *(late)* por la noche? *Los miércoles, viernes y sábados.*
5. ¿____ está el cine? *Delante del Centro Comercial Gigante.*

Cuándo	Por qué
Cómo	Cuál
Dónde	Qué

Fondo cultural

Movies are a popular form of entertainment for teenagers in Spanish-speaking countries. Spain, Mexico, Argentina, Colombia, and Venezuela have important film industries, but movies from the United States are also popular. Spanish-speaking teens tend to go to the movies in groups.

- How do your movie-going habits compare with those of teens in Spanish-speaking countries?
- Are movies from Spanish-speaking countries popular in your community? Why or why not?

En la entrada del cine

Actividad 17 Gramática **Escribir/Hablar**

Los fines de semana

1. Copy a chart like this one on a separate sheet of paper and fill in information on one activity you do on the weekends. Then find out the same information from three classmates.

Modelo

A —*¿Adónde vas los fines de semana?*
B —*Voy al centro comercial.*
A —*¿Con quién vas?*
B —*Voy con Selena.*
o: *Voy solo(a).*

Nombre	¿Adónde vas?	¿Con quién?
yo	a mi lección de guitarra	solo(a)
Laura	al centro comercial	con Selena

2. Tell a classmate or the class where you and each of the three people you interviewed are going and with whom.

Modelo

Yo voy a mi lección de guitarra solo(a).
Laura va al centro comercial con Selena.

Actividad 18 **Escribir/Hablar**

Y tú, ¿qué preguntas?

Habla con otro(a) estudiante sobre *(about)* la foto.

1. Mira la foto y escribe cuatro preguntas sobre el parque, las personas y las actividades.
2. Haz tus preguntas *(ask your questions)* a otro(a) estudiante.

Parque de las Palomas, San Juan, Puerto Rico

Fondo cultural

Old San Juan is a popular and lively part of Puerto Rico's capital, San Juan. Puerto Rican authorities are making great efforts to preserve colonial houses and other buildings and restore them to their original beauty.

- Are there historic areas near your community that have been or that are being restored? How do they compare with those in Old San Juan?

Más práctica

Practice Workbook 4A-6, 4A-7

Go Online PHSchool.com
For: Practice with questions
Visit: www.phschool.com
Web Code: jcd-0404

Leer/Escribir

¡Vamos al Viejo San Juan!

Puerto Rico has been a commonwealth of the United States since 1952. It is an island with a fascinating past. Look at the photos and read about a historic section of Puerto Rico's capital. Then answer the questions below.

Conexiones | La historia

El Viejo[1] San Juan es una zona histórica, pintoresca, colonial y muy popular en la capital de Puerto Rico. Los jóvenes[2] pasan el tiempo con sus amigos en los parques, cafés y plazas. Allí cantan, bailan y comen en los restaurantes típicos.

El Morro Construido en el siglo[5] XVI para combatir los ataques de los piratas ingleses y franceses[6]

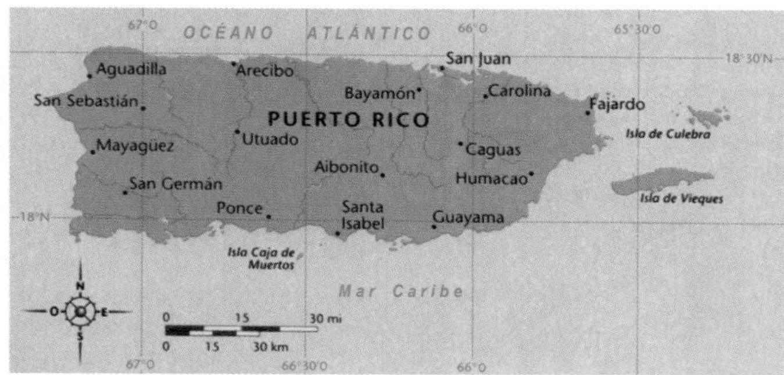

Datos importantes:

- Cristóbal Colón llega[3] aquí durante su segunda visita a las Américas en 1493
- El Viejo San Juan llega a ser[4] la capital de Puerto Rico en 1521

La Catedral de San Juan tiene muchas obras de arte.[7] Allí descansan[8] los restos[9] de Juan Ponce de Léon, famoso explorador de la Florida.

[1]Old [2]young people [3]arrives [4]becomes [5]century [6]French [7]works of art [8]lie [9]remains

1. For how many years has San Juan been the capital of Puerto Rico?
2. On which of his voyages did Christopher Columbus land on Puerto Rico?
3. Why did the Spaniards build El Morro?
4. What are two things you'll see when you visit the cathedral?

¡Adelante!

Objectives

- Read about after-school and weekend activities offered at a mall
- Learn some nursery rhymes
- Role-play a new student's first day at school
- Learn facts about the history of the United States

Lectura

Al centro comercial

Lee las actividades diferentes que puedes hacer en la semana del 11 al 17 de enero durante tu tiempo libre.

Strategy

Using prior knowledge
Think about what you know about special-event weeks at shopping centers. List events that you think might be offered at a mall.

¡Vamos a la Plaza del Sol!

Aquí en la Plaza del Sol, ¡siempre hay algo que hacer!

Actividades para el 11 al 17 de enero

11 *lunes*
7.00 P.M. Música andina

12 *martes*
7.00 P.M. Clase de yoga

13 *miércoles*
8.00 P.M. Noche de jazz

14 *jueves*
7.00 P.M. Clase de repostería[1]

15 *viernes*
8.00 P.M. Música andina

16 *sábado*
1.30 P.M. Exposición de fotografía
2.00 P.M. Show infantil
4.00 P.M. Exhibición de yoga
8.00 P.M. Sábado flamenco

17 *domingo*
1.30 P.M. Exposición de fotografía
2.00 P.M. Show infantil
4.00 P.M. Exhibición de yoga
8.00 P.M. Noche de tango

Música andina
El grupo Sol Andino toca música andina fusionada con bossa nova y jazz el lunes a las 8.00 P.M. Abierto[2] al público.

Clase de yoga
La práctica de yoga es todos los martes desde las 7.00 hasta las 9.00 P.M. La instructora Lucía Gómez Paloma enseña los secretos de esta disciplina. Inscríbase[3] al teléfono 224-24-16. Vacantes limitadas.

[1] pastry making [2] Open [3] Register

Sábado flamenco

El Sábado flamenco es el programa más popular de la semana. María del Carmen Ramachi baila acompañada por el guitarrista Ernesto Hermoza el sábado a las 8.00 P.M. Es una noche emocionante y sensacional de música y danza. Abierto al público.

Clase de repostería

Inscríbase gratis[4] en la clase de repostería programada para el jueves a las 7.00 P.M. Preparamos unos pasteles deliciosos gracias a la Repostería Ideal y al maestro Rudolfo Torres. Inscríbase al teléfono 224-24-16. Vacantes limitadas.

[4] free

¿Comprendes?

1. You will be in town from January 9 through February 2. Will you be able to take part in these activities? In which ones?
2. Which events require you to sign up in advance? Which do not?
3. You have to baby-sit your six-year-old sister. Which day(s) would be best to go with her?
4. Según los intereses de estos chicos, ¿a qué eventos van ellos?

   Raquel: Me gusta mucho hacer ejercicio.

   Roberto: Me encantan los pasteles.

   Teresa: Estudio baile. Tomo lecciones todos los jueves.

   Alejandro: Me gusta escuchar música—toda clase de música.
5. ¿Qué actividad es más interesante para ti?

Andean music has become popular worldwide. This haunting style of music originated in the Andes mountains of Peru, Ecuador, Bolivia, and Chile. Performers sometimes wear typical Andean attire. Instruments commonly used in Andean music include the *quena* flute, *siku* panpipes, and a small guitar called a *charango.*

- The Andean sound is created using a particular set of instruments. What instruments define the music you enjoy?

For: Internet link activity
Visit: www.phschool.com
Web Code: jcd-0405

La cultura en vivo

Rimas infantiles

Niños saltando a la cuerda

Niños jugando en San Sebastián, España

Can you remember the chants and songs you learned as a child? Or do you remember the rhymes you or your friends recited while jumping rope?

Here are some chants and songs that children in the Spanish-speaking world use when they play. The first one is a Spanish-language equivalent to "Eenie, meenie, minie, moe . . ." It is a nonsense rhyme used to select the person who will be "It" in various games.

Tin Marín de dopingüé
cucaramanga titirifuera
yo no fui,
fue Teté.
pégale, pégale,
que ella fue.

Here's a chant for jumping rope:

Salta, salta la perdiz	**The partridge jumps and jumps**
por los campos de maíz.	**Through the cornfields.**
¡Ten cuidado, por favor,	**Be careful, please!**
porque viene el cazador!	**Here comes the hunter!**
	(The jump rope then turns faster.)

Try it out! Here's a traditional game that combines Spanish, math, and hopping over a board. Place a long, narrow board on the floor. Take turns hopping with both feet from one side of the board to the other. Go forward as you hop. When you get to the end of the board, jump and turn in the air, facing the direction you came from. Continue hopping from side to side back to the other end. Be very careful! Try this in an area where you won't hurt yourself. As you are hopping, sing this song:

Brinca la tablita	**Jump over the board**
que yo la brinqué.	**That I already jumped.**
Bríncala tú ahora	**Now you jump**
que yo me cansé.	**Since I'm tired.**
Dos y dos son cuatro,	**Two and two are four,**
cuatro y dos son seis.	**Four and two are six.**
Seis y dos son ocho,	**Six and two are eight,**
y ocho dieciséis,	**And eight are sixteen,**
y ocho veinticuatro,	**And eight are twenty-four,**
y ocho treinta y dos.	**And eight are thirty two.**
Y diez que le sumo	**And ten that I add**
son cuarenta y dos.	**Equals forty-two.**

Think about it! What rhymes and songs do you know? What purpose do they serve in play?

Presentación oral

Un estudiante nuevo

Task

This is a new student's first day at school. You and a partner will play the roles of a new student and a student who has been at the school for awhile. Find out information about the new student.

1 Prepare You will need to prepare for both roles.

Experienced student: Make a list of at least four questions. Find out where the new student is from, activities he or she likes to do and on what days of the week, and where he or she goes and with whom. Plan to greet the new student and introduce yourself.

New student: Look at the questions the experienced student will ask you and jot down answers.

2 Practice Work in groups of four, with two experienced students and two new students. Practice different questions and responses. Be sure you are comfortable in both roles. Go through your presentation several times. You can use your notes in practice, but not during the role play. Try to:

- obtain or provide information
- keep the conversation going
- speak clearly

3 Present Your teacher will tell you which role to play. The experienced student begins the conversation by greeting the new student. Listen to your partner's questions or responses and keep the conversation going.

4 Evaluation Your teacher may give you a rubric for how the presentation will be graded. You probably will be graded on:

- completion of task
- ability to keep the conversation going
- how well you were understood

Strategy

Using models
It helps to go back and review models that prepare you for a task like this role play. Reread *A primera vista* (pp. 172–175). Pay attention to the different questions and answers that will help you with this task.

El mundo hispano

Estados Unidos

Histórico

The oldest permanent European settlement in the United States, St. Augustine, Florida, was established by Spain in 1565—55 years before the Pilgrims landed at Plymouth Rock. For more than two centuries after that, the Spanish controlled a large territory in North America that included what is now Mexico, parts of the southern United States, the states of Texas, New Mexico, Arizona, California, Nevada, and parts of Colorado and Utah.

Constructed as a mission in 1718, the Alamo (in San Antonio, Texas) today is best known as a key battleground in the secession of Texas from Mexico in 1836. The defeat of the Texians at the Alamo became a rallying cry for Texas independence, and Texas gained its freedom from Mexico two months later. ▶

¿Sabes que . . . ?

The language of the Nahua peoples of central Mexico, which included the Aztecs, is related to the languages of the Shoshone, Comanche, and Hopi tribes in the United States. When Spaniards pushed north from the newly conquered central Mexico, they often followed ancient Native American trade routes and used Nahua people as guides.

Para pensar

You can find many Spanish names of cities, counties, and states in the United States. Work with a partner and write a list of at least ten places with Spanish names and then try to guess what they mean in English.

For: Online Atlas
Visit: www.phschool.com
Web Code: jce-0002

The French Quarter in New Orleans was named after the French who first settled here. In spite of its name, most of the buildings date to when Spain ruled Louisiana (1763–1803). Fires ravaged the area in 1788 and 1794, so when the rebuilding was done, the architectural style was Spanish. This can be seen in the landscaped patios and iron grillwork on balconies.

A network of Spanish Catholic missions once extended throughout the Americas. Many cities in the southwestern United States, including San Francisco, San Diego, and Santa Fe, were originally built around Catholic missions, which in turn were often located at Native American villages or religious sites. The Mission San Xavier del Bac, in Arizona, combines the name of a Catholic saint (San Xavier) with the name of the Papago village where it was built (Bac, which means "where the water emerges"). Constructed in the early 1700s, the mission is still used by the Papago people and is considered one of the world's architectural treasures.

Spain built the Castillo de San Marcos to protect both St. Augustine (Florida) and the sea routes for ships returning to Spain from enemy attacks. This fort was started in 1672 and took 23 years to build. When Spain sold Florida to the United States in 1821, the fort was renamed Fort Marion. The Castillo has been a National Monument since 1924.

Repaso del capítulo

Chapter Review

Vocabulario y gramática

To prepare for the test, check to see if you . . .
- know the new vocabulary and grammar
- can perform the tasks on p. 195

to talk about leisure activities

ir de compras	to go shopping
ver una película	to see a movie
la lección de piano	piano lesson (class)
Me quedo en casa.	I stay at home.

to talk about places

la biblioteca	library
el café	café
el campo	countryside
la casa	home, house
en casa	at home
el centro comercial	mall
el cine	movie theater
el gimnasio	gym
la iglesia	church
la mezquita	mosque
las montañas	mountains
el parque	park
la piscina	swimming pool
la playa	beach
el restaurante	restaurant
la sinagoga	synagogue
el templo	temple, Protestant church
el trabajo	work, job

to tell where you go

a	to *(prep.)*
a la, al *(a + el)*	to the
¿Adónde?	(To) Where?
a casa	(to) home

to tell with whom you go

¿Con quién?	With whom?
con mis / tus amigos	with my / your friends
solo, -a	alone

to talk about when things are done

¿Cuándo?	When?
después	afterwards
después (de)	after
los fines de semana	on weekends
los lunes, los martes . . .	on Mondays, on Tuesdays . . .
tiempo libre	free time

to talk about where someone is from

¿De dónde eres?	Where are you from?
de	from, of

to indicate how often

generalmente	generally

other useful words and expressions

¡No me digas!	You don't say!
para + *infinitive*	in order to + *infinitive*

ir *to go*

voy	**vamos**
vas	**vais**
va	**van**

For *Vocabulario adicional,* see pp. 472–473.

Más práctica

Practice Workbook Puzzle 4A-8

Practice Workbook Organizer 4A-9

For: Test preparation
Visit: www.phschool.com
Web Code: jcd-0406

Preparación para el examen

On the exam you will be asked to . . .	Here are practice tasks similar to those you will find on the exam . . .	If you need review . . .
 **1 Escuchar** Listen and understand as people ask questions about weekend events	Two friends are trying to make plans for the weekend. Based on their dialogue, what do they finally agree on? a) Who is going? b) Where are they going? c) When are they going?	**pp. 172–175** *A primera vista* **p. 186** Actividad 17
 **2 Hablar** Talk about places to go and things to do on the weekend	Your parents want to know what you're doing this weekend. Mention at least three places you plan to go or things you plan to do. For example, you might say *Voy de compras con mis amigos.*	**pp. 172–175** *A primera vista* **p. 177** Actividad 6 **p. 178** Actividad 8 **p. 181** Actividad 13 **p. 182** Actividad 14 **p. 186** Actividad 17
3 Leer Read about what a person does on particular days of the week	Someone has left his or her planner at your house. Read the schedule for two days to try to figure out what type of person owns it. Indicate whether you agree or disagree with the statements about the person. MARTES: 6:00 Desayuno 4:00 Lección de piano 5:00 Trabajo 8:30 Clase aeróbica JUEVES: 3:30 Gimnasio 4:30 Piscina 6:00 Trabajo 8:00 Biblioteca *¿Estás de acuerdo o no? a) Es muy perezoso(a); b) Es atlético(a); c) Le gusta ir de compras.*	**pp. 172–175** *A primera vista* **p. 176** Actividad 4 **p. 180** Actividad 11 **pp. 188–189** *Lectura*
 **4 Escribir** Write a short note to a friend to let him or her know where you are going after school	Your friend is taking a make-up test after school, so you need to write her a short note to tell her what you are doing after school today. In the note, tell her where you are going and then at what time you are going home.	**p. 176** Actividad 4 **p. 179** Actividad 10 **p. 181** Actividad 13 **p. 182** Actividad 14 **p. 186** Actividad 18
 **5 Pensar** Demonstrate an understanding of rhymes, songs, and games from Spanish-speaking cultures	Think about your favorite childhood game. How does it compare to the children's games you learned about in this chapter? Describe a traditional game from a Spanish-speaking country.	**p. 190** *La cultura en vivo*

Fondo cultural

Starting with the first **Paralympics Games** in Rome in 1960, the International Paralympics Committee has organized summer and winter games that follow the regular Olympic Games and are hosted by the same city. Athletes with all types of disabilities compete in the Paralympics. More than 160 nations participate in this nonprofit organization, with over 6,000 participants worldwide.

- How do you think athletes with disabilities benefit from competing in the Paralympics or in similar local events?

Capítulo 4B

¿Quieres ir conmigo?

Chapter Objectives

- **Talk about activities outside of school**
- **Extend, accept, and decline invitations**
- **Tell when an event happens**
- **Understand cultural perspectives on after-school activities**

Video Highlights

A primera vista: ***¡A jugar!***
GramActiva Videos: ***ir*** **+** ***a*** **+ infinitive; the verb** ***jugar***

Country Connection

As you learn about after-school activities, you will make connections to these countries and places:

Go Online
PHSchool.com
For: Online Atlas
Visit: www.phschool.com
Web Code: jce-0002

uegos paralímpicos
6, Atlanta, Georgia

A primera vista

Vocabulario y gramática en contexto

Objectives

Read, listen to, and understand information about
- **activities outside of school**

Club Deportivo León

Parque de la Independencia

¿Te gustan los deportes? ¡Puedes practicar con uno de nuestros expertos! ¿Juegas bien o juegas mal? ¡No importa! Hay un deporte para ti.

8.00	el fútbol
8.00	el vóleibol
10.00	el golf
10.00	el tenis
13.00	el béisbol
13.00	el básquetbol
16.00	el fútbol americano

—¿Qué **quieres** hacer **a las ocho de la mañana, jugar al** fútbol o al vóleibol?

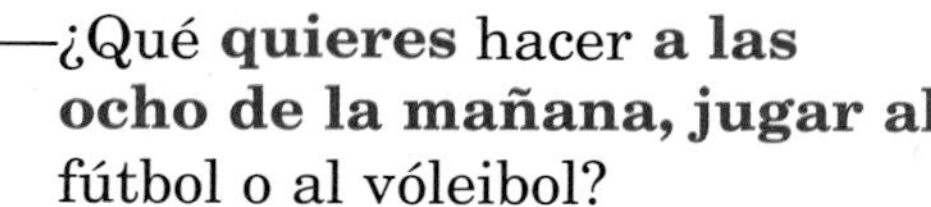

—A ver . . . No **quiero** jugar al fútbol. **Juego** muy **mal.** Prefiero jugar al vóleibol. Necesito practicar más. ¿Y qué **te gustaría** hacer a las cuatro **esta tarde?**

—**Me gustaría** jugar al fútbol americano.

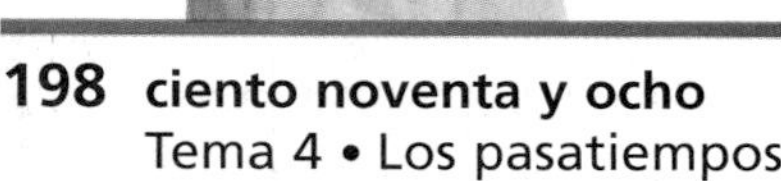

el concierto

la fiesta

el baile

el partido

—¡Hola! ¡Soy Rosa! ¿Quieres hacer algo **conmigo este fin de semana?** Hay un concierto en el parque.

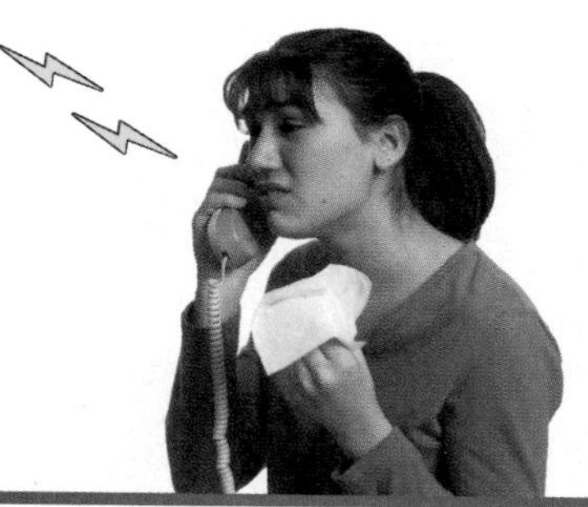

—**Lo siento,** pero no **puedo.** Estoy **demasiado ocupado** y tengo mucha tarea.

—No puedo porque **tengo que** trabajar. Trabajo **esta noche** a las siete y mañana trabajo **a la una de la tarde. Voy a estar** un poco **cansada. ¡Ay! ¡Qué pena!**

—¡Qué **triste!** No, no puedo ir **contigo.** Estoy **un poco enferma.**

ir de cámping

ir de pesca

—**¡Qué buena idea!** Pero no me gustan los conciertos. Prefiero ir de cámping. Siempre estoy muy **contenta** cuando voy de cámping. . . . **¿A qué hora?** ¿Mañana a las cinco de la tarde? **Entonces,** nos vemos.

Escuchar

¡Deportemanía!

Marcela is a sports fanatic! As she lists the days on which she will play the various sports, touch the picture of each sport.

Escuchar

¿Cómo estás?

You will hear how five people are feeling. Act out the adjectives that you hear.

Más práctica

Practice Workbook 4B-1, 4B-2

For: Vocabulary practice
Visit: www.phschool.com
Web Code: jcd-0411

Videohistoria

¡A jugar!

Ignacio, Javier, Ana y Elena están en el Parque del Retiro en Madrid. ¿Qué van a jugar y hacer? ¿De qué hablan? Lee la historia.

Strategy

Looking to find key questions
Before you read the story, skim to find where the characters are asking questions. The answers may point to important information in the story.

- Look at the questions. Which characters are offering invitations? What do you think they will do?

1 *Hoy es sábado y hace buen tiempo. Ignacio, Javier, Ana y Elena están en el parque para jugar al fútbol.*

5 **Ignacio:** Oye, hay una fiesta esta noche. Ana, tú y Elena vais, ¿verdad?

Ana: ¡Claro!

Ignacio : Javier, ¿quieres ir con nosotros a la fiesta?

Elena: ¡Qué buena idea!

6 **Javier:** ¿A qué hora es la fiesta?

Ana: A las nueve **de la noche.** En la escuela.

7 **Javier:** ¿Tengo que bailar?

Ana: Pues, sí. Puedes bailar conmigo y con Elena.

Javier: No **sé** bailar muy bien.

Ana: ¡Vamos, Javier!

Javier: Bien, voy.

2 **Ignacio:** ¡Oye, Javier! ¡Sabes jugar muy bien al fútbol!

Javier: Y tú también . . . Pero necesito practicar más. Ana, ¿quieres jugar?

Ana: ¡Por supuesto! Vamos a jugar.

3 **Elena:** Estoy demasiado cansada y tengo sed. ¿Por qué no tomamos un refresco?

Ignacio: ¡Genial! Yo también estoy un poco cansado.

4 **Ana:** ¿Juegas al vóleibol esta tarde?

Elena: Sí, a las seis.

8 **Javier:** Hasta las nueve, entonces.

Ignacio: ¡Genial! Hasta más tarde.

Escribir/Hablar

¿Comprendes?

¿Quién habla: Ana, Elena, Ignacio o Javier?

1. No sé bailar bien.
2. Necesito practicar más.
3. Necesito beber algo después de jugar al fútbol.
4. Juego al vóleibol a las seis.
5. Voy a la fiesta a las nueve.
6. Estoy cansado.

Más práctica

Practice Workbook 4B-3, 4B-4

For: Vocabulary practice
Visit: www.phschool.com
Web Code: jcd-0412

Manos a la obra

Vocabulario y gramática en uso

Objectives

- Talk about activities outside of school
- Extend, accept, and decline invitations
- Tell when an event happens
- Say what you are going to do
- Learn to use *ir* + *a* + infinitive and the verb *jugar*

Actividad 4 **Hablar**

Me gustaría ir . . .

Say whether or not you would like to do these things this weekend.

Modelo

Me gustaría ir a una fiesta este fin de semana.
o: *No me gustaría ir a una fiesta este fin de semana.*

1. 
2. 
3. 
4. 
5. 

Actividad 5 **Escribir/Hablar**

No sé jugar . . .

Indica si sabes o no sabes jugar estos deportes.

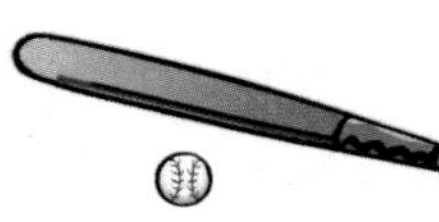

Modelo

Sé jugar al béisbol muy bien.
o: *No sé jugar al béisbol.*

1. 
2. 
3. 
4.  
5. 
6. 

Actividad 6 **Hablar**

¿Qué deportes practicas?

Using the information from Actividad 5, ask and tell about which sports you know, or don't know, how to play.

Modelo

A —*¿Sabes jugar al béisbol?*
B —*¡Por supuesto! Sé jugar al béisbol muy bien.*
o: *No, no sé jugar al béisbol.*

Leer/Escribir

¿Cómo estás?

You've asked your friends how they are. Now read each friend's reply and write the correct form of the missing word from the list.

cansado, -a	contento, -a
enfermo, -a	mal
ocupado, -a	triste

Tú: ¿Cómo estás?

Felipe: Muy __1.__. Voy a un concierto esta noche con mis amigos.

Miguel: ¡ __2.__! Mi clase de ciencias es muy aburrida y no me gusta nada el profesor.

Marta: Estoy __3.__. Me duele la cabeza. Hoy no puedo jugar al tenis ni patinar.

Carlos: Estoy __4.__. Todos mis amigos van a la playa el sábado pero tengo que trabajar.

Gabriela: Un poco __5.__. Todas las noches trabajo en el centro comercial.

Dolores: Demasiado __6.__. Juego al básquetbol después de las clases, tomo lecciones de piano y practico cada día y tengo un trabajo también.

Hablar

Lo siento

Ask your partner if he or she wants to do these activities with you. Your partner can't go, and will offer excuses to explain why.

Modelo

A —*¡Oye! ¿Quieres patinar conmigo esta tarde?*
B —*Lo siento. Hoy no puedo. Estoy demasiado enfermo(a).*

Estudiante A

Estudiante B

muy	ocupado, -a
demasiado	enfermo, -a
un poco	cansado, -a
	triste
	mal

¡Respuesta personal!

Escuchar/Escribir

Escucha y escribe

You will hear three invitations to events and the responses given. On a sheet of paper, write the numbers 1–3. As you listen, write down what each invitation is for and whether the person accepted it (write *sí*) or turned it down (write *no*).

Hablar

¿A qué hora?

Take turns asking and telling what time the following activities take place.

8:00

Modelo

A —*¿A qué hora es la película?*
B —*A las ocho de la noche.*

1.  9:00

2.  2:30

3.  1:30

4.  8:30

5.  7:30

6.  7:00

Hablar

Una invitación para el sábado

Invite your partner to these places, and tell at what time you will go. Your partner will accept or decline. Follow the model.

1:30

Modelo

A —*¿Te gustaría ir al concierto el sábado?*
B —*¿A qué hora?*
A —*A la una y media de la tarde.*
B —*¡Genial! ¡Nos vemos el sábado!*

Nota

To ask and tell what time something happens, you say:

- **¿A qué hora** vas?
- Voy **a la** una.
- Voy **a las** tres y media.

To specify what part of the day, add:

de la mañana* *in the morning (A.M.)*
de la tarde *in the afternoon (P.M.)*
de la noche *in the evening, at night (P.M.)*

**Mañana* means "tomorrow"; *la mañana* means "morning."

Estudiante A

1.  7:30

2.  8:30

3.  5:30

4.  1:00

5.  4:15

6.   11:00

Estudiante B

¡Por supuesto! Me gustaría mucho.

Lo siento, pero no puedo.

¡Ay! ¡Qué pena! Tengo que trabajar.

¡Genial! Nos vemos el sábado.

¡Qué buena idea! ¡Gracias!

¡Respuesta personal!

Exploración del lenguaje

Spanish words borrowed from English

Languages often borrow words from one another. For example, "rodeo" and "patio" are Spanish words that have found their way into English. There are also many examples of English words that have entered Spanish. By recognizing these familiar words, you can increase your vocabulary in Spanish.

Try it out! Read the sentences and identify the "borrowed words." Don't forget to pronounce the words correctly in Spanish.

Quiero hacer videos.
¿Quieres jugar al básquetbol conmigo?
Practico el rugby y el ráquetbol.
Juego al fútbol en el cámping.
¡Me encantan los sándwiches!

Escribir/Hablar

Y tú, ¿qué dices?

1. ¿A qué hora te gusta ir al cine?
2. ¿Estás más contento(a) cuando practicas un deporte o cuando ves la televisión?
3. ¿Qué deportes te gustan más?
4. ¿Este fin de semana tienes que trabajar o puedes pasar tiempo con amigos?

Fondo cultural

La noche de los rábanos is just one of the many kinds of *fiestas* in the Spanish-speaking world. On the evening of December 23, people set up booths around the *zócalo* (town square) of Oaxaca, Mexico, to display and sell radishes *(los rábanos)* sculpted into a fantastic array of shapes. *Oaxaqueños* and visitors alike crowd the square to view the amazing creations.

- Do you know communities or regions in the United States that are known for particular crafts or products?

Rábanos esculpidos *(sculpted)*, Oaxaca, México

Gramática

Ir + a + infinitive

Just as you use "going" + an infinitive in English to say what you are going to do, in Spanish you use a form of the verb ***ir + a*** + an infinitive to express the same thing:

Voy a jugar al tenis hoy.
I'm going to play tennis today.

¿Tú **vas a jugar** al golf esta tarde?
Are you going to play golf this afternoon?

Mis amigas **van a ir de cámping** mañana.
My friends are going camping tomorrow.

Javier: ¿**Van a jugar** conmigo, o no?
Ana: Sí, **vamos a jugar** contigo.

GramActiva VIDEO

Want more help with *ir + a* + infinitive? Watch the **GramActiva** video.

Gramática **Escuchar/Escribir**

Escucha y escribe

Rosario and Pablo have left messages on your answering machine telling you what they are going to do and inviting you to join them. On a sheet of paper, write their names and, under each one, the numbers 1–3. As you listen to each message, write down information to answer these three questions:

1. ¿Adónde quiere ir? **2.** ¿Qué va a hacer? **3.** ¿A qué hora va a ir?

Gramática  **Escribir/Hablar**

Este fin de semana vamos a . . .

¿Qué va a hacer la familia Ríos este fin de semana?

Modelo

Esteban /  / **8:00** ☽ *Esteban va a estudiar a las ocho de la noche.*

1. Angélica /  / **3:30** 

2. Yo /  / **4:00** 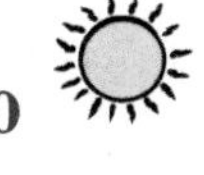

3. Esteban y un amigo / 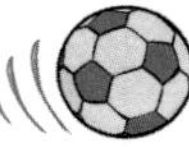 / **10:00** 

4. Angélica y el Sr. Ríos /  / **7:00**

5. Los señores Ríos / / **7:30** ☽

6. Angélica, Esteban y yo /  / **8:00** ☽

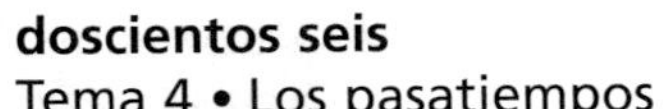

Escribir/Hablar

¿Qué vas a hacer?

1. Make a chart like this one to describe five things you're going to do, when you're going to do them, and with whom. Use the following words to say when you're going to do these things: *esta tarde, esta noche, mañana, el jueves, el fin de semana.*

Modelo

¿Qué?	¿Cuándo?	¿Con quién?
tocar la guitarra	esta tarde	mis amigos

2. Ask your partner what his or her plans are.

Modelo

A —*¿Qué vas a hacer esta tarde?*
B —*Esta tarde mis amigos y yo vamos a tocar la guitarra.*

Mañana voy a tocar la guitarra.

Leer/Escribir/Hablar

El teléfono celular

Lee el anuncio para el teléfono celular y contesta las preguntas.

1. ¿Por qué es bueno tener un teléfono celular?
2. ¿Te gusta hablar por teléfono celular? ¿Con quién?
3. ¿Crees que es bueno o malo usar un teléfono celular en un restaurante? ¿Por qué?

¿Te gustaría . . .
pasar más tiempo con tus amigos?
ir de compras?
ir al cine?
ir a conciertos?
escuchar música?
hablar por teléfono?
¡Por supuesto!
¡Con un teléfono celular puedes hacer planes para hacerlo todo!

Hablar

¿Quieres ir conmigo?

Pretending to use a cell phone, greet a partner and invite him or her to do something with you. Your partner can't go and tells you why.

Modelo

A —*Hola, Sara. Soy Rosa. ¿Quieres jugar al tenis conmigo esta tarde?*
B —*Lo siento, hoy no puedo. Voy a estudiar para la clase de inglés.*
A —*¡Ay! ¡Qué pena!*

Más práctica

Practice Workbook 4B-5, 4B-6

For: Practice with *ir* + *a* + infinitive
Visit: www.phschool.com
Web Code: jcd-0413

Gramática

The verb *jugar*

Use the verb *jugar* to talk about playing a sport or a game. Even though *jugar* uses the same endings as the other *-ar* verbs, it has a different stem in some forms. For those forms, the *-u-* becomes *-ue-*. This kind of verb is called a "stem-changing verb." Here are the present-tense forms:

(yo)	**juego**	(nosotros) (nosotras)	**jugamos**
(tú)	**juegas**	(vosotros) (vosotras)	**jugáis**
Ud. (él) (ella)	**juega**	Uds. (ellos) (ellas)	**juegan**

Nota

Many Spanish speakers always use *jugar a* and the name of the sport or game:

- ¿Juegas **al** vóleibol?

Others do not use the *a:*

- ¿Juegas vóleibol?

GramActiva VIDEO

Use the **GramActiva** video to help you learn more about the verb *jugar.*

Gramática **Escribir**

¿A qué juegan?

Escribe frases para decir qué deportes practican estas personas.

Alex Rodríguez

Modelo

Alex Rodríguez juega al béisbol.

1. 
Sergio García

2.  
Rebecca Lobo y Eduardo Nájera

3. 
Carlos Valderrama

4.  
Sammy Sosa y Edgardo Alfonzo

5. Y tus amigos y tú, ¿a qué juegan Uds.?

También se dice . . .

el básquetbol = el baloncesto *(muchos países)*

el fútbol = el balompié *(muchos países)*

el vóleibol = el balonvolea *(España)*

Actividad 19 Gramática — Dibujar/Escribir/Hablar/GramActiva

Juego

1. On each of two index cards, draw a picture that represents a sport or game and write *muy bien, bien,* or *mal* to show how well you play that sport or game. Don't let your classmates see your cards.

2. Get together with five other students. Put all the cards face down in the center of your group. Choose a card and try to identify who drew it by asking the others how well they play what is pictured. Keep track of what you learn about your classmates.

Modelo

A —*Enrique, ¿juegas bien al tenis?*
B —*No, juego muy mal al tenis.*

3. Write six sentences about the sports and games the students in your group play.

Modelo

Óscar y Nacho juegan muy bien al fútbol. Teresa y yo jugamos bien al golf.

Actividad 20 Leer/Escribir/Hablar

La ciudad deportiva

Lee sobre el sueño *(dream)* de Iván Zamorano y contesta las preguntas.

Mi sueño[1]

Quiero una ciudad[2] dedicada al deporte, a la familia y a los niños.[3] Quiero servicios de calidad internacional, con profesores de excelencia. En mi sueño, los niños y jóvenes juegan y practican deportes para ser mejores.[4] Este sueño ya es realidad y quiero compartirlo contigo.

El lugar[5] para hacer deporte en familia.

Escuelas de Fútbol, Tenis, Hockey

Inicio de Inscripción[6]: 23 de marzo, a las 8
Inicio de Actividades: 1 de abril, a las 14 horas

Avenida Pedro Hurtado 2650, Las Condes, Santiago, Chile
Teléfono: 212 2711

[1]dream
[2]city
[3]children
[4]better
[5]place
[6]Registration

1. ¿Qué es el sueño de Iván Zamorano?
2. ¿Qué deportes juegan en la Ciudad Deportiva de Iván?
3. ¿Qué día empieza *(begins)* la inscripción para las escuelas? ¿A qué hora?
4. ¿A qué hora empiezan las actividades?
5. ¿Te gustaría ir a la Ciudad Deportiva de Iván Zamorano? ¿Por qué?

Más práctica

Practice Workbook 4B-7

For: Practice with *jugar*
Visit: www.phschool.com
Web Code: jcd-0414

Pronunciación

The letter *d*

In Spanish, the pronunciation of the letter *d* is determined by its location in a word. When *d* is at the beginning of a word, or when it comes after *l* or *n,* it sounds similar to the *d* in "dog." Listen, then say these words:

diccionario	doce	donde
domingo	desayuno	día
deportes	calendario	bandera

When *d* comes between vowels and after any consonant except *l* or *n,* it sounds similar to the *th* of "the." Listen, then say these words:

cansado	ocupado	puedes
idea	sábado	partido
tarde	ensalada	atrevido

Try it out! Here is a tongue twister to give you practice in pronouncing the *d,* but also to give you something to think about!

Porque puedo, puedes,
porque puedes, puedo;
Pero si no puedes,
yo tampoco puedo.

Una voluntaria en un hospital

El español en el mundo del trabajo

There are many opportunities to use Spanish in the health care field—in hospitals, emergency rooms, and neighborhood clinics. This young woman volunteers in a California hospital. Since many of the patients come from Spanish-speaking homes, she is able to speak with them and their families in Spanish. *"Para mí, trabajar como voluntaria es una de mis actividades favoritas. Creo que mi trabajo es importante."*

- What opportunities are there in your community to do volunteer work where speaking Spanish is helpful?

Leer/Pensar/Escribir

¡Vamos de cámping!

Tourism is an important industry in Spain. Many tourists prefer to go camping rather than stay in hotels. Read the following brochure about a campground and then answer the questions.

Conexiones | Las matemáticas

Cámping Playa Tropicana

Alcossebre (Castellón)
Teléfono: 462 41 42 73 Fax: 964 01 55 05

240 kilómetros al sur de Barcelona
52 kilómetros al norte de Castellón

- Un cámping verdaderamente recomendable
- Siempre algo nuevo
- La mejor opción para su dinero

Con abundante vegetación y mucha sombra,[1] directamente sobre una fabulosa playa. Ideal para niños. La mejor zona de pesca de la Costa de Azahar.

[1]shade

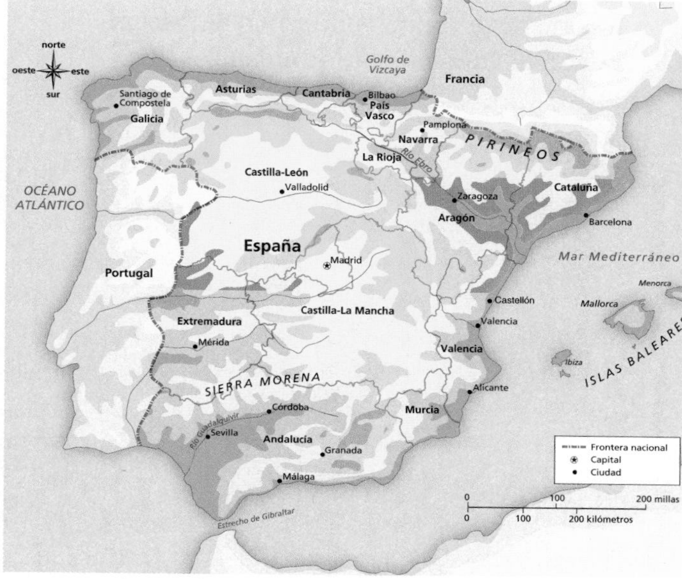

¿Qué distancia en millas[2] hay entre[3] Barcelona y el Cámping Playa Tropicana? ¿Qué distancia hay entre Castellón y el Cámping Playa Tropicana?

Para convertir kilómetros en millas, es necesario dividir el número de kilómetros por 1.6.

[2]miles [3]between

Para decir más . . .
200 = doscientos

Escribir/Hablar

Y tú, ¿qué dices?

1. ¿Con quién te gustaría ir a una fiesta? ¿Por qué?
2. ¿Qué prefieres, ir de pesca o ir a un baile?
3. ¿Qué vas a hacer mañana a las ocho de la noche?
4. ¿Qué vas a hacer este fin de semana?
5. ¿Te gustaría ver un partido de fútbol o ir a un concierto?

¡Adelante!

Objectives

- Read about and compare the lives of two famous golfers
- Recognize specialized sports vocabulary
- Understand cultural perspectives regarding extracurricular activities
- Write an invitation to an event
- Learn facts about the contemporary United States

Lectura

Sergio y Lorena:
El futuro del golf

Lee dos artículos de una revista deportiva. Vas a conocer a[1] Sergio García y a Lorena Ochoa Reyes, dos atletas famosos.

Strategy

Cognates
Use the cognates in the following article to help you understand what is being said about the golfers.

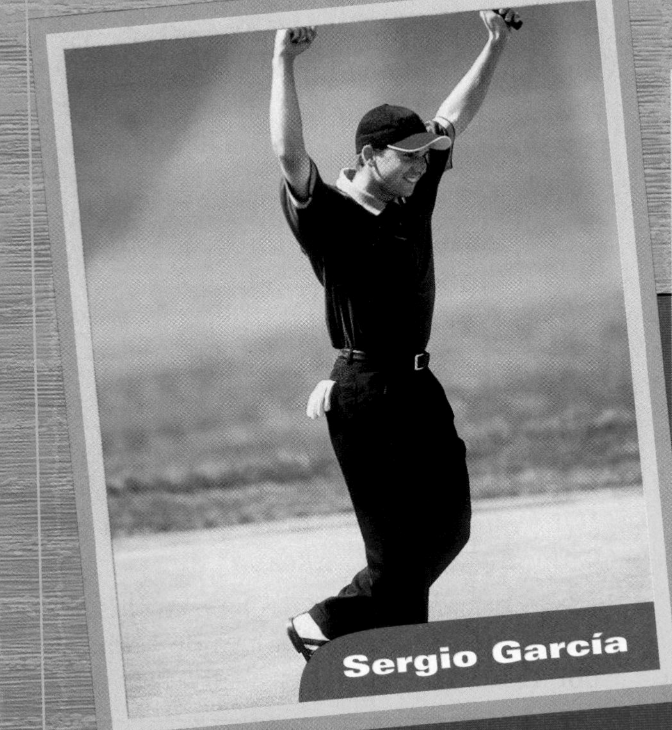

Nombre: Sergio García

Fecha de nacimiento: 9/1/80

Lugar de nacimiento: Borriol, Castellón (España)

Club: Club de Campo del Mediterráneo

Su objetivo: Ser el mejor del mundo

Profesional: Desde abril del 99

Aficiones[2]: Real Madrid, tenis, fútbol, videojuegos

Sergio García es uno de los golfistas más populares en el mundo del golf profesional.

Sergio juega para el Club de Campo del Mediterráneo en Borriol, Castellón, donde su padre Víctor es golfista profesional. Juega al golf desde la edad[3] de tres años y a los 12 años es campeón[4] del Club de Campo. Es el golfista más joven en competir en el campeonato PGA desde Gene Sarazen en 1921 y gana[5] el segundo lugar.[6] Tiene el nombre "El niño." A los 15 años, juega en un torneo del circuito europeo de profesionales. Y a la edad de 17 años gana su primer torneo de profesionales.

Es evidente que este español tiene el talento para realizar su objetivo.

[1] You will meet [2] Interests [3] age [4] champion [5] he wins [6] second place

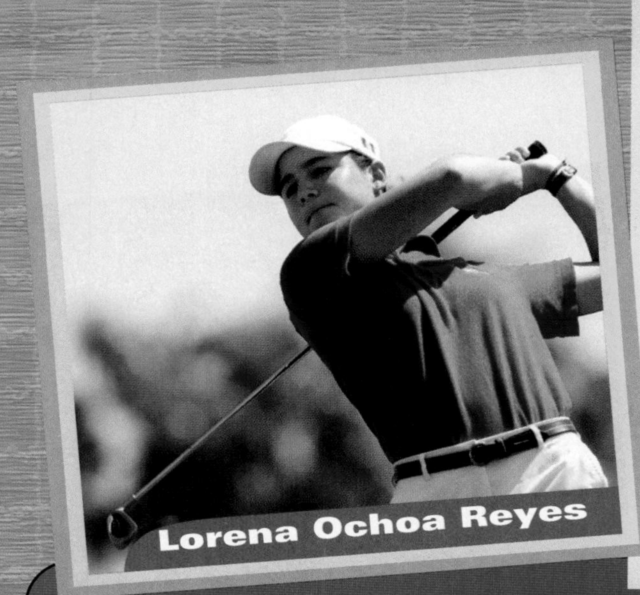

Nombre: Lorena Ochoa Reyes

Fecha de nacimiento: 15/11/81

Lugar de nacimiento: Guadalajara, México

Su objetivo: Ser la golfista número uno del mundo

Universidad: Universidad de Arizona

Aficiones: Básquetbol, tenis, bicicleta de montaña, correr, nadar, comida italiana

Lorena es la mejor golfista de México. Juega al golf desde los seis años de edad. A los 21 años, gana su primer torneo de profesionales. Es la única[7] mexicana en calificar al torneo U.S. Women's Open. Ella dice que está muy emocionada porque quiere jugar mejor[8] y competir en los Estados Unidos. Ella dice que es muy importante practicar y entrenar[9] todos los días. Un día ella quiere ser la golfista número uno del mundo.

[7] only [8] better [9] to train

¿Comprendes?

Copy this Venn diagram on a sheet of paper. Make a list in English of at least eight facts that you learned about Sergio and Lorena. Write the facts on your Venn diagram. Include information about Sergio in the left oval, information about Lorena in the right oval, and any fact that applies to both of them in the overlapping oval.

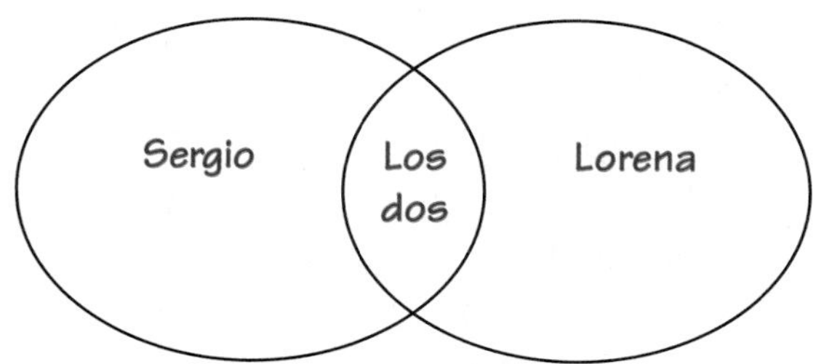

For: Internet link activity
Visit: www.phschool.com
Web Code: jcd-0415

Una jugadora profesional Rebecca Lobo is a professional basketball player. After winning a gold medal in the 1996 Olympics, she became one of the WNBA's original players. Rebecca wrote a book called *The Home Team,* which tells about her life and her mother's struggle against breast cancer. In 2001, she established a college scholarship fund to assist minority students who plan to pursue careers in the healthcare field.

- Rebecca Lobo is a popular motivational speaker. What message do you think she gives to her audiences?

¿Qué haces en tu tiempo libre?

Jugando al hockey en Buenos Aires, Argentina

In many Spanish-speaking countries, extracurricular activities traditionally play a much smaller role in school life than in the United States. Students usually participate in activities such as music and athletics at clubs and institutions outside of school.

Although some schools have teams, many students who are interested in sports attend clubs such as el Club Deportivo General San Martín. At these clubs teens practice and compete on teams. They also participate in individual sports such as tennis. The competition between clubs is sometimes more intense than the competition between schools.

¿Te gusta jugar al ajedrez?

Students with artistic talents often go to a private institute to take music, dance, or art lessons. They might attend el Instituto de Música Clásica or el Instituto de Danza Julio Bocca.

Many students spend their time outside of classes studying a foreign language. They might learn English at la Cultura Inglesa or French at la Alianza Francesa.

In general, students do not hold jobs. They spend their time studying, being with family and friends, and participating in different activities.

Check it out! Take a survey of your friends to find out what they do after school. Do they work a part-time job? Do they participate in a sport with a school team or in extracurricular activities at school? Do they belong to a club or organization outside of school?

Think about it! How do the practices in your community compare with what you have learned about young people's after-school activities in Spanish-speaking countries?

Trabajando después de la clases

Presentación escrita

Una invitación

Task
A special event is coming up on the calendar and you want to invite a friend to go with you.

1. **Prewrite** Think about an event that you'd invite a friend to attend, such as a concert, sporting event, or party. Write an invitation that includes:
   - the name of the event
   - when, where, and at what time the event is taking place
   - who is going

2. **Draft** Use the information from Step 1 to write a first draft of your invitation. Begin your invitation with *¡Hola . . . !* and close with *Tu amigo(a)* and your name.

3. **Revise** Read your note and check for correct spelling and verb forms. Share your invitation with a partner. Your partner should check the following:
   - Did you give all the necessary information?
   - Is there anything you should add or change?
   - Are there any errors?

4. **Publish** Write a final copy of your invitation, making any necessary changes. You may want to give it to your friend or include it in your portfolio.

5. **Evaluation** Your teacher may give you a rubric for how your invitation will be graded. You probably will be graded on:
   - how complete the information was
   - use of vocabulary expressions
   - accuracy of sentence structures

Strategy

Organizing information
Thinking about the correct format and necessary information beforehand will help you create a better invitation.

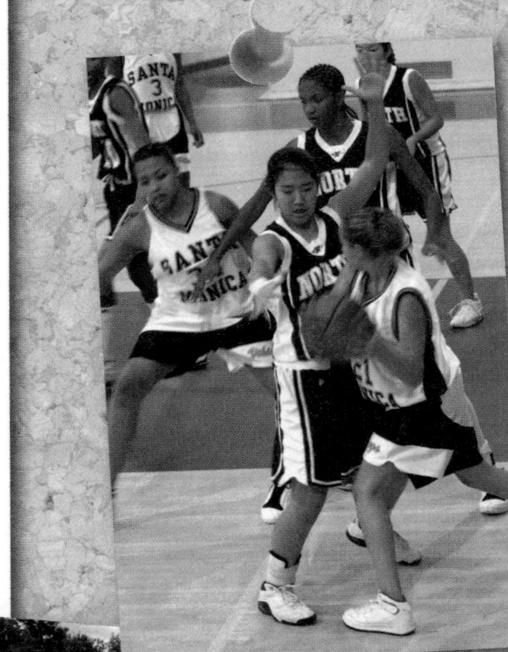

El mundo hispano

Estados Unidos

Contemporáneo

According to the 2000 census, 32,800,000 people (about 12 percent of the total population of the United States) classified themselves as being of Spanish or Hispanic descent. Out of that number, 30,700,800 indicated that they were of either Mexican, Puerto Rican, or Cuban descent. The remaining 2,099,200 people checked "Other Spanish/Hispanic" on their census questionnaires. This broad category included people who came from or who had ancestral ties to other Spanish-speaking countries in the Caribbean, Central and South America, or Spain.

Born in Costa Rica, Dr. Franklin Chang-Díaz (left) was the first Hispanic astronaut to fly in space. He was selected by NASA in 1980 and is a veteran of seven space flights. In 1990, Californian Dr. Ellen Ochoa (right) became the first Hispanic female astronaut. Since then she has logged more than 480 hours in space. Her dream is to help build a space station, which she considers "critical . . . to human exploration in space." Both Dr. Ochoa and Dr. Chang-Díaz are the recipients of many honors for their technical contributions and their scholarship.

¿Sabes que . . . ?

The influence of Spanish-speaking cultures is evident throughout the United States. Musical artists such as Enrique Iglesias, Shakira, and Marc Anthony sell millions of CDs. Actors such as Salma Hayek, Jennifer Lopez, Benjamin Bratt, and Edward James Olmos earn great acclaim for their work. And in politics, Spanish-speaking Americans serve in Congress and top-level Cabinet posts.

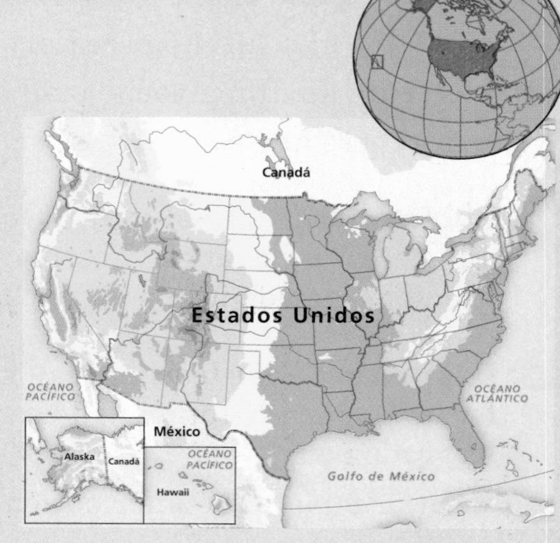

Para pensar

Work with a partner and interview a classmate, friend, or acquaintance who is Spanish-speaking or who has ties to a Spanish-speaking country. What is the person's name? Where did the family come from, and when? Why did the family move to your community? If this person had one thing to say to you and your classmates about the immigrant experience and cultural differences, what might that be? Write a short account of the interview and present it to your class or to a small group.

For: Online Atlas
Visit: www.phschool.com
Web Code: jce-0002

The music and poetry of New York City's Puerto Rican community are a creative blend of English and Spanish. *Nuyoricans* of the *Loisaida* (Lower East Side) rub shoulders with people of diverse ethnic backgrounds creating sounds and rhythms unlike any other in the world. The Nuyorican Poets Café has become an institution on the *Loisaida,* where poets, writers, performance artists, musicians, and visual artists of all nationalities can find an outlet for their work.

More than half of Miami's population is of Spanish-speaking descent. Calle Ocho is the heart of Little Havana, the largest Cuban American community in the United States. The Calle Ocho Festival, which takes place at the end of Carnaval Miami, is a great time to sample Cuban food and dance to some of the world's greatest salsa artists.

More Mexicans visit the border town of Laredo, Texas, than any other city in the United States; and more United States citizens visit the Mexican border town of Tijuana than any other foreign city. Most of the visitors come from nearby areas and stay for only a few hours to visit or shop.

Repaso del capítulo

Vocabulario y gramática

Chapter Review

To prepare for the test, check to see if you . . .
- **know the new vocabulary and grammar**
- **can perform the tasks on p. 219**

to talk about leisure activities

el baile	dance
el concierto	concert
la fiesta	party
el partido	game, match
ir + a + *infinitive*	to be going to + *verb*
ir de cámping	to go camping
ir de pesca	to go fishing
jugar al básquetbol	to play basketball
jugar al béisbol	to play baseball
jugar al fútbol	to play soccer
jugar al fútbol americano	to play football
jugar al golf	to play golf
jugar al tenis	to play tennis
jugar al vóleibol	to play volleyball
(yo) sé	I know (how)
(tú) sabes	you know (how)

to describe how someone feels

cansado, -a	tired
contento, -a	happy
enfermo, -a	sick
mal	bad, badly
ocupado, -a	busy
triste	sad

to tell what time something happens

¿A qué hora?	(At) what time?
a la una	at one (o'clock)
a las ocho	at eight (o'clock)
de la mañana	in the morning
de la noche	in the evening, at night
de la tarde	in the afternoon
este fin de semana	this weekend
esta noche	this evening
esta tarde	this afternoon

to extend, accept, or decline invitations

conmigo	with me
contigo	with you
(yo) puedo	I can
(tú) puedes	you can
¡Ay! ¡Qué pena!	Oh! What a shame!
¡Genial!	Great!
lo siento	I'm sorry
¡Oye!	Hey!
¡Qué buena idea!	What a good / nice idea!
(yo) quiero	I want
(tú) quieres	you want
¿Te gustaría?	Would you like?
Me gustaría	I would like
Tengo que ___.	I have to ___.

other useful words and expressions

demasiado	too
entonces	then
un poco (de)	a little

jugar (a) *to play (games, sports)*

juego	**jugamos**
juegas	**jugáis**
juega	**juegan**

For *Vocabulario adicional,* see pp. 472–473.

Más práctica

Practice Workbook Puzzle 4B-8
Practice Workbook Organizer 4B-9

Go Online PHSchool.com
For: Test preparation
Visit: www.phschool.com
Web Code: jcd-0416

Preparación para el examen

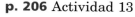

On the exam you will be asked to . . .	Here are practice tasks similar to those you will find on the exam . . .	If you need review . . .
 **1 Escuchar** Listen to and understand messages that give information about when and where to meet someone	On your answering machine, you hear your friend asking if you can go somewhere with her this weekend. Based on her message, try to tell: a) where she is going; b) what she is going to do; and c) what time she wants to go.	**pp. 198–201** *A primera vista* **p. 203** Actividad 9 **p. 206** Actividad 13
 **2 Hablar** Make excuses for not accepting an invitation	You and a friend have planned a camping trip this weekend, but another friend now wants you to do something with him. With a partner, take turns rehearsing excuses for declining his invitation.	**p. 202** Actividad 4 **p. 203** Actividad 8 **p. 204** Actividad 11 **p. 207** Actividad 17
 **3 Leer** Read and understand short messages about accepting or declining invitations	You find notes under your desk that were written to the person who was sitting there before you. Read them to see why people declined an invitation to a party: a) Me gustaría, pero no puedo. Tengo que estudiar para un examen. b) ¡Genial! ¡Una fiesta! Ay, pero no puedo. Voy de cámping. c) ¿A las siete? No puedo. Juego un partido de vóleibol a las siete y media. Lo siento.	**pp. 198–201** *A primera vista* **p. 203** Actividad 7 **pp. 212–213** *Lectura*
 **4 Escribir** Write a short note telling what you are going to do during the week	As a counselor for an after-school program for children, you must write a note to the parents telling them at least three things their children are going to do during the week. (Hint: Start your note with *¡Hola! Esta semana . . .*)	**pp. 198–201** *A primera vista* **p. 206** *ir + a +* infinitive; Actividad 14 **p. 207** Actividad 15 **p. 215** *Presentación escrita*
5 Pensar Demonstrate an understanding of cultural differences regarding extra-curricular activities	Think about what you and your friends typically do after school. Are your activities usually school-related? How would you compare what you do to what some Hispanic teens do in their after-school time?	**p. 214** *Perspectivas del mundo hispano*

¡Viva Texas!

¿Qué quieres hacer en tu tiempo libre?

En la ciudad de Laredo hay muchas actividades para los jóvenes. Después de clases y en los fines de semana, los jóvenes pueden participar en actividades muy divertidas. Laredo tiene muchos lugares[1] interesantes como: gimnasios, parques, teatros y bibliotecas.

[1] places

El Centro de Recreación Cigarroa en Laredo ofrece muchas actividades para jóvenes. Pueden hacer aeróbicos, yoga, levantar pesas y participar en bailes folklóricos.

En la Biblioteca Pública de Laredo hay varios programas y eventos especiales.

En el verano podemos nadar en la piscina.

Teatro

Little Theater
te invita a ver el baile
Encanto Español
este viernes,
el 28 de febrero
a las 8 P.M.
¡Ven[2] con tus amigos!
Little Theater
4802 Thomas Avenue
Laredo, TX 78041

Computadoras

¡OYE!
¿Quieres lecciones de computadoras gratis?[3]
Ven a la **Biblioteca Pública de Laredo** y aprende[4] de computadoras.
Biblioteca Pública de Laredo
1120 E. Calton Rd.

Social

¡**Newcomers and Friends of Laredo** es un club social que tiene actividades diferentes cada mes para todos nuestros amigos de Laredo! Este mes puedes jugar al golf con tu familia y amigos.

Actividades

¿Eres atlético?
¿Te gusta el campo y la diversión?
El **Departamento de Parques y Recreaciones** de Laredo organiza actividades muy divertidas para ti. Ven con tus amigos y participa en: baile folklórico, ajedrez, vóleibol, básquetbol y picnics en el campo.

[2] Come [3] free [4] learn

Ajedrez

El **Club de Ajedrez** de Laredo te invita[5] todos los miércoles de 6 a 9 de la noche.
¡Todos están bienvenidos![6]
Centro de Recreaciones Cigarroa
2201 Zacatecas
Laredo

[5] invites you [6] Everyone is welcome!

¿Comprendes?

Clara and her brother Tomás receive a letter from their friends Elena and Gabriel. Read about their friends and what they enjoy doing in their free time. Then use the information in the newspaper cutouts to answer the questions below.

> *Queridos Clara y Tomás,*
>
> *¿Cómo están? Gabriel y yo vamos a ir a visitar Laredo en una semana. ¿Qué actividades podemos hacer? Sé que a Clara le gusta jugar al golf y al básquetbol. A Tomás le gusta practicar deportes, especialmente el golf y quiere aprender a usar la computadora. A Gabriel y a mí nos gusta practicar deportes y jugar al ajedrez. A todos nos gusta el baile y pasar tiempo con amigos. Vamos a divertirnos mucho.*
>
> *¡Nos vemos!*
> *Elena*

1. ¿A quiénes les gustaría ir al Club de Ajedrez?
2. ¿Dónde puede ir Tomás para aprender a usar la computadora? ¿Con quién puede ir?
3. ¿Quiénes participan en las actividades deportivas del Departamento de Parques y Recreaciones?
4. ¿Qué actividad pueden hacer los jóvenes en el Little Theater?
5. ¿A quiénes les gustaría participar en las actividades del club Newcomers and Friends of Laredo? ¿Por qué?
6. ¿Cuáles actividades pueden hacer todos juntos *(together)*?

Comunicación

Work in groups of three to talk about different after-school activities in your community. Discuss in Spanish the activities you enjoy doing with friends as well as ones you do on your own. Work with your group to design posters for available activities in your town and present them to the class.

Tema 5 • Fiesta en familia

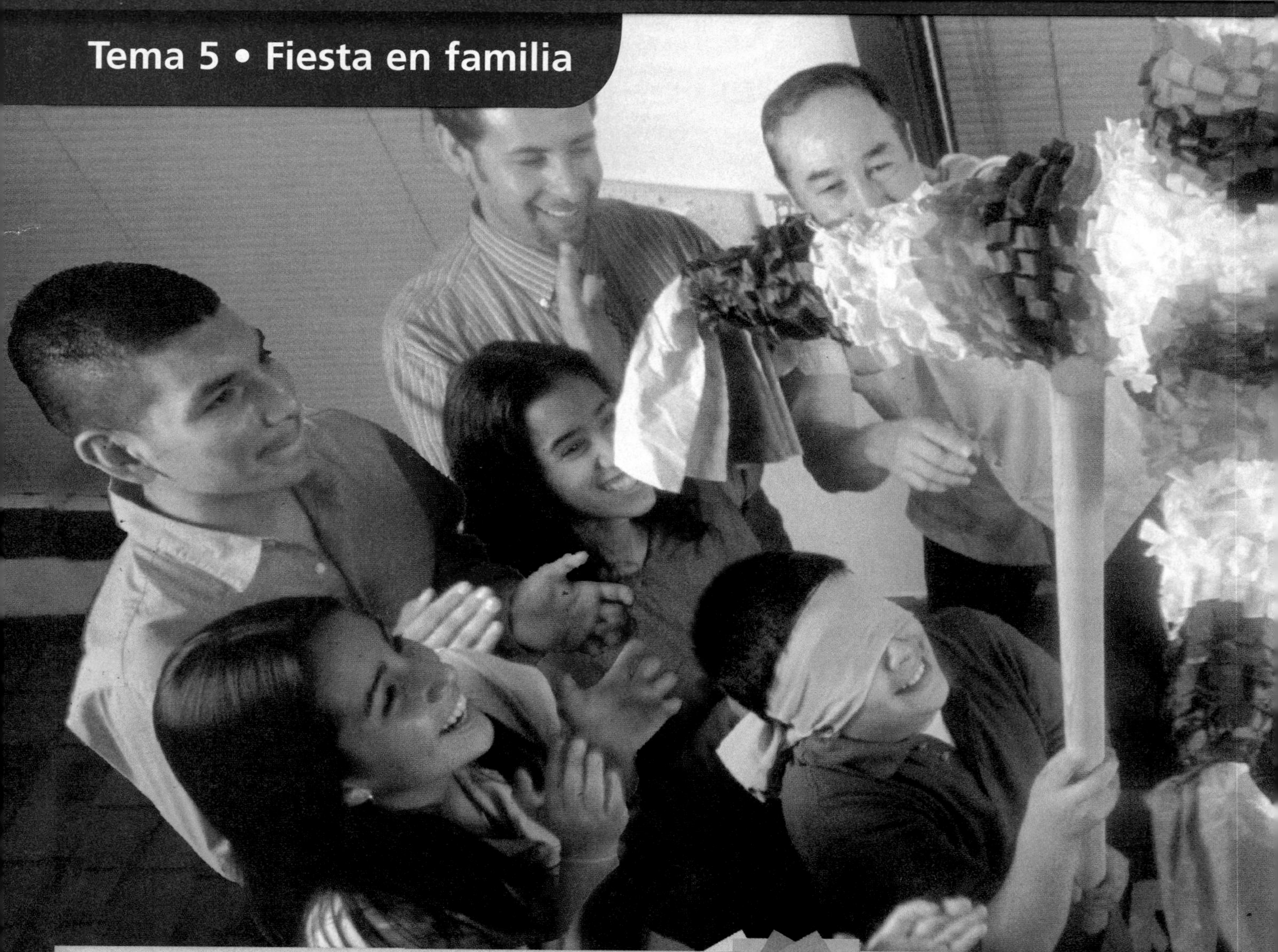

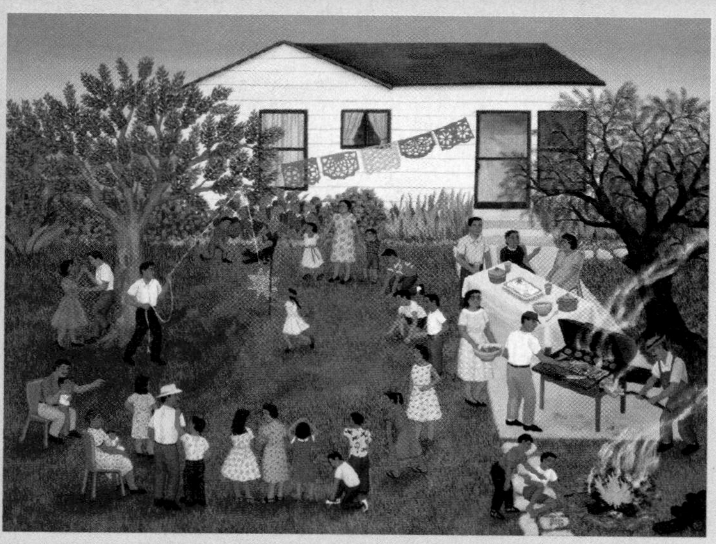

Fondo cultural

Carmen Lomas Garza (1948–) is best known for her paintings that show Mexican American family life in her native South Texas in the 1950s.

- What do you see in the painting that would make this family celebration similar to or different from family parties that you're familiar with?

Barbacoa para cumpleaños / Birthday Party Barbecue (1993), Carmen Lomas Garza
Alkyds on canvas, 36 x 48 inches. © 1993 Carmen Lomas Garza (reg. 1994). Photo credit: M. Lee Fatherree. Collection of Federal Reserve Bank of Dallas.

Capítulo 5A

Una fiesta de cumpleaños

Chapter Objectives

- Describe families
- Talk about celebrations and parties
- Ask and tell ages
- Express possession
- Understand cultural perspectives on family and celebrations

Video Highlights

A primera vista: ***¡Feliz cumpleaños!***

GramActiva Videos: the verb *tener;* possessive adjectives

Videomisterio: ***¿Eres tú, María?,*** **Episodio 1**

Country Connection

As you learn about family celebrations and parties, you will make connections to these countries and places:

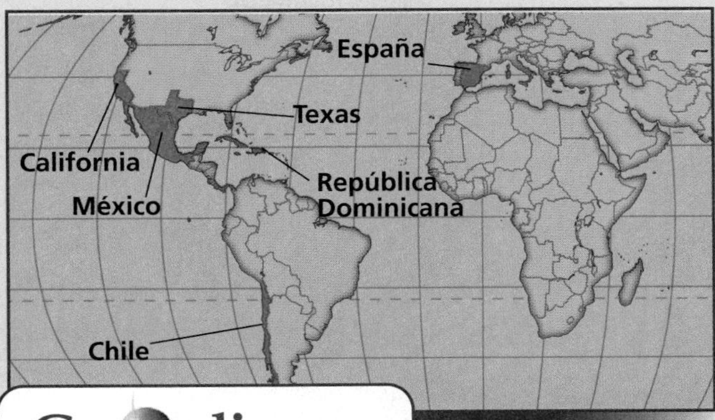

Go Online PHSchool.com

For: Online Atlas
Visit: www.phschool.com
Web Code: jce-0002

fam[ilia] mexicana
bra[ndo] un cumpleaños

A primera vista

Vocabulario y gramática en contexto

Objectives

Read, listen to, and understand information about
- **families**
- **parties and celebrations**

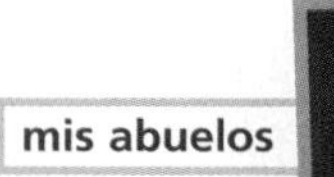

mis abuelos

Ricardo
mi abuelo, 68

Ana María
mi **abuela**, 61

mis **padres**

María
mi **madre**, 39

José Antonio
mi **padre**, 42

Josefina
mi **tía**, 38

Andrés
mi **tío**, 42

mis **tíos**

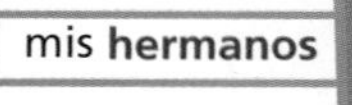

mis **hermanos**

Angélica
mi **hermana**, 16

Esteban
mi **hermano**, 15

Cristina
yo, 13

Carolina
mi **prima**, 17

Gabriel
mi **primo**, 13

mis **primos**

Más vocabulario

el padrastro stepfather
la madrastra stepmother
el hermanastro stepbrother
la hermanastra stepsister

Capitán
mi **perro**

Michi
mi **gato**

“¡Hola! Me llamo Cristina. Hoy es mi **cumpleaños.** Toda mi familia va a **preparar** una fiesta para **celebrar.** ¡Va a ser muy divertido!”

“Aquí está mi familia. Tengo dos hermanos: mi hermana **mayor,** Angélica, **que tiene 16 años,** y mi hermano, Esteban, que tiene 15 años. Y aquí están mis primos: Carolina tiene 17 años. **Su** hermano **menor,** Gabriel, tiene **sólo** 13 años.”

“Mira a **las personas** de **las fotos.** Es la familia de mi tía Josefina. Mi tío Andrés es **el esposo** de Josefina. Ellos tienen dos **hijos: su hijo** Gabriel y su **hija** Carolina.”

el regalo

la cámara

“Hoy es el cumpleaños de Cristina. Tengo un regalo para ella. Es una cámara. A Cristina **le encanta sacar fotos.**”

FIESTAMANÍA
¡Tenemos todo para tu fiesta de cumpleaños!
las luces
la luz
la piñata
el papel picado
la flor
los globos
las flores
¡Feliz Cumpleaños!
el pastel
los dulces
calle Bolívar, 23
Tel. 455-23-19
Abierto de
10h a 20h

Escuchar

La familia de Cristina

Listen as Cristina describes her family. If her statement is true, give a “thumbs-up” sign. If it is false, give a “thumbs-down” sign.

Escuchar

Preparamos la fiesta

Now listen as Cristina and her mother prepare for the birthday party. Look at the items in the party shop ad on this page and touch each item they mention.

Más práctica

Practice Workbook 5A-1, 5A-2

For: Vocabulary practice
Visit: www.phschool.com
Web Code: jcd-0501

Videohistoria

¡Feliz cumpleaños!

¿Qué pasa en la fiesta de Cristina? Lee la historia.

Strategy

Using visuals
Look at the pictures as you read to help you get the details of the story.

1 **Esteban:** Vamos a **hacer un video.** Uno . . . dos . . . tres . . . ¡Acción!

Angélica: Hola, me llamo Angélica. Hoy es el cumpleaños de **nuestra** hermana, Cristina. Todos están aquí para celebrar.

5 **Angélica:** Aquí está mi madre. A **mamá** le gustan **las decoraciones.**

Madre: Sí. A mí me encanta **decorar** con papel picado.

6 **Angélica:** Y aquí está Cristina. Hoy es su cumpleaños. **¡Feliz cumpleaños!**

Cristina: ¿Cuándo puedo **abrir** mis regalos?

Angélica: Ahora no. Primero, la piñata.

7 **Padre:** ¡Vamos, Gabriel! ¿Puedes **romper** la piñata?

Gabriel: ¡Por supuesto!

Todos: *Dale, dale, dale, no pierdas el tino, porque si lo pierdes, pierdes el camino.*

(¡Crac! *Gabriel rompe la piñata y . . .)*

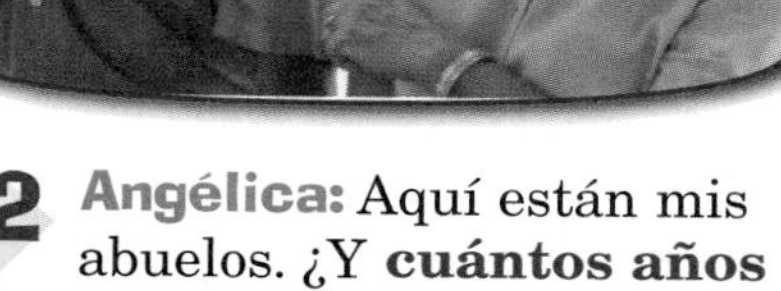

2 **Angélica:** Aquí están mis abuelos. ¿Y **cuántos años tienen Uds.?**

Abuelo: Pues, yo tengo sesenta y ocho años y tu abuela . . .

Abuela: Por favor, Ricardo. Angélica, ¡qué pregunta!

3 **Angélica:** Aquí está Gabriel, mi primo menor. Le gusta mucho el fútbol. Y aquí está mi prima. ¿Cómo te llamas?

Carolina: Pero, Angélica, tú sabes mi nombre.

Angélica: Sí, pero es para el video. Por favor . . .

4 **Angélica:** Él es **nuestro** padre. ¿Qué haces, **papá?**

Padre: Voy a preparar unas hamburguesas y después voy a sacar fotos de la fiesta.

8 **Madre:** ¡Gabriel! ¡La piñata! ¡El pastel! ¡Ay, no!

Actividad 3 **Escribir/Hablar**

¿Comprendes?

1. ¿Quién va a hacer el video, Gabriel o Esteban?
2. ¿Quién tiene sesenta y ocho años, el abuelo o la abuela?
3. ¿A quién le gusta jugar al fútbol, a Esteban o a Gabriel?
4. ¿Qué va a hacer el padre, decorar o preparar hamburguesas?
5. ¿Con qué decora la madre, con globos o con papel picado?
6. ¿Quién rompe la piñata, Cristina o Gabriel?

Más práctica

Practice Workbook 5A-3, 5A-4

For: Vocabulary practice
Visit: www.phschool.com
Web Code: jcd-0502

Manos a la obra

Vocabulario y gramática en uso

Objectives

- Communicate about families and parties
- Ask and tell what people have
- Ask and tell people's ages
- Tell to whom something belongs
- Learn to use the verb *tener* and possessive adjectives

Leer/Escribir/Hablar

¿Quién es?

Completa cada frase con la palabra apropiada.

Modelo

La madre de mi madre es mi abuela.

1. La esposa de mi tío es mi ___.
2. El padre de mi padre es mi ___.
3. El hijo de mi madrastra es mi ___.
4. Paco y Ana son mis tíos. Sus hijos son mis ___.
5. El hermano de mi madre es mi ___.
6. Los padres de mi padre son mis ___.
7. La hija de mi padrastro es mi ___.
8. El hermano de mi prima es mi ___.

Leer/Escribir/Hablar

En la fiesta de cumpleaños

Escribe la palabra apropiada para completar cada frase.

Hoy __1.__ *(celebramos / sacamos)* la fiesta de cumpleaños de mi hermana menor, Cristina. ¿Cuántos años __2.__ *(es / tiene)* ella? Trece.

A nuestra madre __3.__ *(le / me)* encantan las fiestas. Mamá y mi hermana __4.__ *(decoran / rompen)* el patio con __5.__ *(luces / pasteles)* y __6.__ *(fiestas / flores)*.

A __7.__ *(nuestro / nuestra)* hermano le gusta hacer un __8.__ *(regalo / video)* o __9.__ *(abrir / sacar)* fotos de la fiesta. Siempre hay una piñata que nosotros __10.__ *(abrimos / rompemos)*. En la piñata hay __11.__ *(dulces / flores)* sabrosos. Ahora Cristina va a __12.__ *(romper / abrir)* sus regalos.

Fondo cultural

El papel picado Mexican families frequently decorate for celebrations by using *papel picado* (cut paper). It is made by folding and cutting layers of colored tissue paper to create designs or scenes that are then hung as decorations.

- What crafts do you know that use similar techniques?

Haciendo papel picado / Making papel picado (1998), Carmen Lomas Garza

Hablar

Mi familia

Habla de los miembros de tu familia o de otra familia.

Dos hermanos de la República Dominicana

Modelo

hermanos
A —*¿Tienes hermanos?*
B —*Sí, tengo un hermano y una hermana.*
o: *No, no tengo hermanos.*
A —*¿Cómo se llaman?*
B —*Mi hermano se llama David y mi hermana se llama Abby.*

Para decir más . . .

el (la) hijo(a) único(a) only child

Estudiante A

1. tíos
2. primos
3. un abuelo
4. una hermana mayor
5. hermanos menores
6. una tía favorita
7. una abuela
8. un gato o un perro

Estudiante B

¡Respuesta personal!

Hablar

A mi familia le gusta . . .

Habla de las actividades favoritas de los miembros de tu familia o de otra familia.

Modelo

primo
A —*¿Qué le gusta hacer a tu primo?*
B —*Le gusta sacar fotos.*

Estudiante A

1. padre
2. madre
3. abuelo
4. hermana
5. prima o primo favorito(a)
6. tía o tío favorito(a)
7. perro o gato

Estudiante B

¡Respuesta personal!

Escribir/Hablar

Y tú, ¿qué dices?

1. Describe a una persona de tu familia o de otra familia. ¿Cómo se llama? ¿Cuántos años tiene? ¿Cómo es? ¿Qué le gusta hacer?
2. ¿Tienes un perro o un gato? ¿Cómo se llama? ¿Cuántos años tiene?
3. ¿Qué te gusta hacer durante *(during)* una fiesta de cumpleaños?

Gramática

The verb *tener*

The verb *tener* is used to show relationship or possession.

Tengo un hermano mayor. — ***I have** an older brother.*
Tenemos un regalo para Tere. — ***We have** a gift for Tere.*

Some expressions in Spanish use *tener* where English uses "to be."

Mi primo **tiene** dieciséis años. — *My cousin **is** sixteen years old.*
Tengo hambre y sed. — ***I am** hungry and thirsty.*

Here are all the present-tense forms of *tener:*

(yo)	**tengo**	(nosotros) (nosotras)	**tenemos**
(tú)	**tienes**	(vosotros) (vosotras)	**tenéis**
Ud. (él) (ella)	**tiene**	Uds. (ellos) (ellas)	**tienen**

¿Recuerdas?

You have been using the verb *tener* for several chapters.

- **¿Tienes** una bicicleta?
- **Tengo** que hacer ejercicio.

GramActiva VIDEO

Want more help with the verb *tener?* Watch the **GramActiva** video.

Actividad 9 — Gramática — Leer/Escribir/Pensar

Rompecabezas

Escribe la forma apropiada del verbo *tener* para cada frase. Luego *(Then)* resuelve el problema.

El total de las edades *(ages)* de los hijos de nuestra familia es cien. Marta __1.__ 19 años. Paco y yo __2.__ dos años menos que Marta. Laura y Eva __3.__ cinco años menos que Paco y yo. ¿Cuántos años __4.__ nuestro hermano mayor, Enrique?

Actividad 10 — Gramática  Hablar

¿Qué hay para la fiesta?

Pregunta a otro(a) estudiante qué tienen estas personas para la fiesta.

Ana

Modelo

A —*¿Qué tiene Ana?*
B —*Ana tiene la piñata.*

1. David 
2. Yolanda 
3. tu abuela 
4. tú 
5. Uds. 
6. Juan y Marcos 

   Hablar/Escribir

Entrevista

Interview a partner. Find out the answers to the following questions. Your partner may answer based on his or her own family or on a TV family. Write your partner's answers so that you can report your interview to the class.

1. ¿Cómo te llamas y cuántos años tienes? ¿Qué te gusta hacer?
2. ¿Cuántos hermanos mayores o menores tienes?
3. ¿Cómo se llaman tus hermanos(as) y cuántos años tienen?
4. ¿Cómo son tus hermanos(as)?
5. ¿Qué le gusta hacer a uno(a) de tus hermanos(as)?
6. ¿Tienes perros o gatos? ¿Cómo se llama(n)?

Nota

To say that a person likes or loves something, you use *le gusta(n)* or *le encanta(n)*. When you include the name of the person or the pronoun, be sure to add *a:*

- **A Pedro le** gustan los dulces.
- **A ella le** encanta sacar fotos.

 Escribir/Hablar

¡Reportaje!

Based on your notes from Actividad 11, write a report of your interview. Your teacher may ask you to read your report to the class.

Modelo

Anita tiene 13 años y le encanta escuchar música. Anita tiene tres hermanos: un hermano mayor y dos hermanos menores. Su hermano mayor, Peter, tiene 16 años. Sus hermanos menores se llaman Lisa y Kevin. Ellos tienen sólo once y ocho años. Son simpáticos y deportistas. A Kevin le gusta jugar al básquetbol. Anita no tiene ni perros ni gatos.

 Escribir/Hablar

Preparaciones para una fiesta de cumpleaños

Contesta las preguntas.

Cuando tu familia celebra un cumpleaños, ¿quién tiene que . . .

1. . . . decorar la casa? ¿Con qué?
2. . . . preparar la comida y las bebidas?
3. . . . comprar los regalos?
4. . . . hacer el pastel?
5. . . . hacer el video o sacar fotos?

¿Recuerdas?

Remember that *tener que* + infinitive means "to have to" (do something).

- Sofía **tiene que** decorar el pastel.

Celebrando un cumpleaños en un parque en Texas

14 Gramática **Leer/Escribir**

La familia de Pablo

Look carefully at the photograph of Pablo's family, the royal family of Spain, as they celebrate his special day. As Pablo describes this family photo, complete the story with the appropriate forms of the verb *tener*.

Me llamo Pablo Nicolás Urdangarín y de Borbón. Mi cumpleaños es el 6 de diciembre. Nosotros __1.__ muchas fiestas en mi familia.
En la foto celebramos un día muy especial para mí. Es el día de mi bautizo. (Yo) __2.__ un hermano mayor que se llama Juan Valentín. También (yo) __3.__ dos primos: Felipe, que __4.__ dos años, y una prima, Victoria. Victoria __5.__ sólo tres meses más que yo. Felipe y Victoria son los hijos de mis tíos, la infanta[1] Elena y su esposo, Jaime. Están a la derecha en la foto. A la izquierda están mi tío—el príncipe Felipe—y mis padres. Mi hermano está en los brazos de mi padre, Iñaki. Yo estoy en los brazos de mi mamá, la infanta Cristina. Mis abuelos, el rey Juan Carlos y la reina Sofía, __6.__ 62 años. Ellos son los reyes[2] de España. ¿ __7.__ tú tíos y primos? Me encanta tener una familia grande.

[1] In the Spanish royal family, *una infanta* is a princess (*una princesa*) who is not heir to the throne.
[2] Note that *el rey + la reina = los reyes.*

La familia de Juan Carlos I, rey de España

Fondo cultural

La familia real *(royal)* de España Juan Carlos I and Sofía have been king and queen of Spain since 1975.

- What other countries can you name that have monarchies?

Más práctica
Practice Workbook 5A-5

For: Practice with *tener*
Visit: www.phschool.com
Web Code: jcd-0504

15 **Leer/Hablar/Pensar**

¿Quiénes son los miembros de la familia real?

Work with a partner to identify the members of the royal family. Use the photograph and answers from Actividad 14 to help.

Modelo

A —*Creo que el número uno es el tío de Pablo. Se llama Felipe.*
B —*Estoy de acuerdo.*
o: *No estoy de acuerdo.*

Leer

La familia de Carlos IV

Before the age of photography, painted portraits were used to capture the images of people. Look carefully at the painting *La familia de Carlos IV* by Francisco de Goya and then read about the family.

Conexiones El arte

La familia real tiene mucha importancia en la historia de España. Es el año 1800: Carlos IV *(Cuarto)* no es un rey popular y muchas personas creen que es demasiado indeciso.[1] En este cuadro[2] del pintor Francisco de Goya, puedes ver a la familia del rey Carlos IV. Carlos IV reinó[3] de 1788 a 1808.

- El pintor también está en el cuadro. ¿Puedes ver a Goya? ¿Dónde está?

La familia de Carlos IV (1800), Francisco de Goya
Oil on canvas, 110 1/4" x 132 1/4" (280 x 336 cm). Museo Nacional del Prado, Madrid. Photo credit: Scala / Art Resource, NY.

[1] indecisive [2] painting [3] reigned

Pensar/Hablar

Carlos IV y su familia

Work with a partner. Point to different people in Goya's painting of the royal family and ask your partner who he or she thinks they are.

Modelo

A —*¿Quién es?*
B —*Creo que es el hijo menor.*

Fondo cultural

Dos familias reales The family photo of the Spanish royal family on the preceding page was taken in the year 2000, 200 years after Goya painted the portrait of Juan Carlos I's ancestor and his family. Study the two pictures as you answer these questions.

- In what ways are the two pictures similar?
- How are they different?
- How would you compare them to your own family portraits?

Autorretrato (ca. 1815)
Oil on canvas. Academia de San Fernando, Madrid, Spain. Courtesy The Bridgeman Art Library International Ltd.

Francisco de Goya (1746–1828) was one of the greatest Spanish painters and is considered by many to be the "Father of Modern Art." He was known for a wide range of art themes, including portraits of the royal family and other members of the nobility.

Gramática

Possessive adjectives

You use possessive adjectives to tell what belongs to someone or to show relationships. In English, the possessive adjectives are *my, your, his, her, its, our,* and *their.*

Here are the possessive adjectives in Spanish:

¿Recuerdas?

You know that *de* shows possession or relationship and is the equivalent of *-'s* and *-s'*:

- el regalo **de** Ana
- los primos **de** mis amigos

mi(s)	**nuestro(s)** **nuestra(s)**
tu(s)	**vuestro(s)** **vuestra(s)**
su(s)	**su(s)**

Javier y yo con **nuestra** abuela

Mis padres con **su** regalo

Like other adjectives, possessive adjectives agree in number with the nouns that follow them. Only *nuestro* and *vuestro* have different masculine and feminine endings.

mi cámara	mi**s** cámara**s**
nuestr**o** abuelo	nuestr**os** abuel**os**
nuestr**a** hija	nuestr**as** hij**as**

Su and *sus* can have many different meanings: *his, her, its, your,* or *their.* To be more specific, you can use *de* + noun or pronoun.

sus flores = las flores **de ella**

sus regalos = los regalos **de Javier y Carlos**

GramActiva VIDEO

Want to learn more about possessive adjectives? Watch the **GramActiva** video.

Gramática **Leer/Escribir**

La Cenicienta y su familia

Escribe la palabra o los adjetivos posesivos apropiados para completar la historia de la Cenicienta. La Cenicienta es un personaje de un cuento muy famoso. ¿Quién es?

Cenicienta tiene una madrastra y dos hermanastras muy perezosas. **1.** *(Sus / Tus)* hermanastras se llaman Griselda y Anastasia. **2.** *(Nuestra / Su)* madrastra y **3.** *(su / sus)* hermanastras siempre dicen: "¡Cenicienta! Tenemos hambre. ¿Dónde está **4.** *(mi / nuestra)* comida?" Cada mañana Griselda le dice: "Quiero **5.** *(mi / su)* desayuno. ¿Dónde está?" Una noche Cenicienta va al baile del príncipe. Él le pregunta a Cenicienta: "¿Cómo te llamas? ¿Quiénes son **6.** *(tu / tus)* padres?" Las hermanastras **7.** *(de / su)* Cenicienta ven al príncipe cuando baila con Cenicienta. Ellas dicen: "¡ **8.** *(Nuestra / Su)* hermanastra baila con el príncipe! ¡Qué ridículo!"

Actividad 19 Leer/Escribir/Hablar

¿Quién es tu héroe o heroína?

Lee el anuncio y contesta las preguntas.

FIREFIGHTER
7
No es sólo mi padre.
También es mi héroe.
Y es nuestro héroe también.
Gracias.
Patrocinado por la Cámara de Comercio

1. En este anuncio, ¿quién es el héroe? ¿De quiénes es el héroe?
2. Trabaja con otro(a) estudiante. Pregunta quién es su héroe o heroína.

Modelo

A —*¿Quién es tu héroe o heroína? ¿Cómo es?*
B —*Mi heroína es mi madre. Es muy inteligente.*

Actividad 20 Gramática Leer/Pensar

¿Dónde está o dónde están?

Un grupo de estudiantes busca *(is looking for)* sus decoraciones para una fiesta en la escuela. Empareja *(Match)* cada pregunta con la respuesta más apropiada.

1. ¿Dónde están tus flores?
2. ¿Dónde está el papel picado de Clara?
3. ¿Dónde está mi papel picado?
4. ¿Dónde están los globos de Marta y Tere?
5. ¿Dónde están las flores de Teodoro?
6. ¿Dónde están mis globos?

a. Tu papel picado está allí.
b. Sus flores están allí.
c. Mis globos están allí.
d. Mis flores están detrás del escritorio.
e. Tus globos están debajo de la mesa.
f. Su papel picado está debajo de la carpeta.
g. Sus globos están al lado de la computadora.

Actividad 21 Gramática **Hablar/GramActiva**

Juego

1. Working with a partner, make a set of two cubes using the template your teacher will give you.
   - **Cube 1** Write a different subject pronoun on each side.
   - **Cube 2** Write a different classroom object on each side. Make three of them singular and three of them plural.
   - **Both cubes** Write a different point value from 1 to 6 on each side.
2. You and your partner will play against another pair of students. Team 1 rolls both of your cubes and says a sentence using the correct form of the verb *tener,* the appropriate possessive adjective, and the classroom object. If the sentence is correct, Team 1 receives the total points shown on the cubes. Team 2 then rolls the other cubes. Continue until a team reaches 100 points or time is called.

Modelo

Uds. tienen su calculadora.

Actividad 22 **Hablar**

¿Qué tienen y para qué clase?

¿Qué tienen tus compañeros hoy?

1. Escribe cinco cosas *(things)* que usas en la escuela y para qué clases son.
2. Pide *(Ask for)* las respuestas a tres compañeros y escríbelas en una hoja de papel.

Modelo

A —*¿Qué tienes para tus clases hoy?*
B —*Tengo mi calculadora para la clase de matemáticas y mi carpeta para la clase de inglés.*

3. Escribe cinco frases para describir las cosas que tienen los estudiantes para las clases de hoy.

Modelo

Ana tiene su carpeta para la clase de inglés.
Paco y yo tenemos nuestros lápices para la clase de arte.

¿Recuerdas?

You have been using vocabulary for classroom supplies for several chapters.

Más práctica

Practice Workbook 5A-6, 5A-7

For: Practice with possessive adjectives
Visit: www.phschool.com
Web Code: jcd-0505

Exploración del lenguaje

Diminutives

In Spanish you can add the suffix *-ito(a)* to a word to give it the meaning of "small" or "little." It can also be used to show affection. Words with this suffix are called diminutives *(diminutivos)*.

abuelo → abuelito

perros → perritos

hermana → hermanita

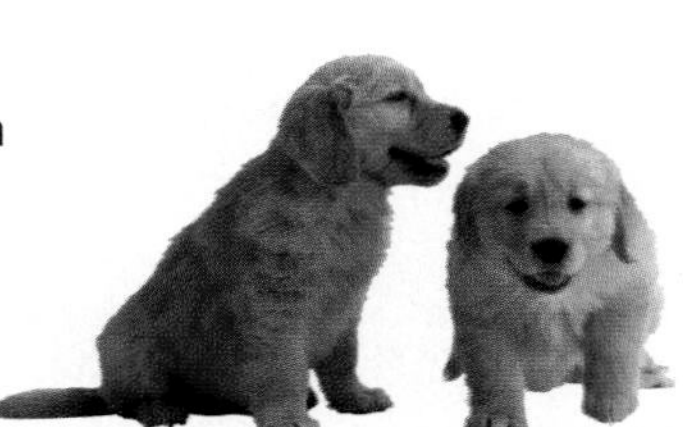

Now that you know what the suffix *-ito(a)* means, can you figure out the meanings of these words?

abuelita gatito Miguelito hijita

Some very popular names are diminutives. What do you think the diminutives of these names are?

Ana Juana Eva Lola

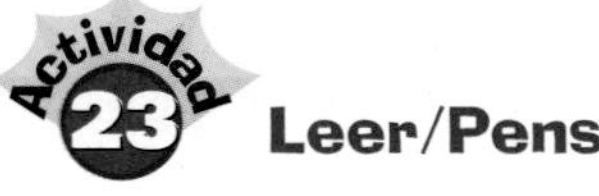

Actividad 23 Leer/Pensar

¡Feliz cumpleaños!

Read the birthday card. Who is it for? Find the diminutives. What words in the poem do you understand? How many objects in the picture can you name in Spanish?

Actividad 24 Escuchar

La fiesta de cumpleaños

En una hoja de papel, escribe los números del 1 al 6. Mira la tarjeta *(card)* de cumpleaños y escucha las frases. Si la frase es cierta, escribe *C*. Si es falsa, escribe *F*.

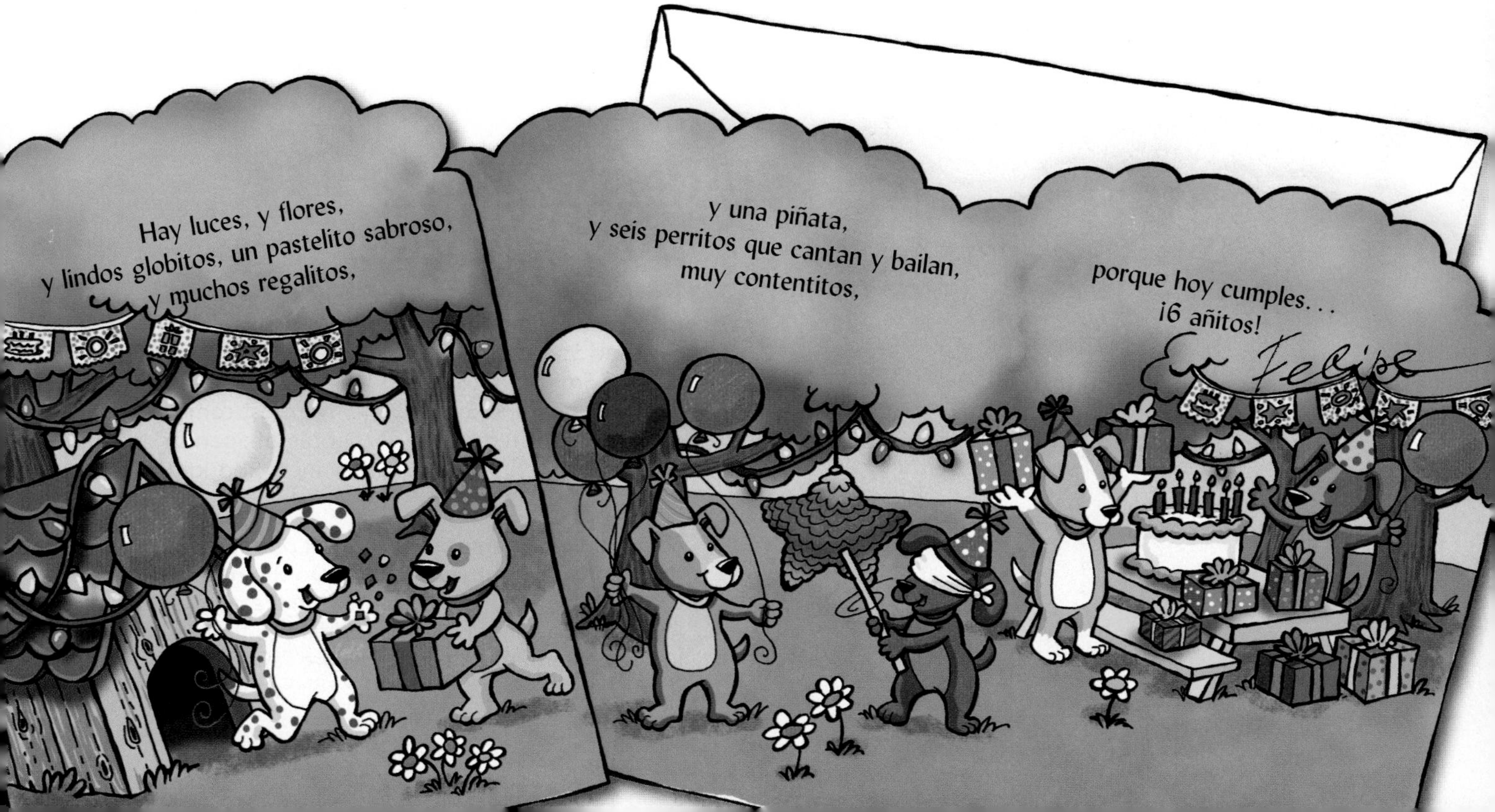

Hay luces, y flores,
y lindos globitos, un pastelito sabroso,
y muchos regalitos,
y una piñata,
y seis perritos que cantan y bailan,
muy contentitos,
porque hoy cumples...
¡6 añitos!
Felipe

Pronunciación

The letters *p, t,* and *q*

In English the consonants *p, t, q,* and the hard *c* sound are pronounced with a little puff of air.

Hold a tissue loosely in front of your mouth as you say these English words. You will notice that the tissue moves.

pan	papa	too	tea
comb	case	park	take

Now say these Spanish words with the tissue in front of your mouth. Try to say the consonants so that there is no puff of air and the tissue does not move.

pan	papá	tú	tía
cómo	queso	parque	taco

Try it out! Listen to this nursery rhyme. Listen particularly for the *p, t,* and *q* sounds. Then repeat the rhyme.

Tortillitas para mamá,
tortillitas para papá.
Las quemaditas,[1] para mamá,
las bonitas,[2] para papá.

[1] The burned ones [2] The pretty ones

Fondo cultural

Diego Rivera (1886–1957) This painting by Mexican muralist Diego Rivera shows a woman grinding maize on a *metate,* a utensil used for grinding grain. This is one of many paintings in which Rivera portrays the daily life of the indigenous peoples of Mexico.

- Through paintings, an artist conveys feelings to the viewer. What do you think Rivera wants you to feel about this woman and her task?

La molendera (1926), Diego Rivera

Oil on canvas, 35 7/16 x 46 1/16 in. Museo Nacional de Arte Moderno, Instituto Nacional de Bellas Artes, México City, D.F., México. © Banco de México Diego Rivera & Frida Kahlo Museums Trust. Av. Cinco de Mayo No. 2, Col. Centro, Del. Cuauhtemoc 06059, México D.F. Reproduction authorized by the *Instituto Nacional de Bellas Artes y Literatura*. Courtesy of Art Resource, NY.

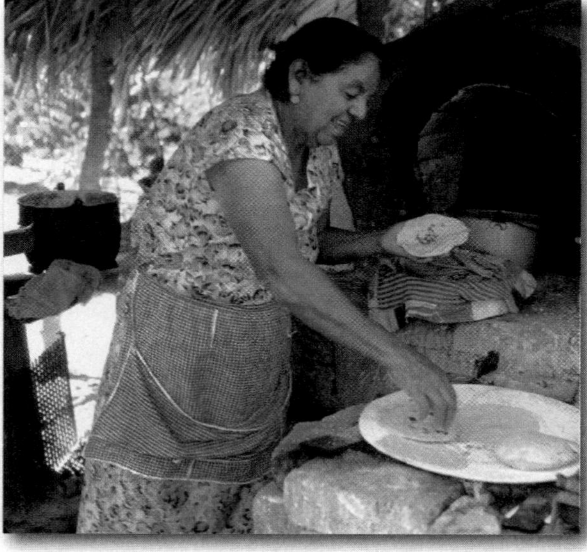

Haciendo tortillas en Chiapas, México

El español en la comunidad

The five most common last names in the United States, in order, are Smith, Johnson, Williams, Jones, and Brown. The five most common last names in the United States for people of Spanish-speaking heritage, in order, are García, Martínez, Rodríguez, Hernández, and López.

- Look up these names in your local phone book. Count the number of entries for each. Do the numbers in your community match the statement made above? Can you identify two other Hispanic last names that are common in your community or that you are familiar with?

Hablar/Escribir

Un cumpleaños divertido

Find out from your classmates what they consider to be a great birthday. Make a chart like the one below on a sheet of paper and complete the first row about yourself. Then survey four classmates to find out what their preferences are and record the information in the chart.

Modelo

¿En qué mes es tu cumpleaños?
¿Cuál es tu actividad y lugar (place) *favorito?*
¿Cuáles son tus comidas favoritas?

	Mes del cumpleaños	Actividad y lugar favorito	Comidas favoritas
yo	julio	comer—un restaurante	pastel y helado
Miguel	enero	abrir regalos—en casa	pizza y ensalada
Anita	julio	bailar—un baile	hamburguesas y helado

Escuchar/Hablar/Escribir/Leer

¿Quién es esta persona?

1. Use your completed chart from Actividad 25 and describe a classmate to the class. Do not give that person's name. The class will try to guess whom you are describing.

Modelo

Su cumpleaños es en enero. Para su cumpleaños le gusta abrir regalos en casa. Sus comidas favoritas en su cumpleaños son pizza y ensalada. ¿Quién es?

2. Write a paragraph describing the person you interviewed whose idea of a great birthday celebration is most like your own. Describe the similarities, but also mention differences.

Modelo

Nuestro cumpleaños es en julio. Nuestra comida favorita es el helado. El lugar favorito para mi cumpleaños es un restaurante porque me gusta comer. Su lugar favorito es un baile porque le gusta bailar. A ella le gustan las hamburguesas pero a mí me gusta el pastel. ¿Quién es la persona? Es Anita.

Un chico chileno con su mejor amigo

¡Adelante!

Objectives

- Read about a *fiesta de quince años*
- Learn to make *papel picado*
- Describe pictures of your family
- Watch *¿Eres tú, María?*, Episodio 1

Lectura

Mis padres te invitan a mi fiesta de quince años

Para muchas jóvenes hispanas, el día de sus quince años es una ocasión muy especial. Toda la familia y muchos amigos van a misa en la iglesia y después celebran con una fiesta. Es una tradición especialmente importante en México, América Central y los países hispanos del Caribe. También es importante entre muchos hispanohablantes en los Estados Unidos.

Aquí está la invitación a la fiesta de quince años de María Teresa Rivera Treviño.

Strategy

Scanning
What information would you expect to find on an invitation? Read quickly through this invitation and find the names of María Teresa's parents and the date and times of the two events to which you are invited.

Felipe Rivera López y
Guadalupe Treviño Ibarra
esperan el honor de su asistencia
el sábado, 15 de mayo de 2004
para celebrar los quince años de su hija,
María Teresa Rivera Treviño

Misa
a las cuatro de la tarde
Iglesia de Nuestra Señora de Guadalupe
2374 Avenida Linda Vista
San Diego, California

Recepción y cena-baile
a las seis de la tarde
Restaurante Luna
7373 Calle Florida
San Diego, California

"Toda mi familia, mis amigos y yo vamos a la iglesia en la tarde. Después vamos a la recepción en un restaurante muy elegante donde comemos y bailamos. Bailo primero con mi padre y después con mis amigos."

"Aquí estoy yo en el día de mis quince años. Es un día muy especial y toda la familia está conmigo para celebrar. Todo está perfecto para mi fiesta—la comida, las decoraciones, la música—¡todo!"

¿Comprendes?

1. ¿Cuál es la fecha de los quince años de María Teresa?
2. Necesitas una hora para ir de tu casa a la Iglesia de Nuestra Señora de Guadalupe. ¿A qué hora tienes que salir *(leave)* de casa?
3. ¿Dónde y a qué hora es la recepción? Según la invitación, ¿qué van a hacer en la recepción?
4. ¿Qué actividad de la fiesta de quince años te gusta más?

¡Vamos a comparar!

The special celebration of a girl's fifteenth birthday is called *la quinceañera, los quince,* or *los quince años.* Think about an event in the lives of your friends that has the importance of a *quince años* celebration. How are the events similar or different?

El nombre completo A person's full name *(nombre completo)* consists of a first name *(nombre),* which often consists of two names, plus two surnames—the father's family name *(apellido paterno),* followed by the mother's family name *(apellido materno).*

For example, look at the *nombres completos* of María Teresa's parents:

Felipe Rivera López y
Guadalupe Treviño Ibarra

- What is Felipe's *apellido paterno*?
- What is Guadalupe's *apellido materno*?
- Can you explain how María Teresa's name is formed?

María Teresa will most often use her first name and her father's family name. If she marries, she may add *de* and her husband's last name to her own name: María Teresa Rivera de García.

- Use the Spanish system to write your *nombre completo.* What advantages or disadvantages do you see to having a name formed this way?

For: Internet link activity
Visit: www.phschool.com
Web Code: jcd-0506

La cultura en vivo

El papel picado

As you've seen in this chapter, *el papel picado* (cut paper) is a well-known Mexican craft. Colored tissue paper is cut into small patterns similar to making paper snowflakes. The cut paper is then hung on string to make a banner to use as decoration at many different celebrations. Here's how to make *papel picado* to decorate your classroom.

Una fiesta con música de mariachi

Materials

- colored tissue paper cut into 12" x 18" sheets
- scissors
- stapler
- string

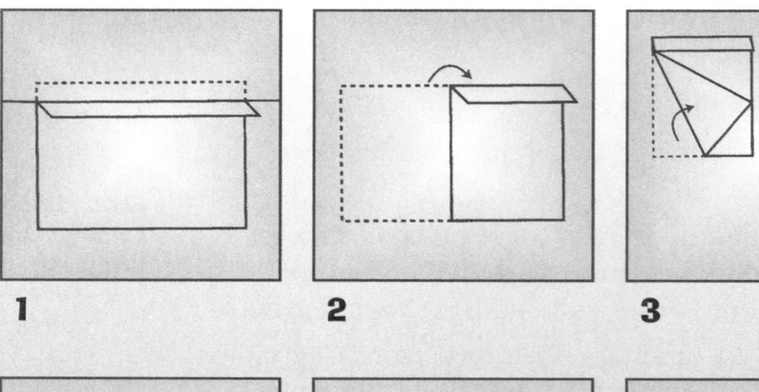

Directions

1. Spread the tissue paper flat. Fold down 1" on the 18" side for making a hanging flap.
2. Fold the paper in half on the 12" side and crease on the fold to make a sharp line.
3. Fold the paper twice, diagonally.

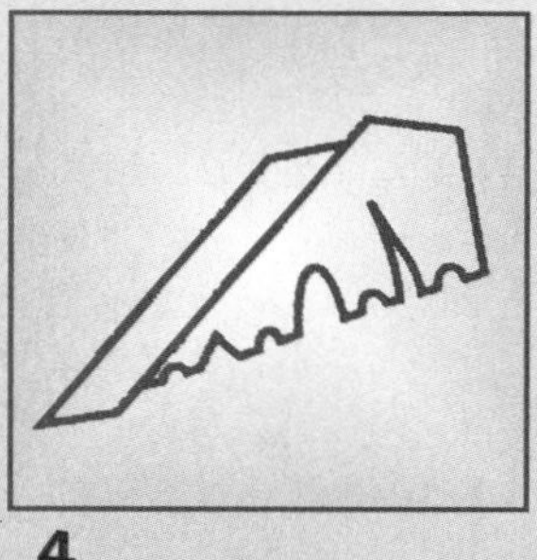

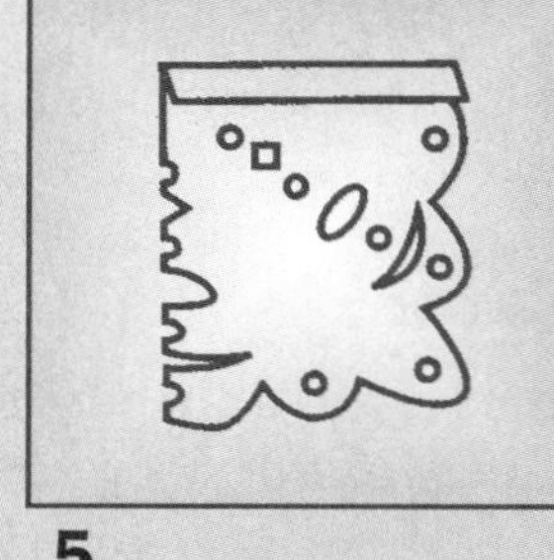

4
5
6

4. Cut out designs along the folded edge. Experiment with snowflake or other geometric designs.

5. Cut a scalloped design on the outside edge.
6. Open the cutout and staple to a string to hang across a room to decorate for a *fiesta*.

Presentación oral

Mi familia

Task
You are on an exchange program in Chile and your host family wants to know about your family back home. Show them photographs of three family members and talk about the people shown.

1 Prepare Bring in three family photos or "create" a family using pictures from a magazine. Use a chart like this one to think through what you want to say about each person.

Nombre	Es mi ...	Edad	Actividad favorita
Isabel	hermana menor	9 años	le gusta cantar

2 Practice Go through your presentation several times. You can use your notes in practice, but not when you present. Try to:

- provide all the information on each family member
- use complete sentences
- speak clearly

Modelo

Se llama Isabel. Ella es mi hermana menor y tiene 9 años. A Isabel le gusta cantar. Es muy artística.

3 Present Show your pictures and give the information about each person.

4 Evaluation Your teacher may give you a rubric for how the presentation will be graded. You probably will be graded on:

- how complete your preparation is
- how much information you communicate
- how easy it is to understand you

Strategy

Using graphic organizers
Simple charts can help you organize your thoughts for a presentation.

Videomisterio

¿Eres tú, María?

Madrid, España

Episodio 1

Antes de ver el video

Personajes importantes

Doña Lupe, portera

Lola Lago, detective

Nota cultural In many apartment buildings in Spain, you will find a *portero* or *portera*. In exchange for a small salary and free apartment (in Spain, an apartment is called *un piso),* this person watches over the building and its residents, doing small chores such as taking messages and receiving packages. Because the *portero* or *portera* knows everyone in the building, he or she is often a good source of information about the residents.

Resumen del episodio

Estamos en el piso de Lola Lago, una detective que trabaja en Madrid, la capital de España. Es la una de la mañana. Desde[1] su balcón, ella ve a dos personas hablando enfrente de un edificio.[2] ¿Qué pasa? Más tarde, Lola encuentra[3] algo muy importante en la calle.[4] Al día siguiente,[5] doña Lupe, la portera del edificio, entra en el piso de doña Gracia y . . .

[1]From [2]building [3]finds [4]street [5]The next day

Palabras para comprender

investigar	to investigate
las llaves	keys
el periódico	newspaper
el piso	apartment; floor *(of a building)*

"¿Qué es esto?
Mañana voy a investigar."

"A ver. Unas llaves . . ."

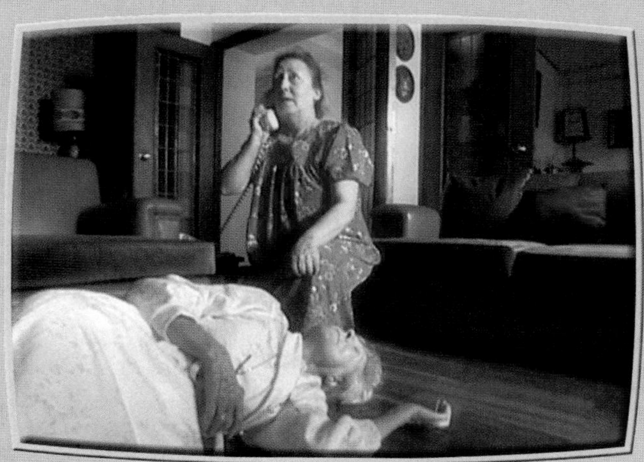

"¡Ay de mí! Necesito una ambulancia. Plaza del Alamillo. Número 8. Tercer piso. ¡Rápido!"

Después de ver el video

¿Comprendes?

Lee las frases y decide si son ciertas o falsas. Si una frase es falsa, escríbela con la información correcta.

1. Es la una de la tarde cuando Lola entra en su piso.
2. Ella está sola en su piso.
3. Lola ve a dos hombres hablando en la calle.
4. Las dos personas están muy contentas.
5. Lola encuentra un llavero con las iniciales "J.R.D."
6. Lola compra *(buys)* una revista en la mañana.
7. Doña Lupe entra en el piso de Lola con el periódico.

For: More on *¿Eres tú, María?*
Visit: www.phschool.com
Web Code: jcd-0507

Repaso del capítulo

Vocabulario y gramática

Chapter Review

To prepare for the test, check to see if you . . .
- know the new vocabulary and grammar
- can perform the tasks on p. 245

to talk about family members

los abuelos	grandparents
el abuelo	grandfather
la abuela	grandmother
el esposo, la esposa	husband, wife
los hermanos	brothers; brother(s) and sister(s)
el hermano	brother
la hermana	sister
el hermanastro	stepbrother
la hermanastra	stepsister
los hijos	children; sons
el hijo	son
la hija	daughter
los padres (papás)	parents
el padre (papá)	father
la madre (mamá)	mother
el padrastro	stepfather
la madrastra	stepmother
los primos	cousins
el primo	(male) cousin
la prima	(female) cousin
los tíos	uncles; aunt(s) and uncle(s)
el tío	uncle
la tía	aunt

to discuss and compare ages

¿Cuántos años tiene(n) ___?	How old is / are ___?
Tiene(n) ___ años.	He / She is / They are ___ (years old).
mayor *pl.* **mayores**	older
menor *pl.* **menores**	younger

to talk about people

la persona	person

to name animals

el gato	cat
el perro	dog

to discuss what someone likes

(a + *person*) **le gusta(n) / le encanta(n)**	he / she likes / loves

For *Vocabulario adicional,* see pp. 472–473.

to describe activities at parties

abrir	to open
celebrar	to celebrate
decorar	to decorate
las decoraciones	decorations
hacer un video	to videotape
el video	video
preparar	to prepare
romper	to break
sacar fotos	to take photos
la foto	photo
la cámara	camera

to discuss celebrations

el cumpleaños	birthday
¡Feliz cumpleaños!	Happy birthday!
los dulces	candy
la flor *pl.* **las flores**	flower
el globo	balloon
la luz *pl.* **las luces**	light
el papel picado	cut-paper decorations
el pastel	cake
la piñata	piñata
el regalo	gift, present

other useful words

que	who, that
sólo	only

to indicate possession or relationship

tener *to have*

tengo	**tenemos**
tienes	**tenéis**
tiene	**tienen**

possessive adjectives

mi(s) my	**nuestro(s), -a(s)** our
tu(s) your	**vuestro(s), -a(s)** your *(pl.)*
su(s) your *(formal),* his, her, its	**su(s)** your *(pl.),* their

Más práctica

Practice Workbook Puzzle 5A-8

Practice Workbook Organizer 5A-9

Go Online
PHSchool.com
For: Test preparation
Visit: www.phschool.com
Web Code: jcd-0508

Preparación para el examen

	On the exam you will be asked to . . .	Here are practice tasks similar to those you will find on the exam . . .	If you need review . . .
	**1 Escuchar** Listen to and understand someone's description of a family member	At a friend's party, a woman is telling you stories about her brother, Jorge. a) How old is her brother? b) Who is older, the woman or her brother? c) What does her brother like to do?	**pp. 222–225** *A primera vista* **p. 226** Actividad 4 **p. 227** Actividades 7–8 **p. 229** Actividad 11
	**2 Hablar** Describe some members of your family and what they like to do	At your first Spanish Club meeting, your teacher requests that all of you try to talk to each other in Spanish. Since you just learned how to talk about your family, you feel confident that you can talk about some of your family members. Tell about: a) how they are related to you; b) their ages; c) what they like to do; d) their personalities.	**pp. 222–225** *A primera vista* **p. 226** Actividad 4 **p. 227** Actividad 7 **p. 229** Actividad 12 **p. 232** *Gramática: Possessive adjectives* **p. 237** Actividad 26
	**3 Leer** Read and understand someone's description of a problem he or she is having with a family member	Read this letter to an advice columnist. Can you describe in English what Ana's problem is? Querida Dolores, Yo soy la hija menor de una familia de seis personas. Uno de mis hermanos mayores, Nacho, siempre habla de mí con mis padres. A él le encanta hablar de mis amigos y de mis actividades. Tenemos una familia muy simpática, pero ¡Nacho me vuelve loca! —Ana	**pp. 222–225** *A primera vista* **p. 226** Actividades 4–5 **p. 232** Actividad 18
	**4 Escribir** Write a brief note telling at least two facts about a friend or family member	The party planner at a local restaurant is helping you plan a birthday party for your cousin. Write a brief note telling her your cousin's name, age, two things he or she likes to do at a party, the kinds of decorations he or she likes, and one thing he or she loves to eat.	**p. 226** Actividad 5 **p. 227** Actividad 8 **p. 229** Actividad 12 **p. 237** Actividad 26
	**5 Pensar** Demonstrate an understanding of some ways that Spanish-speaking families celebrate special occasions	Think about what you would consider your most important birthday. Based on what you know about important family traditions, describe why a fifteenth birthday is important for a young Spanish-speaking girl and what you would expect to see at her celebration.	**pp. 222–225** *A primera vista* **p. 226** *Fondo cultural* **pp. 238–239** *Lectura* **p. 240** *La cultura en vivo*

Orgullo de familia (1997), Simón Silva
Courtesy of Simón Silva.

Fondo cultural

Extended families tend to be close-knit in Spanish-speaking cultures. Parents, children, grandparents, aunts, uncles, and cousins get together often for meals or just to spend time together, and not just on special occasions. In fact, it is not uncommon for three generations to live under one roof or in the same neighborhood.

- How does the idea of extended families in Spanish-speaking cultures compare with what happens with you and your friends?

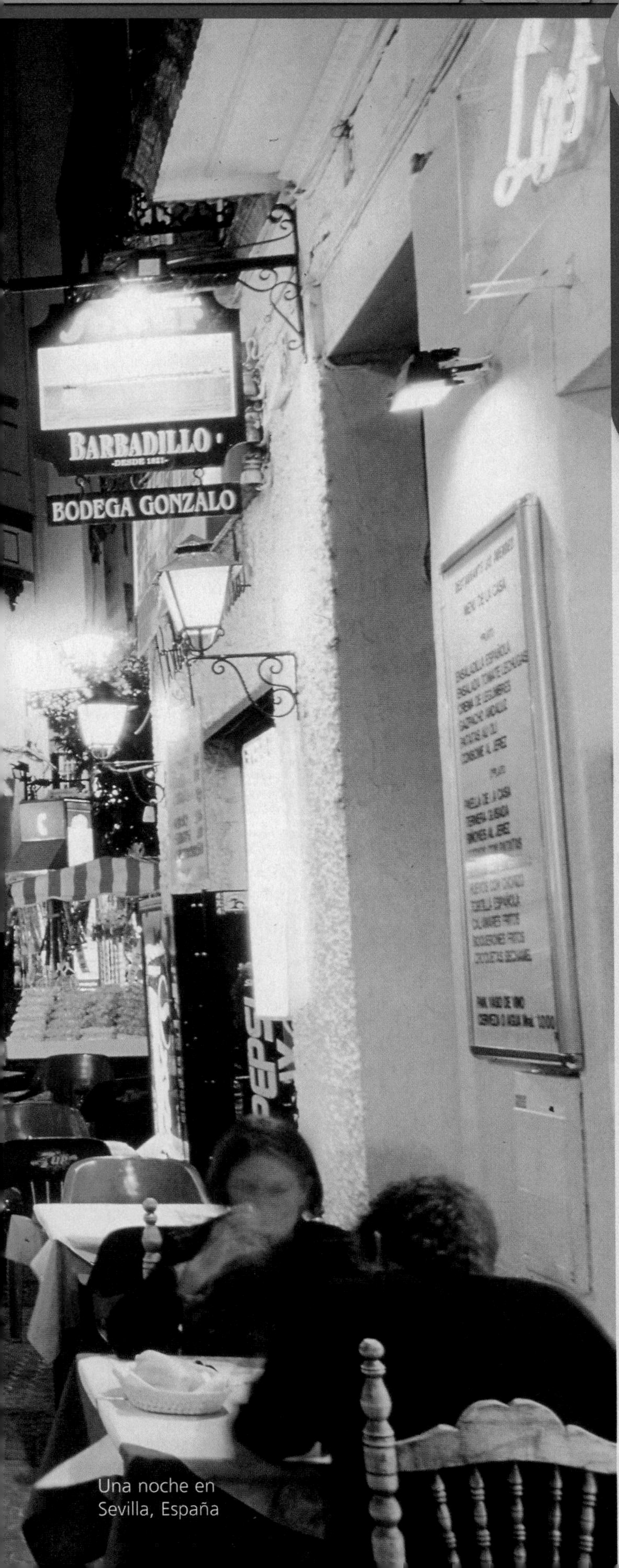

¡Vamos a un restaurante!

Chapter Objectives

- Talk about family celebrations
- Describe family members and friends
- Ask politely to have something brought to you
- Order a meal in a restaurant
- Understand cultural perspectives on family celebrations

Video Highlights

A primera vista: ***En el restaurante Casa Río***

GramActiva Videos: **the verb *venir;* the verbs *ser* and *estar***

Videomisterio: ***¿Eres tú, María?,*** **Episodio 2**

Country Connection

As you learn about family celebrations, describing family members, and restaurants, you will make connections to these countries and places:

For: Online Atlas
Visit: www.phschool.com
Web Code: jce-0002

Una noche en Sevilla, España

A primera vista

Vocabulario y gramática en contexto

Objectives

Read, listen to, and understand information about
- **descriptions of family members**
- **restaurant vocabulary**
- **table settings**

—Abuelito, ¿quiénes son las personas en la foto?

—La mujer es tu abuela y el hombre, soy yo. Y aquí está tu papá. Tiene sólo seis años.

la mujer

el hombre

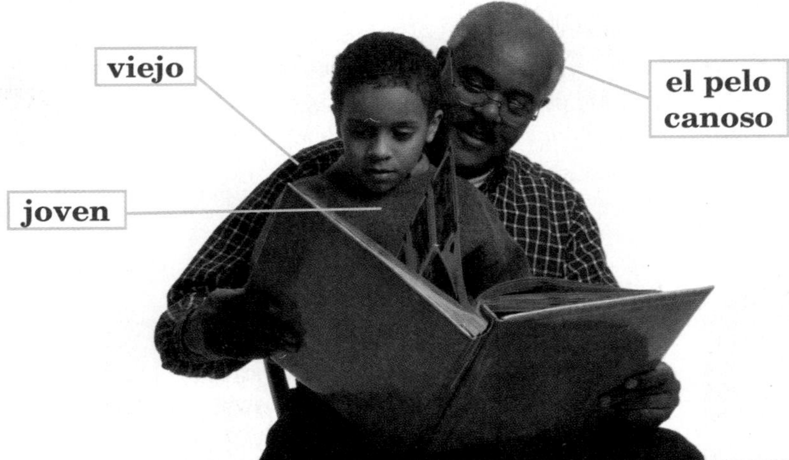

—¿Quién es **el joven** alto y **guapo?**

—Es tu primo Rafael.

—¿Y **la joven** baja al lado del primo Rafael?

—Es su amiga, Sara. Y estas **otras** personas son amigos también.

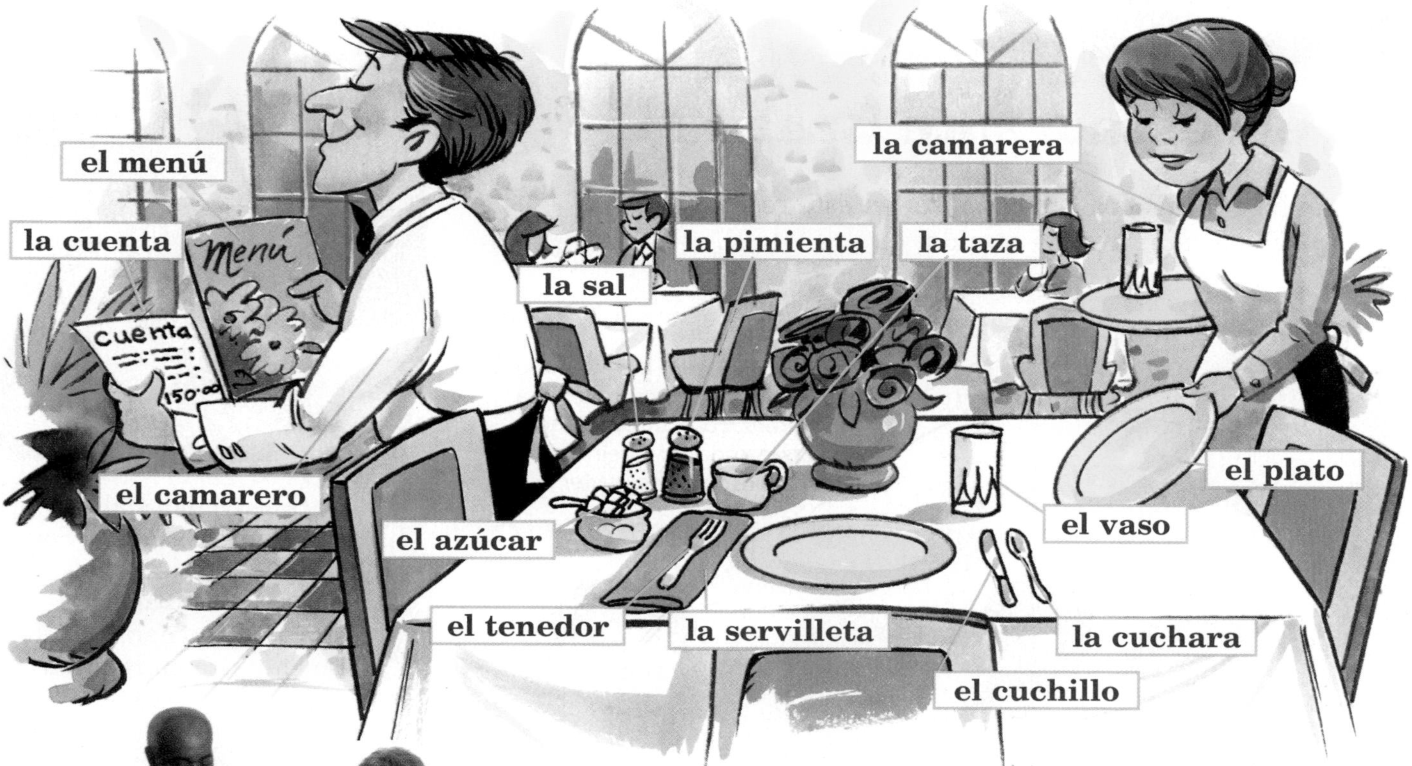

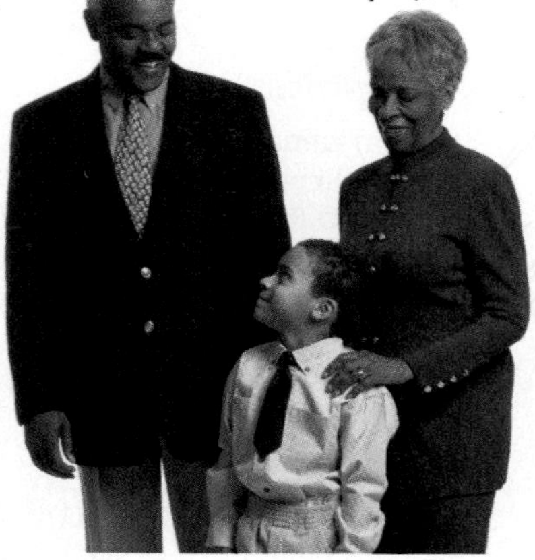

el menú
la cuenta
Menú
Cuenta
150.00
el camarero
la sal
la pimienta
la taza
la camarera
el azúcar
el tenedor
la servilleta
el vaso
el plato
la cuchara
el cuchillo

—Abuela, ¿qué celebramos esta noche?

—Es el cumpleaños de tu abuelo.

—¿Quiénes **vienen** a la fiesta?

—Toda la familia **viene.**

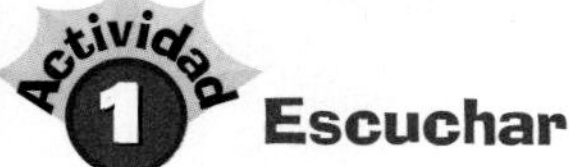

Actividad 1 **Escuchar**

¿Quiénes vienen?

Paquito is showing the family album to a friend. Point to the different pictures as he describes the people in the photographs.

Actividad 2 **Escuchar**

¿Qué necesitas para . . . ?

You will hear seven statements about the table setting. If a statement is correct, indicate *cierto* by raising one hand. If a statement is incorrect, indicate *falso* by raising two hands.

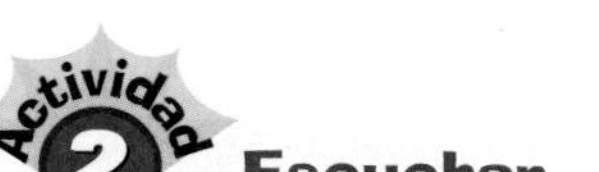

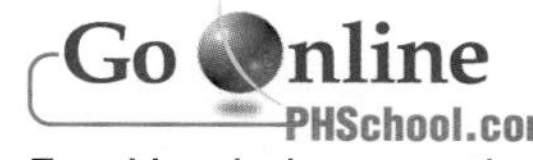

Más práctica
Practice Workbook 5B-1, 5B-2

Go Online PHSchool.com
For: Vocabulary practice
Visit: www.phschool.com
Web Code: jcd-0511

Videohistoria

En el restaurante Casa Río

La familia de Angélica come la cena en este restaurante. Lee lo que pasa durante la comida.

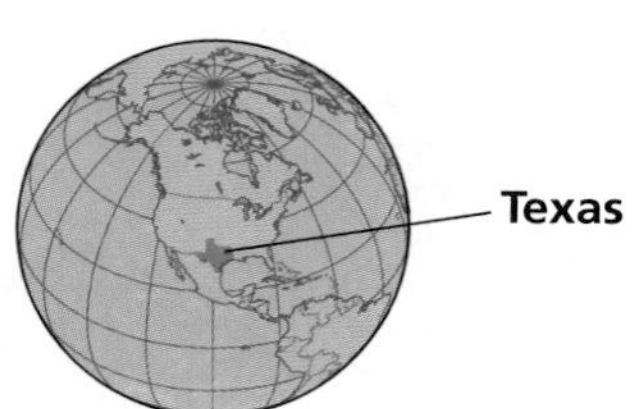

Strategy

Scanning
Think about what a waiter might say to you when you order in a restaurant. Look through the dialogue and find three expressions that the waiter uses.

1 **Luis:** Bienvenidos al restaurante Casa Río. Soy Luis, su mesero. Hoy es mi primer día de trabajo. Estoy un poco nervioso. El menú está en la mesa.

También se dice . . .

el (la) camarero(a) =
el (la) mesero(a) *(México, Puerto Rico);* el (la) mozo(a) *(Argentina, Puerto Rico)*

5 **Esteban:** Señor, **me faltan** un cuchillo y un tenedor.

Luis: ¡Ah, sí! En un momento **le traigo** un cuchillo y un tenedor.

6 **Luis:** ¿Y para quién son las enchiladas?

Angélica: Creo que son para el señor de pelo castaño.

Luis: ¡Oh! ¡Gracias!

Angélica: **De nada.**

7 **Luis:** ¿Necesitan **algo más?** ¿Y cómo está la comida?

Mamá: La comida aquí es **deliciosa. ¡Qué rica!**

2 **Luis:** ¿Qué va a **pedir** Ud. de bebida?

Papá: ¡Uy! **Tengo calor.** Para mí, un té helado.

Mamá: Y yo **tengo frío.** Para mí, café.

3 **Luis:** Y **ahora** . . . , ¿qué **desean** Uds. **de plato principal?**

Angélica: **Quisiera** el arroz con pollo.

Esteban: Para mí, una hamburguesa con papas fritas.

4 **Luis:** ¿Y qué desea Ud.?

Cristina: **¿Me trae** las fajitas de pollo, por favor?

Luis: ¡Muy bien!

8 **Luis:** Ahora, ¿desean **postre?**

Mamá: Pues, sí. Y **otro** café, por favor.

Papá: Para mí, nada. Pero quisiera un café, yo también. Ahora **tengo sueño.**

Escribir/Hablar

¿Comprendes?

1. ¿Cómo se llama el restaurante? ¿Cómo se llama el mesero?
2. ¿Por qué está nervioso Luis?
3. ¿Qué va a beber el padre? ¿Por qué?
4. ¿Quién come las fajitas? ¿La hamburguesa?
5. ¿Quién desea las enchiladas?
6. Según la mamá, ¿cómo es la comida?

Más práctica

Practice Workbook 5B-3, 5B-4

For: Vocabulary practice
Visit: www.phschool.com
Web Code: jcd-0512

Manos a la obra

Vocabulario y gramática en uso

Objectives

- **Describe people and foods**
- **Order a meal in a restaurant**
- **Learn to use the verb *venir***
- **Know some uses of the verbs *ser* and *estar***

Escuchar

¿Quiénes son?

Vas a escuchar descripciones de las personas en el dibujo. En una hoja de papel, escribe los números del 1 al 5. Al lado de cada número escribe el nombre de la persona que describen.

También se dice . . .

pelirrojo(a) = colorado(a) *(Argentina)*; colorín, colorina *(Chile)*

el pelo = el cabello *(muchos países)*

rubio(a) = güero(a) *(México)*

Eduardo, 15

Rosalía, 14

Lucía, 18

Alejandro, 20

María Elena, 60

Jorge, 65

Escribir/Hablar

¿Quién es?

1. Mira los dibujos de la Actividad 4 y escribe frases para describir a cada persona.

Modelo

El joven muy alto es Eduardo. Tiene 15 años. Tiene el pelo castaño. Le gusta jugar al tenis.

2. Describe a uno(a) de tus amigos.

¿Recuerdas?

Adjectives agree in number and gender with the nouns they describe.

  **Leer/Pensar/Escribir**

Las analogías

Many exams test your vocabulary by asking about the logical relationships, or analogies, between words. In analogies, the symbol ":" is used to mean "is to" *(es a)* and the symbol "::" is used to mean "as" *(como)*. For example:

la madre : la hija :: el padre : el hijo

You would read this as *"La madre es a la hija como el padre es al hijo."* Complete these analogies.

Modelo

trabajador : perezoso :: alto : bajo

1. aburrido : interesante :: largo : ________
2. comida : plato :: bebida : ________
3. escuela : profesora :: restaurante : ________
4. chico : joven :: abuelo : ________
5. bistec : plato principal :: pastel : ________
6. amigo : amiga :: hombre : ________
7. ensalada : tenedor :: sopa : ________

  **Escribir**

¿Qué te gusta pedir?

Escribe frases para decir lo que te gusta pedir cuando tienes . . .

Modelo

Cuando tengo hambre, me gusta pedir pizza en un restaurante.

1. 

2. 

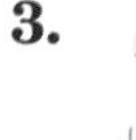

3. 

4. 

5. 

En un restaurante en Cali, Colombia

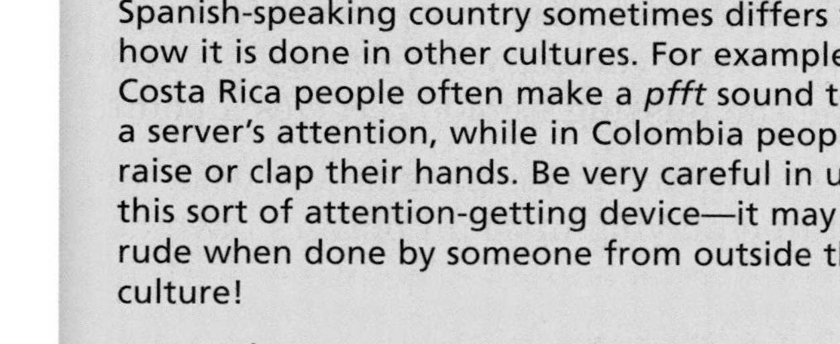

Getting a server's attention at a restaurant in a Spanish-speaking country sometimes differs from how it is done in other cultures. For example, in Costa Rica people often make a *pfft* sound to get a server's attention, while in Colombia people may raise or clap their hands. Be very careful in using this sort of attention-getting device—it may seem rude when done by someone from outside the culture!

- How do you get a server's attention in a restaurant here in the United States? Compare this to what is acceptable in some Spanish-speaking countries.

Leer/Hablar

En el restaurante

Con otro(a) estudiante, lee la conversación entre un camarero y dos jóvenes. Empareja *(Match)* lo que dice el camarero con lo que contestan *(answer)* los jóvenes para crear *(create)* la conversación.

Un restaurante en el Paseo del Río, San Antonio, Texas

El camarero

1. Buenas noches. ¿Qué desean de bebida?
2. ¿Qué desea pedir de plato principal?
3. ¡Ay, señor! Le falta el cuchillo, ¿no?
4. ¿Le gusta la sopa?
5. Señorita, ¿qué desea Ud. de postre?
6. Señor, ¿le traigo otra bebida?
7. ¿Desean Uds. algo más?
8. Gracias por venir a nuestro restaurante.

Los jóvenes

a. Sí, está deliciosa. Umm. ¡Qué rica!
b. No, sólo la cuenta, por favor.
c. Quisiera el arroz con pollo, por favor.
d. De nada. Hasta luego.
e. Un helado, por favor.
f. Sí. ¿Me trae uno, por favor?
g. Para mí, un refresco y, para la señorita, un té helado.
h. Sí, por favor. Tengo mucha sed.

Hablar

Juego

1. Work in groups of three or four. Your teacher will give you copies of pictures of various table items. Cut or tear the pictures apart to make cards.
2. Arrange the pictures in a table setting on a desk. While the other players have their backs turned, hide one or more of the cards. Then ask: *¿Qué me falta?* The first player to say correctly *Te falta(n) . . .* and name the missing item(s) receives a point.
3. Put the hidden items back on the desk and continue playing until all players have had a chance to hide items. The player with the most points is the winner.

Nota

When one item is missing, use *me / te falta*. When more than one item is missing, use *me / te faltan.*

Exploración del lenguaje

Adjectives ending in *-ísimo*

Muy + an adjective can be expressed in another way by adding the correct form of *-ísimo* to the adjective. The *-ísimo* ending conveys the idea of "extremely."

un chico muy guapo = un chico guap**ísimo**
una clase muy difícil = una clase dificil**ísima**

Adjectives that end in *-co* or *-ca* have a spelling change to *-qu-*. The *-o* or *-a* is dropped.

unos pasteles muy ri**cos** = unos pasteles ri**quísimos**

Try it out! Rework the following phrases using the correct *-ísimo* form.

un perro muy perezoso = ¿ ?
dos libros muy interesantes = ¿ ?
una clase muy aburrida = ¿ ?
unas chicas muy simpáticas = ¿ ?

Leer/Pensar/Escribir/Hablar

El Café Buen Libro

Lee la crítica del café y lo que dicen estas *(these)* personas. ¿A quiénes recomiendas el café? ¿A quiénes no?

Café Buen Libro
Nuevo León, 28

✓✓ ++ $ ☺☺

Es un café tranquilo con un ambiente* intelectual donde puedes pasar el tiempo en la compañía de un buen amigo o un buen libro. Los precios son muy razonables. Puedes comer un sándwich, una ensalada, un postre riquísimo o simplemente beber un café. También tienen lo último en libros, videos y música. Un "plus" es la presentación de grupos musicales los fines de semana.

Ambiente
aburrido ✓
tranquilo ✓✓
fantástico ✓✓✓
Comida y bebida
regular +
buena ++
excelente +++
Precios
barato $
medio $$
caro $$$
Servicio
regular ☺
bueno ☺☺
superior ☺☺☺

* atmosphere

1. **Carmen:** "Quisiera comer un bistec sabroso."
2. **Marta:** "Me encanta escuchar música."
3. **Diego:** "Tengo muchísima hambre y poco tiempo."
4. **Lupe:** "Me gusta pasar tiempo con otras personas interesantes y graciosas."
5. **Ana:** "No tengo mucho dinero *(money)* ahora."
6. Y a ti, ¿te gustaría ir al Café Buen Libro? ¿Por qué?

Gramática

The verb *venir*

You use *venir* to say that someone is coming to a place or an event.

¿A qué hora **vienes** al restaurante?
*When **are you coming** to the restaurant?*

Vengo a las cuatro de la tarde.
***I'm coming** at 4:00 in the afternoon.*

Here are all the present-tense forms:

(yo)	**vengo**	(nosotros) (nosotras)	**venimos**
(tú)	**vienes**	(vosotros) (vosotras)	**venís**
Ud. (él) (ella)	**viene**	Uds. (ellos) (ellas)	**vienen**

GramActiva VIDEO

Want more help with *venir?* Watch the **GramActiva** video.

Gramática  Leer/Escribir

¿Cómo vienen?

Tu amigo Antonio invita a tu familia a su casa en el campo. Escribes una nota para explicar cómo y cuándo todos Uds. vienen. Completa la nota con las formas apropiadas del verbo *venir*.

Antonio,

¡Gracias por tu invitación! Yo **1.** en bicicleta con mi amiga, Marta. Nosotros **2.** a las dos porque Marta trabaja hasta la una. Mi abuela **3.** en tren[1] con mis padres. Ellos **4.** a las once para ayudar[2] con la cena. Mis hermanitos también **5.** en tren con mis padres. Mi hermana mayor, Cecilia, **6.** en monopatín. No sé a qué hora va a venir.

¡Nos vemos el sábado!

[1]train [2]to help

Gramática  Escuchar/Escribir

Escucha, escribe y dibuja

Roberto, otro amigo de Antonio, también va a la fiesta con su familia. Vas a escuchar la descripción de su familia. Escribe las cuatro descripciones y después dibuja a la familia. Compara tu dibujo con el dibujo de otro(a) estudiante.

Hablar

¿Qué traen a tu casa?

Estás en casa de un(a) amigo(a). Habla de lo que traen las personas a la casa.

Modelo

A —*Cuando tus tíos vienen a tu casa, ¿traen algo?*
B —*Sí, generalmente traen el postre.*
o: *No, generalmente no traen nada.*

Nota

Traer, "to bring," follows the pattern of *-er* verbs except for the irregular *yo* form: *traigo.*

- Mañana **traigo** pasteles para todos.
- Y tú, **¿traes** bebidas?

Estudiante A

1. tu(s) abuelo(s)
2. tu mejor amigo(a)
3. tus amigos
4. tus tíos
5. tus primos
6. los amigos de tus padres

Estudiante B

el plato principal
un regalo
nada
el postre
flores
¡Respuesta personal!

Pronunciación

The letters *b* and *v*

In Spanish, *b* and *v* are pronounced the same. At the beginning of a word or phrase, *b* and *v* sound like the *b* in "boy." Listen to and say these words:

voy bolígrafo vienen bien viejo video

In most other positions *b* and *v* have a softer "b" sound. The lips barely touch as the *b* or *v* sound is pronounced. Listen to and say these words:

abuelo divertido joven huevos globo Alberto

Try it out! Listen to and say this *trabalenguas:*

Cabral clava un clavo.
¿Qué clavo clava Cabral?

Hablar

¿Quiénes vienen?

Estás en una fiesta en la escuela y hablas con los otros estudiantes.

1. ¿Quiénes vienen a la fiesta? ¿A qué hora vienen?
2. ¿Vienen todos los profesores a la fiesta? ¿Qué traen ellos?
3. ¿Traen los estudiantes pizza o sándwiches? ¿Frutas o pasteles?
4. ¿Quién trae las decoraciones? ¿Qué traes tú?

Más práctica

Practice Workbook 5B-5

For: Practice with *venir*
Visit: www.phschool.com
Web Code: jcd-0513

Gramática

The verbs *ser* and *estar*

You know that both *ser* and *estar* mean "to be." Their uses, however, are different.

(yo)	**soy**	(nosotros) (nosotras)	**somos**
(tú)	**eres**	(vosotros) (vosotras)	**sois**
Ud. (él) (ella)	**es**	Uds. (ellos) (ellas)	**son**

(yo)	**estoy**	(nosotros) (nosotras)	**estamos**
(tú)	**estás**	(vosotros) (vosotras)	**estáis**
Ud. (él) (ella)	**está**	Uds. (ellos) (ellas)	**están**

Use *ser* to talk about characteristics that generally do not change. *Ser* is used for descriptions that are not about conditions or location. For example:

- who a person is or what a person is like
- what something is or what something is like
- where a person or thing is from

Teresa **es** mi prima. **Es** muy graciosa.
Los tacos **son** mi comida favorita. **Son** riquísimos.
Mis tíos **son** de México. **Son** muy simpáticos.

Use *estar* to talk about conditions that tend to change. For example:

- how a person feels
- where a person or thing is

¿Dónde **está** Mariana? No **está** aquí.
No puede venir hoy porque **está** muy enferma.

GramActiva VIDEO

Want more help with *ser* and *estar?* Watch the **GramActiva** video.

Actividad 15 Gramática   Hablar

¿Dónde están las otras personas?

Estás en un café con un(a) amigo(a) y preguntas dónde están los otros amigos. Tu amigo(a) explica dónde están y cómo están.

Modelo

Marcos y Graciela **A** —*¿Dónde están Marcos y Graciela?*
B —*Están en la biblioteca. Están muy ocupados.*

Strategy

Using rhymes
To remember the uses of *estar,* memorize this rhyme:

For how you feel
And where you are,
Always use the verb *estar.*

Estudiante A

1. Yolanda
2. Miguel y Fernando
3. Isabel y Raquel
4. Ana María
5. Federico
6. Enrique

Estudiante B

la escuela
casa
el trabajo
la lección de . . .
la biblioteca

ocupado, -a
enfermo, -a
cansado, -a
triste
mal
contento, -a

¡Respuesta personal!

Gramática

Leer/Escribir

Entrevista con una chef

Lee la entrevista con la chef Ortiz y completa la conversación con la forma apropiada del verbo *estar* o *ser.*

— Bienvenida, Chef Ortiz. ¿Cómo __1.__ Ud. hoy?
— __2.__ muy bien, gracias.
— Ud. trabaja aquí en Asunción ahora pero, ¿de dónde __3.__ Ud. originalmente?
— Mi familia y yo __4.__ del campo.
— ¿Y cuál __5.__ su trabajo aquí?
— Yo __6.__ directora de los chefs en el famoso restaurante La Capital.
— La Capital __7.__ un restaurante muy popular aquí. ¿Dónde __8.__ el restaurante?
— Al lado de la catedral.
— Los platos en su restaurante __9.__ muy típicos de Paraguay, ¿no?
— Sí, y según los clientes, la comida en nuestro restaurante __10.__ deliciosa.
— Y los postres __11.__ muy populares también, ¿no?
— Sí, tenemos pasteles ricos, helados simples con frutas exóticas, un poco de todo.
— ¡Muchas gracias, Chef Ortiz!
— De nada. Siempre __12.__ muy contenta de estar aquí con Uds.

¡Qué rico!

Paraguay

Leer/Pensar

Un postre delicioso

Your grandmother has given you her recipe for *arroz con leche* and you want to try it out. But the ingredients are given in *gramos* and *litros* and you don't know what the customary measure equivalents are. Study the conversion chart, convert the measurements given in the recipe, and answer the question.

ARROZ CON LECHE

Para 8

300 gramos de arroz
3 litros de leche
400 gramos de azúcar
un poco de vainilla
canela[1]

Pon el arroz en remojo[2] con la leche una hora y media. Luego cocina a fuego lento[3] una hora más o menos. Añade[4] el azúcar y la vainilla y cocina unos 5 minutos más. Pon el arroz en el refrigerador y esparce[5] un poco de canela encima.

Conexiones | Las matemáticas

1 kilo (k) = 2,2 libras *(pounds)*
1 gramo (g) = 0,035 onzas *(ounces)*
1 litro (l) = 1,057 cuartos *(quarts)*

Multiplica los kilos, gramos o litros por su medida[6] correspondiente en el sistema que usas.

Calcula las onzas o los cuartos que hay en 300 gramos de arroz, tres litros de leche y 400 gramos de azúcar.

- ¿Cuántas libras hay en dos kilos de arroz?

[1]cinnamon [2]soak [3]cook slowly [4]Add [5]sprinkle [6]measure

Escribir/Hablar

¡Es buenísimo para la salud!

Habla con otro(a) estudiante sobre cómo son las comidas en general.

1. Escribe una lista de diez comidas y bebidas.
2. Usa tu lista y pregunta a un(a) compañero(a) si come lo que le preguntas. Tu compañero(a) va a contestar y decirte por qué come o no come cada una de estas comidas.

Modelo

A —*¿Comes muchas verduras?*
B —*¡Por supuesto! Las verduras son muy buenas para la salud.*
o: *No. ¡Qué asco! Las verduras son horribles.*

Nota

To describe what a food item is like in general, use *ser*. To describe how a food item tastes at a particular time, use *estar*.

bueno (para la salud)
malo (para la salud)
rico
riquísimo
sabroso
delicioso
horrible

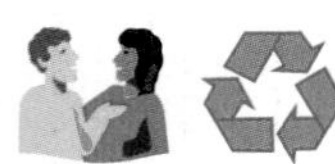

Hablar

¡La sopa está riquísima!

Estás en un restaurante y el (la) camarero(a) te pregunta cómo está todo. Mira el menú para contestar.

Modelo

A —*Señor(ita), ¿cómo está el arroz con pollo?*
B —*Está muy sabroso. Me encanta.*
o: *Lo siento. Está malo. ¿Me trae otro plato principal?*

Restaurante Hidalgo

Menú del día

$20,00

SOPAS Y ENSALADAS
Ensalada de tomates y cebollas
Sopa de verduras
Sopa Hidalgo

VERDURAS
Papas fritas
Papas al horno
Guisantes con jamón

PLATOS PRINCIPALES
Bistec
Pescado
Arroz con pollo

POSTRES
Pastel de chocolate
Helado de mango o papaya
Frutas frescas

In many Spanish-speaking countries, restaurants and cafés often offer *un menú del día* or, as they are called in some parts of Mexico, *una comida corrida.* These daily menus usually offer one to three choices for each course at a reasonable fixed price.

- Do any restaurants that you know offer something similar to *el menú del día?* What would be the advantages and disadvantages of ordering from *un menú del día?*

También se dice . . .

el menú = la carta *(México, España)*

Escribir/Hablar

El menú del día

With a classmate, prepare to play the roles of a server and client *(cliente)* at the Restaurante Hidalgo, which is in San Juan, Puerto Rico. Write five questions that each one could ask. Use the menu in Actividad 19 to help you decide what to ask. Don't forget to use the formal *Ud.* form in your questions and answers.

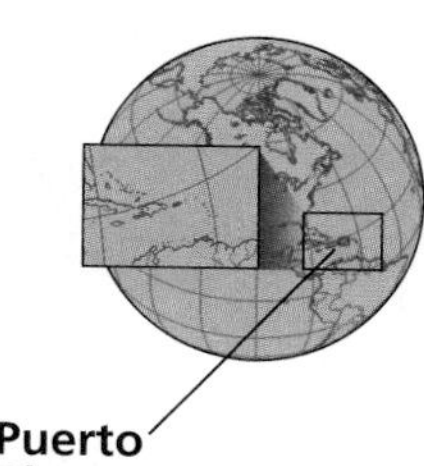

Modelo

el (la) camarero(a)	el (la) cliente
¿Qué desea pedir de plato principal?	¿Cómo está el bistec?

Hablar

En el restaurante

Usa las preguntas y frases de la Actividad 20 para tener una conversación completa. En tu conversación habla de las sopas y ensaladas, verduras, platos principales y postres.

Modelo

A —*¿Qué desea pedir de plato principal?*
B —*No sé. ¿Cómo está el bistec?*
A —*Está muy sabroso.*
B —*¡Genial! Quisiera el bistec, por favor.*

El español en el mundo del trabajo

How can you combine an interest in nutrition and health with skills in Spanish? Here's one example. As you know, the U.S. Department of Agriculture provides the public with a wide range of nutritional information through print materials and Web sites. Much of this information is available in Spanish. There is a need for federal employees who are knowledgeable to translate and work with the Spanish-speaking community on issues related to nutrition.

- What other opportunities can you think of that would combine communication skills with a knowledge of nutrition?

Más práctica

Practice Workbook 5B-6, 5B-7

For: Practice with *ser* vs. *estar*
Visit: www.phschool.com
Web Code: jcd-0514

¡Adelante!

Objectives

- Read a letter about a visit to Santa Fe, New Mexico
- Learn about *la sobremesa*
- Write a review of a restaurant
- Watch *¿Eres tú, María?,* Episodio 2

Lectura

Una visita a Santa Fe

Lee esta carta que escriben Alicia y Pedro. Ellos hablan de una visita que van a hacer sus primos a Santa Fe. ¿Qué cosas interesantes van a hacer? ¿Qué van a visitar?

Strategy

Skimming

Before you read this letter, make a list of three pieces of information you might expect to find. Quickly skim the letter. What information did you find that was on your list?

Queridos Rosario y Luis,

¡Esperamos[1] su visita en agosto! Aquí en Santa Fe vamos a hacer muchas cosas. ¿Saben que es una ciudad[2] con más de 400 años de historia y cultura? Vamos a visitar museos y tiendas, y vamos a comer comida típica. ¡Los cinco días van a pasar rápidamente![3]

Tenemos planes para pasar una noche muy especial en honor de su visita. Vamos a comer en un "restaurante" histórico que se llama Rancho de las Golondrinas.[4] Está a diez millas de nuestra casa, al sur de Santa Fe. El Rancho, en realidad, no es un restaurante; es una casa española.

Durante los días de su visita, el Rancho va a celebrar "un fandango," un baile histórico y típico, con una cena tradicional. Toda la comida es riquísima, pero nuestro plato favorito es el chile con carne y queso. Después de comer, vamos a bailar. ¡No sabemos bailar pero va a ser muy divertido! Mandamos[5] el menú con la carta.

¡Nos vemos en agosto!

Sus primos de Nuevo México,

Alicia y Pedro

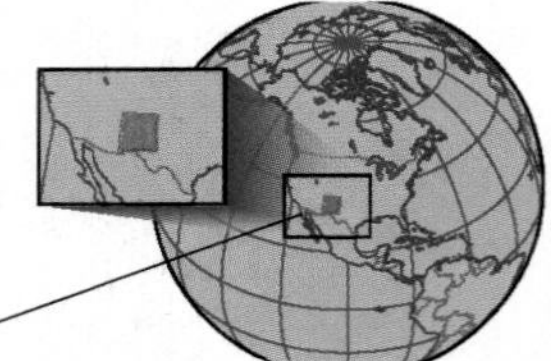

Un paraje[6] en El Camino Real[7] desde la Ciudad de México hasta Santa Fe, es del año 1710. Ahora es un museo.

[1] We're looking forward to [2] city [3] quickly [4] Swallows [5] We're sending [6] stopping place [7] the Royal Highway

Menú del Fandango

Sopas
Sopa de arroz
Garbanzos con chile

Plato principal
Pollo relleno[8]
Chile con carne y queso

Postre
Bizcochitos[9]
Pudín de arroz con leche

Bebidas
Chocolate mexicano
Ponche
Café

[8]Stuffed chicken [9]Cookies

La Capilla de San Miguel, la iglesia más vieja de Santa Fe, del año 1610

El Palacio de los Gobernadores, construido en 1610, es el edificio *(building)* público más viejo de los Estados Unidos que todavía se usa. Ahora es un museo de historia.

¿Comprendes?

1. ¿Cuáles son cuatro actividades que los primos van a hacer durante la visita? ¿Cuál te gustaría hacer en Santa Fe?
2. ¿Por qué es importante Santa Fe?
3. ¿Por qué quieren ir Alicia y Pedro al Rancho de las Golondrinas?
4. Si no te gusta nada la comida picante *(spicy)*, ¿qué debes pedir del menú?
5. ¿Por qué es importante La Capilla de San Miguel?

For: Internet link activity
Visit: www.phschool.com
Web Code: jcd-0515

¡A pensar! Santa Fe was established thirteen years before Plymouth Colony was settled by the Mayflower Pilgrims. It has been a seat of government for Spain, Mexico, and the Confederacy.

- Find out when the oldest building in your community was built. How does it differ in age from the Palacio de los Gobernadores in Santa Fe?

Perspectivas del mundo hispano

A la hora de comer

Una familia en Escazú, Costa Rica

Imagine that you had two hours for lunch every day. Or imagine that every time you ate a meal, you sat down at a table with a friend or family member and had a lengthy conversation. Now imagine that you didn't jump up from dinner as soon as you finished eating. What do these situations have in common?

In many Spanish-speaking cultures, even ordinary mealtimes are considered social events, a time to spend enjoying food and company. People often take time after a meal to relax, to sit around the table and enjoy a good conversation or just to have a laugh. This custom, called the *sobremesa,* is more important in many cultures than getting to the next appointment or saving time and money by buying a quick meal.

A los jóvenes de muchos países hispanos les gusta pasar el tiempo de la sobremesa con amigos o con la familia.

Not surprisingly, most Spanish-speaking countries have very few drive-through restaurants. Since people rarely take food "to go," they might be surprised if you suggested grabbing a sandwich to eat in the car. In fact, many cars don't have cup-holders.

Check it out! Figure out how much time you and your family spend at breakfast, lunch, and dinner on days when you're not in school or at work. Compare your results with those of your classmates. Then complete the following statements about practices among families in your community.

Modelo

En mi comunidad, es común *(common)* comer el desayuno en quince minutos.

1. En mi comunidad, es común comer el desayuno en ______.
2. En mi comunidad, es común comer el almuerzo en ______.
3. En mi comunidad, es común comer la cena en ______.

Think about it! What does your research say about the importance of relaxing and enjoying a leisurely meal with friends and family? How does it compare to what happens during meals in Spanish-speaking countries? Consider the two different attitudes towards mealtime. What benefits might each one have?

Presentación escrita

Un restaurante muy bueno

Task

Your school is developing a community guide for Spanish-speaking residents. Your class is in charge of writing about restaurants. Write a review of your favorite restaurant.

Strategy

Persuasion
Give specific information and concrete examples to persuade your readers to try a restaurant.

1. **Prewrite** Think about the restaurant you and your family like best. Copy the word web. Write the name of the restaurant you are reviewing in the middle circle. Write words and expressions associated with each category inside the appropriate circles.

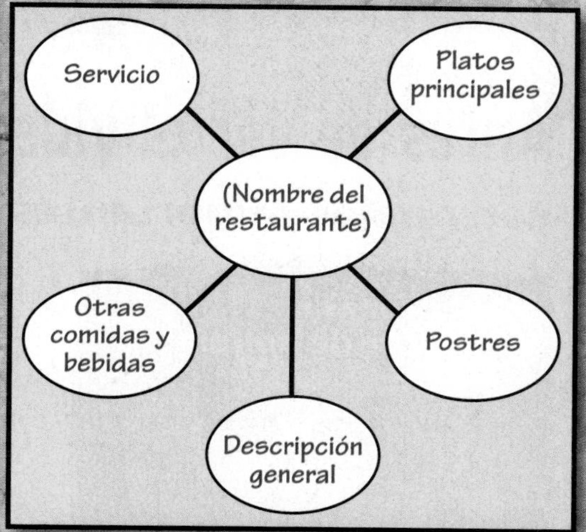

2. **Draft** Write your review of the restaurant using information from the word web. Try to include any information that might persuade others to try the restaurant.

3. **Revise** Read through your review and check for agreement, verb forms, and spelling. Share your review with a partner. Your partner should check the following:
   - Did you provide information about all categories?
   - Did you use the correct forms of the verbs?
   - Do you have any errors in spelling or agreement?
   - Is the review persuasive?

4. **Publish** Write a final copy of your review and make any necessary changes or additions. You may want to add illustrations and include your review in a booklet with your classmates' reviews or in your portfolio.

5. **Evaluation** Your teacher may give you a rubric for grading your review. You may be evaluated on:
   - how complete the task was
   - how you used new and previously learned vocabulary
   - how accurate the agreement, verb forms, and spelling are
   - correct use of verbs

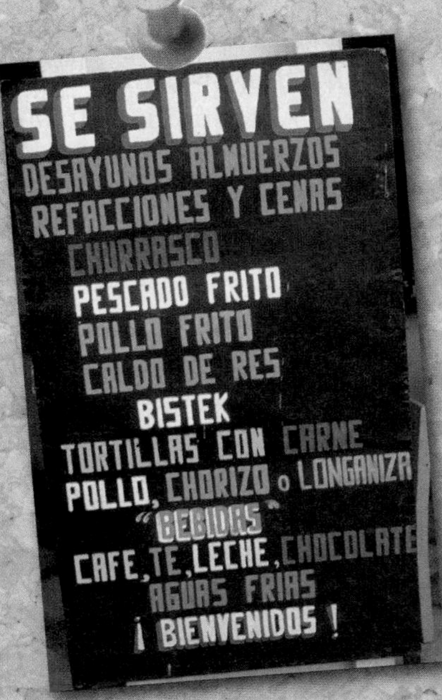

Videomisterio

¿Eres tú, María?

Episodio 2

Antes de ver el video

Personajes importantes

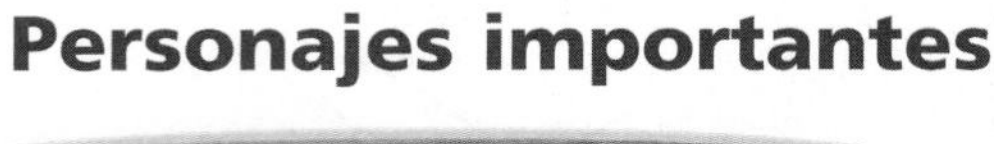

Resumen del episodio

En este episodio, la ambulancia llega[1] y lleva[2] a doña Gracia Requena al hospital. También llegan dos inspectores de policía. Le hablan a doña Lupe, la portera, sobre el incidente en el piso de doña Gracia. Lola se presenta[3] a los dos hombres y les dice[4] lo que sabe del incidente.

[1] arrives [2] takes away [3] introduces herself [4] tells them

Nota cultural In the cities and towns of Spain and many Spanish-speaking countries, you will find *plazas,* open squares that are surrounded by buildings. The *plazas* are the social center of the community or neighborhood. They may contain benches, trees and flowers, statues, and fountains. In the evening, neighbors will spend time in the *plaza* sharing details about families, daily events, politics, and many other topics.

Palabras para comprender

vive *(vivir)*	she lives *(to live)*
la sobrina	niece
esperar	to wait
anoche	last night
vi *(ver)*	I saw *(to see)*
una barba	beard
¿Quién era?	Who was she?
ayudar	to help
saber	to know

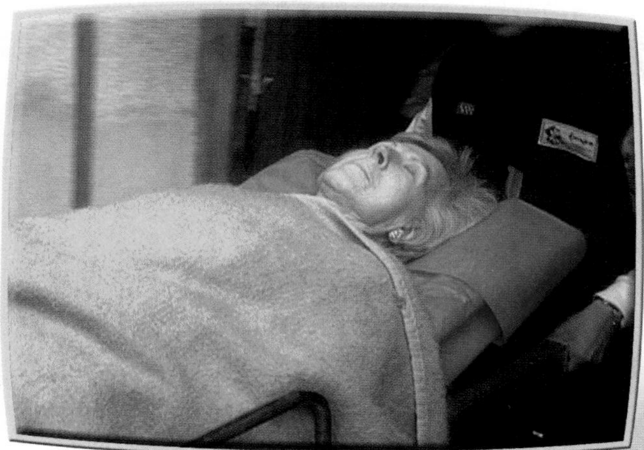

"Es doña Gracia Salazar. Vive en el tercer piso con su sobrina, María."

"Anoche a la una de la mañana, vi a un hombre y a una mujer."

—¿Ud. es detective pero no tiene una descripción exacta ni del hombre ni de la mujer?

—A la una de la mañana es imposible ver mucho, ¿no?

Después de ver el video

¿Comprendes?

A. ¿Quién . . . ?

1. ¿Quién es la víctima?
2. ¿Quiénes viven en el tercer piso?
3. ¿Quién es la sobrina?
4. ¿Quién es doña Lupe?
5. ¿Quiénes llegan para investigar el crimen?
6. ¿Quién espera en la plaza?
7. ¿Quién dice que es imposible ver mucho a la una de la mañana?
8. ¿Quién quiere ayudar a los inspectores?

B. Escoge una de las fotos de esta página y escribe tres frases para describir la foto.

For: More on *¿Eres tú, María?*
Visit: www.phschool.com
Web Code: jcd-0507

Repaso del capítulo

Vocabulario y gramática

Chapter Review

To prepare for the test, check to see if you . . .

- know the new vocabulary and grammar
- can perform the tasks on p. 269

to talk about people

el hombre	man
la mujer	woman
el joven	young man
la joven	young woman

to describe people and things

alto, -a	tall
bajo, -a	short *(stature)*
corto, -a	short *(length)*
guapo, -a	good-looking
joven	young
largo, -a	long
viejo, -a	old
el pelo	hair
canoso	gray
castaño	brown (chestnut)
negro	black
rubio	blond
pelirrojo, -a	red-haired

to describe how someone is feeling

tener calor	to be warm
tener frío	to be cold
tener sueño	to be sleepy

to talk about food

delicioso, -a	delicious
desear	to want
pedir *(e → i)*	to order
el plato principal	main dish
de plato principal	as a main dish
el postre	dessert
de postre	for dessert
rico, -a	rich, tasty

For *Vocabulario adicional,* see pp. 472–473.

to describe table settings

el azúcar	sugar
la cuchara	spoon
el cuchillo	knife
la pimienta	pepper
el plato	plate, dish
la sal	salt
la servilleta	napkin
la taza	cup
el tenedor	fork
el vaso	glass

to talk about eating out

el camarero, la camarera	waiter, waitress
la cuenta	bill
el menú	menu

to express needs

Me falta(n) . . .	I need . . .
Quisiera	I would like
traer	to bring
Le traigo . . .	I will bring you . . .
¿Me trae . . . ?	Will you bring me . . . ?
yo traigo	I bring

other useful words

ahora	now
¿Algo más?	Anything else?
De nada.	You're welcome.
otro, -a	other, another
¡Qué + *adjective!*	How . . . !

venir *to come*

vengo	**venimos**
vienes	**venís**
viene	**vienen**

Más práctica

Practice Workbook Puzzle 5B-8

Practice Workbook Organizer 5B-9

Go Online PHSchool.com
For: Test preparation
Visit: www.phschool.com
Web Code: jcd-0516

Preparación para el examen

On the exam you will be asked to . . .	Here are practice tasks similar to those you will find on the exam . . .	If you need review . . .
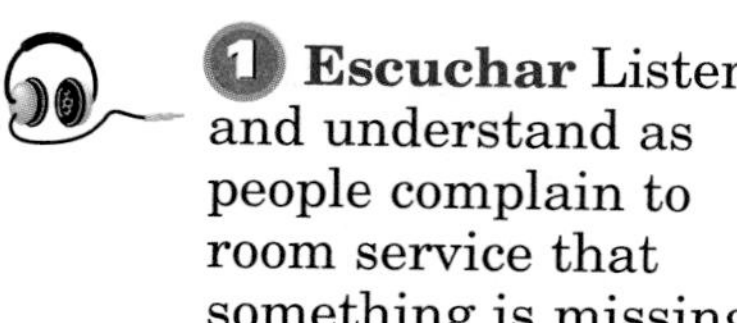 **1 Escuchar** Listen and understand as people complain to room service that something is missing from their order	As you listen to complaints about room service, see if you can tell if there is: a) missing silverware; b) missing food; c) missing condiments; d) all of the above.	**p. 248–251** *A primera vista,* Actividad 2 **p. 254** Actividades 8–9 **p. 260** Actividades 18–19
 **2 Hablar** Describe physical characteristics of family members to another person	Your aunt and uncle are going to celebrate their anniversary with you in a restaurant, but they're late. You describe them to the waiter so that he can recognize them when they arrive. Mention at least two physical characteristics about each person, such as hair color, height, or age.	**pp. 248–251** *A primera vista* **p. 252** Actividades 4–5 **p. 256** Actividad 12
 **3 Leer** Read and understand a letter about an upcoming visit with a relative	As you read part of a letter about an upcoming trip to Santa Fe, can you determine what the writers are most looking forward to in the trip? What questions do they have about it? Queridos Alicia y Pedro, Nosotros también esperamos impacientemente nuestra visita a Santa Fe en el verano. Me encanta la idea de visitar una ciudad con mucha historia. Nuestra ciudad también es muy histórica. ¿Qué es una comida típica del Rancho de las Golondrinas?	**p. 255** Actividad 10 **p. 262** *Lectura*
 **4 Escribir** Write a short report telling whether people are coming to an event and what they are bringing with them	You and your classmates decide to bring either a main dish, dessert, eating utensils, glassware, plates, or condiments for the Spanish Club party. Write a note to the club president indicating who is coming and what they are bringing. For example: *Ryan viene y trae las servilletas.*	**p. 256** Actividad 11 **p. 257** Actividades 13–14 **p. 265** *Presentación escrita*
 **5 Pensar** Demonstrate an understanding of cultural perspectives regarding meals	Think about how you spend lunch or dinner time during the school week. What would be at least three things that would be different at mealtime if you were an exchange student in a Spanish-speaking country? What is a *sobremesa*?	**p. 253** *Fondo cultural* **p. 260** *Fondo cultural* **p. 264** *Perspectivas del mundo hispano*

¡Viva Texas!

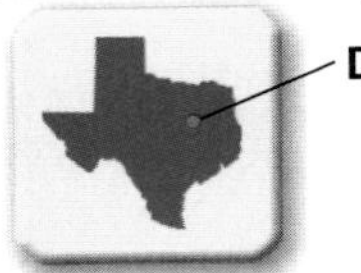

Un restaurante de familia

¿Puedes imaginar el estado de Texas sin enchiladas, salsa o tortillas? Durante cuatro generaciones, la familia Martínez está dedicada a servir esta comida riquísima. Y desde que abrió[1] el restaurante original en 1918, los tejanos (y personas de muchos diferentes lugares[2]) vienen a El Fénix para pedir los platos típicos y deliciosos de la comida que ahora se llama "Tex-Mex."

En el año 1911 Miguel (Mike) Martínez viene de México a los Estados Unidos. En 1915, se casa[3] con Faustina Porras, una inmigrante de Chihuahua, México. Miguel y su esposa trabajan mucho y en 1918 abren un restaurante en la calle McKinney en Dallas. Después abren muchos otros restaurantes que se llaman El Fénix. Faustina ayuda[4] a su esposo en el restaurante y también cría[5] a sus doce hijos. En 1955, ocho de los hijos Martínez comienzan a administrar los restaurantes de sus padres.

La creación de "la combinación," que es muy popular en los restaurantes Tex-Mex, es una de las historias favoritas de la familia Martínez. El padre, Mike, tenía[6] un problema en el restaurante: muchísimos platos que lavar[7] después de la cena sin lavaplatos. La solución: servir los frijoles, el arroz y las enchiladas en un plato que se llama "una combinación." Hoy día, la combinación es uno de los platos más importantes en los menús de los restaurantes Tex-Mex.

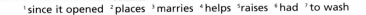

[1]since it opened [2]places [3]marries [4]helps [5]raises [6]had [7]to wash

El Fénix

Combinaciones mexicanas

Plato Juárez

Una deliciosa enchilada de queso sobre chile con carne, un sabroso taco de carne, una crujiente[8] tostada con guacamole, frijoles refritos mexicanos y arroz español $ 9.69

Especial de Monterrey

Una tostada con frijoles, una ensalada, una tostada con guacamole, una tostada con chile y queso y arroz español $ 7.79

El favorito

Un taco en tortilla de harina[9] con queso, una enchilada de queso, frijoles refritos y arroz $ 7.49

Ensalada Rosita

Un generoso plato de carne o pollo picante,[10] frijoles refritos, tomate, lechuga y una combinación de nuestra salsa especial de taco con guacamole y crema fresca[11] servido en una gran tortilla crujiente $ 7.79

Plato Durango

Una enchilada de queso cubierta[12] con chile con carne, un taco con carne, tomate y lechuga combinados con nuestra salsa especial de taco, un taco suave cubierto de chile con queso, frijoles refritos mexicanos y arroz español $ 9.69

Hoy muchos miembros de la familia de Faustina y Mike trabajan en los restaurantes.

[8] crispy [9] flour [10] spicy [11] sour cream [12] covered

¿Comprendes?

1. ¿De dónde viene Faustina Porras? ¿Cómo se llama su esposo?
2. ¿Por qué inventa el padre, Mike, "la combinación"?
3. Mira el menú del restaurante El Fénix. ¿Cuál de los platos te gustaría más? ¿Cuál de los platos no te gustaría? ¿Por qué?
4. ¿Qué trabajo te gustaría hacer más en un restaurante: preparar la comida, ser camarero(a) o lavar los platos?

Comparaciones

Work with a partner and discuss the different cultural influences on the food industry in your community. How many Tex-Mex restaurants can you list? Look at the menu from El Fénix. How does it compare to the menus at the Tex-Mex restaurants on your list? Where in your community can you find foods from other cultures? What typical foods date back to the early settlers in your region? If you visit a local grocery store, which foods will you find from other cultures? Which ones do you usually buy?

Fondo cultural

Salvador Dalí (1904–1989) was a painter born in Figueras, Spain. This is one of his most famous paintings, made when he was only 20. Here he has painted his sister, who appears only from the back.

- Why do you think that Dalí painted her looking out the window rather than facing the viewer?

Muchacha en la ventana (1924), Salvador Dalí

Museo Español de Arte Contemporáneo, Madrid, Spain.

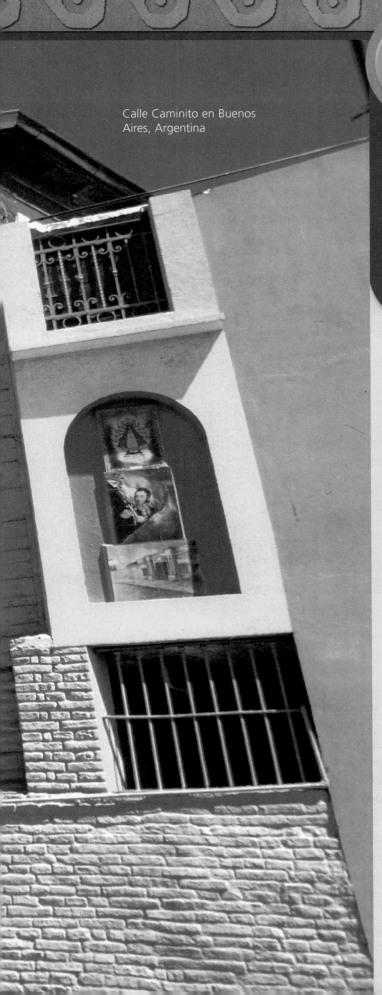

Calle Caminito en Buenos Aires, Argentina

En mi dormitorio

Chapter Objectives

- Talk about your bedroom
- Describe bedroom items and electronic equipment
- Make comparisons
- Understand cultural perspectives on homes

Video Highlights

A primera vista: ***El cuarto de Ignacio***

GramActiva Videos: making comparisons; the superlative; stem-changing verbs: *poder* and *dormir*

Videomisterio: ***¿Eres tú, María?,*** **Episodio 3**

Country Connection

As you learn how to describe your bedroom, you will make connections to these countries and places:

Go Online
PHSchool.com

For: Online Atlas
Visit: www.phschool.com
Web Code: jce-0002

A primera vista

Vocabulario y gramática en contexto

Objectives

Read, listen to, and understand information about
- **bedroom items**
- **electronic equipment**
- **colors**

“Tengo **un dormitorio pequeño.** Las paredes son azules. Tengo carteles de mis grupos musicales favoritos en las paredes. Generalmente mi dormitorio está muy desordenado, pero hoy está ordenado. No comparto el dormitorio con otra persona—es mi **propio** dormitorio.

En mi dormitorio tengo todas mis **posesiones más importantes:** mi guitarra, mis discos compactos, mis fotos, mi computadora. ¿Por qué me gusta mucho mi dormitorio? ¡Está encima del garaje! ¡Es **el mejor** dormitorio para tocar y escuchar música!”

amarillo, -a

negro, -a

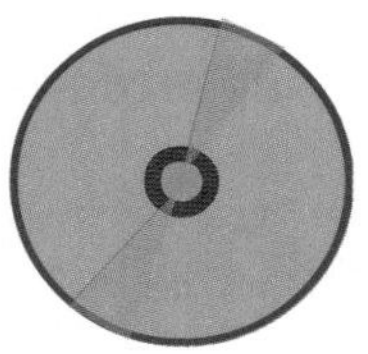
anaranjado, -a

azul

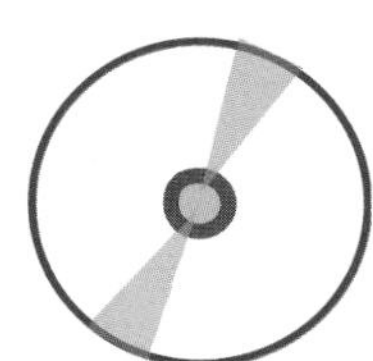
blanco, -a

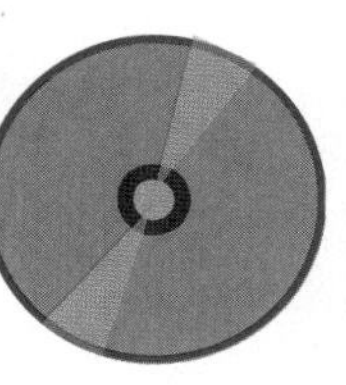
gris

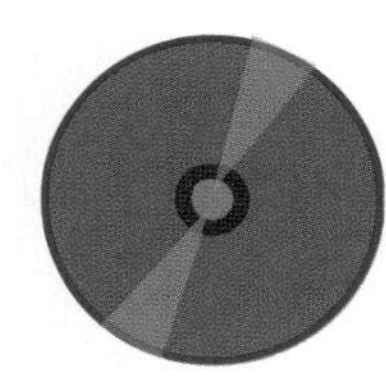
marrón

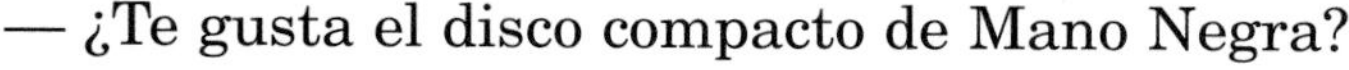

— ¿Te gusta el disco compacto de Mano Negra?

— ¡Por supuesto! Me encanta su música. Pero es **menos** interesante **que** la música de Mecano.

— A mis padres les encanta escuchar música. Me gustaría tener mi propio equipo de sonido.

**El televisor* refers to the actual appliance. *La televisión (tele)* is the programming that is watched.

verde

rojo, -a

morado, -a

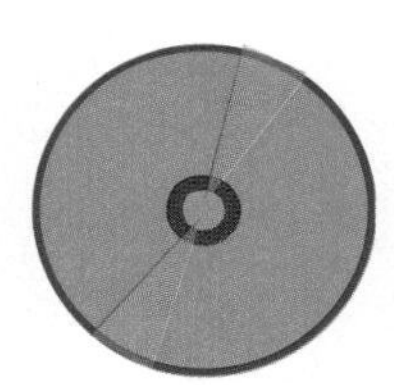
rosado, -a

Escuchar

Las posesiones

Escucha a Marcos describir su dormitorio. Mira el dibujo y toca cada cosa que menciona.

Escuchar

Los colores

Cuando escuches el nombre de un color, señala algo en estas páginas que es de ese color.

Más práctica

Practice Workbook 6A-1, 6A-2

For: Vocabulary practice
Visit: www.phschool.com
Web Code: jcd-0601

Videohistoria

El cuarto de Ignacio

¡El cuarto de Ignacio está muy desordenado!

Strategy

Using prior experience
Have you ever had someone go in and change things around in your room? How did you feel? Look at the photos and guess how Ignacio and his mother feel.

1 **Mamá:** Mira este cuarto . . . ¡qué **feo!** ¡Está muy desordenado! Ignacio, ¿cómo puedes hacer esto?

También se dice . . .

el dormitorio = el *cuarto (España)*

5 **Mamá:** Tu cuarto está mucho más **bonito.** Los libros **grandes** están aquí, y **a la izquierda** están las revistas. Y los discos compactos están **a la derecha de** los libros. Es mejor, ¿no crees?

6 **Ignacio:** Mamá, no es el **mismo** cuarto. **Para ti,** está **mejor que** antes, pero **para mí,** está **peor.** Tengo todas mis posesiones más importantes aquí y ahora no sé dónde están.

7 **Mamá:** Pero Ignacio, ¿cómo puedes **dormir** con todas las cosas encima de la cama?

Ignacio: Mamá, siempre **duermo** bien.

Mamá: ¡Ay! Está bien. Nunca más voy a organizar tu cuarto.

2 **Mamá:** **¿De qué color** es esta camiseta? ¿Gris? ¿Blanca? Y esta camiseta de muchos colores, ¿qué es? ¡Ay, tengo que trabajar mucho en este cuarto!

3 **Mamá:** ¿Qué **podemos** hacer con este cuarto? El cuadro va en la pared y la lámpara va en la mesita. ¡Ay, ay, ay!

4 **Ignacio:** ¡Mamá! ¡Mi cuarto! ¡Mis **cosas!** ¿Dónde están?

8 **Ignacio:** ¡Eres la mejor mamá! Muchas gracias.

Mamá: De nada, Ignacio.

Actividad 3 **Leer/Escribir**

¿Cierto o falso?

Lee las frases y decide si son ciertas o falsas. Si una frase es falsa, escríbela con la información correcta.

1. El cuarto de Ignacio siempre está muy ordenado.
2. La madre de Ignacio no está contenta.
3. La madre de Ignacio trabaja en el cuarto de Ignacio.
4. Ignacio no puede dormir bien en su cama.
5. Ahora Ignacio sabe dónde están todas sus posesiones.
6. A Ignacio no le gusta el trabajo de su madre.
7. Mañana la madre de Ignacio va a organizar el cuarto de Ignacio.

Más práctica

Practice Workbook 6A-3, 6A-4

For: Vocabulary practice
Visit: www.phschool.com
Web Code: jcd-0602

Manos a la obra

Vocabulario y gramática en uso

Objectives

- Name items found in a bedroom
- Talk about electronic equipment
- Use colors to describe things
- Use comparatives and superlatives
- Learn to use the verbs *poder* and *dormir*

Escribir

Las palabras opuestas

Escribe las palabras de la lista y su opuesto *(opposite)*.

Modelo

día *noche*

1. bonito	**3.** derecha	**5.** alto	**7.** ordenado
2. grande	**4.** peor	**6.** negro	**8.** joven

Strategy

Making word associations
Learning vocabulary as opposites helps you make quick associations to other words.

Escuchar/Escribir

Escucha, dibuja y escribe

Copia el dibujo en una hoja de papel. Vas a escuchar a Celia describir su dormitorio. Dibuja las cosas que ella menciona en los lugares *(places)* correctos y escribe las palabras en español para cada cosa.

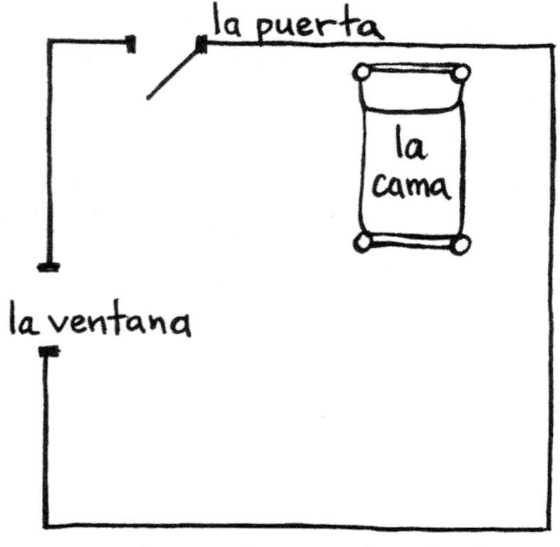

Tocando la guitarra en México

También se dice . . .

el dormitorio = la habitación, la alcoba *(España);* la pieza *(Argentina, Chile);* la recámara *(México)*

bonito = lindo, chulo *(México);* mono *(España)*

marrón = de color café, castaño, de color chocolate *(México, América del Sur)*

la cómoda = el gavetero, el buró *(México, muchos países)*

el armario = el guardarropa, el ropero *(México, muchos países)*

pequeño = chico *(México)*

Dibujar/Escribir

Tu propio dormitorio

1. Dibuja tu propio dormitorio. Escribe el nombre de ocho cosas en el dibujo.
2. Escribe siete frases para describir o *(either)* tu dormitorio o el dormitorio de Celia de la Actividad 5.

Modelo

El espejo está al lado de la cama.
Las cortinas en el dormitorio son largas.

> **¿Recuerdas?**
> Use *estar* to tell the location of items.
> Use *ser* to tell what items are like.

Escuchar/Hablar

¿Qué dormitorio es?

Trabaja con otro(a) estudiante. Muestra *(Show)* los dibujos de tu dormitorio y del dormitorio de Celia a tu compañero(a). Lee una de las frases que escribiste *(that you wrote)* en la Actividad 6. Tu compañero(a) tiene que identificar qué dormitorio describes.

> **Strategy**
> **Labeling**
> Put Spanish labels on the items in your bedroom so that you will see them every day. This will help you learn new words quickly.

Modelo

A —*El espejo está al lado de la cama.*
B —*Es tu propio dormitorio.*
o: *Es el dormitorio de Celia.*

Escuchar/Hablar

Juego

Trabajen en grupos de tres personas. Necesitan una moneda *(coin)* y uno de los dibujos de la Actividad 6. Una persona describe dónde está la moneda en el dormitorio. Los otros dos tratan de colocar *(try to place)* la moneda en el cuarto correctamente. La primera persona que coloca la moneda correctamente recibe un punto.

Modelo

La moneda está debajo de la cama.

Leer/Pensar/Hablar

¿Quién soy yo?

Aquí tienes una adivinanza *(riddle)* popular en las escuelas primarias en México. Trabaja con otro(a) estudiante para resolver la adivinanza.

Cine no soy,
radio tampoco.
Tengo pantalla
y me creen poco.

Gramática

Making comparisons

Just as you can use *más . . . que* to compare two things, you can also use **menos . . . que** *(less . . . than).*

El disco compacto de Los Toros es **menos** popular **que** el disco compacto de Los Lobos.

*The CD by Los Toros is **less** popular **than** the CD by Los Lobos.*

¿Recuerdas?

You have learned to use *más . . . que* to compare two things.

- La clase de inglés es **más** interesante **que** la clase de matemáticas.

The adjectives *bueno(a), malo(a), viejo(a),* and *joven* and the adverbs *bien* and *mal* have their own comparative forms. *Más* and *menos* are not used with these comparative adjectives and adverbs.

Adjective	Adverb	Comparative	
bueno, -a	**bien**	**mejor (que)**	*better than*
malo, -a	**mal**	**peor (que)**	*worse than*
viejo, -a		**mayor (que)**	*older than*
joven		**menor (que)**	*younger than*

Mejor, peor, mayor, and *menor* have plural forms that end in *-es.*

Los discos compactos son **mejores que** los casetes.

GramActiva VIDEO

Want more help with comparisons? Watch the **GramActiva** video.

Gramática **Escuchar/Escribir**

Dos dormitorios

En una hoja de papel, escribe los números del 1 al 6. Escucha las seis comparaciones de los dormitorios de Paco y de Kiko. Escribe *C* si la frase es cierta o *F* si es falsa.

el dormitorio de Paco

el dormitorio de Kiko

Gramática 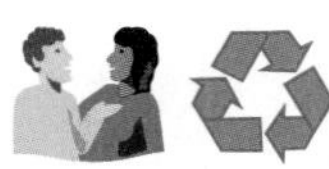 Escribir/Hablar

¡Viva la música!

1. Escribe cinco frases con comparaciones de los varios tipos de música que ves aquí. Usa estos *(these)* adjetivos en la forma correcta con *más . . . que* o *menos . . . que.*

aburrido, -a	interesante
bonito, -a	popular
divertido, -a	serio, -a
feo, -a	triste
importante	

Modelo

Para mí, la salsa es más divertida que la música rap.

2. Lee tus comparaciones a otro(a) estudiante para ver si Uds. están de acuerdo.

Modelo

A —*Para mí, la salsa es más divertida que la música rap.*

B —*Sí, estoy de acuerdo, pero la salsa es menos popular que la música rap.*

Para decir más . . .

los blues	la música rap
la música reggae	el jazz
la música clásica	la música rock
la música folklórica	la salsa
la música hip-hop	

Fondo cultural

Since 2000, the **Latin Grammy** awards have recognized the talent of many Spanish- and Portuguese-speaking artists every year.

- Who are some Latin recording artists you enjoy and what is their music like?

El cantante Juanes de Colombia

Gramática   Escribir/Hablar

¿Cómo se comparan los dos?

Con otro(a) estudiante, escoge dos cosas o personas de cada categoría de la lista. En una hoja de papel, escribe una comparación de las dos. Después, túrnate *(take turns)* con tu compañero(a) para leer tus comparaciones y dar *(give)* tus opiniones.

Modelo

actividades

A —*Para mí, ir al cine es mejor que ver un video.*

B —*Estoy de acuerdo. Ver un video es menos divertido que ir al cine.*

1. actividades
2. deportes
3. comidas
4. clases
5. libros o revistas
6. personas famosas

Más práctica

Practice Workbook 6A-5

Go Online PHSchool.com

For: Practice with unequal comparisons
Visit: www.phschool.com
Web Code: jcd-0603

Gramática

The superlative

To say that someone or something is the "most" or "least," use:

definite article **(el, la, los, las)** + noun + **más / menos** + adjective

La foto de mi familia es **la posesión más importante** para mí.

To say that someone or something is the "best" or the "worst," use:

definite article + **mejor(es) / peor(es)** + noun

Rojo y azul son **los mejores colores** para mi dormitorio.

GramActiva VIDEO

Want more help with the superlative? Watch the **GramActiva** video.

Actividad 13 Gramática   Hablar

Las casas de los ricos y famosos

Un grupo de personas del programa de televisión "Las casas de los ricos y famosos" está en tu casa. Habla con el grupo sobre las cosas especiales en tu casa. Pregunta y contesta según el modelo.

Modelo

cuadro/bonito

A —*Para ti, ¿cuál es el cuadro más bonito?*
B —*Para mí, el cuadro más bonito es el cuadro de las flores rojas y amarillas.*

1. posesión / importante
2. disco compacto / popular
3. video / gracioso
4. foto / bonita
5. videojuego / divertido
6. libro / interesante

Actividad 14 Gramática   Hablar/Escribir

Los premios Héctor

1 En grupos de cuatro estudiantes, pregunta y contesta sobre las mejores y peores cosas del año. Decide el (la) mejor y el (la) peor de cada categoría de la lista y escribe una frase para cada una.

Modelo

el mes

A —*Para ti, ¿cuál es el mejor mes del año?*
B —*Para mí, el mejor mes del año es junio.*
A —*¿Y cuál es el peor mes del año?*
B —*El peor mes del año es enero.*

1. el programa de televisión
2. el video
3. el grupo musical
4. la película
5. el disco compacto

2 Prepara una presentación para la clase para dar un premio *(give a prize)* Héctor para las categorías indicadas.

Modelo

Nuestro grupo da el premio Héctor para el mejor mes del año a junio.
Nuestro grupo da el premio Héctor para el peor mes del año a enero.

Hablar/Escribir

Tus propias cosas

1. Habla con otro(a) estudiante sobre las cosas que tienes en tu dormitorio. Pregunta y contesta según el modelo. Escribe las respuestas en una hoja de papel.

Modelo

A —*¿Tienes tu propia videocasetera?*
B —*Sí, tengo mi propia videocasetera. ¿Y tú?*
A —*No, pero puedo usar la videocasetera de mi familia.*

Estudiante A

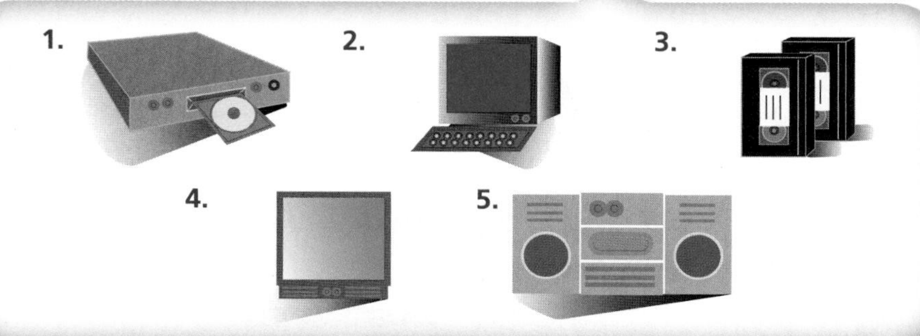

Estudiante B

Sí, tengo mi propio(a) . . .

No, pero comparto . . . con . . .

No, pero puedo usar . . . de mi familia.

No, no tengo . . .

2. Trabajen con otra pareja. Sumen *(Add together)* los resultados del paso *(step)* 1. Escriban frases para presentar los resultados a la clase. Compartan los resultados del grupo de ustedes con los otros grupos y sumen los resultados de toda la clase.

Modelo

Cuatro estudiantes tienen computadoras en sus casas.

3. Determinen un porcentaje *(percentage)* para cada aparato *(appliance)* tecnológico y creen *(create)* una gráfica para demostrar los resultados.

Comparar/Escribir/Hablar

Los aparatos tecnológicos en Cataluña

Estudia la gráfica y contesta las preguntas.

1. ¿Cuáles son los aparatos tecnológicos más populares en las casas en la región de Cataluña en España?
2. Escribe frases para comparar los resultados de tu clase y de los catalanes.

Modelo

Nosotros tenemos más lectores DVD que . . .

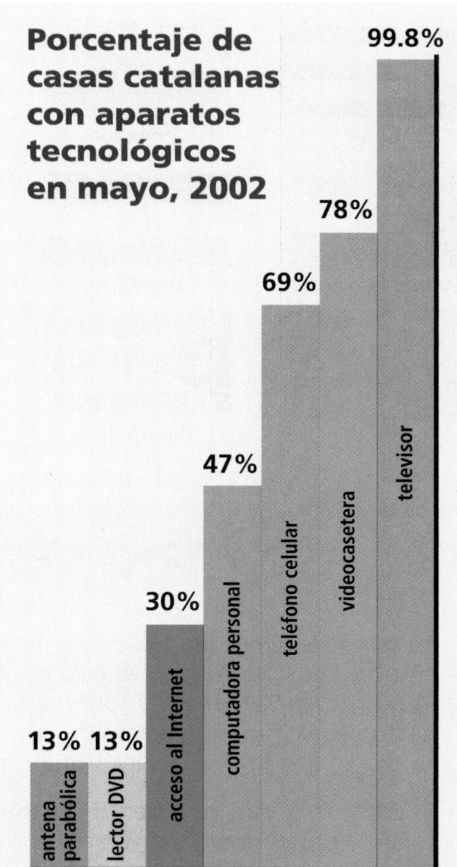

Pensar/Escribir/Hablar

¿De qué color es tu día?

¿Cuáles son los colores que asocias con estas palabras? Escribe los colores.

Modelo

regular *gris*

1. contento **3.** artístico **5.** reservado **7.** frío **9.** gracioso
2. calor **4.** horrible **6.** triste **8.** sociable **10.** aburrido

Y para ti, ¿cuál es el color de tu personalidad?

Hablar

Las banderas

Identifica los colores de las banderas de los países *(countries)* o lugares de habla española. Trabaja con otro(a) estudiante.

Modelo

A —*La bandera tiene los colores rojo, amarillo y verde.*
B —*¿Es la bandera de Bolivia?*
A —*Sí.*

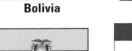

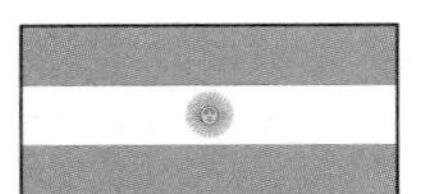
Argentina

Bolivia

Chile

Colombia

Costa Rica

Cuba

Ecuador

El Salvador

España

Guatemala

Guinea Ecuatorial

Honduras

Nicaragua

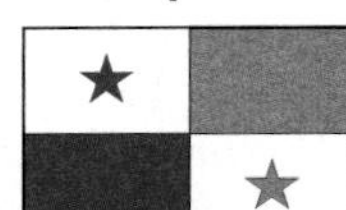
Panamá

Paraguay

Perú

Puerto Rico

República Dominicana

Uruguay

Venezuela

La bandera mexicana has a fascinating history. According to tradition, the Aztecs were to build their capital city, Tenochtitlán, where they found an eagle perched on a cactus and devouring a serpent. This image is what you see in the center of the Mexican flag today.

- What flags can you identify in the United States that also contain a symbol with historical significance?

Leer/Pensar/Escribir

¿Qué significan los colores?

En la psicología, hay un estudio de los significados *(meanings)* de diferentes colores en diferentes culturas. Lee las descripciones aquí para contestar las preguntas.

Conexiones | Las ciencias sociales

En muchas culturas, el verde significa buena salud, la primavera, las plantas y tranquilidad. Es un color de la paz.[1]

El blanco, en las culturas de las Américas, significa generalmente inocencia y paz. En ciertas culturas asiáticas, el blanco significa la muerte.[2]

El color que expresa energía, pasión y acción en muchas culturas diferentes es el rojo.

En muchas culturas, el amarillo significa atención, precaución, el sol y energía. Es muy fácil ver el amarillo y se usa mucho para los taxis.

Un color que expresa protección, autoridad, confianza[3] y armonía es el azul. Vemos este color mucho en los uniformes de la policía y los militares.

[1]peace [2]death [3]confidence

Find words or expressions in the reading to explain the following uses of color:

- yellow traffic light
- green recycling symbol
- blue police uniform
- red roses for Valentine's Day

Escribir/Hablar

Una bandera para ti

Imagina que vas a diseñar *(design)* una bandera para una organización, un club o un equipo *(team)*. ¿Qué colores vas a usar? ¿Por qué?

Escribir/Hablar

Y tú, ¿qué dices?

1. ¿Cuáles son tus colores favoritos? ¿Qué posesiones tienes en tu dormitorio de estos colores?
2. Escribe una lista de cinco cosas que están en tu dormitorio y el color de cada cosa. Por ejemplo: *Tengo una lámpara anaranjada.*
3. ¿De qué colores son los libros y las carpetas que tienes para tus clases?

Más práctica
Practice Workbook 6A-6

For: Practice with superlatives
Visit: www.phschool.com
Web Code: jcd-0604

Gramática

Stem-changing verbs: *poder* and *dormir*

Like *jugar, poder* and *dormir* are stem-changing verbs. They have a change from *o* → *ue* in all forms except *nosotros* and *vosotros*. Here are the present-tense forms:

¿Recuerdas?

You use *puedo* and *puedes* to say what you can or cannot do:

—**¿Puedes** ir a la fiesta conmigo?
—No, no **puedo.**

(yo)	**puedo**	(nosotros) (nosotras)	**podemos**
(tú)	**puedes**	(vosotros) (vosotras)	**podéis**
Ud. (él) (ella)	**puede**	Uds. (ellos) (ellas)	**pueden**

(yo)	**duermo**	(nosotros) (nosotras)	**dormimos**
(tú)	**duermes**	(vosotros) (vosotras)	**dormís**
Ud. (él) (ella)	**duerme**	Uds. (ellos) (ellas)	**duermen**

GramActiva VIDEO

Want more help with these stem-changing verbs? Watch the **GramActiva** video.

Actividad 22 Gramática Leer/Escribir/Pensar

Rompecabezas

¿Cuántas horas duermen las personas en esta familia? Escribe la forma apropiada del verbo *dormir* para cada frase. Después contesta la pregunta.

¡Mis hermanos y yo __1.__ 50 horas al día! Es mucho, ¿no? Tomás, mi hermano mayor, __2.__ menos, seis horas al día. Catalina __3.__ más horas que todos—cuatro horas más que Tomás. Guillermo y yo __4.__ el mismo número de horas. Juntos *(Together)* nosotros __5.__ el mismo número de horas que Tomás y Catalina. Paco y Laura __6.__ el mismo número de horas. ¿Cuántas horas duerme cada persona (Tomás, Catalina, Guillermo, Paco, Laura y yo)?

Nota

When the forms of *poder* are followed by another verb, the second verb is in the infinitive form.

- Ana no **puede hablar** español.

Actividad 23 Escuchar/Escribir/Hablar

El campamento Nadadivertido

Es el primer día en el campamento de verano Nadadivertido. Tu amigo(a) nunca escucha nada. Escucha las reglas *(rules)* del campamento y después contesta las preguntas de tu amigo(a).

1. ¿Podemos usar el equipo de sonido en la tarde?
2. ¿Quiénes no pueden ir a los dormitorios de los chicos?
3. ¿Podemos ver videos en los dormitorios?
4. ¿Cuándo podemos escuchar discos compactos?
5. ¿Podemos beber refrescos en la cama?
6. ¿Podemos dormir hasta *(until)* las nueve?

  Escribir/Hablar

Las reglas

Tienes que cuidar *(baby-sit)* a dos niños y no sabes las reglas de su casa. Primero escribe cinco preguntas para ellos. Después pregunta y contesta según el modelo. Aquí está una lista de verbos que puedes usar:

beber	escuchar	jugar
comer	ir	ver

Modelo

A —*¿Uds. pueden comer helado después de las siete?*

B —*No, nunca podemos comer helado después de las siete.*

o: *¡Por supuesto! Siempre podemos comer helado después de las siete.*

    Hablar

¡Podemos hacer muchas cosas!

Trabaja con otro(a) estudiante para decir qué pueden hacer diferentes personas con las posesiones que tienen.

Modelo

Marcos / sacar fotos

A —*¿Marcos puede sacar fotos?*

B —*¡Por supuesto! Tiene una cámara muy buena.*

o: *No. No tiene una cámara.*

Estudiante A

1. Uds. / ver películas en casa
2. Raquel / hacer la tarea de álgebra
3. tu papá (o tu mamá) / usar el Internet
4. tú / escuchar discos compactos
5. Guillo y Patricio / jugar videojuegos

Estudiante B

Pronunciación

The letters *r* and *rr*

Except at the beginning of a word or after *l* or *n*, the sound of the letter *r* is similar to the *dd* in the English word *ladder.* Listen to and say these words:

derecha	quiero	amarillo	bandera
pero	puerta	alfombra	morado

The sound of *rr* is similar to saying "batter, batter, batter" over and over again very quickly. Listen to and say these words:

perro	correr	guitarra	marrón
aburrido	arroz	pelirrojo	horrible

When *r* is the first letter of a word or comes after *l* or *n*, it is pronounced like the *rr*.

Roberto	Rita	Ricardo	rojo	regalo
rubio	radio	reloj	romper	Enrique

Try it out! Listen to and say this *trabalenguas:*

Erre con erre cigarro,
erre con erre barril.
Rápido corren los carros,
cargados de azúcar del
ferrocarril.

Leer/Escribir/Hablar

¿Duermes bien?

Lee este artículo de una revista y contesta las preguntas.

1. Según el artículo, ¿cuál es el problema?
2. ¿Qué porcentaje de las personas duerme menos de ocho horas diarias durante la semana?
3. ¿El artículo presenta estas ideas? Contesta *sí* o *no.*

   Las personas que duermen poco . . .
   - . . . generalmente están más cansadas.
   - . . . trabajan mejor.
   - . . . juegan mucho y hacen ejercicio.
   - . . . son menos sociables.
4. Y tú, durante los fines de semana, ¿cuántas horas duermes en la noche?

¿Cuántas horas duermes por noche?

Un nuevo estudio indica que muchos adultos no duermen ni[1] seis horas por noche, y afecta mucho a su calidad de vida.[2]

Durante la semana:

Menos de 6: 15%
6 a 6.9: 24%
7 a 7.9: 29%
8 ó más: 30%

Fines de la semana:

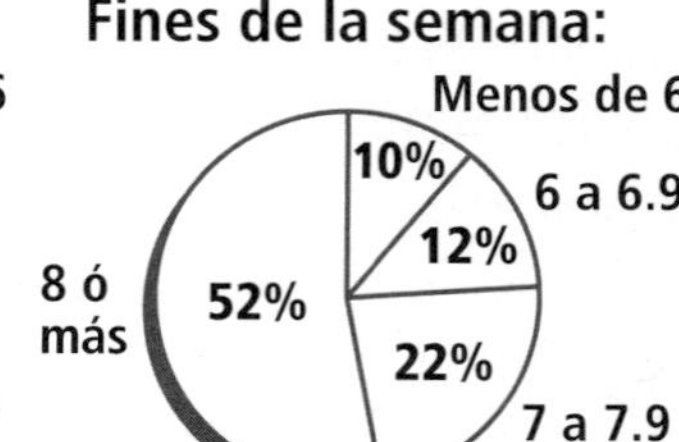

Las personas que duermen menos de seis horas por noche:

- Tienen más estrés y fatiga
- Están más tristes y menos alertas
- Hacen peor su trabajo
- Sufren más lesiones[3]
- Tienen más problemas de relaciones interpersonales
- Comen más de lo usual
- Tienen menos energía

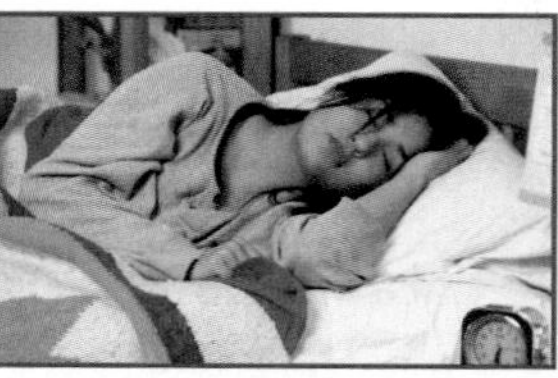

[1]not even [2]quality of life [3]injuries

Exploración del lenguaje

Using root words

You can build your vocabulary, both in Spanish and in English, if you recognize the root of a word and know its meaning.

For example, because you know the root of one word, ***comer***, you can more easily learn another word, *la* ***comida***.

Try it out! Because you know the root of ***beber***, you can easily remember *la* __?__. And since you know *ver la* ***televisión***, you can easily recognize *el* __?__.

Once you learn another language, your mastery of your own language can increase. This is because you begin to use words from your second language to help you understand words in English that are new to you.

Try it out! Since you know *verde*, *azul,* and *gris,* what do you think these words mean?

verdant fields   *azure* sky   a *grizzled* old man

Fondo cultural

La siesta, an afternoon nap after the large midday meal, has been observed in Spain and other Spanish-speaking countries for centuries. However, with modern-day pressures and in larger cities, many people no longer take off work for *la siesta*.

- What do you think would be some advantages and disadvantages of a *siesta* in your daily life?

En España muchas tiendas se cierran entre las 14.00 y las 16.30 horas.

   **Escribir/Hablar**

Juego

Con otro(a) estudiante, describe tres cosas y escribe las descripciones. Lee las frases a otra pareja para ver si ellos pueden identificar las cosas.

Modelo

A —*Es una cosa que toca música. Puede ser grande o pequeño. Está en muchas casas. ¿Qué es?*
B —*Es un equipo de sonido.*

Strategy

Circumlocution
When you don't know or can't remember the word for something, you can describe it. You can tell what it is used for, what size it is, what color it is, where it is often found, and so on.

   **Escribir/Hablar/Dibujar**

Y tú, ¿qué preguntas?

1. Escribe cinco preguntas que puedes hacer *(ask)* a otra persona. Puedes preguntar sobre las actividades que le gustan, cómo es, sus colores favoritos, sus intereses en música y deportes.
2. Haz tus preguntas a otro(a) estudiante. Escribe sus respuestas.
3. Dibuja un dormitorio especial para el (la) estudiante según sus respuestas a tus preguntas. Usa lápices de color. Presenta tu dibujo a tu compañero(a) y explica por qué el dormitorio es especial para él o ella.

Modelo

El dormitorio es especial para ti porque tus colores favoritos son azul y rojo. Hay una foto de Lleyton Hewitt en la cómoda porque te gusta mucho el tenis. Hay muchas fotos en las paredes porque sacas fotos de tus amigos también. Tú eres muy gracioso y desordenado. Hay muchos videos y revistas en la cama. Te gusta escuchar la música hip-hop. Aquí, en el estante, están tus discos compactos.

El español en la comunidad

In many communities in the United States, you can see the influence of Spanish-style architecture. Spanish-style buildings often have tile roofs, stucco exteriors, and interior courtyards or patios.

- Identify houses, buildings, or neighborhoods in your community that feature this style. Draw or take a picture of one example.

Más práctica

Practice Workbook 6A-7

For: Practice with *o*→*ue* verbs
Visit: www.phschool.com
Web Code: jcd-0605

¡Adelante!

Objectives

- Read a letter and response in an advice column
- Learn about *las luminarias*
- Talk about how a person's bedroom reflects his or her personality
- Watch *¿Eres tu, María?*, Episodio 3

Lectura

El desastre en mi dormitorio

Lee esta carta *(letter)* a Querida Magdalena. Ella da soluciones a los problemas de los jóvenes en una revista.

Strategy

Using cognates
As you read the letter and response, look for cognates to help you better understand Rosario's problem. Try to guess the meaning of some of the cognates: *el desorden, la situación, recomendar, considerar.*

Con tu amiga Magdalena

"Querida Magdalena:
Mi problema tiene un nombre: es mi hermana Marta. Compartimos el mismo dormitorio y estoy desesperada. Todo en mi lado del dormitorio está en orden. Pero su lado es un desastre. Ella es la reina del desorden. Le encanta comer en el dormitorio. Hay pizza debajo de la cama. Hay botellas de agua en la mesita. Hay postre en el escritorio. Es horrible. Siempre deja[1] ropa,[2] videos y todas sus posesiones en el suelo,[3] en la mesita, en la cama. ¡No hay ni un libro en el estante!

Y ella no escucha sus propios discos compactos—¡no! Escucha mis discos compactos y sin pedir[4] permiso. Y escucha música a toda hora (y a un volumen muy alto) y ¡yo no puedo dormir!

Las paredes en su lado del dormitorio son negras. Es el peor color y es feísimo. Mi color favorito es el amarillo, claro. Es más bonito que el negro, ¿no?

Estoy cansada de compartir el dormitorio con ella y su desorden.
¿Qué debo hacer?"

Rosario Molino
Montevideo, Uruguay

> Mi problema tiene un nombre: es mi hermana, Marta.

[1]leaves [2]clothing [3]floor [4]asking for

¡Es difícil compartir un dormitorio con otra persona!

Querida Rosario:

¡Qué problema! Es difícil compartir un dormitorio con otra persona, especialmente si la persona es tu hermana. Uds. son muy diferentes, ¿no? Tú eres más ordenada que ella. Ella cree que el color negro es el más bonito.

Necesitas hablar con tu hermana delante de tus padres. Tienes que explicar[5] la situación y recomendar unas soluciones. Es necesario encontrar[6] un punto intermedio.[7] Si la situación no es mejor después de unas semanas, tienes que considerar la posibilidad de separar el dormitorio con una cortina. ¡Pero no debe ser una cortina ni negra ni amarilla!

Tu amiga,
Magdalena

[5]explain [6]find [7]middle ground

¿Comprendes?

Lee las frases y decide quién dice *(says)* la frase. ¿Es Rosario, Marta o su madre?

1. "Pero me gusta comer en la cama y escuchar música."
2. "Soy una persona muy simpática y el color amarillo representa mi personalidad."
3. "Estoy muy ocupada y no tengo tiempo para 'un dormitorio perfecto'."
4. "Uds. tienen que respetar las posesiones de la otra."
5. "Mi color favorito es el negro. No me gustan los colores amarillo, anaranjado o azul."
6. "Ella debe pedir permiso para escuchar mis discos compactos."
7. "Tu hermana no es ordenada como tú. Tienes que ser más paciente."

Y tú, ¿qué dices?

¿Eres desordenado(a) como *(like)* Marta o eres ordenado(a) como Rosario? ¿En qué? Incluye dos ejemplos en tu respuesta.

Los aparatos electrónicos Throughout the Spanish-speaking world you will find the latest electronic devices: DVD players, stereo sound systems, cell phones, computers, etc. In all countries, there is a demand for movies, music, and instant communication.

- What are some advantages and disadvantages of the new global community brought about by these technological innovations?

For: Internet link activity
Visit: www.phschool.com
Web Code: jcd-0606

La cultura en vivo

Las luminarias

En Santa Fe, Nuevo México

To celebrate Christmas in Mexico and the southwest United States, countless bags, tons of sand, and candles are transformed into flickering outdoor lanterns called *luminarias.* They are lined up along window ledges, walkways, and roofs and are lit to welcome visitors.

This tradition dates back more than 300 years, when villagers along the Río Grande built bonfires to light and warm their way to church on Christmas Eve. The luminarias used today go back to the 1820s, when traders introduced brown paper into the region and candles were set in sand in the bottom of the paper bags.

Try it out! Here's how you can make your own luminarias.

Materials

- 12" paper lunch bags
- sand
- small flashlights
- scissors

Figure 1

Figure 2

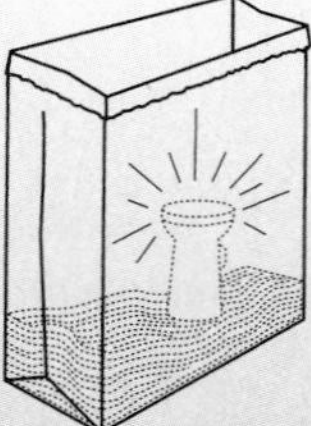
Figure 3

Directions

1. Trace a pattern on the side of the bag, leaving at least 4 inches at the top and 3 inches at the bottom. You may want to use the pattern in Fig. 1 or create your own.
2. Cut out the design, cutting through both sides of the bag. *(Fig. 1)*
3. Open the bag and fold down a 2" cuff around the top. *(Fig. 2)*
4. Fill the bag $\frac{1}{4}$ full of sand.
5. Place a flashlight in the sand. *(Fig. 3)*
6. Place the completed luminarias along your walkway, turn on the small flashlights, and enjoy these symbols of hope and joy for any special occasion.

Variations

1. Use white or brightly colored bags.
2. Paste or glue white or pastel tissue paper behind the cut-out design.
3. Cut a scalloped edge along the top of the bag instead of folding down the cuff.
4. Instead of sand, use soil, cat litter, or gravel to hold the flashlight in place.

Think about it! What kind of decorations do you use for special events? How is light used in different cultures to celebrate events?

Presentación oral

La personalidad de un dormitorio

Task
You are doing a study on how a bedroom can reflect the personality of its owner(s). Use a photograph or drawing of a bedroom and talk about what its contents and colors tell about the personality of the owner.

1 Prepare Bring in a picture of a bedroom. It can be a photo you took, one cut out from a magazine, or a picture that you drew. Use this word web to think through what you want to say about the room and the personality of the person who decorated it. Then answer the questions.

- En tu opinion, ¿cómo es la persona que vive *(lives)* en el dormitorio? ¿Qué le gusta hacer?

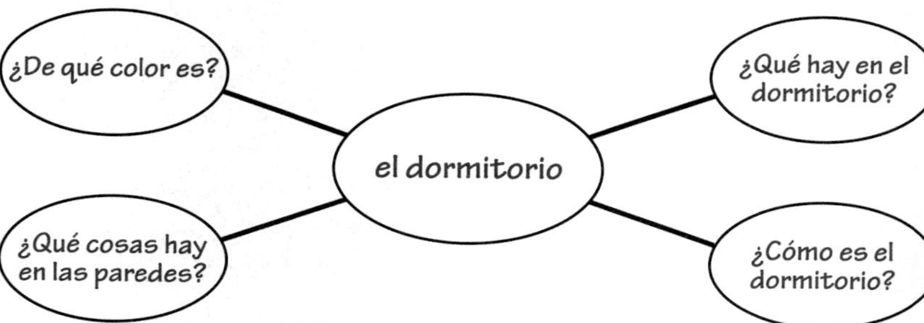

¿De qué color es?
¿Qué hay en el dormitorio?
el dormitorio
¿Qué cosas hay en las paredes?
¿Cómo es el dormitorio?

Strategy
Using graphic organizers
A word web can help you organize your thoughts for a presentation.

2 Practice Go through your presentation several times. You can use your notes in practice, but not when you present. Try to:

- support your statements with examples
- use complete sentences
- speak clearly

3 Present Show your picture and give the information about the bedroom and the personality behind it. Don't forget to stand up straight and project your voice!

4 Evaluation Your teacher may give you a rubric for how your presentation will be graded. You probably will be graded on:

- how complete your presentation is
- how much information you communicate
- how easy it is to understand you

Videomisterio

¿Eres tú, María?

Episodio 3

Antes de ver el video

Personajes importantes

Paco, quien trabaja en la oficina de Lola y la ayuda con las investigaciones

Margarita, la secretaria de la oficina

Nota cultural *El País* is probably Spain's most widely read and influential newspaper. You can consult an electronic version of *El País* on the Internet.

Resumen del episodio

Este episodio es muy importante. Lola le explica a Paco lo que pasó[1] en el incidente del domingo pasado.[2] En otra escena, Lola habla con doña Lupe quien le describe el incidente en el piso de doña Gracia. También doña Lupe le explica a Lola la historia de la familia de doña Gracia. ¿Por qué cree que María va a recibir toda la fortuna de doña Gracia?

[1] what happened [2] last Sunday

Palabras para comprender

dinero money
periodista newspaper reporter
¿Qué pasó . . .? What happened . . .?
No ve casi nada. She can hardly see anything.
abro I open
muerta dead
busco I'm looking for
¿Robaron . . .? Did they steal . . .?
las joyas jewels
accidente de coche car accident
Pasó antes de venir a vivir con doña Gracia. It happened before she came to live with doña Gracia.
Pasó tres meses . . . She spent three months . . .
el nieto grandson
No viene aquí nunca. He never comes here.
No conoce a su abuela. He doesn't know his grandmother.

La familia Requena

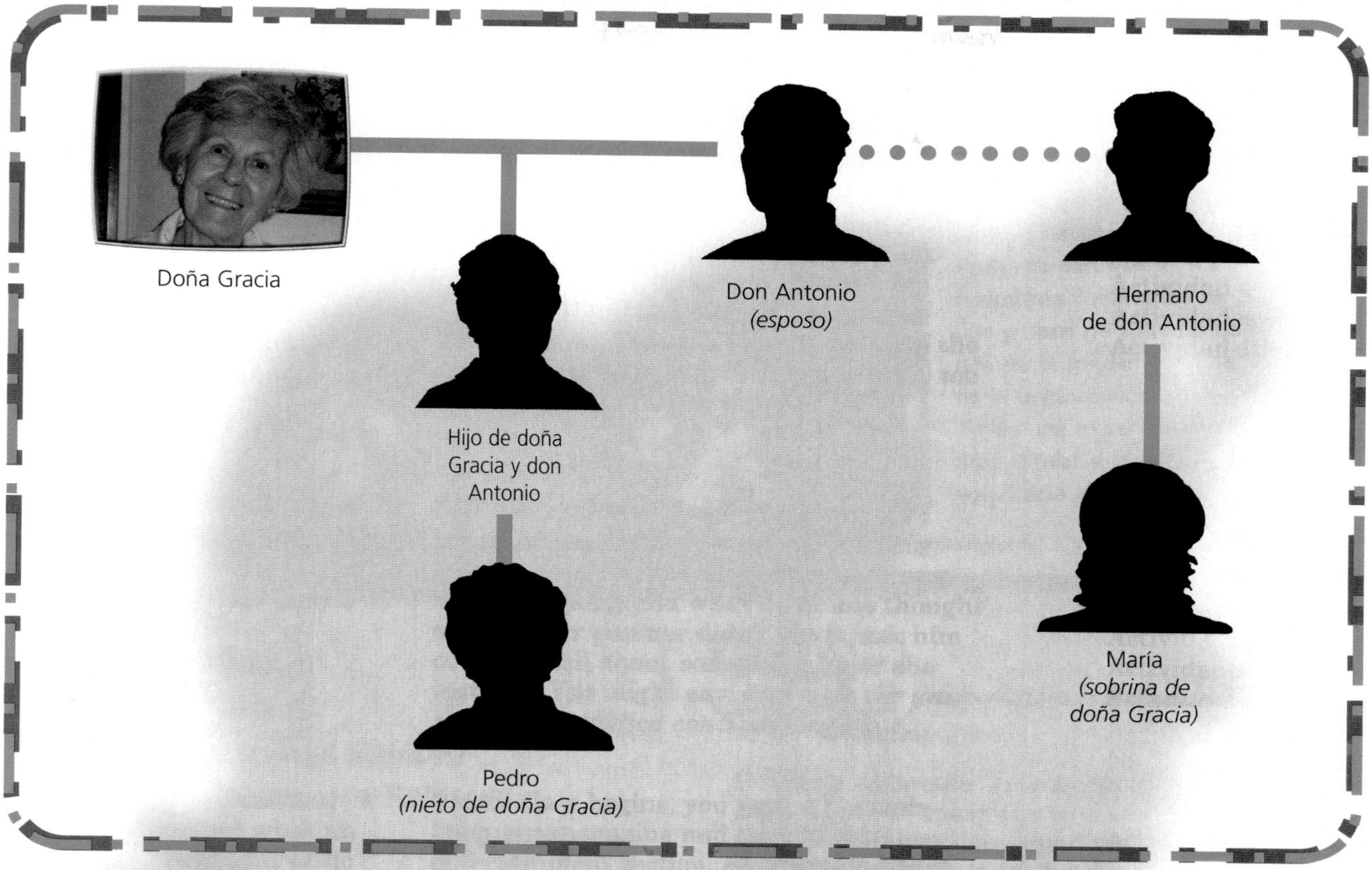

Doña Gracia

Don Antonio
(esposo)

Hermano
de don Antonio

Hijo de doña
Gracia y don
Antonio

María
*(sobrina de
doña Gracia)*

Pedro
(nieto de doña Gracia)

Después de ver el video

¿Comprendes?

Completa cada frase con la palabra apropiada del recuadro.

periodista	hija
fortuna	accidente de coche
joyas	conoce
dinero	sobrina

1. Según Paco, si no hay cliente, si no hay ____, entonces no hay nada.
2. Lola dice que trabaja para *El País,* un periódico importante en España, y es ____.
3. María es la ____ de Lorenzo Requena y la ____ de doña Gracia.
4. Doña Gracia es muy rica. Tiene una fortuna en dinero, ____ y arte.
5. Antes de venir a vivir con doña Gracia, a María le pasó un grave ____.
6. Pedro, el nieto de doña Gracia, vive en Italia y su abuela no lo ____.
7. Según doña Lupe, María va a recibir la ____ de doña Gracia.

For: More on *¿Eres tú, María?*
Visit: www.phschool.com
Web Code: jcd-0507

Repaso del capítulo

Chapter Review

Vocabulario y gramática

To prepare for the test, check to see if you . . .

- know the new vocabulary and grammar
- can perform the tasks on p. 295

to talk about things in a bedroom

la alfombra	rug
el armario	closet
la cama	bed
la cómoda	dresser
las cortinas	curtains
el cuadro	painting
el despertador	alarm clock
el dormitorio	bedroom
el espejo	mirror
el estante	shelf, bookshelf
la lámpara	lamp
la mesita	night table
la pared	wall

to talk about electronic equipment

el disco compacto	compact disc
el equipo de sonido	sound (stereo) system
el lector DVD	DVD player
el televisor	television set
el video	videocassette
la videocasetera	VCR

to talk about colors

¿De qué color . . . ?	What color . . . ?
los colores	colors
amarillo, -a	yellow
anaranjado, -a	orange
azul	blue
blanco, -a	white
gris	gray
marrón	brown
morado, -a	purple
negro, -a	black
rojo, -a	red
rosado, -a	pink
verde	green

For *Vocabulario adicional,* see pp. 472–473.

to describe something

bonito, -a	pretty
feo, -a	ugly
grande	large
importante	important
mismo, -a	same
pequeño, -a	small
propio, -a	own

to indicate location

a la derecha (de)	to the right (of)
a la izquierda (de)	to the left (of)

to compare and contrast

mejor(es) que	better than
el / la mejor; los / las mejores	the best
menos . . . que	less, fewer . . . than
peor(es) que	worse than
el / la peor; los / las peores	the worst

other useful words

la cosa	thing
para mí	in my opinion, for me
para ti	in your opinion, for you
la posesión	possession

stem-changing verbs: *dormir* and *poder*

duermo	**dormimos**
duermes	**dormís**
duerme	**duermen**

puedo	**podemos**
puedes	**podéis**
puede	**pueden**

Más práctica

Practice Workbook Puzzle 6A-8
Practice Workbook Organizer 6A-9

Go Online PHSchool.com
For: Test preparation
Visit: www.phschool.com
Web Code: jcd-0607

Preparación para el examen

On the exam you will be asked to . . .	Here are practice tasks similar to those you will find on the exam . . .	If you need review . . .
 **1 Escuchar** Listen to and understand descriptions of bedrooms	You will be spending a month in a Spanish immersion camp. You go to the camp Web site and click on the audio descriptions of the student rooms. Which items are provided? Which items do you have to bring?	**pp. 272–275** *A primera vista* **p. 276** Actividad 5 **p. 277** Actividad 7 **p. 281** Actividad 15
2 Hablar Ask and answer questions about your bedroom and that of a classmate	You are asked to survey several classmates about their bedrooms to describe the "typical" teenage room for a class project. Ask a partner at least three questions including: a) information about the color of his or her room; b) whether or not there is a TV or sound system; c) whether he or she is able to study well in the room; d) what is on the walls.	**pp. 272–275** *A primera vista* **p. 277** Actividad 7 **p. 281** Actividad 15
 **3 Leer** Read and understand descriptions of bedroom colors that are associated with particular personality types	Decorators say that the colors of a room's walls should match the personality of the person living in it. Based on the descriptions of a "yellow personality" and a "blue personality," what kind of room best suits you? Why or why not? A las personas más sociables les gustan los dormitorios amarillos. Es el color más popular para los jóvenes a quienes les gusta hablar y hablar por teléfono. ¡Ellos son los mejores amigos! Al contrario, a las personas más serias les gustan los dormitorios azules. Ellos son los mejores estudiantes y los peores cómicos.	**p. 282** Actividad 17 **p. 283** Actividad 19 **pp. 288-289** *Lectura*
 **4 Escribir** Write a short paragraph comparing your bedroom to a friend's bedroom	After surveying classmates, you are asked to write a comparison of your room to that of one of the people you surveyed. Use the information from Task 2 to practice. You might compare: a) the colors; b) the sizes; c) the types of furniture; d) the number of different things on the walls.	**p. 277** Actividad 6 **p. 278** Actividad 10 **p. 291** *Presentación oral*
 **5 Pensar** Demonstrate an understanding of cultural perspectives regarding a celebration	Explain the historical significance of *las luminarias.* What is the history of other decorations used in the celebrations of different cultures?	**p. 290** *La cultura en vivo*

Fondo cultural

La arpillera is a popular textile folk art of rough patchwork appliqués created by women in Chile. Done in brilliant colors, the themes show the story of daily life, traditions, and values in the country.

- What other types of crafts have you seen that portray life in a region or country?

Arpillera de Chile

Capítulo 6B

¿Cómo es tu casa?

Chapter Objectives

- Identify rooms in a house
- Name household chores
- Tell where you live
- Understand cultural perspectives on different types of housing

Video Highlights

A primera vista: *Los quehaceres de Elena*

GramActiva Videos: affirmative *tú* commands; the present progressive tense

Videomisterio: *¿Eres tú, María?*, Episodio 4

Country Connection

As you learn about rooms in a house and household chores, you will make connections to these countries and places:

Go Online PHSchool.com
For: Online Atlas
Visit: www.phschool.com
Web Code: jce-0002

A primera vista

Vocabulario y gramática en contexto

Objectives

Read, listen to, and understand information about

- **rooms in a house**
- **household chores**
- **how to tell someone to do something**

la escalera

el despacho

el segundo piso

el primer piso

el baño

el garaje

la planta baja*

el comedor

la cocina

la sala

el sótano

el patio

*In most countries, Spanish speakers call the ground floor in a multi-story building *la planta baja,* the second floor *el primer piso,* the third floor *el segundo piso,* the fourth floor *el tercer piso,* and so on.

Se vende.

Casa particular de dos pisos y sótano. Sala grande, cocina moderna, comedor, despacho, 2 baños, 3 dormitorios, garaje.

Llama al 555-37-89.

—Me gustaría ver esta casa. Es grande y bonita.

—Sí, tiene tres dormitorios y un despacho. También tiene una cocina moderna, **si** te gusta cocinar.

SE VENDE
555-37-89

Más vocabulario

el apartamento	apartment
cerca (de)	close (to), near
lejos (de)	far (from)
bastante	enough, rather

lavar los platos sucios

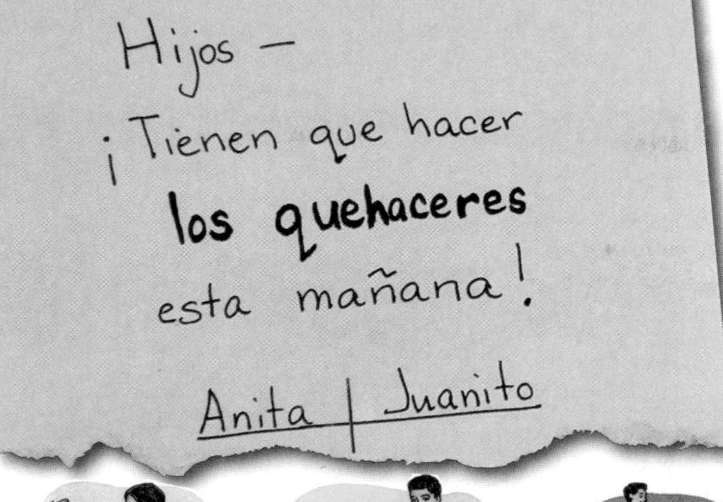
Hijos –
¡Tienen que hacer
los quehaceres
esta mañana!
Anita | Juanito

cortar el césped

poner la mesa

lavar el coche

pasar la aspiradora

dar de comer al perro

lavar la ropa

sacar la basura

cocinar

hacer la cama

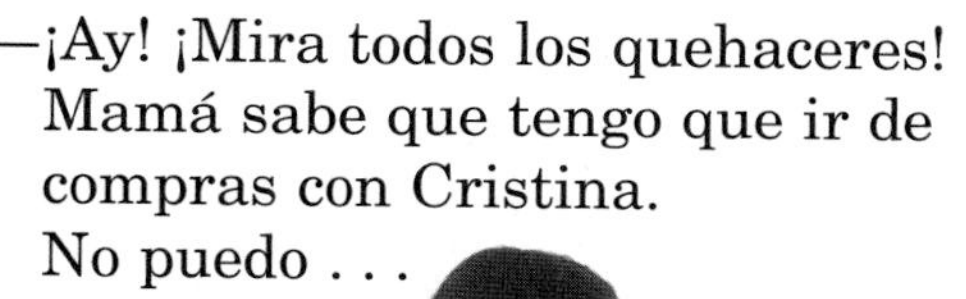
—¡Ay! ¡Mira todos los quehaceres! Mamá sabe que tengo que ir de compras con Cristina. No puedo . . .

—Yo voy a jugar al fútbol a la una. Y tengo más quehaceres que tú.

quitar el polvo

arreglar el cuarto

limpiar el baño

Actividad
1
Escuchar

La casa de Elena

Escucha a Elena describir su casa. Señala cada cuarto que describe.

Actividad
2
Escuchar

¿Es lógico o no?

Escucha cada frase. Si es lógica, haz el gesto del pulgar hacia arriba *("thumbs-up" sign).* Si no es lógica, haz el gesto del pulgar hacia abajo *("thumbs-down" sign).*

Más práctica
Practice Workbook 6B-1, 6B-2

Go Online
PHSchool.com
For: Vocabulary practice
Visit: www.phschool.com
Web Code: jcd-0611

Videohistoria

Los quehaceres de Elena

Elena no quiere hacer sus quehaceres. ¿Qué hace ella?

Strategy

Using language knowledge
You've just learned the infinitives for various household chores. Using what you know, what are the four activities that Elena tells Jorgito to do in Panel 5?

1 **Elena:** ¡Hola! Bienvenidos a mi casa. **Vivo** en el número 12 de la calle Apodaca. Vamos a entrar. Mi casa es su casa.

5 **Jorgito:** **¿Cuáles** son los quehaceres que necesito hacer?

Elena: **Pon** la mesa, lava los platos sucios en la cocina, **haz** la cama en mi dormitorio y da de comer al perro.

6 **Mamá:** Elena, ¡qué trabajadora eres!

Papá: ¡Cómo ayudas en casa! Das de comer al perro, lavas los platos, **pones** la mesa . . .

Elena: Ah, . . . **¿Recibo** mi dinero?

Mamá: **Un momento.** ¿Tu dormitorio está **limpio?**

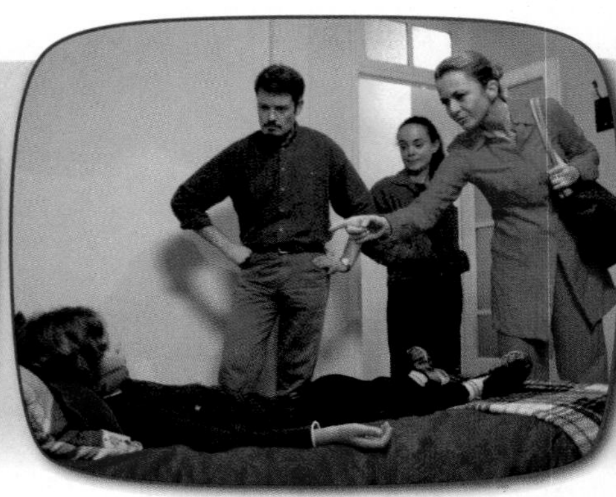

7 **Mamá:** ¡Jorgito! ¡Qué perezoso eres! **¿Qué estás haciendo?**

Jorgito: Pero, . . . pero, . . .

Papá: Ni pero ni nada. ¡Jorgito, a tu dormitorio! Vamos a ver . . .

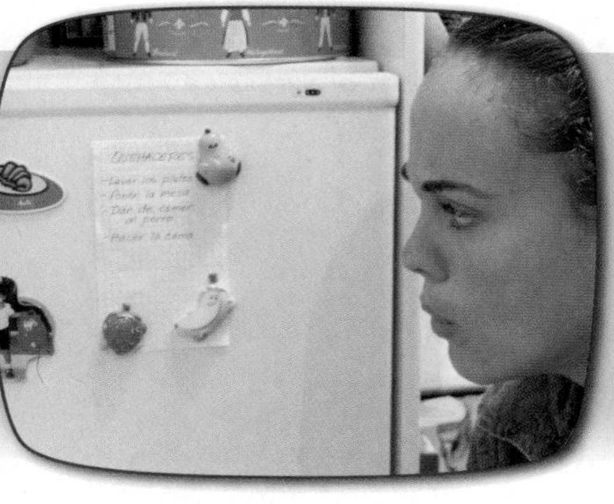

2 **Elena:** ¡Ay, no! Veo que tengo más quehaceres. Siempre lavo los platos sucios y **pongo** la mesa para la cena. ¡Y ahora necesito hacer más trabajo!

3 **Elena:** ¿Me **ayudas** con los quehaceres?

Jorgito: Quiero **dinero.**

Elena: No te **doy** dinero, pero puedes escuchar discos compactos en mi dormitorio.

4 **Jorgito:** A ver. Si hago unos de los quehaceres, me **das** los discos y escucho música por una hora.

Elena: Media hora.

Jorgito: Cuarenta y cinco minutos.

Elena: Está bien.

8 **Mamá:** Elena, tu dinero.

Elena: Gracias, mamá.

Papá: Jorgito, ¿cómo puedes vivir así? Tienes que arreglar tu cuarto, hijo: haz la cama, quita el polvo, pasa la aspiradora . . .

Jorgito: Pero, Elena . . .

Elena: ¡Adiós! ¡Voy al cine!

Escribir/Hablar

¿Comprendes?

Lee las frases y escribe *cierta* si la frase es correcta o *falsa* si es incorrecta. Si la frase es incorrecta, escribe una frase nueva con la información correcta.

1. Elena siempre pone la mesa en su casa.
2. Jorgito está contento de escuchar los discos compactos.
3. Si hace uno de los quehaceres, Jorgito puede escuchar una hora de música.
4. Según los padres, Elena es muy trabajadora.
5. Según los padres, Jorgito es trabajador también.
6. Ahora Jorgito tiene mucho que hacer en su dormitorio.

Más práctica

Practice Workbook 6B-3, 6B-4

For: Vocabulary practice
Visit: www.phschool.com
Web Code: jcd-0612

Manos a la obra

Vocabulario y gramática en uso

Objectives

- Know the rooms of a house
- Talk about chores around the house
- Learn to use familiar *tú* commands and the present progressive tense

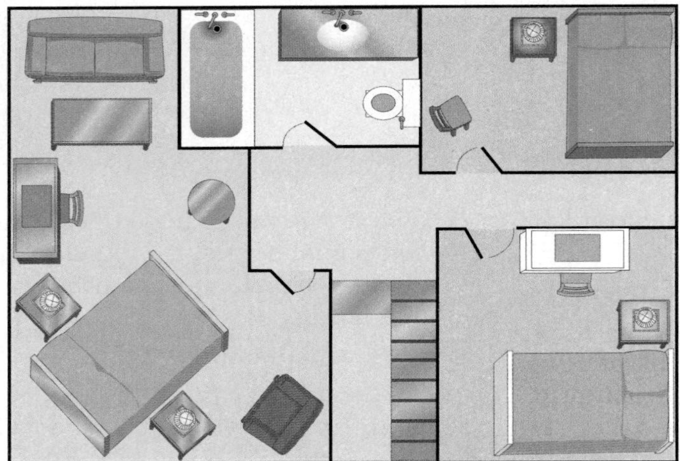

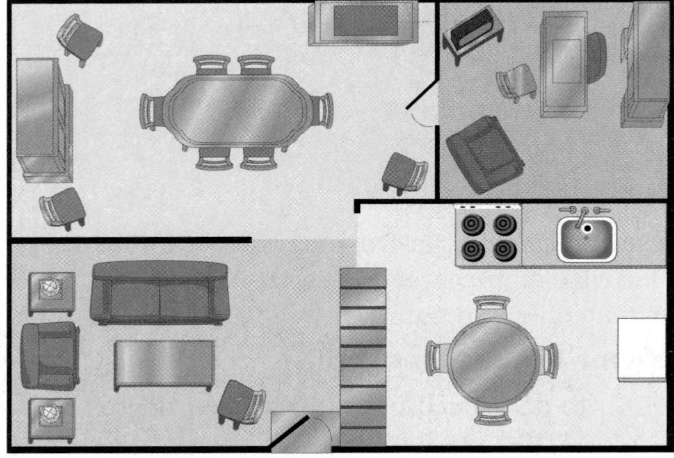

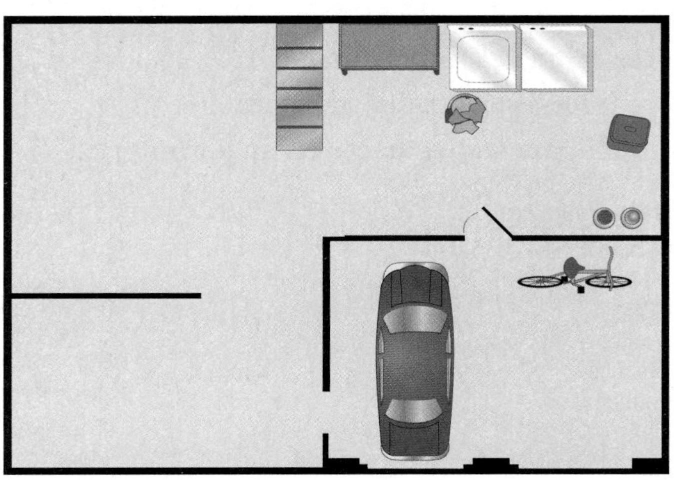

Escuchar/Escribir

La casa de los Ramírez

Los Ramírez van a comprar la casa que ves aquí. En una hoja de papel escribe los números del 1 al 8 y escribe el nombre de cada cuarto que describen.

> **Nota**
>
> *Primero(a)* and *tercero(a)* become *primer* and *tercer* before a masculine singular noun.
>
> - Mi dormitorio está en el **primer** piso.
> - Su apartamento está en el **tercer** piso.

Escribir/Escuchar/Hablar

¿Cierto o falso?

Escribe cinco frases para indicar dónde están los cuartos en la casa de los Ramírez. Las frases pueden ser ciertas o falsas. Lee tus frases a otro(a) estudiante, quien va a indicar si son ciertas o falsas. Si son falsas, tiene que dar la información correcta.

Modelo

A —*La sala está en el primer piso.*
B —*Falso. La sala está en la planta baja.*

> **También se dice . . .**
>
> **la sala** = el salón *(muchos países),* el living *(España)*
>
> **el despacho** = la oficina *(muchos países)*
>
> **el piso** = la planta *(muchos países)*
>
> **el apartamento** = el piso *(España),* el departamento *(muchos países)*

Hablar

¿Dónde pongo la silla?

Ayudas a la familia Ramírez a mudarse *(move)* a su nueva casa pero no sabes dónde poner sus cosas. Otro(a) estudiante te va a explicar dónde tienes que poner todo.

Modelo

A —*¿Dónde pongo la silla?*
B —*Vamos a poner la silla en el comedor.*

Nota

Poner, "to put," is also used in the expression *poner la mesa,* "to set the table." It has an irregular *yo* form: *pongo.*

- En la mañana **pongo** la mesa.

Estudiante A

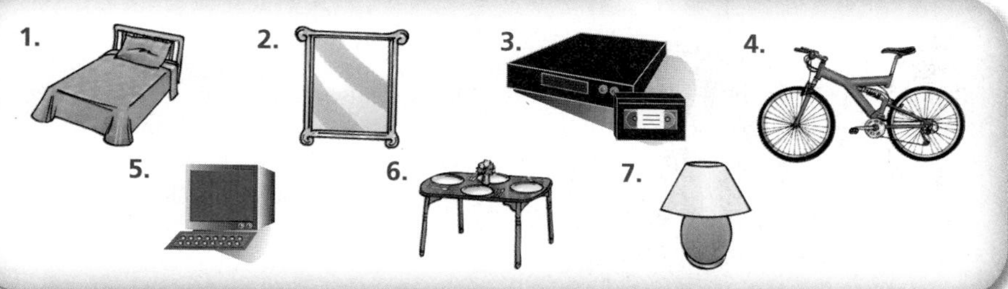

Estudiante B

¡Respuesta personal!

Escribir

¿En qué cuarto?

Ahora los Ramírez están muy contentos en su casa. ¿En qué cuarto hacen los Ramírez estos quehaceres? Escribe las frases.

Modelo

Sacan la basura en el garaje.

1. 
2. 
3. 
4. 
5. 
6. 

Fondo cultural

El patio in an apartment building in a large Spanish city is usually just an open area in the center of the building. In southern Spain, however, houses are often built around *patios,* which may have gardens as well as a fountain. The Moors brought this architectural style to Spain, and the Spaniards then carried it over to the Americas.

- How does the Spanish *patio* differ from what a patio is in your community? How is it similar?

Un patio típico en Córdoba, España

Hablar

¿Cómo ayudas en casa?

¿Ayudas mucho en casa? Habla de tus quehaceres con otro(a) estudiante.

Modelo

A —*¿Tienes que lavar el coche?*
B —*Sí, lavo el coche todos los sábados.*

Estudiante A

1. 
2. 
3. 
4. 

5. 
6. 

Estudiante B

a veces
mucho
todos los días
todos los (sábados)
en el (verano)
los fines de semana
nunca

Nota

Dar means "to give" and is used in the expression *dar de comer,* "to feed." It has an irregular *yo* form: *doy.*

- En mi casa **doy** de comer al perro.

Escribir/Hablar

¿Dónde vives?

Escribe una lista de cinco lugares en tu comunidad, como la escuela, el centro comercial, la biblioteca, etc. Pregunta a otro(a) estudiante si vive cerca o lejos de estos lugares.

Modelo

El cine Rex
A —*¿Vives cerca del cine Rex?*
B —*Sí, vivo bastante cerca del cine.*
o: *No, vivo muy lejos.*

También se dice . . .

cocinar = guisar *(España)*

cortar el césped = cortar la hierba, cortar el pasto *(muchos países),* cortar el zacate *(México)*

lavar los platos = fregar los platos *(España)*

quitar el polvo = sacudir los muebles *(México)*

Actividad 10 **Escribir/Hablar**

Y tú, ¿qué dices?

1. ¿Ayudas mucho o poco en casa? ¿Cuáles son tus quehaceres?
2. ¿Generalmente tu cuarto está sucio o limpio?
3. En tu casa, ¿quién pasa la aspiradora? ¿Quién saca la basura?
4. Para ti, ¿cuáles son los tres peores quehaceres? ¿Y los mejores?
5. Imagina que eres padre o madre. ¿Cuánto dinero recibe tu hijo(a) si hace sus quehaceres?
6. ¿Vives cerca o lejos de tu escuela?

Gramática

Affirmative *tú* commands

When you tell friends, family members, or young people to do something, you use an affirmative *tú* command. To give these commands, use the same present-tense forms that you use for *Ud., él, ella.*

INFINITIVE	*UD. / ÉL / ELLA*	AFFIRMATIVE *TÚ* COMMANDS
hablar	habla	¡Habla!
leer	lee	¡Lee!
escribir	escribe	¡Escribe!

- Certain verbs, like *poner* and *hacer,* have irregular command forms.

Jorgito, ¡**pon** la mesa! Jorgito, ¡**haz** tu cama!

¿Recuerdas?

In the direction lines of many activities, you have already seen many affirmative commands.

- **Habla** con otra persona.
- **Lee** las frases.
- **Escribe** la palabra apropiada.

GramActiva VIDEO

Want more help with the affirmative *tú* commands? Watch the **GramActiva** video.

 Gramática   Escuchar/GramActiva

"Simón dice . . ."

Escucha y sigue *(follow)* las instrucciones de tu profesor(a) o de otro(a) estudiante. Si no dicen *"Simón dice,"* no debes hacer la acción.

 Gramática  Escribir

¡Habla bien!

Un(a) amigo(a) quiere hablar bien el español. ¿Qué recomiendas? Escribe el mandato *(command)* de los siguientes verbos.

Modelo

usar: *usa*
Usa un buen diccionario.

1. estudiar
2. ver
3. escuchar
4. escribir
5. hacer
6. hablar con
7. leer
8. practicar

Instituto de inglés

Aprende con nosotros
¡Cursos de verano!

Nuestro sistema cubre las cuatro habilidades esenciales:
Hablar ✶ *Comprender* ✶ *Leer* ✶ *Escribir*
Grupos reducidos • Cuotas accesibles

TEL/FAX: 212–1234

 Gramática  Leer/Escribir

¿Qué debo hacer?

Tu amiga Carmen tiene un problema y te escribe una carta. Lee su carta y escribe tus recomendaciones en otra carta, usando los verbos de la lista.

Modelo

Mi querida Carmen,
Aquí están mis recomendaciones:
Come menos dulces, . . .

beber	dormir	jugar
comer	hacer ejercicio	¡Respuesta personal!
correr	levantar pesas	

¡Hola!

Tengo un problema grande. Quisiera estar mejor de salud. No estoy muy enferma pero tampoco estoy en buena forma. Siempre tengo mucho sueño y poca energía. Si camino a la escuela, estoy muy cansada. Si hago muchos quehaceres por la casa, también estoy cansada. ¡Y no quiero estar cansada! ¿Qué debo hacer?

Tu amiga desesperada,

Carmen

 Gramática  Hablar

Muchos quehaceres

Debes hacer muchos quehaceres en casa, pero no quieres. ¡A ver si tu hermanito(a) puede hacer todo! Primero di *(say)* lo que está sucio (o lo que no está limpio). Luego di lo que tiene que hacer.

Modelo

Los platos no están limpios. Lava los platos, por favor.

¿Recuerdas?

Adjectives agree in number and gender with the nouns they modify.

- **La** casa está suci**a**.
- **Los** plat**os** están limpi**os**.

1. 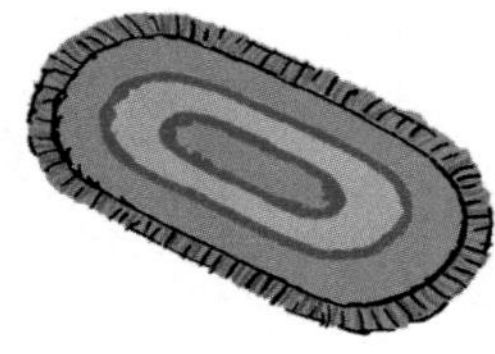

2. 

3. 

4. 

5. 

6. 

Leer/Escribir/Hablar

¿Quién hace los quehaceres?

Un artículo de la revista española *Muy* explica quién hace la mayoría de *(most of)* los quehaceres de la casa. Estudia las gráficas a la derecha y haz comparaciones entre *(between)* las mujeres y los hombres españoles. Después, explica si las mujeres hacen los siguientes quehaceres mucho más, un poco más o menos que los hombres.

Modelo

lavar los platos
Las mujeres lavan los platos mucho más que los hombres.

1. comprar cosas para la familia cada día
2. preparar la comida y la cena
3. cuidar *(take care of)* el coche
4. cuidar a las personas enfermas de la familia
5. lavar y planchar *(iron)* la ropa
6. ir al banco
7. limpiar la casa

¿Quién hace los quehaceres?

	Mujeres	Hombres	Juntos*
Lavar y planchar la ropa	88%	0%	8%
Comprar la comida	73%	4%	19%
Preparar comidas	68%	1%	19%
Cuidar el coche	2%	78%	8%
Limpiar la casa	73%	1%	19%
Ir al banco	37%	26%	36%
Lavar los platos	67%	3%	23%
Cuidar a los enfermos	31%	1%	30%

*Together

Exploración del lenguaje

The endings *-dor* and *-dora*

Every day you use appliances and devices: a calculator, a computer, a stapler, a copier, a dryer, and so on. Many of these words in English add the ending *-er* or *-or* to the verb that tells what the appliance is for. Spanish follows a similar pattern. Look at these words you already know and identify the pattern: **despertador, computadora, calculadora, aspiradora.** Can you guess what the corresponding verbs are and what they mean?

Try it out! Read each statement on the left and decide which appliance is needed.

1. Tengo calor.
2. ¿Dónde está el pan tostado?
3. Mi ropa está sucia.
4. Necesito leche para el cereal.

a. Está en la tostadora.
b. Ponla en la lavadora.
c. Está en el refrigerador.
d. Necesitas el ventilador.

Más práctica

Practice Workbook 6B-5

For: Practice with affirmative *tú* commands
Visit: www.phschool.com
Web Code: jcd-0613

Gramática

The present progressive tense

When you want to emphasize that an action is happening *right now*, you use the present progressive tense.

Paco **está lavando** los platos. — *Paco is washing dishes (now).*
Estoy haciendo la cama. — *I'm making the bed (right now).*

To form the present progressive tense, use the present-tense forms of *estar* + the present participle. The present participle is formed by dropping the ending of the infinitive and adding *-ando* for *-ar* verbs or *-iendo* for *-er* and *-ir* verbs.

(yo)	estoy	lavando comiendo escribiendo	(nosotros) (nosotras)	estamos	lavando comiendo escribiendo
(tú)	estás	lavando comiendo escribiendo	(vosotros) (vosotras)	estáis	lavando comiendo escribiendo
Ud. (él) (ella)	está	lavando comiendo escribiendo	Uds. (ellos) (ellas)	están	lavando comiendo escribiendo

Leer has an irregular spelling in the present participle: *leyendo.*

¿Recuerdas?

You use the present tense to talk about an action that regularly takes place, or that is happening now.

- Paco **lava** los platos.
  *Paco **washes** the dishes.*
  OR
  *Paco **is washing** the dishes.*

GramActiva VIDEO

Want more help with the present progressive? Watch the **GramActiva** video.

Gramática  Escribir

¿Qué están haciendo ahora?

Escribe cinco frases para explicar lo que están haciendo varias personas en tu sala de clases.

Modelo
La profesora está escribiendo algo.

Gramática  Escuchar/Escribir

Escucha y escribe

Estos hermanos tienen muchos quehaceres. Escucha y escribe la pregunta de la madre y las excusas de los hijos.

   Hablar/Escribir

Un momento, por favor

A veces no podemos hacer los quehaceres porque estamos haciendo otras cosas. Trabaja con otro(a) estudiante para dar un mandato y una excusa.

Modelo

A —*Por favor, da de comer al perro.*
B —*No puedo. Estoy estudiando para un examen.*

Estudiante A

1. 
2. 
3. 
4. 
5. 
6. 

Estudiante B

Un momento . . .	beber
No puedo . . .	comer
Lo siento . . .	escribir
Me gustaría pero . . .	escuchar
	estudiar
	hablar
	hacer
	jugar
	tocar

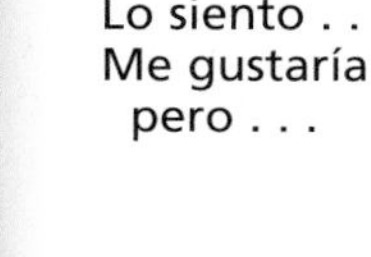

¡Respuesta personal!

   Escribir/Hablar GramActiva

Juego

1. En una hoja de papel *(sheet of paper)*, escribe una frase para explicar lo que está haciendo una persona (usa la forma *tú).* En otra hoja de papel, escribe una frase para explicar lo que están haciendo dos personas (usa la forma *Uds.).*

Modelo

Estás levantando pesas.
Uds. están esquiando.

2. Todas las frases van boca abajo *(face down)* encima de una mesa. Toma una frase. Si la frase usa la forma *tú,* haz la acción solo(a). Si la frase usa la forma *Uds.,* haz la acción con otro(a) estudiante. Los compañeros tienen que adivinar *(guess)* lo que estás (están) haciendo.

   Escribir/Hablar GramActiva

¿Qué están haciendo todos?

Haz un dibujo de tres personas que están haciendo diferentes actividades. En otra hoja de papel, escribe dos preguntas sobre lo que está haciendo cada persona. Trabaja en un grupo de tres. Da tu dibujo a los otros estudiantes y lee tus preguntas. Tus compañeros tienen que contestar.

Modelo

A —*¿Qué está haciendo la chica?*
B/C —*Está lavando los platos sucios.*

Más práctica

Practice Workbook 6B-6, 6B-7

For: Practice with present progressive
Visit: www.phschool.com
Web Code: jcd-0614

Leer/Pensar

¿Qué casa están buscando?

En Santiago, Chile, tres personas están buscando *(looking for)* una nueva casa y leen el anuncio a la derecha. ¿Quién crees que va a comprar *(buy)* la casa?

José Guzmán: "Quiero vivir bastante cerca de mi trabajo. Para mi esposa es importante tener una cocina equipada. Prefiero una casa con sólo un piso porque mis padres van a vivir con nosotros y las escaleras son muy difíciles para ellos."

Alejandro Lara: "Mis padres y yo vivimos en un apartamento ahora. Quiero una casa con tres dormitorios porque mis primos vienen a nuestra casa a veces. No quiero una casa muy grande porque no me gusta ni pasar la aspiradora ni limpiar los baños."

Dora Peña: "Mi familia y yo estamos buscando una casa nueva. Tenemos dos hijas y mi mamá vive con nosotros. Quiero una casa con un dormitorio un poco separado para mi mamá. Prefiero tener alfombra en los dormitorios porque nuestras hijas juegan mucho allí."

Chile

LAS MEJORES CASAS
EN LA AVENIDA LA FLORIDA

CASA VENEZIA: 310 m^2 3 PISOS, DESDE 2.390 UF

Primer piso: Amplia sala • Comedor separado • Cocina y baño de visitas
Segundo piso: Dormitorio principal, más 2 dormitorios y otro baño
Tercer piso: Amplio dormitorio con baño completo y una gran sala de estar

«AHORA VISITE PILOTOS Y COMPRE HOY MISMO»

- Cerámica en el primer piso
- Alfombra en dormitorios
- Cocina equipada
- Papel vinílico en paredes
- Armarios terminados
- Ventanas de aluminio
- Amplio jardín

¡Llame hoy! 232 9980

Pronunciación

The letters *n* and *ñ*

In Spanish, the letter *n* sounds like the *n* in "no." Listen to and say these words:

anaranjado	nieva	nadar	joven	desayuno
necesito	encantado	número	nombre	donde

However, the sound changes when there is a tilde (~) over the *n*. The *ñ* then sounds like the *-ny-* of the English word *canyon*. Listen to and say these words:

señor	otoño	español	enseñar	año
montañas	niña	mañana	piñata	cumpleaños

Try it out! Listen to this *trabalenguas* and then try to say it.

El señor Yáñez come ñames en las mañanas con el niño.

Leer/Pensar

¿Dónde viven?

En la capital de Venezuela, Caracas, analizaron *(they analyzed)* dónde viven unos 2.7 millones de habitantes. Según los estudios, ¿viven más personas en casas o en apartamentos? ¿Viven en casas y apartamentos grandes o pequeños? Estudia las gráficas y luego contesta las preguntas.

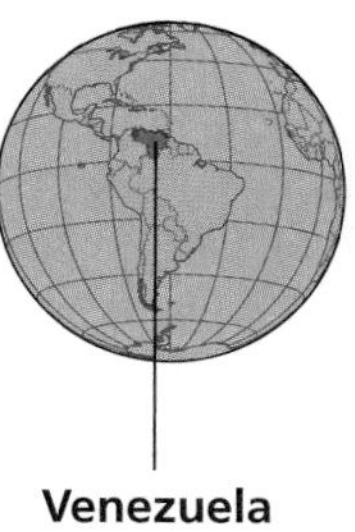

Nota

Do you see the pattern in the following numbers?

100,000 = cien mil
200,000 = doscientos mil
300,000 = trescientos mil

But watch out for 500,000:

542,656 = quinientos cuarenta y dos mil seiscientos cincuenta y seis

1,000,000 = un millón

Conexiones | Las matemáticas

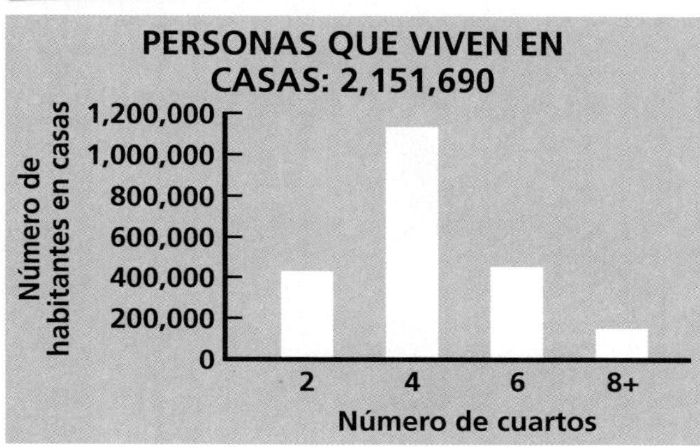

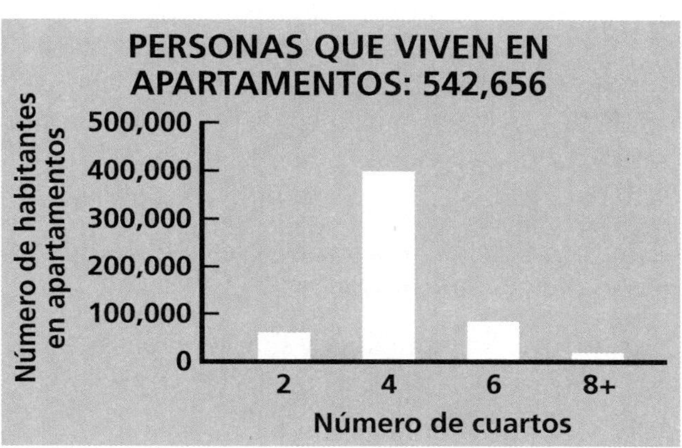

1. ¿Cuántas personas viven en una casa con dos cuartos? ¿Cuántas viven en un apartamento con dos cuartos?
2. ¿Cuántas personas viven en una casa con ocho o más cuartos? ¿Cuántas viven en un apartamento con ocho o más cuartos?
3. Calcula el porcentaje de personas que viven en una casa con cuatro cuartos. Calcula el porcentaje de personas que viven en un apartamento con cuatro cuartos.

Across the country, "For Sale" signs in Spanish are appearing on lawns, in front of apartment buildings, and in office complexes.

- Look for ads in Spanish in the real estate section of your local newspaper.

La Casa J. Knox Corbett en el distrito histórico de Tucson, Arizona.

¡Adelante!

Lectura

Objectives

- Read a version of "Cinderella"
- Learn about houses in the Spanish-speaking world
- Create a flyer to sell a house or apartment
- Watch *¿Eres tú, María?*, Episodio 4

Cantaclara

Lee esta historia sobre una joven que se llama Cantaclara.

Strategy

Skimming
This reading is based on the story of Cinderella. Quickly skim the story and find characters and dialogue that remind you of Cinderella.

Hay una muchacha que se llama Cantaclara. Ella vive con su madrastra y sus dos hermanastras, Griselda y Hortencia. Las cuatro viven en una casa grande y Cantaclara hace todos los quehaceres. Sus dos hermanastras y su madrastra no hacen nada.

—Cantaclara, saca la basura. Y después, pon la mesa —dice la madrastra.

—Cantaclara, haz mi cama y limpia el baño —dice Griselda.

—Haz mi cama también —dice Hortencia.

—Un momento. Estoy lavando los platos ahora mismo —dice Cantaclara.

¡Pobre[1] Cantaclara! Hace todos los quehaceres y cuando trabaja, ella canta. Tiene una voz[2] muy clara y le encanta cantar.

Un día, Cantaclara entra en el dormitorio de Griselda para hacer la cama. Ve en la televisión un anuncio[3] para un programa muy popular que se llama *La estrella[4] del futuro*. En la televisión hay un señor que dice: "¡Hola, amigos! ¿Tienen talento? ¿Cantan bien? ¿Por qué no cantan para nosotros? ¡Pueden tener un futuro fantástico y recibir muchísimo dinero!"

Cantaclara está muy contenta. Ella puede cantar. Ella quiere un futuro fantástico. En este momento, ella decide cantar para el programa *La estrella del futuro*.

[1]Poor [2]voice [3]ad [4]star

Es la noche del programa. Después de hacer todos los quehaceres, Cantaclara está saliendo[5] de casa cuando su madrastra le habla.

—Cantaclara, ¿adónde vas?

—Quiero salir por unas horas, madrastra. ¿Está bien?

—Ahora no. Tienes que limpiar la cocina — contesta la madrastra. —Está muy sucia.

—Pero, madrastra, tengo que . . .

—¡No importa, Cantaclara! ¡Limpia la cocina!

Cantaclara mira su reloj. Sólo tiene una hora. Va a la cocina y limpia todo. Trabaja muy rápidamente. Después de cuarenta y cinco minutos, termina el trabajo.

Cantaclara llega[6] al programa y canta su canción favorita. ¡Por supuesto ella canta mejor que todos![7] Ella va a tener un futuro fantástico y va a recibir muchísimo dinero.

Son las ocho de la noche. La madrastra y las dos hermanastras están en la sala y ven su programa favorito. Pero, ¿qué es esto? ¡Ven a Cantaclara en la pantalla!

—Mira, mamá. ¡Es Cantaclara! —dice Hortencia.

—¡Oh, no! Si Cantaclara es la nueva estrella del futuro, ¿quién va a hacer los quehaceres? —pregunta Griselda.

[5]is leaving [6]arrives [7]anyone else

¿Comprendes?

Pon las frases en orden según la historia.

1. Ella decide cantar en el programa *La estrella del futuro.*
2. Cantaclara es la persona que canta mejor en el programa.
3. Ella está lavando los platos.
4. Ella tiene que limpiar la cocina.
5. Ve el anuncio para *La estrella del futuro.*
6. Griselda no sabe quién va a hacer los quehaceres.
7. Cantaclara vive en una casa grande con su madrastra y sus dos hermanastras.
8. Son las ocho de la noche y la madrastra y las hermanastras están viendo la tele.

La Cenicienta The story of Cinderella is perhaps the best-known fairy tale in the world. Almost every culture seems to have its own version and there may be over 1,500 variations. The tale appears to date back to a Chinese story from the ninth century, "Yeh-Shen."

- What aspects of the story might change from culture to culture?

For: Internet link activity
Visit: www.phschool.com
Web Code: jcd-0615

El patio de una casa en Córdoba, España

Perspectivas del mundo hispano

¿Cómo son las casas en el mundo hispano?

In many Spanish-speaking countries the architectural features of houses are very different from those in the United States. Houses tend to be separated from the outside by a barrier such as a tall wall or fence. The owner would open a gate to enter the property where there may be a carport or small outside area. In many communities, the outside wall of the house is located directly on the sidewalk and the front windows may contain bars or *rejas.* The doors may be large wooden or metal doors. A plain walled exterior gives no hints about what may be a beautiful, comfortable interior.

Inside, a home will often have an open space in the middle called the *patio.* Many rooms of the house open onto the *patio,* and it is a place for the family to meet, eat meals, talk, and spend time together. Privacy is valued, and the home and family activities are shielded from view from the outside.

Homes in Spanish-speaking countries are used for the family and to entertain very close relatives and friends. It is unusual to invite non-family members such as coworkers or casual friends into the home. Parties often take place in restaurants or small reception halls.

Una calle en una zona residencial de San Juan, Puerto Rico

Check it out! Look around your neighborhood. How does the architecture of houses compare with the design of houses in the Spanish-speaking world?

Think about it! If architectural features of houses in Spanish-speaking countries imply a desire for privacy, what do the architectural features of houses in the United States imply? How does the concept of a *patio* compare in these cultures?

Una casa en Caracas, Venezuela

Presentación escrita

Se vende casa o apartamento

Task
You have been asked to create a flyer in Spanish to promote the sale of your family's house or apartment. Create an attractive and inviting flyer that will make your home (or your dream house, if you prefer) appealing to a potential buyer.

Una casa en México, D.F.

1. **Prewrite** Think about the information you want to include in your flyer. Read these questions and jot down what you'd like to say about the house or apartment.
   - En general, ¿cómo es la casa o el apartamento?
   - ¿Cuántos cuartos hay? ¿Cuáles son? ¿Cómo son? ¿De qué colores son?
   - ¿Hay algo especial en la casa (piscina, cuarto especial)?
   - Incluye *(Include)* otra información importante como la dirección *(address)* y el precio *(price)*.
2. **Draft** Look at the ad on p. 310 to help you design your flyer. Use the answers to the Prewrite questions. Include an illustration and other features to make it attractive. Begin with the phrase *Se vende casa* or *Se vende apartamento*.
3. **Revise** Read through your ad to see that you have included all the information that a potential buyer might want. Make sure the words are spelled correctly. Share your flyer with a partner, who will check the following:
   - Is the flyer neat and attractive? Does it include a visual?
   - Is the key information provided?
   - Does it make you want to look at the property?
4. **Publish** Write a final copy of your flyer, making any necessary changes. You may want to include it with your classmates' flyers in a collection called *Se venden casas y apartamentos* or in your portfolio.
5. **Evaluation** Your teacher may give you a rubric for grading your flyer. You probably will be graded on:
   - neatness and attractiveness
   - use of vocabulary
   - amount of information provided

Strategy

Using key questions
Answering key questions can help you think of ideas for writing.

Casa Milá en Barcelona, España

Videomisterio

¿Eres tú, María? Episodio 4

Antes de ver el video

Personajes importantes

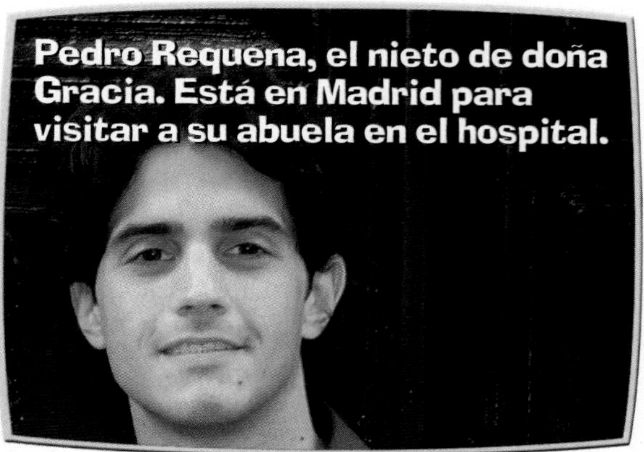

Pedro Requena, el nieto de doña Gracia. Está en Madrid para visitar a su abuela en el hospital.

Nota cultural *Tapas* are popular appetizers in Spain. *Tapas* come in small servings called *raciones,* and can be almost anything: olives, fish, meat, cheese, vegetables, shellfish, or any dish the chef cares to prepare. Eating *tapas* is a social event. Friends eat, drink, and relax as they talk. When you are done, you are charged according to how many platefuls of *tapas* you ate.

Resumen del episodio

Doña Gracia está mucho mejor y puede ir a casa en unos días. Pero no recuerda mucho del incidente. Lola llama por teléfono a su buena amiga, Carmela. Las dos van a un café para hablar y Carmela le dice a Lola que una de sus amigas, Rosalinda, trabaja en el hospital San Carlos. Es el hospital donde está doña Gracia. Deciden ir al hospital para hablar con Rosalinda y ver a doña Gracia. A la mañana siguiente, Lola habla con Pedro Requena.

Palabras para comprender

fui a visitarla I went to visit her
¿Habló del incidente? Did she talk about the incident?
¿Sabe . . .? Does she know . . .?
Lo único que recuerda . . . The only thing she remembers . . .
un golpe hit, blow
ahora mismo right away
preguntar por to ask about
los churros fried dough pastries
No estoy pensando en . . . I'm not planning to . . .
Voy a pensarlo. I'll think about it.

"Lo único que recuerda es un golpe aquí, en la cabeza. ¿La verdad? No sabe nada."

"Soy Pedro Requena. Exacto, el nieto de la Sra. Gracia Requena. Voy ahora mismo para el hospital."

—Si necesita más información, aquí tiene mi número de teléfono.

—Gracias, señorita. Voy a pensarlo.

Después de ver el video

¿Comprendes?

A. Lee las frases y ponlas *(put them)* en orden cronológico.

1. Pedro no sabe si quiere contratar a una detective.
2. Lola y Carmela van al café a comer unas tapas.
3. Lola habla con Pedro y le da su número de teléfono.
4. Paco y Lola hablan en la oficina.
5. Pedro Requena habla por teléfono con el Dr. Sánchez Mata.
6. Doña Lupe dice que fue al hospital y habló con doña Gracia.
7. Carmela dice que su amiga, Rosalinda, trabaja en el hospital San Carlos.

B. Lee las frases y escribe el nombre de la persona que dice cada frase: Pedro, Carmela, Lola, doña Lupe o Paco.

1. No podemos trabajar si no hay cliente y no hay dinero.
2. Buenas noticias. Doña Gracia está mejor.
3. ¿Quieres tomar un café conmigo?
4. Mi amiga trabaja allí. Puedes hablar con doña Gracia.
5. No estoy pensando en contratar a un detective.

For: More on *¿Eres tú, María?*
Visit: www.phschool.com
Web Code: jcd-0507

Repaso del capítulo

Vocabulario y gramática

Chapter Review

To prepare for the test, check to see if you . . .

- **know the new vocabulary and grammar**
- **can perform the tasks on p. 319**

to talk about where someone lives

cerca (de)	close (to), near
lejos (de)	far (from)
vivir	to live

to talk about houses or apartments

el apartamento	apartment
el baño	bathroom
la cocina	kitchen
el comedor	dining room
el cuarto	room
el despacho	home office
la escalera	stairs, stairway
el garaje	garage
el piso	story, floor
la planta baja	ground floor
el primer piso	second floor
la sala	living room
el segundo piso	third floor
el sótano	basement

to name household chores

arreglar el cuarto	to straighten up the room
ayudar	to help
cocinar	to cook
cortar el césped	to cut the lawn
dar (yo doy, tú das)	to give
dar de comer al perro	to feed the dog
hacer la cama	to make the bed
lavar (el coche, los platos, la ropa)	to wash (the car, the dishes, the clothes)
limpiar el baño	to clean the bathroom
pasar la aspiradora	to vacuum
poner (yo pongo, tú pones)	to put, place
poner la mesa	to set the table
los quehaceres	chores
quitar el polvo	to dust
sacar la basura	to take out the trash

to describe household items

limpio, -a	clean
sucio, -a	dirty

other useful words

bastante	enough; rather
¿Cuáles?	which (ones)
el dinero	money
un momento	a moment
¿Qué estás haciendo?	What are you doing?
recibir	to receive
si	if, whether

affirmative *tú* commands

For regular verbs, use the *Ud. / él / ella* form:

-ar:	**habla**
-er:	**lee**
-ir:	**escribe**

For *hacer* and *poner:*

hacer	**haz**
poner	**pon**

present progressive tense

Use the present-tense forms of *estar* + the present participle to say that you are doing something right now.

present participles:

-ar:	stem + **-ando** → **lavando**
-er:	stem + **-iendo** → **comiendo**
-ir:	stem + **-iendo** → **escribiendo**

For *Vocabulario adicional,* see pp. 472–473.

Más práctica

Practice Workbook Puzzle 6B-8
Practice Workbook Organizer 6B-9

For: Test preparation
Visit: www.phschool.com
Web Code: jcd-0616

Preparación para el examen

On the exam you will be asked to . . .	Here are practice tasks similar to those you will find on the exam . . .	If you need review . . .
1 Escuchar Listen to and understand teenagers' excuses for not doing a particular chore at the moment they are asked to do it	As you listen to a teenager explain to his mother why he can't do a particular chore at the moment, identify: a) what the mother wants the teenager to do; b) what the teenager says he is busy doing.	**pp. 298–301** *A primera vista* **p. 303** Actividad 7 **p. 304** Actividad 8 **p. 308** Actividad 17 **p. 309** Actividad 18
 **2 Hablar** Give advice to someone about how to be successful in school	Your school counselors have asked you to participate in an orientation for new Spanish-speaking students. Offer each student in the group a piece of advice. For example, you might say *Escucha bien en clase* or *Haz la tarea.*	**p. 305** Actividad 12 **p. 306** Actividad 13
 **3 Leer** Read and understand ads for apartments that you might find in the classified section of a Spanish-language newspaper	A friend is moving to Spain and asks you to help find an apartment. He wants a two-bedroom, two-bath apartment with a small kitchen. He wants to live near a gym and a library. Read this ad and answer the following: a) Is this a good apartment for him? b) How many of his requested features does it have? c) What other features that are mentioned might he like? Este maravilloso apartamento tiene todo. Está cerca de un parque y un gimnasio moderno. Tiene una cocina pequeña, pero totalmente equipada. Tiene dos dormitorios con estantes y un baño muy grande. También tiene televisión por satélite y un garaje privado. No se permiten animales.	**pp. 298–301** *A primera vista* **p. 302** Actividades 4–5 **p. 310** Actividad 21 **p. 315** *Presentación escrita*
4 Escribir Write a list of household chores that you are willing to do	You and your classmates are offering to do chores to earn money for your Spanish club. Make a list of at least eight chores that you would be willing to do.	**pp. 298–301** *A primera vista* **p. 303** Actividades 6–7 **p. 304** Actividad 8 **p. 306** Actividad 14 **p. 307** Actividad 15
 **5 Pensar** Demonstrate an understanding of cultural perspectives regarding houses	Explain how the architectural features of many homes in the Spanish-speaking world reflect the importance the owners place on privacy. How do these features compare to those in homes in the United States?	**p. 303** *Fondo cultural* **p. 314** *Perspectivas del mundo hispano*

¡Viva Texas!

San Antonio en el siglo XIX

Un palacio en San Antonio

La ciudad[1] de San Antonio de Béjar (Béxar), fundada como un centro de defensa en 1718, es importante en la historia de Texas. Hoy día San Antonio es una ciudad grande y moderna pero en el centro de la ciudad hay una casa fantástica que representa su historia fascinante: el Palacio del gobernador[2] español. Esta casa fue construida[3] en 1749 como residencia para el capitán del presidio[4] de San Antonio.

[1] city [2] governor [3] was built [4] fort, garrison

La casa, una representación auténtica del estilo colonial español, tiene paredes de adobe.

Para una casa del año 1749 es muy grande—tiene diez cuartos. La sala, un cuarto favorito para bailes y otros eventos sociales, tiene cuadros históricos en las paredes. En el despacho del gobernador puedes ver un escritorio antiguo[5] y una cama de la misma época.[6]

[5] old [6] era

En el comedor hay una mesa grande para la familia y los amigos. En la cocina, detrás de la casa, puedes ver utensilios para cocinar de esa época.

Los 10 cuartos del Palacio del gobernador

- la capilla[7]
- la sala de baile
- 3 dormitorios (gobernador, niños e invitados)
- la sala
- la cocina
- el comedor
- el vestíbulo[8]
- la bodega[9]
- También hay una terraza y un patio.

[7] chapel [8] foyer [9] storeroom

El patio bonito y grande es, probablemente, el centro de la vida diaria[10] de la familia. Cuando visitas el palacio del gobernador español, dejas[11] el San Antonio moderno para pasar unos momentos maravillosos en el San Antonio de la época colonial.

[10] daily [11] leave behind

¿Comprendes?

Lee las descripciones y escribe qué parte del palacio describen.

Modelo

Son de adobe. *las paredes*

1. Aquí hay una mesa grande donde comen.
2. A la familia le gusta pasar tiempo aquí cuando no están en la casa.
3. La cama y el escritorio están aquí.
4. Tiene un estilo colonial español.
5. La familia y los amigos bailan y escuchan música aquí.
6. Preparan la comida en este cuarto rústico.
7. Puedes ver cuadros muy antiguos.

Comunicación

Con un(a) compañero(a) compara tu propia casa o la casa de un(a) amigo(a) con la descripción del Palacio del gobernador español. ¿Cuántos cuartos tienen en común las dos casas? ¿Cuáles son diferentes?

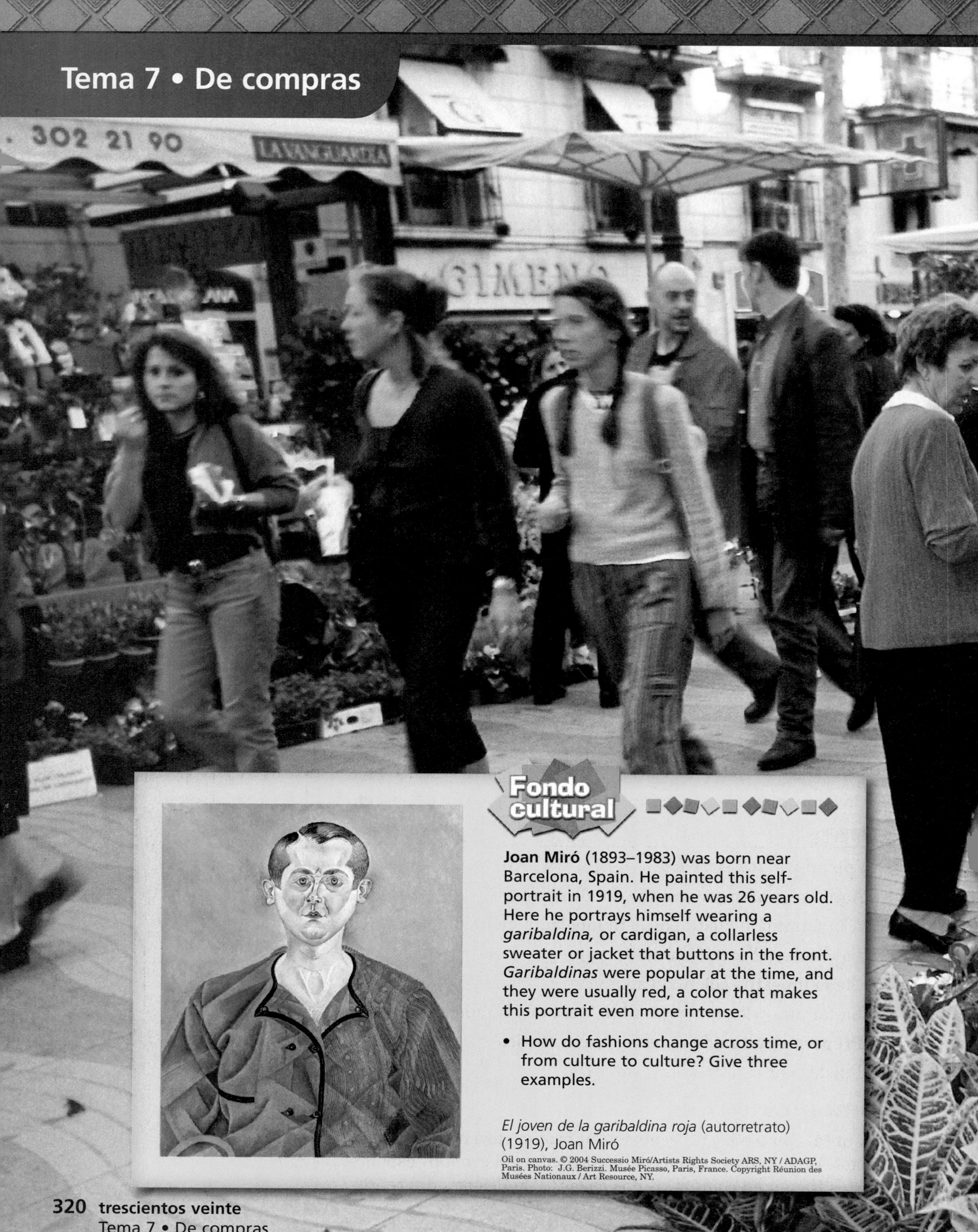

Fondo cultural

Joan Miró (1893–1983) was born near Barcelona, Spain. He painted this self-portrait in 1919, when he was 26 years old. Here he portrays himself wearing a *garibaldina,* or cardigan, a collarless sweater or jacket that buttons in the front. *Garibaldinas* were popular at the time, and they were usually red, a color that makes this portrait even more intense.

- How do fashions change across time, or from culture to culture? Give three examples.

El joven de la garibaldina roja (autorretrato) (1919), Joan Miró

En Las Ramblas, Barcelona, España

¿Cuánto cuesta?

Chapter Objectives

- Talk about clothes, shopping, and prices
- Describe your plans
- Talk about what you want and what you prefer
- Point out specific items
- Understand cultural perspectives on shopping

Video Highlights

A primera vista: *Una noche especial*

GramActiva Videos: stem-changing verbs *pensar, querer,* and *preferir;* demonstrative adjectives

Videomisterio: *¿Eres tú, María?,* Episodio 5

Country Connection

As you learn about clothing and shopping, you will make connections to these countries and places:

Go Online PHSchool.com
For: Online Atlas
Visit: www.phschool.com
Web Code: jce-0002

A primera vista

Vocabulario y gramática en contexto

Objectives

Read, listen to, and understand information about

- shopping for clothes
- plans, desires, and preferences

Tienda de ropa La Preferida

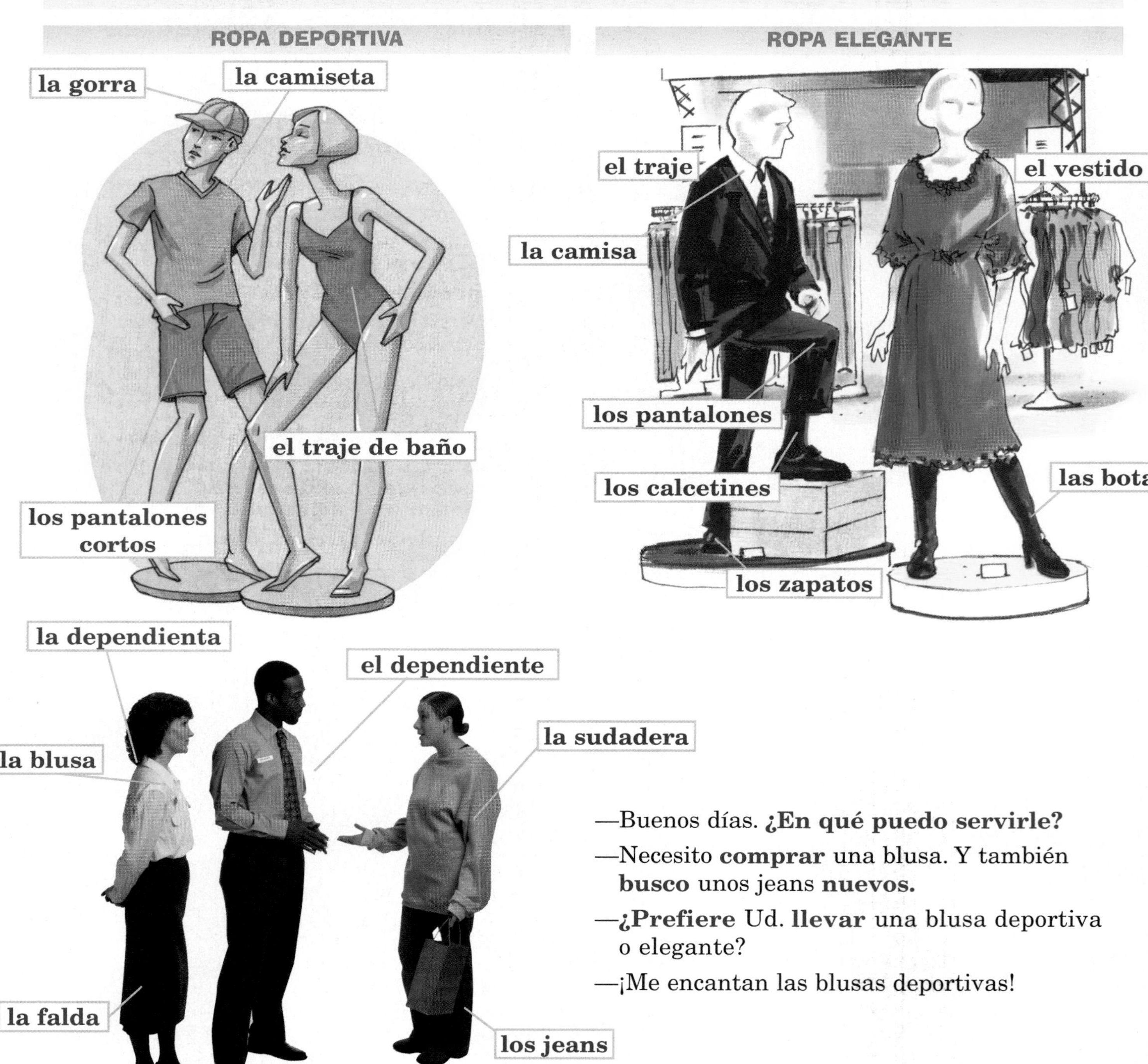

—Buenos días. **¿En qué puedo servirle?**

—Necesito **comprar** una blusa. Y también **busco** unos jeans **nuevos.**

—**¿Prefiere** Ud. **llevar** una blusa deportiva o elegante?

—¡Me encantan las blusas deportivas!

—¿Qué **piensas** comprar hoy?

—Necesito comprar un abrigo. Me gusta **ese** abrigo. **¿Entramos en la tienda?**

—¡Uf! **Me queda mal.**

—**Tienes razón.** Es demasiado grande.

—**¿Cómo me queda** este abrigo?

—**Te queda bien.** Me gusta. ¿Qué piensas?

—Me gusta también. **¿Cúanto cuesta?**

—A ver . . . Cuesta ochocientos pesos. Es un buen **precio,** ¿no?

doscientos **pesos**

trescientos **pesos**

400

cuatrocientos **pesos**

quinientos **pesos**

seiscientos **pesos**

setecientos **pesos**

ochocientos **pesos**

novecientos **pesos**

mil **pesos**

Escuchar

¿Qué ropa llevan?

Escucha qué ropa llevan hoy diferentes personas. Señala en la foto o en los dibujos cada artículo de ropa que escuchas.

Escuchar

¿Verano o invierno?

On a sheet of paper, draw a snowman on one side and the sun on the other. If a statement you hear is most logical for winter, hold up the snowman. If it is most logical for summer, hold up the sun.

Más práctica

Practice Workbook 7A-1, 7A-2

For: Vocabulary practice
Visit: www.phschool.com
Web Code: jcd-0701

Videohistoria

Una noche especial

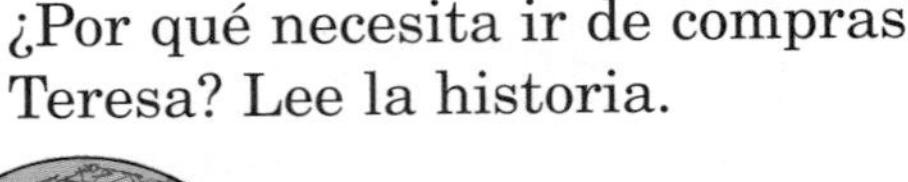

¿Por qué necesita ir de compras Teresa? Lee la historia.

México

Strategy

Reading for key information
Reading the questions at the end of the *Videohistoria* before viewing or reading it will help you focus on key information.

1 **Teresa:** **Esta** falda no me queda bien y **este** vestido no me gusta. No sé qué llevar para la fiesta.

Claudia: Pues, puedes comprar ropa nueva. Hay una tienda de ropa aquí cerca y tienen ropa muy bonita.

Teresa: Sí, **quizás** una falda nueva . . . **¡Vamos!**

5 **Manolo:** Ramón, son las ocho. La fiesta es a las nueve, ¿recuerdas?

Ramón: Sí, sí, tienes razón. Vamos.

6 **Berta:** Ramón, ¿tú piensas llevar esa ropa a la fiesta de Teresa? **¡Esos** jeans y esa camiseta y . . . esa gorra! No, no puedes.

Ramón: ¿Y por qué no?

Berta: Umm . . . Pues, aquí en México no llevamos esa ropa a las fiestas.

7 **Ramón:** ¡Yo quiero llevar mi gorra favorita, y me gustan **estos** jeans!

Manolo y Berta: Te ayudamos.

2 **Claudia:** ¡Mira esta tienda!

Teresa: Mmmm . . . No sé. No tengo mucho dinero y **esa** ropa es muy cara.

Claudia: ¡Vamos! **¡Queremos** ver qué tienen!

3 **Teresa: Perdón,** ¿señora?

Dependienta: ¿Sí? ¿En qué puedo servirle, señorita?

Teresa: Busco ropa para llevar a una fiesta. Me gustaría comprar esta falda y esta blusa.

Claudia: A ver . . . ¿Cuánto **cuestan?**

Teresa: ¡Seiscientos pesos! Pero, ¡es mucho dinero!

4 **Dependienta:** Bueno, aquí hay ropa que no cuesta **tanto.**

Claudia: Mira, Teresa. Esta falda cuesta trescientos pesos. ¿Qué piensas?

Teresa: ¡Genial! Y este suéter cuesta doscientos pesos. **Los dos** no cuestan tanto.

8 **Teresa:** ¡Hola! Buenas noches. Pero, ¿dónde está la gorra?

Actividad 3 **Hablar/Escribir**

¿Comprendes?

1. ¿Por qué no está contenta Teresa? ¿Adónde va ella?
2. Según Claudia, ¿qué puede hacer Teresa?
3. ¿Adónde van las dos?
4. ¿Tiene Teresa mucho o poco dinero?
5. ¿Por qué no compra Teresa la primera falda y blusa?
6. ¿Cuánto cuestan la segunda falda y blusa?
7. ¿Qué quiere llevar Ramón a la fiesta?
8. Cuando Ramón entra en la casa de Teresa, ¿qué lleva?

Más práctica

Practice Workbook 7A-3, 7A-4

For: Vocabulary practice
Visit: www.phschool.com
Web Code: jcd-0702

Manos a la obra

Vocabulario y gramática en uso

Objectives

- Talk about shopping for clothes
- Discuss how clothes fit and how much they cost
- Ask and tell what you or others plan to do
- Ask and tell what you or others want and prefer
- Point things out using demonstrative adjectives

  **Escribir**

¿Qué piensas llevar?

¡Es importante llevar ropa diferente en diferentes ocasiones! ¿Qué ropa piensas llevar a estos lugares o actividades? Escribe las frases.

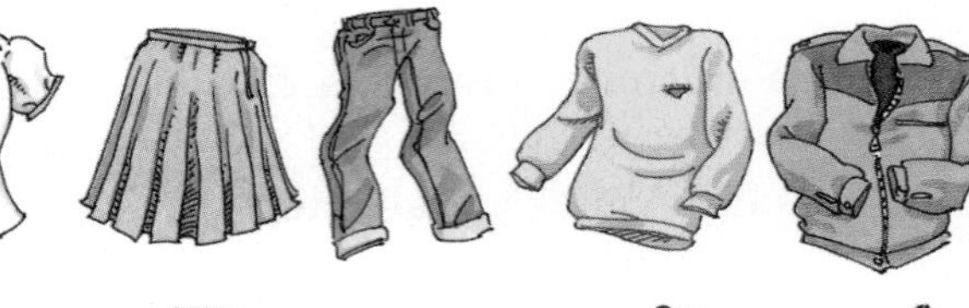

Modelo

la casa de un amigo
Pienso llevar unos jeans y una camiseta.

1. la playa
2. un baile elegante
3. un concierto
4. las montañas
5. un partido de béisbol

 **Escuchar/Escribir**

Escucha y escribe

Trabajas en una tienda de ropa y escuchas los comentarios de diferentes personas que buscan ropa. Escribe los números del 1 al 6 en una hoja de papel y escribe las frases que escuchas. Después indica con (+) o (-) si piensas que las personas van a comprar la ropa.

También se dice . . .

la camiseta = la playera *(México)*; la polera *(Chile)*; la remera *(Argentina)*

la chaqueta = la chamarra *(México)*; la campera *(Argentina, Bolivia, Chile, Paraguay, Uruguay)*

los jeans = los mahones *(el Caribe)*; las mezclillas *(México)*; los vaqueros *(Argentina, España)*; el pantalón vaquero *(España)*

el suéter = el jersey *(España)*; la chompa *(Bolivia, Ecuador, Paraguay, Perú, Uruguay)*

   **Hablar**

¿En qué puedo servirle?

Tú y tu compañero(a) van de compras. Pregunta y contesta según el modelo. Escoge cinco cosas.

Modelo

A —*¿En qué puedo servirle, señor (señorita)?*
B —*Me gustaría comprar una camisa nueva.*
A —*¿De qué color?*
B —*Estoy buscando una camisa amarilla.*

      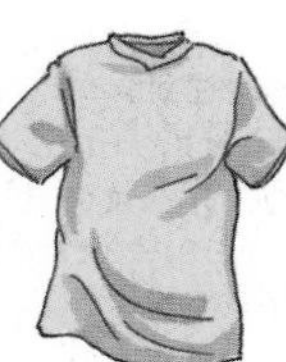 

   **Escribir/Hablar**

Juego

1. Escribe una descripción de la ropa de una persona en tu clase. Incluye dos o más cosas que lleva y los colores de la ropa.
2. Juega con otro(a) estudiante. Lee tu descripción. Tu compañero(a) tiene que identificar a la persona que describes. Antes de decir *(Before saying)* su nombre, él o ella tiene que hacer tres preguntas para saber más cosas. Por ejemplo: *¿Lleva una sudadera azul? ¿Tiene zapatos negros? ¿Sus calcetines son blancos? ¿Es Mateo?*

  **Escribir**

¿Qué ropa llevan en el cuadro?

Escribe cuatro o más frases que describen la ropa que lleva la familia en este cuadro de Fernando Botero.

Modelo

La madre lleva . . .

Fernando Botero (1932–) is a very famous artist from Medellín, Colombia. His paintings and sculptures feature people and objects that are puffed up to an exaggerated size. The figures celebrate life while at the same time making fun of what they represent.

- What statement might an artist like Botero be making when his artwork presents humorous portrayals of politicians and prominent people?

En familia (1983), Fernando Botero

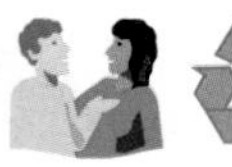

Pensar/Leer/Hablar

En la tienda

Con otro(a) estudiante lee la conversación entre un(a) dependiente(a) y un(a) joven. Empareja lo que dice el (la) dependiente(a) con lo que contesta el (la) joven.

el (la) dependiente(a)

1. Buenas tardes. ¿En qué puedo servirle?
2. ¿Qué color prefiere Ud.?
3. Pues, estos pantalones son muy populares.
4. Sólo 50 dólares.
5. Pues, hay otros pantalones que no cuestan tanto.
6. Creo que le quedan muy bien.

el (la) joven

a. Perdón . . . ese precio es demasiado para mí.
b. Entonces voy a comprar estos pantalones.
c. Quiero comprar unos pantalones nuevos.
d. Son bonitos. A ver si me quedan bien.
e. No sé—quizás negro.
f. Me gustan. ¿Cuánto cuestan?

Escuchar/Escribir

¿Cuánto cuesta en Montevideo?

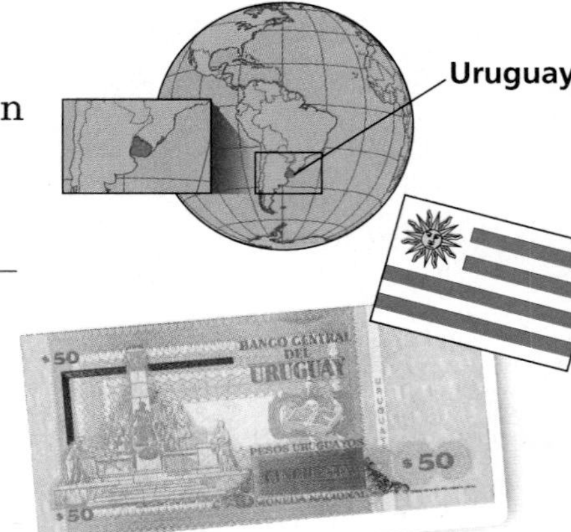

Estás comprando ropa en Montevideo, Uruguay. Escucha los precios en pesos uruguayos. Escribe en tu hoja de papel el precio que escuchas.

Modelo

los zapatos
Escuchas: *Los zapatos cuestan mil ochocientos veinte pesos.*
Escribes: *1820 pesos*

1. la camiseta
2. el suéter
3. la blusa
4. el vestido
5. el traje de baño
6. la chaqueta

The currencies of Bolivia, Peru, and Costa Rica are all different. Latin American countries have special names for their national currency and use different symbols as abbreviations. In Bolivia, the official currency is the *boliviano* (abbreviated BOB). The *nuevo sol* (abbreviated s/) is the official currency of Peru. Costa Rica's money is called the *colón,* and its symbol is a ¢ placed in front of the amount, as in ¢100 (meaning 100 *colones).* Cents are either *céntimos* or *centavos* in most Latin American countries. The images on the printed money honor each country's history and culture.

- How do the images on these currencies compare to those on bills and coins in the United States?

Hablar

¿Cómo me queda?

Estás en una tienda de ropa. Te pruebas *(You're trying on)* la ropa y necesitas la opinión honesta de tu amigo(a). Tu amigo(a) siempre te hace *(gives you)* comentarios. Escoge dos artículos de ropa.

Modelo

A —*¿Me queda bien el traje? ¿Qué piensas?*
B —*Te queda bien. ¡Qué guapo estás!*

Nota

Me / te queda(n) follows the same pattern as *me / te gusta(n).*

- La camisa **me** queda bien pero los jeans **me** qued**an** mal.

Estudiante A

Estudiante B

Te queda(n) bien / mal.

Es / son muy / bastante / demasiado . . .

¡Qué guapo / bonita estás!

(No) me gusta(n) mucho.

Pronunciación

The letter *z*

In most Spanish-speaking countries, the letter *z* sounds like the *s* in *see.* Listen to and say these words:

zapato	arroz	almuerzo	cabeza
izquierda	haz	razón	nariz
	azul	quizás	

In many parts of Spain, however, the letter *z* is pronounced like the *th* in *think.* Listen to the words as a Spaniard says them and practice saying them as if you were in Spain.

Try it out! Listen to *"En la puerta del cielo"* ("At Heaven's Gate"), a traditional poem from Puerto Rico. Then say the poem aloud.

En la puerta del cielo,
venden zapatos
para los angelitos
que andan descalzos.

Escribir/Hablar

Y tú, ¿qué dices?

1. ¿Qué ropa llevas en el verano? ¿Y en el invierno? Incluye tres artículos de ropa para cada estación.
2. ¿Cuáles son tres artículos de ropa que te gustaría comprar? ¿Cuánto cuesta cada uno? ¿Cuál es el total?
3. Describe alguna ropa nueva que tienes.

Gramática

Stem-changing verbs: *pensar, querer,* and *preferir*

Verbs like *pensar* ("to think," "to plan"), *querer* ("to want"), and *preferir* ("to prefer") are *e→ie* stem-changing verbs. The *-e-* of the stem changes to *-ie-* in all forms except *nosotros* and *vosotros.* Here are the forms:

(yo)	**pienso** **quiero** **prefiero**	(nosotros) (nosotras)	**pensamos** **queremos** **preferimos**
(tú)	**piensas** **quieres** **prefieres**	(vosotros) (vosotras)	**pensáis** **queréis** **preferís**
Ud. (él) (ella)	**piensa** **quiere** **prefiere**	Uds. (ellos) (ellas)	**piensan** **quieren** **prefieren**

¿Recuerdas?

You have used *quiero / quieres* and *prefiero / prefieres* to say what you want or prefer.

Use the infinitive for any verb that follows *pensar, querer,* or *preferir.*

¿Piensas comprar esa blusa?
***Do you plan to buy** that blouse?*

GramActiva VIDEO

Want more help with stem-changing verbs? Watch the **GramActiva** video.

Gramática  Escuchar/Escribir

¿Qué prefieren llevar?

1. En una hoja de papel escribe los números del 1 al 6. Escucha lo que quieren o piensan hacer diferentes personas y escribe las frases.
2. Escribe otra frase para decir qué piensan llevar las personas para sus actividades.

Modelo

Mis primas quieren ir a un baile el viernes. Piensan llevar una falda y una blusa.

Gramática 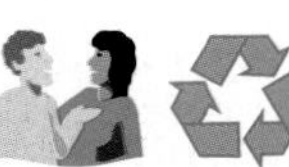 Hablar

¿Qué piensas hacer?

Habla con otro(a) estudiante sobre qué piensas hacer tú y qué piensan hacer otras personas.

Modelo

tu amigo(a) / después de las clases
A —*¿Qué piensa hacer tu amigo después de las clases?*
B —*Mi amigo David piensa montar en monopatín.*

Estudiante A

1. tus amigos(as) / mañana
2. tu familia / este fin de semana
3. tus amigos y tú / esta tarde
4. tú / el domingo
5. tu amigo(a) / esta noche

Estudiante B

¡Respuesta personal!

Actividad 15 Escribir

¿Qué quieren comprar?

Después de dos semanas de trabajo, todos los jóvenes tienen dinero y quieren ir de compras. Escribe frases para decir qué prefieren comprar y cuándo piensan ir de compras.

Catalina / el sábado

Modelo

Catalina quiere ir de compras. Prefiere comprar unos pantalones cortos. Piensa ir a la tienda de ropa el sábado.

1. Isidoro y Lorenzo / esta tarde
2. Julia y yo / mañana
3. Javier / este fin de semana
4. yo / ¿ ?

Actividad 16 Escribir/Hablar

¿Qué piensan hacer Uds.?

1. Copia la gráfica en una hoja de papel y escribe los nombres de tres personas con quienes vas a salir. ¿Adónde quieren ir Uds. y qué piensan hacer?

¿Con quién?	¿Adónde?	¿Qué?
Pepe	el gimnasio	levantar pesas

2. Dile *(Tell)* a otro(a) estudiante adónde quieren ir tú y la otra persona. Tu compañero(a) va a adivinar *(guess)* qué piensan hacer Uds. Puede continuar adivinando hasta *(until)* decir la actividad correcta.

Pensamos comprar algo en el mercado.

Modelo

A —*Pepe y yo queremos ir al gimnasio.*
B —*¿Uds. piensan jugar al básquetbol?*
A —*No, no pensamos jugar al básquetbol.*
B —*¿Uds. piensan levantar pesas?*
A —*Sí, tienes razón. Pensamos levantar pesas.*

Más práctica

Practice Workbook 7A-5

For: Practice with *e→ie* verbs
Visit: www.phschool.com
Web Code: jcd-0704

Gramática

Demonstrative adjectives

You use demonstrative adjectives to point out nouns: ***this** cap, **these** socks, **that** shirt, **those** shoes.* Notice that "this" and "these" refer to things that are close to you, while "that" and "those" refer to things that are at some distance from you.

Here are the corresponding demonstrative adjectives in Spanish. Like other adjectives, demonstrative adjectives agree in gender and number with the nouns that follow them.

	"this," "these"	*"that," "those"*
SINGULAR	**este** suéter **esta** falda	**ese** vestido **esa** chaqueta
PLURAL	**estos** suéteres **estas** faldas	**esos** vestidos **esas** chaquetas

Strategy

Using rhymes to remember meaning
To remember the difference between these demonstrative adjectives that are spelled very similarly, memorize this rhyme:

"This" and "these" both have *t's,*
"that" and "those" don't.

GramActiva VIDEO

Want more help with demonstrative adjectives? Watch the **GramActiva** video.

Leer/Escribir

En la tienda de ropa

Carmen está en una tienda y habla con su amiga sobre la ropa que se están probando *(trying on)*. Escribe la forma correcta de *este(a)* o *estos(as)* para cada número.

Carmen: __1.__ botas son bonitas, ¿no?

Mariel: Sí, pero creo que __2.__ zapatos son bastante feos.

Carmen: ¿Qué piensas de __3.__ blusa? A mí me gusta mucho.

Mariel: A mí también. __4.__ suéter es demasiado grande, ¿no?

Carmen: Tienes razón. Y pienso que __5.__ falda es muy larga también.

Mariel: Quizás. __6.__ jeans no cuestan mucho. ¡Qué bueno!

Gramática

Hablar

¡Un día con tu hermanito!

Tienes que cuidar *(take care of)* a tu hermanito. Tus padres tienen toda la ropa para él encima de la cama, pero ¡tu hermanito tiene sus propias ideas!

Modelo

A (tú)—*Tienes que llevar esta ropa.*
B (tu hermanito)—*¡No! No quiero llevar esa ropa. Prefiero esta ropa que está en el armario.*

Gramática

Escribir/Hablar

Juego

¿Quién en tu clase sabe mejor cuánto cuestan diferentes cosas?

1. Trabaja con otro(a) estudiante. Escojan un objeto o una foto de un objeto. Puede ser ropa, algo de la casa, algo de la escuela, etc. Escriban una descripción de ese objeto y determinen cuánto cuesta.

Modelo

Este suéter azul y amarillo es . . . . Puedes llevar este suéter a . . . . Puedes comprar este suéter en . . . . ¿Cuánto cuesta este suéter? (Cuesta 55 dólares.)

2. Ahora, trabajen en grupos de cuatro parejas (ocho estudiantes). Lean la descripción de su objeto sin decir cuánto cuesta. La pareja que da el precio más aproximado *(closest)* sin exceder *(without exceeding)* el precio, gana.

Modelo

—*Pensamos que el suéter cuesta 50 dólares.*
—*Daniel y Eva, Uds. ganan. El suéter cuesta 55 dólares.*

Exploración del lenguaje

Nonverbal language

You've learned about the gesture *¡Ojo!*, which means "be careful." Another common gesture used by Spanish speakers conveys the meaning of "a lot of money." This gesture is made by holding the hand palm-up and rubbing the fingertips together. It is often accompanied by expressions such as *¡Cuesta muchísimo!* or *Es mucho dinero.* It can even be used when you're describing someone who is rich.

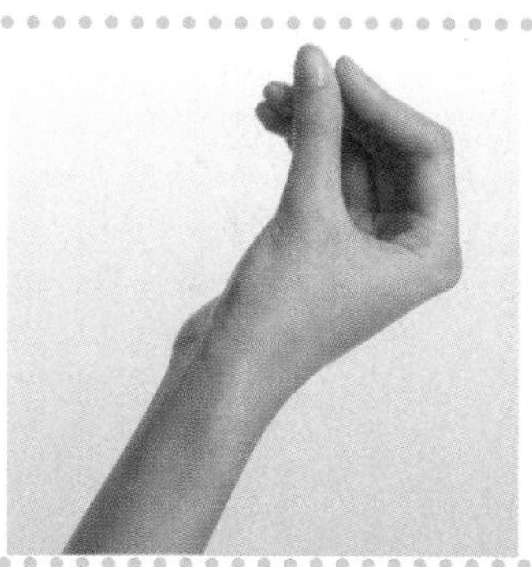

Leer/Hablar

¡Muchos regalos!

Muchas personas en tu familia y unos amigos tienen cumpleaños este mes y tienes que comprar regalos. Tú y un(a) compañero(a) miran este anuncio de una tienda de ropa. Habla con tu compañero(a) sobre qué necesitas comprar.

Modelo

tu tía o tío

A —*Necesito un regalo para mi tía. Voy a buscar un suéter para ella.*

B —*Buena idea. ¿Te gusta este suéter rosado? Sólo cuesta 32 dólares.*

A —*Sí. Vamos a la tienda a buscar este suéter.*

1. tu hermano o amigo
2. tu hermana o amiga
3. tu abuelo o abuela
4. tu mamá o papá

La tienda de ropa Perfección

¡Sólo 1 día!

$35 orig. $50

$25 orig. $38

$19 orig. $28

$11 orig. $18

$18 orig. $30

$32 orig. $45

$16 orig. $24

$8 orig. $14

Pensar/Hablar

En la tienda

Conexiones | Las matemáticas

Estás ahora en la tienda de ropa Perfección de la Actividad 20. Hablas con un(a) dependiente(a) sobre los descuentos que hay en la ropa hoy.

1. Calcula el porcentaje de descuento de la ropa en el anuncio.
2. Pregunta y contesta según el modelo.

Modelo

A —*Perdón, señor (señorita). ¿Cuánto cuesta ese suéter rosado?*

B —*Hoy este suéter cuesta sólo 32 dólares. Es un descuento del 29 por ciento.*

A —*¡Genial! Quiero comprar el suéter. ¡Qué buen precio!*

Escribir/Hablar

Un desfile de modas

Trabajen en grupos de tres. Una persona de los tres va a ser el (la) modelo en un desfile de modas *(fashion show)*. Decidan qué va a llevar el (la) modelo. En una hoja de papel, describan tres o más cosas que lleva el (la) modelo. Puedes incluir los colores, cuánto cuesta, dónde puedes comprar la ropa y en qué ocasión o estación puedes llevar la ropa.

Su modelo va a participar con los otros modelos de la clase en el desfile de modas. Los otros dos leen la descripción de la ropa.

Para decir más . . .

cómodo, -a	comfortable
elegante	elegant
de algodón	cotton
de lana	wool
de seda	silk

Modelo

El (La) modelo que entra en este momento lleva . . .

Fondo cultural

Carolina Herrera is one of the world's leading fashion designers. The clothes, perfume, and accessories by this Venezuelan designer are worn by some of the world's most elegant women. She is one of many creative Spanish-speaking designers who are making their mark in the fashion world.

- Think of the names of some fashion designers from the United States. In what ways do you think they influence everyday culture?

BOUTIQUE GUADALAJARA

Vestidos y accesorios para toda ocasión

Ropa sport y vaquera; sombreros, botas

- *Invitaciones y regalos*
- *Discos y casetes*
- *Libros y revistas*
- *Envío de dinero y tarjetas telefónicas*

1819 First Street Sonora, Arizona

El español en la comunidad

Locate a store in your community or on the Internet that sells products from Spanish-speaking countries. Visit the store or Web site and list the types of items you find there. Are they similar to the items listed in the ad? Bring your list to class and compare it with other students' lists. What are the most common types of items found in these stores?

Más práctica

Practice Workbook 7A-6, 7A-7

For: Practice with demonstrative adjectives
Visit: www.phschool.com
Web Code: jcd-0703

¡Adelante!

Lectura

Objectives

- Read about traditional clothing of Panama
- Learn about and make a *mola*
- Create and perform a skit about buying an article of clothing
- Watch *¿Eres tú, María?*, Episodio 5

Strategy

Predicting
Look at the maps and photos on these pages and read the title to predict what the reading will be about. This will help you anticipate the types of words and expressions you will encounter as you read.

Tradiciones de la ropa panameña

Panamá
Mar Caribe
ISLAS DE SAN BLAS
COSTA RICA
Canal de Panamá
Ciudad de Panamá
Golfo de Panamá
PANAMÁ
Las Tablas
LOS SANTOS
OCÉANO PACÍFICO
COLOMBIA

Una tradición panameña de mucho orgullo[1] es llevar el vestido típico de las mujeres, "la pollera." Hay dos tipos de pollera, la pollera montuna[2] y la pollera de gala, que se lleva en los festivales. La pollera de gala se hace a mano y cuesta muchísimo por la cantidad de joyas[3] que adornan el vestido. ¿Cuánto cuesta una pollera de gala? Puede costar unos 1.850 dólares americanos, y requiere aproximadamente siete meses de trabajo. La pollera es tan importante que en la ciudad de Las Tablas celebran el Día Nacional de La Pollera el 22 de julio.

Si quieres celebrar con los panameños, puedes visitar la ciudad de Las Tablas en la provincia de Los Santos. Las Tablas es famosa por ser el mejor lugar para celebrar los carnavales. Durante el carnaval y en otros festivales, puedes admirar los vestidos y los bailes tradicionales.

El canal de Panamá conecta el océano Pacífico con el mar Caribe y el océano Atlántico.

El istmo de Panamá es la conexión entre dos continentes, y tiene costas sobre el océano Pacífico y el mar Caribe. Es famoso por el canal en el que navegan barcos[4] de todo el mundo. El folklore panameño es muy variado. La música, los bailes y los vestidos son importantes en la vida[5] social, especialmente en las provincias del centro del país.

[1] pride [2] from the mountains [3] jewels [4] ships [5] life

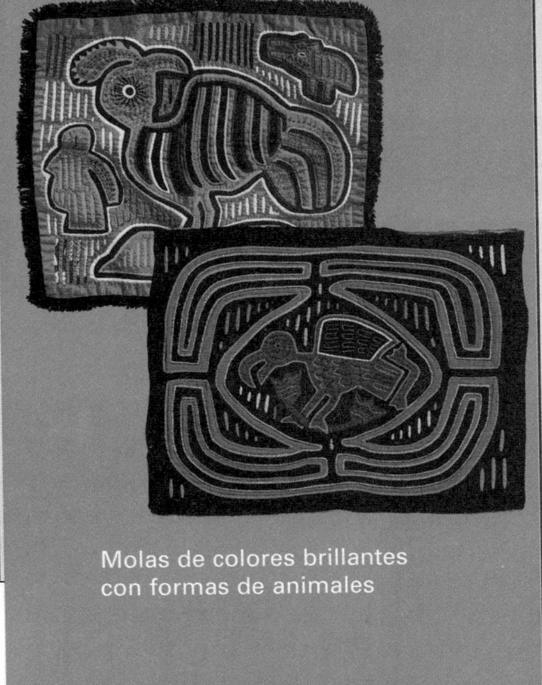

Molas de colores brillantes con formas de animales

Otro tipo de ropa auténtica de Panamá viene de los indios Kuna, un grupo de indígenas que viven en las islas de San Blas. Las mujeres llevan una blusa hecha[6] de molas. Las molas son paneles decorativos que forman la parte de adelante y de atrás de las blusas. Las mujeres demuestran[7] su talento y expresión personal con los diseños[8] originales de las molas. Los diseños representan formas humanas y animales. Hoy día, puedes ver y admirar molas como objetos de arte en muchos museos y colecciones.

[6]made [7]demonstrate [8]designs

¿Comprendes?

1. ¿Por qué es importante Panamá en el comercio global?
2. ¿Cuáles son las dos formas de ropa auténtica de Panamá en el artículo?
3. ¿Qué puedes celebrar si visitas Las Tablas?
4. ¿Cuánto puede costar una pollera de gala? En tu opinión, ¿es mucho o poco dinero?
5. ¿Cómo se llama el grupo de indígenas que viven en las islas de San Blas?
6. ¿Quiénes llevan las molas, los hombres o las mujeres?
7. ¿Por qué es diferente cada mola?

Carnaval is a traditional celebration in many Latin American countries. It takes place in the weeks before the season of Lent. *Carnaval* normally includes the coronation of a beauty queen, parades, elaborate costumes, street music, and dancing. The *Carnaval* in Las Tablas, a town near the Pacific coast in Panama, is very popular and attracts thousands of visitors every year.

- What traditional parades or celebrations take place in your community? How do they compare to the celebration of *carnaval?*

Go Online PHSchool.com
For: Internet link activity
Visit: www.phschool.com
Web Code: jcd-0705

La cultura en vivo

Las molas

Molas are the bright fabric artwork created by the Kuna Indians of the San Blas Islands, a group of islands off the Panama coast in the Caribbean Sea. *Mola* is a Kuna word meaning "blouse." This art form was originally used to make clothing, but today the term *mola* refers to any piece of fabric made using this method.

Kuna women cut out a cloth pattern and sew it onto layers of cloth that have been sewn together. Pieces of the upper layers are cut away to expose the underlying colors and create a design. Later, the women embroider details. Many designs on *molas* represent nature or animals. Each *mola* may take many weeks to complete.

Try it out! Here's how you can make *molas* out of paper.

Materials

- 2 pencils
- rubber bands
- construction paper
- paste or glue
- scissors

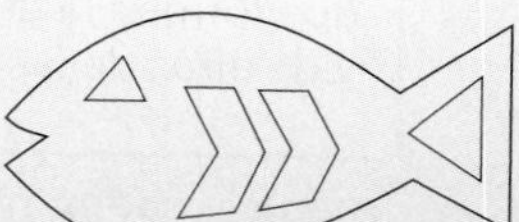

Figure 1

Directions

1 Your teacher will provide a pattern to trace on a piece of construction paper. You may prefer to trace around a cookie cutter or draw a simple design found in nature (for example, a leaf, flower, or fir tree). *(Fig. 1)*

2 Double all the lines by drawing with two pencils fastened together with rubber bands. *(Fig. 2)*

Figure 2

3 Cut out all spaces that do NOT fall between the double lines. *(Fig. 3)*

4 Paste or glue the cutout figure onto construction paper of a contrasting color.

5 Cut around the pasted or glued figure, leaving a border of the second color. *(Fig. 4)*

6 Paste or glue this cutout figure onto another piece of construction paper and cut around it, leaving a border of the new color. Paste the entire piece on a contrasting background.

Figure 3

Think about it! Do you or anyone in your family practice a traditional handicraft? Do you have any clothes or outfits that you have made or customized to express your interests or personality?

Figure 4

Presentación oral

¿En qué puedo servirle?

Task

You and a partner will play the roles of a customer and a salesclerk in a clothing store. You will ask and answer questions about the articles of clothing sold in the store. The customer will then decide whether or not to buy the articles.

1. **Prepare** Work with a partner to prepare the skit. One of you will play the role of the salesperson, and the other will be the shopper. Be prepared to play both roles. Decide the type of clothing the store will sell and bring to class articles of clothing or pictures from a magazine. Give the store a name.

   Cliente: Make a list of expressions and questions you can use to ask about, describe, and say whether you will buy an article of clothing.

   Dependiente(a): Make a list of expressions and questions you can use to help your client, answer his or her questions, and show him or her the clothing.

2. **Practice** Work with your partner and practice both roles. You might want to review *A primera vista,* the *Videohistoria,* and Actividad 9 for ideas. You can use your written notes when you practice, but not during the actual role play.

3. **Present** Your teacher will assign the roles. The clerk will begin the conversation. Keep talking until the customer has made a decision to buy or not to buy the article of clothing.

4. **Evaluation** Your teacher may give you a rubric for how your presentation will be graded. You probably will be graded on:
   - how well you sustain a conversation
   - how complete your preparation is
   - how well you use new and previously learned vocabulary

Strategy

Seeking feedback
As you practice with a partner, seek his or her feedback to correct errors you have made and to improve your overall performance.

Videomisterio

¿Eres tú, María? Episodio 5

DIGESTIVO
GÍA ME
Rosalinda, una amiga de Carmela quien trabaja en el hospital San Carlos

Antes de ver el video

Personaje importante

Resumen del episodio

Lola y Carmela van al hospital para hablar con Rosalinda sobre doña Gracia y María. Aprenden más sobre el accidente de coche de María. Ocurrió entre María y otra joven, Julia. Las dos fueron llevadas[1] al Hospital San Carlos. Desafortunadamente,[2] Julia murió. Rosalinda va a los archivos para buscar los historiales clínicos de Julia y María. Pero hay un problema. . . .

[1] were brought [2] unfortunately

Palabras para comprender

Estuvo aquí . . . She was here . . .
¿Te acuerdas de ella? Do you remember her?
Sí, me acuerdo de María. Yes, I remember María.
Dos coches chocaron . . . Two cars crashed . . .
la carretera highway
murió died
Les ayudó a las dos. He helped the two of them.
No viene a trabajar. He hasn't been coming to work.
el archivo records
los historiales clínicos medical records
los visitantes visitors

"Primero, quiero hablar de una paciente que se llama María Requena. Estuvo aquí, en el hospital."

"Pues, no está su historial clínico. Ni un papel. Nada, absolutamente nada sobre María Requena."

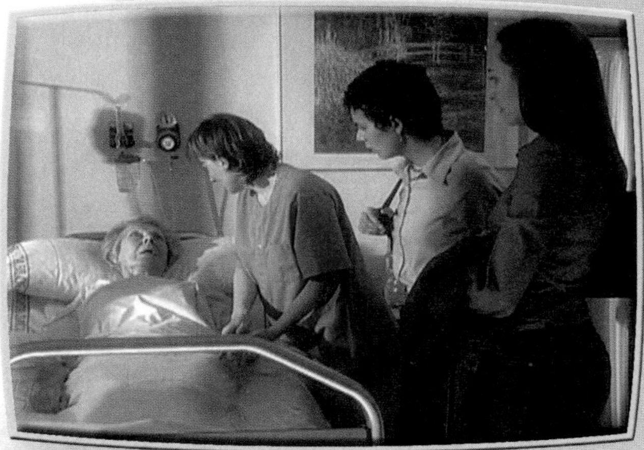

"¿Eres tú, María?"

Después de ver el video

¿Comprendes?

Lee las frases. Decide a quién(es) describe cada frase: Lola, Rosalinda, Carmela, Julia, María o Luis Antonio.

1. Dos coches y dos chicas. Fue muy triste.
2. Ella murió en el accidente.
3. Hay un enfermero que ayudó a las dos.
4. Es muy simpática tu amiga.
5. No hay nada sobre ellas en los archivos.
6. Está bastante mal.
7. Las amigas de Carmela son amigas mías.

Nota gramatical Rosalinda uses two *vosotros* commands when she is talking with Carmela and Lola: *esperad* ("wait") and *venid* ("come"). You will hear this verb form often if you go to Spain.

For: More on *¿Eres tú, María?*
Visit: www.phschool.com
Web Code: jcd-0507

Chapter Review

Repaso del capítulo

Vocabulario y gramática

To prepare for the test, check to see if you . . .

- know the new vocabulary and grammar
- can perform the tasks on p. 343

to talk about shopping

buscar	to look for
comprar	to buy
el dependiente, la dependienta	salesperson
¿En qué puedo servirle?	How can I help you?
entrar	to enter
la tienda	store
la tienda de ropa	clothing store

to talk about clothing

el abrigo	coat
la blusa	blouse
las botas	boots
los calcetines	socks
la camisa	shirt
la camiseta	T-shirt
la chaqueta	jacket
la falda	skirt
la gorra	cap
los jeans	jeans
los pantalones	pants
los pantalones cortos	shorts
la sudadera	sweatshirt
el suéter	sweater
el traje	suit
el traje de baño	swimsuit
el vestido	dress
los zapatos	shoes
¿Cómo me / te queda(n)?	How does it (do they) fit (me / you)?
Me / te queda(n) bien / mal.	It fits (They fit) me / you well / poorly.
llevar	to wear
nuevo, -a	new

other useful words

quizás	maybe
Perdón.	Excuse me.
¡Vamos!	Let's go!

For *Vocabulario adicional,* see pp. 472–473.

to talk about prices

¿Cuánto cuesta(n) . . . ?	How much does (do) . . . cost?
costar *(o → ue)*	to cost
el precio	price
tanto	so much
doscientos, -as	two hundred
trescientos, -as	three hundred
cuatrocientos, -as	four hundred
quinientos, -as	five hundred
seiscientos, -as	six hundred
setecientos, -as	seven hundred
ochocientos, -as	eight hundred
novecientos, -as	nine hundred
mil	a thousand

to indicate if someone is correct

tener razón	to be correct

to indicate specific items

los / las dos	both
este, esta	this
estos, estas	these
ese, esa	that
esos, esas	those

pensar *to think, to plan*

pienso	**pensamos**
piensas	**pensáis**
piensa	**piensan**

preferir *to prefer*

prefiero	**preferimos**
prefieres	**preferís**
prefiere	**prefieren**

querer *to want*

quiero	**queremos**
quieres	**queréis**
quiere	**quieren**

Más práctica

Practice Workbook Puzzle 7A-8

Practice Workbook Organizer 7A-9

For: Test preparation
Visit: www.phschool.com
Web Code: jcd-0706

Preparación para el examen

On the exam you will be asked to . . .	Here are practice tasks similar to those you will find on the exam . . .	If you need review . . .
 **1 Escuchar** Listen and understand why people are returning clothing items	Listen as people explain to the clerk in a department store why they are returning or exchanging clothing they received as gifts. Try to decide if the reason is: a) it doesn't fit well; b) it's the wrong color or style; c) it's too expensive; d) they just didn't like it.	**pp. 322–325** *A primera vista* **p. 326** Actividad 5 **p. 328** Actividad 10 **p. 329** Actividad 11 **p. 332** Actividad 17
 **2 Hablar** Describe what you are planning to buy with gift certificates from your favorite clothing store	You got gift certificates from your favorite clothing store for your birthday. Describe at least four items you would like to buy. You could say something like: *Me gustaría comprar un suéter rojo. Prefiero esos suéteres que me quedan grandes.*	**pp. 322–325** *A primera vista* **p. 327** Actividad 6 **p. 328** Actividad 9 **p. 329** Actividad 12 **p. 330** Actividad 13 **p. 331** Actividad 15 **p. 334** Actividad 20 **p. 339** *Presentación oral*
 **3 Leer** Read and understand an online order form for a popular department store	You want to apply for a job at a department store. They need someone who understands Spanish to interpret the online orders that come in. Read the entries to see if you can tell them: a) the description of the item ordered; b) the color; c) the price.	**pp. 322–325** *A primera vista* **p. 328** Actividad 10 **p. 334** Actividad 20

	Artículo	Color	Precio
A.	sudadera	rojo/azul	355 pesos
B.	abrigo	negro	801 pesos
C.	falda	blanco/marrón/verde	506 pesos

On the exam you will be asked to . . .	Here are practice tasks similar to those you will find on the exam . . .	If you need review . . .
 **4 Escribir** Fill in an order form for specific clothing items you might purchase as gifts	Order the following items using the online order form: a) black boots for your sister, who is very little; b) a blue-and-white baseball cap for your brother, who would need a small size; c) three pairs of gray socks for your dad, who has VERY big feet!	**pp. 322–325** *A primera vista* **p. 327** Actividades 7–8 **p. 329** Actividad 12 **p. 331** Actividad 15

Artículo	Color	Tamaño

On the exam you will be asked to . . .	Here are practice tasks similar to those you will find on the exam . . .	If you need review . . .
 **5 Pensar** Demonstrate an understanding of cultural perspectives on crafts and clothing	Think about something you would consider to be American folk art that has been passed on from one generation to another. How would it be similar to or different from the *molas* made by the Kuna Indians?	**pp. 336–337** *Lectura* **p. 338** *La cultura en vivo*

Tema 7 • De compras

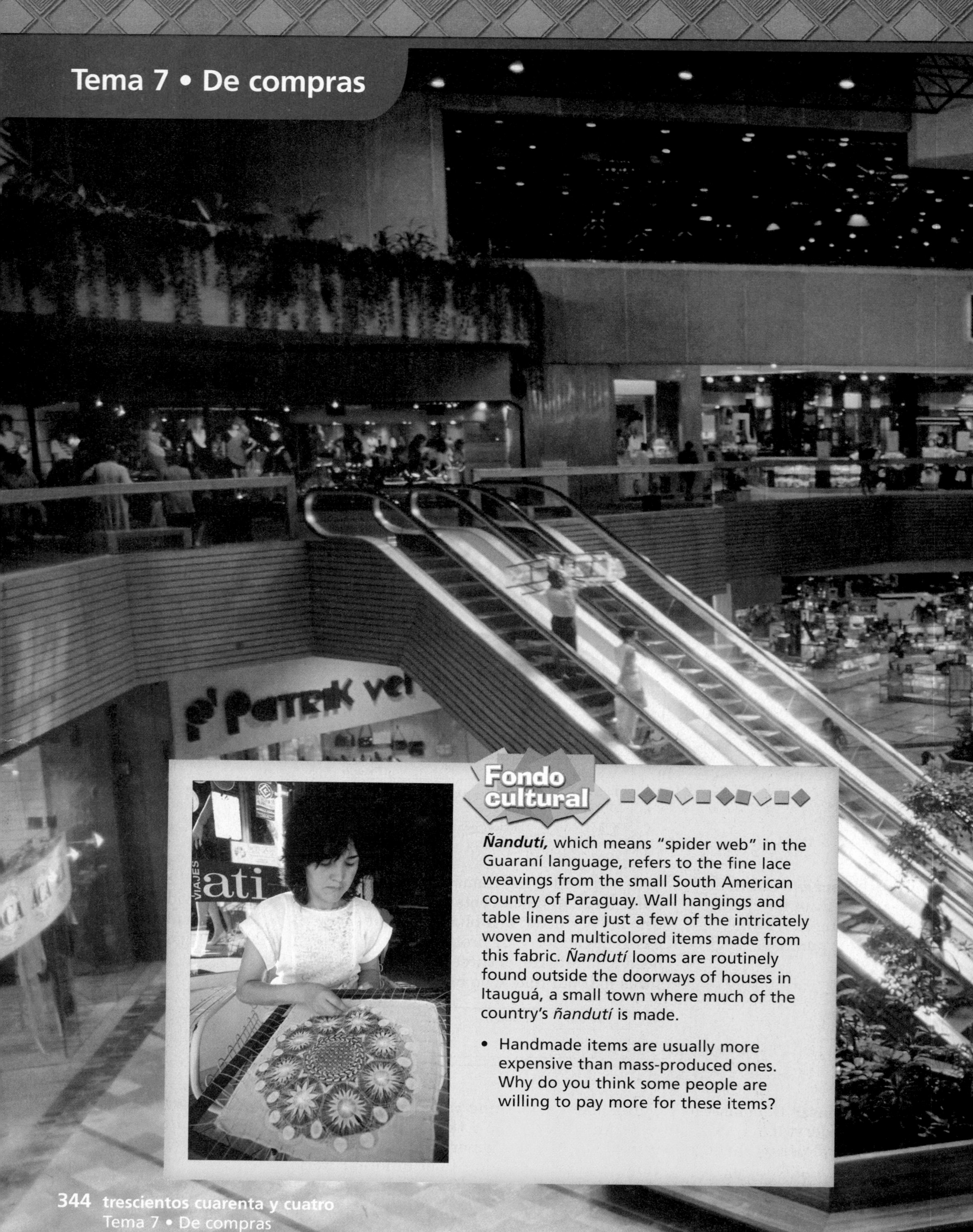

Fondo cultural

Ñandutí, which means "spider web" in the Guaraní language, refers to the fine lace weavings from the small South American country of Paraguay. Wall hangings and table linens are just a few of the intricately woven and multicolored items made from this fabric. *Ñandutí* looms are routinely found outside the doorways of houses in Itauguá, a small town where much of the country's *ñandutí* is made.

- Handmade items are usually more expensive than mass-produced ones. Why do you think some people are willing to pay more for these items?

Capítulo 7B

¡Qué regalo!

El centro comercial Perisur, Ciudad de México, México

Chapter Objectives

- **Talk about buying gifts**
- **Tell what happened in the past**
- **Use direct object pronouns**
- **Understand cultural perspectives on gift-giving**

Video Highlights

A primera vista: ***Un regalo especial***

GramActiva Videos: the preterite of *-ar* verbs; the preterite of verbs ending in *-car* and *-gar;* direct object pronouns

Videomisterio: ***¿Eres tú, María?*, Episodio 6**

Country Connection

As you learn about shopping and buying gifts, you will make connections to these countries and places:

Go Online PHSchool.com

For: Online Atlas
Visit: www.phschool.com
Web Code: jce-0002

A primera vista

Vocabulario y gramática en contexto

Objectives

Read, listen to, and understand information about
- **stores**
- **shopping for gifts and accessories**
- **things done in the past**

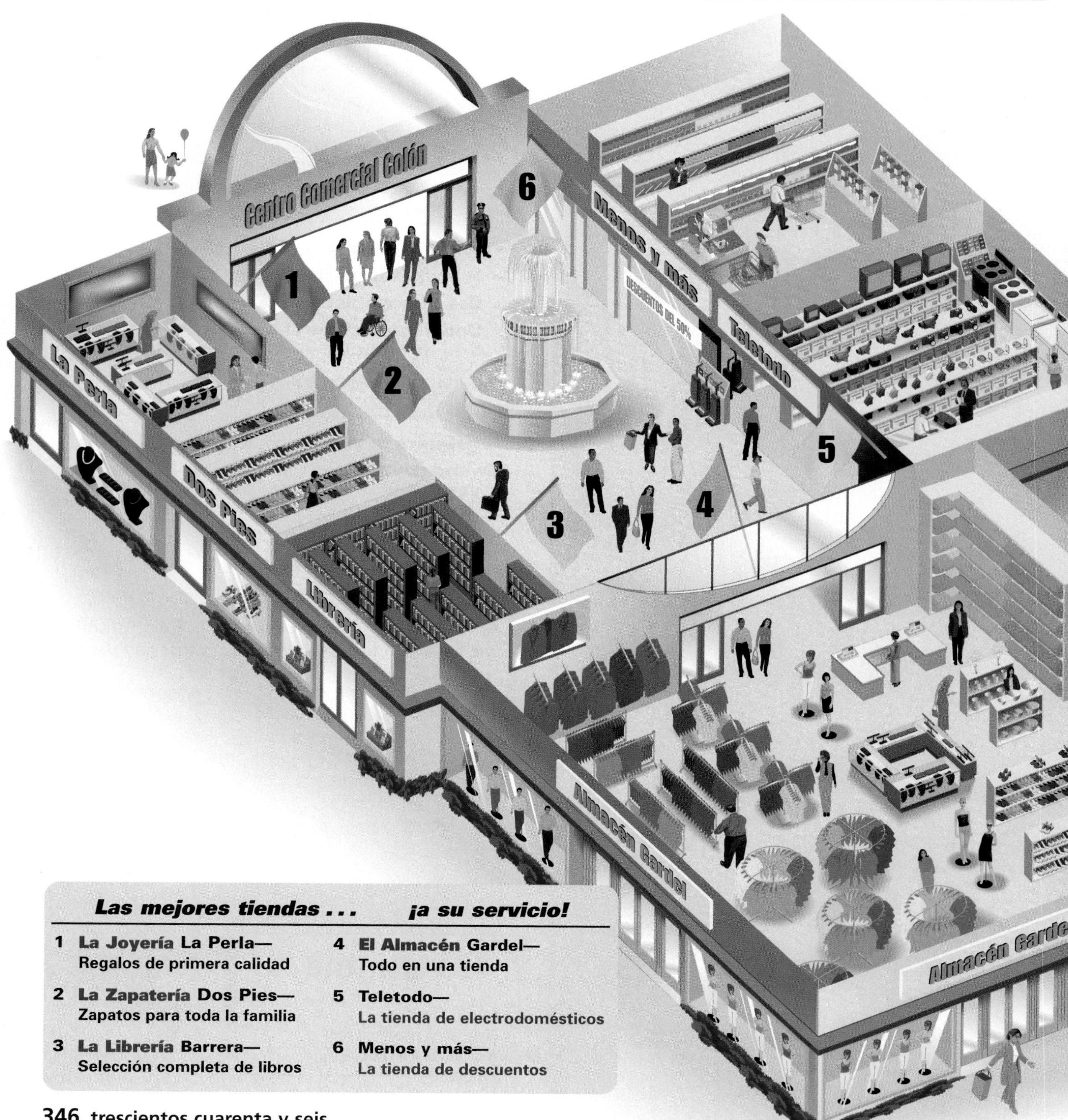

Las mejores tiendas . . . ¡a su servicio!

1. **La Joyería La Perla—** Regalos de primera calidad
2. **La Zapatería Dos Pies—** Zapatos para toda la familia
3. **La Librería Barrera—** Selección completa de libros
4. **El Almacén Gardel—** Todo en una tienda
5. **Teletodo—** La tienda de electrodomésticos
6. **Menos y más—** La tienda de descuentos

—¡**Mira!** Todo cuesta menos aquí. ¡Qué **barato!**

—¡No puede ser! Yo **compré** esta cartera en el Almacén Gardel **hace una semana** y **pagué** mucho más. **¡Uf!**

—Mi **novio** necesita un reloj pulsera.

—¿Por qué no **lo** compras? Cuesta 30 dólares. No es muy **caro.**

—¡Buena idea! Vamos a entrar.

Escuchar

¿Qué vas a hacer?

Estás de compras con tu hermana en un centro comercial. Tu hermana te está diciendo todo lo que quiere hacer, o lo que necesita en el centro comercial. Para cada cosa que dice, señala dónde en el centro comercial tiene que ir.

Escuchar

¿Dónde lo llevas?

Escucha cada una de estas frases. Señala la parte del cuerpo en la que una persona lleva cada artículo que se menciona.

Más práctica

Practice Workbook 7B-1, 7B-2

For: Vocabulary practice
Visit: www.phschool.com
Web Code: jcd-0711

Videohistoria

Un regalo especial

¿Qué pasó cuando Manolo compró un regalo para su tía? Lee la historia.

Strategy

Using visuals
Look at the pictures as you read to help you understand the story.
Can you guess what happens at the end of the story?

1 **Manolo:** Necesito comprar un regalo para mi tía. Mañana es su cumpleaños.

Claudia: ¿Qué compraste **el año pasado?**

Manolo: Compré un libro. Quizás otro libro.

Claudia: ¡Qué aburrido! Vamos al centro comercial . . .

5 *Claudia y Manolo están esperando el autobús. Tienen el regalo para la tía. A su derecha hay otra chica con un perro y otro regalo también.*

6 **Manolo:** ¡Vamos, Claudia! Aquí viene el autobús.

Claudia: Bueno . . . bueno.

7 **Manolo:** ¡Feliz cumpleaños, tía! Te compré este regalo **ayer.**

Tía: ¿Para mí? Ah, es muy bonito, pero . . . sabes que no tenemos perro.

Manolo: ¡No entiendo . . . !

2 Manolo: Aquí **venden** guantes, corbatas . . .

Claudia: ¿Corbatas para tu tía? ¿No tienes otra idea? Mira, aquí hay otras cosas . . .

3 Manolo: ¡Ah! Tengo una idea. **Anoche** compré un videojuego **en la Red** con mi computadora. ¿Quizás podemos comprar **software?**

Claudia: Para un amigo, sí, pero para tu tía, ¡no!

4 Claudia: Yo prefiero la joyería: una pulsera, un collar, un anillo. A ver. Señorita, ¿cuánto cuesta ese collar?

Dependienta: Cuesta 200 pesos con el descuento.

Claudia: ¡Qué barato! **La semana pasada** yo **pagué** 300 pesos **por** un collar.

8 Perro: ¡Me gusta mucho este collar nuevo! Me queda bien, ¿no crees?

Actividad 3 **Escribir/Hablar**

¿Comprendes?

1. ¿Por qué van de compras Manolo y Claudia?
2. ¿Qué compró Manolo para su tía el año pasado?
3. ¿Qué piensa Claudia de comprar otro libro?
4. A Claudia, ¿qué regalos le gustan más?
5. ¿Qué regalo compran y cuánto pagan?
6. ¿A la tía le gusta el collar? ¿Por qué?
7. Al fin *(At the end)*, ¿quién tiene el mejor collar?

Más práctica

Practice Workbook 7B-3, 7B-4

Go Online PHSchool.com

For: Vocabulary practice
Visit: www.phschool.com
Web Code: jcd-0712

Manos a la obra

Vocabulario y gramática en uso

Objectives

- Talk about stores and where they are located
- Ask and tell about shopping and buying
- Talk about the past
- Learn to use the preterite of *-ar* verbs and verbs that end in *-car* and *-gar*
- Use the direct object pronouns *lo, la, los,* and *las*

Actividad 4 **Escuchar/Escribir**

Escucha y escribe

1. Vas a escuchar lo que unos jóvenes dicen de algunas tiendas. En una hoja de papel escribe los números del 1 al 6. Escribe lo que escuchas.
2. Escribe frases para describir lo que crees que van a comprar los jóvenes en cada tienda.

Modelo

Creo que él (ella) va a comprar . . .

Actividad 5 **Escribir/Hablar**

En tu comunidad

1. Para cada tienda de la lista, piensa en una que está en tu comunidad. Escribe una frase para describir dos o más cosas que venden allí.

Modelo

una tienda de ropa
En la tienda de ropa Moda, venden camisas, pantalones y corbatas.

1. una librería
2. una tienda de descuentos
3. una tienda de electrodomésticos
4. una joyería
5. un almacén
6. una zapatería

2. Trabaja con otro(a) estudiante. Lee lo que venden en cada tienda sin decir qué tipo de tienda es. Tu compañero(a) debe identificar qué tipo de tienda es.

Modelo

A —*Venden camisas, pantalones y corbatas allí.*
B —*¿Es una tienda de ropa?*

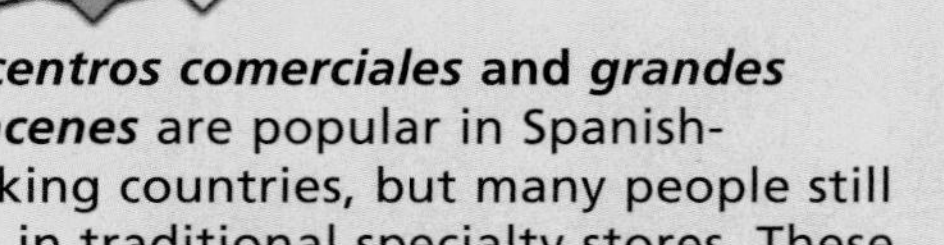

Fondo cultural

Los centros comerciales **and** ***grandes almacenes*** are popular in Spanish-speaking countries, but many people still shop in traditional specialty stores. These stores are often owned and operated by families, and customer loyalty is built over generations.

- Why do you think small specialty stores continue to survive when large, one-stop superstores and malls are very popular? Where do you prefer to shop? Why?

Tienda en España

   Dibujar/Escribir/Hablar

¿Dónde está el almacén La Galería?

Habla con otro(a) estudiante sobre dónde están las tiendas en un centro comercial.

1. Haz un dibujo de un centro comercial. En el dibujo incluye *(include)*:

   una zapatería, un almacén, un restaurante, una librería, una tienda de descuentos, una tienda de regalos, una tienda de ropa, una tienda de electrodomésticos, **¡Respuesta personal!**

2. Inventa un nombre para cada tienda y el restaurante. Escribe los nombres en tu dibujo.

3. Muestra *(Show)* tu dibujo a otro(a) estudiante. Haz seis preguntas sobre el centro comercial. Tu compañero(a) debe contestar.

Modelo

A —*¿Dónde está el restaurante La Mariposa?*
B —*Está detrás de la zapatería y la librería.*
A —*¿Por qué quieres ir allí?*
B —*Quiero comer con mi amigo.*

¿Recuerdas?

To tell the location of something, use *está . . . :*

a la derecha de
a la izquierda de
al lado de
cerca de
delante de
detrás de
lejos de

Para decir más . . .

entre between
enfrente de across from

vas / voy a . . .
quieres / quiero . . .
necesitas / necesito . . .
te / me gustaría . . .
piensas / pienso . . .
comer . . .
buscar . . .
comprar . . .
mirar . . .

   Hablar

Un buen regalo

Habla con otro(a) estudiante sobre los buenos regalos para diferentes personas.

Modelo

un señor que trabaja en una oficina

A —*¿Cuál es un buen* regalo para un señor que trabaja en una oficina?*
B —*Creo que una corbata es el mejor regalo para él.*
A —*¿Sabes dónde venden corbatas?*
B —*Por supuesto. En la tienda de ropa.*

Estudiante A

1. un(a) joven que no es puntual
2. un(a) joven que trabaja en un almacén
3. tu hermano(a) mayor (menor)
4. tu mejor amigo(a)
5. tu novio(a)
6. tu abuelo(a)

Estudiante B

¡Respuesta personal!

**Buen* is used in front of a masculine singular noun.

Hablar

¡Qué barato! ¡Qué caro!

El fin de semana pasado compraste muchas cosas. Ahora un(a) amigo(a) quiere saber dónde compraste todas las cosas y cuánto pagaste.

Modelo

A —*¿Dónde compraste tu suéter nuevo?*
B —*Lo compré en la tienda de ropa.*
A —*¿Cuánto pagaste?*
B —*Pagué 25 dólares.*
A —*¡Qué barato!*
o: *¡Uf! ¡Qué caro!*

Estudiante A

1. 
2.  
3. 
4. 
5. 
6. 

Estudiante B

¡Respuesta personal!

Leer/Escribir/Hablar

Vamos a la joyería

Lee el anuncio de una joyería en Tegucigalpa, Honduras, y luego contesta las preguntas.

1. ¿Qué venden en la tienda?
2. Según el anuncio, ¿las cosas que venden en la tienda cuestan mucho o poco?
3. Además de *(In addition to)* vender, ¿qué otros servicios hay en la joyería?
4. Pregunta a dos personas diferentes:
   - ¿Qué te gustaría comprar en una joyería?
   - ¿Qué joyas tienes?

Strategy

Using cognates and context clues

Try to figure out the meanings of unknown words by looking for cognates or by seeing how other words are used in the sentence.

- Can you guess the meanings of *bajos, diamantes, piedras preciosas, baterías,* and *arreglos* in this ad?

JOYERÍA HERMANOS SILVA

Vendemos relojes variados y todo tipo de joyas para toda ocasión

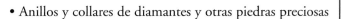

- Anillos y collares de diamantes y otras piedras preciosas
- Baterías de reloj, incluyendo instalación
- Hacemos reparaciones y joyas nuevas de su oro* viejo
- Reparación de cadenas y arreglos de pulseras

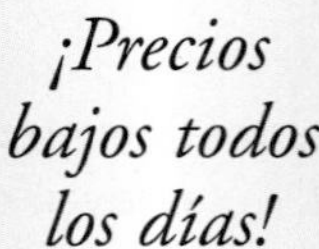

¡Precios bajos todos los días!
MENCIONE ESTE ANUNCIO Y RECIBA UN DESCUENTO DEL 10%

Abierto lunes a sábado de 10:00 hs. a 18:00 hs.

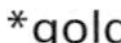

Exploración del lenguaje

Nouns that end in *-ería*

The Spanish word ending, or suffix, *-ería* usually indicates a place where something is sold, made, or repaired. This suffix is added to a form of the word that names the specialty item. For example, if you know that *una joya* is a piece of jewelry, you understand that you can buy jewelry at *la joyería*.

Try it out! You will often see these signs over stores. Tell what each one sells.

heladería	librería	pastelería
papelería	panadería	zapatería

Modelo

joyería
En la joyería venden joyas como anillos, pulseras y collares.

Venden flores para todas las ocasiones en esta florería en Argentina.

Esta joyería vende pulseras, anillos y collares.

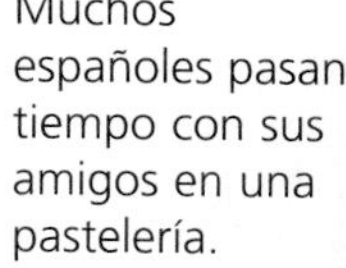

Muchos españoles pasan tiempo con sus amigos en una pastelería.

Muchos mexicanos compran tortillas frescas en una tortillería cerca de su casa.

Actividad 10 **Escribir/Hablar**

Y tú, ¿qué dices?

1. A qué tiendas vas de compras? ¿Qué te gusta comprar?
2. ¿Para quiénes compras regalos? ¿Qué tipo de regalos compras?
3. ¿Qué regalo compraste recientemente? ¿Cuándo y dónde compraste el regalo? ¿Pagaste mucho o poco dinero?

Gramática

The preterite of *-ar* verbs

To talk about actions that were completed in the past, you use the preterite tense. To form the preterite tense of a regular *-ar* verb, add the preterite endings to the stem of the verb. Here are the preterite forms of *comprar:*

(yo)	compr**é**	(nosotros) (nosotras)	compr**amos**
(tú)	compr**aste**	(vosotros) (vosotras)	compr**asteis**
Ud. (él) (ella)	compr**ó**	Uds. (ellos) (ellas)	compr**aron**

Notice the accent marks on the endings *-é* and *-ó*.

The *nosotros* form is the same in the present and preterite tenses. You will need to look for other context clues to tell which tense is intended.

¿Recuerdas?

In Spanish, the endings of verbs identify both who is performing the action (the subject) and when it is being performed (the tense).

GramActiva VIDEO

Need more help with the preterite of *-ar* verbs? Watch the **GramActiva** video.

Actividad 11 Gramática  Escuchar

¿El presente o el pasado?

En una hoja de papel escribe los números del 1 al 8. Vas a escuchar ocho frases que describen los quehaceres de una familia. ¿Ocurren los quehaceres en el presente o el pasado *(past)*? Escribe *presente* o *pasado*.

Actividad 12 Gramática Escribir/Hablar

El dinero es un buen regalo

Tus abuelos les regalaron *(gave)* a todos dinero y cada uno compró algo. Explica lo que compraron todos y cuándo compraron las cosas.

Modelo

Mi hermano ____ hace una semana.
Mi hermano compró un reloj pulsera hace una semana.

1.  Mi madre ____ ayer.
2.  Mis primos ____ anoche.
3.  Mi papá ____ el año pasado.
4. Tú ____ hace tres días.
5.  Mis tíos ____ hace un mes.
6.  Mi hermana y yo ____ ayer.

Gramática

Hablar/GramActiva

Juego

1. Tu profesor(a) va a enseñar a todos cómo deben señalar *(point to)* a diferentes personas *ella, nosotros, tú, ellos,* etc. Practica con tu profesor(a).

2. Trabaja en un grupo de cuatro. Una persona es líder y dice un infinitivo de la lista y un sujeto *(subject)*. Por ejemplo: *cantar / ella*. Los otros tienen que señalar a la persona, o a las personas, y decir el verbo en el pretérito: *ella cantó*. Continúa así con tres sujetos más y el mismo verbo. Después, cambia de *(change)* líderes.

¿Recuerdas?

arreglar	hablar
bailar	lavar
caminar	levantar
cantar	limpiar
cocinar	montar
cortar	nadar
dibujar	pasar
escuchar	patinar
esquiar	trabajar
estudiar	usar

Escribir/Hablar

Hace una semana

Usa el pretérito para escribir y hablar de tus actividades.

1. Copia la tabla en una hoja de papel. Usa los verbos de la lista de la Actividad 13 para escribir seis actividades que hiciste *(you did)* en el pasado. Indica cuándo hiciste cada actividad.

¿Qué?	¿Cuándo?
patiné	la semana pasada

2. Usa la información de la tabla para escribir frases sobre tus actividades. Incluye información para contestar *¿dónde?* y *¿con quién?* Después, lee tus frases a otro(a) estudiante y pregunta: *¿Y tú?* Tu compañero(a) debe contestar. Escribe la respuesta de tu compañero(a).

Modelo

A —*Patiné en el parque con mis amigos la semana pasada. ¿Y tú?*

B —*Monté en monopatín con mi hermana la semana pasada.*

3. Escribe tres frases con la información del paso 2.

Modelo

Patiné en el parque con mis amigos la semana pasada, pero Luisa montó en monopatín con su hermana.

Nota

To say when something happened, use *hace* + a time expression. It's like saying "ago."

- Compré la pulsera **hace un año.** *I bought the bracelet **a year ago.***

Más práctica

Practice Workbook 7B-5

For: Practice with regular preterite *-ar* verbs
Visit: www.phschool.com
Web Code: jcd-0713

Gramática

The preterite of verbs ending in *-car* and *-gar*

Verbs that end in *-car* and *-gar* have a spelling change in the *yo* form of the preterite.

buscar: c → qu yo bus***qué***

Silvia y Rosa bus***caron*** aretes pero yo bus***qué*** un collar.

pagar: g → gu yo pa***gué***

¿Cuánto pa***gaste*** por tu cadena? Pa***gué*** 13 dólares.

Verbs such as *jugar* that have a stem change in the present tense do not have a stem change in the preterite.

El sábado pasado **jugué** al tenis.
Mis hermanos **jugaron** al básquetbol.

¿Recuerdas?

You know these verbs that end in *-car* and *-gar:*

buscar	**practicar**
jugar	**sacar**
pagar	**tocar**

GramActiva VIDEO

Need more help with the preterite of verbs ending in *-car* and *-gar*? Watch the **GramActiva** video.

Actividad 15 Gramática  Escribir/Leer

El viernes pasado

El viernes pasado Juan invitó a unos amigos a su casa. Completa la descripción de sus actividades con la forma apropiada del pretérito de los verbos *jugar, pagar, sacar* y *tocar.*

El viernes pasado mis amigos pasaron tiempo conmigo en mi casa. Tomás y Fernando __1.__ videojuegos en mi dormitorio pero yo no __2.__ con ellos. Yo __3.__ la guitarra en la sala y todos cantamos. Jorge __4.__ el piano un poco también. Después de cantar, nosotros __5.__ al vóleibol. Mi amiga Ana __6.__ fotos de nosotros. ¡Qué graciosas son las fotos! A las nueve fuimos por pizza y ¡mis padres __7.__ la cuenta! ¡Qué bueno porque nunca tengo mucho dinero! Yo __8.__ fotos de todos mis amigos en la pizzería. ¡Qué bien lo pasamos nosotros!

Fondo cultural

El Museo del Oro in Bogotá, Colombia, houses over 33,000 objects of gold, emeralds, and other precious stones made by pre-Columbian cultures—cultures that existed long before the arrival of Columbus in the Americas. These ancient civilizations viewed gold as life-giving energy from the sun.

- What kinds of specialized museums have you visited in your community or in other locations? What did you learn from the types of objects that were included there?

El Museo del Oro en Bogotá, Colombia

Pronunciación

The letter combinations *gue, gui, que,* and *qui*

You know that when the letter *g* appears before the letters *a, o,* or *u,* it is pronounced like the *g* in "go," and that *g* before *e* and *i* is pronounced like the *h* in "he."

To keep the sound of the *g* in "go" before *e* and *i*, add the letter *u*: *gue, gui.* Don't pronounce the *u*. Listen to and say these words:

Guillermo	guitarra	espaguetis
guisantes	hamburguesa	Miguel

You also know that the letter *c* before *a, o,* or *u* is pronounced like the *c* in "cat," while the *c* before *e* and *i* is usually pronounced like the *s* in "Sally."

To keep the sound of the *c* in "cat" before *e* and *i*, words are spelled with *qu: que, qui.* The *u* is not pronounced. Listen to and say these words:

queso	quince	quieres	riquísimo
quehacer	quinientos	quisiera	querer

Try it out! Listen to the first verse of this traditional song from Puerto Rico entitled *"El coquí." El coquí* is a little tree frog found in Puerto Rico, named for the *coquí, coquí* sound that it makes at night. Say the verse.

El coquí, el coquí siempre canta.
Es muy suave el cantar del coquí.
Por las noches a veces me duermo
con el dulce cantar del coquí.
Coquí, coquí, coquí, quí, quí, quí,
coquí, coquí, coquí, quí, quí, quí.

Actividad 16 Escribir/Escuchar/Hablar/GramActiva

Juego

1. Escribe en una hoja de papel una o dos frases para indicar qué regalo compraste, para quién es, dónde lo compraste y cuánto pagaste.

Modelo

Compré un collar para mi novia en la Red. Pagué 45 dólares.

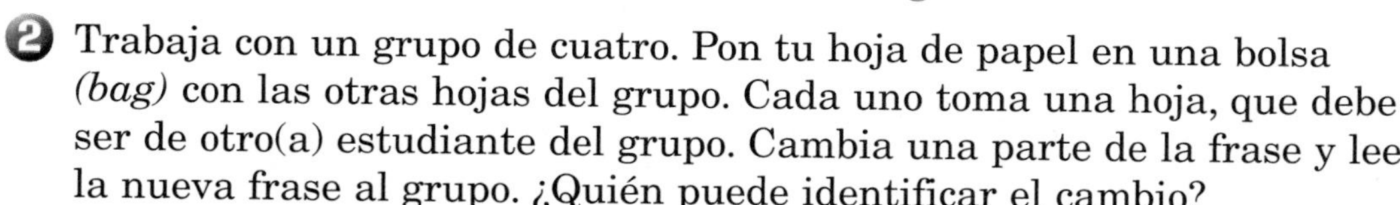

2. Trabaja con un grupo de cuatro. Pon tu hoja de papel en una bolsa *(bag)* con las otras hojas del grupo. Cada uno toma una hoja, que debe ser de otro(a) estudiante del grupo. Cambia una parte de la frase y lee la nueva frase al grupo. ¿Quién puede identificar el cambio?

Modelo

A —*Esta persona compró un collar para su madre en la Red. Pagó 45 dólares.*
B —*No es cierto. Compré un collar para mi novia.*

Gramática **Leer/Pensar/Escribir/Hablar**

Una lección de historia

Estudia la línea cronológica *(timeline)*, los eventos y el mapa. Luego usa el pretérito para emparejar estos eventos históricos con las personas en la línea cronológica.

Nota

Here is how you say dates:

- **1500** mil quinientos
- **1898** mil ochocientos noventa y ocho
- **2005** dos mil cinco

Modelo

1. *En 1492 Cristóbal Colón llegó* (arrived) *a la República Dominicana.*

Conexiones | **La historia**

Los eventos

a. fundar la misión de San Diego de Alcalá
b. pagar 15 millones de dólares a México según el Tratado de Guadalupe Hidalgo
c. empezar la construcción del canal de Panamá
d. explorar la Florida
e. ayudar a Cuba y Puerto Rico a declarar su independencia de España
f. buscar las siete ciudades de Cibola en el suroeste de los Estados Unidos
g. llegar a la República Dominicana

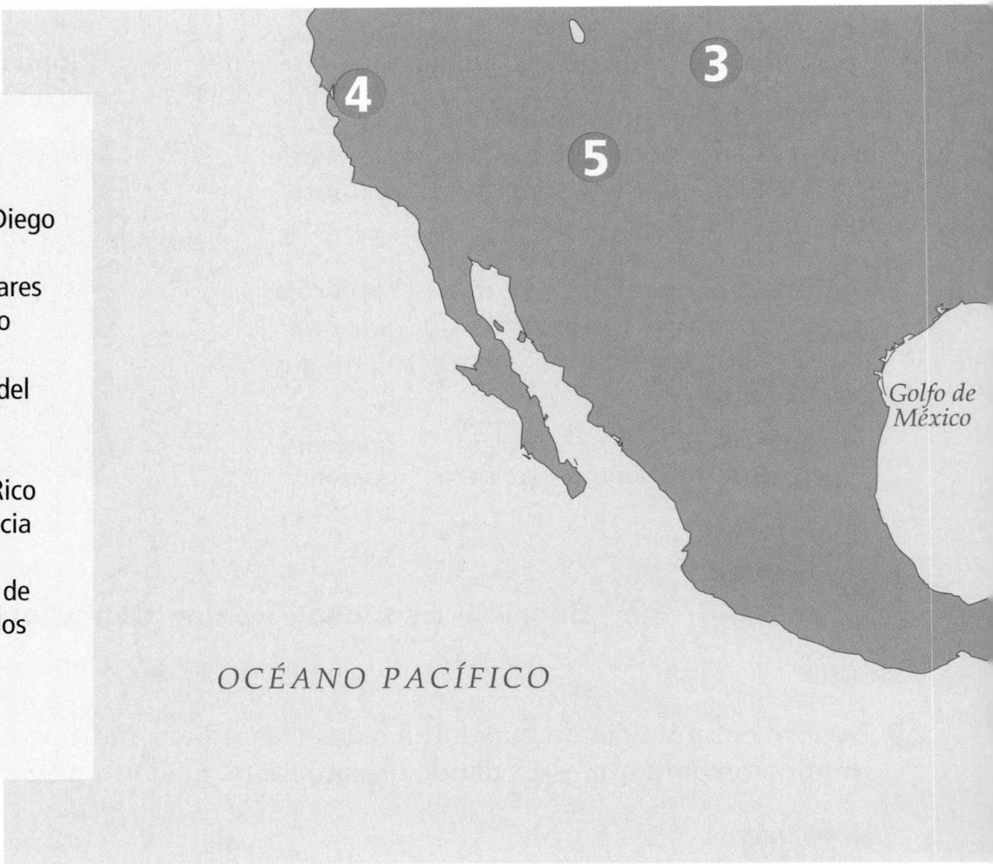

1500 — 1600 — 1700

1492 — **1.** Cristóbal Colón

1513 — **2.** Juan Ponce de León

1540 — **3.** Francisco Vázquez de Coronado

1769 — **4.** Fray Junípero Serra

El edificio más antiguo de los Estados Unidos está en San Agustín, en la Florida.

La misión de San Diego de Alcalá, fundada en 1769

Fray Junípero Serra

OCÉANO ATLÁNTICO

Mar Caribe

1848
5. El presidente James K. Polk y los Estados Unidos

1900

1898
6. El presidente William McKinley y los Estados Unidos

1904
7. El presidente Theodore Roosevelt y los Estados Unidos

Actividad 18 **Escribir/Hablar**

Y tú, ¿qué dices?

1. ¿Qué deportes practicaste el año pasado?
2. ¿Jugaste algún partido de tenis o de fútbol el mes pasado? ¿Cómo jugaste?
3. ¿Tocaste un instrumento musical ayer? ¿Cuál? Si no, ¿te gustaría saber tocar algún instrumento? ¿Cuál?
4. ¿Sacaste fotos durante tus vacaciones? Si no, ¿quién las sacó? ¿De qué?
5. Para el cumpleaños de tu mejor amigo(a), ¿qué compraste? ¿Cuánto pagaste?

Más práctica

Practice Workbook 7B-6

For: Practice with preterite verbs with *-car, -gar*
Visit: www.phschool.com
Web Code: jcd-0714

Gramática

Direct object pronouns

A direct object tells who or what receives the action of the verb.

Busco **una cadena.**

Compré **unos guantes.**

To avoid repeating a direct object noun, you can replace it with a direct object pronoun.

¿Dónde compraste **tus aretes?**
*Where did you buy **your earrings**?*

Los compré en la joyería Sánchez.
*I bought **them** at Sánchez Jewelry.*

	SINGULAR	PLURAL
M.	**lo** *it*	**los** *them*
F.	**la** *it*	**las** *them*

Direct object pronouns agree in gender and number with the nouns they replace.

¿Tienes **mi pulsera?** No, no **la** tengo.

¿Tienes **mis anillos?** No, no **los** tengo.

A direct object noun *follows* the conjugated verb. A direct object pronoun comes *before* the conjugated verb.

When an infinitive follows a conjugated verb, the direct object pronoun can either be placed before the conjugated verb or be attached to the infinitive.

¿Quieres comprar **el llavero?**

Sí, **lo** quiero comprar.

o: Sí, quiero comprar**lo.**

GramActiva VIDEO

For more help with direct object pronouns watch the **GramActiva** video.

Las compré.

Actividad 19

Gramática **Escribir**

¡No compraron nada!

Ayer muchas personas fueron *(went)* al centro comercial y miraron muchas cosas pero ¡no compraron nada! Escribe lo que no compraron.

Modelo

Carlos  

Ayer Carlos miró unas carteras pero no las compró.

1. Juanita 
2. los novios 
3. tú 
4. nosotros 
5. el señor Miró 
6. yo 

También se dice . . .

el anillo = la sortija *(muchos países)*

los aretes = los pendientes *(España)*; los aros *(Argentina, Uruguay)*

la pulsera = el brazalete *(muchos países)*

el bolso = la cartera *(Argentina)*; la bolsa *(Chile, México)*

los anteojos de sol = las gafas de sol *(Argentina, España)*

la cartera = la billetera *(Argentina, Uruguay)*

20 Gramática **Leer/Pensar/Escribir**

¿Quién compró qué?

¿Te gusta ser detective? ¡Vamos a ver si puedes descubrir lo que compraron las personas, dónde compraron las cosas y cuánto costó cada cosa!

1 Lee las pistas *(clues)*. Luego copia la tabla en una hoja de papel y completa la tabla.

Las pistas

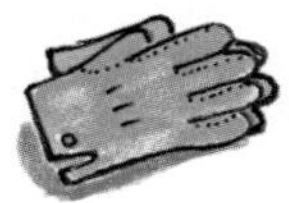

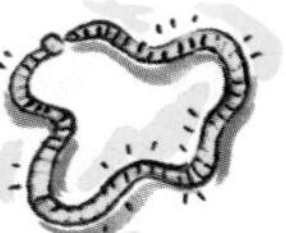

1. José gastó *(spent)* $35 en la joyería.
2. El software costó $45.
3. Paco no compró la novela.
4. Isabel fue *(went)* de compras a la tienda de electrodomésticos.
5. Luisa gastó $20 en la librería.
6. Los guantes costaron $25.
7. Paco fue de compras al almacén, pero no compró el collar.

Nombre	¿Qué compró?	¿Dónde lo compró?	¿Cuánto costó?

2 Usa la información de la tabla y escribe tus frases completas.

Modelo

José compró . . . . Los (Las / Lo / La) compró en . . . . Costaron (Costó) . . . .

21 Gramática   **Hablar**

¡Demasiadas preguntas!

Tu hermanito te hace muchas preguntas. Trabaja con otro(a) estudiante y contesta todas sus preguntas con mucha paciencia.

1. ¿Vas a comprar perritos calientes?
2. ¿Quieres leer este libro?
3. ¿Tienes que hacer la tarea?
4. ¿Quieres jugar videojuegos conmigo?
5. ¿Puedo comer este pastel?
6. ¿Vas a hacer mi cama?

Modelo

A —*¿Necesito llevar mis botas en el invierno?*
B —*Sí, necesitas llevarlas.*
o: *No, no necesitas llevarlas.*

Gramática  **Escribir/Hablar**

¿Cuándo los compró?

1. Escribe cuatro frases para indicar lo que compró una persona y cuándo lo compró.

Modelo

Mi padre compró unos guantes la semana pasada.

2. Lee tus frases a otro(a) estudiante sin decir cuándo la persona compró el artículo. Tu compañero(a) va a preguntar cuándo lo compró.

Modelo

A —*Mi padre compró unos guantes.*
B —*¿Cuándo los compró?*
A —*Los compró la semana pasada.*

Gramática  **Hablar/GramActiva**

Juego

Play this game in groups of five.

1. Each student in a group of five puts an object in the center of the group. The objects must be items for which you have learned the name in Spanish. One student turns around while another hides one of the objects.

2. The student who turned around now guesses who has the object. Correct first guesses are worth five points; correct second guesses are worth three. If the second guess is wrong, the student who has the object must say that he or she has it. All take turns being the "guesser."

Modelo

A —*Marta, ¿tienes el llavero?*
B —*No, no lo tengo.*
A —*Carlos, ¿tienes el llavero?*
C —*No, no lo tengo.*
A —*¿Quién tiene el llavero?*
D —*¡Yo lo tengo!*

Fondo cultural

The Zapotecs and other indigenous groups in the Mexican state of Oaxaca have their own languages and cultures. However, every July they all gather to celebrate the *Guelaguetza*, a Zapotec word that means "offering" or "gift." The *Guelaguetza* was first celebrated more than 3,000 years ago with music, dance, and food products. Today the festivities last two weeks and celebrate regional dances, music, costumes, and foods.

- What celebration in your culture is similar?

La fiesta de la Guelaguetza en Oaxaca, México

Hablar

Pero mamá, necesito . . .

Quieres ir de compras, pero primero debes hablar con tu madre o padre. Explica lo que necesitas y ¡pide *(ask for)* dinero! Tu madre o padre va a explicar por qué no necesitas comprar nada. Tu profesor(a) te dará el papel *(will assign the role)* que vas a hacer.

1. **Hijo(a):** Piensa en lo que quieres comprar y cómo vas a convencer *(convince)* a tu padre o madre.

   Padre (Madre): Tienes que decir a tu hijo(a) que no necesita lo que pide. Piensa en razones *(reasons)* para convencerle de esto.
2. Practica el drama con otro(a) estudiante.
3. Presenta el drama a tus compañeros. Ellos van a decidir quién tiene las mejores razones: los padres o los hijos.

El español en el mundo del trabajo

Large stores and mail-order companies employ buyers who search the world over for goods to offer their customers. Buyers often need to rely on their language skills when looking for products in places where English may not be spoken, and when negotiating prices.

- What stores in your community might employ buyers who travel the world (or the Internet) in search of products from Spanish-speaking countries?

Fondo cultural

Madrid's El Rastro is said to be the world's largest flea market. Located in one of the oldest sections of the city, *el Rastro* attracts thousands of visitors every Sunday of the year. Vendors line the streets with their stalls and offer everything from blue jeans to fine art. Bargain hunters as well as serious antique collectors bargain for the best prices.

- Have you ever gone to a flea market in your community or state? What kinds of things did you find there? How do you think they would differ from the things found in Madrid's *el Rastro?*

El Rastro en Madrid, España

Más práctica

Practice Workbook 7B-7

For: Practice with direct object pronouns
Visit: www.phschool.com
Web Code: jcd-0715

¡Adelante!

Objectives

- Read about shopping in four Hispanic communities in the United States
- Learn about differences between consumers in Chile and the United States
- Write a letter describing a gift that you bought
- Watch *¿Eres tú, María?*, Episodio 6

Lectura

¡De compras!

Lee este artículo de una revista. A Luisa le encanta ir de compras. ¿Qué puede comprar en cada ciudad?

Strategy

Using prior experience
Think about a trip that you took to another city. Did you go shopping? What items did you find that were unique to that city?

De COMPRA$
con Luisa la compradora

¡Me encanta ir de compras! Hay muchos lugares donde me gusta ir de compras en los vecindarios[1] hispanos. Siempre es una experiencia divertida. Hay cosas que uno puede comprar que son muy baratas y que no hay en otros lugares. Voy a hablar de mis aventuras por las comunidades hispanas de Nueva York, Miami, Los Ángeles y San Antonio.

En el Barrio de Nueva York, en la calle[2] 116, venden ropa, comida típica del Caribe, discos compactos, libros y mucho más. Allí compré una camiseta con la bandera de Puerto Rico. En junio siempre hay una celebración grande que se llama el Festival de la calle 116. ¡Me encanta Nueva York!

La Pequeña Habana y la calle Ocho son el corazón[3] de la comunidad cubana en Miami. Hay bodegas[4] que venden productos típicos cubanos: frijoles[5] negros y frutas tropicales como el maguey y la papaya. Allí compré pasta de guayaba, un dulce delicioso que los cubanos comen con queso blanco. ¡Qué rico!

[1]neighborhoods [2]street [3]heart
[4]grocery stores [5]beans

La calle 116 en Nueva York

Tienda en la Pequeña Habana, Miami

Pasta de guayaba

De compras en la calle Olvera, Los Ángeles

El Mercado en San Antonio, Texas

La calle Olvera es la calle más antigua[6] de la ciudad de Los Ángeles y allí uno puede ver la cultura mexicana. Hay muchos restaurantes y muchos lugares para comprar artesanías.[7] Me encanta ir de compras en las joyerías porque las joyas me fascinan. En las joyerías de la calle Olvera, venden joyas de plata:[8] aretes, collares, anillos y mucho más. En una joyería de allí compré una pulsera muy bonita a un precio muy bajo.

¡Ahora vamos a hablar de San Antonio! ¡Qué compras! En esta ciudad bonita de Texas, hay tiendas de artesanías mexicanas que son fabulosas. Mis favoritas están en el Mercado o como dicen en inglés, *Market Square.* Allí compré una piñata para mi hermano, una blusa bordada[9] para mi madre, una cartera para mi padre y un sarape[10] para decorar mi dormitorio... ¡y no pagué mucho!

[6]oldest [7]handicrafts [8]silver [9]embroidered [10]shawl; blanket

¿Comprendes?

1. De los cuatro lugares en *¡De compras!*, ¿adónde debe ir cada persona?

   Ana: Me gustaría comprar algo de Puerto Rico.

   Lorenzo: A mí me fascinan las artesanías mexicanas.

   Miguel: ¿Mi almuerzo favorito? El sándwich cubano.
2. ¿Qué compró Luisa en cada lugar?

For: Internet link activity
Visit: www.phschool.com
Web Code: jcd-0716

Las artesanías Handicrafts from Puerto Rico, Mexico, and other Spanish-speaking countries have been popular for years among tourists looking for gift ideas. Now these handicrafts are receiving recognition as museum quality artwork. At the Mexican Fine Arts Center Museum in the Pilsen neighborhood of Chicago, visitors can see permanent collections of paintings, weavings, sculpture, pottery, and silver jewelry from all over Mexico. Other types of handmade items are for sale in the museum's gift shop.

- Do you think that handicrafts should be displayed in museums along with fine art? Why or why not?

Una caja pintada de El Salvador

¿Por qué vas al centro comercial?

Why do people go to the mall? Note the differences between consumers in Chile and the United States.

In the United States many people go to the mall to see what merchandise is available and to spend time. In Chile, many people go to the mall because they want to make a specific purchase. They decide where to go according to the merchandise they need to buy.

For many in the United States, going to the mall is more than going shopping. The mall offers an opportunity to eat and to spend time with friends. For 50% of United States consumers the atmosphere of a mall is very important. Only 13% of Chilean consumers think that atmosphere is important.

Although their motivation for going to the mall is different, 80% of both Chilean and United States consumers make a purchase once they are in the stores.

Check it out! Interview at least three people your age and at least three adults that you know and find out what their main reasons for going to a mall are, how they decide which mall to go to, and if they usually make a purchase while at the mall. Compare what you find out with the results above for shoppers in the United States and Chile.

Think about it! Why might shoppers in the United States consider the mall atmosphere an important factor in their decision about where to shop? Given what you have read about the reasons Chileans go shopping, what do you think a store clerk in a mall in Chile might expect you to do if you entered his or her store? How might a Chilean exchange student feel if he or she went to the mall with you and your friends?

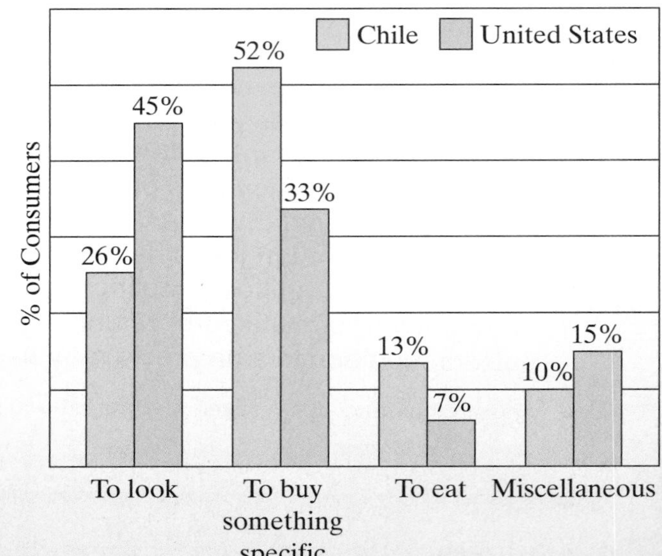

En el centro comercial Galerías Pacífico en Buenos Aires, Argentina

Presentación escrita

Un regalo para mi . . .

Task

You recently bought a gift for a member of your family. Write a letter to a cousin or other relative about the gift so that he or she will not buy the same item.

1. **Prewrite** Amember of your family is celebrating a special birthday. Think about the gift you bought. Answer the following questions to help organize your thoughts.
   - ¿Para quién es el regalo?
   - ¿Qué compraste?
   - ¿Dónde compraste el regalo?
   - ¿Por qué compraste ese regalo?
   - ¿Cuánto pagaste por el regalo?
   - ¿Cuándo es la fiesta de cumpleaños?
2. **Draft** U se the answers to the questions in Step 1 to help you write a first draft of your letter. You may want to begin your letter with *Querido(a)* . . . or *Hola* . . . , and close it with *Tu primo(a)* . . . or *Saludos,* or *Hasta pronto.*
3. **Revise** Read the letter and check spelling, vocabulary choice, verb forms, and agreement. Share the letter with your partner, who will check the following:
   - Is the letter easy to read and understand?
   - Does it provide all the necessary information?
   - Did you use appropriate letter form?
   - Are there any errors?
4. **Publish** Rewrite the letter, making any necessary changes or additions. Share your letter with your teacher. You may also want to add it to your portfolio.
5. **Evaluation** Your teacher may give you a rubric that will be used to grade the letter. You may be evaluated on:
   - how easy the letter is to understand
   - how much information is included about the gift
   - how appropriate the greeting and closing are
   - the accuracy of the use of the preterite

Strategy

Organizing information
Thinking about the correct format and necessary information beforehand will help you write a better letter.

Querido Mauricio,

Compré un reloj pulsera para el abuelito. Lo compré en el almacén Génova que está en el centro comercial Plaza del Río. No pagué mucho por él. Creo que al abuelito le va a gustar. Voy a ver a toda la familia el dos de octubre para la fiesta de cumpleaños del abuelito.

Tu primo,

Luis

Videomisterio

¿Eres tú, María?

Episodio 6

Antes de ver el video

Resumen del episodio

Lola llega a su oficina y hay un recado de Pedro Requena. Él viene a hablar con ella sobre su abuela, doña Gracia. Necesita un detective privado y quiere la ayuda de Lola y Paco. Pedro explica que su abuela es una mujer muy rica y que tiene joyas preciosas. Pero hay un problema. Las joyas de doña Gracia no están en el piso. Pedro cree que un ladrón robó las joyas. Pero, ¿cómo sabe el ladrón que hay joyas en el piso de doña Gracia?

"Por favor, ¿por qué no me tuteas?"

Nota cultural Lola quotes Pedro a price for her agency's services in euros. The euro is the currency in Spain and many other countries in Europe that are part of the European Union.

Nota cultural In Spain, it is customary for adults to speak to new acquaintances using the formal *Ud.* In most cases, the other person will then invite you to address them informally using the *tú* form. This is called *tutear.* In this scene, Pedro invites Lola to speak to him informally. When you visit Spain, you should address new adult acquaintances in the *Ud.* form and wait to be invited to *tutear.*

Palabras para comprender

un recado a message
una cita an appointment
Acabo de venir del hospital. I just came from the hospital.
Vi a su abuela. I saw your grandmother.
necesito saber . . . I need to know . . .
el ladrón robó the burglar stole
nosotros cobramos we charge

"Mi abuela es una mujer rica. Tiene dinero y joyas de valor. Son de la familia."

"María va a recibir todo el dinero, todas las joyas, todo de mi abuela."

"Pedro, vamos a buscar las joyas."

Después de ver el video

¿Comprendes?

Termina las frases con la palabra más apropiada del recuadro.

fotos	recado
joyas	dinero
sobrina	abuela
teléfono	nieto

1. Lola, hay un _____ para ti de un tal Pedro Reteña, Resqueña o Retena. Algo así.
2. El _____ de doña Gracia viene a la una y media.
3. ¡Qué bueno! Un cliente con _____.
4. Acabo de venir del hospital. Vi a su _____.
5. Aquí tengo unas _____ de ella.
6. Mira, las _____ no están en el piso.
7. Aquí está el número de _____: 318 18 02.

For: More on *¿Eres tú, María?*
Visit: www.phschool.com
Web Code: jcd-0507

Chapter Review

Repaso del capítulo

Vocabulario y gramática

To prepare for the test, check to see if you . . .
- know the new vocabulary and grammar
- can perform the tasks on p. 371

to talk about places where you shop

el almacén *pl.* **los almacenes**	department store
en la Red	online
la joyería	jewelry store
la librería	bookstore
la tienda de descuentos	discount store
la tienda de electrodomésticos	household appliance store
la zapatería	shoe store

to talk about gifts you might buy

el anillo	ring
los anteojos de sol	sunglasses
los aretes	earrings
el bolso	purse
la cadena	chain
la cartera	wallet
el collar	necklace
la corbata	tie
los guantes	gloves
el llavero	key chain
el perfume	perfume
la pulsera	bracelet
el reloj pulsera	watch
el software	software

to talk about who might receive a gift

el novio	boyfriend
la novia	girlfriend

to talk about buying or selling

barato, -a	inexpensive, cheap
caro, -a	expensive
mirar	to look (at)
pagar (por)	to pay (for)
vender	to sell

to talk about time in the past

anoche	last night
el año pasado	last year
ayer	yesterday
hace + *time expression*	ago
la semana pasada	last week

other useful expressions

¡Uf!	Ugh! Yuck!

preterite of regular *-ar* verbs

compré	**compramos**
compraste	**comprasteis**
compró	**compraron**

preterite of *-car* and *-gar* verbs

These verbs have a spelling change in the *yo* form of the preterite.

buscar *c → qu*	yo busqué
pagar *g → gu*	yo pagué
jugar *g → gu*	yo jugué

direct object pronouns

	SINGULAR	PLURAL
M.	**lo** *it*	**los** *them*
F.	**la** *it*	**las** *them*

For *Vocabulario adicional,* see pp. 472–473.

Más práctica

Practice Workbook Puzzle 7B-8
Practice Workbook Organizer 7B-9

Go Online
PHSchool.com
For: Test preparation
Visit: www.phschool.com
Web Code: jcd-0717

Preparación para el examen

On the exam you will be asked to . . .	Here are practice tasks similar to those you will find on the exam . . .	If you need review . . .
 **1 Escuchar** Listen as someone describes what she bought as a gift and where she bought it	As a teenager tells what she bought for her friend's *quinceañera,* see if you can tell: a) what she bought; b) where she bought it; c) how much she paid for it.	**pp. 346–349** *A primera vista* **p. 347** Actividad 1 **p. 350** Actividad 4
 **2 Hablar** Exchange opinions about whether certain items are expensive or inexpensive	Think about a gift you've bought. Tell your partner what you bought, for whom you bought it, and how much you paid. Then ask your partner whether he or she thinks the gift was expensive or inexpensive. Your partner will then share the same information and ask the same questions about a gift that he or she bought.	**p. 350** Actividad 5 **p. 351** Actividades 6–7 **p. 352** Actividad 8 **p. 354** Actividad 12
3 Leer Read and understand an online advertisement for a store you might find on the Internet	While surfing on the Internet, you find a Web site for a discount store in Mexico City. Can you list at least two advantages for customers who shop here?	**pp. 346–349** *A primera vista* **p. 352** Actividad 9
 **4 Escribir** Write a short explanation about some items that you have bought this school year with your own money	As an entry for your class journal, explain how you spent your money last month. Describe: a) at least two new clothing items or accessories you bought; b) where you bought the items; c) how much you paid for them.	**p. 354** Actividad 12 **p. 357** Actividad 16 **p. 360** Actividad 19 **p. 361** Actividad 20 **p. 362** Actividad 22 **p. 367** *Presentación escrita*
 **5 Pensar** Demonstrate an understanding of cultural perspectives regarding shopping	Think about what you do when you go to a shopping mall. Based on what you've learned in this chapter, would these be the same things that Chileans do? What similarities and differences would you expect to see in shopping malls and in attitudes of shoppers in both countries?	**p. 366** *Perspectivas del mundo hispano*

Tienda virtual de descuentos

Todos nuestros clientes reciben un descuento del 10%. Tenemos de todo—perfume para su novia, bolsos para su mamá, videojuegos para su hermano y software para Ud. Tenemos los mejores precios y descuentos en la Red. Si paga por algo en la Tienda virtual, va a recibir "ePesos." Puede usarlos en su próxima visita.

¡Viva Texas!

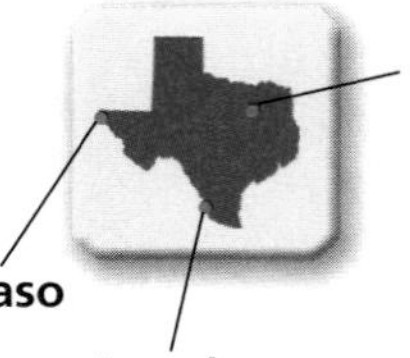

Dos artesanos de Texas

¿Dónde compras la ropa y los accesorios que llevas? Mucha gente los compra en un almacén o en una tienda grande. Pero, ¿qué haces si quieres comprar algo diferente, algo original? ¿Buscas diseños originales en tiendas más particulares o en la Red? Lee sobre estos dos artesanos de Texas que hacen y venden diseños únicos.

Claudette Elizondo

En 2001, Claudette Elizondo comenzó una compañía pequeña de joyería llamada Mexica Chica. Vende sus joyas en más de diez tiendas en Dallas y en algunas tiendas en Massachusetts. Todos los collares, pulseras y aretes están hechos a mano[1] según los diseños de Claudette.

Claudette vive en Dallas, pero es de una familia de rancheros de Laredo, Texas. Dice ella: "Ser de Texas me ayuda porque mis diseños combinan elementos mexicanos con elementos americanos. En Texas, la conexión entre las culturas es muy fuerte."

Claudette es de origen mexicano. Sus joyas son inspiradas por[2] la rica cultura mexicana. "Frida Kahlo [la artista mexicana] es mi inspiración. Diseño cosas que llevaría[3] ella," dice Claudette. Mexica Chica usa metales, piedras,[4] cuero[5] y otros materiales que reflejan los elementos naturales de México, como[6] las playas y las montañas.

[1] hand-made [2] inspired by [3] she would wear [4] stones [5] leather [6] such as

Pedro Muñoz

Pedro Muñoz es un artesano que hace el accesorio más famoso de Texas, las botas. En 1980, Muñoz comenzó Stallion Boot & Belt Co., una botería en El Paso. Todas las botas de Stallion están hechas a mano. Son muy artísticas y originales.

La tradición de hacer botas es muy fuerte en El Paso, una ciudad con conexiones históricas y culturales con su vecino[7] al sur, Juárez, México. Los artesanos que trabajan en Stallion son todos de Juárez. Muchos de los artesanos aprendieron[8] a hacer las botas de sus padres y abuelos. Las técnicas que usa Stallion no pueden ser imitadas por una máquina.[9] "Creo que las botas y los cinturones[10] son arte funcional," dice Pedro. "Yo invento los diseños con mis clientes."

Hacer una bota básica toma aproximadamente 15 horas. Los artesanos de Stallion hacen 60 pares de botas y 70–80 cinturones a la semana.

[7] neighbor [8] learned [9] machine [10] belts

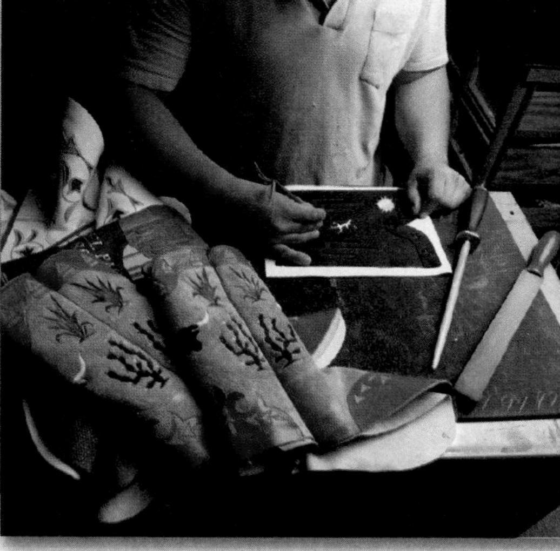

¿Comprendes?

1. ¿Qué hace y vende Claudette Elizondo?
2. ¿Es posible comprar los aretes de Claudette en muchos de los grandes almacenes de los Estados Unidos? ¿Por qué?
3. ¿Cuáles son las influencias de la cultura mexicana en el arte de Claudette?
4. ¿Por qué dice Pedro Muñoz que las botas y cinturones que él hace son "arte funcional"?
5. Pedro trabaja con sus clientes para diseñar las botas perfectas para ellos. Trabaja con un(a) compañero(a) y describe tus botas ideales. Menciona los colores y los diseños que prefieres y explica por qué estas botas te representan.

Conexiones

1. Según Pedro Muñoz, si él trabaja 6 horas al día, ¿cuántas botas puede hacer en 5 días?
2. Si la familia Castillo pide botas para los 6 miembros de su familia y si hay 5 trabajadores en Stallion que las van a hacer, ¿cuántas horas tiene que trabajar cada persona? Si todos trabajan 6 horas al día, ¿cuántos días necesitan trabajar?

Fondo cultural

View of Toledo is one of the most famous paintings by El Greco (the Greek). Born Doménikos Theotokópoulos in 1541 on the island of Crete, El Greco moved to Spain and settled in Toledo, a city south of Madrid. His *View of Toledo,* painted around 1597, was considered radical for its time because of its use of green, blue, and purple hues and its bold style. Instead of being realistic, the painting highlights the city's landmarks and its grandeur. El Greco's style has greatly influenced other painters.

- What would you highlight if you were painting your town or city?

Vista de Toledo (1597), El Greco

Oil on canvas.†Metropolitan Museum of Art, New York/Index/ Bridgeman Art Library, London/New York.

De vacaciones

Chapter Objectives

- Talk about things to do on vacation
- Describe places to visit while on vacation
- Talk about events in the past
- Understand cultural perspectives on travel and vacations

Video Highlights

A primera vista: ***¿Qué te pasó?***

GramActiva Videos: the preterite of *-er* and *-ir* verbs; the preterite of *ir;* the personal *a*

Videomisterio: ***¿Eres tú, María?***, Episodio 7

Country Connection

As you learn about travel and vacations, you will make connections to these countries and places:

Go Online
PHSchool.com
For: Online Atlas
Visit: www.phschool.com
Web Code: jce-0002

El Museo Guggenheim en Bilbao, España

A primera vista

Vocabulario y gramática en contexto

Objectives

Read, listen to, and understand information about
- **travel and vacations**
- **past events**

—**Dime,** ¿adónde **fuiste** el mes pasado?

—**Fui de vacaciones** con mis padres a **un lugar fantástico.**

—¿Qué lugar **visitaste?**

—Fui a Barcelona. Me gusta mucho **viajar** a otros **países como** México, España, Guatemala . . .

—**¿Qué hiciste?**

—Pues, fui al zoológico con mi familia.

—**¿Te gustó?** ¿Qué **viste?**

—**Fue** fantástico. **Vi** muchos **animales** como osos y monos y también muchas otras **atracciones.** También compré **unos recuerdos:** una camiseta, unos aretes y un llavero.

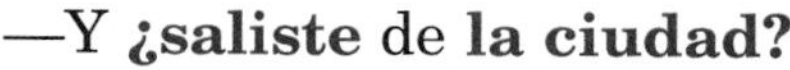

—Y **¿saliste** de **la ciudad?**

—¡Por supuesto! **Salí*** muy **temprano** para ir al mar. **Durante** el día **aprendí a** bucear. Fue muy divertido. **Regresamos** al **hotel** muy **tarde,** como a las diez de la noche.

*The verb *salir* has an irregular *yo* form in the present tense: *salgo*.

el avión

el barco

el tren

el autobús

—¿Cómo prefieres viajar?

—**En** avión.

Escuchar

El viaje de María Luisa

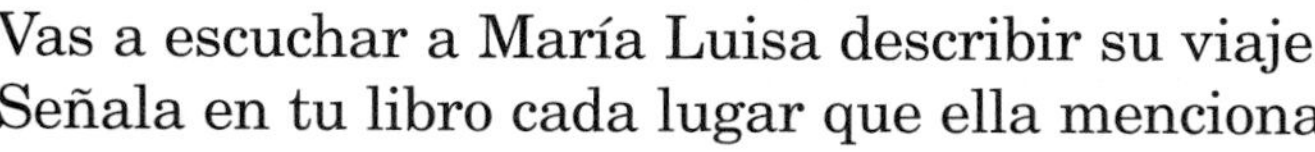

Vas a escuchar a María Luisa describir su viaje. Señala en tu libro cada lugar que ella menciona.

Más práctica

Practice Workbook 8A-1, 8A-2

For: Vocabulary practice
Visit: www.phschool.com
Web Code: jcd-0801

Escuchar

¿Qué piensas? ¿Sí o no?

Vas a escuchar diez frases. Si la frase es lógica, haz el gesto del pulgar hacia arriba *("thumbs-up" sign)*. Si es ilógica, haz el gesto del pulgar hacia abajo *("thumbs-down" sign)*.

Videohistoria

¿Qué te pasó?

¿Qué le pasó a Tomás durante su visita al parque nacional Sarapiquí en Costa Rica?

Strategy

Using visuals to make predictions
Before you read the story, look at the pictures to try to predict what will happen. After you finish reading, see how your predictions compared with what you read.

1 **Raúl:** Aquí están **los boletos** para el autobús.

Tomás: ¿Cuánto dura **el viaje?**

Gloria: El parque está a 82 kilómetros de San José. Es un viaje de hora y media.

5 **Gloria:** Va a ser una foto fantástica, Tomás. Un momento . . . un poco más a la izquierda.

Tomás: ¿Aquí?

Gloria: No, un poco más. Uno, dos . . .

Tomás: ¡Ay!

Raúl: Tomás, ¿dónde estás? ¿Estás bien?

6 **Gloria:** Lo siento, Tomás. ¿Quieres regresar a casa?

Raúl: ¿Quieres **descansar** un poco?

Tomás: No. Estoy bien. ¡Vamos a la catarata* La Paz!

*waterfall

7 **Tomás:** Quiero una foto de la catarata. ¡Es **tremenda, impresionante!** Uno puede estar muy cerca de ella.

Raúl: No, creo que estar un poco lejos de ella es mejor. Voy a ayudarte, Tomás.

Gloria: Un poco más hacia atrás* y a la derecha . . .

*towards the back

2 **Gloria:** Mira este mapa del **parque nacional.** Es mi parque favorito y lo llamamos "bosque lluvioso."* No hace ni frío ni calor, pero llueve mucho.

Tomás: Aquí hay un libro sobre los animales del parque.

*rain forest

3 **Gloria:** ¿Lo viste? Allí en **el árbol.**

Tomás: No, no lo vi. ¿Qué es?

Gloria: Es **un pájaro.** Es un tucán. Hay más de cuatrocientas especies de pájaros en el parque.

4 **Raúl:** Tomás, **¿qué te pasó?**

Tomás: ¡Hay agua en las palmas! Eh . . . ¡no es nada divertido!

Raúl: Pero, Tomás, es un bosque lluvioso y llueve todo el tiempo. Siempre hay agua en las palmas. Pero sólo es un poco de agua.

Gloria: Estás aprendiendo muchas cosas, ¿verdad?

8 **Mamá:** ¡Tomás! **¿Cómo lo pasaste?** ¿Qué te pasó?

Gloria: Pobre* Tomás . . . **fue un desastre.**

Tomás: No fue tan malo. **Me gustó.** Aprendí mucho y vi muchas cosas nuevas. ¡Pero hay mucha agua en el bosque lluvioso y en la catarata!

*Poor

Leer/Escribir

¿Comprendes?

1. Haz una lista de cinco cosas que aprendiste sobre el bosque lluvioso Sarapiquí.
2. ¿A quién se refiere cada frase: a Tomás, a Gloria o a Raúl?
   - **a.** Compró los boletos para el autobús.
   - **b.** Sacó fotos de los otros.
   - **c.** No vio el pájaro.
   - **d.** Sarapiquí es su parque favorito.
   - **e.** Ayudó a Tomás delante de la catarata La Paz.
   - **f.** Vio un libro sobre los animales del parque.
   - **g.** Decidió no descansar.
   - **h.** Cree que el viaje a Sarapiquí fue un desastre.

Más práctica

Practice Workbook 8A-3, 8A-4

Go Online PHSchool.com
For: Vocabulary practice
Visit: www.phschool.com
Web Code: jcd-0802

Manos a la obra

Vocabulario y gramática en uso

Objectives

- **Talk about vacations and trips**
- **Talk about places to visit and how to get there**
- **Learn the preterite tense of *-er* and *-ir* verbs and the preterite of *ir***
- **Learn to use the personal *a***

Escribir/Hablar

Una lista de actividades

1. ¿Qué actividades te gusta hacer cuando vas de vacaciones? ¿Qué actividades no te gusta hacer? En una hoja de papel, haz tres columnas y escribe *me gusta mucho, me gusta* y *no me gusta nada*. Debajo de cada expresión, escribe estas actividades en la columna apropiada.

ver . . .

visitar . . .

sacar fotos de . . .

ir a . . .

ir a . . .

comprar . . .

2. Usa tu lista de actividades y habla con otro(a) estudiante. Pregunta y contesta según el modelo. Haz por lo menos *(at least)* cuatro preguntas.

Modelo

A —*Cuando vas de vacaciones, ¿qué te gusta más: ver una obra de teatro o ir al zoológico?*
B —*Me gusta más ir al zoológico.*

Escuchar/Escribir

Escucha y escribe

Vas a escuchar a una persona describir su viaje a Puerto Rico. Uno de los lugares que visitó es El Yunque. En una hoja de papel escribe los números del 1 al 6 y escribe las frases que escuchas.

El Yunque, un parque nacional en Puerto Rico

Actividad 6 **Hablar**

¿Qué te gustaría hacer?

Habla con otro(a) estudiante sobre adónde les gustaría ir de vacaciones.

Modelo

A —*Dime, ¿te gustaría ir de vacaciones a una ciudad?*
B —*Sí, porque en una ciudad puedes ir de compras y comer en restaurantes fantásticos.*
o: *No, me gustaría más ir a un parque nacional porque puedes ir de cámping.*

Estudiante A

1. una ciudad
2. un parque nacional
3. un lago
4. el mar

Estudiante B

¡Respuesta personal!

Actividad 7 **Leer/Escribir**

El delta del río[1] Paraná

Lee la descripción del delta del río Paraná, a 30 kilómetros de Buenos Aires, y completa las frases con las palabras correctas de los recuadros. Después contesta las preguntas.

tren	ciudad	país	lugar

Al norte de la __1.__ de Buenos Aires, Argentina, está el delta del río Paraná, un laberinto de islas y canales con más de 2.500 kilómetros navegables. Es un __2.__ favorito de los habitantes de Buenos Aires para ir de excursión. Para ir de Buenos Aires al delta, muchas personas viajan en __3.__ hasta[2] el Tigre, un pueblo[3] pequeño.

descansar	regresar	pasear	montar

Aquí las personas pueden __4.__ en bote por los canales, __5.__ y tomar el sol en la orilla,[4] __6.__ a caballo o practicar el esquí acuático.

recuerdos	lagos	pájaros	árboles

El delta del Paraná, Argentina

También pueden comprar comida y __7.__ turísticos en los mercados.[5] Las personas siempre tienen sus cámaras en las excursiones al delta porque hay muchos tipos de animales y __8.__ que viven en los __9.__ muy altos.

- Para ti, ¿es el delta del río Paraná un buen lugar para ir de vacaciones? ¿Por qué?
- ¿Qué actividades te gustaría hacer en este lugar?

[1]river [2]as far as [3]town [4]riverbank [5]markets

   **Hablar**

Cómo puedes viajar

Mira los mapas al principio del libro. Dile a tu compañero(a) que te gustaría viajar de un lugar o país a otro. Tu compañero(a) debe decir cómo puedes viajar entre los dos lugares.

Modelo

A —*Me gustaría viajar de la República Dominicana a Puerto Rico.*
B —*Pues, entonces, puedes viajar en barco o en avión.*

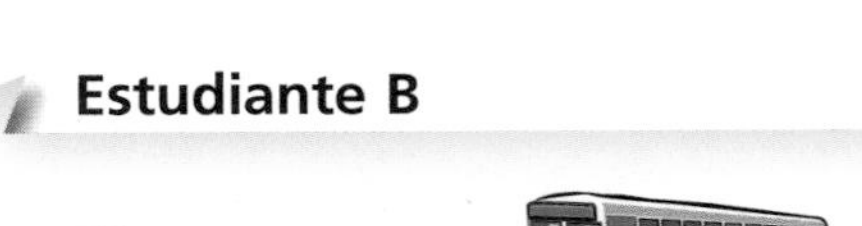

También se dice . . .

el autobús =
el camión *(México);*
el colectivo, el ómnibus *(Argentina);*
la guagua *(Puerto Rico, Cuba);*
el micro *(Bolivia, Perú, Chile)*

Pronunciación

Diphthongs

In Spanish, there are two groups of vowels: "strong" *(a, e* and *o)* and "weak" *(i* and *u).*

When a weak vowel is combined with any other vowel, the individual vowel sounds become blended to form a single sound called a diphthong *(un diptongo).* Listen to and say these words:

limpiar	baile	siete	seis	estadio	ciudad
fuimos	cuarto	juego	aire	piensas	autobús

When two strong vowels are together, each vowel is pronounced as a separate sound. Listen to and say these words:

teatro	museo	pasear	bucear
cereal	video	leer	zoológico
traer	idea	tarea	cumpleaños

If there is an accent mark over a weak vowel, it causes that letter to be pronounced as though it were a strong vowel. Listen to and say these words:

día	frío	tíos	zapatería
joyería	país	esquío	gustaría

Try it out! Listen to some of the lines of *"Cielito lindo,"* a song from Mexico that is very popular with mariachi bands. Can you identify the diphthongs in the lyrics? Try saying the words and then singing the song.

De la sierra morena,
cielito lindo, vienen bajando
un par de ojitos negros,
cielito lindo, de contrabando.
¡Ay, ay, ay, ay!
Canta y no llores,
porque cantando se alegran,
cielito lindo, los corazones.

Leer/Escribir/Hablar

¿Quieres aprender a bucear?

Lee el anuncio y contesta las preguntas.

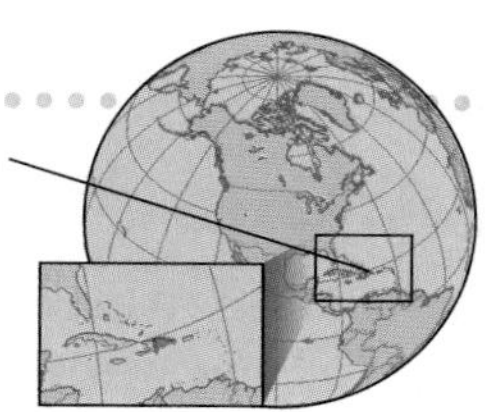

Escuela de buceo "Flor del mar"

Puerto Plata, República Dominicana

Cursos de buceo "Flor del mar"

¡Aprende a bucear en sólo tres cursos!
Ve peces impresionantes y otros animales del mar.
Practica un deporte interesante y divertido.
Pasa tiempo con amigos en un lugar fantástico.

Señales de buceo

Hay un lenguaje especial que permite a los buzos comunicarse en el agua con señales. En los cursos de buceo, puedes aprender estas señales. Así no vas a tener ningún problema practicando este deporte. Algunas de las señales más importantes son:

Si quieres información sobre un curso de buceo en la República Dominicana, comunícate al 555-19-19 con la Dra. María Elena Santos o al 555-02-28 con Marcos Morelos.

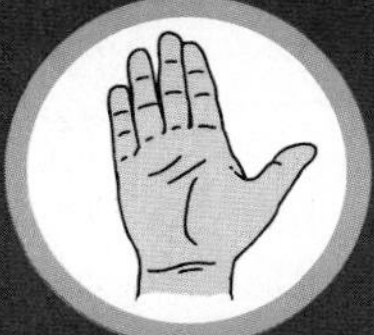
Alto

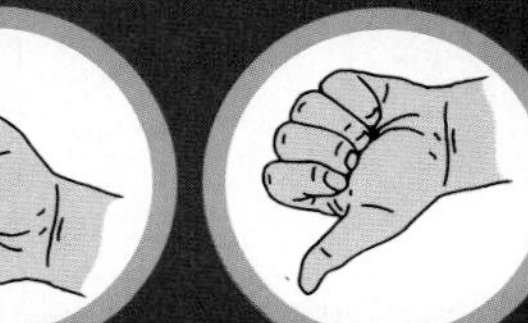
Ir hacia arriba

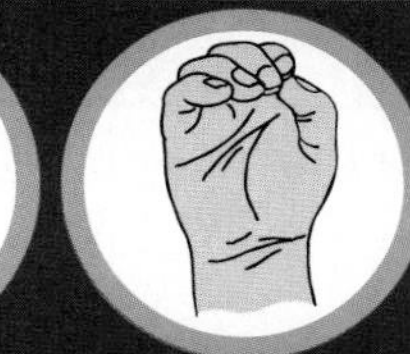
Ir hacia abajo

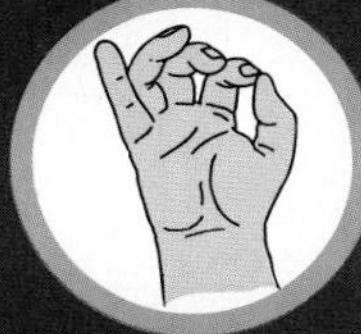
Preguntar si estás bien

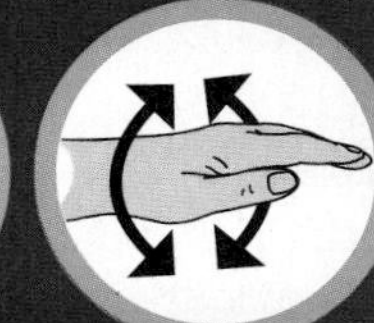
Contestar OK o sí

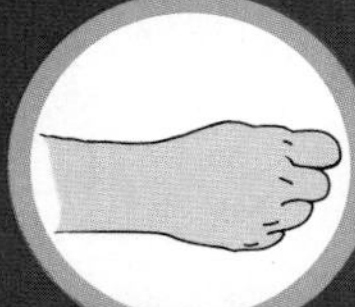
Hay un problema

¡Peligro!

1. ¿Por qué debes estudiar cursos de buceo en la escuela "Flor del mar"?
2. Practica las señales con otro(a) estudiante. ¿Qué puedes comunicar?

Hablar

¿Dónde aprendiste a bucear?

Habla con otro(a) estudiante sobre dónde aprendió a hacer las actividades de la lista.

1. bucear
2. montar a caballo
3. esquiar
4. montar en bicicleta
5. patinar
6. tocar la guitarra

Modelo

nadar

A —*¿Dónde aprendiste a nadar?*
B —*Aprendí a nadar en California.*
o: *No aprendí a nadar nunca pero me gustaría aprender.*
o: *No aprendí a nadar nunca y no quiero aprender.*

Hablar

¿Adónde fuiste?

La primavera pasada fuiste de vacaciones a la Ciudad de México. Ahora tienes tus fotos y hablas con otro(a) estudiante. En la Ciudad de México viste estas cosas:

El Paseo de la Reforma con el monumento del Ángel de la Independencia ¡Impresionante!

un partido de fútbol
muchas atracciones
una obra de teatro
el monumento del Ángel de la Independencia
animales como osos y monos
muchos cuadros interesantes

Modelo

A —*¿Adónde fuiste?*
B —*Fui al Paseo de la Reforma.*
A —*¿Qué viste?*
B —*Vi el monumento del Ángel de la Independencia.*
A —*¿Cómo lo pasaste allí? ¿Te gustó?*
B —*Fue impresionante. Me gustó mucho.*

1.

Museo de arte de Frida Kahlo
¡Fantástico!

2.

El Zoológico del Parque Chapultepec
¡Tremendo!

3.

El parque de diversiones en el Parque Chapultepec
¡Muy divertido!

4.

El Teatro del Auditorio
¡Fenomenal!

5.

El Estadio Azteca
¡Genial!

Escribir/Hablar

Y tú, ¿qué dices?

1. ¿Adónde te gustaría ir de vacaciones en los Estados Unidos? ¿Cómo quieres viajar? ¿Qué te gustaría hacer?
2. ¿Qué ciudades te gustaría visitar? ¿Qué lugares en esas ciudades quieres ver?
3. Cuando viajas, ¿prefieres salir temprano o tarde?
4. Durante un viaje, ¿descansas mucho o regresas a casa muy cansado(a)?

Gramática

The preterite of *-er* and *-ir* verbs

Regular *-er* and *-ir* verbs are similar to one another in the preterite. Here are the preterite forms of *aprender* and *salir.* Notice the accent marks on the endings *-í* and *-ió:*

¿Recuerdas?

You have already learned to talk about completed past actions using regular *-ar* verbs.

(yo)	**aprendí**	(nosotros) (nosotras)	**aprendimos**
(tú)	**aprendiste**	(vosotros) (vosotras)	**aprendisteis**
Ud. (él) (ella)	**aprendió**	Uds. (ellos) (ellas)	**aprendieron**

(yo)	**salí**	(nosotros) (nosotras)	**salimos**
(tú)	**saliste**	(vosotros) (vosotras)	**salisteis**
Ud. (él) (ella)	**salió**	Uds. (ellos) (ellas)	**salieron**

The verb *ver* is regular in the preterite but does not have accent marks in any of its forms:

vi viste vio vimos visteis vieron

GramActiva VIDEO

Want more help with the preterite of *-er* and *-ir* verbs? Watch the **GramActiva** video.

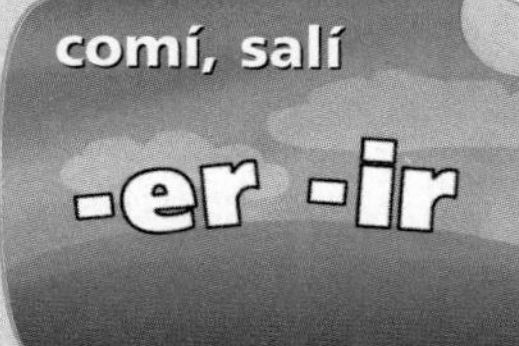

Gramática  Leer/Escribir

Ricitos de Oro y los tres osos

Escribe los verbos apropiados en el pretérito para completar cada frase del cuento de *Ricitos de Oro y los tres osos.*

Un día los tres osos **1.** *(salir / beber)* temprano de su casa para caminar. Ricitos de Oro, una chica muy bonita, **2.** *(comer / ver)* la casa de los tres osos y **3.** *(recibir / abrir)* la puerta. Ella no **4.** *(ver / comprender)* que era[1] la casa de los tres osos y **5.** *(comer / aprender)* toda la comida del oso chiquito. Luego ella **6.** *(beber / decidir)* dormir un poco. Poco después, los tres osos regresaron a su casa, **7.** *(abrir / salir)* la puerta y **8.** *(deber / ver)* a Ricitos de Oro en la cama del osito. Cuando Ricitos de Oro **9.** *(viajar / ver)* a los osos, **10.** *(abrir / salir)* de la casa rápidamente. **11.** *(Comer / Correr)* hasta llegar[2] a su propia casa.

[1]it was [2]until she arrived

Mexico City's *Metro* is one of the most advanced subway systems in the world. It is fast, modern, and very inexpensive. In addition, an extensive bus service crosses the whole city. Smaller green and gray minibuses, called *peseros,* also serve passengers along major routes.

- Why do you think Mexico City has such an advanced and varied public transportation system?

  **Escribir**

Durante las vacaciones

Escribe seis frases para decir qué hicieron *(did)* estas personas durante sus vacaciones. Usa las palabras de la lista.

comer en . . .
compartir una casa en . . .
escribir . . .
correr en . . .
aprender a . . .
ver . . .
salir de casa temprano para . . .
salir con . . .

Modelo

Durante las vacaciones, mi hermana y yo corrimos en la playa de Santa Mónica.

1. mi familia y yo
2. mis amigos
3. yo
4. mis padres
5. mi hermano(a)
6. mi amigo(a) *(nombre)*

   **Escribir/Hablar**

Tú y yo

1. Trabaja con otro(a) estudiante. Lee una frase de la Actividad 14. Tu compañero(a) va a contestar si tiene una idea similar en su hoja de papel.

Modelo

A—*Mi hermana y yo corrimos en la playa de Santa Mónica.*
B—*Mi amigo y yo también corrimos, pero nosotros corrimos en un estadio.*
o: *Yo no corrí en las vacaciones. Escribí cuentos todos los días.*

2. Escribe seis frases para comparar lo que hicieron tú y tu compañero(a) durante las vacaciones.

Modelo

Adela y yo corrimos durante las vacaciones. Ella corrió en un estadio con su amigo. Yo corrí en la playa con mi hermana.

Más práctica

Practice Workbook 8A-5

For: Practice with preterite *-er, -ir* verbs
Visit: www.phschool.com
Web Code: jcd-0803

Fondo cultural

La Patagonia is a vast, windy region of diverse climates and terrains at the southern tip of South America. It lies east of the Andes and spans parts of Chile and nearly a quarter of Argentina. A sparsely populated area, it is home to many species, including a large colony (400,000 breeding pairs) of Magellanic penguins, whose breeding grounds are the eastern and western coasts of Chile and Argentina, as well as offshore islands.

- What regions of the United States can be compared to Patagonia? What types of animals live in those regions?

Pingüinos de Patagonia

Gramática

The preterite of *ir*

Ir is irregular in the preterite. Notice that the preterite forms of *ir* do not have accent marks:

(yo)	**fui**	(nosotros) (nosotras)	**fuimos**
(tú)	**fuiste**	(vosotros) (vosotras)	**fuisteis**
Ud. (él) (ella)	**fue**	Uds. (ellos) (ellas)	**fueron**

The preterite of *ir* is the same as the preterite of *ser*. The context makes the meaning clear.

José **fue** a Barcelona. *José **went** to Barcelona.*
El viaje **fue** un desastre. *The trip **was** a disaster.*

Strategy

Using memory devices
Here's a memory tip to help you remember the subjects of *fui* and *fue:*

The "I" form ends in *-i (fui).*

The "he" and "she" form ends in *-e (fue).*

GramActiva VIDEO

Want more help with the preterite of *ir?* Watch the **GramActiva** video.

Gramática

Hablar

¿Adónde fueron?

Con otro(a) estudiante, di adónde y cómo fueron estas personas a estos lugares.

Óscar y Lourdes

Modelo

A —*¿Adónde fueron Óscar y Lourdes?*
B —*Fueron al teatro.*
A —*¿Cómo fueron?*
B —*Fueron en coche.*

1.

los Sánchez

2.

tus amigos y tú

3.

Liliana

4.

Uds.

5.

Gregorio

6.

¡Respuesta personal!

tú

Escribir/Hablar/GramActiva

Juego

1 Play in groups of four. Each person cuts a sheet of paper to form a perfect square. Fold that square into four smaller squares. Unfold the paper and label the squares *a, b, c,* and *d.* Follow Step a below for the *a* square. Fold the corner of that little square so it covers what you have written. Pass the paper to the person on your left. Follow Step b for the *b* square on the paper you receive from the person on your right, fold down the corner, and pass it to your left. Continue until all the squares have been filled. Do not look at what is written on the paper you receive. Write all of your answers in Spanish.

a. Write a subject plus the correct preterite form of *ir.*

b. Write a destination or place *(a / al / a la . . .).*

c. Write a mode of transportation.

d. Write a reason *(para* + infinitive) for going somewhere.

a. Mis amigos fueron	b. al estadio
c. en barco	d. para ver una obra de teatro

2 When you get your original paper back, unfold each square and read the complete sentence to your group. Let the group decide, *¿Cuál es la frase más tonta* (silly)? Read your silliest sentence to the class. Then make changes to the sentence so it makes sense.

Escribir/Hablar

Tus vacaciones pasadas

1 Piensa en un lugar donde fuiste de vacaciones. Copia la tabla y escribe el lugar, dos o más actividades que hiciste y una descripción del viaje.

¿Adónde fuiste?	¿Qué hiciste?	¿Cómo fue?
San Diego	Visité el zoológico, vi muchos animales, compré recuerdos	fantástico

2 Habla con dos estudiantes sobre sus vacaciones.

Modelo

A —*¿Adónde fuiste de vacaciones?*
B —*Fui a San Diego.*
A —*¿Qué hiciste allí?*
B —*Visité el zoológico y vi muchos animales. Compré recuerdos también.*
A —*¿Cómo lo pasaste? ¿Te gustó?*
B —*Fue fantástico.*

3 Escribe una descripción de los viajes de los dos estudiantes con quienes hablaste.

Modelo

Pedro fue a San Diego. Visitó el zoológico. Vio muchos animales y compró recuerdos. Su viaje fue fantástico.
Miguel fue a . . .

Más práctica

Practice Workbook 8A-6

For: Practice with preterite of *ir*
Visit: www.phschool.com
Web Code: jcd-0804

Gramática

The personal *a*

You know that the direct object is the person or thing that receives the action of a verb. When the direct object is a person or group of people, you usually use the word *a* before the object. This is called the "personal *a*."

Visité **a mi abuela.**	*I visited **my grandmother.***
Vimos **a Juan y Gloria.**	*We saw **Juan and Gloria.***

You can also use the personal *a* when the direct object is a pet.

Busco **a mi perro,** Capitán.

To ask who receives the action of a verb, use *¿A quién?*

¿A quién visitaron Uds.?

GramActiva VIDEO

Watch the **GramActiva** video for more help with the personal *a*.

Actividad 19

Gramática   Leer/Escribir/Hablar

Don Pepito y don José

1. Lee esta rima tradicional.

—Hola, don Pepito.
—Hola, don José.
—¿Pasó* Ud. por mi casa?
—Por su casa no pasé.
—¿Vio Ud. a mi abuela?
—A su abuela no la vi.
—Adiós, don Pepito.
—Adiós, don José.

* Did (you) stop by

2. Ahora escribe las líneas *¿Vio Ud. a mi abuela?* y *A su abuela no la vi* y sustituye estos miembros de la familia por "abuela." Usa el pronombre *(pronoun)* apropiado.

1. tíos **2.** hermano **3.** primas **4.** hermanita

3. Con otro(a) estudiante, lee la rima. Un(a) estudiante va a ser don Pepito y el (la) otro(a), don José. Lean la rima cuatro veces, cada vez con un miembro diferente de la familia.

Nota

You have learned the direct object pronouns *lo*, *la*, *los*, and *las*. These direct object pronouns can refer to people as well as to things. Note that the direct object pronouns do not take the personal *a*.

- ¿Viste **a tus primos** durante tus vacaciones?
- Sí, **los** vi.

En Barcelona, España

 Gramática  Hablar

De visita

Pregunta a otro(a) estudiante si visitó a diferentes personas o diferentes lugares durante las vacaciones.

Modelo

tus tíos
A —*¿Visitaste a tus tíos durante las vacaciones?*
B —*Sí, los visité.*
o: *No, no los visité.*

Estudiante A

1. tus abuelos
2. un(a) amigo(a) que no vive aquí
3. un parque de diversiones
4. tus primos
5. otra ciudad
6. el museo de arte

Estudiante B

¡Respuesta personal!

  Leer/Pensar

Juego de geografía: Las Américas

¿Conoces[1] bien los países de las Américas? Empareja las descripciones con los países apropiados.

Conexiones La geografía

1. Este país es el más grande de América Central. En el suroeste hay un lago muy grande que tiene el mismo nombre que el país. El lago está muy cerca de la frontera[2] con Costa Rica. En el este del país está el mar Caribe donde el clima es tropical y llueve mucho.
2. Este país pequeño tiene dos regiones tropicales—en el este y en el oeste—con montañas en el centro. Un cuarto de las personas en el país son de origen indígena y hablan quechua, el idioma[3] de los incas. Su nombre viene de la línea imaginaria que cruza el país.
3. Las ciudades más grandes de este país, como la capital, están en el centro del país donde hay montañas y volcanes. En el norte hay desiertos extensos y en el sur hay selvas[4] tropicales. Este país comparte una frontera con los Estados Unidos.
4. Este país es el más grande de América del Sur, con el río más grande del mundo.[5] Una gran parte del país es selva tropical con miles de especies de plantas, árboles y animales como monos, jaguares y tucanes. No hablan español aquí—hablan portugués.
5. Es el único[6] país de América del Sur que tiene playas en el mar Caribe y el océano Pacífico. Es un país famoso por su café, que viene de los valles fértiles.

[1] Do you know [2] border [3] language [4] forests [5] world [6] only

Exploración del lenguaje

Nouns that end in *-io* and *-eo*

Latin words for buildings and places have carried into many modern languages, including Spanish. In many place names, the Latin ending *-um* (which remains in a number of words in English today) changed to an *-io* or *-eo* in Spanish. You know some of these words: *el estadio, el museo, el gimnasio.*

Acuario de Madrid, España

Try it out! Based on your knowledge of English and what you have learned about Spanish place names from Latin, match the definitions with the Spanish words in the list.

1. where you stand to deliver a speech
2. usually found in a cemetery
3. where you can see all kinds of sea life
4. where you sit when you see school plays or concerts
5. where you go to learn about stars and planets
6. where the ancient Romans went to see sporting events

a. el auditorio
b. el podio
c. el acuario
d. el planetario
e. el coliseo
f. el mausoleo

Actividad 22 **Escribir/Hablar**

Y tú, ¿qué dices?

1. ¿Qué puedes visitar en tu comunidad? ¿Hay museos, parques de diversiones o monumentos? ¿Cuál prefieres visitar?
2. El año pasado, ¿fuiste a ver una obra de teatro en tu comunidad o en tu escuela? ¿Te gustó? ¿Por qué? ¿Cuestan mucho los boletos de teatro?
3. El año pasado, ¿visitaste un museo o un zoológico en tu comunidad? ¿Cómo lo pasaste?
4. ¿Prefieres viajar a otros países o ciudades, o prefieres visitar lugares en tu comunidad?

El español en la comunidad

POR FAVOR NO LES DE COMIDA A LOS ANIMALES

Your community may have some of the tourist destinations you learned about in this chapter, such as *un museo, un teatro, un zoológico,* or *un parque de diversiones*. Think of different opportunities to use your Spanish at each of the locations. As you learn more Spanish, perhaps you could provide tours to visitors who speak Spanish. You could help write brochures and maps in Spanish to assist Spanish-speaking visitors. Can you think of other opportunities?

- Visit one of these locations in person or online and see what written resources are available in Spanish. Bring these materials to class to share with other students.

Más práctica

Practice Workbook 8A-7

For: Practice with personal *a*
Visit: www.phschool.com
Web Code: jcd-0805

¡Adelante!

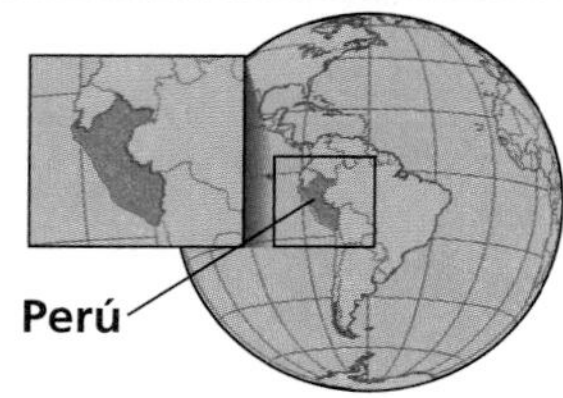

Lectura

Objectives

- Read journal entries about a trip to Peru
- Learn about *los ojos de Dios*
- Describe a trip you have taken
- Watch *¿Eres tú, María?*, Episodio 7

Álbum de mi viaje a Perú

Por Sofía Porrúa

Strategy

Using context clues
If you don't recognize a word, use the other words in the sentence to guess its meaning. Can you guess the meaning of *antigua, altura, construyeron,* and *nivel?*

domingo, 25 de julio
Estoy en Perú con mis amigos Beto y Carmen. Vamos en autobús a Cuzco, antigua capital del imperio inca. Hoy día es una ciudad pequeña y una atracción turística. Beto está sacando muchas fotos con su cámara digital. Carmen está dibujando todo lo que ve. Las montañas son fantásticas.

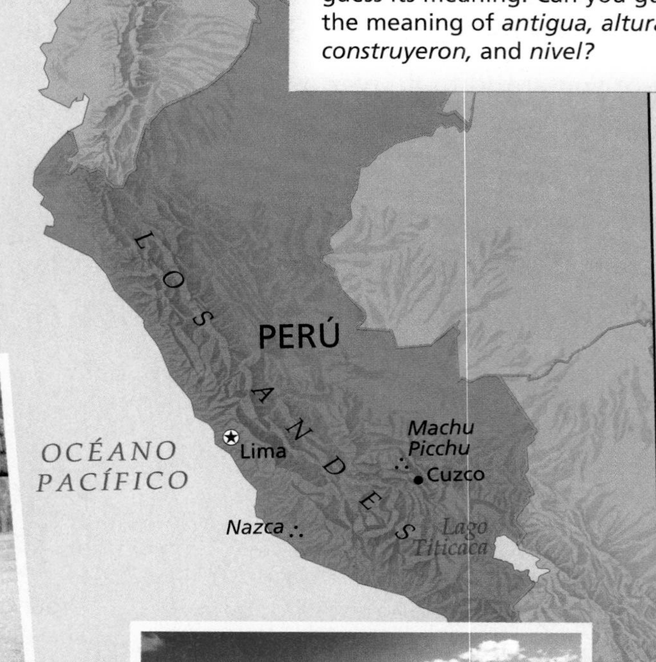

miércoles, 28 de julio
Hoy es el Día de la Independencia peruana. En esta fecha en 1821, José de San Martín proclamó la independencia de Perú. En Lima, una gran ciudad moderna y capital del país, hay grandes celebraciones.

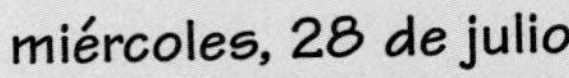

jueves, 29 de julio
Hoy estamos en Machu Picchu, ruinas impresionantes de una ciudad antigua de los incas. A más de 2.000 metros de altura en los Andes, los incas construyeron calles, casas, acueductos, palacios, templos y terrazas para cultivar. Hiram Bingham, un arqueólogo de la Universidad de Yale, descubrió[1] Machu Picchu en 1911.

[1]discovered

sábado, 31 de julio
Estamos paseando en bote por el lago Titicaca, en la frontera de Perú y Bolivia. Es el lago más grande de estos países y el más alto del mundo.[2] ¡Estamos a más de 3.800 metros sobre el nivel del mar!

miércoles, 4 de agosto
Ahora estamos en un avión pequeño. Sobre la tierra[3] podemos ver algo muy misterioso: hay un desierto donde vemos enormes dibujos de animales y figuras geométricas. Estos dibujos se llaman las líneas de Nazca. Miden[4] más de 300 metros y tienen más de dos mil años. ¿Quiénes los dibujaron—y por qué? Es necesario estar en un avión para verlos. ¿Cómo dibujaron los artistas algo tan[5] grande sin poder verlo?

Mañana regresamos a Cuzco y el domingo salimos de Perú. ¡Un viaje muy interesante! Beto tiene sus fotos y Carmen, sus dibujos. Yo no soy ni fotógrafa ni artista, por eso voy a comprar tarjetas postales como recuerdos.

[2] world [3] ground [4] They measure [5] so

¿Comprendes?

1. ¿Cómo va a recordar Sofía su viaje a Perú? ¿Y Beto y Carmen?
2. Pizarro y los españoles descubrieron muchas de las ciudades de los incas. ¿Por qué piensas que no descubrieron Machu Picchu? ¿Quién lo descubrió?
3. Para muchos turistas que visitan el lago Titicaca es difícil caminar y respirar *(breathe)*. ¿Por qué piensas que tienen estos problemas?
4. ¿Cuáles son los misterios de las líneas de Nazca?
5. Copia la tabla en una hoja de papel. Usa la información de la lectura para comparar Perú con los Estados Unidos.

	Perú	Estados Unidos
a. Dos lugares históricos y turísticos		
b. Día de la Independencia		
c. Año de la proclamación de la independencia		
d. Capital del país hoy		
e. Héroe nacional		

Go Online PHSchool.com
For: Internet link activity
Visit: www.phschool.com
Web Code: jcd-0806

La cultura en vivo

Los ojos de Dios

Mujer tarahumara en San Rafael, México

Traveling in the Spanish-speaking world you will encounter a marvelous variety of artwork and crafts, many of which have their origins in the time before the Spaniards came to the Americas. One form of art that is popular among visitors to parts of Mexico is the *ojo de Dios.*

The *ojo de Dios* is a diamond-shaped weaving. As a gift, it symbolizes good wishes from one person to another. *Ojos de Dios* may have originated in Peru about 300 B.C. The people best known for making these today are the Indians of Mexico's Sierra Madre region. The Cora, Huichol, Tarahumara, and Tepehuane all make and use these weavings in their daily lives.

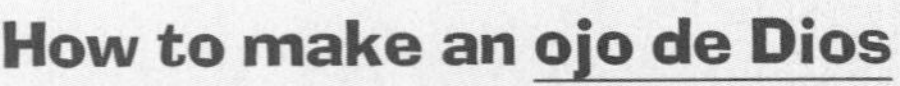

How to make an ojo de Dios

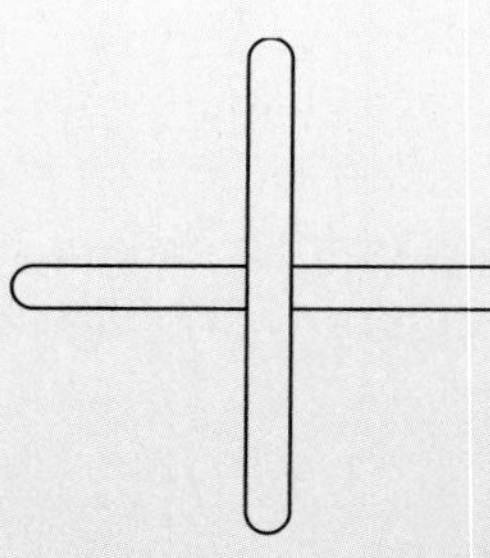
Figure 1

Materials

- yarn
- scissors
- two sticks of the same size
- optional: feathers, beads, or tassels for finishing touches

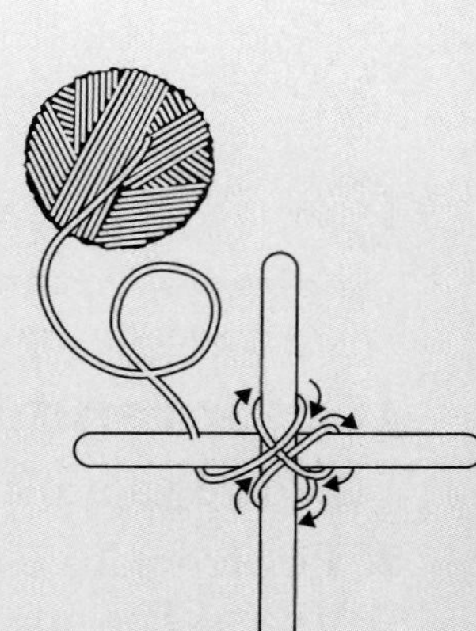
Figure 2

Directions

1. Tie the sticks together to form a cross. *(Fig. 1)*
2. Tie the end of the yarn to the center of the cross.
3. Weave the yarn over and around each stick, keeping the yarn pulled tight. *(Fig. 2)* To change color, knot together two ends of different-colored yarn. The knot should fall on the back side. Continue wrapping until the sticks are covered with yarn. Tie a small knot at the back and leave enough yarn to make a loop for hanging.
4. You may want to add feathers, beads, or tassels to the ends of the sticks. Hang your decorative piece for everyone to enjoy.

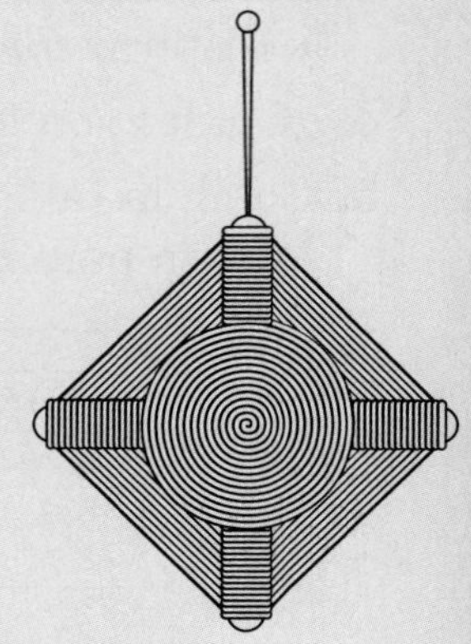
Figure 3

Think about it! What are some of the traditional handicrafts in the United States? What is the ethnic heritage of these crafts?

Presentación oral

Mi viaje

Task
Tell a friend about a trip you took. It could be a vacation or a trip to visit family members, or you can make up a trip. Use photographs or drawings to make your talk more interesting.

1 Prepare Use the word web to help you think about what you did on your trip. Think of information and events to include in each circle. Bring in photos from the trip or draw pictures to illustrate each part of the trip represented on the word web. Design the illustration of your trip so it looks appealing.

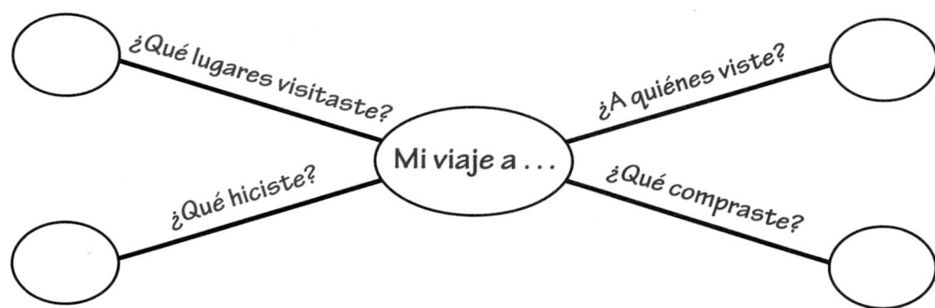

Strategy

Using graphic organizers
Using a graphic organizer such as a word web will help you think through what you want to say in your presentation.

2 Practice Work with a partner and use the information in your word web to tell about your trip. Go through your story several times using the photographs or illustrations. You can use your notes in practice, but not when you present. End your presentation by saying how you felt about the trip.

Modelo

En marzo, fui a Florida para visitar a mi abuelita y a mis primos. Tomamos el sol en la playa y nadamos mucho. Aprendí a bucear y vi animales muy interesantes en el mar. Me gusta mucho Florida. Es un lugar fantástico. El viaje fue muy divertido.

3 Present Talk about your trip to a small group or the whole class. Use your photos or drawings to help you present.

4 Evaluation Your teacher may give you a rubric for how your presentation will be graded. You may be evaluated on:

- how much information you provide
- how well you use photographs or visuals to illustrate your story
- how well you are understood

Videomisterio

¿Eres tú, María?

Episodio 7

Antes de ver el video

Resumen del episodio

Lola y Pedro visitan el piso elegante de doña Gracia. Entran en la habitación[1] de María. Hay ropa, libros, unas fotos y una tarjeta postal. Lola y Pedro leen algo muy interesante en la tarjeta postal. Después, van al piso de Julia. Allí vive un hombre que no conoce a Julia. Pero antes vivía[2] una chica en el piso. Todavía hay unas cosas de esa chica: ropa, unas cartas y unos papeles. ¿Y qué más?

[1] bedroom [2] used to live

Nota cultural Addresses in Spain are written differently than in the United States. For example, the name of Julia's street is Calle Norte. The building number is 23. The 1° *(primero)* indicates the apartment is on the first floor (not the ground floor, but what we would call the second floor), and Julia lives in apartment D.

"Lola, te llamo porque tengo información sobre la otra chica en el accidente. Tengo la dirección de su piso. Es Calle Norte, 23, 1°, D."

Palabras para comprender

¡Suerte! Good luck!

No la conozco. I don't know her.

tenía un secretario had a secretary

tuvo problemas con él had problems with him

¡Qué casualidad! What a coincidence!

"¿Sabes, Pedro? En mi profesión la casualidad no existe."

"Mira esta tarjeta postal. Interesante, ¿no?"

"¿A quién buscáis? Antes aquí vivía una chica . . ."

Después de ver el video

¿Comprendes?

Pon las frases en orden según el episodio.

1. Pedro recuerda el nombre de Luis Antonio Llamas, un secretario de su papá.
2. Leen la tarjeta postal de Luis Antonio.
3. Pedro llama a Lola para invitarla a visitar el piso de su abuela.
4. El joven en el piso de Julia no está nada contento.
5. Rosalinda llama a Lola para darle la dirección de Julia.
6. Quieren ver la habitación de María.
7. Deciden visitar el piso de Julia.

Nota gramatical In this episode you will hear a few more examples of the *vosotros* form: *queréis, sois, podéis, buscáis.* Remember that in Spain you use *vosotros* or *vosotras* when talking to more than one person whom you would address individually as *tú.*

For: More on *¿Eres tú, María?*
Visit: www.phschool.com
Web Code: jcd-0507

Repaso del capítulo

Vocabulario y gramática

Chapter Review

To prepare for the test, check to see if you . . .
- **know the new vocabulary and grammar**
- **can perform the tasks on p. 397**

to talk about places to visit on vacation

la ciudad	city
el estadio	stadium
el lago	lake
el lugar	place
el mar	sea
el monumento	monument
el museo	museum
el país	country
el parque de diversiones	amusement park
el parque nacional	national park
el teatro	theater
la obra de teatro	play
el zoológico	zoo

to talk about things to see on vacation

el animal	animal
el árbol	tree
la atracción *pl.* **las atracciones**	attraction(s)
el mono	monkey
el oso	bear
el pájaro	bird

to talk about things to do on vacation

aprender (a)	to learn
bucear	to scuba dive / snorkel
(comprar) recuerdos	(to buy) souvenirs
descansar	to rest, to relax
montar a caballo	to ride horseback
pasear en bote	to go boating
tomar el sol	to sunbathe
visitar	to visit

to talk about ways to travel

en	by
el autobús	bus
el avión	airplane
el barco	boat, ship
el tren	train

For *Vocabulario adicional,* see pp. 472–473.

to talk about your vacation

el boleto	ticket
como	like, such as
¿Cómo lo pasaste?	How was it (for you)?
dime	tell me
fantástico, -a	fantastic
Fue un desastre.	It was a disaster.
el hotel	hotel
impresionante	impressive
ir de vacaciones	to go on vacation
Me gustó.	I liked it.
¿Qué hiciste?	What did you do?
¿Qué te pasó?	What happened to you?
regresar	to return
salir	to leave, to go out
¿Te gustó?	Did you like it?
tremendo, -a	tremendous
vi	I saw
¿viste . . . ?	Did you see . . . ?
viajar	to travel
el viaje	trip

to express time

durante	during
tarde	late
temprano	early

preterite of *-er* and *-ir* verbs

aprendí **salí**	**aprendimos** **salimos**
aprendiste **saliste**	**aprendisteis** **salisteis**
aprendió **salió**	**aprendieron** **salieron**

preterite of *ir*

fui	**fuimos**
fuiste	**fuisteis**
fue	**fueron**

● **Más práctica**

Practice Workbook Puzzle 8A-8
Practice Workbook Organizer 8A-9

Go Online PHSchool.com
For: Test preparation
Visit: www.phschool.com
Web Code: jcd-0807

Preparación para el examen

On the exam you will be asked to . . .	Here are practice tasks similar to those you will find on the exam . . .	If you need review . . .
 **1 Escuchar** Listen to and understand what someone says he did and where he went during his last vacation	As part of a presentation in Spanish class, a student talked about his last vacation. As you listen, see if you can determine: a) where he went; b) one thing he did; c) one thing he saw.	**pp. 374–377** *A primera vista* **p. 375** Actividad 1 **p. 378** Actividades 4–5
 **2 Hablar** Tell about your best trip or vacation	Find out where your partner went on his or her best vacation, and what he or she did and saw. As you listen, make a drawing that includes details of the trip. Then your partner will ask you to describe your best vacation. Do your drawings match the descriptions?	**p. 379** Actividad 6 **p. 380** Actividad 8 **p. 382** Actividad 11 **p. 385** Actividad 16 **p. 386** Actividad 18 **p. 393** *Presentación oral*
 **3 Leer** Read and understand a vacation postcard	Read the postcard Javier sent to his friend last summer during his family vacation. Which things does he say he liked? Was there anything he didn't like? *¡Hola! Salí de vacaciones la semana pasada y ahora estamos aquí en Puerto Rico. Visitamos a nuestra tía en San Juan. Ayer fuimos al Viejo San Juan, donde vi muchos monumentos. También vi El Morro, un lugar muy famoso. ¡Fue fabuloso! Hoy fui a la playa de Luquillo y tomé el sol. Los otros bucearon por tres horas, pero a mí no me gusta el mar. Después, comimos arroz con pollo en un restaurante. ¡Uf! ¡Siempre arroz con pollo aquí! Regreso el sábado. ¡Hasta luego! Javier*	**p. 379** Actividad 7 **p. 381** Actividad 9 **p. 388** Actividad 21 **pp. 390–391** *Lectura*
 **4 Escribir** Write a brief narrative about an imaginary character's trip	You have been asked by a first-grade teacher to write a story in Spanish for her students. She has a stuffed bear in her room, *el Oso Teo,* so you decide to write the story about him and his trip. Tell where he went, what he did, what he saw, and what he ate. Begin with something like, *"El Oso Teo fue de viaje a su parque favorito . . ."*	**p. 378** Actividad 4 **p. 384** Actividades 14–15 **p. 386** Actividad 18 **p. 389** Actividad 22 **pp. 390–391** *Lectura*
 **5 Pensar** Demonstrate an understanding of cultural perspectives regarding artwork and crafts	Think about a gift you might give someone to symbolize good luck and good fortune in our culture. Compare it to a traditional craft from Mexico that is given for the same reason. Describe its significance and history in the Spanish-speaking world.	**p. 392** *La cultura en vivo*

Fondo cultural

The United States Peace Corps has programs in countries throughout the world. The volunteer in this photo is working on a project in Guatemala, where more than 4,000 United States volunteers have served since the establishment of the Peace Corps program. Since 1963, Peace Corps volunteers have been helping rural communities through projects in agriculture, the environment, health, and business development.

- How do you think your language skills could help you serve other people? What types of projects might you want to work on if you were a Peace Corps volunteer?

Un proyecto del Cuerpo de Paz en Guatemala

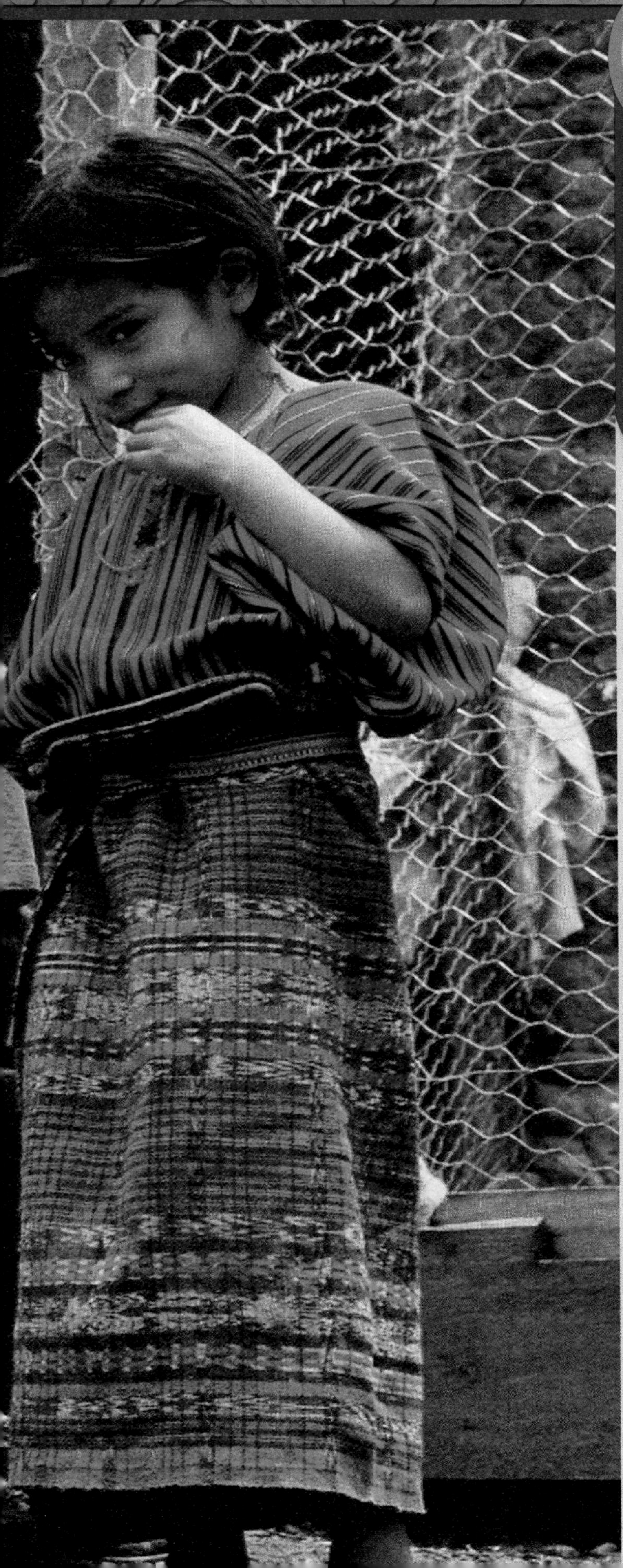

Ayudando en la comunidad

Chapter Objectives

- **Discuss volunteer work and ways to protect the environment**
- **Talk about what people say**
- **Talk about what people did for others**
- **Understand cultural perspectives on volunteer work**

Video Highlights

A primera vista: ***Cómo ayudamos a los demás***

GramActiva Videos: the present tense of *decir;* indirect object pronouns; the preterite of *hacer* and *dar*

Videomisterio: ***¿Eres tú, María?,*** **Episodio 8**

Country Connection

As you learn about volunteer work and ways to protect the environment, you will make connections to these countries and places:

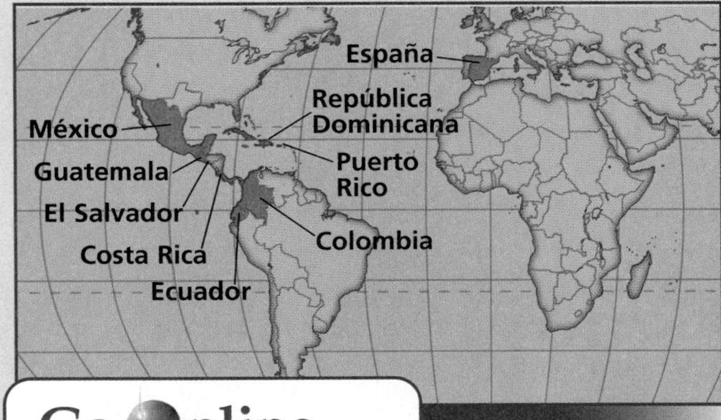

For: Online Atlas
Visit: www.phschool.com
Web Code: jce-0002

A primera vista

Vocabulario y gramática en contexto

Objectives

Read, listen to, and understand information about
- **volunteer work**
- **community-service tasks**
- **what people did to help others**

¿Quieres ayudar a los demás?

¡Trabaja como voluntario en tu comunidad!

¡Habla con los Amigos del barrio hoy! ¡Tú puedes ser la diferencia!

ayudar en un jardín

trabajar en un proyecto de construcción

hacer trabajo voluntario en una escuela primaria

trabajar en un campamento de deportes

—Mira el cartel. Hay **problemas*** en nuestra comunidad. Debemos trabajar como voluntarios.

—Tienes razón. ¿Cómo puedes **decidir** qué hacer? Es la primera **vez** que trabajo como voluntario.

—Quiero enseñar**les** a **los niños** a leer. **Es necesario** poder leer, ¿no crees?

*Even though *problema* ends in *-a*, it is a masculine noun: *Tengo **un problema**.*

—¿Me ayudas a **reciclar** la basura del río y de las calles? Son cosas que se pueden usar **otra vez. Dicen** que tenemos que **separar**las.

—Bueno, te ayudo. ¿Adónde vamos a **llevar**las?

—Al centro de reciclaje en la calle Bolívar.

Escuchar

El trabajo voluntario

Gloria investiga *(is researching)* los trabajos voluntarios en la comunidad. Señala cada lugar que ella menciona.

For: Vocabulary practice
Visit: www.phschool.com
Web Code: jcd-0811

Escuchar

¿Qué puedes reciclar?

Estás separando unos artículos en dos cajas: una es para el papel y la otra es para todos los demás artículos. Levanta una mano si debes poner el artículo en la caja para papel. Levanta dos manos si debes ponerlo en la otra caja.

Más práctica
Practice Workbook 8B-1, 8B-2

Videohistoria

Cómo ayudamos a los demás

Gloria, Raúl y Tomás hacen trabajo voluntario. ¿Por qué les gusta ser voluntarios?

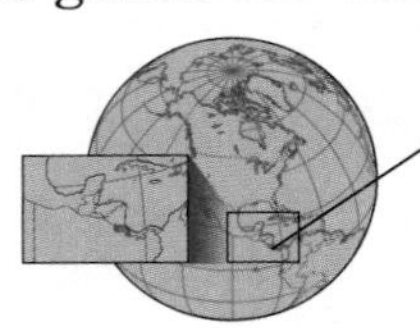

Costa Rica

Strategy

Activating prior knowledge
Before you read this selection, think about what you know about the topic of volunteer work. In what ways can one volunteer in your community?

1 **Gloria:** Raúl y yo trabajamos como voluntarios en **el Hospital** Nacional de Niños. ¿Quieres venir con nosotros?

Tomás: Sí. Me encanta el trabajo voluntario. Es **increíble** la satisfacción que **nos** da cuando ayudamos a los demás.

5 **Raúl:** El año pasado yo trabajé en un centro para **ancianos.** Pasé mucho tiempo con ellos.

6 **Tomás:** Soy miembro de un club que se llama "Casa latina." El año pasado recogimos ropa **usada.** ¿Sabes que **hay que** separar la ropa y después lavarla?

Gloria: **¿Qué más hicieron** Uds.?

Tomás: Luego le **dimos** la ropa a **la gente pobre.**

7 **Raúl:** Aquí podemos reciclar el papel y las botellas.

Gloria: Mira, para el plástico, el papel y el vidrio.

Tomás: En mi comunidad también reciclamos.

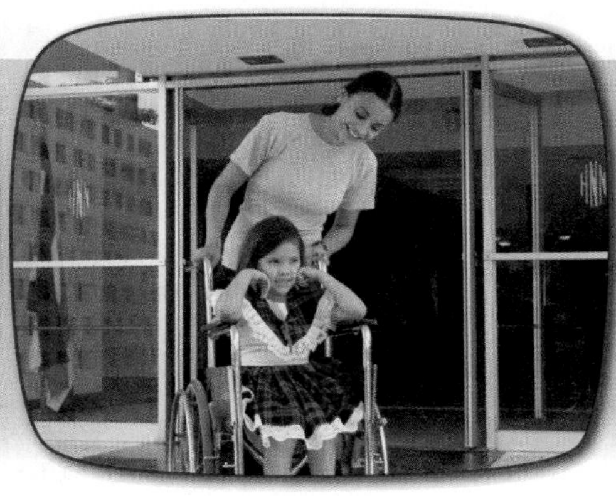

2 **Papá:** Un momento. ¿Pueden Uds. reciclar este papel y estas botellas?

Tomás: ¡Por supuesto! Dame la bolsa de plástico.

3 **Tomás:** ¿Y qué hacen Uds. en el hospital?

Gloria: Ayudamos con los niños. Leemos libros y cantamos y jugamos con ellos. **A menudo** les traemos **juguetes.**

4 **Gloria:** A veces es difícil porque los niños están muy enfermos. Pero es **una experiencia inolvidable.**

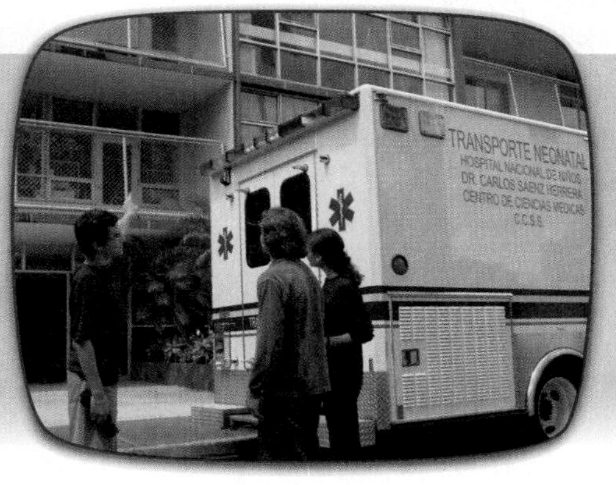

8 **Raúl:** Mira. Aquí está el hospital. ¿Entramos?

Leer/Hablar

¿Comprendes?

¿A quién describe cada frase: a Gloria, a Tomás o a Raúl? ¡Ojo! Una frase puede describir a más de una persona.

1. "Me gusta mucho el trabajo voluntario."
2. "Trabajo en un hospital para niños."
3. "Ayudar a los demás me da mucha satisfacción."
4. "Trabajo con los niños y les traigo juguetes."
5. "Me gusta pasar tiempo con los ancianos. Les leo el periódico y hablo con ellos."
6. "Recojo* la ropa usada."
7. "Es importante reciclar las botellas y latas."

**Recoger* is a regular *-er* verb with a spelling change in the *yo* form of the present tense: *recojo.*

Más práctica

Practice Workbook 8B-3, 8B-4

For: Vocabulary practice
Visit: www.phschool.com
Web Code: jcd-0812

Manos a la obra

Vocabulario y gramática en uso

Objectives

- **Talk about helping your community**
- **Ask and tell about recycling**
- **Ask and tell about volunteering**
- **Learn the present tense of *decir* and the preterite of *hacer* and *dar***
- **Learn to use indirect object pronouns**

Actividad 4 **Escuchar/Escribir**

Escucha y escribe

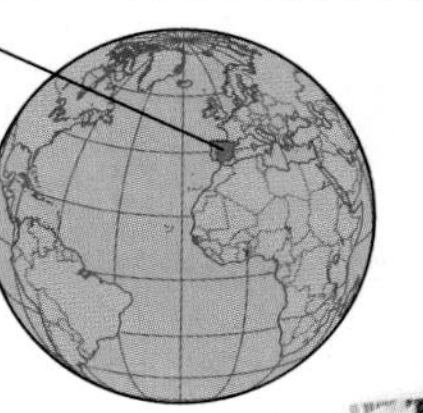

En la región de Cataluña en España, hay un sistema para reciclar que usan muchas personas.

1. En una hoja de papel, escribe los números del 1 al 6. Escucha la descripción de este sistema y escribe las frases.
2. Escribe tres frases para describir el sistema de reciclaje que usan, o que deben usar, en tu comunidad o barrio. Si quieres, usa las frases sobre Cataluña como modelo.

También se dice . . .

la lata = el bote *(España, Puerto Rico)*

En Cataluña, España

Actividad 5 **Hablar**

El reciclaje

Habla con otro(a) estudiante sobre el reciclaje.

Modelo

A —*En nuestra comunidad, ¿hay que reciclar el papel?*
B —*¡Por supuesto! Lo separamos y lo ponemos en la caja azul.*
o: *No sé. Nosotros no lo reciclamos.*

¿Recuerdas?

The direct object pronouns *lo, la, los,* and *las* replace nouns. They have the same gender and number as the nouns they replace.

1. 
2. 
3. 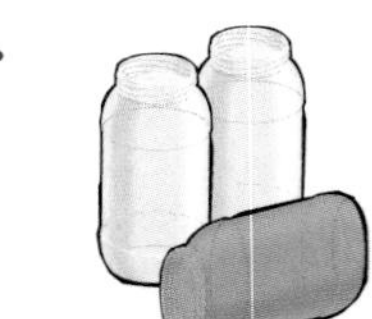
4. 
5. 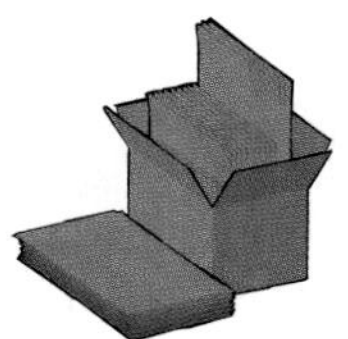
6. 

Leer/Pensar/Escribir/Hablar

El trabajo voluntario

Según las preferencias de los jóvenes de las fotos, explica dónde debe trabajar cada uno de ellos.

Modelo

Samuel debe trabajar en un hospital.

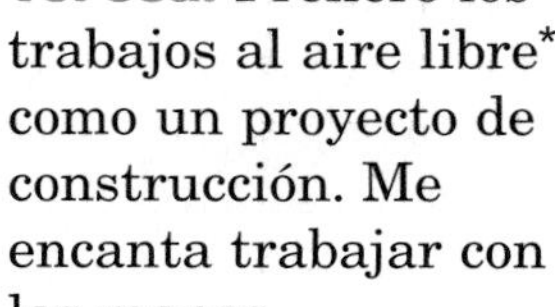

Teresa: Prefiero los trabajos al aire libre* como un proyecto de construcción. Me encanta trabajar con las manos.

*outdoors

Rafael: Mi trabajo voluntario favorito es estar con niños—en un campamento o una escuela primaria. Para mí es una experiencia inolvidable ver cómo aprenden tanto.

Samuel: Me gusta mucho ayudar a la gente pobre o a las víctimas de los desastres. Sus problemas son muy importantes para mí.

Bárbara: Me gusta mucho pasar tiempo con los ancianos. Son muy interesantes y simpáticos y me enseñan muchas cosas.

1. 
2.  
3.  
4. 
5.  
6.  

El reciclaje Spain is one of the leading European countries in recycling. Spain's glass recycling program is called *Ecovidrio,* from the Spanish words for ecology *(ecología)* and glass *(vidrio). Ecovidrio* started in the late 1990s and has been very successful. Glass recycling is an excellent way of reducing waste and protecting the environment.

- How do efforts in your community compare to glass recycling in Spain? What other efforts are available in your community?

Reciclaje en Cataluña, España

Exploración del lenguaje

Nouns that end in *-dad, -tad, -ción,* and *-sión*

You know that *actividad* means "activity" and that *comunidad* means "community." In Spanish, nouns that end in *-dad* or *-tad* usually correspond to nouns in English that end in "-ty." Nouns that end in *-dad* or *-tad* are feminine.

In a similar way, nouns in Spanish that end in *-ción* or *-sión* frequently correspond to nouns in English that end in "-tion" or "-sion." These nouns are also feminine. You know that *construcción* means "construction" and that *posesión* means "possession."

Try it out! Figure out the meanings of these Spanish words.

la generosidad	la comunicación
la responsabilidad	la comisión
la variedad	la vegetación
la tranquilidad	la información
la libertad	la organización
la universidad	la presentación

Los médicos *(doctors)* de Interplast, una organización voluntaria, ayudan a la comunidad ecuatoriana de Azogues, en los Andes.

El arte de vidrio Mexico is known for its production of beautiful glassware. Many of these works of art—including a wonderful variety of drinking glasses, bowls, and vases—are made from recycled bottles or car windshields. The glass is melted and hand-blown into new forms. Artisans also make trays and decorative windows by cutting different pieces of colored glass into a collage, then melting them together into a single piece. Each recycled glass artwork is unique.

- What everyday items or art objects are you familiar with that are made from recycled materials?

Arte de vidrio de México

Escribir/Hablar

Y tú, ¿qué dices?

1. ¿Qué cosas reciclas en casa? ¿Y en la escuela? ¿Qué más podemos reciclar?
2. ¿Qué puede hacer la gente para tener un barrio más limpio?
3. ¿Qué tipo de trabajo voluntario te gustaría hacer?
4. Escribe dos recomendaciones sobre cómo debemos ayudar a los demás.
5. ¿Qué organizaciones en tu comunidad reciben ropa usada o juguetes como donación? ¿Qué más podemos darles a las personas que necesitan ayuda?

Leer/Hablar/Escribir

La protección de las áreas naturales

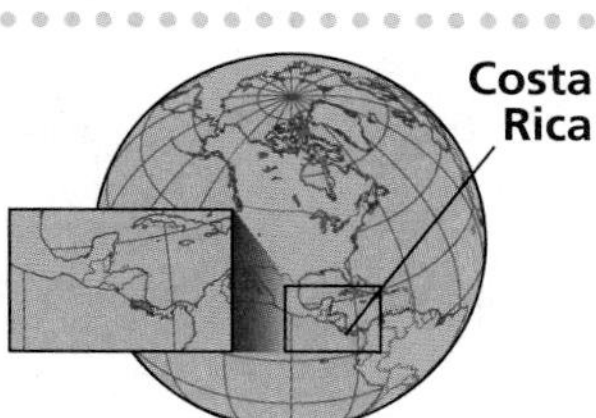

Costa Rica es un país increíble con mucha vegetación y una gran variedad de animales. La conservación de estas áreas naturales del país es muy importante. Por eso hay muchas áreas protegidas[1] en el país.

Conexiones | Las matemáticas

1. Mira el mapa de Costa Rica. Las áreas protegidas (como parques nacionales y reservas) están indicadas en verde. Estima qué porcentaje del área total del país es el área protegida.

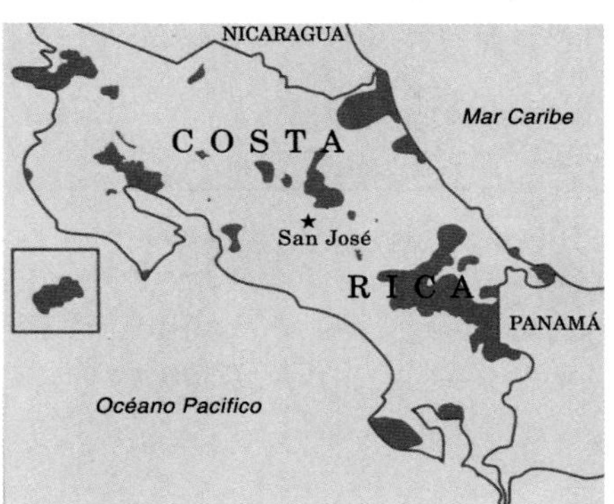

Áreas protegidas	Área total
4.459 millas cuadradas	19.652 millas cuadradas

2. Mira la tabla que compara las áreas protegidas con el área total del país. Trabaja con otro(a) estudiante para:
   - calcular qué porcentaje del área total es el área protegida.
   - comparar la respuesta con las estimaciones que hicieron Uds.
3. Averigua[2] cuántas millas cuadradas tiene los Estados Unidos y cuántas de estas millas son parques nacionales o estatales y, por lo tanto,[3] áreas protegidas. Busca la información en una enciclopedia o en el Internet.
4. Calcula qué porcentaje del área total de los Estados Unidos son estos parques. Preparen un informe sobre los resultados.

Modelo

El área total de los Estados Unidos es de ___ millas cuadradas.
___ millas cuadradas son parques nacionales o estatales.
Estos parques representan el ___ por ciento del país.

[1] protected [2] Figure out [3] therefore

La Asociación conservacionista de Monteverde in Costa Rica helps protect the rain forest in the Monteverde Cloud Forest Preserve. Young people from around the world come to help preserve the natural forest. Volunteers maintain trails and help in preservation projects.

- What programs in your community or state are similar to the program in Costa Rica?

Gramática

The present tense of *decir*

The verb *decir* means "to say" or "to tell." Here are all its present-tense forms:

(yo)	**digo**	(nosotros) (nosotras)	**decimos**
(tú)	**dices**	(vosotros) (vosotras)	**decís**
Ud. (él) (ella)	**dice**	Uds. (ellos) (ellas)	**dicen**

The *yo* form is irregular: ***digo.***

Notice that the *e* of *decir* changes to *i* in all forms except *nosotros* and *vosotros.*

¿Recuerdas?

You have used forms of *decir* in the questions *¿Cómo se dice?* and *Y tú, ¿qué dices?*

GramActiva VIDEO

Need more help with the verb *decir?* Watch the **GramActiva** video.

Gramática **Escribir**

Hay que reciclar

Escribe las formas apropiadas del verbo *decir* para completar las opiniones de diferentes personas sobre cómo tener una comunidad limpia.

1. Mis padres ____ que es necesario recoger la basura en las calles.
2. La gente ____ que es importante llevar los periódicos a un centro de reciclaje.
3. Las personas en mi comunidad ____ que tenemos que separar la basura.
4. Mi profesor de biología ____ que es necesario reciclar el vidrio y el plástico.
5. Nosotros ____ que debemos limpiar nuestro barrio y comunidad.
6. Yo ____ que el reciclaje es muy importante.
7. ¿Qué ____ tú?

Nota

Use the *él/ella* form of the verb with *la gente.*

To tell *what* people say, use ***que*** after *decir.*

- La gente **dice que** . . .

Gramática **Leer/Escribir**

¿Qué dices tú?

Lee las frases del 1 al 5 de la Actividad 9. Escribe otras para decir si haces estas mismas actividades a menudo, a veces o nunca.

Más práctica

Practice Workbook 8B-5

For: Practice with present-tense *decir*
Visit: www.phschool.com
Web Code: jcd-0813

Escribir/Hablar

¿Cómo debemos participar más?

1. Forma un grupo con cuatro estudiantes. Comparen las frases que escribieron para la Actividad 10 y digan con qué frecuencia *(how often)* todos hacen las cosas. Cada grupo va a presentar sus frases a la clase.
2. Cada estudiante debe anotar las respuestas de todos los grupos.

Modelo

En nuestro grupo, una persona dice que recoge la basura en las calles a menudo. Tres personas dicen que no la recogen nunca.

3. Después de escuchar y anotar las frases de todos los grupos, calcula el porcentaje de estudiantes que hacen estas actividades a menudo, a veces o nunca. Escribe frases sobre los resultados.

Modelo

En esta clase, el 10 por ciento de las personas dicen que recogen la basura en las calles a menudo; el 70 por ciento dicen que la recogen a veces; y el 20 por ciento dicen que no la recogen nunca.

Leer/Hablar/Escribir

Las 3 Rs

Lee el anuncio que está abajo *(below)*. Habla de Puerto Rico y la importancia de la conservación. Luego contesta las preguntas.

¡Tú puedes ser parte de la solución del problema de la basura en nuestra isla!

Recuerda esta guía práctica de las 3Rs

Reduce: Cuando vas de compras, decide no comprar cosas que no son necesarias.

Reusa: Usa un producto, objeto o material varias veces.[1] No debes tirar[2] a la basura las cosas que puedes usar otra vez.

Recicla: Usa los mismos materiales otra vez o usa un proceso natural o industrial para hacer el mismo o nuevos productos.

Lo que compras, comes, cultivas o tiras puede ser la diferencia entre un buen futuro o un futuro de destrucción para Puerto Rico.

Fundación Puertorriqueña de Conservación

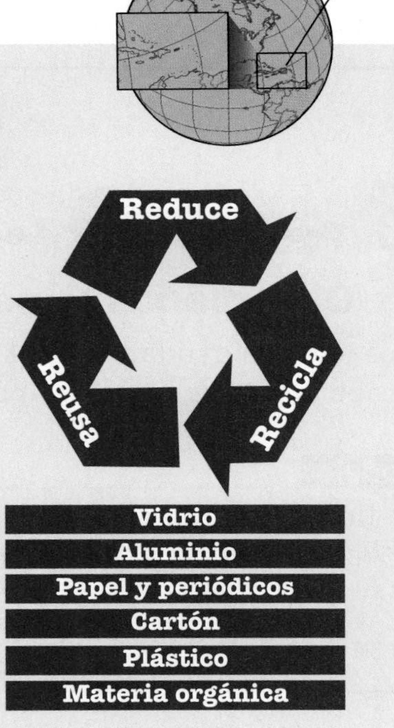

[1] several times [2] throw away

1. ¿Cómo puedes "reducir"? ¿Qué cosas compras o usas a veces que no son necesarias?
2. ¿Cómo puedes reciclar o reusar cosas en casa o en la escuela?
3. Según las frases que escribiste para la Actividad 11, escribe tres recomendaciones para cuidar *(take care of)* más tu comunidad.

Gramática

Indirect object pronouns

An indirect object tells *to whom* or *for whom* an action is performed. Indirect object pronouns are used to replace an indirect object noun.

Les doy dinero.	*I give money to them.*
Te llevo el vidrio y las latas.	*I'll bring **you** the glass and the cans.*
¿**Nos** reciclas estas botellas, por favor?	*Will you please recycle these bottles for **us**?*

The indirect object pronoun comes right before the conjugated verb. Here are the different indirect object pronouns:

SINGULAR		PLURAL	
me	(to / for) me	nos	(to / for) us
te	(to / for) you	os	(to / for) you
le	(to / for) him, her; you *(formal)*	les	(to / for) them; you *(formal)*

When an infinitive follows a conjugated verb, the indirect object pronoun can be attached to the infinitive or be placed before the conjugated verb.

Quiero **darle** un juguete al niño.
o: Le quiero dar un juguete al niño.

Because *le* and *les* have more than one meaning, you can make the meaning clear, or show emphasis, by adding *a* + the corresponding name, noun, or pronoun.

Les damos lecciones **a Miguel y a Felipe.**
Les damos lecciones **a los niños.**
Les damos lecciones **a ellos.**

GramActiva VIDEO

Need more help with indirect object pronouns? Watch the **GramActiva** video.

Actividad 13 Gramática  **Leer/Escribir**

Las Olimpiadas Especiales

Unos jóvenes ayudan con las Olimpiadas Especiales. Escribe *me, te, le, nos* o *les* para completar cada frase.

Modelo

___ llevan comida a los padres de los niños.
Les llevan comida a los padres de los niños.

1. ___ dan naranjas y jugo a los participantes.
2. ___ hacen una donación a la señora que organizó el evento.
3. ___ traen agua a mis compañeros porque tienen sed.
4. ___ dan lecciones de varios deportes a los participantes.
5. ___ dicen a nosotros que debemos preparar los concursos *(contests)*.
6. ___ traen a mí un sándwich porque tengo hambre.
7. ___ dicen a nosotros que necesitan más ayuda.

Lanzador de bala *(shotputter)*

Hablar/GramActiva

Juego

1. Tu profesor(a) va a dividir a los estudiantes en grupos de cinco. Cada grupo forma una fila *(line)*. Las primeras personas de cada fila van al frente de la clase y el (la) profesor(a) les dice una frase.
2. Las personas regresan a sus grupos y le dicen a la primera persona en la fila, *"Me dice que . . . "* y repite la frase del (de la) profesor(a). Luego la primera persona repite la frase a la segunda persona de la fila.
3. Cada grupo continúa hasta decir la frase a la última *(last)* persona. Esta persona escribe la frase que escucha en una hoja de papel. El grupo más rápido y que dice la frase más correcta gana *(wins)* el juego.

 **Gramática**  **Escribir**

¿Cómo ayuda la gente a los demás?

Escribe frases para decir cómo la gente ayuda a los demás. Usa las palabras de las listas y *a menudo, a veces* o *nunca.*

dar	dinero	ropa usada	los pobres
enseñar	flores	juguetes	los niños
comprar	cuentos	periódicos	las personas enfermas
llevar	comida	revistas	los ancianos
leer	una lección de . . .		

Modelo

A veces la gente les lleva comida a los ancianos.

Escribir/Hablar

Regalos

1. En una hoja de papel, haz dos listas. En la primera, escribe los nombres de cinco personas. En la segunda, escribe un regalo para cada una de estas personas.
2. Habla con otro(a) estudiante sobre los regalos que vas a comprar.

Modelo

A —*¿A quién vas a comprar un regalo?*
B —*Le voy a comprar un regalo a mi abuela.*
A —*¿Qué le vas a comprar?*
B —*Le voy a comprar flores.*

Más práctica

Practice Workbook 8B-6

For: Practice with indirect object pronouns
Visit: www.phschool.com
Web Code: jcd-0815

Gramática

The preterite of *hacer* and *dar*

Hacer and *dar* are irregular verbs in the preterite. Notice that these verbs do not have any accent marks in the preterite.

¿Recuerdas?

You used the preterite *tú* form of *hacer* when you asked, *¿Qué hiciste?*

- The preterite stem for *hacer* is *hic-*. In the *Ud. / él / ella* form, the *-c-* changes to a *-z-* so that it keeps the "s" sound: *hizo*.
- The preterite stem for *dar* is *di-*. The same stem is used for all the preterite forms.

(yo)	**hice**	(nosotros) (nosotras)	**hicimos**
(tú)	**hiciste**	(vosotros) (vosotras)	**hicisteis**
Ud. (él) (ella)	**hizo**	Uds. (ellos) (ellas)	**hicieron**

(yo)	**di**	(nosotros) (nosotras)	**dimos**
(tú)	**diste**	(vosotros) (vosotras)	**disteis**
Ud. (él) (ella)	**dio**	Uds. (ellos) (ellas)	**dieron**

GramActiva VIDEO

Watch the **GramActiva** video to learn more about the preterite of *hacer* and *dar.*

Actividad 17 Gramática  Leer/Escribir

En un hospital

Una joven habla de su experiencia como voluntaria en un hospital. Escribe los verbos en el pretérito para completar las frases.

Mis amigos y yo __1.__ *(dar / decidir)* hacer un trabajo voluntario en un hospital. Nosotros __2.__ *(ir / hacer)* dibujos para los ancianos en el hospital. La semana pasada una amiga y yo __3.__ *(llevar / hablar)* los dibujos al hospital. La enfermera[1] nos __4.__ *(dar / decidir)* permiso para entrar en los cuartos de varios ancianos. Nosotros __5.__ *(llevar / visitar)* a los ancianos y les __6.__ *(decidir / dar)* los dibujos. Los ancianos nos __7.__ *(hablar / llevar)* de sus familias y nos __8.__ *(decidir / dar)* abrazos.[2] Ésta fue la primera vez que yo __9.__ *(hacer / llevar)* un trabajo voluntario. Fue una experiencia inolvidable para nosotros. Vamos a regresar al hospital otra vez.

[1] nurse [2] hugs

Fondo cultural

El Hospital de la Caridad, a hospice in Seville, Spain, was founded in the 1600s by the monks of *la Hermandad de la Caridad* (Charity Brotherhood). Today, the brothers still look after people who are old or poor, as part of a long tradition of caring for the needy.

- What programs in your community provide support for people in need?

El Hospital de la Caridad en Sevilla, España

Gramática Escuchar/Escribir

Las donaciones

Vas a escuchar cómo varias personas y organizaciones, como la Cruz Roja, ayudaron a las víctimas de un desastre en El Salvador. En una hoja de papel, escribe los números del 1 al 6. Escribe las frases que escuchas.

La Cruz Roja ayuda en El Salvador

Gramática  Escribir/Hablar

¿Qué hicieron el sábado pasado?

1. Escribe lo que hicieron estas personas el fin de semana pasado.

tu mejor amigo(a)	tu madre (padre)
tú y tus amigos	tu profesor(a) de . . .
tus amigos(as)	tú

2. Habla con otro(a) estudiante sobre lo que hicieron las personas.

Modelo

tus amigos
A —*¿Qué hicieron tus amigos el fin de semana pasado?*
B —*Mis amigos fueron al río. Y tus amigos, ¿qué hicieron ellos?*
A —*Vieron una película en el cine.*
o: *No sé qué hicieron ellos.*

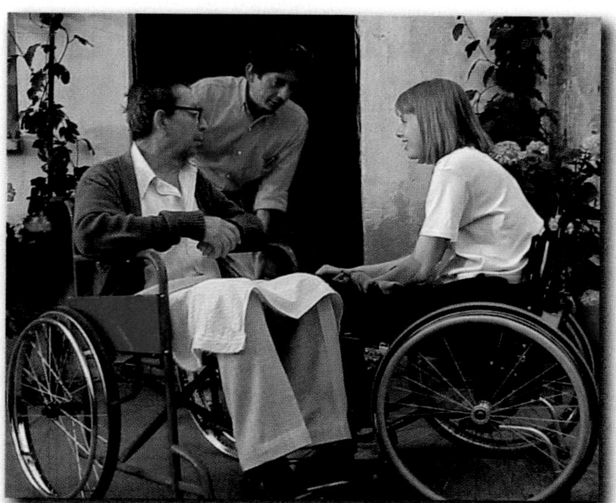
Una voluntaria de The Mobility Project de Colorado Springs, CO, conversando con dos amigos en Villa Guerrero, México

Actividad 20 Escribir/Hablar

Y tú, ¿qué dices?

1. ¿Qué hiciste el viernes pasado? ¿Qué hicieron tus amigos?
2. ¿Qué hizo tu familia el verano pasado?
3. ¿Qué les diste a tus hermanos o a tus amigos para su cumpleaños? ¿Qué te dieron a ti?
4. ¿Qué hizo la gente de tu comunidad el año pasado para ayudar a los pobres o a las víctimas de un desastre?
5. ¿Hizo tu barrio algo para ayudar a los ancianos o a los niños? ¿Qué?

Más práctica
Practice Workbook 8B-7

For: Practice with preterite of *hacer, dar*
Visit: www.phschool.com
Web Code: jcd-0814

Escribir/Hablar

Juego

1. En grupos de cuatro, deben pensar en diferentes premios *(prizes)* que reciben las personas: por ejemplo, el premio Nobel, el Heisman, el Óscar, el Emmy, el Golden Globe o el Grammy. Cada uno escribe una pregunta que tu grupo va a hacerle a otro grupo sobre los premios que dieron el año pasado.

2. Tu grupo debe leer una de las preguntas a otro grupo, que tiene 30 segundos para contestarla. Si el grupo contesta bien la primera vez, recibe tres puntos. Si contesta bien la segunda vez, recibe un punto. Si contesta mal, tu grupo debe decirles la respuesta.

Modelo

A —*¿A quién le dieron el Óscar por ser la mejor actriz el año pasado?*
B —*Le dieron el premio a . . .*

Para decir más . . .

la actriz	actress
el actor	actor
el / la cantante	singer
el / la atleta	athlete

Al colombiano Gabriel García Márquez le dieron el premio Nobel de Literatura.

Pronunciación

The letter *x*

The letter *x* is pronounced several ways. When it is between vowels or at the end of a word, it is pronounced "ks." Listen to and say these words:

examen	taxi	aproximadamente
exactamente	dúplex	éxito

When the *x* is at the beginning of a word, it is usually pronounced "s." At the end of a syllable, the *x* can be pronounced "s," "ks," or "gs." Listen to and say these words:

xilófono	explicar	experiencia
exploración	experimento	experto

Try it out! Work with a partner to ask and answer these questions, paying special attention to how you pronounce the letter *x*.

1. ¿En qué clase son más difíciles los exámenes?
2. ¿Qué clase tienes durante la sexta hora?
3. ¿En qué clase haces experimentos? ¿Qué tipo de experimentos haces?
4. ¿En qué clase hablas o escribes mucho de tus experiencias personales?

In the 1500s, the *x* represented the "h" sound of the Spanish letter *j*. That is why you see some words, like México, Oaxaca, and Texas written with *x*, even though the *x* is pronounced like the letter *j*.
In words from indigenous languages of Mexico and Central America, the *x* has the "sh" sound, as with the Mayan cities of Xel-há and Uxmal.

Una familia en Xochimilco, México

Leer/Escribir/Hablar

Las tortugas tinglar

Lee esta información sobre las tortugas tinglar. Luego contesta las preguntas.

¡La tortuga tinglar es enorme! Es la tortuga marina más grande del mundo.[1] Los tinglares adultos pueden ser de hasta siete pies de largo y pesar[2] hasta 1.400 libras.[3] Cada año, entre febrero y julio, esta tortuga sale del mar en la noche y pone sus huevos en playas tropicales, como las de la República Dominicana, Costa Rica o de la isla de Culebra cerca de Puerto Rico. Después regresa a aguas frías.

Desde 1970 el tinglar está en peligro[4] de extinción. Por eso, en la primavera voluntarios de diferentes países van a las playas como las de la isla de Culebra. Llevan trajes de baño, jeans, sudaderas, camisetas, cámaras, binoculares, linternas,[5] repelente contra mosquitos y muchas ganas de[6] ayudar a las tortugas. Patrullan[7] las playas buscando las tortugas.

Después de poner las tortugas los huevos, los voluntarios los llevan a un nido artificial. Aproximadamente 60 días después, las tortuguitas salen de los huevos. Los voluntarios llevan a las tortuguitas al mar donde nadan contínuamente por unas 28 horas. Estos voluntarios son muy importantes para la preservación de la tortuga tinglar.

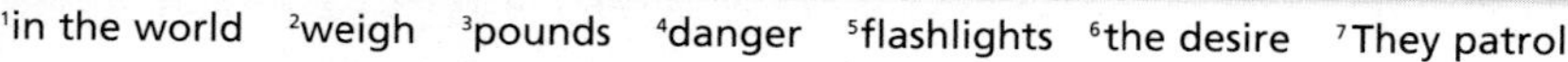

[1]in the world [2]weigh [3]pounds [4]danger [5]flashlights [6]the desire [7]They patrol

1. Para ti, ¿cuáles son los hechos *(facts)* más increíbles sobre la tortuga tinglar?
2. Escribe una lista, en orden, del trabajo que hacen los voluntarios en la playa.
3. ¿Te gustaría trabajar como voluntario en una de las playas donde están las tortugas tinglar? ¿Por qué?

Protegiendo a las tortugas en las Islas Cayman

El español en el mundo del trabajo

There may be community service organizations in your neighborhood where knowing Spanish is helpful. These organizations include medical clinics, food kitchens, senior centers, career counseling and job training, and after-school programs. Volunteering your skills for these agencies is the first step to finding out if you would be interested in pursuing work in the nonprofit sector.

- Check with local agencies to find out which ones offer services in Spanish (or in other languages). Develop a class list of volunteer opportunities in your community in which you could use your Spanish skills.

¡Adelante!

Lectura

Lee este artículo sobre una organización que hace proyectos de construcción en muchos países del mundo.

Objectives

- **Read about an international volunteer organization**
- **Learn about volunteer work in Spanish-speaking countries**
- **Create a poster announcing a community-service project**
- **Watch *¿Eres tú, María?*, Episodio 8**

Strategy

Recognizing cognates
Recognizing cognates in the following article can help improve your understanding of the reading.

Hábitat para la Humanidad Internacional

Hábitat es una organización internacional que ayuda a la gente pobre a tener casa. Su objetivo es construir casas seguras[1] que no cuestan mucho para las personas que no tienen mucho dinero. Hábitat trabaja con las familias pobres, con los grupos de voluntarios y con las personas que les dan dinero. Esta organización tiene más de 2.500 proyectos en muchas comunidades de los Estados Unidos y otros 1.600 proyectos en más de 83 países diferentes. Hábitat ha construido[2] unas 125.000 casas en todo el mundo.

Guatemala tiene catorce afiliados de Hábitat. Cada afiliado tiene su propio dinero y hace su plan de construcción y sus proyectos. Los afiliados de Guatemala tienen mucho éxito.[3] Han construido más de 10.000 casas y tienen planes para construir 15.000 más en los años que vienen. Según Hábitat, las personas pobres tienen que ayudar a construir sus casas. Es una manera positiva de ayudar a los demás. Hábitat les da los materiales de construcción y los trabajadores voluntarios. Cuando la casa está construida, el nuevo propietario[4] paga una pequeña hipoteca[5] cada mes. Después, los nuevos propietarios tienen que ayudar a otros futuros propietarios a construir sus casas.

[1] safe [2] has built [3] success [4] owner [5] mortgage

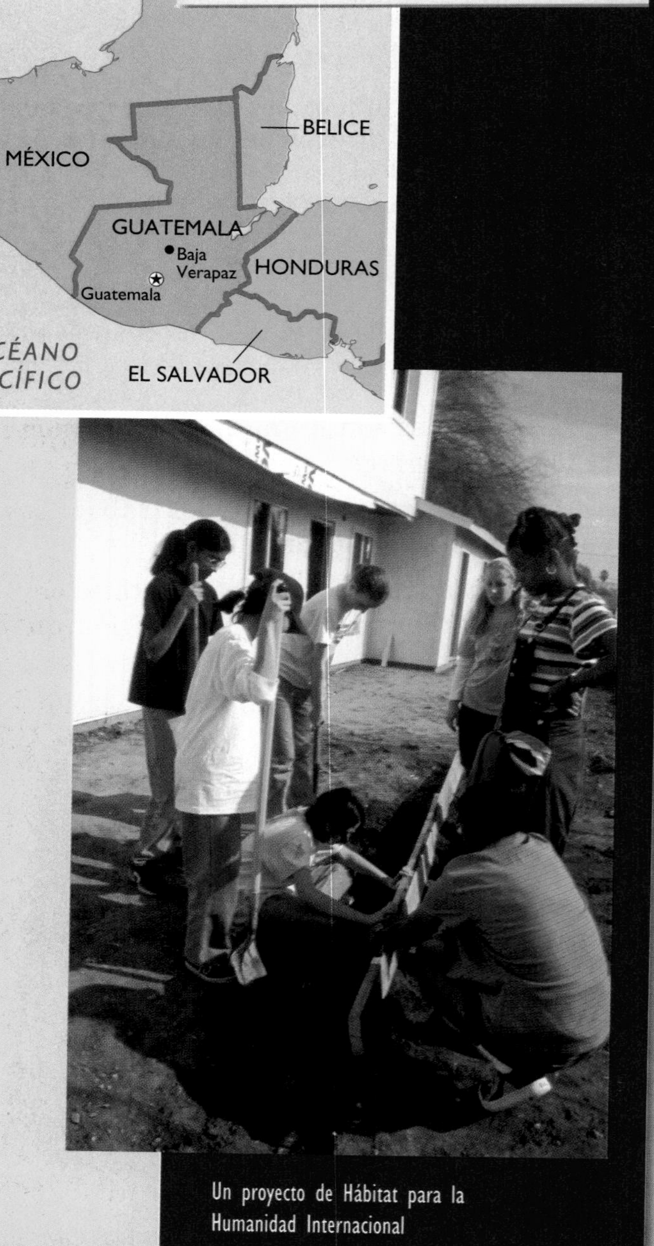

Un proyecto de Hábitat para la Humanidad Internacional

Para todos, es una experiencia increíble.

Trabajadores de Hábitat para la Humanidad Internacional

—Ayer fue mi cumpleaños y recibí el mejor regalo de mi vida, mi propia casa —dijo una señora de la comunidad de Baja Verapaz.

La mayoría[6] del dinero viene de donaciones privadas y del trabajo voluntario de muchísimas personas.

¿Sabes que el ex-presidente Jimmy Carter y su esposa Rosalynn son dos de los primeros miembros voluntarios de Hábitat? Los grupos de voluntarios son una parte fundamental del éxito de la organización.

—Es una experiencia inolvidable para ayudar a los demás —dijo un voluntario en Guatemala.

[6] the majority

¿Comprendes?

1. ¿Qué hace Hábitat?
2. ¿Con quiénes trabaja Hábitat?
3. ¿En cuántos países está Hábitat?
4. ¿Cuántas casas construyeron los afiliados de Guatemala?
5. ¿Qué tienen que pagar los nuevos propietarios?
6. ¿Qué tienen que hacer los nuevos propietarios?
7. ¿De dónde viene el dinero para construir las casas?
8. Y a ti, ¿te gustaría trabajar con Hábitat? ¿Por qué?

For: Internet link activity
Visit: www.phschool.com
Web Code: jcd-0816

Fondo cultural

El trabajo voluntario AmeriCorps is an organization of volunteers who work in urban and rural communities throughout the United States. They teach children to read, assist victims of natural disasters, and participate in other activities that benefit needy people.

One of the advantages of serving as an AmeriCorps volunteer is learning skills that can be used later in the workplace.

- What are some of the skills a volunteer might learn? Why are they important?

Doctores de las Naciones Unidas en Santa Cruz, Perú

¿Trabajas como voluntario?

Throughout the Spanish-speaking world students are involved in volunteer activities and organizations. In many private schools students are encouraged to serve their community for two to three hours per week to help them learn responsibilities that will make them good citizens. Community service also provides a good occasion to explore different professions such as education, medicine, or social work. For example, many young people work with local branches of the *Cruz Roja* (Red Cross) and learn how to respond in times of emergency. Courses are offered by the organization, and some students even study for a degree in health services.

In many Spanish-speaking countries, students are involved in causes dealing with the environment. In these countries, the natural beauty of the land is not only a source of national pride, it is also an economic resource and important to the well-being of the country. Students work at recycling centers collecting paper, glass, and plastic and collect trash along roadsides and in parks.

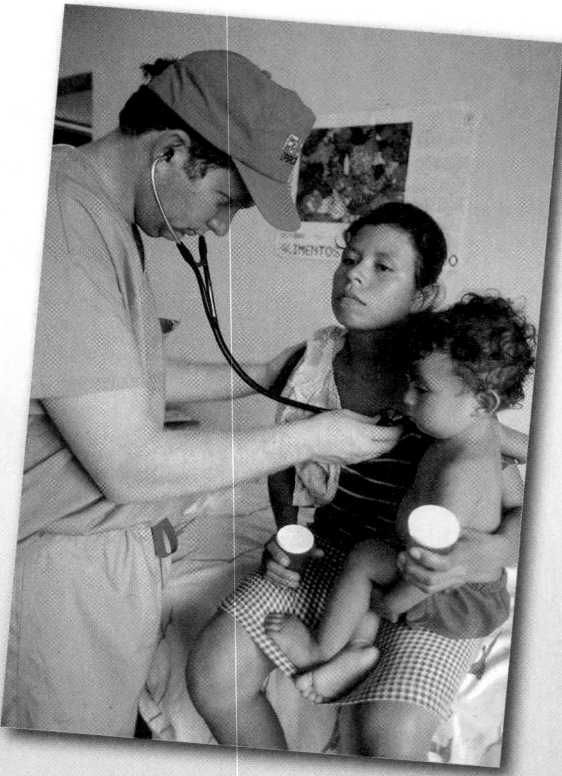

En una clínica en Trinidad, Honduras

Check it out! Survey the students in your class. Who does volunteer work? What kind of work do they do? How often are they involved in community service activities?

Think about it! How does the involvement in volunteerism among teenagers in many Spanish-speaking countries compare with the involvement of teenagers in your community?

En la Reserva Ecológica El Ángel, Ecuador

Presentación escrita

¿Puedes ayudarnos?

Task
Your school sponsors community-service projects every year, so you want to organize a clean-up campaign for a park, recreation center, school playground, or other place in your community. Make a poster announcing the project and inviting students to participate.

1. **Prewrite** Answer the following questions about your project:
   - ¿Qué van a limpiar?
   - ¿Qué tienen que hacer?
   - ¿Dónde está el lugar?
   - ¿Cuándo van a trabajar?
   - ¿Cuántas horas van a trabajar?
   - ¿Quién(es) puede(n) participar?

2. **Draft** Prepare a first draft using the answers to the questions. Organize the information in a clear and logical manner. Remember that you want students to stop and read the poster.

3. **Revise** Check your poster idea for spelling, accent marks, punctuation, and vocabulary usage. Share your work with a partner, who will check the following:
   - Is the information presented clearly and easy to understand?
   - Is it arranged logically?
   - Is there anything that you should add or change?
   - Are there any errors?

4. **Publish** Prepare a final version of the poster making any necessary changes. Add visuals to make the poster appealing. Display it in the classroom, cafeteria, or school library, or add it to your portfolio.

5. **Evaluation** Your teacher may give you a rubric for grading the poster. You may be evaluated on:
   - how complete the information is
   - the accuracy of the language in the poster
   - the visual presentation

Strategy
Using key questions
Answering key questions can help you think of ideas for writing.

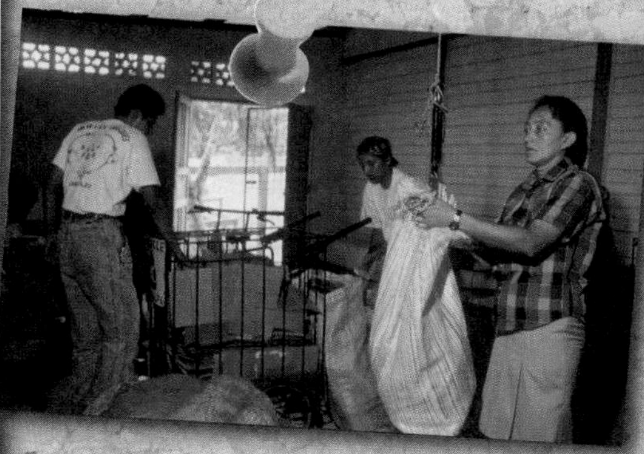

Videomisterio

¿Eres tú, María? Episodio 8

Antes de ver el video

"A ver. Esta foto. Yo conozco a este hombre. Pero no sé de qué. ¡Qué problema!"

Resumen del episodio

Después de visitar el piso de Julia, Lola y Pedro van a un café a tomar unos refrescos. Hablan de las cosas de Julia que el joven acaba de darles:[1] la ropa, las fotos, los papeles. Cuando Lola llega a su piso en la noche, ve que una mujer entra en el edificio número 8. Lola cree que es María. Sale rápidamente de su piso y espera[2] enfrente. Una mujer sale del edificio y Lola le pregunta, "¿Eres tú, María?"

[1] just gave them [2] waits

Palabras para comprender

María tenía las llaves. María had the keys.

Ella las perdió. She lost them.

¡No me sigas! Don't follow me!

Acabo de ver . . . I just saw . . .

Acabo de hablar con . . . I just spoke with . . .

—¿Eres María Requena?
—¿Por qué quieres saberlo?

—Acabo de hablar con María Requena delante del piso de doña Gracia.

—Srta. Lago, esto es cosa de la policía.

Después de ver el video

¿Comprendes?

A. ¿Quién lo dice: Lola, Carmela, Pedro, el Inspector Gil, la camarera o María?

1. ¿Qué desean Uds.?
2. Y yo, un agua mineral.
3. ¿Cómo es que tienes las llaves del piso de Julia?
4. ¿Sabes algo más sobre el caso de doña Gracia?
5. Las diez y media. ¡Por fin!
6. ¿Qué quieres? ¿Quién eres?
7. ¡No me sigas! ¡No me sigas!
8. Acabo de ver a María Requena.
9. Ahora trabajo para Pedro Requena, el nieto de doña Gracia.
10. Hay que decirlo todo a la policía.

B. Escribe dos frases que describan cada foto de esta página.

For: More on *¿Eres tú, María?*
Visit: www.phschool.com
Web Code: jcd-0507

Repaso del capítulo

Vocabulario y gramática

Chapter Review

To prepare for the test, check to see if you . . .
- **know the new vocabulary and grammar**
- **can perform the tasks on p. 423**

to talk about recycling

la bolsa	bag, sack
la botella	bottle
la caja	box
el cartón	cardboard
el centro de reciclaje	recycling center
la lata	can
llevar	to take; to carry
el periódico	newspaper
el plástico	plastic
reciclar	to recycle
recoger	to collect; to gather
separar	to separate
usado, -a	used
el vidrio	glass

to talk about places in a community

el barrio	neighborhood
la calle	street, road
la comunidad	community
el jardín	garden, yard
el río	river

to discuss possibilities for volunteer work

los ancianos	older people
el anciano	older man
la anciana	older woman
el campamento	camp
los demás	others
la escuela primaria	primary school
la gente	people
el hospital	hospital
el juguete	toy
los niños	children
el niño	young boy
la niña	young girl
pobre	poor
el problema	problem
el proyecto de construcción	construction project
el trabajo voluntario	volunteer work
el voluntario, la voluntaria	volunteer

other useful expressions

a menudo	often
decidir	to decide
Es necesario.	It's necessary.
la experiencia	experience
Hay que . . .	One must . . .
increíble	incredible
inolvidable	unforgetable
¿Qué más?	What else?
la vez *pl.* **las veces**	time
otra vez	again

decir *to say, to tell*

digo	**decimos**
dices	**decís**
dice	**dicen**

indirect object pronouns

SINGULAR	PLURAL
me (to / for) me	**nos** (to / for) us
te (to / for) you	**os** (to / for) you
le (to / for) him, her; you *(formal)*	**les** (to / for) them; you *(formal)*

preterite of *dar*

di	**dimos**
diste	**disteis**
dio	**dieron**

preterite of *hacer*

hice	**hicimos**
hiciste	**hicisteis**
hizo	**hicieron**

For *Vocabulario adicional,* see pp. 472–473.

Más práctica

Practice Workbook Puzzle 8B-8
Practice Workbook Organizer 8B-9

For: Test preparation
Visit: www.phschool.com
Web Code: jcd-0817

Preparación para el examen

On the exam you will be asked to . . .	Here are practice tasks similar to those you will find on the exam . . .	If you need review . . .
1 Escuchar Listen and understand as someone describes what he did in his community	A radio station is sponsoring a contest to encourage people to help in the community. Listen as a teen tells the announcer what he did. Identify whether he: a) helped older people; b) worked on a recycling project; c) contributed money; d) volunteered in a hospital or school.	**pp. 400–403** *A primera vista* **p. 401** Actividades 1–2 **p. 404** Actividad 4 **p. 413** Actividad 18
 **2 Hablar** Ask and answer questions about what you or someone you know did to help others in the past few months	Many organizations offer scholarships to students who help others. With a partner, practice asking and answering the following questions for the scholarship interviews with a local agency that works in the Spanish-speaking community: a) What did you do to help others? b) Why did you decide to do volunteer work?	**p. 404** Actividad 5 **p. 405** Actividad 6 **p. 406** Actividad 7
 **3 Leer** Read and understand what people gave as donations to various people or groups	The Spanish Club treasurer's report about charitable contributions is ready for the members. Read one line item from the report. Indicate whether the member(s) donated: a) cash; b) lessons for an individual or group; c) clothing; d) furniture. For example, you might read: *Scott y Jamie le dieron una cama y una cómoda a una familia pobre.*	**p. 412** Actividad 17 **p. 415** Actividad 22 **pp. 416–417** *Lectura*
 **4 Escribir** Write a list of things teenagers can do to help in your community	To encourage your classmates to participate in *La semana de la comunidad,* make a poster for your classroom with at least five suggestions for activities. For example: *Recicla las botellas. Ayuda a los niños de la escuela primaria.*	**p. 408** Actividades 9–10 **p. 409** Actividad 12 **p. 410** Actividad 13 **p. 411** Actividad 15 **p. 412** Actividad 17 **p. 419** *Presentación escrita*
 **5 Pensar** Demonstrate an understanding of cultural perspectives regarding volunteer work	Think about the volunteer activities in which you and your friends participate. Based on what you've learned in this chapter, compare these to the type of work teenage volunteers do in Spanish-speaking countries.	**pp. 400–403** *A primera vista* **p. 407** *Fondo cultural* **p. 416–417** *Lectura* **p. 417** *Fondo cultural* **p. 418** *Perspectivas del mundo hispano*

¡Viva Texas!

Voluntarios tejanos

Amigos de las Américas es una organización de voluntarios basada en Texas. Fue establecida[1] en 1965 cuando un grupo de jóvenes de Houston, Texas, viajó a Honduras para pasar el verano ayudando en la lucha contra[2] el polio. Hoy día, hay casi 600 voluntarios de Amigos de las Américas que participan en programas en Latinoamérica cada año. Los servicios incluyen ayuda médica, proyectos de construcción, proyectos para recoger basura y muchos más. Para ser voluntario hay que tener 16 años y haber tomado[3] dos años de español en la escuela secundaria o el equivalente. También hay voluntarios que ya hablan español con fluidez.[4] Lee las descripciones de algunos voluntarios de Texas que participaron en el programa.

[1] was established [2] fight against [3] have taken [4] fluently

Bolivia

Lauren — Bolivia

Lauren pasó ocho semanas en Bolivia y dice que fue increíble. La vida es un poco diferente para los voluntarios en Bolivia. En Nicaragua y Costa Rica hace calor en verano, pero en Bolivia hace frío. En Bolivia las estaciones son diferentes a las estaciones de los Estados Unidos. El verano aquí es el invierno en Bolivia. En Zanja Honda, Lauren y los otros voluntarios decidieron ayudar a la gente a implementar un sistema para recoger basura. También enseñaron inglés y con la ayuda de todos los niños y profesores, hicieron un jardín para la escuela.

Rachel — Costa Rica

Rachel pasó ocho semanas en Costa Rica trabajando con miembros de la comunidad. Durante su tiempo allí, ayudó a construir una casa para uno de los profesores de la escuela local. Construir la casa era el proyecto principal, pero Rachel y sus compañeros también participaron en charlas[5] educativas en la escuela sobre temas como higiene dental, nutrición y reforestación. Rachel tuvo un verano increíble. Tuvo la oportunidad de aprender español, jugar vóleibol con sus nuevos amigos de la comunidad y caminar por el bosque lluvioso. También comió mucho aguacate, ¡le encanta!

Costa Rica

[5] talks

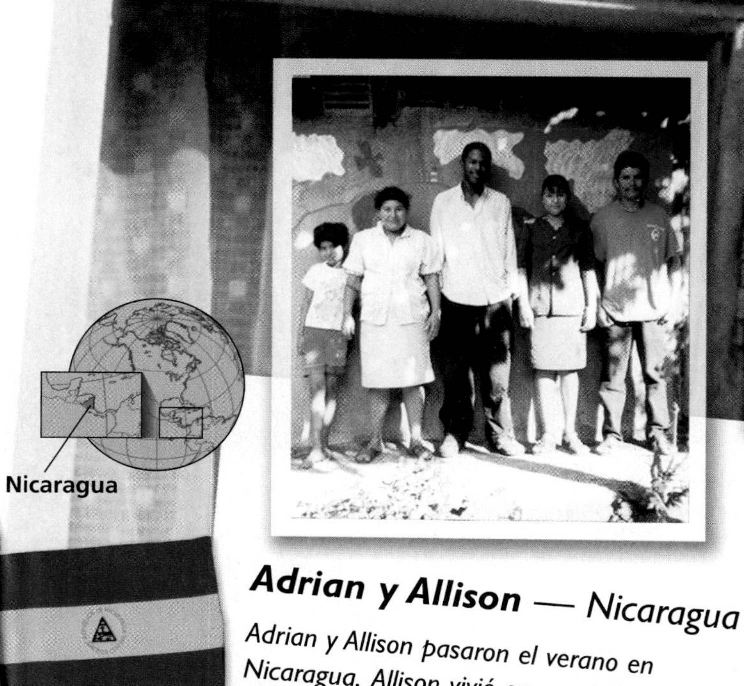

Adrian y Allison — Nicaragua

Adrian y Allison pasaron el verano en Nicaragua. Allison vivió en un pequeño pueblo[6] que se llama María del Pilar y Adrian vivió en la comunidad de Guanacastal Norte. Los dos participaron en proyectos de construcción para mejorar la salud de la gente del pueblo. Allison también pintó murales y participó en un proyecto para recoger basura. Para los dos jóvenes, fue una experiencia inolvidable. Como voluntarios, ellos ayudaron mucho a la gente de estos pueblos, pero esta gente también les dio a los voluntarios algo muy importante: una experiencia inolvidable que puede cambiarles la vida.

[6] town

Comunicación

1. ¿Qué tipo de trabajo hacen los voluntarios de Amigos de las Américas?
2. Según los voluntarios, la experiencia de participar en Amigos de las Américas les cambió la vida. ¿Cómo crees que ser voluntario(a) en Latinoamérica puede cambiarte?
3. ¿En cuál de los proyectos de los voluntarios de Amigos de las Américas te gustaría participar? ¿Por qué?
4. Compara los trabajos de los voluntarios de Amigos de las Américas con trabajos voluntarios que tú hiciste o que hay en tu comunidad. ¿Cómo son diferentes? ¿Cómo son similares?

Comunidades

Para hacer trabajo voluntario con Amigos de las Américas, es necesario hablar español. ¿Hay organizaciones similares donde tú vives? Busca oportunidades en tu comunidad de hacer trabajo voluntario usando el español. Escribe una carta a la organización pidiendo más información. Incluye una descripción de quién eres, el trabajo que prefieres hacer y cuántas horas a la semana puedes dedicar *(to dedicate)* al trabajo voluntario.

Tema 9 • Medios de comunicación

Fondo cultural

Portrait of Luis Buñuel Luis Buñuel (1900–1983) was a Spanish-born film director. He made films in Spain, the United States, Mexico, and France. His films were often controversial because of their strong imagery and difficult topics. Buñuel made two surrealist films with artist Salvador Dalí (1904–1989), Spain's most famous surrealist painter. The films mixed reality and dreams. This portrait of Buñuel was painted by Dalí in 1924 when the painter was 20 years old and Buñuel was 24.

- Who are some young film directors today whose films are considered to be "cutting edge"?

Retrato de Luis Buñuel (1924), Salvador Dalí

Oil on canvas, .70 x .60 m. Coll. Luis Buñuel, México City, D.F., México. © 2004 Salvador Dalí, Gala-Salvador Dalí Foundation/Artists Rights Society (ARS), NY. Photo credit: Bridgeman-Giraudon / Art Resource, NY.

El cine y la televisión

Chapter Objectives

- Describe movies and television programs
- Express opinions about media entertainment
- Talk about things you have done recently
- Understand cultural perspectives on common gestures

Video Highlights

A primera vista: *¿Qué dan en la tele?*
GramActiva Videos: *acabar de* + infinitive; *gustar* and similar verbs
Videomisterio: *¿Eres tú, María?*, Episodio 9

Country Connection

As you learn about movies and television programs, you will make connections to these countries and places:

Go Online
PHSchool.com
For: Online Atlas
Visit: www.phschool.com
Web Code: jce-0002

Presentadoras de Primer Impacto, un programa de Univisión

A primera vista

Vocabulario y gramática en contexto

Objectives

Read, listen to, and understand information about
- **movies and television programs**
- **opinions on media entertainment**

¡Le damos el mundo en *el Canal 9!*

¿Qué le interesa? Un programa . . .

¿ . . . de entrevistas?

Pablo Ramírez habla con personas **fascinantes.**

Entre tú y yo

¿ . . . de noticias?

Presentamos todo lo que necesita saber del mundo en 30 minutos.

Las noticias de hoy

¿ . . . educativo?

Explora el mundo de los animales.

Nuestro planeta

¿ . . . de dibujos animados?

Una presentación **cómica** para todos los niños.

Patito y Paquito

¿ . . . de concursos?

¡Los participantes pueden recibir mucho dinero!

¡Una fortuna para ti!

¿ . . . deportivo?

Hay fútbol, fútbol y más fútbol.

Fútbol hoy

¿ . . . musical?

Le presenta música de **más de** 20 países diferentes.

Ritmos latinos

¿Quizás una telenovela?

¿Qué va a pasar con Rosario y Felipe en este programa **emocionante?**

Secretos de amor

—¿Qué quieres ver en la tele?

—¿La verdad? **Me aburre** la televisión. No me interesan nada los programas que **dan.**

—No estoy de acuerdo. Pienso que la televisión presenta muchos programas interesantes y divertidos.

CINE FLORIDA

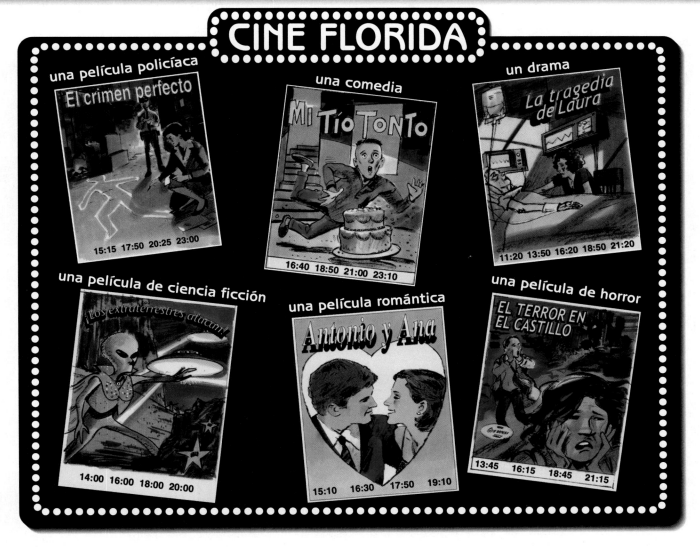

una película policíaca
El crimen perfecto
15:15 17:50 20:25 23:00

una comedia
Mi Tío Tonto
16:40 18:50 21:00 23:10

un drama
La tragedia de Laura
11:20 13:50 16:20 18:50 21:20

una película de ciencia ficción
¡Los extraterrestres atacan!
14:00 16:00 18:00 20:00

una película romántica
Antonio y Ana
15:10 16:30 17:50 19:10

una película de horror
EL TERROR EN EL CASTILLO
13:45 16:15 18:45 21:15

—¿Qué dan en el Cine Florida?

—Hay seis películas. Mis amigos dicen que esta película policíaca es muy **violenta.** No quiero verla. Me interesan más las películas románticas como *Antonio y Ana*.

—Yo también quiero verla. ¿A qué hora va a **empezar?**

—**Empieza** a las cuatro y media, y **termina antes de** las seis. **Dura menos de** una hora y **media.**

—**¿De veras?** Son **casi** las cuatro. ¡Vamos ahora!

Más práctica
Practice Workbook 9A-1, 9A-2

For: Vocabulary practice
Visit: www.phschool.com
Web Code: jcd-0901

Escuchar

¿Qué dan en la tele hoy?

Vas a escuchar información sobre ocho programas del Canal 9. Señala cada tipo de programa en tu libro.

Escuchar

¿Qué película vamos a ver?

Vas a escuchar siete frases sobre las películas que dan en el Cine Florida. Si una frase es lógica, haz el gesto del pulgar hacia arriba. Si no es lógica, haz el gesto del pulgar hacia abajo.

Videohistoria

¿Qué dan en la tele?

¿Qué programa de televisión van a ver los chicos? Lee la historia.

Strategy

Scanning
Looking for details prior to reading can help with comprehension. Scan the reading and look for instances in which one or more people disagree about something. What do they disagree about and what are some expressions used?

1 **Ignacio:** ¿Qué dan en la televisión? Elena, ¿dónde está el mando a distancia?*

Elena: Está encima de la mesita, al lado de la lámpara.

Ignacio: ¡Ah, sí! Lo veo. Vamos a ver lo que hay . . .

*remote control

5 **Ignacio:** No me gustan estos programas **infantiles.** ¿Qué más hay?

Elena: Un momento . . . este programa de entrevistas es mi favorito. Hablan de todo. Ohhh, **¡acaban de** hablar con mi actor favorito!

Ignacio: Sí, y ya terminaron. **Por eso** no tenemos que verlo.

6 **Ignacio:** Podemos ver un programa de concursos.

Javier: ¿O un programa educativo? ¿O las noticias?

Todos: ¡Nooo!

Ignacio: ¡Tantos canales y no hay nada que ver!

Ana: ¿Por qué no vamos al cine?

7 **Ana:** Quiero ver una comedia.

Elena: Yo prefiero ver una película romántica.

Ignacio: No, son tontas. ¿Qué tal una película de ciencia ficción?

Todos: ¡Nooo!

Javier: Dan un drama nuevo en el Cine Capitol.

Todos: ¡Nooo!

2 **Ana:** ¡Fabuloso! Mi telenovela favorita.

Elena: Sí, me encanta. Es muy emocionante. **El actor** y **la actriz** principales son muy guapos.

Ignacio: ¡No! Me aburren las telenovelas. Vamos a ver otro canal.

Ana y Elena: Ignacio, ¡nuestra telenovela, por favor!

3 **Elena:** ¿Qué más hay? Mmmm. **¿Qué clase de** programa es éste?

Ana: Es **un programa de la vida real.** Es muy **realista.**

Ignacio: No son realistas. Pienso que son **tontos.** ¿Verdad, Javier?

Javier: Pues, no sé mucho **sobre** esta clase de programas.

4 **Jorgito:** Elena, quiero ver dibujos animados. **Ya** son las cuatro.

Elena: Jorgito, ¿no ves que estoy con mis amigos? Tú puedes ver la tele más tarde. Mira, puedes escuchar música en mi dormitorio.

Jorgito: Está bien, pero sólo hoy.

Todos: Adiós, Jorgito.

8 **Jorgito:** Ahora puedo ver los dibujos animados, **especialmente** mi favorito, *Rin, ran, run.* ¡Qué bien!

Escribir/Hablar

¿Comprendes?

¿A quién(es) se refiere *(refers)* cada frase: Ana, Elena, Ignacio, Javier o Jorgito? Una frase puede referirse a más de una persona.

1. No me interesan nada las telenovelas.
2. No veo mucho los programas de la vida real.
3. Me encanta este programa. Hablan con actores.
4. Me encantan las telenovelas.
5. Voy a escuchar música.
6. Yo prefiero ver una película romántica.
7. Ahora no hay nadie aquí. Puedo ver mi programa favorito.

Más práctica

Practice Workbook 9A-3, 9A-4

For: Vocabulary practice
Visit: www.phschool.com
Web Code: jcd-0902

Manos a la obra

Vocabulario y gramática en uso

Objectives

- Talk about different kinds of movies and television programs
- Express opinions and preferences about entertainment
- Use *acabar de* + infinitive to talk about things you have just done
- Tell why you don't do something
- Learn to use *gustar* and similar verbs

Escuchar/Escribir/Hablar

Muchas opiniones

Un programa de radio les pregunta a sus oyentes *(listeners)* qué piensan de los diferentes programas de televisión.

1. En una hoja de papel copia la tabla y escribe los números del 1 al 6. Vas a escuchar las opiniones de unas personas. Escribe la clase de programa en la primera columna y la descripción en la segunda columna. Luego escribe frases para expresar tu opinión.

Programa de televisión	Descripción
1. las comedias	muy cómicas

Modelo

Me encantan las comedias porque son muy cómicas.

2. Habla con otro(a) estudiante. Di si estás de acuerdo con sus opiniones.

Modelo

Estoy de acuerdo. Las comedias son muy cómicas.

o: *No estoy de acuerdo. Las comedias son muy tontas.*

Escribir

Buenos ejemplos

Escoge seis de los siguientes programas de televisión. Luego escribe frases para dar un buen ejemplo de los diferentes programas.

Modelo

Frasier *es una comedia.*

   **Hablar**

¿Te gustaría ver . . . ?

Usa la información que escribiste en la Actividad 5 y habla con otro(a) estudiante sobre qué clase de programas le gustaría ver. Él o ella puede usar las siguientes palabras.

me aburren	tontos, -as	fascinantes
me gustan	emocionantes	cómicos, -as
me interesan	violentos, -as	infantiles
me encantan	realistas	**¡Respuesta personal!**

Modelo

A —*¿Te gustaría ver una comedia como Frasier?*
B —*¡Uf! Me aburren las comedias. Son tontas.*
o: *¡Por supuesto! Me encantan las comedias. Son cómicas.*

 **Escuchar/Escribir**

Escucha y escribe

Escucha y luego escribe en una hoja de papel lo que dice un joven sobre un programa de televisión que ve.

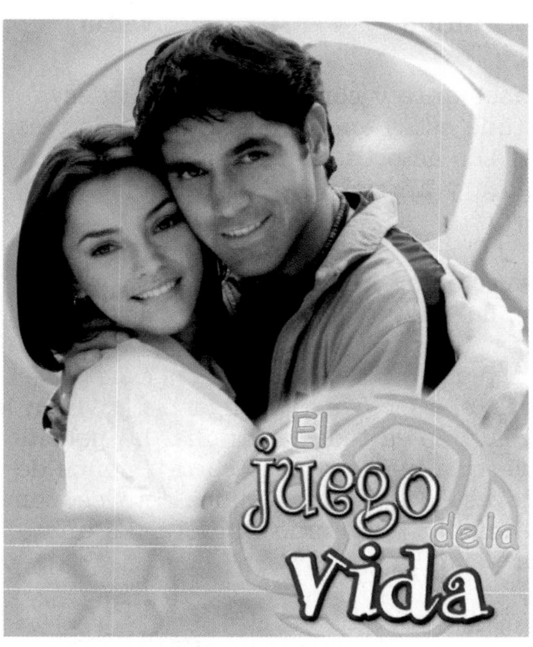

El juego de la vida, una telenovela popular de Televisa (México)

  **Escribir/Hablar**

¿Qué programa ves tú?

1. Usa la descripción del programa de televisión de la Actividad 7 como modelo y escribe sobre un programa que tú ves. No debes nombrar el programa en la descripción.
2. Lee tu descripción a otros(as) estudiantes de la clase. Ellos deben identificar el programa que describes.

Las telenovelas Venezuela, Mexico, Argentina, and Spain produce many soap operas that are popular with people of all ages. Unlike soap operas in the United States that continue for years with the same characters, the *telenovelas* frequently last only a matter of months. They are then replaced with new shows and different characters.

- What are the advantages of stories that continue for years versus stories that are new every several months? Which would you prefer?

Leer/Hablar

¿Qué dicen los críticos?

Lee el artículo abajo que escribieron los críticos Guillo y Nadia. Luego trabaja con otro(a) estudiante para decidir qué película van a ver. Contesta las preguntas en el recuadro.

Nota

Use *más / menos* **de** with numbers.

- más **de** tres horas
- menos **de** diez personas

Modelo

A —*Acabo de leer un artículo sobre la película . . . ¿Te gustaría verla?*

B —*¿Qué clase de película es?*

¿Qué clase de película es?	¿Cuánto tiempo dura?
¿De veras? ¿Cómo es?	¿Quiénes son los actores principales?
¿Sí? ¿Qué pasa en la película?	Pues, ¿quieres verla?

En nuestra opinión

¿Piensas ir al cine este fin de semana? Nadia y Guillo te dan sus impresiones de tres nuevas películas . . .

Guillo

Nadia

★★★ **recomendable**
★★ **más o menos**
★ **no la recomiendo**

Cuando el amor llega Con Cristina Campos y Rafael Montenegro. Una película romántica sobre un joven rico enamorado de una chica pobre. Ante la oposición de sus padres, el amor de los jóvenes es imposible. Esta película, de dos horas y media, es similar a las viejas fórmulas de las telenovelas—un poco tonta y aburrida. Los protagonistas son buenos, pero los actores secundarios son demasiado dramáticos. Recomendable para personas que no tienen nada que hacer. (★)

Mis padres son de otro planeta Unos chicos descubren que sus padres son originarios de otra galaxia y que están en este planeta para explorar y planear una invasión. Una producción para toda la familia que combina elementos de comedia y ciencia ficción. Es tan fascinante y cómica que no puedes creer que estás en el cine por más de tres horas. Los actores principales, Javier Zaragoza y Miguel Vilar, son fantásticos. (★★★)

Mi perro es mi héroe Un drama para toda la familia—no es violenta y es bastante realista. Un poco infantil, pero con mucha acción y emoción. El mejor amigo del hombre, el perro, con inteligencia y valor, le salva la vida* a toda la familia. La película es divertida pero un poco corta (menos de dos horas). Tiene muy buenos actores, como Ana Jiménez y Antonio Barrera. Es una buena película. (★★★)

*saves the life

Pensar/Hablar/Escribir

¿Cuántas horas de tele?

Vas a calcular el promedio *(average)* de horas que tus compañeros ven la tele.

Conexiones | Las matemáticas

1. Escribe el número de horas que viste la tele cada día de la semana pasada. Suma *(Add up)* estas horas. Calcula el promedio de horas para cada día.

   ____ *(total de horas)* dividido por 7

2. Trabaja con un grupo de cuatro personas. Pregunta a tus compañeros(as) el tiempo promedio que vieron la televisión cada día. Escribe la información que recibes de tu grupo.

Modelo

A —*Como promedio, ¿cuántas horas viste la tele cada día?*
B —*La vi casi dos horas cada día.*

3. Calcula el promedio de horas que tu grupo vio la tele cada día la semana pasada. Escribe una frase para presentar la información a la clase.

Pensar/Leer/Hablar

La tele en tu vida

En un estudio reciente, se dio a conocer que, como promedio, las personas de los Estados Unidos ven casi cuatro horas de tele al día. ¡La suma de estas horas equivale a casi dos meses al año frente a la televisión!

1. Usa el promedio de horas de tu grupo de la Actividad 10 y calcula el número total de horas que vieron la tele en un año.
   - 365 días al año por *(promedio de horas)* son *(total de horas)* al año
2. Usa el total de horas al año para contestar estas preguntas. *(Nota: Hay aproximadamente 720 horas en un mes.)*
   1. ¿Tu grupo ve la tele más de un mes al año o menos?
   2. ¿La ven Uds. más que el promedio de personas en los Estados Unidos o menos? ¿Y de las personas en los otros países de la gráfica?
   3. ¿Crees que las personas en los países de la gráfica ven demasiada tele? ¿Por qué?

Fuente: Red de los que apagan la tele

Gramática

Acabar de + infinitive

When you want to say that something just happened, use the present tense of *acabar de* + infinitive.

Acabo de ver un programa musical.	***I just saw** a music program.*
Mis padres **acaban de ir** al cine.	*My parents **just went** to the movies.*
Acabamos de hablar de esa película.	***We just talked** about that movie.*

Although the action took place in the past, the present-tense forms of *acabar* are used.

GramActiva VIDEO

Want more help with *acabar de* + infinitive? Watch the **GramActiva** video.

Gramática  Escribir

¡Acaban de hacer muchas cosas!

La familia Martínez acaba de hacer muchas cosas esta mañana antes de ir a estudiar y trabajar. Lee la lista de quehaceres y escribe quién acaba de hacer qué cosa.

Modelo

mamá / preparar el desayuno de sus hijos
Mamá acaba de preparar el desayuno de sus hijos.

Quehaceres ...

1. mamá / preparar el desayuno de sus hijos ✓
2. Carlitos / comer el desayuno ✓
3. Mariel / limpiar su dormitorio ✓
4. Ezequiel / sacar la basura ✓
5. Ezequiel, Carlitos y Mariel / terminar su tarea ✓
6. papá / pasar la aspiradora en la sala ✓
7. Elena / dar de comer al gato ✓
8. todos / buscar sus abrigos ✓

Sábado gigante is one of the longest running shows in television history. Its popular host, Don Francisco, started this unique variety program in his native Chile in 1962. It now airs from Miami every Saturday night and brings comedy, celebrity guests, musical performances, games, and contests to its more than 100 million viewers in 42 countries.

- What television shows do you know that have enjoyed continued success over the years?

El famosísimo Don Francisco

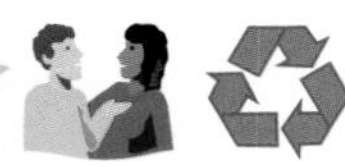

Escribir/Hablar

Acabo de ver . . .

1. Copia la gráfica en una hoja de papel. Escribe tres clases de programas de televisión, obras de teatro o películas que acabas de ver. Da el nombre y haz una descripción.

Acabo de ver . . .	Nombre	Descripción
Una película romántica	*¡No puedo vivir sin ti!*	*demasiado triste*

2. Trabaja con otro(a) estudiante para hablar sobre lo que acaban de ver.

Modelo

A —*Acabo de ver una película romántica.*
B —*¿De veras? ¿Cómo se llama?*
A —¡No puedo vivir sin ti!
B —*¿Te gustó?*
A —*No, no me gustó porque es demasiado triste.*

¿Recuerdas?

Some adverbs you can use in descriptions are:

bastante	muy
demasiado	un poco

Más práctica

Practice Workbook 9A-5

For: Practice with *acabar de*
Visit: www.phschool.com
Web Code: jcd-0903

Exploración del lenguaje

Words of Greek and Arabic origin

Languages change when regions and nations interact with, or are conquered or colonized by, people who speak a different language. Long before the Romans brought Latin to Spain, certain Greek words had entered the Latin language. Words like *el problema, el programa,* and *el drama* originally were masculine nouns in Greek. When they came into Latin and then Spanish, they kept their masculine gender even though they end in *a.*

Try it out! Which of these new words would you use in the following sentences?

el clima   el sistema   el poema

1. No comprendo _____ de clasificación de películas en ese país.
2. Me gustaría visitar Panamá porque _____ allí es tropical.
3. Me gusta _____ que acabo de leer.

Arabic also had a large influence on Spanish. Around A.D. 700 the Arabic-speaking Moors invaded Spain from northern Africa. They ruled for 800 years and played a major role in the development of the Spanish language and culture. Words that came from Arabic often begin with the letters *al-*. Many words in Spanish that have a *z* or a *j* in them are also of Arabic origin. You know these words that came from Arabic: *alfombra, azúcar, naranja.*

Try it out! You also know these words that are from Arabic. Fill in the missing letters.

a_ul   __macén   _anahoria

Gramática

Gustar and similar verbs

Even though we usually translate the verb *gustar* as "to like," it literally means "to please." So when you say, *Me gustan los programas deportivos,* you're actually saying, "Sports programs are pleasing to me." *Programas deportivos* is the subject of the sentence, and *me* is the indirect object. Here's the pattern:

indirect object + form of *gustar* + subject

> **¿Recuerdas?**
>
> You have used *me gusta(n), te gusta(n),* and *le gusta(n)* to talk about what a person likes.
>
> - A mí **me gusta** el cine pero a mi hermano **le gusta** más la televisión.

The subject in a sentence with *gustar* usually follows the verb. You need to know if the subject is singular or plural to know which form of *gustar* to use. If the subject is singular, use *gusta.* If it's plural, use *gustan.* If it's an infinitive, use *gusta.*

Me gust**a** **el actor** en la telenovela pero no me gust**an** **las actrices.**

A mis amigos les gust**a** **ver** películas.

To emphasize or clarify *who* is pleased, you can use an additional *a* + pronoun:

A mí me gustan los dibujos animados, pero **a él** no le gustan.

Here are the other verbs you know that are similar to *gustar:*

aburrir	A mí **me aburren** las películas románticas.
doler *(o→ue)*	A Fernando **le duelen** los pies.
encantar	A mis padres **les encanta** el teatro.
faltar	**Me faltan** un cuchillo y un tenedor.
interesar	**Nos interesan** mucho los programas musicales.
quedar	¿No **te queda** bien el vestido?

> **GramActiva** VIDEO
>
> Want more help with *gustar* and other similar verbs? Watch the **GramActiva** video.

Gramática **Escuchar/Escribir**

Escucha y escribe

Escucha las opiniones de la familia Linares sobre los programas que dan en la televisión. En una hoja de papel, escribe los números del 1 al 6 y escribe las frases que escuchas.

Mirando la tele en familia.

  **Escribir/Hablar**

A mí y a ti

1. Trabaja con otro(a) estudiante. Copia el diagrama Venn en una hoja de papel. Escribe el nombre de tu compañero(a) encima del óvalo a la derecha. En el óvalo indicado con *A mí* escribe cinco clases de películas o programas de televisión que te gustan.

2. Pregunta a tu compañero(a) si le gustan las clases de programas y películas que tú escribiste. Si a él o a ella le gusta la clase de programa o película, escribe el nombre en el óvalo de la derecha. (Vas a usar el diagrama Venn en la Actividad 16.)

Modelo

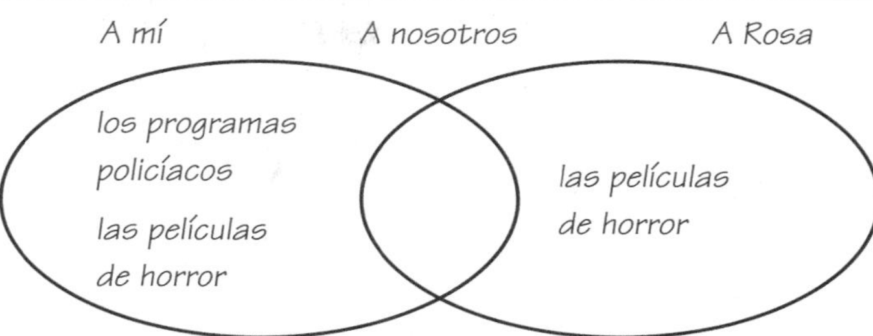

Modelo

A —*¿Te gustan los programas policíacos?*
B —*A ver . . . no, no me gustan mucho.*
A —*Pues, ¿te gustan las películas de horror?*
B —*Sí, me gustan mucho.*

 **Escribir**

A nosotros nos gusta . . .

Compara los dos lados de tu diagrama. Escribe las clases de programas y películas que a los dos les gustan en el centro de ese diagrama. Escribe al menos cinco frases completas para describir qué les gusta a Uds.

Modelo

A nosotros nos gustan las películas de horror.
A mí me gustan los programas policíacos pero a Rosa no le gustan.

Modelo

A mí — A nosotros — A Rosa

los programas policíacos
las películas de horror

las películas de horror

las películas de horror

Fondo cultural 

Cable television The cable and satellite television industry in Latin America has grown tremendously. Hundreds of channels are available to viewers. Some cable channels specialize in news or sports, and offer their programming to other countries as well. Among the sports, soccer is the one that attracts the most viewers. The World Cup is enormously popular in Latin America and around the world.

- What Latin American programs can you find in your local cable or satellite listings? Watch some of them to find out where these programs are produced.

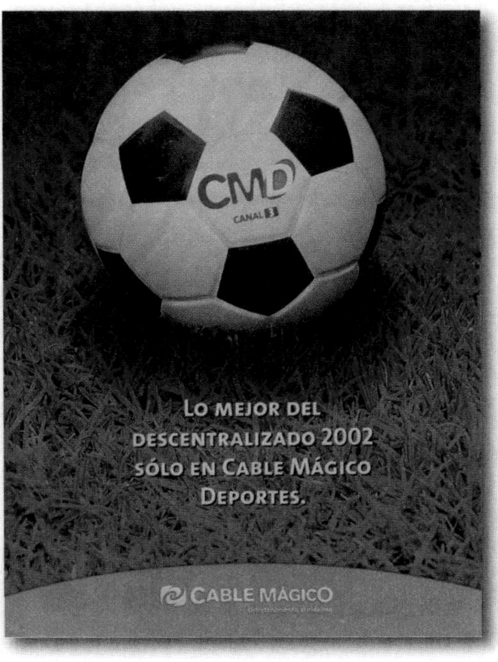

Escribir/Hablar/GramActiva

Juego

1. Trabaja en grupos de cuatro personas. Necesitas 20 tarjetas de tres colores. Debes tener cinco tarjetas de un color para la columna 1, cinco de otro color para la columna 2 y diez del tercer color para la columna 3. En cada tarjeta, escribe una de las palabras o expresiones de las dos primeras columnas. Para la tercera columna, escribe dos palabras para cada categoría (por ejemplo, para "cuerpo" puedes escribir *el brazo* en una tarjeta, y *la pierna* en otra).

1	2	3
a mí	encanta(n)	cuerpo
a mi amigo(a)	duele(n)	películas
a nosotros	interesa(n)	clases
a mis amigos	aburre(n)	ropa
a Uds.	queda(n) bien	comidas

2. Baraja *(Shuffle)* las tarjetas de cada columna y ponlas boca abajo *(face down)* en sus tres grupos. Toma una tarjeta de cada grupo, forma una frase completa y di la frase. *Importante:* Para las palabras del primer grupo, vas a tener que escoger una de estas palabras: *me, te, le, nos, les.* Si tu grupo decide que la gramática de tu frase es correcta, recibes 1 punto. Recibes otro punto si la frase es lógica. Si puedes cambiar la frase para hacerla lógica, recibes 2 puntos.

Modelo

A mi amigo le duele el pescado. (1 punto)
A mi amigo le duele la pierna. (2 puntos)

Pronunciación

Linking words

In Spanish just as in English, you don't pronounce a sentence as completely separate words. Instead, the words flow together in phrases. That is why it often seems that phrases or sentences sound as if they are one long word.

How the words flow together depends on the last sound of a word and the beginning sound of the following word. The flow of sounds is usually created by two of the same vowels, two different vowels, or a consonant followed by a vowel. Listen to and say these word combinations:

me‿encanta	de‿entrevistas	le‿aburre
nos‿interesa	dibujos‿animados	de‿horror

Try it out! Listen to and say these sentences. Be careful not to break the flow of sound where you see "‿".

Me‿interesa‿ese programa de‿entrevistas.

A‿Ana le‿aburre‿ese programa‿educativo.

La película de‿horror dura‿una‿hora‿y media.

Vamos‿a ver lo que‿hay‿en la tele.

Me‿encanta‿el‿actor y la‿actriz de‿esa telenovela.

Escribir/Hablar

¿Qué hay en la tele?

A veces decimos, "¡Hay tantos canales y programas en la tele pero no hay nada interesante!" Ahora tienes la oportunidad de planear seis horas de televisión para el sábado, desde las 17.00 horas hasta las 23.00 horas, para un concurso que se llama "Tus propias seis horas en la tele."

1. Trabaja en un grupo de tres. Escriban una lista de programas o películas que les gustaría incluir *(include)* en las seis horas. Den esta información para cada programa o película:
   - la clase de programa
   - el nombre
   - cómo es
   - cuánto tiempo dura
   - para quiénes es recomendable
   - por qué le va a interesar al público

2. Preparen una presentación para la clase. Pueden hacer algo visual para acompañar su presentación.

3. Después de escuchar a los diferentes grupos, cada grupo va a votar por la mejor presentación. ¡No pueden votar por la suya *(your own)*! Los grupos tienen que escribir cuatro frases para explicar su decisión. El grupo que recibe más votos gana el concurso.

Modelo

Nosotros votamos por la presentación del grupo de Ana, David y Kathy. Tienen muchos programas que nos interesan a nosotros.

El español en la comunidad

While many television networks are losing viewers, the number of viewers watching Spanish-language networks is growing. Look in your newspaper's TV guide and find listings for a Spanish-language network. Find the name of a program for each kind of show on p. 426. Watch a few minutes of one of the programs. Although you might find it difficult to understand, tune in from time to time. You'll be amazed at how much you'll learn!

- How are the listings similar to or different from those for the networks you usually watch? Write your impressions of the television show you watched.

Más práctica

Practice Workbook 9A-6, 9A-7

For: Practice with verbs like *gustar*
Visit: www.phschool.com
Web Code: jcd-0904

¡Adelante!

Lectura

Objectives

- **Read about TV-watching habits of teens**
- **Learn to use gestures**
- **Present a summary of a movie or TV show**
- **Watch *¿Eres tú, María?*, Episodio 9**

Una semana sin televisión

Strategy

Reading for comprehension
Read without stopping at unknown words. Then go back, decide if the words are important, and see if you can guess their meanings.

¿Sabes que los niños estadounidenses pasan más horas al año pegados a la pantalla de su televisión que haciendo cualquier otra cosa, a excepción de dormir?

Hay estudios que dicen que ver demasiado la televisión puede causar malos hábitos de comida, falta de ejercicio y obesidad. En cuatro horas de dibujos animados el sábado por la mañana los niños pueden ver 202 anuncios sobre refrescos, dulces y cereales azucarados. Esta comida combinada con las horas frente a la pantalla resulta en que uno de cada ocho niños estadounidenses tenga exceso de peso.

También hay estudios que dan nuevas pruebas de la relación entre la televisión y la violencia. Uno de estos estudios indica que niños que ven más de una hora de televisión al día tienen más probabilidad de ser violentos y agresivos de adultos.

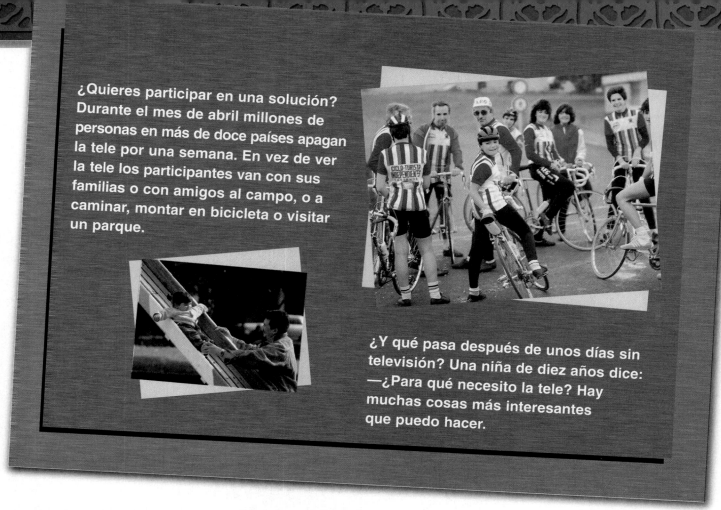

¿Quieres participar en una solución? Durante el mes de abril millones de personas en más de doce países apagan la tele por una semana. En vez de ver la tele los participantes van con sus familias o con amigos al campo, o a caminar, montar en bicicleta o visitar un parque.

¿Y qué pasa después de unos días sin televisión? Una niña de diez años dice: —¿Para qué necesito la tele? Hay muchas cosas más interesantes que puedo hacer.

¿Comprendes?

Prepara información para un debate sobre la cuestión: ¿Es bueno o malo ver la televisión?

1. Escribe una lista de cuatro razones *(reasons)* en favor de no ver la tele. Usa información que leíste en el artículo.
2. Escribe una lista de cuatro razones en favor de ver la tele.

Y tú, ¿qué dices?

1. Usa la información en tu lista para expresar tu opinión: ¿Es bueno o malo ver la televisión? ¿Por qué?
2. Para ti, ¿va a ser fácil o difícil pasar una semana sin ver la televisión? ¿Por qué?
3. En Chile, a una persona que ve mucha televisión se le llama "un(a) tevito(a)." ¿Qué puedes decirle a un(a) tevito(a) para persuadirlo(a) a hacer otras cosas que son mejores para la salud?

For: Internet link activity
Visit: www.phschool.com
Web Code: jcd-0905

La cultura en vivo

Comunicación sin palabras

Every culture has gestures that communicate a message. You've already seen gestures for *¡ojo!* and *más o menos.* Here are a few more gestures used in many Spanish-speaking countries to communicate a message.

mucha gente

¡Hay mucha gente en la fiesta!

(Place your fingertips together, then open your hand. Repeat this motion in a rhythmic gesture.)

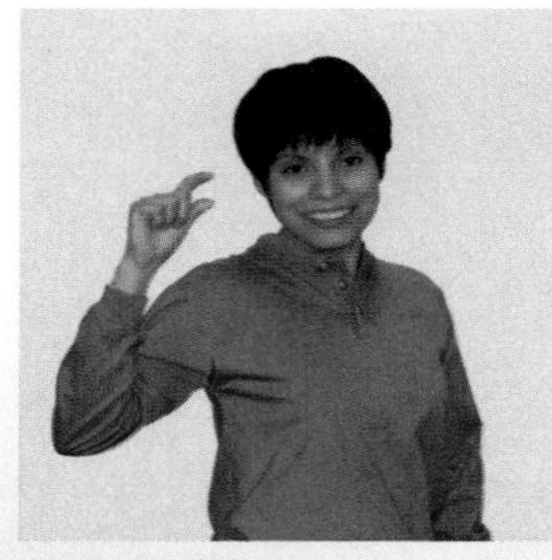

un poco

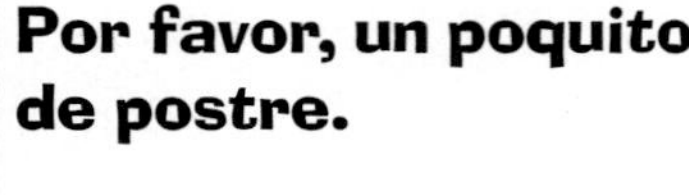

Por favor, un poquito de postre.

¡a comer!

¡Vamos a comer!

(With your fingertips bunched, bring your hand up close to your mouth, then extend it forward, bending your arm at the elbow. Repeat the motion two or three times.)

¡qué rico!

¡Este plato está muy rico!

(Kiss the bunched fingertips of one hand, then quickly pull your hand away, extending your fingers.)

no sé

No sé dónde está el libro.

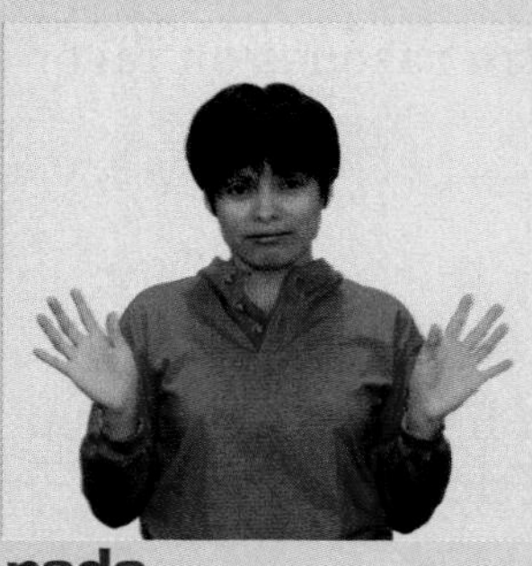

nada

No tengo nada.

Try it out! Work with a partner and create a short skit in which you use one of these gestures. Present it for the class.

Think about it! What gestures do you use most often? Do you ever use gestures that are the same as or similar to the ones shown on this page? Do you think you would understand some of the gestures on this page even without an explanation?

Presentación oral

¿Qué dan esta semana?

Task

You are reviewing a movie or television show you have just seen for your school's closed-circuit TV system. Prepare a summary of the movie or show.

1. **Prepare** Choose a movie or TV show to talk about. Cut out ads or photos about it from a newspaper or TV guide or download them from the Internet. Copy the chart below on a sheet of paper and provide the information for the movie or show you have chosen.

Nombre	
Clase de película o programa	
Actor / actores	
Actriz / actrices	
Cómo es	
Cuánto tiempo dura	
Para quiénes es	
Tus impresiones	

2. **Practice** Use your notes from the chart for your presentation. Create a poster with the visuals you have collected. Go through your presentation several times. You may use your notes in practice, but not when you present. Try to:
   - provide all key information about the film or show
   - use complete sentences in your presentation
   - speak clearly

3. **Present** Present your chosen movie or television show to a small group or the class. Use your poster to help guide you through the presentation.

4. **Evaluation** Your teacher may give you a rubric for how your presentation will be graded. You probably will be graded on:
   - how complete your presentation is
   - how much information you communicate
   - how easy it is to understand you

Strategy

Using charts
Create a chart to help you think through the key information you will want to talk about. This will help you speak more effectively.

Videomisterio

¿Eres tú, María?

Episodio 9

Antes de ver el video

"Paco, te digo que te necesito ahora mismo. Por favor, rápido. Y a Margarita, también."

Nota gramatical What's a good mystery without an expression like "Follow her!"? In this episode you'll hear several uses of the verb to follow: *seguir.*

sigo	**seguimos**
sigues	**seguís**
sigue	**siguen**

Resumen del episodio

Al día siguiente Lola va a su trabajo, cuando ve a María. ¡Qué suerte! Lola la sigue y llama a Paco y a Margarita. Ella necesita a los dos ahora mismo para ayudarla. Vigilan[1] a María y a un hombre en el café, y Margarita muestra[2] sus talentos de detective. Es evidente que María y el hombre no están nada contentos. Pero, ¿quién es este hombre misterioso y por qué quiere irse de Madrid?

[1] They watch [2] shows

Palabras para comprender

¡Venid! Come!
ve a sentarte go sit
aparece appears
quiere irse wants to go away
vengan en seguida come right away
sigue vigilando continue watching

—¡Ay de mí!
—Cálmate, Lola.

"Lola, ¿quién es ese hombre? ¿De qué están hablando?"

"Ahora lo comprendo todo. Voy a llamar al Inspector Gil."

Después de ver el video

¿Comprendes?

A. Contesta las preguntas.

1. ¿Quiénes ayudan a Lola con la investigación?
2. ¿Quién va al café para escuchar a María y al hombre?
3. ¿Está Lola tranquila o nerviosa? ¿Por qué?
4. Según Lola, ¿quién es el hombre en el café?
5. Según Margarita, ¿quién es la chica en el café?
6. Según Margarita, ¿el hombre quiere quedarse *(stay)* en Madrid o quiere irse?

B. Lola dice, "Ahora lo comprendo todo." En tu opinión, ¿qué comprende Lola? ¿Cuál es la solución del misterio?

For: More on *¿Eres tú, María?*
Visit: www.phschool.com
Web Code: jcd-0507

Repaso del capítulo

Vocabulario y gramática

Chapter Review

To prepare for the test, check to see if you . . .

- **know the new vocabulary and grammar**
- **can perform the tasks on p. 447**

to talk about television shows

el canal	channel
el programa de concursos	game show
el programa deportivo	sports show
el programa de dibujos animados	cartoon show
el programa de entrevistas	interview program
el programa de la vida real	reality program
el programa de noticias	news program
el programa educativo	educational program
el programa musical	musical program
la telenovela	soap opera

to talk about movies

la comedia	comedy
el drama	drama
la película de ciencia ficción	science fiction movie
la película de horror	horror movie
la película policíaca	crime movie, mystery
la película romántica	romantic movie

to give your opinion of a movie or program

cómico, -a	funny
emocionante	touching
fascinante	fascinating
infantil	for children; childish
realista	realistic
tonto, -a	silly, stupid
violento, -a	violent
me aburre(n)	it bores me (they bore me)
me interesa(n)	it interests me (they interest me)

to ask and tell about movies or programs

el actor	actor
la actriz	actress
dar	to show
durar	to last
empezar *(e → ie)*	to begin
terminar	to end
más / menos de	more / less than
medio, -a	half
¿Qué clase de . . . ?	What kind of . . . ?

to talk about what has just happened

acabar de + *infinitive*	to have just . . .

verbs similar to *gustar*

aburrir	to bore
doler *(o → ue)*	to hurt, to ache
encantar	to please very much, to love
faltar	to be missing
interesar	to interest
quedar	to fit

other useful expressions

antes de	before
casi	almost
¿De veras?	Really?
especialmente	especially
por eso	therefore, for that reason
sobre	about
ya	already

Más práctica

Practice Workbook Puzzle 9A-8
Practice Workbook Organizer 9A-9

For *Vocabulario adicional,* see pp. 472–473.

For: Test preparation
Visit: www.phschool.com
Web Code: jcd-0906

Preparación para el examen

On the exam you will be asked to . . .	Here are practice tasks similar to those you will find on the exam . . .	If you need review . . .
 **1 Escuchar** Listen and understand as people express opinions about movies and TV programs	Listen as you hear a phone pollster ask people about TV programs they have watched on the new Spanish-language cable station. For each viewer, decide if the shows were: a) boring; b) interesting; c) too violent; d) too childish or silly.	**pp. 426-429** *A primera vista* **p. 430** Actividad 4 **p. 431** Actividades 6–7 **p. 435** Actividad 13
 **2 Hablar** Ask and answer questions about the types of movies and TV programs people prefer	Tell your partner about a movie or TV program you just saw and express your opinion about it. Ask if your partner saw the same thing and what he or she thought of it. If your partner didn't see it, ask him or her to tell about something he or she just saw. You might say: *Acabo de ver una película fantástica con Tom Cruise . . .*	**pp. 426-429** *A primera vista* **p. 430** Actividad 4 **p. 431** Actividad 6 **p. 432** Actividad 9 **p. 435** Actividad 13 **p. 437** Actividad 15 **p. 443** *Presentación oral*
3 Leer Read and understand what an entertainment critic writes about a new TV program	Before class begins, you grab a Spanish-language magazine and turn to the entertainment section. After reading part of the entertainment critic's review, see if you can determine his opinion of a new soap opera series, *Mi secreto.* Does he like it? Why or why not? En el primer episodio de ***Mi secreto,*** nos aburren con una historia infantil y con actores sin talento que quieren ser emocionantes pero no pueden. ¡Pienso que este programa es para las personas que no tienen nada que hacer!	**pp. 426-429** *A primera vista* **p. 432** Actividad 9
 **4 Escribir** Write about a movie you recently saw	You are keeping a journal to practice writing in Spanish. Today you are going to write about a movie you saw recently. Mention the name of the movie, the type of movie it is, and what you liked or disliked about it.	**p. 431** Actividad 8 **p. 435** Actividad 13 **p. 437** Actividades 15–16 **p. 443** *Presentación oral*
 **5 Pensar** Demonstrate an understanding of common gestures	You have learned that almost all cultures can communicate without words. With a partner, see if you can demonstrate the six gestures you have learned in this chapter from the Spanish-speaking world. Are these gestures similar to those in our culture?	**p. 442** *La cultura en vivo*

Fondo cultural

Reading the Letter is from painter Pablo Picasso's Neo-Classical period, when he was influenced by ancient Roman sculpture. He used simplified color and heavy lines. The thickness of the hand over the man's shoulder on the right can remind you of weighty, unmoving, ancient statuary.

- What other characteristics of statuary do you see in the painting?

Reading the Letter (1921), Pablo Picasso

Oil on canvas, 184 x 105 cm. Photo: J.G. Berizzi. Musée Picasso, Paris, France. Photo credit: Réunion des Musées Nationaux/Art Resource, NY.

Edificio de Correos, Madrid, España

La tecnología

Chapter Objectives

- Talk about computers and the Internet
- Learn to ask for something and to tell what something is used for
- Talk about knowing people or knowing how to do things
- Understand cultural perspectives on using technology

Video Highlights

A primera vista: ***¿Cómo se comunica?***
GramActiva Videos: **the present tense of *pedir* and *servir; saber* and *conocer***
Videomisterio: ***¿Eres tú, María?,* Episodio 10**

Country Connection

As you learn about different means of communication and how technology changes people's lives, you will make connections to these countries and places:

For: Online Atlas
Visit: www.phschool.com
Web Code: jce-0002

A primera vista

Vocabulario y gramática en contexto

Objectives

Read, listen to, and understand information about
- computers and ways to use computers
- ways to communicate

"En **el laboratorio** en nuestra escuela, los estudiantes **saben** usar las computadoras para hacer muchas cosas. A muchos estudiantes les gusta . . .

. . . **crear documentos** o escribir **una composición,**

. . . hacer **gráficos,**

la diapositiva

la computadora portátil

. . . y preparar **presentaciones** con diapositivas.

Otros estudiantes **están en línea** para **navegar en la Red.** Pueden **buscar un sitio Web** o **bajar información** para **un informe.**

una canción

A otros les interesa **grabar un disco compacto.** Esta chica graba canciones."

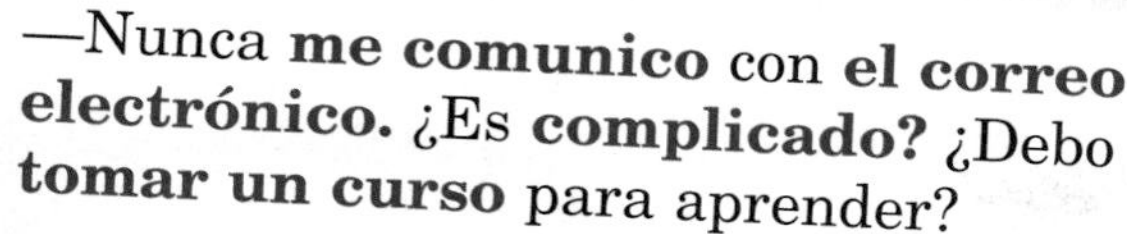

—Nunca **me comunico** con **el correo electrónico.** ¿Es **complicado?** ¿Debo **tomar un curso** para aprender?

—No, abuelito, puedes aprender fácilmente. No debes **tener miedo de** usar la computadora. Y siempre me puedes **pedir** ayuda. ¿Cómo **te comunicas** con tus amigos que no viven cerca?

—Prefiero **enviarles** una carta o una tarjeta o puedo visitarlos para hablar cara a cara. Es mucho más personal.

la carta

la tarjeta

hablar **cara a cara**

Actividad 1 **Escuchar**

¿Sí o no?

Vas a escuchar siete frases. Si una frase es cierta, haz el gesto del pulgar hacia arriba. Si una frase es falsa, haz el gesto del pulgar hacia abajo.

Más práctica
Practice Workbook 9B-1, 9B-2

For: Vocabulary practice
Visit: www.phschool.com
Web Code: jcd-0911

Actividad 2 **Escuchar**

¿Es lógico?

Primero lee las respuestas. Luego escucha cada conversación y escoge el comentario más lógico.

1. **a.** Al papá le gusta usar la Red.
   b. El papá no sabe usar la Red.
2. **a.** El estudiante quiere grabar un disco compacto.
   b. El estudiante quiere bajar información.
3. **a.** Va a enviarle una carta.
   b. Va a enviarle una tarjeta.

Videohistoria

¿Cómo se comunica?

Ana sabe usar una cámara digital y una computadora. Ella puede navegar en la Red y tiene su propia página Web. ¿Qué le va a enseñar a Javier?

Strategy

Recognizing cognates
Recognizing cognates in the following dialogue can help improve your understanding. Skim the reading and make a list of the cognates.

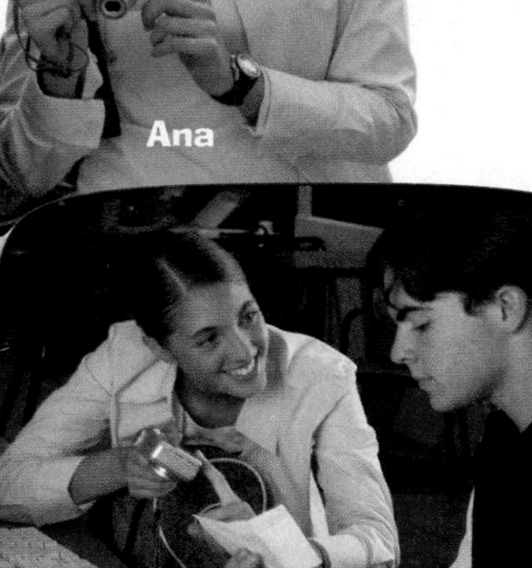

1 **Javier:** Hola, Ana. ¿Cómo estás?

Ana: Muy bien, ¿y tú? Mira. Acabo de comprar esta **cámara digital.** Es fascinante. ¿La **conoces?**

Javier: A ver. No **conozco** ese tipo de cámara. ¡Qué interesante!

5 **Ana:** Aquí puedes navegar en la Red o **visitar salones de chat.** Mira, mi **página Web.** Yo la hice.

Javier: ¿Tú la hiciste? ¡Qué bien! Pero . . . **¿para qué sirve?**

Ana: El Internet **sirve para** mucho. Puedes **escribir por** correo electrónico, buscar información, jugar juegos . . .

6 **Ana:** Tengo una idea. Tu amigo Esteban tiene **dirección electrónica,** ¿no?

Javier: Creo que sí. ¡Ah! Aquí está en su carta.

7 **Javier:** Hola, Esteban. Saludos desde un cibercafé en Madrid . . .

Ana: ¡Eso es! Tú vas a escribirle por correo electrónico. Y le vamos a enviar esta foto de nosotros.

2 **Ana:** ¿Adónde vas?

Javier: Voy a enviar una tarjeta a Esteban, mi amigo en San Antonio. Mira, tengo una foto de él.

Ana: Mmmm. Es muy simpático, ¿no? Si quieres, te acompaño.

3 **Ana:** Vamos, Javier. Uno, dos, tres. Y mira, aquí estás. **¿Qué te parece?**

Javier: Muy bien. Sacaste las fotos muy **rápidamente.** Veo que no es complicado.

4 **Javier:** Un momento, voy a enviar mi tarjeta.

Ana: ¿Por qué no te comunicas con Esteban por correo electrónico?

Javier: Porque no tengo ordenador.

Ana: No importa. En Madrid hay muchos cibercafés. Vamos a uno.

8 **Javier:** . . . y aquí estoy con mi buena amiga, Ana. ¿Qué tal la familia? Y el cumpleaños de Cristina, ¿cómo lo pasaste?

Esteban: Es evidente que Javier está muy contento en Madrid.

También se dice . . .

la computadora = el ordenador *(España)*

Leer/Escribir

¿Comprendes?

En cada frase hay un error. Lee la frase y después escribe la frase con la información correcta.

1. Ana acaba de comprar una computadora portátil.
2. Javier quiere enviarle a Esteban una carta.
3. Javier no le escribe por correo electrónico porque no le gusta usar las computadoras.
4. Javier saca las fotos con la cámara digital.
5. Según Ana, la Red no sirve para mucho.
6. Ana le escribe a Esteban por correo electrónico.
7. Javier le pregunta a Esteban sobre el cumpleaños de Angélica.

Más práctica

Practice Workbook 9B-3, 9B-4

For: Vocabulary practice
Visit: www.phschool.com
Web Code: jcd-0912

Manos a la obra

Vocabulario y gramática en uso

Objectives

- Talk about traditional and electronic forms of communication
- Talk about how computers are used
- Express opinions about computers
- Learn e→*i* stem-changing verbs: *pedir* and *servir*
- Know when to use *saber* and *conocer*

Leer/Pensar/Hablar

La computadora y tú

1. Toma esta prueba *(test)* sobre cómo usas la computadora. Determina tu evaluación y lee la recomendación del Centro de Computación.
2. Pregunta a otro(a) estudiante qué curso debe tomar según los resultados de la prueba. Tiene que darte tres razones *(reasons)* para justificar el curso.

Modelo

A —*¿Qué curso debes tomar?*
B —*Debo tomar un curso avanzado.*
A —*¿Por qué?*
B —*Porque ya navego en la Red y busco sitios Web. Sé crear un sitio Web.*

Las cuevas de Altamira Long before people were able to write, they drew pictures on cave walls. These are the first record we have of communication. Spectacular paintings of bison, deer, horses, and wild boars were discovered in 1879 in the caves of Altamira in northern Spain. These drawings are more than 14,000 years old.

- Why do you think the cave dwellers drew pictures of animals? What would you draw?

Un bisonte en la cueva de Altamira

La computadora y tú

1. ¿Cómo te comunicas más con otras personas?
   a. Les hablo cara a cara.
   b. Les envío cartas o tarjetas.
   c. Les escribo por correo electrónico.
   d. Visito salones de chat.
2. ¿Cómo buscas información cuando escribes informes?
   a. Voy a la biblioteca por un libro.
   b. Les pido ayuda a mis amigos.
   c. Navego en la Red y busco sitios Web.
   d. Bajo documentos que me sirven mucho.
3. ¿Qué sabes hacer en la computadora?
   a. Sé encender* la computadora.
   b. Sé escribir una composición.
   c. Sé crear una presentación usando diapositivas.
   d. Sé crear un sitio Web.
4. ¿Para qué te sirve la computadora?
   a. No me sirve para nada.
   b. Me sirve para jugar juegos.
   c. Me sirve para navegar en la Red.
   d. Me sirve para buscar y bajar información.
5. ¿Cuál es tu opinión de las computadoras?
   a. Tengo miedo de las computadoras.
   b. Las computadoras son demasiado complicadas.
   c. Las computadoras me ayudan a hacer cosas más rápidamente.
   d. Las computadoras son necesarias para la comunicación.

Evaluación
Cada a = 1 punto
Cada b = 3 puntos
Cada c = 4 puntos
Cada d = 6 puntos

El Centro de Computación tiene cursos ideales para ti. Según el resultado de la prueba, debes tomar uno de estos cursos:

Puntos	Tu curso ideal
de 5 a 10	Básico 1
de 11 a 16	Básico 2
de 17 a 23	Intermedio
de 24 a 30	Avanzado

*turn on

Escuchar/Escribir

Opiniones diferentes

1. Vas a escuchar las opiniones de cuatro personas sobre cómo prefieren comunicarse. En una hoja de papel, escribe los números del 1 al 4 y escribe lo que escuchas.
2. Después de escuchar sus opiniones, indica si crees que las personas que tienen estas opiniones están en la sala o en el laboratorio de computadoras.

Leer/Escribir

Definiciones

Lee las definiciones y escribe la palabra correspondiente.

Modelo

Es cómo puedes enviar una carta por computadora.
el correo electrónico

1. Es una foto que podemos proyectar durante una presentación.
2. Es una composición musical que podemos cantar.
3. Es una forma de comunicación que usa bolígrafo y papel. *(Hay dos posibilidades.)*
4. Es un lugar en la Red que da información sobre una organización o una persona.
5. Es una computadora pequeña que puedes llevar a diferentes lugares.
6. Es un lugar en la escuela donde hay muchas computadoras que los estudiantes pueden usar.
7. Es una forma de comunicación bonita o cómica que le envías* a una persona para su cumpleaños.
8. Es algo visual que puedes crear o ver en la computadora.
9. Es algo que escribes sobre un tópico para una clase. *(Hay dos posibilidades.)*

**Enviar* has an accent mark on the *i* in all present-tense forms except *nosotros* and *vosotros.*

La Real Academia Española was founded in Spain in 1713 with a mission to preserve the quality, elegance, and purity of the Spanish language. There are now *Academias* in all the Spanish-speaking countries, including the Philippines and the United States. Today the *Academias* ensure that changes in Spanish reflect the needs of its more than 360 million native speakers. La Real Academia Española publishes the most complete, authoritative dictionary of the Spanish language.

- Why do you think that it's important to preserve the quality and purity of a language?

La Real Academia Española en Madrid

Escribir/Hablar

¿Cómo te comunicas?

1 Mira cada dibujo y escribe qué forma de comunicación es. Luego escribe por qué se usa esta forma de comunicación.

Modelo

hablar por teléfono
Casi todos tienen teléfonos. Es fácil.

1. 

2. 

3.

4. 

2 Trabaja con un grupo de cinco personas y pregunta a tus compañeros cómo se comunican con otras personas y por qué. Escriban sus respuestas.

Modelo

A —*¿Cómo te comunicas con otras personas?*
B —*Les hablo por teléfono.*
A —*¿Por qué?*
B —*Porque casi todos tienen teléfonos y es fácil.*

3 Una persona de cada grupo va a escribir en la pizarra la forma preferida de comunicación de su grupo. Según esta información, ¿cuál es la forma de comunicación preferida de la clase?

¿Recuerdas?

You use the indirect object pronoun *les* to mean "to them" or "for them."

Para decir más . . .

eficiente efficient
íntimo, -a personal
rápido, -a quick, fast

Leer/Escribir/Hablar

¿Quiénes están en línea?

Lee el anuncio y luego contesta estas preguntas.

1. ¿Quiénes usan más el Internet: los estadounidenses o los españoles? ¿Los estadounidenses o los suecos?
2. ¿Usas tú el Internet a menudo, a veces o nunca?
3. Entre *(Among)* las personas que conoces, ¿quién usa más el Internet? ¿Para qué lo usa?

A sus teclados[1], listos . . . ¡a navegar!

¿Usas el Internet? En el mundo hay más de 400 millones de internautas. El récord lo tienen los suecos:[2] siete de cada diez personas usan la Red. En los Estados Unidos, seis de cada diez estadounidenses[3] la usan. En España la gente está muy lejos de esa cifra.[4] Sólo dos de cada diez españoles están conectados al Internet.

[1]keyboards [2]Swedes [3]Americans [4]figure

Escribir/Hablar

Y tú, ¿que dices?

1. ¿Tienes tú, o tiene tu familia o un(a) amigo(a), una computadora portátil? ¿Qué te parece?
2. ¿A veces tienes miedo de las computadoras? ¿Por qué?
3. ¿Tienes tu propia dirección electrónica? Crea una nueva dirección electrónica "inolvidable" para las personas que nunca recuerdan *(remember)* tu dirección.
4. ¿Qué sabes crear en la computadora?
5. ¿Qué sitio Web conoces mejor? ¿Qué te parece?

Exploración del lenguaje

Using *-mente* to form an adverb

Adverbs are words that describe verbs. They often tell *how* an action is performed. Many adverbs in English end in the letters *-ly*: *slowly, frequently, happily,* and so on. To form similar adverbs in Spanish, add the ending *-mente* to the feminine singular form of an adjective. This *-mente* ending is equivalent to the *-ly* ending in English.

rápida → rápidamente	fácil → fácilmente	general → generalmente
práctica → prácticamente	feliz → felizmente	especial → especialmente

Note that if the adjective has a written accent, as with *rápida, fácil,* and *práctica,* the accent appears in the same place in the adverb form.

Try it out! Give the adverb for each of the adjectives in the list. Then use each adverb in one of the sentences. Some sentences have more than one possible answer.

normal   total   completo   frecuente   reciente

1. El laboratorio de nuestra escuela es ____ nuevo.
2. ____ les escribo a mis amigos por correo electrónico pero hoy les envío una carta.
3. ____ mis padres nos compraron una nueva computadora.
4. Mi hermano está ____ contento cuando está usando la computadora.
5. ____ grabamos canciones en un disco compacto.

Gramática

The present tense of *pedir* and *servir*

Pedir and *servir* are stem-changing verbs in which the *e* in the stem of the infinitive changes to *i* in all forms except *nosotros* and *vosotros.*

Here are the present-tense forms of *pedir* and *servir:*

(yo)	**pido**	(nosotros) (nosotras)	**pedimos**
(tú)	**pides**	(vosotros) (vosotras)	**pedís**
Ud. (él) (ella)	**pide**	Uds. (ellos) (ellas)	**piden**

(yo)	**sirvo**	(nosotros) (nosotras)	**servimos**
(tú)	**sirves**	(vosotros) (vosotras)	**servís**
Ud. (él) (ella)	**sirve**	Uds. (ellos) (ellas)	**sirven**

Pedir means "to ask for."

Juan **pide** la dirección electrónica.

Pedimos más información sobre la Red.

Servir means "to serve" or "to be useful for."

Servimos refrescos después de la clase.

Las computadoras **sirven** para mucho.

GramActiva VIDEO

Need more help with *pedir* and *servir*? Watch the **GramActiva** video.

Gramática **Escribir**

En la clase de tecnología

En la clase de tecnología hay muchas cosas que los estudiantes no pueden hacer. Por eso le piden ayuda al profesor. Escribe las frases.

Modelo

Fernando (no poder / bajar los gráficos)

Fernando le pide ayuda al profesor porque no puede bajar los gráficos.

1. Mario (no saber / grabar un disco compacto)
2. nosotros (no comprender / por qué hay un error)
3. tú (querer / crear una canción)
4. Marisol y Elena (no poder / abrir el documento)
5. yo (desear / enviar una foto por correo electrónico)
6. Vicente y yo (no poder / crear nuestro sitio Web)

Nota

In English you say that you ask *for* help. In Spanish, "for" is implied in the meaning of *pedir* and a separate word is *not* used.

Hablar

¿Pides muchas cosas?

Habla con otro(a) estudiante sobre las cosas que les pides a diferentes personas.

> **¿Recuerdas?**
> The indirect object pronouns *le* and *les* mean "to him, her, you *(pl.)*, them." With *pedir,* they refer to the person whom you ask for something.

Modelo

dinero

A —*¿A quién le pides dinero?*
B —*Le pido dinero a mi mejor amiga, Luisa.*
o: *Les pido dinero a mis padres.*

1. ropa nueva
2. tiempo libre sin tarea
3. ayuda con . . .
4. tu propio(a) . . .
5. tiempo libre sin quehaceres
6. **¡Respuesta personal!**

Hablar/Escribir

Los mejores restaurantes

1. Piensa en los restaurantes que conoces. ¿Qué sirven allí que te gusta? Con otro(a) estudiante, habla sobre los restaurantes y la comida que sirven.

Modelo

A —*¿En qué restaurante comes?*
B —*Como en el restaurante . . . . A menudo pido . . . allí. Es muy . . . . Lo sirven con . . . .*

2. Ahora hablen con otra pareja de los restaurantes donde Uds. comen, lo que piden y con qué sirven las comidas. Preparen tres o más recomendaciones de restaurantes para presentar a la clase.

Modelo

Si Uds. quieren comer bien, recomendamos el restaurante Las Palmeras. Siempre pedimos el pescado . . . ¡es delicioso! Lo sirven con arroz. . . .

Escribir/Hablar

Juego

Con otro(a) estudiante, escriban descripciones de tres cosas y expliquen para qué sirven. Lean las frases a otra pareja para ver si ellos pueden identificar las cosas.

Modelo

A —*Es una cosa bastante pequeña. Puede estar en tu mochila o pupitre. No cuesta mucho dinero.*
B —*¿Para qué sirve?*
A —*Sirve para escribir cartas o composiciones.*
B —*Es un bolígrafo.*

Escribir/Hablar

Y tú, ¿qué dices?

1. ¿A quién le pides ayuda con la computadora? ¿Le pides ayuda a menudo o sólo a veces?
2. ¿Qué haces cuando tus amigos te piden ayuda con la computadora? ¿Para qué cosas te piden ayuda?

Más práctica
Practice Workbook 9B-5

For: Practice with present-tense $e \rightarrow i$ verbs
Visit: www.phschool.com
Web Code: jcd-0913

Gramática

Saber and *conocer*

Sé and *sabes* come from the verb *saber,* "to know." There is another verb in Spanish that also means "to know": *conocer.* Use *conocer* to talk about people, places, and things that you are familiar with.

Here are the present-tense forms of *saber* and *conocer.* Except for the *yo* forms, they are regular in the present tense.

¿Recuerdas?

You have used *(yo) sé* and *(tú) sabes* to talk about knowing a fact and to say what you know how to do.

- **¿Sabes** dónde está la biblioteca?
- Yo **sé** esquiar bastante bien.

(yo)	**sé**	(nosotros) (nosotras)	**sabemos**
(tú)	**sabes**	(vosotros) (vosotras)	**sabéis**
Ud. (él) (ella)	**sabe**	Uds. (ellos) (ellas)	**saben**

(yo)	**conozco**	(nosotros) (nosotras)	**conocemos**
(tú)	**conoces**	(vosotros) (vosotras)	**conocéis**
Ud. (él) (ella)	**conoce**	Uds. (ellos) (ellas)	**conocen**

- *Conocer* is followed by the personal *a* when the direct object is a person. Direct object pronouns can also be used with *conocer.*

¿Conocen Uds. **a la señora** que trabaja en el laboratorio?

Sí, **la** conocemos bien. ¿Quieres **conocerla?**

GramActiva VIDEO

Watch the **GramActiva** video to learn more about using the verbs *saber* and *conocer.*

Gramática   Hablar

Lo que sabemos hacer

Habla con otro(a) estudiante sobre quiénes saben hacer las diferentes actividades en los dibujos.

Modelo

A —*¿Quién sabe esquiar?*
B —*Mario sabe esquiar. Lo hace a menudo.*

1. 

2. 

3. 

4. 

5. 

6. 

  **Escribir/Hablar**

¿Qué lugares conoces? ¿Y a qué personas?

Si una persona visita tu comunidad y tu escuela, ¿puedes ayudarla a conocer a diferentes personas y lugares? Escribe frases completas con las formas apropiadas del verbo *conocer* y la información necesaria. Después lee tus frases a otro(a) estudiante. ¿Conocen Uds. a las mismas personas y los mismos lugares?

1. (Yo) ____ a muchos de los estudiantes en la clase de . . .
2. Mis amigos y yo (no) ____ a la secretaria de la escuela. Es la Sra. . . .
3. Mi hermano(a) / amigo(a) ____ bastante bien al (a la) profesor(a) de . . .
4. Mis amigos ____ bien el parque de diversiones . . .
5. (Yo) ____ la tienda . . . donde me gusta comprar . . .
6. Mi madre (padre) ____ bien *(un lugar en tu ciudad)* . . .
7. Si la persona necesita usar la computadora, nosotros ____ el programa de software . . .

¿Conoces este museo en Austin, Texas?

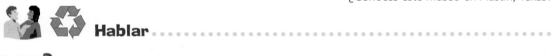

 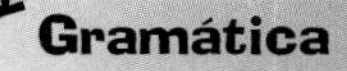   **Hablar**

¿Saber o conocer?

Trabaja con otro(a) estudiante para ver lo que sabe y conoce.

Modelo

la persona que trabaja en la biblioteca de la escuela
A —*¿Conoces a la persona que trabaja en la biblioteca de la escuela?*
B —*Sí, la conozco. Es la Sra. Wilton. Es muy simpática.*
o: *No, no la conozco.*

bailar salsa
A —*¿Sabes bailar salsa?*
B —*Sí, sé bailar salsa. Me encanta.*
o: *No, no sé bailar salsa.*

1. la hermana de . . .
2. bajar información de la Red
3. el nombre de una canción en español
4. las cámaras digitales
5. España o México
6. la dirección electrónica de . . .
7. un sitio Web interesante
8. enviar fotos por la Red

Pronunciación

Dividing words into syllables

Knowing how to divide words into syllables will help you sound out a new word. Just as in English, all syllables in Spanish include a vowel. When there is a consonant between two vowels, you divide the word into syllables before the consonant. The letter combinations *ch, ll,* and *rr* are never divided in Spanish.

Listen to and say these words:

ju-gar	pá-gi-na	la-bo-ra-to-rio	na-ve-gar
ca-lle	no-ti-cias	co-mu-ni-dad	a-bu-rri-do

When there are two consonants between vowels, you divide the word between the consonants. Exceptions are the blends *pr, pl, br, bl, fr, fl, tr, dr, cr, cl, gr,* and *gl.* These blends are never divided and go with the following vowel: *pro-ble-ma.* Listen to and say these words:

car-ta	in-fan-til	con-cur-sos	jar-dín
par-que	a-bri-go	des-can-sar	pa-dres

When there are three or more consonants between vowel sounds, the first two go with the vowel that precedes them and the third goes with the vowel that follows them: *trans-por-te.* When the second and third consonants form a blend, however, the first consonant goes with the vowel before it and the other consonants go with the vowel that follows them: *en-tre.*

Listen to and say these words:

es-cri-to-rio	com-pli-ca-do
en-tre-vis-tas	com-pras-te

Try it out! See if you can separate the following words into the correct syllables.

1. emocionante
2. rápidamente
3. computadora
4. anaranjado
5. electrónico
6. comunicamos

Leer/Escribir

Los tres cerditos

Lee el anuncio y contesta las preguntas.

1. ¿Conocen los cerditos a la "persona" que está en la ventana? ¿Saben ellos lo que quiere?
2. ¿Tiene tu familia un servicio de identificación de llamadas en su teléfono? ¿Te gusta este servicio, o te gustaría tener este servicio? ¿Por qué?
3. ¿Te parece bien saber quién llama por teléfono? ¿Por qué?
4. ¿Te gusta hablar por teléfono? ¿Con quién te gusta hablar más?

¿Sabes quién es?

Pide el servicio de identificación de llamadas.
Si eres cliente de Teléfonos Caribe, es completamente gratis.

Así, siempre vas a saber quién está llamando.
¡Pídelo hoy! Llama al teléfono 20-05-617.

Actividad 19 Leer/Pensar/Escribir/Dibujar

¿Qué inventos conoces?

Mucho antes de la invención de la computadora personal, había *(there were)* otros inventos que nos ayudaron a comunicar y que seguimos *(keep)* usando. Mira la línea cronológica y lee la lista de inventos. Luego contesta las preguntas.

la máquina de escribir	el televisor de color	el sello
el teléfono móvil	la pluma	el código Morse
el alfabeto Braille	la primera película con sonido	el teléfono
el televisor	el telégrafo	el walkie talkie

1. Identifica cada invento según el año en que se inventó y explica qué impacto tiene sobre la comunicación.
2. Busca información en la Red o en la biblioteca para identificar los inventores de cada invento de la lista.
3. ¿Cuál de estos inventos te parece el más importante? ¿Por qué?
4. Piensa en un invento que quieres hacer. ¿Para qué sirve? Escribe un párrafo y haz un dibujo para explicar tu invento.

El español en el mundo del trabajo

The need to share information will be crucial in the 21st century. Innovations from medicine, science, technology, engineering, manufacturing, and social services need to be communicated across the globe. With a partner, make a list of six ways in which information can be spread. For each, tell how knowing Spanish would be beneficial. Share your ideas with the class.

Más práctica

Practice Workbook 9B-6, 9B-7

For: Practice with *saber* vs. *conocer*
Visit: www.phschool.com
Web Code: jcd-0914

¡Adelante!

Lectura

La invasión del ciberspanglish

Lee este artículo sobre el Internet. El Internet sirve para muchas cosas aquí en los Estados Unidos y también en los otros países donde hablan español. Pero no es siempre fácil traducir[1] los términos técnicos.

Objectives

- Read about the Internet and its impact on the Spanish language
- Learn about *cibercafés*
- Write an e-mail message defending your use of the computer
- Watch *¿Eres tú, María?*, Episodio 10

Strategy

Using prior knowledge
Use what you know about a topic to help you understand what you read. This article is on the Internet and its impact on the Spanish language. List five things you know about the Internet that might help you with this reading.

La invasión del ciberspanglish

¿Te gusta usar el Internet? Actualmente[2] hay gente en todos los países del mundo que usa el Internet. Sirve para muchas cosas: para hacer compras, divertirse, educarse, trabajar, buscar información, hacer planes para un viaje y mucho más. Hoy en día uno no puede pensar en una vida sin computadoras o el Internet.

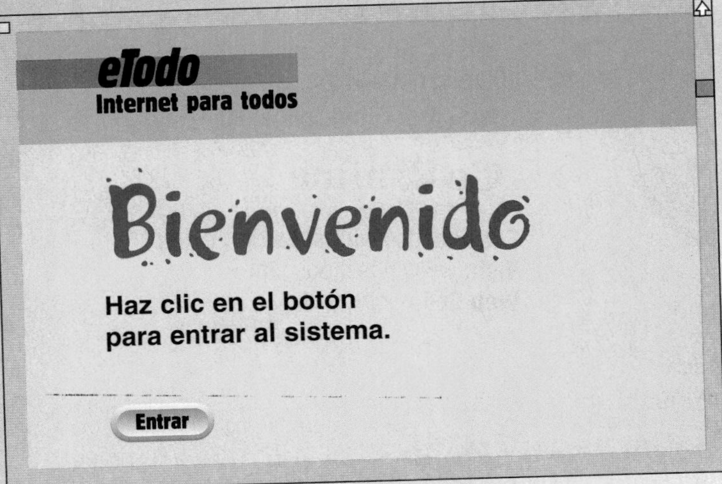

eTodo
Internet para todos
Bienvenido
Haz clic en el botón
para entrar al sistema.
Entrar

Si quieres explorar el Internet en español, hay una explosión de portales (sitios que sirven como puerta al Internet) en los Estados Unidos, España y América Latina. Como puedes imaginar, hay una rivalidad[3] grande entre estos portales para atraer[4] a los hispanohablantes. Algunos portales dan la misma información en inglés y español; sólo tienes que hacer clic para cambiarla.

[1] to translate [2] Nowadays
[3] rivalry [4] to attract

Juntos,[5] el inglés y el español en el Internet dieron origen al "ciberspanglish." A algunas personas no les gusta nada este nuevo "idioma."[6] Piensan que el español es suficientemente rico para poder traducir los términos del inglés. Hay otros que dicen que no hay problema con mezclar[7] los idiomas para comunicarse mejor. Piensan que el "ciberspanglish" es más fácil y lógico porque los términos técnicos vienen del inglés y expresarlos en español es bastante complicado.

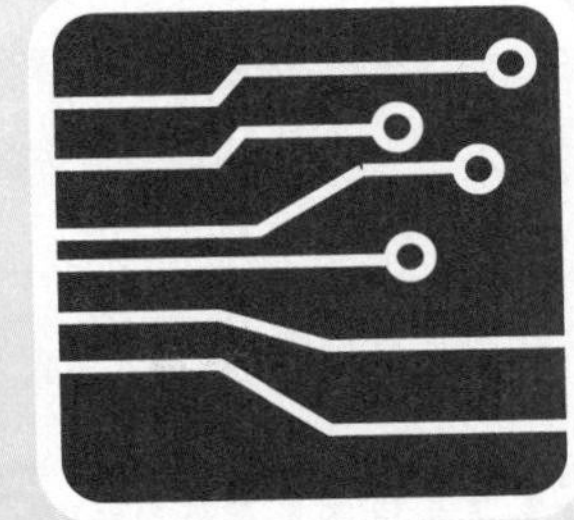

Éste es un debate que va a durar[8] mucho tiempo, y no presenta grises.

Términos de ciberspanglish	Términos en español
emailear	mandar por correo electrónico
espam	un bombardeo de grandes cantidades de correo electrónico
chatear	conversar
hacer clic	picar con el ratón
hacer doble clic	picar dos veces con el ratón
rebootear	rearrancar
linkear	enlazar con una página en Internet
crashear	quebrar o chocar
formatear	hacer un formato
programar	escribir un programa
escanear	rastrear o digitalizar
surfear	explorar o navegar
hacer un upgrade	actualizar o subir un grado
el clipart	dibujos artísticos
hacer un exit	salir
printear	imprimir

[5]Together [6]language [7]mixing

¿Comprendes?

1. Look at the list you created for the Strategy "Using prior knowledge." Place a check mark next to any pieces of information mentioned in the article.
2. According to the article, how could the Internet help you learn more Spanish?
3. Summarize briefly the two sides of the argument related to *ciberspanglish.*
4. You have already learned that Spanish borrowed words from languages such as Greek and Arabic. Is *ciberspanglish* different? Why or why not?
5. What do you think the statement *Éste es un debate que . . . no presenta grises* means? Why is it appropriate as the closing statement for this article?

For: Internet link activity
Visit: www.phschool.com
Web Code: jcd-0915

Perspectivas del mundo hispano

¿Para qué usas una computadora?

In many Spanish-speaking countries, the use of computers and access to the Internet are often not as widespread as in the United States. Many homes don't have telephones, computers cost more money, and in many cases, the Internet is not as accessible. Schools and libraries may not have computers and the same access to the Internet as they do in most communities in the United States. For these reasons, many cybercafés have opened. Cybercafés are nice places for students to meet after school and work on assignments, do research, or e-mail friends. They offer very inexpensive access to the Internet.

Usando computadoras para estudiar en Quito, Ecuador

In recent years, the number of *portales* (portals) that serve as access points to the Internet has increased and many of these are offered in Spanish as well as English. The number of *buscadores* (search engines) has also increased, making it easier for Spanish speakers to search for information or just surf the Internet.

Check it out! Survey your friends. Over the course of one week, how much time do they spend using a computer and for what reasons?

Think about it! Name three ways that you think Spanish-language Internet sites could help you learn more Spanish and understand the perspectives of Spanish speakers.

Haciendo la tarea en la computadora

Presentación escrita

La computadora en mi vida

Task
Your parents think that you are spending too much time on the computer and you disagree. Send an e-mail message (of course!) to your best friend in Mexico explaining your position and how you plan to defend your computer use to your parents.

1. **Prewrite** Create a chart. In the first column, list at least three ways you use the computer. In the second column, write the benefit *(la ventaja)* to you.

Cómo uso la computadora	La ventaja
Busco información para mis clases en Internet.	Aprendo mucho y es muy interesante.

2. **Draft** Use the information from the chart to write the first draft of your e-mail. Here are some expressions you might include:

   pienso que . . . tengo que . . .
   creo que . . . primero (segundo, tercero), . . .

3. **Revise** Check for spelling, accent marks, verb forms, pronouns, and vocabulary use. Share the e-mail with a partner. Your partner should check the following:

   - Is the paragraph easy to read and understand?
   - Does it provide good reasons and support for your position?
   - Is there anything that you could add to give more information or change to make it clearer?
   - Are there any errors?

4. **Publish** Rewrite the e-mail, making necessary changes. Make a copy for your teacher and add it to your portfolio.

5. **Evaluation** Your teacher may give you a rubric for grading the paragraph. You may be evaluated on:

   - the amount of information provided
   - how well you presented each reason and its benefit
   - use of vocabulary and accuracy of spelling and grammar

Strategy

Using supporting examples
When preparing a persuasive argument, you should first clearly state your position and then provide examples to support it. Making a list of your arguments will help you make a strong statement.

¿Eres tú, María? Episodio 10

Antes de ver el video

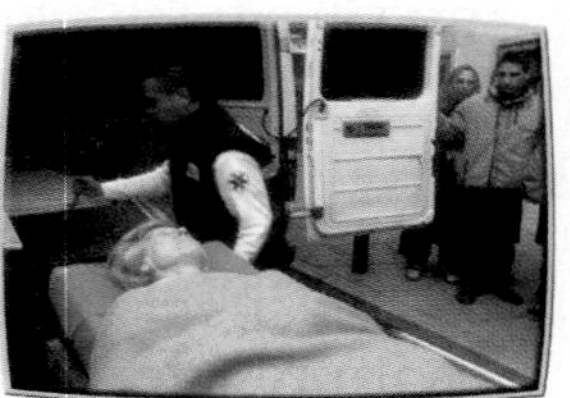

Resumen del episodio

Es el último episodio y Lola y el Inspector Gil van a solucionarlo todo. En realidad, ¿quién es María? ¿Qué importancia tiene Luis Antonio? ¿Quién tiene las joyas? ¿Cómo y por qué ocurrió el crimen? ¿Quién va a la cárcel? ¿Quién va a necesitar un buen abogado? ¿Qué pasa cuando Pedro ve a su abuela por primera vez?

Palabras para comprender

Deténgala. Arrest her.
No quería. I didn't want to.
las reconoció recognized them
los novios boyfriend and girlfriend
tomó took
mucha suerte a lot of luck
robarlas to steal them
no quería esperar didn't want to wait
Parece que . . . It seems like . . .
la cárcel jail
un abogado lawyer

Y tú, ¿qué piensas?

¿Sabes lo que va a pasar en este episodio? Escribe tus respuestas a las preguntas en el Resumen del episodio. Ahora, mira el episodio y compara tus respuestas con lo que pasó. ¿Tenías razón?

Después de ver el video

¿Comprendes?

A. ¿A quién(es) describe cada frase: Lola, María, Julia, Luis Antonio, Pedro o doña Gracia?

1. Pues, señorita, es evidente que Ud. sabe mucho.
2. Las reconoció en el hospital.
3. Es evidente en la foto que son novios.
4. Murió en el hospital.
5. No puede ver muy bien.
6. Viene a Madrid para vivir con ella.
7. Tiene ochenta y cinco años y está en buena salud.
8. Entra en el piso y ataca a la señora.
9. Ud. no va a París, señor. Ud. va a la cárcel.
10. La mejor detective de Madrid.

B. Con un grupo de tres o cuatro estudiantes, escoge una escena del video. Tu profesor(a) les va a dar el guión *(script)* de la escena. Representen la escena para la clase. Hay que aprender de memoria el papel *(the part),* llevar la ropa del personaje y representar la escena de una manera bien profesional.

For: More on *¿Eres tú, María?*
Visit: www.phschool.com
Web Code: jcd-0507

Repaso del capítulo

Vocabulario y gramática

Chapter Review

To prepare for the test, check to see if you . . .

- **know the new vocabulary and grammar**
- **can perform the tasks on p. 471**

to talk about communication

cara a cara	face-to-face
la carta	letter
comunicarse **(yo) me comunico** **(tú) te comunicas**	to communicate (with)
enviar	to send
la tarjeta	card

to talk about computer-related activities

bajar	to download
buscar	to search (for)
la cámara digital	digital camera
la canción, *pl.* **las canciones**	song
la composición, *pl.* **las composiciones**	composition
la computadora portátil	laptop computer
crear	to create
el curso **tomar un curso**	course to take a course
la diapositiva	slide
la dirección electrónica	e-mail address
el documento	document
escribir por correo electrónico	to send an e-mail message
estar en línea	to be online
grabar un disco compacto	to burn a CD
los gráficos	graphics
la información	information
el informe	report
el laboratorio	laboratory
navegar en la Red	to surf the Web
la página Web	Web page
la presentación, *pl.* **las presentaciones**	presentation
el sitio Web	Web site
visitar salones de chat	to visit chat rooms

For *Vocabulario adicional,* see pp. 472–473.

other useful expressions

complicado, -a	complicated
¿Para qué sirve?	What's it (used) for?
¿Qué te parece?	What do you think?
rápidamente	quickly
Sirve para . . .	It's used for . . .
tener miedo (de)	to be afraid (of)

pedir (e → i) *to ask for*

pido	**pedimos**
pides	**pedís**
pide	**piden**

servir (e → i) *to serve, to be useful for*

sirvo	**servimos**
sirves	**servís**
sirve	**sirven**

saber *to know (how)*

sé	**sabemos**
sabes	**sabéis**
sabe	**saben**

conocer *to know, to be acquainted with*

conozco	**conocemos**
conoces	**conocéis**
conoce	**conocen**

Más práctica

Practice Workbook Puzzle 9B-8
Practice Workbook Organizer 9B-9

Go Online PHSchool.com
For: Test preparation
Visit: www.phschool.com
Web Code: jcd-0916

Preparación para el examen

On the exam you will be asked to . . .	Here are practice tasks similar to those you will find on the exam . . .	If you need review . . .
 **1 Escuchar** Listen and understand as people talk about how they use computers	You overhear some people expressing their opinions about computers. Tell whether each person likes or dislikes using computers.	**pp. 450–454** *A primera vista* **p. 451** Actividades 1–2 **p. 455** Actividad 5
 **2 Hablar** Ask and answer questions about what you know about computers and the Internet	A local Internet company wants to interview you to work as a telephone tech support assistant. To prepare, you and your partner take turns interviewing each other. Ask if your partner: a) knows how to surf the Web; b) is familiar with Web sites for teens; c) knows how to use the computer to create music; d) knows how to make graphics. Then switch roles.	**pp. 450–454** *A primera vista* **p. 454** Actividad 4 **p. 457** Actividad 9 **p. 459** Actividad 14 **p. 460** Actividad 15 **p. 461** Actividad 17
 **3 Leer** Read and understand part of an online conversation in a chat room	A teen in the chat room *Mis padres y yo* is upset. According to the teenager, what do his parents not understand? What is his parents' opinion? ¡Yo soy muy impaciente! Para hacer la tarea, me gusta tener la información que necesito rápidamente. Mis padres dicen que puedo ir a la biblioteca y buscar libros allí para hacer mi tarea, pero me gustaría tener mi propia computadora. Ellos piensan que las computadoras sólo sirven para jugar videojuegos. ¿Qué hago?	**pp. 450–454** *A primera vista* **p. 454** Actividad 4 **p. 455** Actividad 6 **p. 456** Actividad 8 **pp. 464–465** *Lectura*
 **4 Escribir** Write your personal profile *(perfil)* for a Web survey	You are completing a Web survey online for *MundoChat*. Provide answers to the following questions: a) what you like to do; b) your favorite Web site; c) how often you visit chat rooms; d) how much time you spend online each day.	**p. 458** Actividad 10 **p. 459** Actividad 14 **p. 461** Actividad 16 **p. 467** *Presentación escrita*
 **5 Pensar** Demonstrate an understanding of cultural perspectives regarding technology	Explain why cybercafés are so popular in many Spanish-speaking countries. Compare how you use computers to the way in which teenagers might use them in these countries. If you were to live in one of these countries, how might you approach homework differently?	**p. 466** *Perspectivas del mundo hispano*

¡Viva Texas!

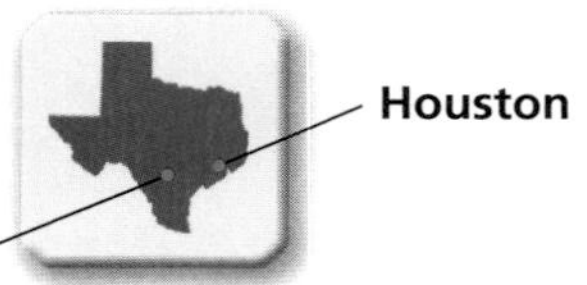

Tres generaciones de televisión

En la familia de Emilio Nicolás, el gerente[1] de KAZH-57 en Houston, hay tres generaciones de líderes en la telecomunicación en español. En 1945 su abuelo, Raúl Cortez, fundó la primera estación de radio en español en San Antonio, Texas. En esta misma ciudad en 1955, el Sr. Cortez fundó KCOR-TV, el primer canal de televisión en español en los Estados Unidos. Económicamente, los años de KCOR-TV no fueron fáciles.

[1]director

La primera estación de radio en San Antonio, Texas fue KCOR. Usaron las letras "COR" por el fundador de la estación, Raúl Cortez.

Raúl Cortez

En 1961 el padre de Emilio, también llamado Emilio Nicolás, compró KCOR con la ayuda de tres otras personas. Cambiaron el nombre de la estación a KWEX y empezaron otra vez. Emilio Nicolás, el padre, comprendió muy bien este medio de comunicación y con la motivación de servir a la comunidad latina en San Antonio, tuvo mucho éxito.[2] Hoy día, KWEX Univisión 41 continúa su programación en español para el público de San Antonio.

Emilio Nicolás

[2] was very successful

KAZH-57 en Houston es una estación afiliada con Azteca América de México. Para el Sr. Nicolás, el gerente de esta estación de televisión independiente, los programas tienen que ser fascinantes, informativos y deben servir a la comunidad. Algunos de los programas locales que puedes ver en KAZH-57 son:

Fuerza musical:
Un programa de vídeos musicales que presenta música tejana y bandas regionales.

Memorias de oro:
La celebración de las quinceañeras es muy importante para muchos en la comunidad latina de Houston. En KAZH-57 dan los momentos preciosos de las celebraciones que toman lugar en Houston. Las familias y las chicas que captan sus quinceañeras en vídeo pueden compartir este día especial con todos.

Salvadoreños de corazón:

En Houston hay 1.5 millones de hispanos y 120,000 de ellos vienen de El Salvador. Para servirles, hay un programa de música y entrevistas con temas de alto interés para los salvadoreños.

Estrenando[3] casas:

Para mucha gente comprar una casa es un poco confuso, especialmente si una persona llegó a este país recientemente. En muchos países latinoamericanos el proceso de comprar una casa es muy diferente. A veces la idea de un hipoteca[4] es completamente nueva. Este programa informativo le ayuda al público hispano de Houston a encontrar y comprar la casa de sus sueños.[5]

[3] Premiering [4] mortgage [5] dreams

Comunicación

1. Raúl Cortez es considerado uno de los pioneros de la televisión y radio en español. ¿Por qué?
2. Lee las descripciones de estas personas y escribe el nombre del programa que les puede interesar. Explica por qué.
   - **a.** Laura y su esposo Alejandro viven en un apartamento pero es demasiado pequeño y quieren un lugar con dos pisos, un sótano, dos baños, cuatro dormitorios, una sala grande y un jardín.
   - **b.** Miguel es un estudiante en Houston. Toca la guitarra en una banda local y acaba de hacer un video con los otros miembros de la banda.
   - **c.** Alicia tiene quince años. El domingo pasado fue su cumpleaños y sus padres le hicieron una celebración grande y filmaron el evento.

Comparaciones

Trabaja con un(a) compañero(a) para hablar de los programas de televisión en español. ¿En qué canal dan programas en español en tu comunidad? ¿Hay programas locales? ¿Cómo son similares o diferentes a los programas de KAZH-57?

Vocabulario adicional

Las actividades

coleccionar sellos / monedas to collect stamps / coins

jugar al ajedrez to play chess

patinar sobre hielo to ice-skate

practicar artes marciales *(f.)* to practice martial arts

tocar to play *(an instrument)*

- **el bajo** bass
- **la batería** drums
- **el clarinete** clarinet
- **el oboe** oboe
- **el saxofón** *pl.* **los saxofones** saxophone
- **el sintetizador** synthesizer
- **el trombón** *pl.* **los trombones** trombone
- **la trompeta** trumpet
- **la tuba** tuba
- **el violín** *pl.* **los violines** violin

Las clases

el alemán German

el álgebra *(f.)* algebra

el anuario yearbook

la banda band

la biología biology

el cálculo calculus

el drama drama

la fotografía photography

el francés French

la geografía geography

la geometría geometry

el latín Latin

la química chemistry

la trigonometría trigonometry

Las cosas para la clase

la grapadora stapler

las grapas staples

el sacapuntas *pl.* **los sacapuntas** pencil sharpener

el sujetapapeles *pl.* **los sujetapapeles** paper clip

las tijeras scissors

Las comidas

Las frutas

el aguacate avocado

la cereza cherry

la ciruela plum

el coco coconut

el durazno peach

la frambuesa raspberry

el limón *pl.* **los limones** lemon

el melón *pl.* **los melones** melon

la pera pear

la sandía watermelon

la toronja grapefruit

Las verduras

el apio celery

el brócoli broccoli

la calabaza pumpkin

el champiñón *pl.* **los champiñones** mushroom

la col cabbage

la coliflor cauliflower

los espárragos asparagus

las espinacas spinach

el pepino cucumber

La carne

la chuleta de cerdo pork chop

el cordero lamb

la ternera veal

Los condimentos

la mayonesa mayonnaise

la mostaza mustard

la salsa de tomate ketchup

Otro tipo de comidas

los fideos noodles

Los lugares y actividades

el banco bank

el club club

el equipo de . . . ___ team

la farmacia pharmacy

la oficina office

la práctica de . . . ___ practice

la reunión *pl.* **las reuniones de . . .** ___ meeting

el supermercado supermarket

Los animales

el conejillo de Indias guinea pig

el conejo rabbit

el gerbo gerbil

el hámster *pl.* **los hámsters** hamster

el hurón *pl.* **los hurones** ferret

el loro parrot

el pez *pl.* **los peces** fish

la serpiente snake

la tortuga turtle

Los miembros de la familia

el bisabuelo, la bisabuela great-grandfather, great-grandmother

el nieto, la nieta grandson, granddaughter

el sobrino, la sobrina nephew, niece

Las descripciones de personas

llevar anteojos to wear glasses
ser
- **calvo, -a** bald
- **delgado, -a** thin
- **gordo, -a** fat

tener
- **la barba** beard
- **el bigote** moustache
- **las pecas** freckles
- **el pelo lacio** straight hair
- **el pelo rizado** curly hair
- **las trenzas** braids

Las partes de la casa y cosas en la casa

el balcón *pl.* **los balcones** balcony
la estufa stove
el jardín *pl.* **los jardines** garden
el lavadero laundry room
la lavadora washing machine
el lavaplatos *pl.* **los lavaplatos** dishwasher
el microondas *pl.* **los microondas** microwave oven
los muebles furniture
el patio patio
el refrigerador refrigerator
la secadora clothes dryer
el sillón *pl.* **los sillones** armchair
el sofá sofa
el tocador dressing table

Los quehaceres

quitar
- **la nieve con la pala** to shovel snow
- **los platos de la mesa** to clear the table

rastrillar las hojas to rake leaves

Los colores

(azul) claro light (blue)
(azul) marino navy (blue)
(azul) oscuro dark (blue)

Las expresiones para las compras

ahorrar to save
el dinero en efectivo cash
gastar to spend
la(s) rebaja(s) sale(s)
regatear to bargain
se vende for sale

La ropa

la bata bathrobe
el chaleco vest
las pantimedias pantyhose
el paraguas *pl.* **los paraguas** umbrella
el pijama pajamas
la ropa interior underwear
el saco loose-fitting jacket
los tenis tennis shoes
las zapatillas slippers
los zapatos atléticos athletic shoes
los zapatos de tacón alto high-heeled shoes

Las expresiones para los viajes

el aeropuerto airport
la agencia de viajes travel agency
los cheques de viajero travelers' checks
el equipaje luggage
hacer una reservación to make a reservation
el lugar de interés place of interest
el pasaporte passport
volar *(o → ue)* to fly

Los animales del zoológico

el ave *(f.) pl.* **las aves** bird
el canguro kangaroo
la cebra zebra
el cocodrilo crocodile
el delfín *pl.* **los delfines** dolphin
el elefante elephant
la foca seal
el gorila gorilla
el hipopótamo hippopotamus
la jirafa giraffe
el león *pl.* **los leones** lion
el oso bear
el oso blanco polar bear
el pingüino penguin
el tigre tiger

Las expresiones para las computadoras

la búsqueda search
comenzar *(e → ie)* **la sesión** to log on
el disco duro hard disk
la impresora printer
imprimir to print
el marcapáginas *pl.* **los marcapáginas** bookmark
multimedia multimedia
la página inicial home page
la tecla de borrar delete key
la tecla de intro enter key

Resumen de gramática

Grammar Terms

Adjectives describe nouns: *a* ***red*** *car.*

Adverbs usually describe verbs; they tell when, where, or how an action happens: *He read it* ***quickly.*** Adverbs can also describe adjectives or other adverbs: ***very*** *tall,* ***quite well.***

Articles are words in Spanish that can tell you whether a noun is masculine, feminine, singular, or plural. In English, the articles are *the, a,* and *an.*

Commands are verb forms that tell people to do something: ***Study!, Work!***

Comparatives compare people or things.

Conjugations are verb forms that add endings to the stem in order to tell who the subject is and what tense is being used: *escrib****o****, escrib****iste****.*

Conjunctions join words or groups of words. The most common ones are ***and, but,*** and ***or.***

Direct objects are nouns or pronouns that receive the action of a verb: *I read the* ***book.*** *I read* ***it.***

Gender in Spanish tells you whether a noun, pronoun, or article is masculine or feminine.

Indirect objects are nouns or pronouns that tell you to whom / what or for whom / what something is done: *I gave* ***him*** *the book.*

Infinitives are the basic forms of verbs. In English, infinitives have the word "to" in front of them: ***to walk.***

Interrogatives are words that ask questions: ***What*** *is that?* ***Who*** *are you?*

Nouns name people, places, or things: ***students, Mexico City, books.***

Number tells you if a noun, pronoun, article, or verb is singular or plural.

Prepositions show relationship between their objects and another word in the sentence: *He is* ***in*** *the classroom.*

Present tense is used to talk about actions that always take place, or that are happening now: *I always* ***take*** *the bus; I* ***study*** *Spanish.*

Present progressive tense is used to emphasize that an action is happening *right now: I* ***am doing*** *my homework; he* ***is finishing*** *dinner.*

Preterite tense is used to talk about actions that were completed in the past: *I* ***took*** *the train yesterday; I* ***studied*** *for the test.*

Pronouns are words that take the place of nouns: ***She*** *is my friend.*

Subjects are the nouns or pronouns that perform the action in a sentence: ***John*** *sings.*

Superlatives describe which things have the most or least of a given quality: *She is the* ***best*** *student.*

Verbs show action or link the subject with a word or words in the predicate (what the subject does or is): *Ana* ***writes;*** *Ana* ***is*** *my sister.*

Nouns, Number, and Gender

Nouns refer to people, animals, places, things, and ideas. Nouns are singular or plural. In Spanish, nouns have gender, which means that they are either masculine or feminine.

Singular Nouns	
Masculine	**Feminine**
libro	carpeta
pupitre	casa
profesor	noche
lápiz	ciudad

Plural Nouns	
Masculine	**Feminine**
libros	carpetas
pupitres	casas
profesores	noches
lápices	ciudades

Definite Articles

El, la, los, and *las* are definite articles and are the equivalent of "the" in English. *El* is used with masculine singular nouns; *los* with masculine plural nouns. *La* is used with feminine singular nouns; *las* with feminine plural nouns. When you use the words *a* or *de* before *el,* you form the contractions *al* and *del: Voy **al** centro; Es el libro **del** profesor.*

Masculine	
Singular	**Plural**
el libro	los libros
el pupitre	los pupitres
el profesor	los profesores
el lápiz	los lápices

Feminine	
Singular	**Plural**
la carpeta	las carpetas
la casa	las casas
la noche	las noches
la ciudad	las ciudades

Indefinite Articles

Un and *una* are indefinite articles and are the equivalent of "a" and "an" in English. *Un* is used with singular masculine nouns; *una* is used with singular feminine nouns. The plural indefinite articles are *unos* and *unas.*

Masculine	
Singular	**Plural**
un libro	unos libros
un escritorio	unos escritorios
un baile	unos bailes

Feminine	
Singular	**Plural**
una revista	unas revistas
una mochila	unas mochilas
una bandera	unas banderas

Pronouns

Subject pronouns tell who is doing the action. They replace nouns or names in a sentence. Subject pronouns are often used for emphasis or clarification: *Gregorio escucha música. **Él** escucha música.*

A direct object tells who or what receives the action of the verb. To avoid repeating a direct object noun, you can replace it with a *direct object pronoun*. Direct object pronouns have the same gender and number as the nouns they replace: *¿Cuándo compraste **el libro? Lo** compré ayer.*

An indirect object tells to whom or for whom an action is performed. *Indirect object pronouns* are used to replace an indirect object noun: ***Les** doy dinero. (I give money to them.)* Because *le* and *les* have more than one meaning, you can make the meaning clear, or show emphasis, by adding *a* + the corresponding name, noun, or pronoun: ***Les** doy el dinero a **ellos.***

After most prepositions, you use *mí* and *ti* for "me" and "you." The forms change with the preposition *con: conmigo, contigo.* For all other persons, you use subject pronouns after prepositions.

The personal a

When the direct object is a person, a group of people, or a pet, use the word *a* before the object. This is called the "personal *a*": *Visité **a** mi abuela. Busco **a** mi perro, Capitán.*

Subject Pronouns		Direct Object Pronouns		Indirect Object Pronouns		Objects of Prepositions	
Singular	**Plural**	**Singular**	**Plural**	**Singular**	**Plural**	**Singular**	**Plural**
yo	nosotros, nosotras	me	nos	me	nos	(para) mí, conmigo	nosotros, nosotras
tú	vosotros, vosotras	te	os	te	os	(para) ti, contigo	vosotros, vosotras
usted (Ud.)	ustedes (Uds.)	lo, la	los, las	le	les	Ud.	Uds.
él, ella	ellos, ellas					él, ella	ellos, ellas

Adjectives

Words that describe people and things are called adjectives. In Spanish, most adjectives have both masculine and feminine forms, as well as singular and plural forms. Adjectives must agree with the noun they describe in both gender and number. When an adjective describes a group including both masculine and feminine nouns, use the masculine plural form.

Masculine	
Singular	**Plural**
alto	altos
inteligente	inteligentes
trabajador	trabajadores
fácil	fáciles

Feminine	
Singular	**Plural**
alta	altas
inteligente	inteligentes
trabajadora	trabajadoras
fácil	fáciles

Shortened Forms of Adjectives

When placed before masculine singular nouns, some adjectives change into a shortened form.

bueno	buen chico
malo	mal día
primero	primer trabajo
tercero	tercer plato
grande	gran señor

One adjective, ***grande,*** changes to a shortened form before any singular noun: *una gran señora, un gran libro.*

Possessive Adjectives

Possessive adjectives are used to tell what belongs to someone or to show relationships. Like other adjectives, possessive adjectives agree in number with the nouns that follow them.

Only *nuestro* and *vuestro* have different masculine and feminine endings. *Su* and *sus* can have many different meanings: *his, her, its, your,* or *their.*

Singular	Plural
mi	mis
tu	tus
su	sus
nuestro, -a	nuestros, -as
vuestro, -a	vuestros, -as
su	sus

Demonstrative Adjectives

Like other adjectives, demonstrative adjectives agree in gender and number with the nouns that follow them. Use *este, esta, estos, estas* ("this" / "these") before nouns that name people or things that are close to you. Use *ese, esa, esos, esas* ("that" / "those") before nouns that name people or things that are at some distance from you.

Singular	Plural
este libro	estos libros
esta casa	estas casas

Singular	Plural
ese niño	esos niños
esa manzana	esas manzanas

Interrogative Words

You use interrogative words to ask questions. When you ask a question with an interrogative word, you put the verb before the subject. All interrogative words have a written accent mark.

¿Adónde?	¿Cuándo?	¿Dónde?
¿Cómo?	¿Cuánto, -a?	¿Por qué?
¿Con quién?	¿Cuántos, -as?	¿Qué?
¿Cuál?	¿De dónde?	¿Quién?

Comparatives and Superlatives

Comparatives Use *más . . . que* or *menos . . . que* to compare people or things: *más interesante que . . . , menos alta que . . .*

When talking about number, use *de* instead of *que: Tengo más de cien monedas en mi colección.*

Superlatives Use this pattern to express the idea of "most" or "least."

el
la + noun + más / menos + adjective
los
las

Es la chica más seria de la clase.
Son los perritos más pequeños.

Several adjectives are irregular when used with comparatives and superlatives.

older	mayor
younger	menor
better	mejor
worse	peor

Affirmative and Negative Words

To make a sentence negative in Spanish, *no* usually goes in front of the verb or expression. To show that you do not like either of two choices, use *ni . . . ni.*

Alguno, alguna, algunos, algunas and *ninguno, ninguna* match the number and gender of the noun to which they refer. *Ningunos* and *ningunas* are rarely used. When *alguno* and *ninguno* come before a masculine singular noun, they change to *algún* and *ningún.*

Affirmative	Negative
algo	nada
alguien	nadie
algún	ningún
alguno, -a, -os, -as	ninguno, -a, -os, -as
siempre	nunca
también	tampoco

Adverbs

To form an adverb in Spanish, *-mente* is added to the feminine singular form of an adjective. This *-mente* ending is equivalent to the "-ly" ending in English. If the adjective has a written accent, such as *rápida, fácil,* and *práctica,* the accent appears in the same place in the adverb form.

- general → generalmente
- especial → especialmente
- fácil → fácilmente
- feliz → felizmente
- rápida → rápidamente
- práctica → prácticamente

Verbos

Regular Present and Preterite Tenses

Here are the conjugations for regular *-ar, -er,* and *-ir* verbs in the present and preterite tense.

Infinitive	Present		Preterite	
estudiar	estudio estudias estudia	estudiamos estudiáis estudian	estudié estudiaste estudió	estudiamos estudiasteis estudiaron
correr	corro corres corre	corremos corréis corren	corrí corriste corrió	corrimos corristeis corrieron
escribir	escribo escribes escribe	escribimos escribís escriben	escribí escribiste escribió	escribimos escribisteis escribieron

Present Progressive

When you want to emphasize that an action is happening *right now,* you use the present progressive tense.

estudiar	estoy estás está	estudiando estudiando estudiando	estamos estáis están	estudiando estudiando estudiando
correr	estoy estás está	corriendo corriendo corriendo	estamos estáis están	corriendo corriendo corriendo
escribir	estoy estás está	escribiendo escribiendo escribiendo	estamos estáis están	escribiendo escribiendo escribiendo

Affirmative tú Commands

When telling a friend, a family member, or a young person to do something, use an affirmative *tú* command. To give these commands for most verbs, use the same present-tense forms that are used for *Ud., él, ella.* Some verbs have an irregular affirmative *tú* command.

Regular	Irregular	
¡Estudia! ¡Corre! ¡Escribe!	decir hacer ir poner salir ser tener venir	di haz ve pon sal sé ten ven

Stem-changing Verbs

Here is an alphabetical list of the stem-changing verbs. You will learn the verb forms that are in italic type next year.

Infinitive and Present Participle	Present		Preterite	
costar (o → ue) costando	cuesta	cuestan	costó	costaron
doler (o → ue) doliendo	duele	duelen	dolió	dolieron
dormir (o → ue) *durmiendo*	duermo duermes duerme	dormimos dormís duermen	dormí dormiste *durmió*	dormimos dormisteis *durmieron*
empezar (e → ie) empezando	empiezo empiezas empieza	empezamos empezáis empiezan	*empecé* empezaste empezó	empezamos empezasteis empezaron
jugar (u → ue) jugando	juego juegas juega	jugamos jugáis juegan	jugué jugaste jugó	jugamos jugasteis jugaron
llover (o → ue) lloviendo	llueve		llovió	
nevar (e → ie) nevando	nieva		nevó	
pedir (e → i) *pidiendo*	pido pides pide	pedimos pedís piden	pedí pediste *pidió*	pedimos pedisteis *pidieron*
pensar (e → ie) pensando	pienso piensas piensa	pensamos pensáis piensan	pensé pensaste pensó	pensamos pensasteis pensaron
preferir (e → ie) *prefiriendo*	prefiero prefieres prefiere	preferimos preferís prefieren	preferí preferiste *prefirió*	preferimos preferisteis *prefirieron*
sentir (e → ie) *sintiendo*	*See* preferir			
servir (e → i) *sirviendo*	*See* pedir			

Spelling-changing Verbs

These verbs have spelling changes in different tenses. The spelling changes are indicated in black.

You will learn the verb forms that are in italic type next year.

Infinitive and Present Participle	Present		Preterite	
buscar (c → qu) buscando	*See regular verbs*		**busqué** buscaste buscó	buscamos buscasteis buscaron
comunicarse (c → qu) *comunicándose*	*See reflexive verbs*		*See reflexive verbs and* **buscar**	
conocer (c → zc) conociendo	**conozco** conoces conoce	conocemos conocéis conocen	*See regular verbs*	
creer (i → y) *creyendo*	*See regular verbs*		creí creíste ***creyó***	creímos creísteis ***creyeron***
empezar (z → c) empezando	*See stem-changing verbs*		**empecé** empezaste empezó	empezamos empezasteis empezaron
enviar (i → í) enviando	**envío** **envías** **envía**	enviamos enviáis **envían**	*See regular verbs*	
esquiar (i → í) esquiando	*See* **enviar**		*See regular verbs*	
jugar (g → gu) jugando	*See stem-changing verbs*		**jugué** jugaste jugó	jugamos jugasteis jugaron
leer (i → y) leyendo	*See regular verbs*		*See* **creer**	
pagar (g → gu) pagando	*See regular verbs*		*See* **jugar**	
parecer (c → zc) pareciendo	*See* **conocer**		*See regular verbs*	
practicar (c → qu) practicando	*See regular verbs*		*See* **buscar**	
recoger (g → j) recogiendo	**recojo** recoges recoge	recogemos recogéis recogen	*See regular verbs*	
sacar (c → qu) sacando	*See regular verbs*		*See* **buscar**	
tocar (c → qu) tocando	*See regular verbs*		*See* **buscar**	

Irregular Verbs

These verbs have irregular patterns. You will learn the verb forms that are in italic type next year.

Infinitive and Present Participle	Present		Preterite	
dar dando	doy das da	damos dais dan	di diste dio	dimos disteis dieron
decir *diciendo*	digo dices dice	decimos decís dicen	*dije* *dijiste* *dijo*	*dijimos* *dijisteis* *dijeron*
estar estando	estoy estás está	estamos estáis están	*estuve* *estuviste* *estuvo*	*estuvimos* *estuvisteis* *estuvieron*
hacer haciendo	hago haces hace	hacemos hacéis hacen	hice hiciste hizo	hicimos hicisteis hicieron
ir *yendo*	voy vas va	vamos vais van	fui fuiste fue	fuimos fuisteis fueron
poder *pudiendo*	puedo puedes puede	podemos podéis pueden	*pude* *pudiste* *pudo*	*pudimos* *pudisteis* *pudieron*
poner poniendo	pongo pones pone	ponemos ponéis ponen	*puse* *pusiste* *puso*	*pusimos* *pusisteis* *pusieron*
querer queriendo	quiero quieres quiere	queremos queréis quieren	*quise* *quisiste* *quiso*	*quisimos* *quisisteis* *quisieron*
saber sabiendo	sé sabes sabe	sabemos sabéis saben	*supe* *supiste* *supo*	*supimos* *supisteis* *supieron*
salir saliendo	salgo sales sale	salimos salís salen	salí saliste salió	salimos salisteis salieron
ser siendo	soy eres es	somos sois son	fui fuiste fue	fuimos fuisteis fueron
tener teniendo	tengo tienes tiene	tenemos tenéis tienen	*tuve* *tuviste* *tuvo*	*tuvimos* *tuvisteis* *tuvieron*

Irregular Verbs (continued)

You will learn the verb forms that are in italic type next year.

Infinitive and Present Participle	Present		Preterite	
traer *trayendo*	traigo traes trae	traemos traéis traen	*traje* *trajiste* *trajo*	*trajimos* *trajisteis* *trajeron*
venir *viniendo*	vengo vienes viene	venimos venís vienen	*vine* *viniste* *vino*	*vinimos* *vinisteis* *vinieron*
ver viendo	veo ves ve	vemos veis ven	vi viste vio	vimos visteis vieron

Reflexive Verbs

You will learn the verb forms that are in italic type next year.

Infinitive and Present Participle	Present	
comunicarse *comunicándose*	me comunico te comunicas *se comunica*	*nos comunicamos* *os comunicáis* *se comunican*
Affirmative Familiar *(tú)* Command	**Preterite**	
comunícate	me comuniqué te comunicaste *se comunicó*	*nos comunicamos* *os comunicasteis* *se comunicaron*

Expresiones útiles para conversar

The following are expressions that you can use when you find yourself in a specific situation and need help to begin, continue, or end a conversation.

Greeting someone

Buenos días. Good morning.

Buenas tardes. Good afternoon.

Buenas noches. Good evening. Good night.

Making introductions

Me llamo . . . My name is . . .

Soy . . . I'm . . .

¿Cómo te llamas? What's your name?

Éste es mi amigo ***m.*** **. . .** This is my friend . . .

Ésta es mi amiga ***f.*** **. . .** This is my friend . . .

Se llama . . . His / Her name is . . .

¡Mucho gusto! It's a pleasure!

Encantado, -a. Delighted.

Igualmente. Likewise.

Asking how someone is

¿Cómo estás? How are you?

¿Cómo andas? How's it going?

¿Cómo te sientes? How do you feel?

¿Qué tal? How's it going?

Estoy bien, gracias. I'm fine, thank you.

Muy bien. ¿Y tú? Very well. And you?

Regular. Okay. Alright.

Más o menos. More or less.

(Muy) mal. (Very) bad.

¡Horrible! Awful!

¡Excelente! Great!

Talking on the phone

Aló. Hello.

Diga. Hello.

Bueno. Hello.

¿Quién habla? Who's calling?

Habla . . . It's [name of person calling].

¿Está . . . , por favor? Is . . . there, please?

¿De parte de quién? Who is calling?

¿Puedo dejar un recado? May I leave a message?

Un momento. Just a moment.

Llamo más tarde. I'll call later.

¿Cómo? No le oigo. What? I can't hear you.

Making plans

¿Adónde vas? Where are you going?

Voy a . . . I'm going to . . .

¿Estás listo, -a? Are you ready?

Tengo prisa. I'm in a hurry.

¡Date prisa! Hurry up!

Sí, ahora voy. OK, I'm coming.

Todavía necesito . . . I still need . . .

¿Te gustaría . . . ? Would you like to . . . ?

Sí, me gustaría . . . Yes, I'd like to . . .

¡Claro que sí (no)! Of course (not)!

¿Quieres . . . ? Do you want to . . . ?

Quiero . . . I want to . . .

¿Qué quieres hacer hoy? What do you want to do today?

¿Qué haces después de las clases? What do you do after school (class)?

¿Qué estás haciendo? What are you doing?

Te invito. It's my treat.

¿Qué tal si . . . ? What about . . . ?

Primero . . . First . . .

Después . . . Later . . .

Luego . . . Then . . .

Making an excuse

Estoy ocupado, -a. I'm busy.

Lo siento, pero no puedo. I'm sorry, but I can't.

¡Qué lástima! What a shame!

Ya tengo planes. I already have plans.

Tal vez otro día. Maybe another day.

Being polite

Con mucho gusto. With great pleasure.

De nada. You're welcome.

Disculpe. Excuse me.

Lo siento. I'm sorry.

Muchísimas gracias. Thank you very much.

Te (Se) lo agradezco mucho. I appreciate it a lot.

Muy amable. That's very kind of you.

Perdón. Pardon me.

¿Puede Ud. repetirlo? Can you repeat that?

¿Puede Ud. hablar más despacio? Can you speak more slowly?

Keeping a conversation going

¿De veras? Really?

¿Verdad? Isn't that so? Right?

¿En serio? Seriously?

¡No lo puedo creer! I don't believe it!

¡No me digas! You don't say!

Y entonces, ¿qué? And then what?

¿Qué hiciste? What did you do?

¿Qué dijiste? What did you say?

¿Crees que . . . ? Do you think that . . .?

Me parece bien. It seems alright.

Perfecto. Perfect.

¡Qué buena idea! What a good idea!

¡Cómo no! Of course!

De acuerdo. Agreed.

Está bien. It's all right.

Giving a description when you don't know the name of someone or something

Se usa para . . . It's used to / for . . .

Es la palabra que significa . . . It's the word that means . . .

Es la persona que . . . It's the person who . . .

Ending a conversation

Bueno, tengo que irme. Well, I have to go.

Chao. (Chau.) Bye.

Hasta pronto. See you soon.

Hasta mañana. See you tomorrow.

Vocabulario español-inglés

The *Vocabulario español–inglés* contains all active vocabulary from the text, including vocabulary presented in the grammar sections.

A dash (—) represents the main entry word. For example, **pasar la —** after **la aspiradora** means **pasar la aspiradora.**

The number following each entry indicates the chapter in which the word or expression is presented. The letter *P* following an entry refers to the *Para empezar* section.

The following abbreviations are used in this list: *adj.* (adjective), *dir. obj.* (direct object), *f.* (feminine), *fam.* (familiar), *ind. obj.* (indirect object), *inf.* (infinitive), *m.* (masculine), *pl.* (plural), *prep.* (preposition), *pron.* (pronoun), *sing.* (singular).

A

a to *(prep.)* (4A)
- **— ...le gusta(n)** he/she likes (5A)
- **— ...le encanta(n)** he/she loves (5A)
- **— casa** (to) home (4A)
- **— la derecha (de)** to the right (of) (6A)
- **— la izquierda (de)** to the left (of) (6A)
- **— la una de la tarde** at one (o'clock) in the afternoon (4B)
- **— las ocho de la mañana** at eight (o'clock) in the morning (4B)
- **— las ocho de la noche** at eight (o'clock) in the evening / at night (4B)
- **— menudo** often (8B)
- **— mí también** I do (like to) too (1A)
- **— mí tampoco** I don't (like to) either (1A)
- **¿— qué hora?** (At) what time? (4B)
- **— veces** sometimes (1B)
- **— ver** Let's see (2A)

el abrigo coat (7A)

abril April (P)

abrir to open (5A)

la abuela, el abuelo grandmother, grandfather (5A)

los abuelos grandparents (5A)

aburrido, -a boring (2A)

me aburre(n) it bores me (they bore me) (9A)

aburrir to bore (9A)

acabar de + *inf.* to have just ...(9A)

el actor actor (9A)

la actriz *pl.* **las actrices** actress (9A)

acuerdo:
- **Estoy de —.** I agree. (3B)
- **No estoy de —.** I don't agree. (3B)

¡Adiós! Good-bye! (P)

¿Adónde? (To) where? (4A)

agosto August (P)

el agua *f.* water (3A)

ahora now (5B)

al *(a + el),* **a la,** to the (4A)
- **al lado de** next to (2B)

la alfombra rug (6A)

algo something (3B)
- **¿— más?** Anything else? (5B)

allí there (2B)

el almacén *pl.* **los almacenes** department store (7B)

el almuerzo lunch (2A)
- **en el —** for lunch (3A)

alto, -a tall (5B)

amarillo, -a yellow (6A)

el amigo male friend (1B)

la amiga female friend (1B)

anaranjado, -a orange (6A)

la anciana, el anciano older woman, older man (8B)

los ancianos older people (8B)

el anillo ring (7B)

el animal animal (8A)

anoche last night (7B)

los anteojos de sol sunglasses (7B)

antes de before (9A)

el año year (P)
- **el — pasado** last year (7B)
- **¿Cuántos años tiene(n) ...?** How old is/are ...? (5A)
- **Tiene(n) ... años.** He/She is / They are ... (years old). (5A)

el apartamento apartment (6B)

aprender (a) to learn (to) (8A)

aquí here (2B)

el árbol tree (8A)

los aretes earrings (7B)

el armario closet (6A)

arreglar el cuarto to straighten up the room (6B)

el arroz rice (3B)

el arte:
- **la clase de —** art class (2A)

artístico, -a artistic (1B)

asco:
- **¡Qué —!** How awful! (3A)

la atracción *pl.* **las atracciones** attraction(s) (8A)

atrevido, -a daring (1B)

el autobús *pl.* **los autobuses** bus (8A)

el avión *pl.* **los aviones** airplane (8A)

¡Ay! ¡Qué pena! Oh! What a shame/pity! (4B)

ayer yesterday (7B)

ayudar to help (6B)

el azúcar sugar (5B)

azul blue (6A)

B

bailar to dance (1A)

el baile dance (4B)

bajar (información) to download (9B)

bajo, -a short (5B)

la bandera flag (2B)

el baño bathroom (6B)
- **el traje de —** swimsuit (7A)

barato, -a inexpensive, cheap (7B)

el barco boat, ship (8A)

el barrio neighborhood (8B)

el básquetbol: jugar al — to play basketball (4B)

bastante enough, rather (6B)
beber to drink (3A)
las bebidas beverages (3B)
béisbol: jugar al — to play baseball (4B)
la biblioteca library (4A)
bien well (P)
el bistec beefsteak (3B)
blanco, -a white (6A)
la blusa blouse (7A)
la boca mouth (P)
el boleto ticket (8A)
el bolígrafo pen (P)
la bolsa bag, sack (8B)
el bolso purse (7B)
bonito, -a pretty (6A)
las botas boots (7A)
el bote: pasear en — to go boating (8A)
la botella bottle (8B)
el brazo arm (P)
bucear to scuba dive, to snorkel (8A)
bueno (buen), -a good (1B)
Buenas noches. Good evening. (P)
Buenas tardes. Good afternoon. (P)
Buenos días. Good morning. (P)
buscar to look for (7A); to search (for) (9B)

C

el caballo: montar a — to ride horseback (8A)
la cabeza head (P)
cada día every day (3B)
la cadena chain (7B)
el café coffee (3A); café (4A)
la caja box (8B)
los calcetines socks (7A)
la calculadora calculator (2A)
la calle street, road (8B)
calor:
Hace —. It's hot. (P)
tener — to be warm (5B)

la cama bed (6A)
hacer la — to make the bed (6B)
la cámara camera (5A)
la — digital digital camera (9A)
el camarero, la camarera waiter, waitress (5B)
caminar to walk (3B)
la camisa shirt (7A)
la camiseta T-shirt (7A)
el campamento camp (8B)
el campo countryside (4A)
el canal (TV) channel (9A)
la canción *pl.* **las canciones** song (9B)
canoso: pelo — gray hair (5B)
cansado, -a tired (4B)
cantar to sing (1A)
cara a cara face-to-face (9B)
la carne meat (3B)
caro, -a expensive (7B)
la carpeta folder (P)
la — de argollas three-ring binder (2A)
la carta letter (9B)
el cartel poster (2B)
la cartera wallet (7B)
el cartón cardboard (8B)
la casa home, house (4A)
a — (to) home (4A)
en — at home (4A)
casi almost (9A)
castaño: pelo — brown (chestnut) hair (5B)
catorce fourteen (P)
la cebolla onion (3B)
celebrar to celebrate (5A)
la cena dinner (3B)
el centro:
el — comercial mall (4A)
el — de reciclaje recycling center (8B)
cerca (de) close (to), near (6B)
el cereal cereal (3A)
los cereales grains (3B)

cero zero (P)
la chaqueta jacket (7A)
la chica girl (1B)
el chico boy (1B)
cien one hundred (P)
las ciencias:
la clase de — naturales science class (2A)
la clase de — sociales social studies class (2A)
cinco five (P)
cincuenta fifty (P)
el cine movie theater (4A)
la ciudad city (8A)
la clase class (2A)
la sala de clases classroom (P)
¿Qué — de...? What kind of ...? (9A)
el coche car (6B)
la cocina kitchen (6B)
cocinar to cook (6B)
el collar necklace (7B)
el color *pl.* **los colores** (6A)
¿De qué — ...? What color ...? (6A)
la comedia comedy (9A)
el comedor dining room (6B)
comer to eat (3A)
cómico, -a funny, comical (9A)
la comida food, meal (3A)
como like, as (8A)
¿cómo?:
¿— eres? What are you like? (1B)
¿— es? What is he/she like? (1B)
¿— está Ud.? How are you? *formal* (P)
¿— estás? How are you? *fam.* (P)
¿— lo pasaste? How was it (for you)? (8A)
¿— se dice ...? How do you say ...? (P)
¿— se escribe ...? How is ... spelled? (P)

¿**— se llama?** What's his/her name? (1B)

¿**— te llamas?** What is your name? (P)

¿**— te queda(n)?** How does it (do they) fit (you)? (7A)

la cómoda dresser (6A)

compartir to share (3A)

complicado, -a complicated (9B)

la composición *pl.* **las composiciones** composition (9B)

comprar to buy (7A)

comprar recuerdos to buy souvenirs (8A)

comprender to understand (3A)

la computadora computer (2B)

la — portátil laptop computer (9B)

usar la — to use the computer (1A)

comunicarse to communicate (9B)

(tú) te comunicas you communicate (9B)

(yo) me comunico I communicate (9B)

la comunidad community (8B)

con with (3A)

— mis/tus amigos with my/your friends (4A)

¿**— quién?** With whom? (4A)

el concierto concert (4B)

conmigo with me (4B)

conocer to know, to be acquainted with (9B)

contento, -a happy (4B)

contigo with you (4B)

la corbata tie (7B)

correr to run (1A)

cortar el césped to cut/to mow the lawn (6B)

las cortinas curtains (6A)

corto, -a short (5B)

los pantalones cortos shorts (7A)

la cosa thing (6A)

costar (o → ue) to cost (7A)

¿Cuánto cuesta(n) ...? How much does (do) ... cost? (7A)

crear to create (9B)

creer to think (3B)

Creo que ... I think ... (3B)

Creo que no. I don't think so. (3B)

Creo que sí. I think so. (3B)

el cuaderno notebook (P)

el cuadro painting (6A)

¿Cuál? Which?, What? (3A)

¿**— es la fecha?** What is the date? (P)

¿Cuándo? When? (4A)

¿cuánto?: ¿— cuesta(n) ... ? How much does (do) ... cost? (7A)

¿cuántos, -as? how many? (P)

¿Cuántos años tiene(n) ...? How old is/are ...? (5A)

cuarenta forty (P)

el cuarto room (6B)

cuarto, -a fourth (2A)

y — *(time)* quarter past (P)

menos — *(time)* quarter to (P)

cuatro four (P)

cuatrocientos, -as four hundred (7A)

la cuchara spoon (5B)

el cuchillo knife (5B)

la cuenta bill (5B)

el cumpleaños birthday (5A)

¡Feliz —! Happy birthday! (5A)

el curso: tomar un curso to take a course (9B)

D

dar to give (6B)

— + *movie or TV program* to show (9A)

— de comer al perro to feed the dog (6B)

de of (2B); from (4A)

¿**— dónde eres?** Where are you from? (4A)

— la mañana/la tarde/la noche in the morning /afternoon / evening (4B)

— nada. You're welcome. (5B)

— plato principal as a main dish (5B)

— postre for dessert (5B)

¿**— qué color ...?** What color ...? (6A)

¿**— veras?** Really? (9A)

debajo de underneath (2B)

deber should, must (3B)

decidir to decide (8B)

décimo, -a tenth (2A)

decir to say, to tell (8B)

¿Cómo se dice ...? How do you say ...? (P)

dime tell me (8A)

¡No me digas! You don't say! (4A)

¿Qué quiere — ...? What does ... mean? (P)

Quiere — ... It means ... (P)

Se dice ... You say ... (P)

las decoraciones decorations (5A)

decorar to decorate (5A)

el dedo finger (P)

delante de in front of (2B)

delicioso, -a delicious (5B)

los demás, las demás others (8B)

demasiado too (4B)

el dependiente, la dependienta salesperson (7A)

deportista sports-minded (1B)

derecha: a la — (de) to the right (of) (6A)

el desayuno breakfast (3A)

en el — for breakfast (3A)

descansar to rest, to relax (8A)

los descuentos: la tienda de — discount store (7B)

desear to wish (5B)

¿Qué desean (Uds.)? What would you like? (5B)

desordenado, -a messy (1B)

el despacho office (home) (6B)

el despertador alarm clock (6A)

después afterwards (4A)

después (de) after (4A)
detrás de behind (2B)
el día day (P)
Buenos —s . Good morning. (P)
cada — every day (3B)
¿Qué — es hoy? What day is today? (P)
todos los —s every day (3A)
la diapositiva slide (9B)
dibujar to draw (1A)
el diccionario dictionary (2A)
diciembre December (P)
diecinueve nineteen (P)
dieciocho eighteen (P)
dieciséis sixteen (P)
diecisiete seventeen (P)
diez ten (P)
difícil difficult (2A)
digital: la cámara — digital camera (9B)
dime tell me (8A)
el dinero money (6B)
la dirección electrónica e-mail address (9B)
el disco compacto compact disc (6A)
grabar un disco compacto to burn a CD (9B)
el disquete diskette (2B)
divertido, -a amusing, fun (2A)
doce twelve (P)
el documento document (9B)
doler (o → ue) to hurt (9A)
domingo Sunday (P)
dónde:
¿—? Where? (2B)
¿De — eres? Where are you from? (4A)
dormir (o → ue) to sleep (6A)
el dormitorio bedroom (6A)
dos two (P)
los/las dos both (7A)
doscientos, -as two hundred (7A)
el drama drama (9A)
los dulces candy (5A)
durante during (8A)
durar to last (9A)

E

la educación física: la clase de — physical education class (2A)
el ejercicio: hacer — to exercise (3B)
el the *m. sing.* (1B)
él he (1B)
los electrodomésticos: la tienda de — household appliance store (7B)
electrónico, -a: la dirección — e-mail address (9B)
ella she (1B)
ellas they *f. pl.* (2A)
ellos they *m. pl.* (2A)
emocionante touching (9A)
empezar (e → ie) to begin, to start (9A)
en in, on (2B)
— + *vehicle* by, in, on (8A)
— casa at home (4A)
— la ... hora in the ... hour class period) (2A)
— la Red online (7B)
¿— qué puedo servirle? How can I help you? (7A)
encantado, -a delighted (P)
encantar to please very much, to love (9A)
a él/ella le encanta(n) he/she loves (5A)
me/te encanta(n) ... I/you love ... (3A)
encima de on top of (2B)
enero January (P)
enfermo, -a sick (4B)
la ensalada salad (3A)
la — de frutas fruit salad (3A)
enseñar to teach (2A)
entonces then (4B)
entrar to enter (7A)
enviar (i → í) to send (9B)
el equipo de sonido sound (stereo) system (6A)
¿Eres...? Are you ...? (1B)
es is (P); (he/she/it) is (1B)
— el *(number)* **de** *(month)* it is the ... of ... *(in telling the date)* (P)
— el primero de *(month)*. It is the first of ... (P)
— la una. It is one o'clock. (P)
— necesario. It's necessary. (8B)
— un(a) ... it's a ... (2B)
la escalera stairs, stairway (6B)
escribir:
¿Cómo se escribe ...? How is ... spelled? (P)
— cuentos to write stories (1A)
— por correo electrónico to write e-mail (9B)
Se escribe ... It's spelled ... (P)
el escritorio desk (2B)
escuchar música to listen to music (1A)
la escuela primaria primary school (8B)
ese, esa that (7A)
eso: por — that's why, therefore (9A)
esos, esas those (7A)
los espaguetis spaghetti (3B)
el español: la clase de — Spanish class (2A)
especialmente especially (9A)
el espejo mirror (6A)
la esposa wife (5A)
el esposo husband (5A)
esquiar (i → í) to ski (1A)
la estación *pl.* **las estaciones** season (P)
el estadio stadium (8A)
el estante shelf, bookshelf (6A)
estar to be (2B)
¿Cómo está Ud.? How are you? *formal* (P)
¿Cómo estás? How are you *fam.* (P)

— + *present participle* to be + *present participle* (6B)

— en línea to be online (9B)

Estoy de acuerdo. I agree. (3B)

No estoy de acuerdo. I don't agree. (3B)

este, esta this (7A)

esta noche this evening (4B)

esta tarde this afternoon (4B)

este fin de semana this weekend (4B)

el estómago stomach (P)

estos, estas these (7A)

Estoy de acuerdo. I agree. (3B)

el/la estudiante student (P)

eestudiar to study (2A)

estudioso, -a studious (1B)

la experiencia experience (8B)

F

fácil easy (2A)

la falda skirt (7A)

faltar to be missing (9A)

la familia family (1B)

fantástico, -a fantastic (8A)

fascinante fascinating (9A)

favorito, -a favorite (2A)

febrero February (P)

la fecha: ¿Cuál es la —? What is the date? (P)

¡Feliz cumpleaños! Happy birthday! (5A)

feo, -a ugly (6A)

la fiesta party (4B)

el fin de semana:

este — this weekend (4B)

los fines de semana on weekends (4A)

la flor *pl.* **las flores** flower (5A)

la foto photo (5A)

las fresas strawberries (3A)

frío:

Hace —. It's cold. (P)

tener — to be cold (5B)

fue it was (8A)

— un desastre. It was a disaster. (8A)

el fútbol: jugar al — to play soccer (4B)

el fútbol americano: jugar al — to play football (4B)

G

la galleta cookie (3A)

el garaje garage (6B)

el gato cat (5A)

generalmente generally (4A)

¡Genial! Great! (4B)

la gente people (8B)

el gimnasio gym (4A)

el globo balloon (5A)

el golf: jugar al — to play golf (4B)

la gorra cap (7A)

grabar un disco compacto to burn a CD (9B)

gracias thank you (P)

gracioso, -a funny (1B)

los gráficos computer graphics (9B)

grande large (6A)

los grasas fats (3B)

gris gray (6A)

los guantes gloves (7B)

guapo, -a good-looking (5B)

los guisantes peas (3B)

gustar:

a él/ella le gusta(n) he/she likes (5A)

(A mí) me gusta ... I like to ... (1A)

(A mí) me gusta más ... I like to ... better (I prefer to ...) (1A)

(A mí) me gusta mucho ... I like to ... a lot (1A)

(A mí) no me gusta ... I don't like to ... (1A)

(A mí) no me gusta nada ... I don't like to ... at all. (1A)

Le gusta ... He/She likes ... (1B)

Me gusta ... I like ... (3A)

Me gustaría ... I would like ... (4B)

Me gustó. I liked it. (8A)

No le gusta ... He/She doesn't like ... (1B)

¿Qué te gusta hacer? What do you like to do? (1A)

¿Qué te gusta hacer más? What do you like better (prefer) to do? (1A)

Te gusta ... You like ... (3A)

¿Te gusta ...? Do you like to ...? (1A)

¿Te gustaría ...? Would you like ... ? (4B)

¿Te gustó? Did you like it? (8A)

H

hablar to talk (2A)

— por teléfono to talk on the phone (1A)

hacer to do (3B)

hace + *time expression* ago (7B)

Hace calor. It's hot. (P)

Hace frío. It's cold. (P)

Hace sol. It's sunny. (P)

— ejercicio to exercise (3B)

— la cama to make the bed (6B)

— un video to videotape (5A)

haz *(command)* do, make (6B)

¿Qué hiciste? What did you do? (8A)

¿Qué tiempo hace? What's the weather like? (P)

(yo) hago I do (3B)

(tú) haces you do (3B)

hambre: Tengo —. I'm hungry. (3B)

la hamburguesa hamburger (3A)

hasta:

— luego. See you later. (P)

— mañana. See you tomorrow. (P)

Hay There is, There are (P, 2B)

— que one must (8B)

el helado ice cream (3B)

el hermano, la hermana brother, sister (5A)

el hermanastro, la hermanastra stepbrother, stepsister (5A)

los hermanos brothers; brother(s) and sister(s) (5A)

el hijo, la hija son, daughter (5A)

los hijos children; sons (5A)

la hoja de papel sheet of paper (P)

¡Hola! Hello! (P)

el hombre man (5B)

la hora:

en la ... — in the ... hour (class period) (2A)

¿A qué hora? (At) what time? (4B)

el horario schedule (2A)

horrible horrible (3B)

el horror: la película de — horror movie (9A)

el hospital hospital (8B)

el hotel hotel (8A)

hoy today (P)

los huevos eggs (3A)

I

la iglesia church (4A)

igualmente likewise (P)

impaciente impatient (1B)

importante important (6A)

impresionante impressive (8A)

increíble incredible (8B)

infantil childish (9A)

la información information (9B)

el informe report (9B)

el inglés: la clase de — English class (2A)

inolvidable unforgettable (8B)

inteligente intelligent (1B)

interesante interesting (2A)

interesar to interest (9A)

me interesa (n) it interests me (they interest me) (9A)

el invierno winter (P)

ir to go (4A)

— a + *inf.* to be going to + *verb* (4B)

— a la escuela to go to school (1A)

— de cámping to go camping (4B)

— de compras to go shopping (4A)

— de pesca to go fishing (4B)

— de vacaciones to go on vacation (8A)

¡Vamos! Let's go! (7A)

izquierda: a la — (de) to the left (of) (6A)

J

el jardín *pl.* **los jardines** garden, yard (8B)

los jeans jeans (7A)

el joven, la joven young man, young woman (5B)

joven *adj.* young (5B)

la joyería jewelry store (7B)

las judías verdes green beans (3B)

jueves Thursday (P)

jugar (a) (u → ue) to play (games, sports) (4B)

— al básquetbol to play basketball (4B)

— al béisbol to play baseball (4B)

— al fútbol to play soccer (4B)

— al fútbol americano to play football (4B)

— al golf to play golf (4B)

— al tenis to play tennis (4B)

— al vóleibol to play volleyball (4B)

— videojuegos to play video games (1A)

el jugo:

— de manzana apple juice (3A)

— de naranja orange juice (3A)

el juguete toy (8B)

julio July (P)

junio June (P)

L

la the *f. sing.* (1B); it, her *f. dir. obj. pron.* (7B)

el laboratorio laboratory (9B)

lado: al — de next to, beside (2B)

el lago lake (8A)

la lámpara lamp (6A)

el lápiz *pl.* **los lápices** pencil (P)

largo, -a long (5B)

las the *f. pl.* (2B); them *f. dir. obj. pron.* (7B)

— dos, los dos both (7A)

la lata can (8B)

lavar to wash (6B)

— el coche to wash the car (6B)

— la ropa to wash the clothes (6B)

— los platos to wash the dishes (6B)

le (to/for) him, her, *(formal)* you *sing. ind. obj. pron.* (8B)

— gusta ... He/She likes ... (1B)

— traigo ... I will bring you ... (5B)

No — gusta ... He/She doesn't like ... (1B)

la lección *pl.* **las lecciones de piano** piano lesson (class) (4A)

la leche milk (3A)

la lechuga lettuce (3B)

el lector DVD DVD player (6A)

leer revistas to read magazines (1A)

lejos (de) far (from) (6B)

les (to/for) them, *(formal)* you *pl. ind. obj. pron.* (8B)

levantar pesas to lift weights (3B)

la librería bookstore (7B)

el libro book (P)

la limonada lemonade (3A)

limpiar el baño to clean the bathroom (6B)

limpio, -a clean (6B)

línea: estar en — to be online (9B)

llamar:

¿Cómo se llama? What's his/her name? (1B)

¿Cómo te llamas? What is your name? (P)

Me llamo ... My name is ... (P)

el llavero key chain (7B)

llevar to wear (7A); to take, to carry, to bring (8B)

llover (o → ue): Llueve. It's raining. (P)

lo it, him *m. dir. obj. pron.* (7B)

— siento. I'm sorry. (4B)

los the *m. pl.* (2B); them *m. dir. obj. pron* (7B)

— dos, las dos both (7A)

— fines de semana on weekends (4A)

— lunes, los martes ... on Mondays, on Tuesdays ... (4A)

el lugar place (8A)

lunes Monday (P)

los lunes on Mondays (4A)

la luz *pl.* **las luces** light (5A)

M

la madrastra stepmother (5A)

la madre (mamá) mother (5A)

mal bad, badly (4B)

malo, -a bad (3B)

la mano hand (P)

mantener: para — la salud to maintain one's health (3B)

la mantequilla butter (3B)

la manzana apple (3A)

el jugo de — apple juice (3A)

mañana tomorrow (P)

la mañana:

a las ocho de la — at eight (o'clock) in the morning (4B)

de la — in the morning (4B)

el mar sea (8A)

marrón *pl.* **marrones** brown (6A)

martes Tuesday (P)

los martes on Tuesdays (4A)

marzo March (P)

más:

¿Qué —? What else? (8B)

— ... que more ... than (2A)

— de more than (9A)

— o menos more or less (3A)

las matemáticas: la clase de — mathematics class (2A)

mayo May (P)

mayor older (5A)

me (to/for) me *ind. obj. pron.* (8B)

— aburre(n) it/they bore(s) me (9A)

— falta(n) ... I need ... (5B)

— gustaría I would like (4B)

— gustó. I liked it. (8A)

— interesa(n) it/they interest(s) me (9A)

— llamo ... My name is ... (P)

— queda(n) bien/mal. It/They fit(s) me well/poorly. (7A)

— quedo en casa. I stay at home. (4A)

¿— trae ...? Will you bring me ...? (5B)

media, -o half (P)

y — thirty, half-past (P)

mejor:

el/la —, los/las —es the best (6A)

—(es) que better than (6A)

menor younger (5A)

menos:

más o — more or less (3A)

— ... que less/fewer ... than (6A)

— de less/fewer than (9A)

el menú menu (5B)

menudo: a — often (8B)

el mes month (P)

la mesa table (2B)

poner la — to set the table (6B)

la mesita night table (6A)

la mezquita mosque (4A)

mi, mis my (2B, 5A)

mí:

a — también I do (like to) too (1A)

a — tampoco I don't (like to) either (1A)

para — in my opinion, for me (6A)

miedo: tener — (de) to be scared (of), to be afraid (of) (9B)

miércoles Wednesday (P)

mil a thousand (7A)

mirar to look (at) (7B)

mismo, -a same (6A)

la mochila bookbag, backpack (2B)

el momento: un — a moment (6B)

el mono monkey (8A)

las montañas mountains (4A)

montar:

— a caballo to ride horseback (8A)

— en bicicleta to ride a bicycle (1A)

— en monopatín to skateboard (1A)

el monumento monument (8A)

morado, -a purple (6A)

mucho a lot (2A)

— gusto pleased to meet you (P)

muchos, -as many (3B)

la mujer woman (5B)

el museo museum (8A)

muy very (1B)

— bien very well (P)

N

nada nothing (P)

(A mí) no me gusta — ... I don't like to ... at all. (1A)

De —. You're welcome. (5B)

nadar to swim (1A)

la naranja: el jugo de — orange juice (3A)

la nariz *pl.* **las narices** nose (P)
navegar en la Red to surf the Web (9B)
necesario: Es —. It's necessary. (8B)
necesitar:
(yo) necesito I need (2A)
(tú) necesitas you need (2A)
negro, -a black (6A)
el pelo — black hair (5B)
nevar (e → ie) Nieva. It's snowing. (P)
ni … ni neither … nor, not … or (1A)
el niño, la niña young boy, young girl (8B)
los niños children (8B)
No estoy de acuerdo. I don't agree. (3B)
¡No me digas! You don't say! (4A)
no soy I am not (1A)
noche:
a las ocho de la — at eight (o'clock) in the evening, at night (4B)
Buenas —s. Good evening. (P)
de la — in the evening, at night (4B)
esta — this evening (4B)
nos (to/for) us *ind. obj. pron.* (8B)
¡— vemos! See you later! (P)
nosotros, -as we (2A)
novecientos, -as nine hundred (7A)
noveno, -a ninth (2A)
noventa ninety (P)
noviembre November (P)
el novio, la novia boyfriend, girlfriend (7B)
nuestro(s), -a(s) our (5A)
nueve nine (P)
nuevo, -a new (7A)
nunca never (3A)

O

o or (1A)
la obra de teatro play (8A)
ochenta eighty (P)
ocho eight (P)
ochocientos, -as eight hundred (7A)
octavo, -a eighth (2A)
octubre October (P)
ocupado, -a busy (4B)
el ojo eye (P)
once eleven (P)
ordenado, -a neat (1B)
os (to/for) you *pl. fam. ind. obj. pron.* (8B)
el otoño fall, autumn (P)
otro, -a other, another (5B)
otra vez again (8B)
¡Oye! Hey! (4B)

P

paciente patient (1B)
el padrastro stepfather (5A)
el padre (papá) father (5A)
los padres parents (5A)
pagar (por) to pay (for) (7B)
la página Web Web page (9B)
el país country (8A)
el pájaro bird (8A)
el pan bread (3A)
el — tostado toast (3A)
la pantalla (computer) screen (2B)
los pantalones pants (7A)
los — cortos shorts (7A)
las papas potatoes (3B)
las — fritas French fries (3A)
el papel picado cut-paper decorations (5A)
la papelera wastepaper basket (2B)
para for (2A)
— + *inf.* in order to + *inf.* (4A)
— la salud for one's health (3B)
— mantener la salud to maintain one's health (3B)
— mí in my opinion, for me (6A)
¿ — qué sirve? What's it (used) for? (9B)
— ti in your opinion, for you (6A)
la pared wall (6A)
el parque park (4A)
el — de diversiones amusement park (8A)
el — nacional national park (8A)
el partido game, match (4B)
pasar:
¿Cómo lo pasaste? How was it (for you)? (8A)
— la aspiradora to vacuum (6B)
— tiempo con amigos to spend time with friends (1A)
¿Qué pasa? What's happening? (P)
¿Qué te pasó? What happened to you? (8A)
pasear en bote to go boating (8A)
el pastel cake (5A)
los pasteles pastries (3B)
patinar to skate (1A)
pedir (e → i) to order (5B); to ask for (9B)
la película film, movie (9A)
la — de ciencia ficción science fiction movie (9A)
la — de horror horror movie (9A)
la — policíaca crime movie, mystery (9A)
la — romántica romantic movie (9A)
ver una — to see a movie (4A)
pelirrojo, -a red-haired (5B)
el pelo hair (5B)
el — canoso gray hair (5B)
el — castaño brown (chestnut) hair (5B)
el — negro black hair (5B)
el — rubio blond hair (5B)

pensar (e → ie) to plan, to think (7A)

peor:

el/la —, los/las —es the worst (6A)

—(es) que worse than (6A)

pequeño, -a small (6A)

Perdón. Excuse me. (7A)

perezoso, -a lazy (1B)

el perfume perfume (7B)

el periódico newspaper (8B)

pero but (1B)

el perrito caliente hot dog (3A)

el perro dog (5A)

la persona person (5A)

pesas: levantar — to lift weights (3B)

el pescado fish (3B)

el pie foot (P)

la pierna leg (P)

la pimienta pepper (5B)

la piñata piñata (5A)

la piscina pool (4A)

el piso story, floor (6B)

primer — second floor (6B)

segundo — third floor (6B)

la pizza pizza (3A)

la planta baja ground floor (6B)

el plástico plastic (8B)

el plátano banana (3A)

el plato plate, dish (5B)

de — principal as a main dish (5B)

el — principal main dish (5B)

la playa beach (4A)

pobre poor (8B)

poco: un — (de) a little (4B)

poder (o → ue) to be able (6A)

(yo) puedo I can (4B)

(tú) puedes you can (4B)

policíaca: la película — crime movie, mystery (9A)

el pollo chicken (3B)

poner to put, to place (6B)

pon *(command)* put, place (6B)

— la mesa to set the table (6B)

(yo) pongo I put (6B)

(tú) pones you put (6B)

por:

— eso that's why, therefore (9A)

— favor please (P)

¿— qué? Why? (3B)

— supuesto of course (3A)

porque because (3B)

la posesión *pl.* **las posesiones** possession (6A)

el postre dessert (5B)

de — for dessert (5B)

practicar deportes to play sports (1A)

práctico, -a practical (2A)

el precio price (7A)

preferir (e → ie) to prefer (7A)

(yo) prefiero I prefer (3B)

(tú) prefieres you prefer (3B)

preparar to prepare (5A)

la presentación *pl.* **las presentaciones** presentation (9B)

la primavera spring (P)

primer (primero), -a first (2A)

— piso second floor (6B)

el primo, la prima cousin (5A)

los primos cousins (5A)

el problema problem (8B)

el profesor, la profesora teacher (P)

el programa program, show (9A)

el — de concursos game show (9A)

el — de dibujos animados cartoon (9A)

el — de entrevistas interview program (9A)

el — de la vida real reality program (9A)

el — de noticias news program (9A)

el — deportivo sports program (9A)

el — educativo educational program (9A)

el — musical musical program (9A)

propio, -a own (6A)

el proyecto de construcción construction project (8B)

puedes: (tú) — you can (4B)

puedo: (yo) — I can (4B)

la puerta door (2B)

pues well *(to indicate pause)* (1A)

la pulsera bracelet (7B)

el reloj — watch (7B)

el pupitre student desk (P)

Q

que who, that (5A)

qué:

¿Para — sirve? What's it (used) for? (9B)

¡— + adj.! How ...! (5B)

¡— asco! How awful! (3A)

¡— buena idea! What a good/nice idea! (4B)

¿— clase de ...? What kind of ...? (9A)

¿— desean (Uds.)? What would you like? (5B)

¿— día es hoy? What day is today? (P)

¿— es esto? What is this? (2B)

¿— hiciste? What did you do? (8A)

¿— hora es? What time is it? (P)

¿— más? What else? (8B)

¿— pasa? What's happening? (P)

¡— pena! What a shame/pity! (4B)

¿— quiere decir ... ? What does ... mean? (P)

¿— tal? How are you? (P)

¿— te gusta hacer? What do you like to do? (1A)

¿— te gusta más? What do you like better (prefer) to do? (1A)

¿— te parece? What do you think (about it)? (9B)

¿— te pasó? What happened to you? (8A)

¿— tiempo hace? What's the weather like? (P)

quedar to fit (7A), to stay (4A)

¿Cómo me queda? How does it fit (me)? (7A)

Me / te queda bien. It fits me / you well. (7A)

Me quedo en casa. I stay home. (4A)

el quehacer (de la casa) (household) chore (6B)

querer (e → ie) to want (7A)

¿Qué quiere decir ...? What does ... mean? (P)

Quiere decir ... It means ... (P)

quisiera I would like (5B)

(yo) quiero I want (4B)

(tú) quieres you want (4B)

el queso cheese (3A)

¿Quién? Who? (2A)

quince fifteen (P)

quinientos, -as five hundred (7A)

quinto, -a fifth (2A)

quisiera I would like (5B)

quitar el polvo to dust (6B)

quizás maybe (7A)

R

rápidamente quickly (9B)

el ratón *pl.* **los ratones** (computer) mouse (2B)

razón: tener — to be correct (7A)

realista realistic (9A)

recibir to receive (6B)

reciclar to recycle (8B)

los recuerdos souvenirs (8A)

comprar recuerdos to buy souvenirs (8A)

la Red:

en la — online (7B)

navegar en la — to surf the Web (9B)

recoger (g → j) to collect, to gather (8B)

el refresco soft drink (3A)

el regalo gift, present (5A)

regresar to return (8A)

regular okay, so-so (P)

el reloj clock (2B)

el — pulsera watch (7B)

reservado, -a reserved, shy (1B)

el restaurante restaurant (4A)

rico, -a rich, tasty (5B)

el río river (8B)

rojo, -a red (6A)

romántico, -a: la película — romantic movie (9A)

romper to break (5A)

la ropa: la tienda de — clothing store (7B)

rosado, -a pink (6A)

rubio, -a blond (5B)

S

sábado Saturday (P)

saber to know (how) (9B)

(yo) sé I know (how to) (4B)

(tú) sabes you know (how to) (4B)

sabroso, -a tasty, flavorful (3B)

el sacapuntas pencil sharpener (2B)

sacar:

— fotos to take photos (5A)

— la basura to take out the trash (6B)

la sal salt (5B)

la sala living room (6B)

la sala de clases classroom (P)

la salchicha sausage (3A)

salir to leave, to go out (8A)

la salud:

para la — for one's health (3B)

para mantener la — to maintain one's health (3B)

el sándwich de jamón y queso ham and cheese sandwich (3A)

sé: (yo) — I know (how to) (1B)

sed: Tengo —. I'm thirsty. (3B)

según according to (1B)

— mi familia according to my family (1B)

segundo, -a second (2A)

— piso third floor (6B)

seis six (P)

seiscientos, -as six hundred (7A)

la semana week (P)

este fin de — this weekend (4B)

la — pasada last week (7B)

los fines de — on weekends (4A)

señor (Sr.) sir, Mr. (P)

señora (Sra.) madam, Mrs. (P)

señorita (Srta.) miss, Miss (P)

separar to separate (8B)

septiembre September (P)

séptimo, -a seventh (2A)

ser to be (3B)

¿Eres ...? Are you ...? (1B)

es he/she is (1B)

fue it was (8A)

no soy I am not (1B)

soy I am (1B)

serio, -a serious (1B)

la servilleta napkin (5B)

servir (e → i) to serve, to be useful (9B)

¿En qué puedo servirle? How can I help you? (7A)

¿Para qué sirve? What's it (used) for? (9B)

Sirve para ... It's used for ... (9B)

sesenta sixty (P)

setecientos, -as seven hundred (7A)

setenta seventy (P)

sexto, -a sixth (2A)

si if, whether (6B)

sí yes (1A)

siempre always (3A)

siento: lo — I'm sorry (4B)

siete seven (P)
la silla chair (2B)
simpático, -a nice, friendly (1B)
sin without (3A)
la sinagoga synagogue (4A)
el sitio Web Web site (9B)
sobre about (9A)
sociable sociable (1B)
el software software (7B)
el sol:
Hace —. It's sunny. (P)
los anteojos de — sunglasses (7B)
tomar el — to sunbathe (8A)
sólo only (5A)
solo, -a alone (4A)
Son las ... It's ... *(time)* (P)
la sopa de verduras vegetable soup (3A)
el sótano basement (6B)
soy I am (1B)
su, sus his, her, your *formal,* their (5A)
sucio, -a dirty (6B)
la sudadera sweatshirt (7A)
sueño: tener — to be sleepy (5B)
el suéter sweater (7A)
supuesto: por — of course (3A)

T

tal: ¿Qué — ? How are you? (P)
talentoso, -a talented (1B)
también also, too (1A)
a mí — I do (like to) too (1A)
tampoco: a mí — I don't (like to) either (1A)
tanto so much (7A)
tarde late (8A); afternoon (4B)
a la una de la — at one (o'clock) in the afternoon (4B)
Buenas —s. Good afternoon. (P)
de la tarde in the afternoon (4B)
esta — this afternoon (4B)
la tarea homework (2A)
la tarjeta card (9B)
la taza cup (5B)
te (to/for) you *sing. ind. obj. pron.* (8B)
¿— gusta ...? Do you like to ... ? (1A)
¿— gustaría ...? Would you like ...? (4B)
¿— gustó? Did you like it? (8A)
el té tea (3A)
el — helado iced tea (3A)
el teatro theater (8A)
el teclado (computer) keyboard (2B)
la tecnología technology/computers (2A)
la clase de — technology/ computer class (2A)
la telenovela soap opera (9A)
el televisor television set (6A)
el templo temple; Protestant church (4A)
temprano early (8A)
el tenedor fork (5B)
tener to have (5A)
(yo) tengo I have (2A)
(tú) tienes you have (2A)
¿Cuántos años tiene(n) ...? How old is/are ... ? (5A)
— calor to be warm (5B)
— frío to be cold (5B)
— miedo (de) to be scared (of), to be afraid (of) (9B)
— razón to be correct (7A)
— sueño to be sleepy (5B)
Tengo hambre. I'm hungry. (3B)
Tengo que ... I have to ... (4B)
Tengo sed. I'm thirsty. (3B)
Tiene(n) ... años. He/She is/ They are ... (years old). (5A)
el tenis: jugar al — to play tennis (4B)
tercer (tercero), -a third (2A)
terminar to finish, to end (9A)
ti you *fam. after prep.*
¿Y a —? And you? (1A)
para — in your opinion, for you (6A)
el tiempo:
el — libre free time (4A)
pasar — con amigos to spend time with friends (1A)
¿Qué — hace? What's the weather like? (P)
la tienda store (7A)
la — de descuentos discount store (7B)
la — de electrodomésticos household appliance store (7B)
la — de ropa clothing store (7A)
Tiene(n) ... años. He/She is / They are ... (years old). (5A)
el tío, la tía uncle, aunt (5A)
los tíos uncles; aunt(s) and uncle(s) (5A)
tocar la guitarra to play the guitar (1A)
el tocino bacon (3A)
todos, -as all (3B)
— los días every day (3A)
tomar:
— el sol to sunbathe (8A)
— un curso to take a course (9B)
los tomates tomatoes (3B)
tonto, -a silly, stupid (9A)
trabajador, -ora hardworking (1B)
trabajar to work (1A)
el trabajo work, job (4A)
el — voluntario volunteer work (8B)
traer:
Le traigo ... I will bring you ... (5B)
¿Me trae ...? Will you bring me ...? (5B)
el traje suit (7A)
el — de baño swimsuit (7A)
trece thirteen (P)
treinta thirty (P)

treinta y uno thirty-one (P)

tremendo, -a tremendous (8A)

el **tren** train (8A)

tres three (P)

trescientos, as three hundred (7A)

triste sad (4B)

tu, tus your (2B, 5A)

tú you *fam.* (2A)

U

Ud. (usted) you *formal sing.* (2A)

Uds. (ustedes) you *formal pl.* (2A)

¡Uf! Ugh!, Yuck! (7B)

un, una a, an (1B)

un poco (de) a little (4B)

la **una: a la —** at one o'clock (4B)

uno one (P)

unos, -as some (2B)

usado, -a used (8B)

usar la computadora to use the computer (1A)

usted (Ud.) you *formal sing.* (2A)

ustedes (Uds.) you *formal pl.* (2A)

las **uvas** grapes (3B)

V

las **vacaciones: ir de —** to go on vacation (8A)

¡Vamos! Let's go! (7A)

el **vaso** glass (5B)

veinte twenty (P)

veintiuno (veintiún) twenty-one (P)

vender to sell (7B)

venir to come (5B)

la **ventana** window (2B)

ver to see (8A)

a — ... Let's see (2A)

¡Nos vemos! See you later! (P)

— la tele to watch television (1A)

— una película to see a movie (4A)

el **verano** summer (P)

veras: ¿De —? Right? (9A)

¿Verdad? Right? (3A)

verde green (6A)

el **vestido** dress (7A)

la **vez,** *pl.* **las veces** time (8B)

a veces sometimes (1B)

otra — again (8B)

vi I saw (8A)

viajar to travel (8A)

el **viaje** trip (8A)

el **video** videocassette (6A)

la **videocasetera** VCR (6A)

los **videojuegos: jugar —** to play video games (1A)

el **vidrio** glass (8B)

viejo, -a old (5B)

viernes Friday (P)

violento, -a violent (9A)

visitar to visit (8A)

— salones de chat to visit chat rooms (9B)

¿Viste? Did you see? (8A)

vivir to live (6B)

el **vóleibol: jugar al —** to play volleyball (4B)

el **voluntario, la voluntaria** volunteer (8B)

vosotros, -as you *pl.* (2A)

vuestro(s), -a(s) your (5A)

Y

y and (1A)

¿— a ti? And you? (1A)

— cuarto quarter past (P)

— media thirty, half-past (in telling time) (P)

¿— tú? And you? *fam.* (P)

¿— usted (Ud.)? And you? *formal* (P)

ya already (9A)

yo I (1B)

el **yogur** yogurt (3A)

Z

las **zanahorias** carrots (3B)

la **zapatería** shoe store (7B)

los **zapatos** shoes (7A)

el **zoológico** zoo (8A)

English-Spanish Vocabulary

The *English-Spanish Vocabulary* contains all active vocabulary from the text, including vocabulary presented in the grammar sections.

A dash (—) represents the main entry word. For example, **to play —** after **baseball** means **to play baseball.**

The number following each entry indicates the chapter in which the word or expression is presented. The letter *P* following an entry refers to the *Para empezar* section.

The following abbreviations are used in this list: *adj.* (adjective), *dir. obj.* (direct object), *f.* (feminine), *fam.*(familiar), *ind. obj.* (indirect object), *inf.* (infinitive), *m.* (masculine), *pl.* (plural), *prep.* (preposition), *pron.* (pronoun), *sing.* (singular).

A

a, an un, una (1B)
a little un poco (de) (4B)
a lot mucho, -a (2A)
a thousand mil (7A)
able: to be — poder (o → ue) (6A)
about sobre (9A)
according to según (1B)
— my family según mi familia (1B)
acquainted: to be —with conocer (9B)
actor el actor (9A)
actress la actriz *pl.* las actrices (9A)
address: e-mail — la dirección electrónica (9B)
afraid: to be — (of) tener miedo (de) (9B)
after después (de) (4A)
afternoon:
at one (o'clock) in the afternoon a la una de la tarde (4B)
Good —. Buenas tardes. (P)
in the — de la tarde (4B)
this — esta tarde (4B)
afterwards después (4A)
again otra vez (8B)
ago hace + *time expression* (7B)
agree:
I —. Estoy de acuerdo. (3B)
I don't —. No estoy de acuerdo. (3B)
airplane el avión *pl.* los aviones (8A)
alarm clock el despertador (6A)
all todos, -as (3B)
almost casi (9A)
alone solo, -a (4A)
already ya (9A)
also también (1A)
always siempre (3A)
am:
I — (yo) soy (1B)
I — not (yo) no soy (1B)
amusement park el parque de diversiones (8A)
amusing divertido, -a (2A)
and y (1A)
¿— you? ¿Y a ti? *fam.* (1A); ¿Y tú? *fam.* (P); ¿Y usted (Ud.)? *formal* (P)
animal el animal (8A)
another otro, -a (5B)
Anything else? ¿Algo más? (5B)
apartment el apartamento (6B)
apple la manzana (3A)
— juice el jugo de manzana (3A)
April abril (P)
Are you ... ? ¿Eres ... ? (1B)
arm el brazo (P)
art class la clase de arte (2A)
artistic artístico, -a (1B)
as como (8A)
— a main dish de plato principal (5B)
to ask for pedir (e → i) (9B)
at:
— eight (o'clock) a las ocho (4B)
— eight (o'clock) at night a las ocho de la noche (4B)
— eight (o'clock) in the evening a las ocho de la noche (4B)
— eight (o'clock) in the morning a las ocho de la mañana (4B)
— home en casa (4A)
— one (o'clock) a la una (4B)
— one (o'clock) in the afternoon a la una de la tarde (4B)
— what time? ¿A qué hora? (4B)
attraction(s) la atracción *pl.* las atracciones (8A)
August agosto (P)
aunt la tía (5A)
aunt(s) and uncle(s) los tíos (5A)
autumn el otoño (P)

B

backpack la mochila (2B)
bacon el tocino (3A)
bad malo, -a (3B); mal (4B)
badly mal (4B)
bag la bolsa (8B)
balloon el globo (5A)
banana el plátano (3A)
baseball: to play — jugar al béisbol (4B)
basement el sótano (6B)
basketball: to play — jugar al básquetbol (4B)
bathroom el baño (6B)
to be ser (3B); estar (2B)
He/She is / They are ... (years old). Tiene(n) ... años. (5A)
How old is/are ... ? ¿Cuántos años tiene(n) ... ? (5A)
to — + *present participle* estar + *present participle* (6B)
to — able poder (o → ue) (6A)
to — acquainted with conocer (9B)
to — afraid (of) tener miedo (de) (9B)
to — cold tener frío (5B)

to — **correct** tener razón (7A)
to — going to + *verb* ir a + *inf.* (4B)
to — online estar en línea (9B)
to — scared (of) tener miedo (de) (9B)
to — sleepy tener sueño (5B)
to — useful servir (e → i) (9B)
to — warm tener calor (5B)
beach la playa (4A)
bear el oso (8A)
because porque (3B)
bed la cama (6A)
to make the — hacer la cama (6B)
bedroom el dormitorio (6A)
beefsteak el bistec (3B)
before antes de (9A)
to begin empezar (e → ie) (9A)
behind detrás de (2B)
best: the — el/la mejor, los/las mejores (6A)
better than mejor(es) que (6A)
beverages las bebidas (3B)
bicycle: to ride a — montar en bicicleta (1A)
bill la cuenta (5B)
binder: three-ring — la carpeta de argollas (2A)
bird el pájaro (8A)
birthday el cumpleaños (5A)
Happy —! ¡Feliz cumpleaños! (5A)
black negro (6A)
black hair el pelo negro (5B)
blond hair el pelo rubio (5B)
blouse la blusa (7A)
blue azul (6A)
boat el barco (8A)
boating: to go — pasear en bote (8A)
book el libro (P)
bookbag la mochila (2B)
bookshelf el estante (6A)
bookstore la librería (7B)
boots las botas (7A)
to bore aburrir (9A)
it/they —(s) me me aburre(n) (9A)
boring aburrido, -a (2A)
both los dos, las dos (7A)
bottle la botella (8B)
box la caja (8B)
boy el chico (1B)
—friend el novio (7B)
young — el niño (8B)
bracelet la pulsera (7B)
bread el pan (3A)
to break romper (5A)
breakfast el desayuno (3A)
for — en el desayuno (3A)
to bring traer (5B); llevar (8B)
I will — you ... Le traigo ... (5B)
Will you — me ... ? ¿Me trae ... ? (5B)
brother el hermano (5A)
brothers; brother(s) and sister(s) los hermanos (5A)
brown marrón *pl.* marrones (6A)
— (chestnut) hair el pelo castaño (5B)
to burn a CD grabar un disco compacto (9B)
bus el autobús *pl.* los autobuses (8A)
busy ocupado, -a (4B)
but pero (1B)
butter la mantequilla (3B)
to buy comprar (7A)
to — souvenirs comprar recuerdos (8A)
by + *vehicle* en + *vehicle* (8A)

C

café el café (4A)
cake el pastel (5A)
calculator la calculadora (2A)
camera la cámara (5A)
digital — la cámara digital (9B)
camp el campamento (8B)
can la lata (8B)
can:
I — (yo) puedo (4B)
you — (tú) puedes (4B)
candy los dulces (5A)
cap la gorra (7A)
car el coche (6B)
card la tarjeta (9B)
cardboard el cartón (8B)
carrots las zanahorias (3B)
to carry llevar (8B)
cartoon el programa de dibujos animados (9A)
cat el gato (5A)
CD: to burn a CD grabar un disco compacto (9B)
to celebrate celebrar (5A)
cereal el cereal (3A)
chain la cadena (7B)
chair la silla (2B)
channel (TV) el canal (9A)
cheap barato, -a (7B)
cheese el queso (3A)
chicken el pollo (3B)
childish infantil (9A)
children los hijos (5A); los niños (8B)
chore: household — el quehacer (de la casa) (6B)
church la iglesia (4A)
Protestant — el templo (4A)
city la ciudad (8A)
class la clase (2A)
classroom la sala de clases (P)
clean limpio, -a (6B)
to clean the bathroom limpiar el baño (6B)
clock el reloj (2B)
close (to) cerca (de) (6B)
closet el armario (6A)
clothing store la tienda de ropa (7A)
coat el abrigo (7A)
coffee el café (3A)

cold:

It's —. Hace frío. (P)

to be — tener frío (5B)

to collect recoger (g → j) (8B)

color:

What — ...? ¿De qué color ...? (6A)

—s los colores (6A)

to come venir (5B)

comedy la comedia (9A)

comical cómico, -a (9A)

to communicate comunicarse (9B)

I — (yo) me comunico (9B)

you — (tú) te comunicas (9B)

community la comunidad (8B)

compact disc el disco compacto (6A)

to burn a — grabar un disco compacto (9B)

complicated complicado, -a (9B)

composition la composición *pl.* las composiciones (9B)

computer la computadora (2B)

— graphics los gráficos (9B)

— keyboard el teclado (2B)

— mouse el ratón (2B)

— screen la pantalla (2B)

—s/technology la tecnología (2B)

laptop — la computadora portátil (9B)

to use the — usar la computadora (1A)

concert el concierto (4B)

construction project el proyecto de construcción (8B)

to cook cocinar (6B)

cookie la galleta (3A)

correct: to be — tener razón (7A)

to cost costar (o → ue) (7A)

How much does (do) ... — ? ¿Cuánto cuesta(n)? (7A)

country el país (8A)

countryside el campo (4A)

course: to take a course tomar un curso (9B)

cousin el primo, la prima (5A)

—s los primos (5A)

to create crear (9B)

crime movie la película policíaca (9A)

cup la taza (5B)

curtains las cortinas (6A)

to cut the lawn cortar el césped (6B)

cut-paper decorations el papel picado (5A)

D

dance el baile (4B)

to dance bailar (1A)

daring atrevido, -a (1B)

date: What is the —? ¿Cuál es la fecha? (P)

daughter la hija (5A)

day el día (P)

every — todos los días (3A); cada día (3B)

What — is today? ¿Qué día es hoy? (P)

December diciembre (P)

to decide decidir (8B)

to decorate decorar (5A)

decorations las decoraciones (5A)

delicious delicioso, -a (5B)

delighted encantado, -a (P)

department store el almacén *pl.* los almacenes (7B)

desk el pupitre (P); el escritorio (2B)

dessert el postre (5B)

for — de postre (5B)

dictionary el diccionario (2A)

Did you like it? ¿Te gustó? (8A)

difficult difícil (2A)

digital camera la cámara digital (9B)

dining room el comedor (6B)

dinner la cena (3B)

dirty sucio, -a (6B)

disaster: It was a — . Fue un desastre. (8A)

discount store la tienda de descuentos (7B)

dish el plato (5B)

as a main — de plato principal (5B)

main — el plato principal (5B)

diskette el disquete (2B)

to do hacer (3B)

— *(command)* haz (6B)

— you like to ...? ¿Te gusta ...? (1A)

I — (yo) hago (3B)

What did you —? ¿Qué hiciste? (8A)

you — (tú) haces (3B)

document el documento (9B)

dog el perro (5A)

to feed the — dar de comer al perro (6B)

door la puerta (2B)

to download bajar (información) (9B)

drama el drama (9A)

to draw dibujar (1A)

dress el vestido (7A)

dresser la cómoda (6A)

to drink beber (3A)

during durante (8A)

to dust quitar el polvo (6B)

DVD player el lector DVD (6A)

E

e-mail:

— address la dirección electrónica (9B)

to write an — message escribir por correo electrónico (9B)

early temprano (8A)

earrings los aretes (7B)

easy fácil (2A)

to eat comer (3A)

educational program el programa educativo (9A)

eggs los huevos (3A)

eight ocho (P)

eight hundred ochocientos, -as (7A)

eighteen dieciocho (P)

eighth octavo, -a (2A)

eighty ochenta (P)

either tampoco (1A)
I don't (like to) — a mí tampoco (1A)
eleven once (P)
else:
Anything —? ¿Algo más? (5B)
What —? ¿Qué más? (8B)
to end terminar (9A)
English class la clase de inglés (2A)
enough bastante (6B)
to enter entrar (7A)
especially especialmente (9A)
evening:
Good —. Buenas noches. (P)
in the — de la noche (4B)
this — esta noche (4B)
every day cada día (3B); todos los días (3A)
Excuse me. Perdón. (7A)
to exercise hacer ejercicio (3B)
expensive caro, -a (7B)
experience la experiencia (8B)
eye el ojo (P)

F

face-to-face cara a cara (9B)
fall el otoño (P)
family la familia (1B)
fantastic fantástico, -a (8A)
far (from) lejos (de) (6B)
fascinating fascinante (9A)
fast rápidamente (9B)
father el padre (papá) (5A)
fats las grasas (3B)
favorite favorito, -a (2A)
February febrero (P)
to feed the dog dar de comer al perro (6B)
fewer:
— ... than menos ... que (6A)
— than ... menos de ... (9A)
fifteen quince (P)
fifth quinto, -a (2A)
fifty cincuenta (P)
film la película (9A)
finger el dedo (P)
to finish terminar (9A)
first primer (primero), -a (2A)
fish el pescado (3B)
to go —ing ir de pesca (4B)
to fit:
How does it (do they) fit me / you? ¿Cómo me / te queda(n)? (7A)
It / They —(s) me well / poorly. Me queda(n) bien / mal. (7A)
five cinco (P)
five hundred quinientos, -as (7A)
flag la bandera (2B)
flavorful sabroso, -a (3B)
floor el piso (6B)
ground — la planta baja (6B)
second — el primer piso (6B)
third — el segundo piso (6B)
flower la flor *pl.* las flores (5A)
folder la carpeta (P)
food la comida (3A)
foot el pie (P)
football: to play — jugar al fútbol americano (4B)
for para (2A)
— breakfast en el desayuno (3A)
— lunch en el almuerzo (3A)
— me para mí (6A)
— you para ti (6A)
fork el tenedor (5B)
forty cuarenta (P)
four cuatro (P)
four hundred cuatrocientos, -as (7A)
fourteen catorce (P)
fourth cuarto, -a (2A)
free time el tiempo libre (4A)
French fries las papas fritas (3A)
Friday viernes (P)
friendly simpático, -a (1B)
from de (4A)
Where are you —? ¿De dónde eres? (4A)
fruit salad la ensalada de frutas (3A)
fun divertido, -a (2A)
funny gracioso, -a (1B); cómico, -a (9A)

G

game el partido (4B)
— show el programa de concursos (9A)
garage el garaje (6B)
garden el jardín *pl.* los jardines (8B)
to gather recoger (g → j) (8B)
generally generalmente (4A)
gift el regalo (5A)
girl la chica (1B)
—friend la novia (7B)
young — la niña (8B)
to give dar (6B)
glass el vaso (5B); el vidrio (8B)
gloves los guantes (7B)
to go ir (4A)
Let's —! ¡Vamos! (7A)
to be —ing to + *verb* ir a + *inf.* (4B)
to — boating pasear en bote (8A)
to — camping ir de cámping (4B)
to — fishing ir de pesca (4B)
to — on vacation ir de vacaciones (8A)
to — shopping ir de compras (4A)
to — to school ir a la escuela (1A)
to — out salir (8A)
golf: to play — jugar al golf (4B)
good bueno (buen), -a (1B)
— afternoon. Buenas tardes. (P)
— evening. Buenas noches. (P)
— morning. Buenos días. (P)
Good-bye! ¡Adiós! (P)
good-looking guapo, -a (5B)
grains los cereales (3B)
grandfather el abuelo (5A)
grandmother la abuela (5A)
grandparents los abuelos (5A)
grapes las uvas (3B)
graphics los gráficos (9B)
gray gris (6A)
— hair el pelo canoso (5B)
Great! ¡Genial! (4B)

green verde (6A)

— beans las judías verdes (3B)

ground floor la planta baja (6B)

guitar: to play the — tocar la guitarra (1A)

gym el gimnasio (4A)

H

hair el pelo (5B)

black — el pelo negro (5B)

blond — el pelo rubio (5B)

brown (chestnut) — el pelo castaño (5B)

gray — el pelo canoso (5B)

half media, -o (P)

— -past y media (P)

ham and cheese sandwich el sándwich de jamón y queso (3A)

hamburger la hamburguesa (3A)

hand la mano (P)

happy contento, -a (4B)

— birthday! ¡Feliz cumpleaños! (5A)

hardworking trabajador, -ora (1B)

to have tener (5A)

to — just ... acabar de + *inf.* (9A)

I — to ... tengo que + *inf.* (4B)

he él (1B)

he/she is es (1B)

He/She is / They are ... (years old). Tiene(n) ... años. (5A)

head la cabeza (P)

health:

for one's — para la salud (3B)

to maintain one's — para mantener la salud (3B)

Hello! ¡Hola! (P)

to help ayudar (6B)

How can I — you? ¿En qué puedo servirle? (7A)

her su, sus *possessive adj.* (5A); la *dir. obj. pron.* (7B); le *ind. obj. pron.* (8B)

here aquí (2B)

Hey! ¡Oye! (4B)

him lo *dir. obj. pron.* (7B); le *ind. obj. pron.* (8B)

his su, sus (5A)

home la casa (4A)

at — en casa (4A)

— office el despacho (6B)

(to) — a casa (4A)

homework la tarea (2A)

horrible horrible (3B)

horror movie la película de horror (9A)

horseback: to ride — montar a caballo (8A)

hospital el hospital (8B)

hot:

— dog el perrito caliente (3A)

It's —. Hace calor. (P)

hotel el hotel (8A)

hour: in the ... — en la ... hora (class period) (2A)

house la casa (4A)

household:

— chore el quehacer (de la casa) (6B)

— appliance store la tienda de electrodomésticos (7B)

how:

— + *adj.*! ¡Qué + *adj.*! (5B)

— awful! ¡Qué asco! (3A)

how? ¿cómo? (P)

— are you? ¿Cómo está Ud.? *formal* (P); ¿Cómo estás? *fam.* (P); ¿Qué tal? *fam.* (P)

— can I help you? ¿En qué puedo servirle? (7A)

— do you say ... ? ¿Cómo se dice ...? (P)

— does it (do they) fit (you)? ¿Cómo te queda(n)? (7A)

— is ... spelled? ¿Cómo se escribe ...? (P)

— many? ¿cuántos, -as? (P)

— much does (do) ... cost? ¿Cuánto cuesta(n) ...? (7A)

— old is/are ... ? ¿Cuántos años tiene(n) ...? (5A)

— was it (for you)? ¿Cómo lo pasaste? (8A)

hundred: one — cien (P)

hungry: I'm —. Tengo hambre. (3B)

to hurt doler (o → ue) (9A)

husband el esposo (5A)

I

I yo (1B)

— am soy (1B)

— am not no soy (1B)

— do too a mí también (1A)

— don't either a mí tampoco (1A)

— don't think so. Creo que no. (3B)

— stay at home. Me quedo en casa. (4A)

— think ... Creo que ... (3B)

— think so. Creo que sí. (3B)

— will bring you ... Le traigo ... (5B)

— would like ... Me gustaría (4B); quisiera (5B)

—'m hungry. Tengo hambre. (3B)

—'m sorry. Lo siento. (4B)

—'m thirsty. Tengo sed. (3B)

ice cream el helado (3B)

iced tea el té helado (3A)

if si (6B)

impatient impaciente (1B)

important importante (6A)

impressive impresionante (8A)

in en (P, 2B)

— front of delante de (2B)

— my opinion para mí (6A)

— order to para + *inf.* (4A)

— the ... hour en la ... hora (class period) (2A)

— your opinion para ti (6A)

incredible increíble (8B)

inexpensive barato, -a (7B)

information la información (9B)

intelligent inteligente (1B)

to interest interesar (9A)

it/they interest(s) me me interesa(n) (9A)

interesting interesante (2A)

interview program el programa de entrevistas (9A)

is es (P)

he/she — es (1B)

it la, lo *dir. obj. pron.* (7B)

— fits (they fit) me well/poorly. Me queda(n) bien/mal. (7A)

— is … Son las *(in telling time)* (P)

— is one o'clock. Es la una. (P)

— is the … of … Es el *(number)* de *(month) (in telling the date)* (P)

— is the first of … Es el primero de *(month)*. (P)

— was fue (8A)

— was a disaster. Fue un desastre. (8A)

—'s a … es un/una ... (2B)

—'s cold. Hace frío. (P)

—'s hot. Hace calor. (P)

—'s necessary. Es necesario. (8B)

—'s raining. Llueve. (P)

—'s snowing. Nieva. (P)

—'s sunny. Hace sol. (P)

J

jacket la chaqueta (7A)

January enero (P)

jeans los jeans (7A)

jewelry store la joyería (7B)

job el trabajo (4A)

juice:

apple — el jugo de manzana (3A)

orange — el jugo de naranja (3A)

July julio (P)

June junio (P)

just: to have — (done something) acabar de + *inf.* (9A)

K

key chain el llavero (7B)

keyboard (computer) el teclado (2B)

kind: What — of … ? ¿Qué clase de …? (9A)

kitchen la cocina (6B)

knife el cuchillo (5B)

to know saber (4B, 9B); conocer (9B)

I — (yo) conozco (9B)

I — (how to) (yo) sé (4B)

you — (tú) conoces (9B)

you — (how to) (tú) sabes (4B)

L

laboratory el laboratorio (9B)

lake el lago (8A)

lamp la lámpara (6A)

laptop computer la computadora portátil (9B)

large grande (6A)

last:

— night anoche (7B)

— week la semana pasada (7B)

— year el año pasado (7B)

to last durar (9A)

late tarde (8A)

later: See you — ¡Hasta luego!, ¡Nos vemos! (P)

lazy perezoso, -a (1B)

to learn aprender (a) (8A)

to leave salir (8A)

left: to the — (of) a la izquierda (de) (6A)

leg la pierna (P)

lemonade la limonada (3A)

less:

less … than menos … que (6A)

less than menos de (9A)

Let's go! ¡Vamos! (7A)

Let's see A ver … (2A)

letter la carta (9B)

lettuce la lechuga (3B)

library la biblioteca (4A)

to lift weights levantar pesas (3B)

light la luz *pl.* las luces (5A)

like como (8A)

to like:

Did you — it? ¿Te gustó? (8A)

Do you — to …? ¿Te gusta …? (1A)

He/She doesn't — … No le gusta … (1B)

He/She —s … Le gusta … (1B); A él/ella le gusta(n) … (5A)

I don't — to … (A mí) no me gusta … (1A)

I don't — to … at all. (A mí) no me gusta nada … (1A)

I — … Me gusta ... (3A)

I — to … (A mí) me gusta … (1A)

I — to … a lot (A mí) me gusta mucho … (1A)

I — to … better (A mí) me gusta más … (1A)

I —d it. Me gustó. (8A)

I would — Me gustaría (4B); quisiera (5B)

What do you — better (prefer) to do? ¿Qué te gusta más? (1A)

What do you — to do? ¿Qué te gusta hacer? (1A)

What would you —? ¿Qué desean (Uds.)? (5B)

Would you —? ¿Te gustaría? (4B)

You — … Te gusta … (3A)

likewise igualmente (P)

to listen to music escuchar música (1A)

little: a — un poco (de) (4B)

to live vivir (6B)

living room la sala (6B)

long largo, -a (5B)

to look:

to — (at) mirar (7B)

to — for buscar (7A)

lot: a — mucho, -a (2A)

to love encantar (9A)

He/She —s … A él/ella le encanta(n) … (5A)

I/You — … Me/Te encanta(n)... (3A)

lunch el almuerzo (2A)

for — en el almuerzo (3A)

M

madam (la) señora (Sra.) (P)

main dish el plato principal (5B)

as a — de plato principal (5B)

to maintain one's health para mantener la salud (3B)

make *(command)* haz (6B)
to make the bed hacer la cama (6B)
mall el centro comercial (4A)
man el hombre (5B)
older — el anciano (8B)
many muchos, -as (3B)
how — ¿cuántos, -as? (P)
March marzo (P)
match el partido (4B)
mathematics class la clase de matemáticas (2A)
May mayo (P)
maybe quizás (7A)
me me *ind. obj. pron* (8B)
for — para mí (6A), me (8B)
— too a mí también (1A)
to — me (8B)
with — conmigo (4B)
meal la comida (3A)
to mean:
It —s ... Quiere decir ... (P)
What does ... — ? ¿Qué quiere decir ... ? (P)
meat la carne (3B)
menu el menú (5B)
messy desordenado, -a (1B)
milk la leche (3A)
mirror el espejo (6A)
miss, Miss (la) señorita (Srta.) (P)
missing: to be — faltar (9A)
moment: a — un momento (6B)
Monday lunes (P)
on Mondays los lunes (4A)
money el dinero (6B)
monkey el mono (8A)
month el mes (P)
monument el monumento (8A)
more:
— ... than más ... que (2A)
— or less más o menos (3A)
— than más de (9A)
morning:
Good —. Buenos días. (P)
in the — de la mañana (4B)
mosque la mezquita (4A)
mother la madre (mamá) (5A)
mountains las montañas (4A)
mouse (computer) el ratón (2B)
mouth la boca (P)
movie la película (9A)
to see a — ver una película (4A)
— theater el cine (4A)
to mow the lawn cortar el césped (6B)
Mr. (el) señor (Sr.) (P)
Mrs. (la) señora (Sra.) (P)
much: so — tanto (7A)
museum el museo (8A)
music:
to listen to — escuchar música (1A)
—al program el programa musical (9A)
must deber (3B)
one — hay que (8B)
my mi (2B); mis (5A)
— name is ... Me llamo ... (P)
mystery la película policíaca (9A)

N

name:
My — is ... Me llamo ... (P)
What is your —? ¿Cómo te llamas? (P)
What's his/her —? ¿Cómo se llama? (1B)
napkin la servilleta (5B)
national park el parque nacional (8A)
near cerca (de) (6B)
neat ordenado, -a (1B)
necessary: It's —. Es necesario. (8B)
necklace el collar (7B)
to need
I — necesito (2A)
I — ... Me falta(n) ... (5B)
you — necesitas (2A)
neighborhood el barrio (8B)
neither ... nor ni ... ni (1A)
never nunca (3A)
new nuevo, -a (7A)
news program el programa de noticias (9A)
newspaper el periódico (8B)
next to al lado de (2B)
nice simpático, -a (1B)
night:
at — de la noche (4B)
last — anoche (7B)
night table la mesita (6A)
nine nueve (P)
nine hundred novecientos, -as (7A)
nineteen diecinueve (P)
ninety noventa (P)
ninth noveno, -a (2A)
nose la nariz *pl.* las narices (P)
not ... or ni ... ni (1A)
notebook el cuaderno (P)
nothing nada (P)
November noviembre (P)
now ahora (5B)

O

o'clock:
at eight — a las ocho (4B)
at one — a la una (4B)
It's one —. Es la una. (P)
It's ... — Son les ... (P)
October octubre (P)
of de (2B)
— course por supuesto (3A)
office (home) el despacho (6B)
often a menudo (8B)
Oh! What a shame/pity! ¡Ay! ¡Qué pena! (4B)
okay regular (P)
old viejo, -a (5B)
He/She is / They are ... years —. Tiene(n) ... años. (5A)
How — is/are ... ? ¿Cuántos años tiene(n) ... ? (5A)
—er mayor (5A)
—er man el anciano (8B)
—er people los ancianos (8B)
—er woman la anciana (8B)

on en (2B)
— Mondays, on Tuesdays ... los lunes, los martes ... (4A)
— top of encima de (2B)
— weekends los fines de semana (4A)
one uno (un), -a (P)
at — (o'clock) a la una (4B)
one hundred cien (P)
one must hay que (8B)
onion la cebolla (3B)
online en la Red (7B)
to be — estar en línea (9B)
only sólo (5A)
to open abrir (5A)
opinion:
in my — para mí (6A)
in your — para tí (6A)
or o (1A)
orange anaranjado, -a (6A)
— juice el jugo de naranja (3A)
to order pedir (e → i) (5B)
other otro, -a (5B)
others los/las demás (8B)
our nuestro(s), -a(s) (5A)
own propio, -a (6A)

P

painting el cuadro (6A)
pants los pantalones (7A)
paper: sheet of — la hoja de papel (P)
parents los padres (5A)
park el parque (4A)
amusement — el parque de diversiones (8A)
national — el parque nacional (8A)
party la fiesta (4B)
pastries los pasteles (3B)
patient paciente (1B)
to pay (for) pagar (por) (7B)
peas los guisantes (3B)
pen el bolígrafo (P)
pencil el lápiz *pl.* los lápices (P)
— sharpener el sacapuntas (2B)
people la gente (8B)
older — los ancianos (8B)
pepper la pimienta (5B)
perfume el perfume (7B)
person la persona (5A)
phone: to talk on the — hablar por teléfono (1A)
photo la foto (5A)
to take —s sacar fotos (5A)
physical education class la clase de educación física (2A)
piano lesson (class) la lección *pl.* las lecciones de piano (4A)
pink rosado, -a (6A)
piñata la piñata (5A)
pizza la pizza (3A)
place el lugar (8A)
to place poner (6B)
to plan pensar (e → ie) (7A)
plastic el plástico (8B)
plate el plato (5B)
play la obra de teatro (8A)
to play jugar (a) (u → ue) (4B); tocar (1A)
to — baseball jugar al béisbol (4B)
to — basketball jugar al básquetbol (4B)
to — football jugar al fútbol americano (4B)
to — golf jugar al golf (4B)
to — soccer jugar al fútbol (4B)
to — sports practicar deportes (1A)
to — tennis jugar al tenis (4B)
to — the guitar tocar la guitarra (1A)
to — video games jugar videojuegos (1A)
to — volleyball jugar al vóleibol (4B)
please por favor (P)
to please very much encantar (9A)
pleased to meet you mucho gusto (P)
pool la piscina (4A)
poor pobre (8B)
possession la posesión *pl.* las posesiones (6A)
poster el cartel (2B)
potatoes las papas (3B)
practical práctico, -a (2A)
to prefer preferir (e → ie) (7A)
I — (yo) prefiero (3B)
I — to ... (a mí) me gusta más ... (1A)
you — (tú) prefieres (3B)
to prepare preparar (5A)
present el regalo (5A)
presentation la presentación *pl.* las presentaciones (9B)
pretty bonito, -a (6A)
price el precio (7A)
primary school la escuela primaria (8B)
problem el problema (8B)
program el programa (9A)
purple morado, -a (6A)
purse el bolso (7B)
to put poner (6B)
I — (yo) pongo (6B)
— *(command)* pon (6B)
you — (tú) pones (6B)

Q

quarter past y cuarto (P)
quarter to menos cuarto
quickly rápidamente (9B)

R

rain: It's —ing. Llueve. (P)
rather bastante (6B)
to read magazines leer revistas (1A)
realistic realista (9A)
reality program el programa de la vida real (9A)
Really? ¿De veras? (9A)
to receive recibir (6B)
to recycle reciclar (8B)
recycling center el centro de reciclaje (8B)

red rojo, -a (6A)

—-haired pelirrojo, -a (5B)

to relax descansar (8A)

report el informe (9B)

reserved reservado, -a (1B)

to rest descansar (8A)

restaurant el restaurante (4A)

to return regresar (8A)

rice el arroz (3B)

rich rico, -a (5B)

to ride:

to — a bicycle montar en bicicleta (1A)

to — horseback montar a caballo (8A)

right: to the — (of) a la derecha (de) (6A)

Right? ¿Verdad? (3A)

ring el anillo (7B)

river el río (8B)

road la calle (8B)

romantic movie la película romántica (9A)

room el cuarto (6B)

to straighten up the — arreglar el cuarto (6B)

rug la alfombra (6A)

to run correr (1A)

S

sack la bolsa (8B)

sad triste (4B)

salad la ensalada (3A)

fruit — la ensalada de frutas (3A)

salesperson el dependiente, la dependienta (7A)

salt la sal (5B)

same mismo, -a (6A)

sandwich: ham and cheese — el sándwich de jamón y queso (3A)

Saturday sábado (P)

sausage la salchicha (3A)

to say decir (8B)

How do you —? ¿Cómo se dice? (P)

You — ... Se dice ... (P)

You don't —! ¡No me digas! (4A)

scared: to be — (of) tener miedo (de) (9B)

schedule el horario (2A)

science:

— class la clase de ciencias naturales (2A)

— fiction movie la película de ciencia ficción (9A)

screen: computer — la pantalla (2B)

to scuba dive bucear (8A)

sea el mar (8A)

to search (for) buscar (9B)

season la estación *pl.* las estaciones (P)

second segundo, -a (2A)

— floor el primer piso (6B)

to see ver (8A)

Let's — A ver ... (2A)

— you later! ¡Nos vemos!, Hasta luego. (P)

— you tomorrow. Hasta mañana. (P)

to — a movie ver una película (4A)

to sell vender (7B)

to send enviar (i → í) (9B)

to separate separar (8B)

September septiembre (P)

serious serio, -a (1B)

to serve servir (e → i) (9B)

to set the table poner la mesa (6B)

seven siete (P)

seven hundred setecientos, -as (7A)

seventeen diecisiete (P)

seventh séptimo, -a (2A)

seventy setenta (P)

to share compartir (3A)

she ella (1B)

sheet of paper la hoja de papel (P)

shelf el estante (6A)

ship el barco (8A)

shirt la camisa (7A)

T- — la camiseta (7A)

shoe store la zapatería (7B)

shoes los zapatos (7A)

short bajo, -a; corto, -a (5B)

shorts los pantalones cortos (7A)

should deber (3B)

show el programa (9A)

to show + *movie or TV program* dar (9A)

shy reservado, -a (1B)

sick enfermo, -a (4B)

silly tonto, -a (9A)

to sing cantar (1A)

sir (el) señor (Sr.) (P)

sister la hermana (5A)

site: Web — el sitio Web (9B)

six seis (P)

six hundred seiscientos, -as (7A)

sixteen dieciséis (P)

sixth sexto, -a (2A)

sixty sesenta (P)

to skate patinar (1A)

to skateboard montar en monopatín (1A)

to ski esquiar (i fi í) (1A)

skirt la falda (7A)

to sleep dormir (o → ue) (6A)

sleepy: to be — tener sueño (5B)

slide la diapositiva (9B)

small pequeño, -a (6A)

to snorkel bucear (8A)

snow: It's —ing. Nieva. (P)

so much tanto (7A)

so-so regular (P)

soap opera la telenovela (9A)

soccer: to play — jugar al fútbol (4B)

sociable sociable (1B)

social studies class la clase de ciencias sociales (2A)

socks los calcetines (7A)

soft drink el refresco (3A)

software el software (7B)

some unos, -as (2B)

something algo (3B)

sometimes a veces (1B)

son el hijo (5A)

—s; —(s) and daughter(s) los hijos (5A)

song la canción *pl.* las canciones (9B)

sorry: I'm —. Lo siento. (4B)

sound (stereo) system el equipo de sonido (6A)

soup: vegetable — la sopa de verduras (3A)

souvenirs los recuerdos (8A)

to buy — comprar recuerdos (8A)

spaghetti los espaguetis (3B)

Spanish class la clase de español (2A)

to spell:

How is ... spelled? ¿Cómo se escribe ... ? (P)

It's spelled ... Se escribe ... (P)

to spend time with friends pasar tiempo con amigos (1A)

spoon la cuchara (5B)

sports:

to play — practicar deportes (1A)

— -minded deportista (1B)

— show el programa deportivo (9A)

spring la primavera (P)

stadium el estadio (8A)

stairs, stairway la escalera (6B)

to start empezar (e → ie) (9A)

to stay: I — at home. Me quedo en casa. (4A)

stepbrother el hermanastro (5A)

stepfather el padrastro (5A)

stepmother la madrastra (5A)

stepsister la hermanastra (5A)

stereo system el equipo de sonido (6A)

stomach el estómago (P)

store la tienda (7A)

book— la librería (7B)

clothing — la tienda de ropa (7A)

department — el almacén *pl.* los almacenes (7B)

discount — la tienda de descuentos (7B)

household appliance — la tienda de electrodomésticos (7B)

jewelry — la joyería (7B)

shoe — la zapatería (7B)

story el piso (6B)

stories: to write — escribir cuentos (1A)

to straighten up the room arreglar el cuarto (6B)

strawberries las fresas (3A)

street la calle (8B)

student el/la estudiante (P)

studious estudioso, -a (1B)

to study estudiar (2A)

stupid tonto, -a (9A)

sugar el azúcar (5B)

suit el traje (7A)

summer el verano (P)

to sunbathe tomar el sol (8A)

Sunday domingo (P)

sunglasses los anteojos de sol (7B)

sunny: It's —. Hace sol. (P)

to surf the Web navegar en la Red (9B)

sweater el suéter (7A)

sweatshirt la sudadera (7A)

to swim nadar (1A)

swimming pool la piscina (4A)

swimsuit el traje de baño (7A)

synagogue la sinagoga (4A)

T

T-shirt la camiseta (7A)

table la mesa (2B)

to set the — poner la mesa (6B)

to take llevar (8B)

to — a course tomar un curso (9B)

to — out the trash sacar la basura (6B)

to — photos sacar fotos (5A)

talented talentoso, -a (1B)

to talk hablar (2A)

to — on the phone hablar por teléfono (1A)

tall alto, -a (5B)

tasty sabroso, -a (3B); rico, -a (5B)

tea el té (3A)

iced — el té helado (3A)

to teach enseñar (2A)

teacher el profesor, la profesora (P)

technology/computers la tecnología (2A)

technology/computer class la clase de tecnología (2A)

television: to watch — ver la tele (1A)

television set el televisor (6A)

to tell decir (8B)

— me dime (8A)

temple el templo (4A)

ten diez (P)

tennis: to play — jugar al tenis (4B)

tenth décimo, -a (2A)

thank you gracias (P)

that que (5A); ese, esa (7A)

—'s why por eso (9A)

the el, la (1B); los, las (2B)

— best el/la mejor, los/las mejores (6A)

— worst el/la peor, los/las peores (6A)

theater el teatro (8A)

movie — el cine (4A)

their su, sus (5A)

them las, los *dir. obj. pron.* (7B); les *ind. obj. pron.* (8B)

then entonces (4B)

there allí (2B)

— is/are hay (P, 2B)

therefore por eso (9A)

these estos, estas (7A)

they ellos, ellas (2A)

thing la cosa (6A)

to think creer (3B) pensar (e → ie) (7A)

I don't — so. Creo que no. (3B)

I — … Creo que … (3B)

I — so. Creo que sí. (3B)

What do you — (about it)? ¿Qué te parece? (9B)

third tercer (tercero), -a (2A)

third floor el segundo piso (6B)

thirsty: I'm —. Tengo sed. (3B)

thirteen trece (P)

thirty treinta (P); y media *(in telling time)* (P)

thirty-one treinta y uno (P)

this este, esta (7A)

— afternoon esta tarde (4B)

— evening esta noche (4B)

— weekend este fin de semana (4B)

What is — ? ¿Qué es esto? (2B)

those esos, esas (7A)

thousand: a — mil (7A)

three tres (P)

three hundred trescientos, -as (7A)

three-ring binder la carpeta de argollas (2A)

Thursday jueves (P)

ticket el boleto (8A)

tie la corbata (7B)

time la vez *pl.* las veces (8B)

At what —? ¿A qué hora? (4B)

free — el tiempo libre (4A)

to spend — with friends pasar tiempo con amigos (1A)

What — is it? ¿Qué hora es? (P)

tired cansado, -a (4B)

to a *(prep.)* (4A)

in order — para + *inf.* (4A)

— the a la, al (4A)

— the left (of) a la izquierda (de) (6A)

— the right (of) a la derecha (de) (6A)

toast el pan tostado (3A)

today hoy (P)

tomatoes los tomates (3B)

tomorrow mañana (P)

See you —. Hasta mañana. (P)

too también (1A); demasiado (4B)

I do (like to) — a mí también (1A)

me — a mí también (1A)

top: on — of encima de (2B)

touching emocionante (9A)

toy el juguete (8B)

train el tren (8A)

to travel viajar (8A)

tree el árbol (8A)

tremendous tremendo, -a (8A)

trip el viaje (8A)

Tuesday martes (P)

on —s los martes (4A)

TV channel el canal (9A)

twelve doce (P)

twenty veinte (P)

twenty-one veintiuno (veintiún) (P)

two dos (P)

two hundred doscientos, -as (7A)

U

Ugh! ¡Uf! (7B)

ugly feo, -a (6A)

uncle el tío (5A)

uncles; uncle(s) and aunt(s) los tíos (5A)

underneath debajo de (2B)

to understand comprender (3A)

unforgettable inolvidable (8B)

us: (to/for) — nos *ind. obj. pron.* (8B)

to use:

to — the computer usar la computadora (1A)

What's it —d for? ¿Para qué sirve? (9B)

used usado, -a (8B)

useful:

to be — servir (9B)

is — for sirve para (9B)

V

vacation: to go on — ir de vacaciones (8A)

to vacuum pasar la aspiradora (6B)

VCR la videocasetera (6A)

vegetable soup la sopa de verduras (3A)

very muy (1B)

— well muy bien (P)

video games: to play — jugar videojuegos (1A)

videocassette el video (5A, 6A)

to videotape hacer un video (5A)

violent violento, -a (9A)

to visit visitar (8A)

to — chat rooms visitar salones de chat (9B)

volleyball: to play — jugar al vóleibol (4B)

volunteer el voluntario, la voluntaria (8B)

— work el trabajo voluntario (8B)

W

waiter, waitress el camarero, la camarera (5B)

to walk caminar (3B)

wall la pared (6A)

wallet la cartera (7B)

to want querer (e → ie) (7A)

I — (yo) quiero (4B)

you — (tú) quieres (4B)

warm: to be — tener calor (5B)

was fue (8B)

to wash lavar (6B)

to — the car lavar el coche (6B)

to — the clothes lavar la ropa (6B)

to — the dishes lavar los platos (6B)

wastepaper basket la papelera (2B)

watch el reloj pulsera (7B)

to watch television ver la tele (1A)

water el agua f. (3A)

we nosotros, -as (2A)

to wear llevar (7A)

weather: What's the — like? ¿Qué tiempo hace? (P)

Web:

to surf the — navegar en la Red (9B)

— page la página Web (9B)

— site el sitio Web (9B)

Wednesday miércoles (P)

week la semana (P)

last — la semana pasada (7B)

weekend:

on —s los fines de semana (4A)

this — este fin de semana (4B)

welcome: You're —. De nada. (5B)

well bien (P); pues ... *(to indicate pause)* (1A)

very — muy bien (P)

what? ¿cuál? (3A)

— are you like? ¿Cómo eres? (1B)

(At) — time? ¿A qué hora? (4B)

— color ... ? ¿De qué color ... ? (6A)

— day is today? ¿Qué día es hoy? (P)

— did you do? ¿Qué hiciste? (8A)

— do you like better (prefer) to do? ¿Qué te gusta hacer más? (1A)

— do you like to do? ¿Qué te gusta hacer? (1A)

— do you think (about it)? ¿Qué te parece? (9B)

— does ... mean? ¿Qué quiere decir ... ? (P)

— else? ¿Qué más? (8B)

— happened to you? ¿Qué te pasó? (8A)

— is she/he like? ¿Cómo es? (1B)

— is the date? ¿Cuál es la fecha? (P)

— is this? ¿Qué es esto? (2B)

— is your name? ¿Cómo te llamas? (P)

— kind of ... ? ¿Qué clase de...? (9A)

— time is it? ¿Qué hora es? (P)

— would you like? ¿Qué desean (Uds.)? (5B)

—'s happening? ¿Qué pasa? (P)

—'s his/her name? ¿Cómo se llama? (1B)

—'s it (used) for? ¿Para qué sirve? (9B)

—'s the weather like? ¿Qué tiempo hace? (P)

what!:

— a good/nice idea! ¡Qué buena idea! (4B)

— a shame/pity! ¡Qué pena! (4B)

When? ¿Cuándo? (4A)

Where? ¿Dónde? (2B)

— are you from? ¿De dónde eres? (4A)

(To) —? ¿Adónde? (4A)

whether si (6B)

which? ¿cuál? (3A)

white blanco, -a (6A)

who que (5A)

Who? ¿Quién? (2A)

Why? ¿Por qué? (3B)

wife la esposa (5A)

Will you bring me ... ? ¿Me trae ... ? (5B)

window la ventana (2B)

winter el invierno (P)

with con (3A)

— me conmigo (4B)

— my/your friends con mis/tus amigos (4A)

— whom? ¿Con quién? (4A)

— you contigo (4B)

without sin (3A)

woman la mujer (5B)

older woman la anciana (8B)

work el trabajo (4A)

volunteer — el trabajo voluntario (8B)

to work trabajar (1A)

worse than peor(es) que (6A)

worst: the — el/la peor, los/las peores (6A)

Would you like ...? ¿Te gustaría ...? (4B)

to write:

to — e-mail escribir por correo electrónico (9B)

to — stories escribir cuentos (1A)

Y

yard el jardín *pl.* los jardines (8B)

year el año (P)

He/She is / They are ... —s old. Tiene(n) ... años. (5A)

last — el año pasado (7B)

yellow amarillo, -a (6A)

yes sí (1A)

yesterday ayer (7B)

yogurt el yogur (3A)

you fam. *sing.* tú (2A); *formal sing.* usted (Ud.) (2A); *fam. pl.* vosotros, -as (2A); *formal pl.* ustedes (Uds.) (2A); *fam. after prep.* ti (1A); *sing. ind. obj. pron.* te (8B); *pl. fam. ind. obj. pron.* os (8B); *ind. obj. pron.* le, les (8B)

And — ? ¿Y a ti? (1A)

for — para ti (6A)

to/for — *fam. pl.* os (8B)

to/for — *fam. sing.* te (8B)

with — contigo (4B)

— don't say! ¡No me digas! (4A)

— say ... Se dice ... (P)

You're welcome De nada (5B)

young joven (5B)

— boy/girl el niño, la niña (8B)

— man el joven (5B)

— woman la joven (5B)

—er menor (5A)

your *fam.* tu (2B); *fam.* tus, vuestro(s), -a(s) (5A); *formal* su, sus (5A)

Yuck! ¡Uf! (7B)

Z

zero cero (P)

zoo el zoológico (8A)

Grammar Index

Structures are most often presented first in *A primera vista*, where they are practiced lexically. They are then explained later in a *Gramática* section or a *Nota*. Light-face numbers refer to the pages where structures are initially presented or, after explanation, where student reminders occur. **Bold-face numbers** refer to pages where structures are explained or are otherwise highlighted.

Acknowledgments

Cover Design Tamada Brown & Associates
Program Graphic Development Herman Adler Design
Maps Mapping Specialists
Technical Illustration/Additional Graphics Herman Adler Design; New England Typographic Services; Publicom; John Reece; Joseph Taylor

Illustrations Wilkinson Studios Artists; Bob Brugger: pp. 136, 167, 210, 257, 285, 307, 329, 383; Donna Catanese: pp. 235; Dennis Dzielak: pp. 8, 67, 81, 96, 100, 101, 133, 136, 205, 323, 373, 380; George Hamblin: p. 382; Seitu Hayden: pp. 6, 12, 16, 27, 32, 36, 37, 77, 172, 173, 176, 199, 202, 203, 204, 276, 303, 306, 329, 331, 355, 430, 448; Reggie Holladay: pp. 18, 27, 37, 58, 86, 188, 189, 246, 256, 257; Tim Jones: pp. 18, 26, 31, 32, 54, 56, 58, 63, 74, 79, 199, 206, 252, 253, 278, 293, 299, 308, 310, 311, 322, 326, 327, 373, 376, 428, 456, 460; Victor Kennedy: pp. 39, 84, 254, 257, 329, 409; Gary Krejca: pp. 27, 37; Miguel Luna: pp. 7, 12, 86, 155, 378; Jonathan Massie: pp. 102, 149, 298, 302, 346, 401, 404, 406, 457, 460; Tom McKee: pp. 2, 4, 15, 54, 58, 115, 154, 190, 209, 248, 249, 312, 313, 323, 332, 335, 352, 372, 392, 397, 426, 427, 453; Donna Perrone: pp. 86, 128, 130, 131, 148, 153, 159, 272; Jud Stead: pp. 3, 18, 60, 79, 105, 198, 204, 223, 273, 280, 282, 350, 352, 354, 359, 449; Nicole Wong: pp. 8, 172, 173, 176, 334, 347, 361, 383, 463

Photography Front and back covers: Dancers from the state of Jalisco, Mexico, Jose Carrillo/PhotoEdit. Inc.; (front cover inset) Cliff Hollenbeck/IS. Photographers who contributed to the studio/location photography: Bill Burlingham, Burlingham Photography and John Morrison, Morrison Photography.

vi, ©LWA-Stephen Welstead/CORBIS; vii, © Bo Zaunders/Corbis; xvi-xvii, ©José Fuste Raga/CORBIS; xvi inset, ©Danny Lehman/CORBIS, xvii inset, ©Phil Schermeister/CORBIS; xvii-xix, ©Danny Lehman/CORBIS; xx-xxi, ©David Zimmerman/CORBIS; xx inset, ©Stuart Westmorland/CORBIS; xxii-xix, ©Jim Erickson/CORBIS; xxiv-xxv ©Galen Rowell/CORBIS; xxvi-xxvii ©Paul Hardy/CORBIS, xxvi inset, ©Mark L. Stephenson, xxvii br inset ©José Fuste Raga/CORBIS; xxvii inset, ©Strauss/Curtis/CORBIS; xxviii ©Craig Tuttle/CORBIS; xxviii, © Bob Daemmrich/ The Image Works, Inc.; xxix br inset, ©Ron Watts/CORBIS, xxix bl inset Royalty– Free/Corbis; xxx, background, © Jim Zuckermann/Corbis; xxx,l, © Corbis; xxx,r, © Bob Daemmrich/The Image Works, Inc.; xxxi, © Joel Salcido/Bob Daemmrich Photography; xxxii tl, Pablo Picasso (1881-1973) a ARS, NY aErich Lessing/Art Resource, NY; xxxii tr, ©Paul Barton/CORBIS; xxxii bm, ©aS.P. Gillette/CORBIS; xxxiv ©Robert Frerck/Odyssey/Chicago; 1 t, ©Robert Frerck/Odyssey/Chicago; 1 b, H. Huntly Hersch/DDB; 3 (1), Bob Daemmrich/SB; 3 (2), Spencer Grant/SB; 3 (3), David Young-Wolff/PhotoEdit; 3 (4), M. Ferguson/PhotoEdit; 3 (5), Bachmann/SB; 3 (6), Mary Kate Denny/PhotoEdit; 5, Mary Kate Denny/PhotoEdit; 8, A.K.G., Berlin/SuperStock; 11, Michael Newman/PhotoEdit; 13, Bridgeman Art Library International, Ltd./Museo Nacional de Antropología, Mexico City, Mexico; 15, David Young-Wolff/PhotoEdit; 16, A. Ramey/PhotoEdit; 17, Peter Wilson/Dorling Kindersley Media Library ©CONACULTA-INAH-MEX. Authorized reproduction by the Instituto Nacional de Antropología e Historia; 18 (1-4), George Gold/SuperStock, Inc.; 19 (1), ©Gordon R. Gainer/CORBIS; 19 (2), Rocio Escobar; 19 (3), Joseph Nettis/Photo Researchers, Inc.; 19 (4), Causes and effects, Philip Steele; 20 tl, Spencer Swanger/Tom Stack & Associates, Inc.; 20 tr, Ann Duncan/Tom Stack & Associates, Inc.; 20 bl, J. Schulte/DDB; 20 br, Ricardo Carrasco/DDB; 20 m, ©ESA/ELI/CORBIS; 24a, b, © Randy Mallory; 24a, t, © Viesti Associates, Inc; 24a, l, © 2004, OSU SCAS; 24b, l, © Bob Daemmrich/Bob Daemmrich Photography; 24b, m, © Darrell Gulin/Corbis; 24b, r, © Viesti Associates, Inc.; 24-25, Latin Focus.com; 24 inset, Picasso, Pablo (1881–1973). (c) ARS, NY. Three musicians. 1921. Oil on canvas, 6'7" x 7'3 3/4". Mrs. Simon Guggenheim Fund. (55.1949). Museum of Modern Art, New York, N.Y., U.S.A./The Bridgeman Art Library International, Ltd.; 28 tm, Roberto M. Arakaki/ImageState/International Stock Photography Ltd.; 28 bm, ©Danny Lehman/CORBIS; 29 tm, SuperStock, Inc.; 29 bm, Buddy Mays/IS; 31 bl, Peter Menzel/StockBoston; 34 m, Museo Bellapart; 35 tl, Bonnie Kamin/PhotoEdit; 35 tr, Blaine Harrington; 35, Jeff Greenberg/PhotoEdit; 35 bl, David Young-Wolff/PhotoEdit; 35 br, PictureQuest; 40 t, David Young-Wolff/PhotoEdit; 40 b, Marison Diaz/LF; 41, ©Robert Frerck/Odyssey/ Chicago; 41 t, Blaine Harrington; 41 b, Myrleen Ferguson Cate/PhotoEdit Inc.; 42, Danilo Boschung/eStock Photography LLC; 43 t, Bob Daemmrich Photography, Inc.; 43 b, Kathy Ferguson-Johnson/PhotoEdit; 44-45, ©Mark L. Stephenson/CORBIS; 45, ©José Fuste Raga/CORBIS; 45, ©Owen Franken/CORBIS; 45, ©Adam Woolfitt/CORBIS; 46, Robert Frerck/OP; 48 inset, Albright-Knox Art Gallery; 48, © Bob Daemmrich/The Image Works, Inc.; 51 br, Paul Mark Smith/Panos Pictures; 57, David Simson/SB; 58 b, The Bridgeman Art Library International, Ltd.; 59 b, David Sanger Photography; 60, b, © Richard Cummins/Corbis; 62, ©Robert Fried/Stock Boston; 65, ©Robert Frerck/OP; 66 tr, Huntly Hersch/D. Donne Bryant Stock Photography; 66 br, David Simson/SB; 66 tl, Tony Arruza/CORBIS; 66 bl, RFP; 67 t and b, David Young-Wolff/PhotoEdit; 68-69, ©Reinhard Eisele/CORBIS; 69 inset t, ©Richard Bickel/CORBIS; 69 inset m, ©Roger Ressmeyer/CORBIS; 69 inset b, ©Jan Butchofsky-Houser/CORBIS; 72a, t, © PhotoDisc; 72a, m, © Danny Lehman/Corbis; 72a, b, © Bob Daemmrich/The Image Works, Inc.; 72b, m, © Bob Daemmrich/The Image Works, Inc.; 72b, t, © Bob Daemmrich/The Image Works, Inc.; 72-73, ©Robert Fried/Stock Boston; 72 inset, Marlborough Gallery, Inc.; 80, Jeff Greenberg/PhotoEdit; 81, Dave Bartruff/SB; 83 (1,8), ©Robert Frerck/OP; 83 (2,6), RFP; 83 (3), Charlie Marsden/Panos Pictures; 83 (4), Jeff Greenberg/PhotoEdit; 83 (5), Owen Franken/SB; 83 (7), Richard Pasley/SB; 85, Carlos S. Pereyra/DDB; 86 lt, Ulrike Welsch/PhotoEdit; 86 lb, Paul Conklin/PhotoEdit; 88, Charlie Marsden/Panos Pictures; 89, br, © Larry Kolvoord/The Image Works, Inc.; 90, ©José Fuste Raga/CORBIS; 90 inset, Bob Daemmrich/SB; 91 t, ©2004 Ulrike Welsch/SB; 91 b, RFP; 92 t, RFP; 92 b, Joe Viesti/VC; 93 t, ©2004 Ulrike Welsch/SB; 93 b, Jeff Greenberg/PhotoEdit; 94-95, José Fuste Raga/CORBIS;

95 inset tr, ©Lindsay Hebberd/CORBIS; 95 inset mr, ©Danny Lehman/CORBIS, 95 inset br, ©Randy Faris/CORBIS; 98 inset, Instituto Amatller de Arte Hispánico; 98, Carlos S. Pereyra/D. Donne Bryant Stock Photography; 98-99, DDB; 104, H. Huntly Hersch/DDB, 106, June Conord/D. Donne Bryant Stock Photography; 108 b, Carlos S. Pereyra/DDB; 111 br, © Mary Kate Denny/PhotoEdit; 112, Ulrike Welsch/PhotoEdit; 113 t, Ulrike Welsch Photography; 113 b, Ulrike Welsch Photography; 114 t, Wolfgang Kaehler Photography; 114 b, Jeremy Horner/Panos Pictures; 115 tl, Jeremy Horner/Panos Pictures; 115 bm, Jon Spaul/Panos Pictures; 115 bl, Sean Sprague/Panos Pictures; 115 br, Jean-Leo Dugast/Panos Pictures; 115 tr, Sean Sprague/Panos Pictures; 116 t, Jeff Greenberg/PhotoEdit; 116 b, Carlos S. Pereyra/DDB; 117, Beryl Goldberg; 118-119, Gail Shumway/Getty Images, 118 inset, ©Kennan Ward/CORBIS; 119 inset tr, ©Shepard Sherbell/CORBIS SABA; 119 inset m, ©Bill Gentile/CORBIS; 119 inset br, José Ángel Murillo; 122a, l, Courtesy of the Ysleta Independent School District; 122a, r, Courtesy of Del Valle High School; 122a, background, © Spencer Jones/Getty Images; 122b, Courtesy of Del Valle High School;122-123, Bob Daemmrich/SB; 122 inset, Murillo, Bartolomeo Esteban. (1618–1682) aARS, NY. Children Eating Sweets. Copyright Scala/Art Resource, NY. Alte Pinakothek, Munich, Germany; 132, Ivonne Barreto/LF; 133, Robert Fried Photography; 134, Morgan Cain & Associates; 137, ©Robert Frerck/Odyssey/Chicago; 139, M. Barlow/Trip/The Viesti Collection, Inc.; 140 t, Richard Hutchings/PhotoEdit; 140 tm, David Young-Wolff/PhotoEdit; 141 t, PatrickRamsey/IS; 141 b, David Shopper/SB; 142-143, ©James Sparshatt/CORBIS; 143, ©Royalty-Free/CORBIS; 143 inset tr, ©Jim Zuckerman/CORBIS; 143 inset ml, ©Caroline Penn/CORBIS; 143 inset bl, S.Am-turtle-Owen Franken/SB; 146-147, Steve Vidler/eStock Photography LLC; 146 inset, Robert Frerck/OP; 152, Carlos Goldwin/Focus/DDB; 156, Robert Arakaki/ImageState/International/Stock Photography Ltd.; 158 m, AGE FotoStock America, Inc.; 158 b, Look GMBH/eStock Photography, LLC; 160 t, James Nelson/Tony Image Studio; 160 b, AP/Wide World Photos; 161, Ulrike Welsch/PhotoEdit; 163 tl, AP/Wide World Photos; 163 br, David Cannon/Hulton Archive/GettyImages; 164 tr, Martin Rogers/SB; 164 br, ©Robert Frerck/OP; 165 tr, The Stock Market; 165 br, Jimmy Dorantes/Latin Focus Photo Agency; 166-167, ©Larry Lee/CORBIS; 167 inset tr, ©Hubert Stadler/CORBIS; 167 inset ml, ©Yann Arthus-Bertrand/CORBIS; 167 inset br, ©Pablo Corral/CORBIS; 170a, t, © Brian Hagiwara/Foodpix; 170a © Corbis; 170b, t, © Melanie Acevedo/PictureArts/Corbis; 170b, © Corbis; 170-171, ©Patrick Ward/CORBIS; 170 inset, Paul Conklin/PhotoEdit; 177, Art Museum of The Americas/Audio Visual Program; 179, ©Daniel Rivadamar/Odyssey/Chicago; 180, Fernando Pastene/Latin Focus Photo Agency; 181, Bob Daemmrich Photography, Inc.; 181, Latin Focus.com; 182 bl,Vic Bider/Photo Edit Inc.; 182 br, Vic Bider/Photo Edit Inc.; 185, Paul Conklin/PhotoEdit; 186, Robert Fried Photography; 187 t and b, ©Robert Frerck/OP; 189, Malcolm Fife/eStock Photogaphy, LLC; 190 t and b, RFP; 191 t and b, Latin Focus.com; 192-193, ©Wolfgang Kaehler/CORBIS; 192-193 inset tm, ©Alan Schein Photography/CORBIS; 192 inset ml, ©D. Boone/CORBIS; 193 bl, ©Richard Cummins/CORBIS; 194, ©Robert Frerck/OP; 196-197, AFPPhoto/Phillipe Huguen/CORBIS; 196 inset, ©AFP/Greg Wood/CORBIS; 205, ©Robert Frerck/OP; 207 t, © Tony Savino/The Image Works, Inc.; 208 (2 & 8), Rob Tingali Jr./SportsChrome-USA; 208 (3), Chris Trotman/Duomo Photography, Inc.; 208 (4), Michael Zito/SportsChrome-USA; 208 (5), AP/Wide World Photos; 208 (6), Henri Szwarc/SportsChrome-USA; 208 (7), Ron J. Bernard/Duomo Photography Inc.; 209, ©Reuters NewMedia Inc.CORBIS; 210 bl and br, Myrleen Ferguson Cate/PhotoEdit; 211, Robert Frerck/Woodfin Camp & Associates; 212, Chris Trotman/Duomo Photography Incorporated; 213 t, AP/Wide World Photos; 213 b, Chris Trotman/Duomo Photography Incorporated; 214 t, Robert Frerck/Odyssey; 214, Pearson Education Corporate Digital Archive; 214 b, Jimmy Corantes/LF; 215 t, Bob Daemmrich/SB; 215 m, David Young-Wolff/PhotoEdit; 215 b, Richard V. Procopio/SB; 216-217, ©Nik Wheeler/CORBIS; 216 inset tl, ©TiziouJacques/CORBIS/Sygma; 216 inset tr, ©CORBIS; 217 inset tr, ©Kevin Fleming/CORBIS; 217 inset mr, ©Randy Faris/CORBIS; 220a, mr, © Tony Freeman/PhotoEdit; 220a, bl, Courtesy of the Laredo Public Library; 220a, t, m, Courtesy of the City of Laredo Texas Parks & Recreation Department; 220 inset, M. Lee Fatherree. Collection of Federal Reserve Bank of Dallas; 226, Carmen Lomas Garza; 228, Dorling Kindersley Media Library; 229, © Tony Freeman/PhotoEdit; 230 t, ©CORBIS/Sygma; 231 tl, Goya, Francisco (1746-1828). Ritratto della famiglia di Carlo IV. Prado Madrid./Art Resource, N.Y.; 231 br, The Bridgeman Art Library International, Ltd.; 235 t, Steve Shott/Dorling Kindersley Media Library; 236 tr, Rivera, Diego (1866–1957). The grinder (La molendera). 1926. Oil on canvas, 35 7/16 x 46 1/16 in. Museo Nacional de Arte Moderno, Instituto Nacional de Bellas Artes, Mexico City, D.F., Mexico./Art Resource, N.Y.; 236 bl, DDB; 238, RFP; 239, Robert Fried Photography; 240, ©David Seawell/CORBIS; 241 t, Mark Bolster/Image State/International Stock Photography Ltd.; 241 m, Patrick Ramsey/Image State International Stock Photography Ltd.; 241 b, Steve Whalen/Image State/International Stock Photography Ltd.; 246-247, John Hicks/eStock Photo; 246 inset, Simón Silva; 253, Englebert Photography, Inc.; 254, t, © Richard Cummins/Corbis; 255, Ilene Perlman/SB; 256 b, Joe Viesti/VC; 259 t, David Young-Wolffe/PhotoEdit; 259 b, Jimmy Dorantes LF; 260, Comnet Ltd./eStock Photography; 261, Bob Nichols/U.S. Department of Agriculture; 261, Image State/International Stock Photography Ltd.; 262, Megan Bowers/LF; 263 t, ©Buddy Mays/CORBIS; 263 m, ©Danny Lehman/CORBIS; 264 t, Robert Frerck/Odyssey Productions; 264 m, ©2004 Ulrike Welsch/PhotoEdit; 265, RFP; 270a, m, Courtesy of El Fenix Restaurants; 270a, r, © Roberto M. Sanchez/Dallas Morning News; 270a, l, © Nan Coulter/Dallas Morning News; 270b, © Dallas Morning News; 270-271, Robert Fried/SB; 270 inset, Dalí, Salvador (1904-89), Young girl looking out of the window. Museo Español de Arte Contemporáneo, Madrid, Spain. The Bridgeman Art Library International, Ltd.; 276, Joe Viesti/VC; 279, AP/Wide World Photos; 286 t, Bob Daemmrich/SB; 286 b, Jimmy Dorantes/LF; 287, Patti McConville/IS; 290, Jeff Greenberg/SB;

291 t, Rhoda Sidney/SB; 291 m, Bonnie Kamin/Photo Edit; 291 b, Reuters NewMedia Inc./CORBIS; 296-297, ©Robert Frerck/Odyssey Productions; 303, Robert Frerck/Woodfin Camp & Associates; 306, RFP; 311, Alan Keohane/Dorling Kindersley Media Library; 314 t, Kim Newton/WC; 314 m, Bob Krist/eStock Photography, LLC; 314 b, Rob Crandall/SB; 315 t, Kal Muller/WC; 315 b, RFP; 320a, tr, © Bettmann/CORBIS; 320a, l, © Bettmann/CORBIS; 320a, r, © Rolf Nussbaumer;

320b, © Lee Boltin/Time Life Pictures/Getty Images Editorial; 320-321, ©Robert Frerck/Odyssey/Chicago; 320 inset, Miró, Joan (1893–1983). Self-portrait, 1919. Oil on canvas. (c)ARS, NY. PHoto: J.G. Berizzi. Musée Picasso, Paris, France./Art Resource, N.Y.; 326, Robert Frerck/Woodfin Camp & Associates; 327, Marlborough Gallery, Inc.; 328 money, Jimmy Dorantes/Latin Focus.com; 331,b, © David Young-Wolff/PhotoEdit; 335, ©Mitchell Gerber/CORBIS; 336 bl, t, Joe Viesti/VC; 336 m, IFA Bilderteam/eStock Photography LLC; 337 tl, IFA Bilderteam/eStock Photography; 337 b, Joe Viesti/VC; 338, Wolfgang Kaehler Photography; 339 t, RFP; 339 b, Robert Frerck/WC; 344-345, Robert Frerck/WC; 344 inset, Englebert Photography, Inc.; 350, ©2004 Ulrike Welsch Photography; 353 tl and tr, RFP; 353 bl, H. Huntly Hersch/DDB; 353 br, Bonnie Kamin/PhotoEdit; 356, Robert Frerck/WC; 357, Thomas R. Fletcher/SB; 359 tl, SuperStock, Inc.; 359 tm, San Diego Historical Society; 359 tr, Richard Pasley/SB; 362, Joe Viesti/VC; 363, Robert Frerck/ Woodfin Camp & Associates; 363, ©Robert Frerck/OP; 364 t, Spencer Grant/PhotoEdit; 364 m, Leslye Borden/PhotoEdit; 365 tl, Richard Carroll/Ambient Images; 365 tr, Joe Viesti/VC; 366, Walter Bibikow/SB; 367, David young-Wolff/PhotoEdit; 372a, l, m, r, Courtesy of Claudette Elizondo/www.mexicachica.com; 372b, tl, Courtesy of Stallion Boot & Belt Company; 372b, mr, ml, © J.W. Cooper/Courtesy of Stallion Boot & Belt Company; 372-373, ©Robert Frerck/OP; 372 inset, El Greco, View of Toledo, Metropolitan Museum of Art, New York/Index/Bridgeman Art Library, London/New York; 377 bl, Michael Sewell/Peter Arnold; 378, ©Wolfgang Kaehler/CORBIS; 379, Robert Fried/DDB; 380 b, Suzanne Murphy Larronde/DDB; 381, Art Womack/IS; 382 t, ©Danny Lehman/CORBIS; 382 (1), Salatiel Barragan/LF; 382 (2), Ulrike Welsch/PhotoEdit; 382 (3), RFP; 382 (4), Salatiel Barragan/Latin Focus.com; 382 (5), Russell Gordon/Danita Delimont, Agent; 384, Mireille Vautier/Woodfin Camp & Associates; 387, Steve Bly/Bly Photography; 389 t, ©Robert Frerck/Odyssey/ Chicago; 389 b, Jimmy Dorantes/LF; 390 tl, Michele Burgess/SB; 390 m, Gisela Damm/eStock Photography, LCC; 390 br, ©Robert Frerck/OP; 391 t, John Neubauer/PhotoEdit; 391 b, ©Robert Frerck/OP; 392 t, Steve Bly/Bly Photography; 393 t, ©Robert Frerck/OP; 393 b, DDB; 393, b, © Lake County Museum/Corbis; 398-399, Courtesy of the Peace Corps; 404, AGE Fotosctock America, Inc.; 405 (1), David Young-Wolff/PhotoEdit; 405 (2, 3, 4,), Michael Newman/PhotoEdit; 405 b, ©2004 Ulrike Welsch Photography; 406 tr, Jimmy Dorantes/Latin Focus.com; 406 bl, Courtesy of Interplast; 407, Gary Braasch/Woodfin Camp & Associates; 409 bl, Puerto Rican Foundation For Conservation; 410, Chris Hamilton/CORBIS; 412, ©Fernando Alda/CORBIS; 413 t, Steve Raymer/NGS Image Collection; 413 b, Courtesy of the Mobility Project Organization, www.mobilityproject.org; 414 t, Marcelo Salinas/LF; 414 b, SuperStock, Inc.; 415, W. Lynn Seldon Jr./D.Donne Bryant Stock Photography; 415 t, Ro De La Harpe/Animals Animals/Earth Scenes; 415 br, Jeremy Horner/Panos Pictures; 416 b, Mary Kate Denny/PhotoEdit; 417 t, A. Ramey/PhotoEdit; 417 b, SuperStock, Inc.; 418 t, Bob Daemmrich/SB; 418 b, Bruce Farnsworth/Chuch Place Photography; 419 t, Jonathan Nourok/PhotoEdit; 419 b, Peter Chartrand/DDB; 424a, m, mr, www.amigoslink.org/Courtesy of Amigos de las Américas volunteers; 424a, l, br, r, © Corbis; 424b, br, r, tl, www.amigoslink.org/Courtesy of Amigos de las Américas volunteers; 424b, ml, © Corbis; 424b l, © Jay Dickman/Corbis; 424-425, Courtesy of Bizbirije/Primer Impacto; ©Univisión Communications Inc. 2002, All rights reserved; 424 inset, Dalí, Salvador, Portrait of Luis Buñuel, 1924. Oil on canvas, .70 x .60 m. Coll. Luis Buñuel, Mexico City, D.F., Mexico./Art Resource, N.Y.; 430, Reuters NewMedia Inc./CORBIS; 431, Courtesy El Juego De La Vida, ©Televisa 2002, All rights reserved; 432 l, David Young-Wolff/PhotoEdit; 432 r, Michael Newman/PhotoEdit; 434 b, REUTERS/David Friedman/CORBIS BETTMAN; 436 b, Steve Chenn/CORBIS; 439 b, Noticiero Univisión; 440 t, Scott Barrow/IS; 440 b, Tony Freeman/PhotoEdit; 441 l, Russell Gordon; 441 r, Joe Viesti/The Viesti Collection, Inc.; 443 t, ©Robert Frerck/ OP; 443 m, David Young-Wolff/PhotoEdit; 443 b, Robert Fried/SB; 448-449, ©Robert Frerck/Odyssey/Chicago; 448 inset, Picasso, Pablo (1881-1973). Reading the Letter, 1921. Oil on canvas, 184 x 105 cm. Photo: J.G. Berizzi. (c) ARS, N.Y. Musée Picasso, Paris. France/Art Resource, N.Y.; 454 b, ©Robert Frerck/OP; 455 b, Candida Höfer/Biblioteca de la Real Academia de la Lengua Madrid IV; 461, t, © J. Griffis Smith/Texas Department of Transportation;; 463 bl, Jeff Greenberg/IS; 463 br, ©Robert Frerck/OP; 463, ©John Vachon/CORBIS; 466 t, ©2004 Ulrike Welsch Photography; 466 b, Najlah Feanny/SB; 467 t, James Davis/IS; 467 b, ©Robert Frerck/OP; 472a, mr, ml, Courtesy of Emilio Nicolás/Azteca América, KAZH – Houston; 472a, tr, © Benson Latin American Collection, Rare Books and Manuscripts, University of Texas at Austin; 472a, br, © Bob Daemmrich/The Image Works, Inc.; 472a, bm, © Luis Delgadillo; 472b, tl, © Jack Vartoogian; 472b, tr, © PhotoDisc.

Text 4B, p. 211: Playa Tropicana. Chapter 6B, p. 307: "¿Quién hace las tareas?" by Matilde de la Vara from *Muy Interesante*. Marzo 2002, No. 250. Published by G Y J España Ediciones, S.L., S. en C. Chapter 8B, p. 409: "Reduce-Reusa-Recicla" from La Fundación Puertorriqueña de Conservación & Logo of Fundación Puertorriqueña de Conservación. Copyright © 2001. Used by permission of Fundación Puertorriqueña de Conservación. Chapter 9A, p. 437: Cable Mágico Guía de Programación Mensual. Abril 2002, No. 107. Chapter 9A, p. 404: Adapted from ¡Apágala! from *Time For Kids*. April 12, 2002, Vol. 7, No. 22. Copyright 2002 Time Inc. All rights reserved. Chapter 9B, p. 456: Adapted from "A sus teclados, listos...¡a navegar!" from *Image Doc*. Marzo 2002, No. 159, p. 48.

Video *¿Eres tú, María?* is based on the novel *¿Eres tú, María?* (from the "Lola Lago, Detective" series) by Lourdes Miguel and Neus Sans, Difusión Centro de Investigación y Publicaciones de Idiomas, S. L. Barcelona, Spain, 1989.

Key D. Donne Bryant Stock Photography = DDB: Image State/international Stock Photography, Ltd. = IS; Latin Focus Photo Agency = LF; Odyssey Productions, In. = OP; The Viesti Collection, Inc. = VC; Woodfin Camp & Associates = WC; Robert Fried Photography = RFP; Stock Boston = SB

Note: Every effort has been made to locate the copyright owner of material used in this textbook. Omissions brought to our attention will be corrected in subsequent editions.

Advanced

Guide to

Program

Design

Microsoft® Excel/Visual Basic® Programmer's Guide

PUBLISHED BY
Microsoft Press
A Division of Microsoft Corporation
One Microsoft Way
Redmond, Washington 98052-6399

Library of Congress Cataloging-in-Publication Data
Microsoft Excel / Visual Basic for Windows 95 programmer's guide.
p. cm.
Includes index.
ISBN 1-55615-819-X
1. Microsoft Windows 95. 2. Microsoft Excel (Computer file)
3. Microsoft Visual BASIC.
QA76.76.O63M48913 1995
005.369--dc20 95-23192
CIP

Printed and bound in the United States of America.

1 2 3 4 5 6 7 8 9 MLML 0 9 8 7 6 5

Distributed to the book trade in Canada by Macmillan of Canada, a division of Canada Publishing Corporation.

A CIP catalogue record for this book is available from the British Library.

Microsoft Press books are available through booksellers and distributors worldwide. For further information about international editions, contact your local Microsoft Corporation office. Or contact Microsoft Press International directly at fax (206) 936-7329.

Acquisitions Editor: Casey D. Doyle
Project Editor: Brenda L. Matteson

Contents

Introduction

Welcome to Visual Basic® for applications—the programming language used in Microsoft® Excel. Using Visual Basic, you can automate everyday tasks, add custom features and functions to suit your needs, and even create complete applications.

In Microsoft Excel, you automate tasks with macros. A *macro* is a sequence of instructions, written in Visual Basic, that tells Microsoft Excel what to do.

Microsoft Excel provides a feature called the macro recorder, which writes macros for you by storing the actions you take and the commands you choose as you work with Microsoft Excel. Later you can play back, or *run*, the macro to repeat your recorded actions automatically, saving yourself time and effort.

After you learn to record and run macros, you'll discover how useful they can be, and you'll want to make them even more powerful by adding your own Visual Basic code and improving the recorded code.

Whether you're a new user or an experienced macro developer, Visual Basic can make you more productive. With Visual Basic, you can create custom commands, menus, dialog boxes, messages, and buttons—and you can display custom Help topics for all of these items. From automating repetitive tasks to developing powerful, full-featured applications, Visual Basic's tools enable you to customize Microsoft Excel so that it fits your specific needs.

Getting Started

This introduction describes the printed and online documentation you'll use as you learn more about Visual Basic. The following sections will help you determine how this book can best serve your needs.

Where Are You?

This book assumes that you already know how to use Microsoft Excel. If you're new to Microsoft Excel, you should set this book aside for now. For general information about Microsoft Excel, see *Getting Results with Microsoft Excel for Windows 95* or *Getting Results with Microsoft Office for Windows 95.*

You can record and use macros in Microsoft Excel without learning Visual Basic. If you've never recorded or run a Visual Basic macro, see the topics listed under "Recording and Running Macros" on the Contents tab in Help.

Note If you clicked Typical when you installed Microsoft Excel, you'll need to run Setup again to install the Visual Basic Help file. For more information, see "Using Online Help" later in this introduction.

This book is designed for intermediate users of Visual Basic in Microsoft Excel. It provides information based on subject area rather than specific tasks. If you're new to Visual Basic in Microsoft Excel, or if you prefer a more task-oriented approach, you might want to start by reading *Microsoft Excel Visual Basic Step by Step*, a self-paced tutorial available from Microsoft Press®; then you can use this book to customize and optimize what you've learned.

Note You can order *Microsoft Excel Visual Basic Step by Step* and the *Microsoft Excel Visual Basic Reference* (a printed version of the online Visual Basic Help) directly from Microsoft Press. To place a credit card order, call 615-793-5090, or call 1-800-MS-PRESS toll-free. Please be sure to have your reference code FXL ready for faster order processing. CompuServe® subscribers can also order through the Microsoft Press Electronic Book Store by typing **GO MSP**.

Tips on How to Learn Visual Basic

The following are suggestions for getting the most from the time you spend learning Visual Basic.

Learn Microsoft Excel first

The more you know about Microsoft Excel, the better prepared you'll be to venture into Visual Basic. Most macros perform a sequence of actions in Microsoft Excel, and most instructions in a macro are equivalent to commands or actions in Microsoft Excel. Consequently, working with Visual Basic is a little like working with Microsoft Excel without a user interface; instead of commands and dialog boxes, you use Visual Basic instructions. The statements and functions you use to write instructions are much easier to understand if you're familiar with the features they represent in Microsoft Excel.

Also, if you know Microsoft Excel well, you can better answer the question you're most likely to ask when writing a macro: "What's the best way to do this?" People have been known to write long macros for tasks that could have been handled by a single Microsoft Excel command.

Learn what you need, when you need it

Learn what you need for the task at hand. Visual Basic can seem overwhelming at first, particularly if you haven't had experience with a macro programming language. A great way to learn the language is to investigate how to implement a particular macro idea you have. As you gain experience writing different types of macros, you'll cover a lot of ground.

Use the macro recorder

The macro recorder can record the Visual Basic instruction for virtually every action you take in Microsoft Excel. You can use the macro recorder to see how actions in Microsoft Excel translate into Visual Basic instructions, and vice versa. Also, you'll find that recording part of a macro is often faster and easier than writing out the instructions.

Use Visual Basic Help

Help is a powerful tool for learning Visual Basic. In a Visual Basic module, you can type a Visual Basic keyword and—with the insertion point somewhere in the keyword—press F1 to immediately display Visual Basic Help for that keyword. The Visual Basic Help topic for most keywords includes an example you can copy and paste into your macro. For more information, see "Using Online Help" later in this introduction.

How This Book Is Organized

The chapters in this book describe major feature areas of Visual Basic and techniques for using those features. The first three chapters—"Modules and Procedures," "Variables, Constants, and Data Types," and "Controlling Program Flow"—provide an introduction to the mechanics of writing Visual Basic code.

Chapter 4, "Objects and Collections," discusses the Microsoft Excel object model in detail and gives useful examples of manipulating and referencing objects to accomplish tasks in Visual Basic macros.

Chapter 5, "Optimizing for Size and Speed," shows you several easy techniques that can make your Visual Basic code faster and more concise.

Chapter 6, "Debugging," and Chapter 7, "Handling Run-Time Errors," show you how to find and eliminate bugs in your code before you run it and how to handle errors that occur while your code is running.

Chapter 8, "Controls and Dialog Boxes," and Chapter 9, "Menus and Toolbars," show you how to add custom user-interface elements to your Visual Basic macros.

Chapter 10, "Communicating with Other Applications," details using OLE Automation to communicate with and control other applications.

Chapter 11, "Automatic Procedures and OnEvent Procedures," shows you how to write procedures that run whenever a specific event—such as opening a workbook or clicking a control—occurs.

Chapter 12, "Creating Add-Ins," provides information about creating and using add-ins to distribute your macros.

Chapter 13, "Accessing External Data," discusses using Data Access Objects (DAOs) to import and export information stored in a database.

Appendixes A through D explain how to write international applications, provide helpful information for experienced Microsoft Excel users who are switching to Visual Basic, list all the toolbar buttons in Microsoft Excel, and diagram the Microsoft Excel object model.

Code Samples

Your Microsoft Excel package includes code samples you can open and run. You can copy any part of the samples into your own applications, modifying them as necessary. These code samples are located in the Samples.xls workbook in the Examples folder in your Microsoft Excel folder.

Using Online Help

Microsoft Excel provides an extensive Help system for the Visual Basic language, the objects that Microsoft Excel supports, and the properties and methods of those objects.

If you clicked Typical when you installed Microsoft Excel, you'll need to run Setup again to install Help forVisual Basic for Microsoft Excel.

You can access Visual Basic Help in any of the following four ways:

- In a Visual Basic module, place the insertion point anywhere in an object, property, method, function, or other keyword, and then press F1 to get context-sensitive Help.
- On the Help menu, click Microsoft Excel Help Topics. You can then either click "Getting Started with Visual Basic" on the Contents tab, look up a specific topic or Visual Basic term on the Index tab, or perform a full-text search from the Find tab.
- On the Help menu, click Microsoft Excel Help Topics. You can then ask a question on the Answer Wizard tab and read the topics displayed in the Programming and Language Reference section of the dialog box.

- With a Visual Basic module active, click Object Browser on the View menu, and then click the Element Help button (appears as a question mark below the Objects/Modules box) for information about an object, method, property, or function.

Document Conventions

This book uses the typographic conventions shown in the following table. You might not recognize all the terms or Visual Basic keywords, but you'll learn more about them later.

Example of convention	Description
setup	Words or characters you're instructed to type appear in bold.
Sub, **If**, **ChDir**, **MsgBox**, **True**, **Add**, **Height**, **Application**, **Range**, **Row**	Words in bold with the initial letter capitalized indicate a a language-specific term: a property, method, or object name; or another Visual Basic keyword.
object	In text, italic type indicates important new terms, usually the first time they occur in the book.
propertyname	In code syntax, italic type indicates placeholders for information you supply.
ENTER	Small capital letters are used for the names of keys and key combinations, such as ENTER and CTRL+R.
CTRL+V	A plus sign (+) between key names indicates a combination of keys. For example, CTRL+V means to hold down the CTRL key while pressing the V key.
DOWN ARROW	Individual arrow keys are referred to by the direction of the arrow on the key (LEFT, RIGHT, UP, or DOWN). The phrase "arrow keys" is used when describing these keys collectively.
BACKSPACE, HOME	Other navigational keys are referred to by their specific names.
`myVar`	This font is used for example code.

`Sub StockSale ( )`
`.`
`.`
`.`
`End Sub`
	A column or row of three periods tells you that part of an example program has been intentionally omitted.

Programming Style

This book uses the following programming style guidelines for code examples. For more information about Visual Basic code, see Chapter 1, "Modules and Procedures."

- The following font is used for code.

```
Sub HelloWorld
    Cells(1,1).Value = "Hello, world!"
End Sub
```

- An apostrophe (') introduces comments in code.

```
' This is a comment; these two lines
' are ignored when the program is running.
```

- Names of macros and user-defined functions appear with initial letters capitalized throughout this book. Note that macro and function names cannot include spaces, so if a name consists of more than one word, the other words in the name also have their initial letters capitalized.

```
' The AuditResult user-defined function is in the Finance module.
Function AuditResult(latestIncome, expenses, taxes, commissions)
```

  Argument and variable names appear with initial letters lowercase (to distinguish them from macro, function, property, method, and object names).

- Keywords appear with initial letters capitalized, whereas built-in constants appear with an initial lowercase "xl" or "vb."

```
' Sub is a keyword.
Sub Title(titleText)

' xlManual is a built-in constant.
Application.Calculation = xlManual
```

- Control-flow blocks and statements in **Sub** and **Function** procedures are indented within the code that surrounds them.

```
Sub CheckRecordSound
    SoundRecordCapable = Application.CanRecordSounds
    If SoundRecordCapable Then
        Cells(1,1).SoundNote.Record
    End If
End Sub
```

- The line-continuation character—an underscore (_)—indicates that code continued from one line to the next is part of the same logical line. You can type these statements all on one line in the Visual Basic module. You can also divide lines of code and add the line-continuation character yourself.

```
ActiveSheet.Rectangles.Add _
    width:=200, _
    height:=200, _
    left:=50, _
    top:=50
```

Microsoft Product Support Services

Microsoft offers a variety of support options to help you get the most from your Microsoft product. For more information about Microsoft Product Support Services, see *Getting Results with Microsoft Excel for Windows 95* or *Getting Results with Microsoft Office for Windows 95.*

Outside the United States, contact Microsoft Product Support Services at the Microsoft subsidiary office that serves your area. Microsoft subsidiary offices and the countries they serve are listed in *Getting Results with Microsoft Excel for Windows 95* and *Getting Results with Microsoft Office for Windows 95.*

CHAPTER 1

Modules and Procedures

Modules and procedures are the basic structural units of a Visual Basic program. By learning how to break complex tasks down into a set of simple procedures, how to invoke one procedure from within another procedure, and how to pass data between procedures, you can create modular code that's easy to write, read, debug, and modify.

Contents

Structuring a Visual Basic Program

One of the goals in modern programming is to produce *modular* programs—that is, programs composed of small, discrete units of code, each of which acts independently to accomplish a particular task. Toward this end, Visual Basic enables you to organize your code into procedures, modules, and workbooks.

A program built from small, reliable components has many advantages over a program built as a single structure. Well-structured modular programs are:

- Easy to write, because complex problems are broken down into a series of discrete, easy-to-understand tasks.
- Easy to read, because a top-level procedure typically contains only a series of calls to descriptively named lower-level procedures.
- Easy to debug, because each task is accomplished in one procedure, and you can easily isolate the source of a problem.
- Efficient, because code that accomplishes a common task appears in only one procedure that's called many times, rather than being duplicated in many places throughout a program.

- Easy to modify, because code that accomplishes a specific task appears in only one place in a program. Therefore, if you need to modify this code, you need only make the change in one place.
- Reliable, because you can build up a library of dependable procedures and then construct your programs using these tested, proven components.
- Robust, because you can hide data from all parts of a program that don't require access to the data, and thereby reduce the risk of accidentally making changes to the data.
- Easy to manage and distribute, because you can store and distribute sets of related or frequently used procedures as a unit.

The rest of this chapter will describe how to organize your code into these components and how to control the interaction among procedures stored in different parts of a program.

Breaking Code Down into Procedures

A *procedure* is a unit of code enclosed either between the **Sub** and **End Sub** statements or between the **Function** and **End Function** statements. A procedure should accomplish a simple, well-defined task. Procedures are often used for performing repeated or shared tasks.

If your code contains a procedure that performs a complicated task, break that procedure down into several smaller procedures, and then write a separate procedure to call these procedures in order. Continue to examine and break down each procedure in your code until each procedure is simple and specific. The simpler the task performed by a procedure, the easier it will be for you to write and debug it. The more specific the task performed by a procedure, the more versatile the procedure will be.

Understanding the Structure of a Module

Modules are workbook sheets that contain code. Each module can contain a declarations section, followed by procedures. The declarations section at the top of the module can contain:

- **Option statements**. If your module contains any **Option** statements, which set various module-level options, these statements must appear before any procedures. For more information, see "option" in Help.
- **User-defined type definitions**. If your module contains any user-defined types, their definitions must appear before any procedures. For more information about user-defined types, see Chapter 2, "Variables, Constants, and Data Types."

- **Declarations**. Any variable or constant declarations that aren't contained within a procedure must be placed before any procedures in the module. For more information about declaring variables and constants, see Chapter 2, "Variables, Constants, and Data Types."

Except for **Option** statements, user-defined type definitions, and declarations, all code in Visual Basic must be contained within procedures; Visual Basic modules cannot contain free-floating (uncontained) commands.

Grouping Procedures into Modules and Workbooks

So that you can easily find a particular procedure or set of procedures that access common data or provide a cohesive set of services, you can group procedures into modules with descriptive names. For example, if you've written a set of procedures that perform various accounting tasks, you could group them into a module and name the module "Accounting_Procedures." You would then know where to find any accounting procedure.

You can further group related modules into a single workbook. This makes it easier to turn the program into an add-in and distribute it. For more information about creating add-ins, see Chapter 12, "Creating Add-Ins."

Although you may want to store procedures in different modules or workbooks for organizational reasons, you may still want to be able to exchange information between them. To support data exchange across modules and workbooks, Visual Basic allows a procedure to access code and data stored in another module or workbook. For more information about accessing data in other modules or workbooks, see Chapter 2, "Variables, Constants, and Data Types." For more information about accessing code in other modules or workbooks, see "Calling Procedures in Other Modules" later in this chapter.

Simple applications can consist of just a single module; all of the code in the application resides in that module. As your applications get larger and more sophisticated, you add additional modules. Eventually you might find that there's common code you want to execute in several modules. You don't want to duplicate the code in both modules, so you create a separate module containing a procedure that implements the common code. Over time, you can build up a library of modules containing shared procedures, as described in the following section.

Creating Library Workbooks

You can organize frequently used procedures into modules you store in *libraries*—workbooks that contain only modules—and make these procedures visible throughout a program without having to copy them into every module or workbook that calls them. You can make the procedures in a library workbook visible to procedures in another workbook by creating a reference from the workbook that contains the calling procedure to the library workbook. For more information about creating a reference to a library workbook, see "Creating a Reference to a Workbook" later in this chapter.

After you've created a reference to the library workbook, procedures in other workbooks can call procedures stored in the library workbook. For more information about calling procedures in other modules and workbooks, see "Calling Procedures in Other Modules" later in this chapter.

Creating Procedures

When you create a procedure, you must decide how widely accessible you want the procedure to be, what you want to name the procedure, what task you want the procedure to perform, what sort of information the procedure will need to perform this task, what types of data you want the procedure to accept and return, and whether you want the procedure to affect data in other parts of the program. The following sections describe how Visual Basic allows you to specify this information for each procedure you write.

Specifying Procedure Scope

The term *scope* means the areas in a program from which a particular program item—such as a variable, constant, user-defined data type, or procedure—is accessible, or "visible." Procedures in Visual Basic can have either private or public scope. A procedure with private scope is visible only to the other procedures in the module where it's declared; a procedure with public scope is visible to all procedures in every module in the workbook in which the procedure is declared, and in all workbooks that contain a reference to that workbook. If you don't specifically indicate otherwise, procedures have public scope.

If you want to limit the availability of a procedure to the module in which it's declared, use the **Private** keyword. Because procedures are public by default, you don't need to use the **Public** keyword to declare a public procedure; however, doing so makes it easier to see immediately which program elements have public scope and which ones have private scope. The following code declares two public procedures and one private procedure.

```
Public Sub CalcPayments()
    ' place statements here
    MsgBox "I'm public!"
End Sub

Sub CalcIncome()    ' Public by default
    ' place statements here
    MsgBox "I'm public, too!"
End Sub

Private Sub CalcSavings()
    ' place statements here
    MsgBox "I'm private!"
End Sub
```

Note A procedure that's declared as **Private** cannot run as a stand-alone procedure. It can be called only from another procedure.

To limit the availability of a procedure to the workbook in which it's declared, declare the procedure itself as **Public**, but make the module private by adding the **Option Private Module** statement to the declarations section of the module.

Naming Procedures

When naming your procedures, you must follow certain guidelines. A procedure name:

- Must begin with a letter.
- Cannot contain embedded periods, mathematical or comparison operators, or type-declaration characters.
- Must not exceed 255 characters.
- Must be unique within its scope.
- Cannot be the name of a Visual Basic method, property, function, argument name, or other restricted keyword. For a list of restricted keywords, see "restricted keywords" in Help.

Tip To avoid having to use module qualifiers when calling procedures, use each procedure name only once.

Types of Procedures

Visual Basic allows you to create two types of procedures: **Sub** procedures and **Function** procedures.

A **Sub** procedure is a unit of code enclosed between the **Sub** and **End Sub** statements that performs a task but doesn't return a value.

A **Function** procedure is a unit of code enclosed between the **Function** and **End Function** statements. Like a **Sub** procedure, a **Function** procedure performs a specific task. However, a **Function** procedure also returns a value you can use in an expression, as shown in the following example.

```
totalSales = CalculateTotal(x)   'CalculateTotal is a Function procedure
```

You can also use **Function** procedures in place of complex worksheet formulas, just as you use built-in Visual Basic functions such as **Sqr**, **Cos**, and **Chr**.

Note A **Function** procedure you call from a formula on a worksheet shouldn't make changes to the data in a workbook or change the Microsoft environment in any way. For more information, see "Using Function Procedures on Worksheets" later in this chapter.

Returning a Value from a Function

For a function to return a value, it must include a function assignment statement that assigns a value to the name of the function, as shown in the following example. The value assigned to ConeSurface will be the value returned by the function.

```
Function ConeSurface(radius, height)
    Const Pi = 3.14159
    coneBase = Pi * radius ^ 2
    coneCirc = 2 * Pi * radius
    coneSide = Sqr(radius ^ 2 + height ^ 2) * coneCirc / 2
    ConeSurface = coneBase + coneSide
End Function
```

When the **Function** procedure returns a value, this value can then become part of a larger expression. For example, the following line in another procedure incorporates the return value of the ConeSurface and ScoopSurface functions into its calculations.

```
totalSurface = ConeSurface(3, 11) + 2 * ScoopSurface(3)
```

The information that must be supplied to a procedure for it to perform its task (`radius` and `height` in the preceding example) is passed in the form of arguments. For more information about arguments, see "Communicating with Procedures Using Arguments" later in this chapter.

Specifying the Data Type for a Function's Return Value

If you want to restrict the return value of a **Function** procedure to a particular data type, declare the return value's type using the **As** keyword after the parentheses that follow the function name.

```
Function CalcPay(hours, rate) As Currency
```

In the absence of an **As** clause, the return value will have the **Variant** type by default.

Note You can also use the **As** keyword within the parentheses enclosing the argument list to specify the data types of procedure arguments, as in this example: `Function CalcPay(hours As Integer, rate As Currency) As Currency`. For more information, see "Specifying Argument Data Types" later in this chapter.

Using Function Procedures on Worksheets

Function procedures you can use to replace long worksheet formulas in a worksheet cell—just as you use built-in worksheet functions—are called *user-defined worksheet functions.*

For example, suppose that the workbook named "MyBook" contains the function ConeSurface, which was defined in "Returning a Value from a Function" earlier in this chapter. If you want a cell on a worksheet in MyBook—a cell in any workbook that has a reference to MyBook—to contain the surface area of a cone with a radius of 5 and a height of 10, you should place the formula `=ConeSurface(5,10)` in the cell. If you want to use the ConeSurface function in a worksheet cell in a workbook that doesn't contain a reference to MyBook, you should precede the function name with the name of the workbook and an exclamation mark—for example, `=MYBOOK.XLS!ConeSurface(5,10)`—and MyBook must be open.

Note You can call functions in loaded add-ins without opening the add-in workbook and without specifying the workbook name. For information about creating add-ins, see Chapter 12, "Creating Add-Ins."

A user-defined worksheet function must not change any data in a workbook or change the Microsoft Excel environment in ways such as the following:

- Inserting, deleting, or formatting cells
- Changing cell values
- Moving, renaming, deleting, or adding sheets
- Changing the calculation mode or screen view

In addition, names of procedures you intend to use as user-defined functions in Microsoft Excel cannot have names that resemble A1-style or R1C1-style cell addresses.

If you cannot remember the exact name of a user-defined function or the name or number of its arguments, you can use the Function Wizard to examine the function and its arguments.

► **To insert a user-defined function using the Function Wizard**

1. On the Insert menu, click Function.
2. In the Function Category box, click User Defined.
3. In the Function Name box, click the name of the function you want to insert.
4. Follow the rest of the Wizard steps. Where appropriate, the Wizard will give you a chance to fill in arguments.

If you want a user-defined function to appear in a category other than User Defined, assign it to a different function category.

► **To specify a user-defined function's category**

1. With a module active, click Object Browser on the View menu.
2. In the Methods/Properties box, click the function you want to specify a category for.
3. Click Options to display the Macro Options dialog box.
4. In the Function Category box, click the category where you want the function to appear.

Calling Procedures

The simplest way to call a procedure is to name it in your code, just as you do with built-in keywords. The following sections describe how to call **Sub** and **Function** procedures from other procedures.

Note If you want a particular procedure to run automatically, without being called explicitly, at every occurrence of a specific event—such as opening a file, clicking an object, or activating a sheet—you should make the procedure an automatic procedure or an OnEvent procedure. For information about creating automatic and OnEvent procedures, see Chapter 11, "Automatic Procedures and OnEvent Procedures."

Calling Sub Procedures

There are two ways to call a **Sub** procedure:

```
' Both of these statements call a Sub named MyProc.
Call MyProc (firstArgument, secondArgument)
MyProc firstArgument, secondArgument
```

Note that when you use the **Call** syntax, arguments must be enclosed in parentheses. If you omit the **Call** keyword, you must also omit the parentheses around the arguments. For more information about arguments, see "Communicating with Procedures Using Arguments" later in this chapter.

Unlike a **Function** procedure, a **Sub** procedure cannot be called by using its name within an expression, and it doesn't return a value.

Calling Function Procedures

Usually, you call a function procedure you've written yourself the same way you call a built-in Visual Basic function such as **Abs**—that is, by using its name in an expression. For example, the following is a function that calculates the rate of single-occupancy vehicle users in a community.

```
Function PercentSOV(SOV, sharedMotorized, nonMotorized)
    Const nmFactor = 0.2
    totalSOV = SOV - nmFactor * nonMotorized
    totalPossibleTrips = SOV + sharedMotorized + nonMotorized
    PercentSOV = (totalSOV / totalPossibleTrips) * 100
End Function
```

All of the following statements call the PercentSOV function.

```
If PercentSOV(SOV, Bus, BikeOrWalk) > 72 Then Debug.Print "Too high"
Application.StatusBar = 100 - PercentSOV(SOV, Bus, BikeOrWalk)
X = PercentSOV(SOV, Bus, BikeOrWalk)
```

The information that must be supplied to a procedure for it to perform its task—`SOV`, `Bus`, and `BikeOrWalk` in the preceding example—is passed in the form of arguments. For more information about arguments, see "Communicating with Procedures Using Arguments" later in this chapter.

Calling Procedures in Other Modules

For a procedure to be called from outside the module in which it resides, two conditions must be met:

- The workbook that contains the calling procedure must contain a reference to the workbook that contains the called procedure.
- The called procedure must be visible outside the module in which it's declared; that is, the procedure must have public scope.

If procedures with duplicate names exist in different modules or workbooks, you may also need to include a module qualifier in front of the procedure name to distinguish between procedures.

The following sections describe how to create a reference to a workbook and how to use module qualifiers. For more information about specifying procedure scope, see "Specifying Procedure Scope" earlier in this chapter.

Creating a Reference to a Workbook

If you want to call a procedure in another workbook, you must create a reference to the workbook that contains the procedure. A referenced workbook need not be visible, or even open, for you to be able to call procedures in it.

▶ **To create a reference to a workbook**

1. Open the workbook that contains the calling procedure, and activate a module sheet.
2. On the Tools menu, click References.
3. The Available References box shows all open workbooks and all workbooks referenced by an open workbook.
4. Select the check box next to the name of the workbook you want to create a reference to.
5. To select a workbook that's not listed in the Available References box, click Browse, and then locate the workbook you want to create a reference to.

If one workbook has an indirect reference link to another workbook, Visual Basic allows the procedures in the first workbook to call procedures in the other workbook by specifying the name of the referenced workbook in the calling statement. For example, suppose that the workbook FirstBk has a reference link to SecondBk, which has a reference link to ThirdBk. A procedure in FirstBk could call the procedure TestProc in ThirdBk using the code in the following example.

```
[THIRDBK.XLS].TestProc
```

You cannot have circular references to workbooks. That is, a workbook that references another workbook cannot in turn be referenced by that other workbook.

Tip You cannot create a link to a workbook programmatically; you must manually create a reference link in each workbook that needs access to procedures in another workbook. One way around this is to create a template that contains a link to the library workbook and then create new workbooks based on that template. Each new workbook will already contain a link to the library workbook.

If you want every new workbook you create to contain a reference link to a certain workbook, create a template that contains a link to that workbook, and save the template as Book.xlt in your Xlstart folder or your alternate startup folder. Every new workbook you create will then be based on this template by default.

Using Module Qualifiers

If there are procedures with duplicate names in different modules or in different workbooks, you may need to include a module qualifier before the procedure name when calling the procedure. If the procedures are in different modules in the same workbook, the module qualifier should have the syntax shown in the following line.

[*modulename*].*procedurename*

For example, the following code calls two procedures—both named "TotalToDate"—stored in different modules in the same workbook.

```
[East Coast].TotalToDate
MidWest.TotalToDate
```

The square brackets around the module name are optional if the module name obeys Visual Basic naming conventions (no spaces, no periods, and so on).

If the procedures are in different workbooks, the module qualifier has the syntax shown in the following line.

[*workbookname*].[*modulename*].*procedurename*

For example, the following code calls two procedures—both named "TotalToDate"—stored in different workbooks.

```
[REGION.XLS].[Total Sales].TotalToDate
[STATE.XLS].[Total Sales].TotalToDate
```

A module qualifier must refer to a module in a workbook referenced by the workbook that contains the calling procedure.

If you don't include a module qualifier to indicate which of the identically named procedures you want to run, Visual Basic searches through modules in the following order, running the first module with that name that it finds: the current module, then other modules in the current workbook, and then modules in referenced workbooks.

Communicating with Procedures Using Arguments

If you need to supply a procedure with information so that it can perform its task, you pass that information in the form of arguments. When you declare an argument, you can specify the data type of the argument, whether or not the procedure can change the argument's value, and whether an argument is required or optional. For more information, see the following sections.

To indicate that a given procedure takes arguments, include an argument list between the parentheses that follow the procedure name in the procedure declaration. The argument list can contain multiple argument declarations, separated by commas.

The following example shows the declaration line of a **Sub** procedure that takes two arguments.

```
Sub UpdateRecord(custId, custName)
```

The following code calls UpdateRecord.

```
Dim newId As Integer
Dim newName As String

newId = 3452
newName = "Mary Boyd"
UpdateRecord newId, newName
```

Note that the name of the variable you pass from the calling procedure doesn't have to match the name of the argument declared in the called procedure.

If you pass an array as an argument, you must include empty parentheses after the array name. Because you don't specify the dimensions of the array, the procedure can accept arrays of any size. The following example shows a declaration line for a **Sub** procedure that takes an array as an argument.

```
Sub PrintList(custArray())
```

Arguments have the same scope as variables declared within a procedure—that is, local (procedure-level) scope. They're not accessible outside the procedure in whose argument list they're declared.

Specifying Argument Data Types

Procedure arguments have the **Variant** data type by default. However, you can declare other data types for arguments, using the **As** keyword in the argument declaration. For example, the following function accepts a string and an integer:

```
Function Reverse (S As String, ByVal n As Integer)
    ' Reverses the first n characters in S.
    Dim Temp As String, i As Integer
    If n > Len(S) Then n = Len(S)
    For i = n To 1 Step -1
        Temp = Temp & Mid(S, i, 1)
    Next
    Reverse = Temp & Right(S, Len(S) - n)
End Function
```

You can declare a procedure argument with a user-defined data type, as shown in the following code.

```
Type custInfo
    custName As String
    custCompany As String
    custId As Integer
End Type

Sub PrintList(newCust As custInfo)
    'place statements here
End Sub
```

Note that you can pass an argument with a user-defined data type only by reference. For more information, see the following section. For more information about fundamental data types and user-defined data types, see Chapter 2, "Variables, Constants, and Data Types," or see the specific data type in Help.

Passing Arguments by Reference

If you pass an argument by reference when calling a procedure, the procedure has access to the actual variable in memory. As a result, the variable's value can be changed by the procedure. Passing by reference is the default in Visual Basic, so if you don't explicitly specify to pass an argument by value, Visual Basic will pass it by reference. Each of the following lines indicates that an argument is passed by reference.

```
Sub AddThree(ByRef passedVar As Integer)
Sub AddThree(passedVar As Integer)      'ByRef is the default
```

The AddThree procedure accepts arguments passed by reference. Because the AddThree procedure changes the value stored in the `varToPass` variable that's passed to the procedure, the **MsgBox** function in TestPassingArgs will display the value 10.

```
Sub TestPassingArgs()
    Dim varToPass As Integer
    varToPass = 7
    AddThree varToPass
    MsgBox varToPass     ' displays 10
End Sub


Sub AddThree(ByRef passedVar As Integer)
    passedVar = passedVar + 3
End Sub
```

Note that if you specify a data type for an argument passed by reference, you must pass a value of that type for the argument. Failure to do this will result in a type mismatch error. For more information about declaring data types, see Chapter 2, "Variables, Constants, and Data Types."

Passing a variable by reference requires less memory and time than passing by value but increases accessibility to the value stored in the variable and therefore increases the chance that the value will be accidentally changed.

Passing Arguments by Value

If you pass an argument by value when calling a procedure, the called procedure only receives a copy of the variable passed from the calling procedure. If the called procedure changes the value, the change affects only the copy and not the variable in the calling procedure. Passing by value therefore protects data from being accidentally changed by the called procedure. Use the **ByVal** keyword to indicate that a variable is passed by value. For example, the following AddThree procedure accepts arguments passed by value. Because the AddThree procedure can only work with a copy of the `varToPass` variable and cannot access the actual value stored in the `varToPass` variable, the **MsgBox** function in TestPassingArgs will display the value 7.

```
Sub TestPassingArgs()
    varToPass = 7
    AddThree varToPass
    MsgBox varToPass     ' displays 7
End Sub


Sub AddThree(ByVal passedVar As Integer)
    passedVar = passedVar + 3
End Sub
```

Note that if you specify a data type for an argument passed by value, you don't need to pass a value of that type for the argument. In the preceding example, the `varToPass` variable is a **Variant** variable (because it hasn't been assigned any other data type), but Visual Basic passes a copy of it to the AddThree procedure as an integer. For more information about declaring data types, see Chapter 2, "Variables, Constants, and Data Types."

Note that your code cannot pass an argument with a user-defined type by value.

Using Parentheses to Pass an Argument by Value

You may at some point want to pass a variable to a procedure by value, even though the procedure indicates that the argument is passed by reference. You can do this by enclosing the variable to pass in parentheses. For example, the following AddThree procedure accepts arguments passed by reference. However, by enclosing the `varToPass` variable in parentheses in the calling procedure, you cause the variable to be passed by value. Therefore, in this example, the **MsgBox** function in TestPassingArgs will display the value 7 instead of the value 10.

```
Sub TestPassingArgs()
    varToPass = 7
    AddThree (varToPass)
    MsgBox varToPass     ' displays 7
End Sub


Sub AddThree(ByRef passedVar As Integer)
    passedVar = passedVar + 3
End Sub
```

Note Make sure that you don't accidentally pass a variable by value when you mean to pass it by reference. If you accidentally use parentheses around an argument when the syntax doesn't require it—that is, if you use parentheses around an argument to a procedure you call without the **Call** keyword, or around an argument to a **Function** procedure whose return value you're not using—you'll pass the variable by value. For more information about the syntax for calling procedures, see "Calling Procedures" earlier in this chapter.

Using Optional Arguments

You can specify that arguments to a procedure be optional by using the **Optional** keyword in the argument list. If you specify an optional argument, all subsequent arguments in the argument list must also be optional and must be declared with the **Optional** keyword. Optional arguments must be of the **Variant** data type.

For example, the following procedure takes two required arguments and two optional arguments. The procedure selects a range of cells on the worksheet named "SampleText" and then optionally makes the text red and sorts the range by the values in the first column.

```
Sub FormatList(startRow As Integer, startCol As Integer, _
        Optional redText, Optional sortList)
    If IsMissing(redText) Then
        redText = False
    Else
        redText = CBool(redText)
    End If
    If IsMissing(sortList) Then
        sortList = False
    Else
        sortList = CBool(sortList)
    End If
    Set myCells = Worksheets("SampleText") _
        .Cells(startRow, startCol).CurrentRegion
    If redText Then
        textColor = 3
    Else
        textColor = xlAutomatic
    End If
    myCells.Font.ColorIndex = textColor
    If sortList Then myCells.Sort key1:=myCells.Cells(1, 1)
End Sub
```

The **IsMissing** function is used to determine whether an optional argument was passed to the procedure. For more information, see "IsMissing" in Help.

The following example calls FormatList, providing both the required and optional arguments.

```
Sub DoList()
    FormatList 2, 2, False, True
End Sub
```

The following example provides the second optional argument.

```
Sub DoList()
    FormatList 2, 2, , True
End Sub
```

If your procedure has several optional arguments, you may want to use named arguments so that you can provide any or all of the arguments, in any order. For more information, see the following section.

Note **Sub** procedures with optional arguments won't appear in the Macro dialog box (Tools menu). (No **Function** procedures appear in the Macro dialog box.) You can, however, see procedures with optional arguments in the Object Browser.

Using Named Arguments

Many built-in functions, statements, and methods take more than one argument. For example, the **Open** method, which opens a workbook, takes 12 arguments. If you want to write code that opens the workbook Book2.xls, which has the protection password "drowssap", you could write the following code.

```
Workbooks.Open "BOOK2.XLS", , , , "drowssap"
```

However, this code is difficult to write correctly without introducing bugs, because you have to count the number of commas to insert between the arguments. The code is also very difficult to read, and it gives no clues about what the arguments represent. The following example shows a better way to write this code.

```
Workbooks.Open fileName:="BOOK2.XLS", password:="drowssap"
```

Because every argument has a name, you can use the name and the := operator to assign a value to an argument. When you use named arguments, you don't have to remember the order of the arguments. For example, the preceding code could have been written with the order of the arguments reversed, as in the following example.

```
Workbooks.Open password:="drowssap", fileName:="BOOK2.XLS"
```

You can use named arguments with the procedures you create, too. Visual Basic automatically associates argument names with their corresponding procedures. For example, the FormatList procedure in the preceding section takes two required arguments and two optional arguments, as shown in the following declaration line.

```
Sub FormatList(startRow As Integer, startCol As Integer, _
        Optional redText, Optional sortList)
```

The following DoList procedure calls the FormatList procedure using named arguments.

```
Sub DoList()
    FormatList redText:=True, startCol:=2, startRow:=2
End Sub
```

The arguments are given out of order, and one of the optional arguments was omitted. Using named arguments is especially useful if your procedures have several optional arguments you don't always need to specify.

Note You cannot use named arguments to avoid entering required arguments.

Using an Indefinite Number of Arguments

Generally, the number of arguments in the procedure call must be the same as in the procedure specification. Using the **ParamArray** keyword with an argument allows you to specify that a procedure will accept an arbitrary number of arguments. The argument used with **ParamArray** must be an array of **Variant** variables. For example, you could write the following AddInts procedure, using the **ParamArray** keyword with the array argument `intNums()` to allow the procedure to handle any number of arguments passed to it.

```
Function AddInts(ParamArray intNums())
    Dim x As Integer
    Dim y As Variant

    For Each y In intNums
        x = x + y
    Next y
    AddInts = x
End Function
```

Note that a **For Each** control variable in an array—`y` in the preceding example—must be a **Variant** variable.

You can subsequently call AddInts with any number of arguments, as shown in the following example.

```
Sub ShowSum()
    MsgBox AddInts(1, 3, 5)
    MsgBox AddInts(1, 3, 5, 7, 8, 9, 34, 98, 123)
End Sub
```

You can use the **ParamArray** keyword only with the last argument in an argument list.

Inserting Procedures and Arguments with the Object Browser

If you forget the names of your arguments or would like to paste them in rather than type them, you can use the Object Browser. The Object Browser lists all the **Sub** procedures and **Function** procedures in all currently open workbooks, including hidden workbooks.

▶ **To locate and insert a procedure using the Object Browser**

1. On the View menu, click Object Browser.
2. In the Libraries/Workbooks box, click the name of a workbook.
3. In the Objects/Modules box, click the name of the module, and then click the name of the procedure in the Methods/Properties box.
4. To view the code for a procedure, click Show.

   This is the easiest way to view the code for a function without actually opening the module that contains it. (You can view and execute procedures from the Macro dialog box, but not functions. The Macro dialog box lists only **Sub** procedures with no optional arguments. It doesn't list **Sub** procedures with optional arguments or any **Function** procedures.)
5. To paste the procedure into your code, click Paste.

It may help you remember details about a procedure if you enter a description that will appear at the bottom of the Object Browser dialog box when you click that procedure.

▶ **To enter a procedure description**

1. With a procedure selected in the Object Browser, click Options.
2. In the Macro Options dialog box, type a description in the Description box.

CHAPTER 2

Variables, Constants, and Data Types

This chapter describes a variety of strategies for managing data storage that enhance different aspects of macro performance:

- Using constants, variables, or structured groups of variables instead of literal values in code. This technique allows you to make single-point changes, and it makes code easier to read, modify, and debug.
- Specifying the parts of a program where specific data is available by defining the scope of the data. This technique reduces the number of procedures from which data can be manipulated and therefore reduces both the possibility that the data can be corrupted and the number of places you must look for the cause of a particular problem.
- Specifying the length of time to keep data in a variable or constant by defining the lifetime of the data. This technique prevents unexpected reinitialization of variables and allows retention of a variable's value between calls to a procedure.
- Specifying the amount of space to allocate in memory for the data and how to organize the data by declaring the data type. This technique makes your macros use less memory and run faster.
- Grouping related data together by creating an array or user-defined data type. Grouping data makes it easier to work with many related variables at once. User-defined types can also make your code easier to read and modify.

This chapter first discusses the basic data storage concepts mentioned above and then describes in detail how to put these concepts to work in your macros.

Contents

Variables

Variables are named areas in memory where you store data while the workbook containing your code is open. If you've written Visual Basic code, you've probably already used variables without really thinking about it. Variables can be useful for keeping track of running counts, storing input from a user or another source, or storing a value that subsequent macro instructions will change.

Choosing Variable Names

There are a few simple rules to follow when naming your variables. A variable name:

- Must begin with a letter.
- Cannot contain an embedded period, mathematical or comparison operator, or type-declaration character.
- Must not exceed 255 characters.
- Must be unique within its scope.
- Cannot be the name of a Visual Basic method, property, function, argument name, or other reserved keyword.

Tip To reduce the amount of time you spend deciphering and debugging code, use each variable for only one purpose.

Using Variables Without Declaring Them

Unless you specify otherwise, Visual Basic allows you to create variables simply by using them in your code (other programming languages, such as C and Pascal, require that you explicitly declare variables before you use them). The following example assigns the value of cell A1 to the variable `tempVal`.

```
tempVal = Worksheets(1).Range("A1").Value
```

This is called an *implicit* variable declaration. When you use this feature, Visual Basic automatically creates a variable and gives it the **Variant** data type. Variables with the **Variant** data type can contain any data, including strings, numbers, and dates. Until you assign a value to the new **Variant** variable, it has the special value **Empty**. As soon as you assign the **Variant** variable a value, it takes the data type of the assigned value. You'll learn more about **Variant** variables, data types, and the **Empty** value later in this chapter.

A **Variant** variable works well in this example because you may not know what kind of information cell A1 contains. Keep in mind that although it's convenient to allow Visual Basic to create variables whenever you use them, this can lead to subtle errors in your macro if you misspell a variable name, as shown in the following example.

```
Sub SwapCells()
    With Worksheets(1)
        tempVal = .Range("a1").Value
        .Range("a1").Value = .Range("a2").Value
        .Range("a2").Value = temVal
    End With
End Sub
```

At first glance, it looks as if this procedure should swap the contents of cells A1 and A2, but if you look carefully, you'll see that the `tempVal` variable is misspelled the second time it's used. Visual Basic doesn't know that you made a mistake and assumes that you meant to introduce a new variable, `temVal`. Visual Basic creates this new (empty) variable and assigns the value of cell A2 to it. After you run this procedure, the value that was in cell A2 has been moved into cell A1, and cell A2 is empty.

Declaring Variables

Whereas implicit variable declaration can initially make your code easier to write, *explicit* variable declaration ultimately makes the code easier to read, modify, debug, and run. To explicitly declare a variable, you use the **Dim**, **Private**, **Public**, or **Static** keyword to specify the variable's scope (what parts of your macro can use the variable), lifetime (how long Visual Basic keeps data in the variable), and data type (what kind of information the variable contains).

Explicit variable declaration:

- Makes code easier to understand by grouping all variable names at the beginning of modules and procedures, where you can keep track of them.
- Helps prevent you from inadvertently creating a new variable by misspelling the name of an existing variable.
- Helps prevent you from inadvertently using an existing variable when meaning to create a new one, thereby erasing the initial value stored in the variable.
- Speeds code execution by specifying the exact data type of each variable. Your code runs faster when Visual Basic doesn't have to determine the data type for each variable while the code is running.
- Matches the capitalization of each variable to the capitalization of the variable in the declaration statement and makes your code easier to read.

Tip To reduce the amount of time you spend deciphering, debugging, and running code, explicitly declare each variable and specify as much information as you can about the data to be stored in it.

The simplest form of explicit variable declaration creates a new variable with the **Variant** data type and procedure-level scope. The value in the variable is preserved only while the procedure is running. The following example declares two variables—`radius` and `area`.

```
Sub CircleArea()
    Dim radius, area
    radius = InputBox("Circle Radius?")
    area = 3.14159 * radius ^ 2
    MsgBox "The area is " & area
End Sub
```

You'll learn more about using declaration statements to specify variable scope, lifetime, and data type later in this chapter.

Requiring Explicit Variable Declarations

To avoid the problem of inadvertently creating new variables by misspelling the names of existing variables, you can stipulate that Visual Basic generate an error message whenever it encounters a name used as a variable but not previously declared explicitly as a variable. To require explicit variable declarations, place the following statement at the top of each module in which you want Visual Basic to enforce explicit declarations.

```
Option Explicit
```

You must manually add this line to the top of each existing module in which you want this option to be turned on, but you can have Visual Basic automatically add the line to new modules.

▶ **To have Visual Basic automatically add the Option Explicit statement to new modules**

- On the Tools menu, click Options, and then select the Require Variable Declaration check box on the Module General tab.

With **Option Explicit** in effect for the module containing the **SwapCells** procedure, Visual Basic requires that variables be declared before you can use them. The following example shows the procedure with the added variable declaration.

```
Sub SwapCells()
    Dim tempVal
    With Worksheets(1)
        tempVal = .Range("a1").Value
        .Range("a1").Value = .Range("a2").Value
        .Range("a2").Value = temVal
    End With
End Sub
```

When you try to run this procedure, Visual Basic generates an error message telling you that the `temVal` variable is undeclared. Recognizing that this error means you've misspelled the variable name, you can fix the name before it causes the procedure to fail.

Tip Because the **Option Explicit** statement helps you catch errors in variable names, and because it encourages you to use explicit data types, you should use it all the time.

Specifying Variable Scope and Lifetime

When you declare a variable within a procedure, only code within that procedure can access or change the value of that variable—that is, the variable has a *scope* that's local to that procedure. Sometimes, however, you need to use a variable with a broader scope, such as one whose value is available to all the procedures within the same module, or even to all the procedures in your entire application. Visual Basic allows you to specify the scope of a variable when you declare it.

Depending on how it's declared, a variable is scoped in one of three ways, as shown in the following table.

Scope	Declaration
Procedure	**Dim** or **Static** within the procedure
Private	**Dim** or **Private** at the top of the module
Public	**Public** at the top of the module

Tip It's generally a good idea to use the narrowest possible scope for your variables. For example, if you're using a temporary variable inside a procedure, use procedure (local) scope instead of private scope or public scope. Limiting the scope of your variables makes your macros more modular and helps reduce bugs.

A variable's *lifetime* is the time during which Visual Basic preserves the value in the variable. The values in private and public variables are preserved while the workbook is open, unless you edit a Visual Basic module in that workbook. When you edit a Visual Basic module, all modules in that workbook are recompiled and all variables are reset.

Although variables declared inside a procedure have the same scope level whether they're declared with **Dim** or **Static**, they have different lifetimes. Local variables declared with **Static** exist the entire time that the workbook where they're declared is open; that is, the variables retain their values between calls to the procedure. Local variables declared with **Dim** exist only while the procedure where they're declared is running. When a procedure ends, the values of its local variables aren't preserved and the memory used by the local variables is reclaimed. The next time the procedure runs, all its local variables are reinitialized.

Procedure-Level Variables

Procedure-level (or *local*) variables are recognized only in the procedure where they're declared. Local variables are a good choice for any kind of temporary calculation. All implicitly declared variables have local scope. You declare local variables explicitly by using the **Dim** or **Static** keyword inside the procedure, as shown in the following example.

```
Sub DoTheWork
    Dim intTemp As Integer
    Static intPermanent As Integer
.
.
.
End Sub
```

Tip Although you can use local variables with the same name in several procedures, it's usually best to use unique variable names. Using the same name in several procedures can make your macro harder to debug.

Preserving the Value of a Local Variable

If you want to preserve the value stored in a local variable between calls to the procedure that contains it, you should declare the variable using the **Static** keyword, as in the following example.

```
Static depth
```

The following function calculates a running total by adding a new value to the total of previous values stored in the static variable `accumulate`.

```
Function RunningTotal(num)
    Static accumulate
    accumulate = accumulate + num
    RunningTotal = accumulate
End Function
```

If `accumulate` were declared with **Dim** instead of **Static**, the previously accumulated values would not be preserved across calls to the function, and the function would simply return the value it was called with.

You could produce the same result by declaring `accumulate` in the declarations section of the module, making it available to any procedure in the module. After you've changed the scope of a variable in this way, however, the procedure no longer has exclusive access to it. Because other procedures can access and change the value of the variable, the running totals might be unreliable and the macro is more difficult to maintain.

Tip Use static variables if you need to preserve the value of a local variable each time a procedure is called. For example, you could use a static variable to record the number of times the procedure has been called or to record a running total, as shown in the preceding example.

Declaring All Local Variables as Static

To make *all* local variables in a procedure static, place the **Static** keyword at the beginning of a procedure heading, as in the following example.

```
Static Function RunningTotal(num)
```

This makes all local variables in the procedure static, regardless of whether they're declared explicitly with **Static** or **Dim** or declared implicitly. You can place **Static** in front of any **Sub** or **Function** procedure heading.

Note After you edit a module, Visual Basic recompiles all modules in the workbook and resets all variables the next time you run any Visual Basic procedure or function. If you need to preserve values when the workbook is compiled or saved, use a hidden worksheet to store the values.

Private Variables

Private variables are available to all the procedures in the module where they're declared, but not to code in other modules. You create private variables by declaring them with **Dim** or **Private** in the declarations section of a module (the top section, above procedure definitions), as in the following example.

```
Dim intTemp As Integer
Private intTemp2 As Integer
```

Tip Because variables declared at the top of a module are private by default, there is no difference between variables declared with **Private** and those declared with **Dim**. However, **Private** is preferred because it readily contrasts with **Public** and makes your macros easier to read. You cannot declare variables in a procedure using the **Private** keyword.

Public Variables

Public variables are available to every procedure in every module in the workbook where they're declared, as well as in all other workbooks that contain a reference link to the workbook where those variables are declared. (For information about creating a reference link to a workbook, see Chapter 1, "Modules and Procedures.")

You use the **Public** keyword to declare a public variable. Like private variables, public variables are declared in the declarations section at the top of the module; you cannot declare private or public variables inside a procedure.

```
Public intX As Integer
```

A public variable exists and retains its value from the time a value is assigned to the variable until the workbook closes (or until you edit a procedure, thus causing Visual Basic to recompile).

Note To create a variable that's available to all modules in a given workbook but not to any other workbooks, make the variable public by declaring it with the **Public** keyword, but make the module itself private to the workbook that contains it by using the **Option Private Module** statement in the module.

Specifying Variable Data Type

When you declare a variable, you can also supply a data type for it. The data type specifies the kind of information you can store in the variable. If you don't supply a data type, Visual Basic automatically gives the variable the **Variant** data type.

The **Variant** data type handles all types of fundamental data and converts between them automatically. If you want to create concise, fast macros, however, use other data types whenever you know that a variable will always contain the same type of data. For example, if a variable always contains small integer values, you can save several bytes (and speed up your macro significantly when performing arithmetic operations on the variable) by declaring that variable as **Integer** instead of **Variant**. For information about specific data types, see "Data Types" later in this chapter.

Before you can use a non-variant variable, you must explicitly declare it using the **As** keyword in a declaration statement. For example, the following statements declare variables as **Long**, **Integer**, **Double**, **String**, and **Currency**, respectively.

```
Dim x as Long
Private i As Integer
Private amt As Double
Static yourName As String
Public billsPaid As Currency
```

A declaration statement can combine multiple type declarations, separated by commas, as in the following statements.

```
Private i As Integer, amt As Double
Private yourName As String, billsPaid As Currency
Private test, amount, j As Integer   ' test and amount are Variants
```

Note If you don't specify a data type for a variable, Visual Basic assigns the **Variant** data type. In the preceding example, the variables `test` and `amount` have the **Variant** data type. This may surprise you if your experience with other programming languages leads you to expect all the variables in one declaration statement to have the same specified data type (in this case, **Integer**).

Arrays

If you've programmed in other languages, you're probably familiar with the concept of arrays. An *array* is a named collection of variables of the same data type. Each array element can be distinguished from other elements by one or more integer indexes. For example, if the `sheetNames` array contains three names, you can set and return the names as shown in the following example.

```
sheetNames(1) = "sheet1"
sheetNames(2) = "module1"
sheetNames(3) = "sheet2"

MsgBox sheetNames(2)
```

Arrays allow you to group related variables in a way that makes it easier for you to keep track of, access, and manipulate them all at once, while still being able to access each variable individually. This helps you create smaller and simpler macros in many situations, because you can set up loops using index numbers to deal efficiently with any number of cases.

When you create an array, its size is determined by the number of dimensions it has and the by the upper and lower bounds for the index numbers in each dimension. Arrays in Visual Basic can have up to 60 dimensions; the number of elements is limited by the amount of available memory. The `sheetNames` array in the earlier example has one dimension and three elements; the lower bound is one and the upper bound is three.

Because Visual Basic allocates space for every possible element in a declared array, whether or not you actually store a value in that element, you should avoid declaring an array any larger than is necessary. If you know ahead of time what size your array needs to be, you can declare a fixed-size array, or *static* array, and stipulate the exact dimensions and upper and lower bounds from the outset. If you don't know how many values you'll need to store in an array, you can declare a *dynamic* array without specifying the number of dimensions or the size of each dimension.

All the elements in an array must have the same data type. If you want to create an array whose elements can contain different kinds of data (objects, strings, numbers, and so on), you should declare an array of the **Variant** type. You can declare an array of any of the fundamental data types, including user-defined types (described in "User-Defined Data Types" later in this chapter) and object variables (described in Chapter 4, "Objects and Collections").

Declaring Arrays

You must explicitly declare an array before you can use it; you cannot implicitly declare an array. The procedure for declaring an array is very similar to the procedure for declaring a variable. You use the **Private**, **Public**, **Dim**, and **Static** keywords to specify the array scope and lifetime, you use integer values to specify the upper and lower bounds for each dimension, and you use the **As** keyword to specify the data type for the array elements.

The rules for determining the scope of an array are identical to those for variables. For more information, see "Specifying Variable Scope and Lifetime" earlier in this chapter.

Setting Upper and Lower Bounds

When you declare an array, you specify the upper and lower bounds for each dimension within the parentheses following the array name. The upper and lower bounds must be integers. The values can be positive, negative, or 0 (zero). You must use constant values to specify the bounds of fixed-size arrays (for information about using variables to specify the bounds of a dynamic array, see "Creating Dynamic Arrays" later in this chapter).

If you specify only one value for a dimension, Visual Basic interprets the value as the upper bound and supplies a default lower bound. The default lower bound is 0 (zero) unless you set it to 1 using the **Option Base** statement. For example, the following code declares one-dimensional arrays containing 15 and 21 elements, respectively.

```
Dim counters(14) As Integer
Dim sums(20) As Double
```

If you haven't changed the default lower bound, the index numbers in these arrays range from 0 to 14 and from 0 to 20, respectively. If you wish the index numbers to start at 1 instead of 0, you can change the default lower bound to 1 by placing an **Option Base** statement in the declarations section of a module:

```
Option Base 1
```

Tip You should always include `Option Base 1` in your modules. Microsoft Excel collections are always 1-based, and any arrays that Microsoft Excel methods or properties return are also 1-based. If you assign a 1-based array to a 0-based array, the same information exists in both arrays, but each element is off by one index. This can make your macros confusing and hard to debug.

You can also specify the lower bound of a dimension explicitly. To do this, separate the lower and upper bounds with the **To** keyword, as in the following examples.

```
Dim counters(1 To 15) As Integer
Dim sums(100 To 120) As String
```

In the preceding declarations, the index numbers of `counters` range from 1 to 15, and the index numbers of `sums` range from 100 to 120.

Tip You can use the Visual Basic **LBound** and **UBound** functions to determine the existing lower and upper bounds of an array.

Using Arrays

After you've declared an array, you can use it in your code. You access each individual element in the array by using the element's index value. For example, the following code fills a 10-element array with random numbers and then displays the fourth element in the array.

```
Sub RandomArray()
    Dim i As Integer, rnums(10) As Integer

    For i = 1 To 10
        rnums(i) = Int(Rnd() * 6) + 1
    Next
    MsgBox rnums(4)
End Sub
```

Creating Dynamic Arrays

If you don't know how large to make an array, or if you want to be able to change the size of the array at run time, you can use a dynamic array. A dynamic array can be resized at any time. Dynamic arrays are among the most flexible and convenient features in Visual Basic, helping you manage memory efficiently. For example, you can use a large dynamic array for a short time and then free up system memory when you're no longer using the array.

▶ **To create a dynamic array**

1. Declare the array just as you would declare a fixed-size array, but without specifying dimension sizes within the parentheses following the array name. For example:

   ```
   Dim dynArray()
   ```

2. Later in the macro, allocate the actual number of elements with a **ReDim** statement, as in the following example.

   ```
   ReDim dynArray(X + 1)
   ```

The **ReDim** statement can appear only in a procedure. Unlike the **Dim** and **Static** statements, **ReDim** is an executable statement—that is, it makes the application carry out an action at run time. Each **ReDim** statement can change the number of elements, the lower and upper bounds for each dimension, and the number of dimensions in the array.

The following example first declares the dynamic array `ovalLeftCoords`, allocates space in the array based on the number of ovals on Worksheet 1, and fills the array with the left coordinates of the ovals.

```
Sub FillArray()
    Dim ovalLeftCoords() As Integer
    Dim i As Integer, ovalCount As Integer, ovs As Ovals
    Set ovs = Worksheets(1).Ovals
    ovalCount = ovs.Count
    ReDim ovalLeftCoords(ovalCount)
    For i = 1 To ovalCount
        ovalLeftCoords(i) = ovs(i).Left
    Next
End Sub
```

Preserving the Contents of Dynamic Arrays

Each time you use the **ReDim** statement, all the values currently stored in the array are lost. Visual Basic resets the values to the **Empty** value (for **Variant** arrays), to 0 (zero) (for numeric arrays), to a zero-length string (for string arrays), or to **Nothing** (for arrays of objects).

This is useful when you want to prepare the array for new data, or when you want to reduce the size of the array so that it occupies minimal memory. However, sometimes you may want to change the size of the array without losing the data in it. You can do this by using **ReDim** with the **Preserve** keyword. For example, you can enlarge an array by one element without losing the values of the existing elements.

```
ReDim Preserve myArray(UBound(myArray) + 1)
```

The **UBound** function returns the value of the upper bound for the specified dimension of an array. For more information, see "UBound" in Help.

Only the upper bound of the last dimension in a multidimensional array can be changed when you use the **Preserve** keyword; if you change either bound of any of the other dimensions, or the lower bound of the last dimension, a run-time error occurs. Thus, you can do the following:

```
ReDim Preserve matrix(10, UBound(matrix, 2) + 1)
```

But you cannot do this:

```
ReDim Preserve matrix(UBound(matrix, 1) + 1, 10)
```

Creating Multidimensional Arrays

With Visual Basic, you can declare arrays of up to 60 dimensions simply by specifying the size of each dimension within the parentheses following the array name. Separate the sizes of different dimensions with commas. For example, the following statement declares a two-dimensional, 10-by-10 array within a procedure.

```
Static matrixA(10, 10) As Double
```

Either dimension, or both, can be declared with explicit lower bounds.

```
Static matrixA(1 To 10, 1 To 10) As Double
```

You can extend this to more than two dimensions, as in the following example.

```
Dim multiD(4, 1 To 10, 1 To 15)
```

The preceding declaration creates an array with three dimensions, whose sizes are 4, 10, and 15. The total number of elements is the product of these three dimensions, or 600.

Tip When you start adding dimensions to an array, the total storage needed by the array increases dramatically, so use multidimensional arrays with care. Be especially careful with **Variant** arrays, because they're larger than arrays of other data types.

Using Loops to Manipulate Multidimensional Arrays

You can efficiently process a multidimensional array by using nested **For...Next** loops. For example, these statements initialize every element in `matrixA` to a value based on its location in the array.

```
Dim i As Integer, j As Integer
Static matrixA(1 To 10, 1 To 10) As Double
For i = 1 To 10
    For j = 1 To 10
        matrixA(i, j) = I * 10 + J
    Next j
Next i
```

Constants

Often, you'll find that your macro contains constant values that reappear again and again. Or you may find that the macro depends on certain numbers that are difficult to remember—numbers that, in and of themselves, have no obvious meaning.

In these cases, you can greatly improve the readability of your macro—and make it easier to maintain—by using constants. A *constant* is a meaningful name that takes the place of a number or string that doesn't change. Although a constant somewhat resembles a variable, you cannot modify a constant or assign a new value to it as you can do with a variable. There are two sources for constants:

- *Built-in* constants—also called *intrinsic* or *system-defined* constants—are provided by applications. Microsoft Excel constants are listed in the Microsoft Excel object library in the Object Browser. Other applications that provide object libraries, such as Microsoft Access and Microsoft Project, also provide a list of constants you can use with their objects, methods, and properties. For information about using the Object Browser, see Chapter 4, "Objects and Collections."

Intrinsic constant names have a mixed-case format, with a two-character prefix indicating the object library that defines the constant. Constants from the Microsoft Excel object library are prefaced with "xl"—for instance, xlAbsolute. Constants from the data access object library are prefaced with "db"—for instance, dbRelationUnique.

- *Symbolic* constants, or *user-defined* constants, are declared with the **Const** statement. User-defined constants are described in the next section, "Declaring User-Defined Constants."

Tip Use constants when you need to use the same value several times in your macro, or when you want to make your macro more readable by assigning a meaningful name to a value that doesn't change.

Declaring User-Defined Constants

You declare a constant using the **Const** statement. You can specify private or public scope and assign a value to the constant. If you don't specify scope, the constant has private scope by default. When naming constants, you must follow the same rules as when naming variables (for more information, see "Choosing Variable Names" earlier in this chapter).

A constant can represent data of any type, as shown in the following examples.

```
Const conPi = 3.14159265358979
Const conMaxPlanets = 9
Const conReleaseDate = #1/1/95#
Const conCodeName As String = "Enigma"
```

You can place two or more constant declarations on a single line if you separate them with commas.

```
Const conPi = 3.14, conMaxPlanets = 9, _
    conWorldPop = 6000000000#
```

The expression on the right side of the equal sign (=) is often a numeric value or string literal, but it can also be an expression that results in a number or string (although that expression cannot contain calls to functions). You can even define constants in terms of previously defined constants, as in the following example.

```
Const conPi2 = conPi * 2
```

After you've defined a constant, you can place it in your macro to make the macro more readable, as in the following example.

```
Static solarSystem(1 To conMaxPlanets)
If numPeople > conWorldPop Then Exit Sub
```

Specifying Constant Scope

A **Const** statement can specify scope the same way a variable declaration can, and the same rules apply:

- To create a constant that exists only within a procedure, declare it within that procedure, using only the **Const** keyword.

  ```
  Const conPi = 3.14159
  ```

- To create a constant that's available to all procedures within a given module but not to any code outside that module, declare it in the declarations section of the module, using the **Private** keyword before **Const**.

  ```
  Private Const conMax = 4096
  ```

- To create a constant that's available to all modules in all workbooks, declare it in the declarations section of the module, using the **Public** keyword.

  ```
  Public Const conMin = 0
  ```

  As with any other type of data, public constants are available only in the workbook where they're declared and in any workbooks with a reference link to the workbook where they're declared. In addition, you can limit the scope of a public constant to a single workbook by using the **Option Private Module** statement in the module where the constant is declared.

Specifying Constant Data Type

If you don't explicitly specify a data type when you declare a constant, Visual Basic gives the constant the data type that best matches the expression assigned to the constant. You may occasionally want to override a constant's default data type to improve the efficiency or accuracy of your calculations. For example, Visual Basic treats constants containing real numbers with a fractional component as **Double** values by default. If you want to speed up your code execution, you could explicitly declare a constant as **Single**; if you want to avoid rounding errors, you could declare it as **Currency**. You may also need to declare a constant as a particular data type to ensure that the result of a computation has a specific data type.

You declare a data type for a constant the same way you declare a type for a variable, using the **As** keyword.

```
Const conTemp As Currency = 3.45
```

Avoiding Circular References

Because constants can be defined in terms of other constants, you must be careful not to set up a circular reference between two or more constants. A circular reference occurs when you have two or more public constants that are defined in terms of each other, as in the following example.

```
' In Module 1:
Public Const conA = conB * 2

' In Module 2:
Public Const conB = conA / 2
```

Visual Basic generates an error when you attempt to run a macro that contains a circular reference. You cannot run the macro until you resolve the circular reference. To avoid creating a circular reference, restrict all your public constants to a single module or a small number of modules. This way, it will be easier for you to keep track of your constants and catch this kind of mistake.

Data Types

Visual Basic recognizes a number of fundamental data types, such as **Integer**, **Currency**, **String**, and **Boolean**. Each data type takes up a specific amount of memory, allows a specific range of values, and is best suited for storing specific kinds of data. All data must have a type in order for Visual Basic to work with it.

If you don't explicitly declare a type, Visual Basic assigns a default type. For variables, the default type is **Variant**; for constants, it's the data type that most closely matches the value assigned to the constant.

You can improve macro performance in several ways by specifying data types yourself. You can make your code run faster by specifying the exact type of each variable, as Visual Basic won't have to spend time examining each **Variant** variable to detect the exact type of the value stored there. You can save memory, because the specific data types use less memory than the **Variant** type. You can avoid rounding and overflow errors by specifying a data type appropriate to the values you'll be using and the calculations you'll be making. For more information about selecting data types to improve performance, see Chapter 5, "Optimizing for Size and Speed."

The fundamental data types in Visual Basic, including **Variant**, are shown in the following table. For more information about the specific types, see the following sections of this chapter.

Type name	Storage size	Range
Integer	2 bytes	–32,768 to 32,767
Long	4 bytes	–2,147,483,648 to 2,147,483,647
Single	4 bytes	–3.402823E38 to –1.401298E-45 (negative values) 1.401298E-45 to 3.402823E38 (positive values)
Double	8 bytes	–1.79769313486232E308 to –4.94065645841247E–324 (negative values) 4.94065645841247E–324 to 1.79769313486232E308 (positive values)
Currency	8 bytes	–922337203685477.5808 to 922337203685477.5807
String	1 byte per character	0 to approximately 65,500 characters 0 to 2E32 on 32-bit systems
Boolean	2 bytes	**True** or **False**
Date	8 bytes	January 1, 100 to December 31, 9999
Object	4 bytes	Any **Object** reference
Variant	16 bytes + 1 byte for each character	**Null**, **Error**, any numeric value valid for any numeric data type, or any text, object, or array.

Numeric Data Types

If you know that a variable will always contain whole numbers (such as 12) rather than fractional numbers (such as 3.57), declare it as an **Integer** or **Long** type.

```
Private memSize As Long
Dim loopCounter As Integer
```

Operations are faster with **Integer** variables, which consume less memory than **Variant** variables. **Integer** variables are especially useful as the counter variables in **For...Next** loops. For more information about **For...Next** loops and other control structures, see Chapter 3, "Controlling Program Flow."

If a variable will always contain fractional numbers, declare it as a **Single**, **Double**, or **Currency** type.

```
Public radius As Single
Private area As Double
Dim costOfGoods As Currency
```

The **Currency** data type supports up to four digits to the right of the decimal separator and 15 digits to the left of it, making **Currency** an accurate fixed-point data type suitable for monetary calculations. Floating-point (**Single** and **Double**) numbers have much larger ranges than **Currency**, but can be subject to small rounding errors.

Note Floating-point values can be expressed as *mmmEeee* or *mmmDeee*, where *mmm* is the mantissa and *eee* is the exponent (a power of 10). The highest positive value of a **Single** data type is 3.402823E+38, or 3.4 times 10 to the 38th power; the highest positive value of a **Double** data type is 1.79769313486232D+308, or about 1.8 times 10 to the 308th power. Using *D* to separate the mantissa and exponent in a numeric literal causes the value to be treated as a **Double** data type. Likewise, using *E* in the same fashion causes the value to be treated as a **Single** data type.

A variable or constant of any numeric data type (or the **Variant** data type) can contain any numeric data. For example, assigning the value 3.14 to a variable of the **Integer** data type doesn't generate an error, even though 3.14 isn't an integer. Visual Basic rounds off rather than truncates the fractional part of a floating-point number before assigning it to an integer.

A variable with one of the numeric data types is initialized to 0 (zero) after it's declared and before you assign another value to it. When you edit any Visual Basic module, all variables in the workbook that contains that module are reinitialized. Procedure-level variables are reinitialized when the procedure starts running.

The String Data Type

A variable that will always contain a string and never a numeric value can be declared with the **String** data type.

```
Private dataName As String
```

Before you assign data, a string variable contains an empty string (""). You can then assign strings to this variable and manipulate it using string functions. You use string literals in Visual Basic by enclosing the string within double quotation marks.

```
dataName = "Database"
dataName = Left(dataName, 4)
```

By default, a string variable or argument is a *variable-length string*; the string grows or shrinks as you assign new data to it. You can also declare strings that have a fixed length. You specify a *fixed-length string* with the following syntax.

String * *size*

For example, to declare a string that's always 50 characters long, use code such as the following:

```
Dim empName As String * 50
```

If you assign a string of fewer than 50 characters, `empName` is padded with enough trailing spaces to total 50 characters (before any assignment, the variable contains 50 spaces). If you assign a string that's too long for the fixed-length string, Visual Basic truncates the characters, as in the following example.

```
Dim tempString As String * 4, dataName As String

dataName = "Database"
tempString = dataName
MsgBox tempString & " : " & dataName
```

The preceding code produces the following output.

```
Database : Data
```

Because fixed-length strings are padded with trailing spaces, you may find the **Trim**, **LTrim**, and **RTrim** functions useful when working with fixed-length strings. For more information, see "Trim," "LTrim," or "RTrim" in Help.

The Boolean Data Type

A variable that contains a logical value (simple true/false, yes/no, or on/off information) can be declared with the **Boolean** data type. The default value for the **Boolean** type is **False**. In the following example, `creditExceeded` is a **Boolean** variable that stores a yes/no setting.

```
Dim creditExceeded as Boolean

' Ask if the credit limit is exceeded.
If amt > Limit Then creditExceeded = True
```

The Date Data Type

A variable that contains date and time values should be declared with the **Date** data type.

```
Private today As Date
```

You can perform calculations on date/time values. Adding or subtracting integers adds or subtracts whole days; adding or subtracting fractions adds or subtracts fractions of days (expressed in hours and minutes). Thus, adding 20 adds 20 days, and subtracting 1/24 subtracts one hour.

You can use date/time literals in a macro by enclosing them within number signs (#), the same way you enclose string literals within double quotation marks. Visual Basic accepts a wide variety of date and time formats in literals. The following are all valid date/time values.

```
someDate = #3-6-93 13:20#
someDate = #March 27, 1993 1:20am#
someDate = #Apr-2-93#
someDate = #4 April 1993#
```

Date variables are initialized to 12:00:00 A.M. (midnight) on December 30, 1899. If you don't include a time in a date/time literal, Visual Basic sets the time part of the value to midnight (the beginning of the day). If you don't include a date in a date/time literal, Visual Basic sets the date part of the value to December 30, 1899. For more information about the various date/time functions and formats, see "Date" and "date formats" in Help.

The Object Data Type

A variable that contains a reference to an object within Microsoft Excel or within some other application can be declared with the **Object** data type. You can assign an object variable (using the **Set** statement) to represent any actual object recognized by the application.

```
Dim wk As Object
Set wk = Worksheets(1)
```

Object variables are initialized to the special value **Nothing**. You can test for this value using the **Is** function.

```
If wk Is Nothing Then    'object variable not set
```

Whenever possible, declare data as the most specific object type possible. For example, declare a variable that will represent a collection of ovals as **Ovals** instead of **DrawingObjects**; or, in the preceding code , declare the variable that will represent a worksheet as **Worksheet** instead of **Object**. Visual Basic can resolve references to the properties and methods of objects with specific types before you run the application (properties and methods for objects declared with the **Object** type must be resolved at run time; this slows down your macro). Specific object types are listed in the Object Browser.

When working with objects contained in other applications, instead of using the **Variant** type or the generic **Object** type, declare objects as they're listed in the Objects/Modules box in the Object Browser. This ensures that Visual Basic recognizes the specific type of object you're referencing, allowing the reference to be resolved at compile time.

For more information about creating and assigning objects and object variables, see Chapter 4, "Objects and Collections."

The Variant Data Type

The **Variant** data type allows you to store most types of data. You don't have to convert between these data types when assigning them to a **Variant** variable; Visual Basic automatically performs any necessary conversion, as in the following example.

```
Private someValue        ' Variant by default.
someValue = "17"
    ' someValue contains "17" (a two-character string).
someValue = someValue - 15
    ' someValue now contains the numeric value 2.
someValue = "U" & someValue
    ' someValue now contains "U2" (a two-character string).
```

Tip A **Variant** variable isn't a variable with no data type; rather, it's a variable that can freely change its type to accommodate the data stored in the variable. An uninitialized **Variant** variable contains the special **Empty** value. As soon as you assign data to the **Variant** variable, the variable assumes the data type most appropriate for the assigned data.

Storing Values in Variant Variables

The **Variant** data type maintains an internal representation of stored values. This internal representation corresponds to one of the non-variant data types discussed earlier in this chapter, and it determines how Visual Basic treats the stored value when performing comparisons and other operations.

Numeric Values Stored in Variant Variables

When you store numbers in a **Variant** variable, Visual Basic uses the most compact representation possible. For example, if you store a small number without a decimal fraction, the variant uses an **Integer** representation for the value. If you then assign a larger number, Visual Basic uses a **Long** value. If the value is very large or has a fractional component, Visual Basic uses a **Double** value. (Visual Basic automatically uses the **Double** internal representation instead of the **Single** or **Currency** type to store a number with a fractional component in a variant.)

Sometimes you want to use a specific representation for a number. For example, you might want a variant to store a numeric value as **Currency** to avoid round-off errors in later calculations. Visual Basic provides several conversion functions that you can use to convert values into a specific type (see "Converting Data Types" later in this chapter). To convert a value to **Currency**, for example, you use the **CCur** function:

```
payPerWeek = CCur(hours * hourlyPay)
```

An error occurs if you attempt to perform a mathematical operation or function on a **Variant** variable that doesn't contain a number or something that can be interpreted as a number. For example, you cannot perform any arithmetic operations on the value "U2" even though it contains a numeric character, because the entire value isn't a valid number. Likewise, you cannot perform any calculations on the value "1040EZ." However, you can perform calculations on the values "+10" and "–1.7E6" because they're valid numbers. For this reason, you'll often want to determine whether a variant contains a value that can be used as a number. The **IsNumeric** function performs this task, as shown in the following example.

```
Do
    anyNumber = InputBox("Enter a number")
Loop Until IsNumeric(anyNumber)
MsgBox "The square root is: " & Sqr(anyNumber)
```

If you assign a **Variant** variable containing a number to a **String** variable, Visual Basic automatically converts the representation of the number to a string. If you want to explicitly convert a number to a string, use the **CStr** function. You can also use the **Format** function to convert a number to a string that includes formatting such as currency, thousands separator, and decimal separator symbols.

For more information, see "Format" in Help. For information about writing macros for applications that will be distributed in foreign markets, see Appendix A, "Writing Code for International Use."

Strings Stored in Variant Variables

Generally, storing and using strings in **Variant** variables poses few problems. However, the result of the **+** operator can be ambiguous when it's used with two **Variant** values. If both of the **Variant** variables contain numbers, the **+** operator performs addition. If both of the **Variant** variables contain strings, the **+** operator performs string concatenation.

If one of the values is represented as a number and the other is represented as a string, the situation becomes more complicated. Visual Basic first attempts to convert the string into a number. If the conversion is successful, the **+** operator adds the two values; if the conversion is unsuccessful, it generates a "Type mismatch" error message.

To make sure that concatenation occurs, regardless of the representation of the value in the variables, use the & operator, as shown in the following example.

```
Sub StringCat()
    Dim x, y

    x = "6"
    y = "7"
    With Worksheets(1)
        .Range("a1") = x + y     'concatenates values
        .Range("b1") = x & y     'concatenates values
        x = 6
        .Range("a2") = x + y     'adds values
        .Range("b2") = x & y     'concatenates values
    End With
End Sub
```

The preceding example produces the following result on the worksheet:

```
67      67
13      67
```

When you type your code, make sure that you leave a space between any variable name and the & operator. If you don't leave a space, Visual Basic assumes you intended to use the ampersand (&) as the type-declaration character for the variable name. For more information about type-declaration characters, see "type-declaration character" in Help.

Date/Time Values Stored in Variant Variables

Variant variables can also contain date/time values. Several functions return date/time values. For example, the **Now** function returns the current date and time.

In the same way that you can use the **IsNumeric** function to determine whether a **Variant** variable contains a value that can be considered a valid numeric value, you can use the **IsDate** function to determine whether a **Variant** variable contains a value that can be considered a valid date/time value. You can then use the **CDate** function to convert the value into a date/time value. For more information, see "The Date Data Type" earlier in this chapter.

Objects Stored in Variant Variables

Variant variables can contain objects. This can be useful when you need to gracefully handle a variety of data types, including objects. For example, all the elements in an array must have the same data type. Setting the data type of an array to **Variant** allows you to store objects along with other data types in an array.

Errors Stored in Variant Variables

If you create your own error values using the **CVErr** function a store them in variables, those variables must be of the **Variant** typ assigned error values to those **Variant** variables, the variables have the **Erro** subtype (**Error** is a subtype because there is no explicit **Error** data type). In the following example, `myError` is a **Variant** variable of subtype **Error**.

```
Dim myError
myError = CVErr(2010)
```

Even though `myError` is a **Variant** variable, if you use it as an argument to the **TypeName** function, **TypeName** returns "Error," not "Variant." Using the **TypeName** function in this situation tells you whether a variable contains a user-defined error. You can also use the **IsError** function to test for error values.

For more information about user-defined errors, see Chapter 7, "Handling Run-Time Errors," or see "CVErr" or "IsError" in Help.

The Empty Value

A **Variant** variable contains the **Empty** value until it's assigned a value. The **Empty** value is a special value that's different from 0 (zero), a zero-length string (""), or the **Null** value. You can test for the **Empty** value using the **IsEmpty** function.

```
If IsEmpty(z) Then z = 0
```

When a **Variant** variable contains the **Empty** value, you can use it in expressions; it's treated as either 0 (zero) or a zero-length string (""), depending on the expression.

The **Empty** value in a **Variant** variable disappears as soon as any value is assigned to that variable (including the value of 0 (zero), the zero-length string, and the **Null** value). You can set a **Variant** variable back to the **Empty** value by assigning the keyword **Empty** to the **Variant** variable.

```
z = Empty
```

The Null Value

The **Variant** data type can contain one other special value: **Null. Null** is commonly used in database applications to indicate unknown or missing data. Because of the way it's used in databases, **Null** has some unique characteristics:

- Expressions involving **Null** always result in **Null**; **Null** "propagates" through expressions. If any part of an expression evaluates to **Null**, the entire expression evaluates to **Null**.

- Passing **Null**, a **Variant** variable containing **Null**, or an expression that evaluates to **Null** as an argument to most functions causes the function to return **Null**.
- **Null** values propagate through intrinsic functions that return **Variant** data types.

You can also assign **Null** with the **Null** keyword.

```
z = Null
```

You can use the **IsNull** function to test for whether a **Variant** variable contains **Null**.

```
If IsNull(x) And IsNull(y) Then
    z = Null
Else
    z = 0
End If
```

Note Variables aren't set to **Null** unless you explicitly assign **Null** to them, so if you don't use **Null** in your application, you don't have to write code that tests for it and handles it.

For more information about using **Null** in expressions, see "Null" in Help.

Determining the Data Type of a Variant

Most of the time, you don't have to be concerned with what internal representation Visual Basic is using for a particular stored value; Visual Basic handles conversions automatically. If you want to know what representation Visual Basic is using, however, you can use the **TypeName** or **VarType** function. The **TypeName** function returns a string for the data type; the **VarType** function returns a numeric value.

For example, if you store values with decimal fractions in a **Variant** variable, Visual Basic always uses the **Double** internal representation. If you know that your application doesn't need the high degree of accuracy (and slower speed) that a **Double** value entails, you can speed up your calculations by converting the values to **Single**, or even to **Currency**.

```
If TypeName(x) = "Double" Then x = CSng(x) ' Convert to Single.
```

For information about converting data types, see the following section, "Converting Data Types." For more information about the **TypeName** and **VarType** functions, see "TypeName" and "VarType" in Help.

Converting Data Types

Visual Basic provides several conversion functions you can use to convert values into specific data types. To convert a value to **Currency**, for example, you use the **CCur** function.

```
payPerWeek = CCur(hours * hourlyPay)
```

Conversion function	Converts an expression to
CBool	**Boolean**
CCur	**Currency**
CDate	**Date**
CDbl	**Double**
CInt	**Integer**
CLng	**Long**
CSng	**Single**
CStr	**String**
CVar	**Variant**
CVErr	**Error**

For more information, see the specific conversion function in Help.

User-Defined Data Types

You can combine variables of several different data types to create user-defined data types (known as *structures* in the C programming language). A user-defined type is useful when you want to create a single variable that records several related pieces of information. The user-defined type encapsulates the information and makes it easier to process; for example, you can pass the entire structure to a procedure or assign all the values at once by assigning one variable to another if they're both of the same user-defined type.

Tip Because the **Variant** data type can store many different types of data, a **Variant** array can be used in many situations where you might expect to use a user-defined type. A **Variant** array is actually more flexible than a user-defined type because you can change the type of data you store in each element at any time, and you can make the array dynamic so that you can change its size as necessary. However, a **Variant** array always uses more memory than an equivalent user-defined type.

Declaring a User-Defined Data Type

You create a user-defined type using the **Type** statement, which must be placed in the declarations section of a module. User-defined types can be declared as either **Private** or **Public** with the appropriate keyword, as in the following example.

```
Private Type yourDataType
Public Type myDataType
```

For example, you could create a user-defined type that records information about a computer system.

```
Private Type systemInfo
    cpu As Variant
    memory As Long
    videoColors As Integer
    cost As Currency
    purchaseDate As Variant
End Type
```

Declaring Variables That Have a User-Defined Type

You can declare local, private, or public variables of the same user-defined type.

```
Dim mySystem As systemInfo, yourSystem As systemInfo
```

The rules for determining the scope and lifetime of a variable with a user-defined type are identical to those for other types of variables. For more information, see "Specifying Variable Scope and Lifetime" earlier in this chapter.

Note Notice the difference between declaring the user-defined data type (using the **Type** statement) and declaring a variable of the user-defined type (using the **Dim** statement). Declaring the user-defined type simply tells Visual Basic how the data type is structured; declaring a variable actually reserves space for information organized according to the user-defined type. The scope of the **Type** declaration and the scope of the declared variable are completely independent; for example, you can declare a local variable using a data type that has been declared as **Public**.

Using Variables That Have a User-Defined Type

You access an individual variable within a structure by writing the name of the variable that has a user-defined type, followed by a period and the name of the individual variable.

```
mySystem.cpu = "486"
If mySystem.purchaseDate > #1/1/92# Then
```

You can also assign one variable to another if they're both of the same user-defined type. This assigns all the elements of one variable to the same elements in the other variable, as in the following example.

```
yourSystem = mySystem
```

User-Defined Types That Contain Arrays

A user-defined type can contain a static (fixed-size) array, as in the following example.

```
Type systemInfo
    cpu As Variant
    memory As Long
    diskDrives(25) As String      ' Fixed-size array.
    videoColors As Integer
    cost As Currency
    purchaseDate As Variant
End Type
```

It can also contain a dynamic array.

```
Type systemInfo
    cpu As Variant
    memory As Long
    diskDrives() As String        ' Dynamic array.
    videoColors As Integer
    cost As Currency
    purchaseDate As Variant
End Type
```

You can access an array within a user-defined type just as you access any individual variable within the user-defined type, that is, by writing the name of the structured variable that contains the array, followed by a period and then the name of the array. You can then specify an individual element in the array with index numbers, just as you normally access an array member.

```
Dim mySystem As systemInfo
mySystem.diskDrives(0) = "1.44 MB"
```

You can also declare an array of user-defined types.

```
Dim allSystems(100) As systemInfo
```

Follow the same rules to access the components of this data structure.

```
allSystems(5).CPU = "386SX"
allSystems(X).DiskDrives(2) = "100M SCSI"
```

User-Defined Types That Contain Objects

User-defined types can contain objects.

```
Private Type inputData
    wkInput as Worksheet
    rInput as Range
End Type
```

Nesting User-Defined Types

User-defined types can contain other user-defined types, as shown in the following example. To make your macros more readable and easier to debug, try to keep all the code that defines user-defined data types in one module.

```
Type driveInfo
    type As String
    size As Long
End Type

Type systemInfo
    cpu As Variant
    memory As Long
    diskDrives(26) As driveInfo
    cost As Currency
    purchaseDate As Variant
End Type

Dim allSystems(100) As systemInfo
allSystems(1).diskDrives(0).type = "Floppy"
```

CHAPTER 3

Controlling Program Flow

In this chapter, you'll learn about *decision making*—how to write procedures that test conditions and then run only certain statements based on the results of those tests. You'll also learn about *looping*, or running a group of statements several times; and you'll learn about *nesting*, or placing one control structure inside another.

The statements that control decision making and looping in Visual Basic are called *control structures*. Without control structures, a procedure's logic flows through statements from left to right and from top to bottom. Although you can write some very simple procedures with this unidirectional flow, most of the power and flexibility of any programming language comes from its ability to use control structures to change the order in which statements are run.

Contents

Making Decisions

Visual Basic procedures can test conditions and then, depending on the results of that test, perform different operations. Visual Basic decision structures include the following statements.

To test	Use
A single condition and run a single statement or a block of statements	**If...Then**
A single condition and choose between two statement blocks	**If...Then...Else**
More than one condition and run one of several statement blocks	**If...Then...ElseIf**
A single condition and run one of several statement blocks	**Select Case**

If...Then

Use the **If...Then** statement to run one or more statements when a specified condition is **True**. You can use either a single-line syntax or a multiple-line "block" syntax; the following pair of examples illustrates both of these types of syntax.

```
If thisVal < 0 Then thisVal = 0

If thisVal > 5 Then
    thatVal = thisVal + 25
    thisVal = 0
End If
```

Notice that the single-line form of the **If...Then** statement doesn't use an **End If** statement. If you want to run more than one line of code when the condition is **True**, you must use the multiple-line **If...Then...End If** syntax.

Note When the condition you're evaluating contains two expressions joined by an **Or** operator—for example, `If (thisVal > 5 Or thatVal < 9)`—both expressions are tested, even if the first one is **True**. In rare circumstances, this behavior can affect the outcome of the statement; for example, it can cause a run-time error if a variable in the second expression contains an error value.

If...Then...Else

Use the **If...Then...Else** statement to define two blocks of statements; one of them runs when a specified condition is **True**, and the other one runs when the condition is **False**.

```
If age < 16 Then
    MsgBox "You are not old enough for a license."
Else
    MsgBox "You can be tested for a license."
End If
```

If...Then...ElseIf

You can add **ElseIf** statements to test additional conditions without using nested **If...Then** statements, making your code shorter and easier to read. For example, suppose that you need to calculate employee bonuses using bonus rates that vary according to job classification. The following **Function** procedure uses a series of **ElseIf** statements to test the job classification before calculating the bonus.

```
Function Bonus(jobClass, salary, rating)
    If jobClass = 1 Then
        Bonus = salary * 0.1 * rating / 10
    ElseIf jobClass = 2 Then
        Bonus = salary * 0.09 * rating / 10
    ElseIf jobClass = 3 Then
        Bonus = salary * 0.07 * rating / 10
    Else
        Bonus = 0
    End If
End Function
```

The **If...Then...ElseIf** statement block is very flexible. You can start with a simple **If...Then** statement and add **Else** and **ElseIf** clauses as necessary. However, this approach is unnecessarily tedious if each **ElseIf** statement compares the same expression with a different value. For this situation, you can use the **Select Case** statement.

Select Case

You can use the **Select Case** statement instead of multiple **ElseIf** statements in an **If...Then** structure when you want to compare the same expression with several different values. A **Select Case** statement provides a decision-making capability similar to the **If...Then...Else** statement, but it makes code more efficient and readable.

For instance, to add several more job classifications to the example in the preceding section, you can add more **ElseIf** statements, or you can write the function using a **Select Case** statement, as in the following code.

```
Function Bonus(jobClass, salary, rating)
    Select Case jobClass
        Case 1
            Bonus = salary * 0.1 * rating / 10
        Case 2
            Bonus = salary * 0.09 * rating / 10
        Case 3
            Bonus = salary * 0.07 * rating / 10
        Case 4, 5   'The expression list can contain several values...
            Bonus = salary * 0.05 * rating / 5
        Case 6 To 8 '...or be a range of values
            Bonus = 150
        Case Is > 8 '...or be compared to other values
            Bonus = 100
        Case Else
            Bonus = 0
    End Select
End Function
```

Notice that the **Select Case** structure evaluates a single expression at the top of the structure. In contrast, the **If...Then...ElseIf** structure can evaluate a different expression for each **ElseIf** statement. You can replace an **If...Then...ElseIf** structure with a **Select Case** structure only if each **ElseIf** statement evaluates the same expression.

Looping

You can use loop structures to repeatedly run a section of your macro. Visual Basic loop structures include the following statements.

To	Use
Test a condition at the start of the loop, run the loop only if the condition is **True**, and continue until the condition becomes **False**	**Do While...Loop**
Test a condition at the start of the loop, run the loop only if the condition is **False**, and continue until the condition becomes **True**	**Do Until...Loop**
Always run the loop once, test a condition at the end of the loop, continue while the condition is **True**, and stop when the condition becomes **False**	**Do...Loop While**
Always run the loop once, test a condition at the end of the loop, continue while the condition is **False**, and stop when the condition becomes **True**	**Do...Loop Until**

To	Use
Run a loop a set number of times, using a loop counter that starts and ends at specified values and that changes value by a specified amount each time through the loop	**For...Next**
Run a loop once for each object in a collection	**For Each...Next**

Do...Loop

Use a **Do...Loop** statement to run a block of statements an indefinite number of times. There are several variations of the **Do...Loop** statement, but each one evaluates a condition to determine whether or not to continue running. As with an **If...Then** statement, the condition must be a value or an expression that evaluates to **True** or **False**. The different variations are described in this section. For more information about the **Do...Loop** statement, see "Do...Loop" in Help.

Do While...Loop

Use the **Do While...Loop** statement when you want to test a condition before you run the loop and then continue to run the loop while the condition is **True**.

Do While *condition*
    statements
Loop

The statements must eventually cause the condition to become **False**, or the loop will run forever (this is called an *infinite loop*). To stop an infinite loop, press ESC or CTRL+BREAK.

The following **Function** procedure counts the occurrences of a target string within another string by looping as long as the target string is found. Because the test is at the beginning of the loop, the loop runs only if the string contains the target string.

```
Function CountStrings(longstring, target)
    position = 1
    Do While InStr(position, longstring, target) 'Returns True/False
        position = InStr(position, longstring, target) + 1
        Count = Count + 1
    Loop
    CountStrings = Count
End Function
```

Do Until...Loop

Use the **Do Until** statement if you want to test the condition at the beginning of the loop and then run the loop until the test condition becomes **True**. If the condition is initially **True**, the statements inside the loop never run.

Do Until *condition*
    statements
Loop

With the test at the beginning of the loop in the following example, the loop doesn't run if **Response** is equal to **vbNo**.

```
Response = MsgBox("Do you want to process more data?", vbYesNo)
Do Until Response = vbNo
    ProcessUserData 'Call procedure to process data
    Response = MsgBox("Do you want to process more data?", vbYesNo)
Loop
```

Do...Loop While

When you want to make sure that the loop will run at least once, you can put the test at the end of the loop. The statements run as long as the condition is **True**.

Do
    statements
Loop While *condition*

This variation guarantees that your procedure will run the loop at least once.

```
Sub MakeBlue()
    Set rSearch = Worksheets("sheet1").Range("a1:a10")
    Set c = rSearch.Find("test")
    If Not c Is Nothing Then
        first = c.Address
        Do
            c.Font.ColorIndex = 5
            Set c = rSearch.FindNext(c)
        Loop While (Not c Is Nothing) And (c.Address <> first)
    Else
        MsgBox "not found"
    End If
End Sub
```

Do...Loop Until

With the **Loop Until** test at the end of the loop, the loop runs at least once and stops running when the condition becomes **True**.

Do
    statements
Loop Until *condition*

```
Do
    ProcessUserData 'Call procedure to process data
    response = MsgBox("Do you want to process more data?", vbYesNo)
Loop Until response = vbNo
```

For...Next

When you don't know how many times you need to run the statements in a loop, use a **Do** loop. When you know that you must run the statements a specific number of times, use a **For...Next** loop. Unlike a **Do** loop, a **For...Next** loop uses a counter variable that increases or decreases in value during each repetition of the loop. Whereas a **Do** loop ends when a test condition becomes **True** or **False**, a **For...Next** loop ends when the counter variable reaches a specified value.

For example, the following **Sub** procedure sounds a tone however many times you specify.

```
Sub BeepSeveral()
    numBeeps = InputBox("How many beeps?")
    For counter = 1 To numBeeps
        Beep
    Next counter
End Sub
```

Because you didn't specify otherwise, the counter variable in the preceding example increases by 1 each time the loop repeats. You can use the **Step** keyword to specify a different increment for the counter variable (if you specify a negative number, the counter variable decreases by the specified value each time through the loop). In the following **Sub** procedure, which replaces every other value in an array with 0 (zero), the counter variable increases by 2 each time the loop repeats.

```
Sub ClearArray(ByRef ArrayToClear())
    For i = LBound(ArrayToClear) To UBound(ArrayToClear) Step 2
        ArrayToClear(i) = 0
    Next i
End Sub
```

Note The variable name after the **Next** statement is optional, but it can make your code easier to read, especially if you have several nested **For** loops.

For Each...Next

A **For Each...Next** loop is similar to a **For...Next** loop, except that it repeats a group of statements for each element in a collection of objects or in an array, instead of repeating the statements a specified number of times. This is especially useful if you don't know how many elements are in a collection, or if the contents of the collection might change as your procedure runs.

For Each *element* **In** *group*
    statements
Next *element*

When Visual Basic runs a **For Each...Next** loop, it follows these steps:

1. It defines *element* as naming the first element in *group* (provided that there is at least one element).
2. It runs the *statements.*
3. It tests to see whether *element* is the last element in *group.* If so, Visual Basic exits the loop.
4. It defines *element* as naming the next element in *group.*
5. It repeats steps 2 through 4.

Keep the following restrictions in mind when using the **For Each...Next** statement:

- For collections, *element* can only be a **Variant** variable, a generic **Object** variable, or any specific OLE Automation object variable. (For information about OLE Automation objects, see Chapter 10, "Communicating with Other Applications.") For arrays, *element* can only be a **Variant** variable.
- You cannot use the **For Each...Next** statement with an array of user-defined types because a **Variant** variable cannot contain a user-defined type. For more information about data types, see Chapter 2, "Variables, Constants, and Data Types."

The following example examines each cell in the current region for cell A1 on the worksheet named "sheet3" and deletes the cell if its value is less than -1.

```
For Each c In Worksheets("sheet3").Range("a1").CurrentRegion.Cells
    If c.Value < -1 Then c.Delete
Next c
```

For more information about collections and more examples of the **For Each...Next** statement, see Chapter 4, “Objects and Collections.”

Note The variable name after the **Next** statement is optional, but it can make your code easier to read, especially if you have several nested **For** loops.

Nesting Control Structures

As the preceding example demonstrates, you can place control structures inside other control structures (for instance, an **If...Then** block within a **For Each...Next** loop within another **If...Then** block, and so on). A control structure placed inside another control structure is said to be *nested.*

The following example searches the range of cells you specify with an argument and counts the number of cells matching the value you specify.

```
Function CountValues(rangeToSearch, searchValue)
    If TypeName(rangeToSearch) <> "Range" Then
        MsgBox "You can search only a range of cells."
    Else
        For Each c in rangeToSearch.cells
            If c.Value = searchValue Then
                counter = counter + 1
            End If
        Next c
    End If
    CountValues = counter
End Function
```

Notice that the first **End If** statement closes the inner **If...Then** block and that the last **End If** statement closes the outer **If...Then** block. Likewise, in nested **For...Next** and **For Each...Next** loops, the **Next** statements automatically apply to the nearest prior **For** or **For Each** statement. Nested **Do...Loop** structures work in a similar fashion, with the innermost **Loop** statement matching the innermost **Do** statement.

Exiting Loops and Procedures

Usually, your macro will run through loops and procedures from beginning to end. There may be situations, however, when leaving a loop or procedure earlier than normal can save you time by avoiding unnecessary repetition.

For example, if you're searching for a value in an array using a **For...Next** loop and you find the value the first time through the loop, there's no reason to search the rest of the array—you can stop repeating the loop and continue with the rest of the procedure immediately. If an error occurs in a procedure that makes the remainder of the procedure unnecessary, you can leave the procedure immediately. You can cut a control structure off early by using one of the **Exit** statements.

While the **Exit** statements can be convenient, you should use them only where absolutely necessary and only as a response to an extraordinary condition (not in the normal flow of a loop or procedure). Overusing **Exit** statements can make your code difficult to read and debug.

There may be better ways to avoid portions of your macro. For example, instead of using an **Exit** statement inside a **For...Next** loop searching for a value in an array, you could use a **Do** loop to search the array only while an incremented index value is smaller than the array's upper bound and a Boolean variable value is **False**. When you find the array value, setting the Boolean value to **True** causes the loop to stop.

```
i = LBound(searchArray)
ub = UBound(searchArray)
foundIt = False
Do
    If searchArray(i) = findThis Then foundIt = True
    i = i + 1
Loop While i <= ub And Not foundIt
```

You use the **Exit For** statement to exit directly from a **For** loop, and you use the **Exit Do** statement to exit directly from a **Do** loop.

```
For Each c in rangeToSearch
    If c.Value = searchValue Then
        found = True
        Exit For
    End If
Next
```

You use the **Exit Sub** and **Exit Function** statements to exit a procedure.

```
For Each c in rangeToSearch
    If c.Value = searchValue Then
        counter = counter + 1
    ElseIf c.Value = "Bad Data" Then
        countValues = Null
        Exit Function   'Stop testing and exit immediately.
    End If
Next c
```

CHAPTER 4

Objects and Collections

Objects are the fundamental building blocks of Visual Basic; nearly everything you do in Visual Basic involves manipulating objects. Every element in Microsoft Excel—each workbook, worksheet, chart, cell, and so on—can be represented by an object in Visual Basic. By creating procedures that manipulate these objects, you automate tasks in Microsoft Excel.

Contents

Introduction to Objects

An *object* is a special type of variable that contains both data and code and that represents a specific element in Microsoft Excel. Objects exist only in the memory of the computer; they don't appear in the code you write.

Objects have types, just as other kinds of variables have data types. Object types are called *classes*; **Workbook**, **Worksheet**, and **Range** are a few of the Microsoft Excel object classes. When you know an object's class, you can use Help to find the object's properties and methods.

Visual Basic supports a set of objects that correspond directly to elements in Microsoft Excel, most of which you're familiar with from the user interface. For example, the **Workbook** object represents a workbook, the **Worksheet** object represents a worksheet, and the **Range** object represents a range of cells. To perform a task using Visual Basic, you return an object that represents the appropriate Microsoft Excel element and then manipulate it using that object's properties and methods. For example, the following illustration shows how Visual Basic sets the value of a cell, using the **Value** property of the **Range** object.

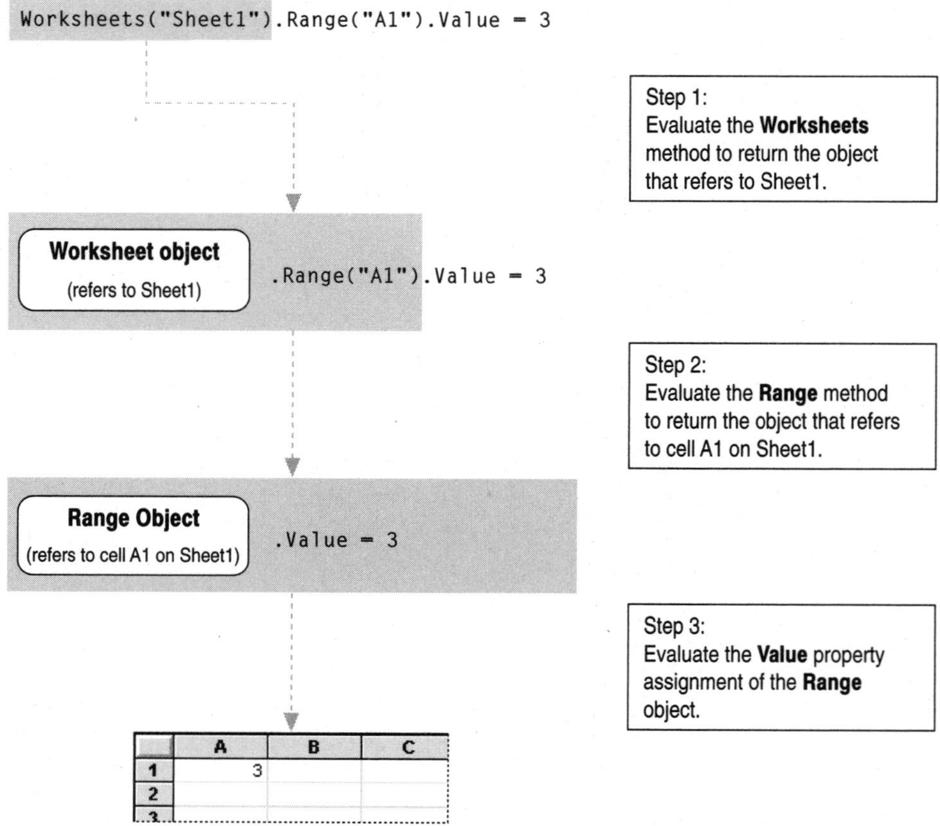

It's important to remember that the **Worksheet** and **Range** objects in this example never appear in the Visual Basic code—they exist only in the memory of the computer. However, the **Worksheets** method and the **Range** method, which return the objects, do appear in the code.

Understanding Collections

A *collection* is an object that contains a group of related objects. For example, the **Worksheets** collection object contains **Worksheet** objects. Each object within a collection is called an *element* of that collection. Because collections are objects, they have properties and methods, just as singular objects do.

In the preceding illustration, the **Worksheets** method returns a **Worksheet** object. The method actually returns one member of the **Worksheets** collection. When you want to work with a single object, you usually return one from a collection. The property or method you use to return the object is called an *accessor*.

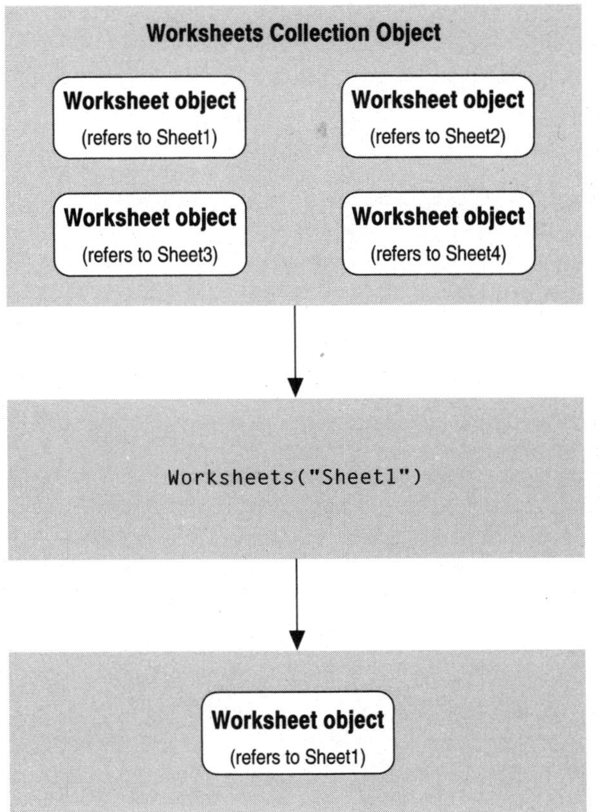

The **Worksheets** method (an accessor) returns a single object from the **Worksheets** collection.

Many accessors take an argument that chooses, or *indexes*, an object in the collection. For example, the **Worksheets** method takes an argument that refers to a single worksheet. The argument can be a worksheet name, or it can be a number that corresponds to the position of the worksheet tabs in a workbook, as shown in the following illustration.

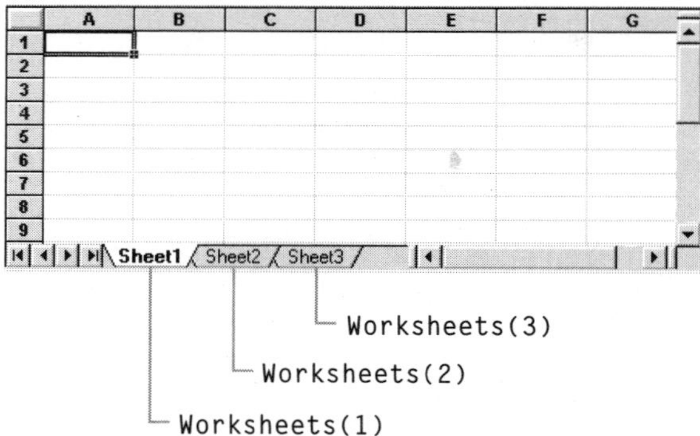

The numeric index always corresponds to the position of the worksheet tab in the workbook. If you rearrange the worksheets, then `Worksheets("Sheet1")` is no longer the same object as `Worksheets(1)`.

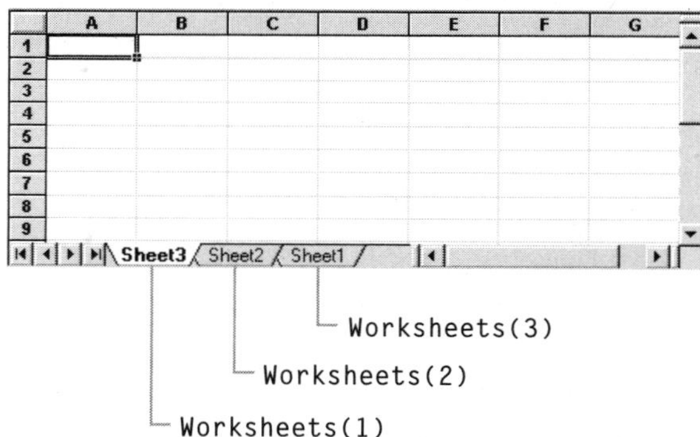

Understanding the Object Hierarchy

Objects can contain other objects, just as elements in Microsoft Excel can contain other elements. For example, a workbook contains worksheets and charts, and a **Workbook** object contains a **Worksheets** collection and a **Charts** collection. This hierarchical arrangement of objects is called the object hierarchy, or the *object model*. For the complete object model, see "Microsoft Excel Object Model" in Help.

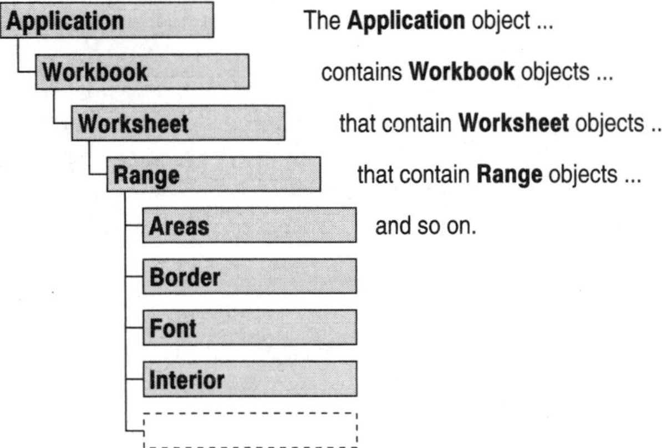
Application
Workbook
Worksheet
Range
Areas
Border
Font
Interior
The **Application** object ...
contains **Workbook** objects ...
that contain **Worksheet** objects ...
that contain **Range** objects ...
and so on.

Building an Expression to Return an Object

There are two ways to build an expression to return an object. The first method is to write the expression from scratch, using Help to navigate the object model. The second method is to use the macro recorder to record an expression and then to modify the expression as necessary.

Building an Expression from Scratch

A few simple rules will help you build expressions from scratch. You can use Help to see the object model and to find the accessors for the objects you want to return. Remember the following guidelines when you build expressions from scratch:

- Many accessors have the same name as the collection they apply to (**Workbooks** collection and **Workbooks** method, for example).
- Each object topic in Help contains a partial view of the object model so that you can locate the object in the hierarchy. The topics also contain information about the accessors, plus sample code showing how to use the object.
- The **Application** property (which returns the **Application** object) is usually optional.
- If you omit the **Workbooks** accessor method, the expression uses the active workbook.
- If you omit the **Worksheets** (or **Sheets**) accessor method as well as the **Workbooks** accessor method, the expression uses the active sheet in the active workbook.

Using the Macro Recorder to Build an Expression

The macro recorder is probably the best way to learn how to build expressions that return objects. The recorder is especially useful when you work with the complex object hierarchies of charts, charts embedded on worksheets, and PivotTables®. Use the macro recorder to build an expression that contains the properties and methods you need, and then modify the expression if necessary.

For example, suppose that you need help building an expression that changes the font style and font size for the title of a chart. You don't remember the object model, so you use the recorder to produce the following code.

```
Sub Macro1()
    ActiveChart.ChartTitle.Select
    With Selection.Font
        .Name = "Times New Roman"
        .FontStyle = "Bold"
        .Size = 24
        .Strikethrough = False
        .Superscript = False
        .Subscript = False
        .OutlineFont = False
        .Shadow = False
        .Underline = xlNone
        .ColorIndex = xlAutomatic
        .Background = xlAutomatic
    End With
End Sub
```

The recorder navigated the object model for you, recording the accessors for the **Chart**, **ChartTitle**, and **Font** objects. You can now modify the recorded code to:

- Change the **ActiveChart** property to the **Charts** method and use a chart name as the argument. This allows you to run the macro from any sheet in the workbook, not just from the chart sheet.
- Remove the selection-based code. You don't need the **Select** method or the **Selection** property. You also need to move the **With** keyword after you make this change.
- Remove the properties of the **Font** object that the macro should not change (it should change only the **FontStyle** property and the **Size** property; it should not change any other property).
- Change the procedure name.

The following example shows the code after modification.

```
Sub FormatChartTitle()
    With Charts("Chart1").ChartTitle.Font
        .FontStyle = "Bold"
        .Size = 24
    End With
End Sub
```

When you record actions on cells and ranges, be sure to record using relative references (on the Tools menu, point to Record Macro, and then click Use Relative References). This ensures that the recorded code contains offsets to cells instead of absolute references to cells, which makes the code more general and more easily adaptable to your specific requirements.

Applying Properties and Methods to an Object

You change attributes of an object by setting its properties. For example, you can set the **Formula** property of the **Range** object that refers to cell A1, which sets the formula in the cell.

You can also get the value of a property. For example, you can get the **Value** property of the **Range** object that refers to cell A1. This returns the value of cell A1 to your code, where you can use the value to make decisions or perform calculations.

Methods perform actions on objects. For example, you can save the active workbook by applying the **SaveAs** method to the **Workbook** object that refers to the active workbook. The difference between properties and methods is that properties have values you set or return, whereas methods are actions you want an object to perform.

Accessors are properties and methods you use to return an object. For example, the **ActiveWorkbook** property returns a **Workbook** object that refers to the active workbook, and the **Range** method returns a **Range** object that refers to a range of cells.

Note In some object-oriented programming languages, distinguishing a property from a method is very straightforward. In Visual Basic, the distinction isn't so clear in some cases. For example, properties generally don't take arguments, but in Microsoft Excel the **International** property does take an argument. Don't worry about whether a keyword is a property or a method; instead, concentrate on finding the correct keyword for the task you want to accomplish.

Setting and Getting Properties

With most properties, you can either set or return their values; these are called read-write properties. With other properties, you can only return their values; these properties are called read-only properties. Each property description in Help tells you whether a property is read-write or read-only.

Setting a Property Value

For an assignment statement to set the value of a property, the expression that contains the property must appear on the left side of the equal sign. For example, to set the **Value** property of the **Range** object that refers to cell A1 on Sheet1, you would write the following code.

```
Worksheets("Sheet1").Range("A1").Value = 3.14159
```

You can also set a property value to another property value, as shown in the following code. This example copies the value from cell B2 on Sheet2 to cell A1 on Sheet1.

```
Worksheets("Sheet1").Range("A1").Value = _
    Worksheets("Sheet2").Range("B2").Value
```

Getting a Property Value

For an assignment statement to get the value of a property, the expression that contains the property must appear on the right side of the equal sign. A variable typically appears on the left side of the equal sign.

For example, the following code gets the **Value** property of the **Range** object that refers to cell A1 on Sheet1 and assigns it to the variable `myValue`.

```
myValue = Worksheets("Sheet1").Range("A1").Value
```

You can also get a property value without assigning the property to a variable. For example, the following code gets the **Value** property of the **Range** object that refers to cell A1 on Sheet1 and then passes this value to the **MsgBox** function.

```
MsgBox Worksheets("Sheet1").Range("A1").Value
```

Using Built-in Constants as Property Values

Many properties have built-in constants as their values. For example, you can set the **HorizontalAlignment** property to **xlCenter**, **xlLeft**, **xlRight**, and so on. The Help topic for any given property contains a list of built-in constants you can use. You should always use the built-in constant, not the value that the constant represents, because the value may change in future versions of Visual Basic.

Using Methods

When you use a method in your procedure, the expression that contains the method can have several different forms. Some methods, such as the **AutoFit** method, take no arguments, whereas other methods take several arguments. These variations are described in the following sections.

Methods That Take No Arguments

To use a method that takes no arguments, build an expression to return the object, and then apply the method. For example, to automatically adjust the column width of columns A through D on Sheet1 to fit the contents of the cells, you could write the following code.

```
Worksheets("Sheet1").Columns("A:D").AutoFit
```

Methods That Take Arguments

When a method takes arguments, the way you write your code depends on whether you want to use the value returned by the method. If you don't want to use the return value of a method, don't enclose the arguments in parentheses. For example, to sort the contents of cells A1:A10 on Sheet1, you could write the following code.

```
Worksheets("Sheet1").Range("A1:A10").Sort _
    Worksheets("Sheet1").Range("A1")
```

In the preceding code, the first argument to the **Sort** method is the expression `Worksheets("Sheet1").Range("A1")`; it isn't enclosed in parentheses because you aren't using the **Sort** method's return value.

On the other hand, if you use the return value, you must enclose the argument in parentheses. Suppose that you use the **CheckSpelling** method to check the spelling of a single word. The word becomes the argument to the method, which returns **True** if the word is spelled correctly or **False** if it isn't. You could write the following procedure.

```
Sub CheckWord()
    returnValue = Application.CheckSpelling("recieve")
    If returnValue = True Then
        MsgBox "The word is spelled correctly"
    Else
        MsgBox "The word is misspelled!"
    End If
End Sub
```

Notice that the argument is enclosed in parentheses. If you run this code, you will get the second message box, because the word is intentionally misspelled.

Using Named Arguments in Methods

Many methods take more than one argument. For example, the **Open** method, which opens a workbook, takes 12 arguments. If you want to write code that opens the workbook BOOK2.XLS, which has the protection password "drowssap", you could write the following code.

```
Workbooks.Open "BOOK2.XLS", , , , "drowssap"
```

However, this code is difficult to write correctly without introducing bugs, because you have to count the number of commas to insert between the arguments. The code is also very difficult to read, and it gives no clues about what the arguments represent. The following example shows a better way to write this code.

```
Workbooks.Open fileName:="BOOK2.XLS", password:="drowssap"
```

Because every argument has a name, you can use the name and the := operator to assign a value to an argument. When you use named arguments, you don't have to remember the order of the arguments. For example, the preceding code could have been written with the order of the arguments reversed.

```
Workbooks.Open password:="drowssap", fileName:="BOOK2.XLS"
```

The preceding section's rules about parentheses apply to named arguments also. For example, the CheckWord procedure could use a named argument for the **CheckSpelling** method, as shown in the following code.

```
Sub CheckWord()
    returnValue = Application.CheckSpelling(word:="recieve")
    If returnValue = True Then
        MsgBox "The word is spelled correctly"
    Else
        MsgBox "The word is misspelled!"
    End If
End Sub
```

Using Built-in Constants as Argument Values

Many methods take built-in constants as their argument values. For example, the **ActivateMicrosoftApp** method takes as its argument values **xlMicrosoftAccess**, **xlMicrosoftWord**, and so on. The Help topic for any given method contains a list of built-in constants you can use for argument values. You should always use the built-in constant, not the value that the constant represents, because the value may change in future versions of Visual Basic.

Using Properties and Methods That Are Unique to Collections

Collections have a **Count** property, an **Add** method, and an **Item** method. This section describes how to use these language elements.

Using the Count Property

The **Count** property returns the number of elements in a collection. For example, the following code uses the **Count** property to display the number of worksheets in the active workbook.

```
Sub NumWorksheets()
    MsgBox "Number of worksheets in this workbook: " & _
        ActiveWorkbook.Worksheets.Count
End Sub
```

The **Count** property is useful when you want to loop on the elements in a collection, although in most cases a **For Each...Next** loop is recommended instead. The following example shows how you can use the **Count** property to loop on the worksheets in the active workbook, hiding every other worksheet.

```
Sub HideEveryOther()
    For i = 1 To Worksheets.Count
        If i Mod 2 = 0 Then
            Worksheets(i).Visible = False
        End If
    Next i
End Sub
```

Using the Add Method

The **Add** method creates a new element in a collection. This results in a new element in Microsoft Excel also. For example, when you use the **Add** method on the **Worksheets** collection, Visual Basic adds a new **Worksheet** object to the collection, and Microsoft Excel adds a new worksheet to the workbook.

The **Add** method takes different arguments, depending on the collection it's applied to. For example, the **Add** method for the **Workbooks** collection takes one argument (***template***), but the **Add** method for the **Worksheets** collection takes four arguments (***before***, ***after***, ***count***, and ***type***). You can find the arguments for the **Add** method in the Object Browser or in Help.

Using the Add Method's Return Value

The **Add** method returns a reference to the new object it creates. If you need to refer to the new object in your code, you should set an object variable to the return value and then use the object variable to refer to the new object.

For example, the first procedure in the following code creates a new worksheet in the active workbook and then hides the worksheet by setting its **Visible** property to the constant **xlVeryHidden**. The public object variable `newSheet` is set to the return value of the **Add** method. The variable `newSheet` can be used by any procedure in any module of the active workbook. Hidden worksheets are an excellent place for a macro to temporarily store numbers and other data, as shown in the other two procedures in the following example.

```
Public newSheet As Object

Sub CreateScratchWorksheet()
    Set newSheet = Worksheets.Add
    newSheet.Visible = xlVeryHidden
End Sub

Sub FillRanges()
    newSheet.Range("F9").Value = "some text"
    newSheet.Range("A1:D4").Formula = "=RAND()"
End Sub

Sub ShowValue()
    MsgBox newSheet.Range("A1").Value
End Sub
```

Using the Item Method

Most of the code you see in this book and in Help uses a shorthand syntax for accessor methods. The following two lines of code, which perform the same action in Microsoft Excel, demonstrate the shorthand syntax.

```
Worksheets("Sheet1").Range("A1").Value = 3       ' shorthand

Worksheets.Item("Sheet1").Range("A1").Value = 3  ' same action
```

You may see the **Item** method used occasionally in other books about Visual Basic. For brevity in code, you can always omit the **Item** method and use the shorthand syntax. The shorthand syntax occurs because the **Item** method is the default method for a collection object.

Using Default Properties and Methods

Many objects in Microsoft Excel have a default property or method. Visual Basic applies the default property or method to a given object to resolve an expression that would not be valid otherwise. For example, the following code would not be valid if the **Range** object did not have a default property, because you cannot set an object equal to a number.

```
Worksheets("Sheet1").Range("A1") = 3
```

Because the **Range** object's default property is the **Value** property, the preceding expression correctly sets the value of cell A1 on Sheet1 to the number 3. The preceding code is equivalent to the following code.

```
Worksheets("Sheet1").Range("A1").Value = 3
```

Although you can use the default property or method to save yourself some typing, this may create code that's difficult to debug and maintain. Using fully qualified expressions instead of using default properties and methods is highly recommended.

Using Microsoft Excel Objects

This section describes some very common programming tasks, such as using object variables, looping on the objects in a collection, and setting multiple properties of an object. This section also describes how to use two of the most common objects in Microsoft Excel—the **Range** and **Workbook** objects.

Using Object Variables

In addition to storing values, a variable can store a reference to an object. You assign an object to a variable for the same reasons you assign any other value to a variable:

- Variable names are often shorter and easier to remember than the values they contain (or, in this case, the objects they refer to).
- Variables can be changed to refer to other objects while your code is running.
- Referring to a variable that contains an object is more efficient than repeatedly referring to the object itself.

Declaring Object Variables

You declare an object variable the same way you declare other types of variables. For example, to declare the object variable `mySheet`, you could write the following code.

```
Dim mySheet As Object
```

This declaration uses the generic **Object** type specifier. Generic object variables are useful when you don't know the specific type of object the variable will contain, or when the variable must at different times contain objects from several different classes. For example, if you set `mySheet` to an object returned from the **Sheets** collection, it could be one of four classes: **Worksheet**, **Chart**, **Module**, or **DialogSheet**.

You can also declare an object variable using a specific class name, as shown in the following code.

```
Dim mySheet As Worksheet
```

In this example, if the code tries to set `mySheet` to an object other than a **Worksheet** object, a run-time error occurs (error 13, "Type mismatch"). You can see this by running the following **Sub** procedure.

```
Sub ListSheetTypes()
    Dim mySheet As Worksheet
    For Each mySheet In ActiveWorkbook.Sheets
        MsgBox TypeName(mySheet)
    Next
End Sub
```

The run-time error occurs when the **For Each...Next** loop tries to set `mySheet` to a member of the **Sheets** collection that's not a **Worksheet** object.

Declaring object variables as specific classes can help you find bugs in your code, because the run-time error indicates that the code is doing something other than what you expected.

Assigning Object Variables

You assign an object to an object variable using the **Set** statement.

Set *variable* = *object*

For example, the following code sets the object variable `myRange` to the object that refers to cell A1 on Sheet1.

```
Set myRange = Worksheets("Sheet1").Range("A1")
```

You must use the **Set** statement whenever you want an object variable to refer to an object. If you forget the **Set** statement, several different errors can occur. For example, if you previously declared the object variable, a run-time error occurs (error 91, "Object variable not set") when you run the following code.

```
Dim myRange As Object
myRange = Worksheets("Sheet1").Range("A1")   ' error 91 occurs here
```

If you haven't previously declared the object variable, it will be a **Variant** variable by default. In this case, if you forget the **Set** statement, Visual Basic attempts to use the default property of the object to assign a value to the variable. For example, the following code causes Visual Basic to use the default property of the **Range** object (which is the **Value** property) to assign `myRange` the value of cell A1.

```
myRange = Worksheets("Sheet1").Range("A1")   ' forgot the Set statement!
```

In this example, no error occurs in the line of code in which you forgot the **Set** statement. However, several different run-time errors can occur later, depending on how your code uses the variable `myRange`. The most common errors in this case will be error 424, "Object required" and error 13, "Type mismatch." When you see either of these errors, check your code for missing **Set** statements.

Looping on a Collection

[illegible]ere are several different ways you can loop on the elements of a collection. [illegible]ever, the recommended method for looping on a collection is to use the [illegible]Each...Next** loop. In this structure, Visual Basic automatically sets an object [illegible]ble to return every object in the collection. The following illustration shows [illegible]ssential components of the **For Each...Next** loop.

– The loop begins with **For Each**.

– The loop automatically sets this object variable to each element in the **Worksheets** collection.

– The **Worksheets** method returns the **Worksheets** collection.

```
[illegible] Each ws In ActiveWorkbook.Worksheets
  MsgBox ws.Name
[illegible] ws
```

– You use the object variable inside the loop.

– The loop ends with **Next**; the object variable (ws) is optional here.

[illegible]ollowing procedure shows how you could use a **For Each...Next** loop to [illegible] every workbook except the workbook that contains the running procedure.

```
[illegible] CloseWorkbooks()
    Dim wb As Workbook
    For Each wb In Application.Workbooks
        If wb.Name <> ThisWorkbook.Name Then
            wb.Close
        End If
    Next wb
[illegible] Sub
```

The **For Each...Next** loop is also the recommended method for looping on a range of cells; for more information, see "Looping on a Range of Cells" later in this chapter. For more information about looping in Visual Basic, see Chapter 3, "Controlling Program Flow."

Performing Multiple Actions on an Object

Procedures often need to perform several different actions on the same object. For example, you might need to set several properties for the same cell. One way to do this is to use several statements, as in the following example.

```
ActiveSheet.Cells(1, 1).Formula = "=SIN(180)"
ActiveSheet.Cells(1, 1).Font.Name = "Arial"
ActiveSheet.Cells(1, 1).Font.Bold = True
ActiveSheet.Cells(1, 1).Font.Size = 8
```

Notice that all these statements use the same object reference. You can make this code easier to enter, easier to read, and more efficient by using the **With...End With** statement.

```
With ActiveSheet.Cells(1, 1)
    .Formula = "=SIN(180)"
    .Font.Name = "Arial"
    .Font.Bold = True
    .Font.Size = 8
End With
```

You can also nest **With...End With** statements. The following example shows how you can rewrite the preceding code using one **With...End With** statement nested inside another one.

```
With ActiveSheet.Cells(1, 1)
    .Formula = "=SIN(180)"
    With .Font
        .Name = "Arial"
        .Bold = True
        .Size = 8
    End With
End With
```

The object reference following the **With...End With** statement can be a reference to either a single object or a collection. The following example sets the font properties of all the text boxes on the active sheet.

```
With ActiveSheet.TextBoxes
    .Font.Name = "Arial"
    .Font.Size = 8
End With
```

Working with the Range Object

The **Range** object can represent a single cell, a range of cells, an entire row or column, a selection containing multiple areas, or a 3-D range. The **Range** object is somewhat unusual in that it can represent both a single cell and multiple cells. There is no separate collection object for the **Range** object; you can think of it as being both a single object and a collection. There are many different properties and methods that return a **Range** object, as shown in the following list.

ActiveCell	**DirectDependents**	**RowFields**
BottomRightCell	**DirectPrecedents**	**RowRange**
Cells	**EntireColumn**	**Rows**
ChangingCells	**EntireRow**	**Selection**
CircularReference	**Next**	**TableRange1**
Columns	**Offset**	**TableRange2**
CurrentArray	**PageRange**	**TopLeftCell**
CurrentRegion	**Precedents**	**UsedRange**
Dependents	**Range**	**VisibleRange**

For more information about these properties and methods, see the individual property and method topics in Help.

Using the Range Method

One of the most common ways to return a **Range** object is to use the **Range** method. The argument to the **Range** method is a string that's either an A1-style reference or the name of a range. The examples in the following table show several different ways to use the **Range** method.

To do this	Use the following code
Set the value of cell A1 on Sheet1	`Worksheets("Sheet1").Range("A1").Value = 3`
Set the formula for cell B1 on the active sheet	`Range("B1").Formula = "=5-10*RAND()"`
Set the value of each cell in the range C1:E3 on the active sheet	`Range("C1:E3").Value = 6`
Clear the contents of the range A1:E3 on the active sheet	`Range("A1", "E3").ClearContents`
Set the font for the range named "myRange" (a workbook-level name) to bold	`Range("myRange").Font.Bold = True`

To do this	Use the following code
Set the value of each cell in the range named "yourRange" (a sheet-level name) to bold	`Range("Sheet1!yourRange").Value = 3`
Set an object variable to refer to a range	`Set objRange = Range("myRange")`

Remember that expressions such as `Range("C1:E3").Value = 6` assume that the **Range** method operates on the active sheet. If you try to run this code from the module that contains it, a run-time error occurs (error 1004, "Range method of Application class failed").

Another cause for errors can be using the **Range** method in an argument to another method, without fully qualifying the **Worksheet** object to which the **Range** method applies. For example, the following code, which is supposed to sort a range of cells on Sheet1, also causes run-time error 1004.

```
Sub SortRange()
Worksheets("Sheet1").Range("A1:B10").Sort _
    key1:=Range("A1"), order1:=xlDescending
End Sub
```

This error is more difficult to find, because the line that contains the **Sort** method is correct. The error is caused by the second line, which contains the ***key1*** argument. This code will run correctly if Sheet1 is the active sheet, but it will fail when it's run from another worksheet or from a module. To correct the error, use the **Worksheets** method in the argument.

```
Sub SortRange()
    Worksheets("Sheet1").Range("A1:B10").Sort _
        key1:=Worksheets("Sheet1").Range("A1"), order1:=xlDescending
End Sub
```

Using the Cells Method

The **Cells** method is similar to the **Range** method except that it takes numeric arguments instead of string arguments. When you use this method to return a single cell, the first argument is the row number of the cell, and the second argument is the column number of the cell. The examples in the following table show several different ways to use the **Cells** method.

To do this	Use the following code
Set the value of cell A1 on Sheet1	`Worksheets("Sheet1").Cells(1, 1).Value = 3`
Set the formula for cell B1 on the active sheet	`Cells(1, 2).Formula = "=5-10*RAND()"`
Set an object variable	`Set objRange = Worksheets("Sheet1").Cells(1, 1)`

The **Cells** method is very useful when you want to refer to cells using loop counters. For example, the following code loops through cells A1:D10 on Sheet1. If any of the cells has a value less than 0.01, the example replaces the value with 0 (zero).

```
Sub RoundToZero()
    For rwIndex = 1 to 4
        For colIndex = 1 to 10
            If Worksheets("Sheet1").Cells(rwIndex, colIndex) < .01 Then
                Worksheets("Sheet1").Cells(rwIndex, colIndex).Value = 0
            End If
        Next colIndex
    Next rwIndex
End Sub
```

The following example shows a quick and easy way to display items in a multicolumn list. The code creates a new worksheet and sets the object variable `newSheet` to refer to the worksheet. The code then creates a list of all the names in the active workbook and shows their formulas in A1-style notation.

```
Sub ListNames()
    Set newSheet = Worksheets.Add
    i = 1
    For Each nm In ActiveWorkbook.Names
        newSheet.Cells(i, 1).Value = nm.Name
        newSheet.Cells(i, 2).Value = "'" & nm.RefersTo
        i = i + 1
    Next nm
    newSheet.Columns("A:B").AutoFit
End Sub
```

Combining the Range and Cells Methods

In some situations, you may need to create a **Range** object based on a top row, a bottom row, a left column, and a right column, given as numbers. You can return **Range** objects by combining the **Range** and **Cells** methods in a single statement. The following code returns a **Range** object that refers to cells A1:D10 on Sheet1. The two **Cells** method calls define cells A1 and D10, and then the **Range** method call returns an object bounded by these two cells.

```
Set myObj = Worksheets("Sheet1").Range(Cells(1, 1), Cells(10, 4))
```

The following code uses a **Range** object that refers to the range bounded by row 1 and column 1 at the upper left and by row 10 and column 6 at the lower right. The range bounds are variables in this example (`rwMin`, `rwMax`, and so on).

```
Sub DemoCells()
    rwMin = 1    ' the top row
    rwMax = 10   ' the bottom row
    colMin = 1   ' the left column
    colMax = 6   ' the right column
    Set TLCell = Worksheets("Sheet1").Cells(rwMin, colMin)
    Set BRCell = Worksheets("Sheet1").Cells(rwMax, colMax)
    Set myRange = Worksheets("Sheet1").Range(TLCell, BRCell)
    myRange.Value = "abc"
End Sub
```

Using the Offset Method

You often need to return a range of cells that's a certain number of rows or columns from another range of cells. The **Offset** method takes an input **Range** object, a ***RowOffset*** argument, and a ***ColumnOffset*** argument to return a new range. For example, the following code determines the type of data in each cell of a range. The code writes the data types in the column to the right of the input cells.

```
Sub ScanColumn()
    For Each c In Worksheets("Sheet1").Range("A1:A10").Cells
        If Application.IsText(c.Value) Then
            c.Offset(0, 1).Formula = "Text"
        ElseIf Application.IsNumber(c.Value) Then
            c.Offset(0, 1).Formula = "Number"
        ElseIf Application.IsLogical(c.Value) Then
            c.Offset(0, 1).Formula = "Boolean"
        ElseIf Application.IsError(c.Value) Then
            c.Offset(0, 1).Formula = "Error"
        ElseIf c.Value = "" Then
            c.Offset(0, 1).Formula = "(blank cell)"
        End If
    Next c
End Sub
```

Using the CurrentRegion and UsedRange Properties

These two properties are very useful when your code operates on ranges whose size you have no control over. The current region is a range of cells bounded by empty rows and empty columns, or by a combination of empty rows, empty columns, and the edges of the worksheet.

The **CurrentRegion** property applies to a **Range** object. There can be many different current regions on a worksheet, depending on the **Range** object to which you apply the **CurrentRegion** property.

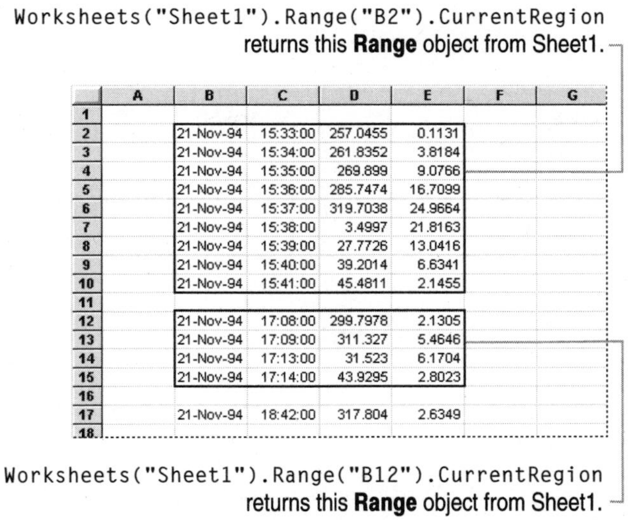

`Worksheets("Sheet1").Range("B2").CurrentRegion`
returns this **Range** object from Sheet1.

	A	B	C	D	E	F	G
1							
2		21-Nov-94	15:33:00	257.0455	0.1131		
3		21-Nov-94	15:34:00	261.8352	3.8184		
4		21-Nov-94	15:35:00	269.899	9.0766		
5		21-Nov-94	15:36:00	285.7474	16.7099		
6		21-Nov-94	15:37:00	319.7038	24.9664		
7		21-Nov-94	15:38:00	3.4997	21.8163		
8		21-Nov-94	15:39:00	27.7726	13.0416		
9		21-Nov-94	15:40:00	39.2014	6.6341		
10		21-Nov-94	15:41:00	45.4811	2.1455		
11							
12		21-Nov-94	17:08:00	299.7978	2.1305		
13		21-Nov-94	17:09:00	311.327	5.4646		
14		21-Nov-94	17:13:00	31.523	6.1704		
15		21-Nov-94	17:14:00	43.9295	2.8023		
16							
17		21-Nov-94	18:42:00	317.804	2.6349		
18							

`Worksheets("Sheet1").Range("B12").CurrentRegion`
returns this **Range** object from Sheet1.

Suppose that Sheet1 contains a list to which you want to apply a number format. The only thing you know about the list is that it begins at cell A1—you don't know how many rows or columns it contains. The following code shows how to format the list using the **CurrentRegion** property.

```
Sub FormatRange()
    Set myRange = Worksheets("Sheet1").Range("A1").CurrentRegion
    myRange.NumberFormat = "0.0"
End Sub
```

The used range is bounded by the upper-left and lower-right nonempty cells on a worksheet. It's a range that contains every nonempty cell on the worksheet, as well as all the empty cells that are interspersed among them. There can be only one used range on a worksheet; the **UsedRange** property applies to a **Worksheet** object, not to a **Range** object.

`Worksheets("Sheet1").UsedRange` returns this **Range** object from Sheet1.

	A	B	C	D	E	F	G
1							
2		21-Nov-94	15:33:00	257.0455	0.1131		
3		21-Nov-94	15:34:00	261.8352	3.8184		
4		21-Nov-94	15:35:00	269.899	9.0766		
5		21-Nov-94	15:36:00	285.7474	16.7099		
6		21-Nov-94	15:37:00	319.7038	24.9664		
7		21-Nov-94	15:38:00	3.4997	21.8163		
8		21-Nov-94	15:39:00	27.7726	13.0416		
9		21-Nov-94	15:40:00	39.2014	6.6341		
10		21-Nov-94	15:41:00	45.4811	2.1455		
11							
12		21-Nov-94	17:08:00	299.7978	2.1305		
13		21-Nov-94	17:09:00	311.327	5.4646		
14		21-Nov-94	17:13:00	31.523	6.1704		
15		21-Nov-94	17:14:00	43.9295	2.8023		
16							
17		21-Nov-94	18:42:00	317.804	2.6349		
18							

Suppose that the active worksheet contains data from a timed experiment. The used range contains the dates in the first column, the times in the second column, and the measurements in the third and fourth columns. You want to write code that combines each separate date and time into a single value, converts that value from Greenwich Mean Time (GMT) to Pacific Standard Time, and then applies a date format. The raw data appears as in the following example.

	A	B	C	D	E	F
1						
2		9-Feb-95	13:26:00	168.9019	12.2089	
3		9-Feb-95	13:27:00	158.9633	6.9121	
4		9-Feb-95	13:28:00	152.7701	2.7073	
5						
6		10-Feb-95	12:31:00	135.5225	2.7125	
7						
8		10-Feb-95	14:04:00	200.4457	3.9705	
9		10-Feb-95	14:05:00	189.9157	1.6707	
10						
11						
12						

Notice that the table can contain empty rows and columns. You can use the **UsedRange** property to return the entire used range, including the two embedded blank rows. The following code shows one way to convert and format the dates and times.

```
Sub ConvertDates()
    Set myRange = ActiveSheet.UsedRange
    myRange.Columns("C").Insert
    Set dateCol = myRange.Columns("C")
    For Each c In dateCol.Cells
        If c.Offset(0, -1).Value <> "" Then
            c.FormulaR1C1 = "=RC[-2]+RC[-1]-(8/24)"
        End If
    Next c
    dateCol.NumberFormat = "mmm-dd-yyyy hh:mm"
    dateCol.Copy
    dateCol.PasteSpecial Paste:=xlValues
    myRange.Columns("A:B").Delete
    dateCol.AutoFit
End Sub
```

The formatted worksheet appears as in the following example.

	A	B	C	D	E	F
1						
2		Feb-09-1995 05:26	168.9019	12.2089		
3		Feb-09-1995 05:27	158.9633	6.9121		
4		Feb-09-1995 05:28	152.7701	2.7073		
5						
6		Feb-10-1995 04:31	135.5225	2.7125		
7						
8		Feb-10-1995 06:04	200.4457	3.9705		
9		Feb-10-1995 06:05	189.9157	1.6707		
10						
11						
12						

Notice that the code uses the expression `ActiveSheet.UsedRange.Columns("C")` to return the third column from the used range (although this is the third column in the used range, it appears in column D on the worksheet because column A is empty). You can use other **Range** object properties and methods in a similar way to build complex expressions that return sub-ranges or super-ranges of an input **Range** object. Some properties and methods commonly used in this way are **Areas**, **Cells**, **Columns**, **EntireColumn**, **EntireRow**, **Range**, and **Rows**.

Looping on a Range of Cells

There are several different ways to loop on the cells in a range. This section shows examples of the **For Each...Next** statement and the **Do...Loop** statement applied to looping on a range of cells.

Using For Each...Next

The recommended way to loop on the cells in a range is to use the **For Each...Next** loop, which is also the recommended way to loop on the elements in a collection.

The following example shows how to loop through the range A1:D10 on Sheet1, setting any number whose absolute value is less than 0.01 to 0 (zero).

```
Sub RoundToZero()
    For Each r In Worksheets("Sheet1").Range("A1:D10").Cells
        If Abs(r.Value) < 0.01 Then
            r.Value = 0
        End If
    Next r
End Sub
```

Suppose that you want to modify this code to loop over a range of cells that a user selects. One way of doing this is to use the **InputBox** method to prompt the user to select a range of cells. The **InputBox** method returns a **Range** object that represents the selection. By using the ***type*** argument and error handling, you can ensure that the user selects a valid range of cells before the input box is dismissed.

```
Sub RoundToZero()
    Worksheets("Sheet1").Activate
    On Error GoTo PressedCancel
    Set r = Application.InputBox( _
            prompt:="Select a range of cells", _
            Type:=8)
    On Error GoTo 0
    For Each c In r.Cells
        If Abs(c.Value) < 0.01 Then
            c.Value = 0
        End If
    Next c
    Exit Sub

PressedCancel:
    Resume
End Sub
```

If you don't want the user to select the range, you may be able to use the **CurrentRegion** property or the **UsedRange** property to return a **Range** object. For example, if you know that the data on Sheet1 begins at cell A1 and has no empty rows or columns, you can use the **CurrentRegion** property to return the entire range automatically.

```
Sub RoundToZero()
    Set r = Worksheets("Sheet1").Range("A1").CurrentRegion
    For Each c In r.Cells
        If Abs(c.Value) < 0.01 Then
            c.Value = 0
        End If
    Next c
End Sub
```

The following two examples show two different ways to hide every other column in the used range on Sheet1. The first example shows a **For Each...Next** loop in which the **Column** property of the object variable is tested.

```
Sub HideColumns()
    Set r = Worksheets("Sheet1").UsedRange
    For Each col In r.Columns
        If col.Column Mod 2 = 0 Then
            col.Hidden = True
        End If
    Next col
End Sub
```

The second example shows a **For Each...Next** loop using a loop counter in which the loop counter is tested.

```
Sub HideColumns()
    Set r = Worksheets("Sheet1").UsedRange
    For i = 1 To r.Columns.Count
        If i Mod 2 = 0 Then
            r.Columns(i).Hidden = True
        End If
    Next i
End Sub
```

Using Do...Loop

Occasionally, the **For Each...Next** loop isn't the best way to loop on a range. Suppose that you have a column of data and you want to write a macro that sorts the data and then deletes rows that contain duplicate data. You could try to use a **For Each...Next** loop, as shown in the following code.

```
Sub BuggyRemoveDuplicates()    ' DON'T USE THIS CODE!
    Worksheets("Sheet1").Range("A1").Sort _
        key1:=Worksheets("Sheet1").Range("A1")
    Set r = Worksheets("Sheet1").Range("A1").CurrentRegion.Columns("A")
    For Each c In r.Cells
        If c.Offset(1, 0).Value = c.Value Then
            c.Offset(1, 0).EntireRow.Delete
        End If
    Next c
End Sub
```

Unfortunately, this code doesn't work correctly because the **Delete** method is modifying the range over which the **For Each...Next** loop is iterating. This causes duplicates not to be deleted in some cases.

A better solution is to use a **Do...Loop** structure, as shown in the following code.

```
Sub GoodRemoveDuplicates()
    Worksheets("Sheet1").Range("A1").Sort _
            key1:=Worksheets("Sheet1").Range("A1")
    Set currentCell = Worksheets("Sheet1").Range("A1")
    Do While Not IsEmpty(currentCell)
        Set nextCell = currentCell.Offset(1, 0)
        If nextCell.Value = currentCell.Value Then
            currentCell.EntireRow.Delete
        End If
        Set currentCell = nextCell
    Loop
End Sub
```

The loop tests the object variable `currentCell`, exiting when it encounters an empty cell at the bottom of the column of data. You could build an equivalent loop by testing the value in `currentCell` against an empty string, as shown in the following code.

```
    Do While currentCell.Value <> ""
        ' code here
    Loop
```

In either case, don't forget to increment the cell (`Set currentCell = nextCell`, for example) at the bottom of the **Do...Loop** structure.

Using the Address Property to Debug Range Object Code

You can apply the **Address** property to any **Range** object. The **Address** property returns the cell address of a range, as a string. The following example shows how to use the **Address** property to debug the HideColumns code.

```
Sub HideColumns()
    Set r = Worksheets("Sheet1").UsedRange
    MsgBox r.Address  ' debugging only!
    For i = 1 To r.Columns.Count
        If i Mod 2 = 0 Then
            r.Columns(i).Hidden = True
            MsgBox r.Columns(i).Address  ' debugging only!
        End If
    Next i
End Sub
```

You can also set watch expressions instead of using message boxes. For the preceding example, you could set two watch expressions—`r.Address` and `r.Columns(i).Address`—and then examine the values of the watch expressions in the Immediate pane of the Debug window. For more information about debugging, see Chapter 6, "Debugging."

Working with the Workbook Object

When you open or save a file in Microsoft Excel, you're actually opening and saving a workbook. In Visual Basic, the methods for manipulating files are methods of the **Workbook** object or its collection.

Opening Workbooks

When you open a workbook, you use the **Open** method. The **Open** method always applies to the **Workbooks** collection, which you return using the **Workbooks** method. The following code opens the file BOOK1.XLS (in the current folder) and then displays the value that's in cell A1 of the first worksheet in the workbook.

```
Sub OpenBook1()
    Set myBook = Workbooks.Open(Filename:="BOOK1.XLS")
    MsgBox myBook.Worksheets(1).Range("A1").Value
End Sub
```

Notice that the return value of the **Open** method is a **Workbook** object that refers to the workbook that was just opened.

The filename in this example doesn't contain a path; therefore, the file is assumed to be in the current folder. This is guaranteed to cause a run-time error, because as soon as the user changes the current folder, Visual Basic can no longer find the file.

There are two relatively safe places to store a workbook you want to open programmatically. One place is the folder that contains the executable file for Microsoft Excel. The other place is the Library folder, which is created automatically during setup; this folder is one level down from the folder that contains the executable file.

If you want to open a workbook that's saved in the folder that contains the executable file, you can use the **Path** property to return a string that specifies the folder. The **PathSeparator** property returns the correct separator character for the current file system (for example, "\" for MS-DOS®/Windows® FAT or ":" for the Macintosh®). The following example shows file-system-independent code you can use to open BOOK1.XLS, assuming that BOOK1.XLS is saved in the executable file's folder.

```
Sub OpenBook1()
    EXEPath = Application.Path & Application.PathSeparator
    fName = EXEPath & "BOOK1.XLS"
    Set myBook = Workbooks.Open(Filename:=fName)
    MsgBox myBook.Worksheets(1).Range("A1").Value
End Sub
```

The other relatively safe place to store a workbook is in the Library folder. You can use the **LibraryPath** property instead of the **Path** property to return a string that specifies the Library folder. The following code shows how you would alter the preceding example to use the **LibraryPath** property.

```
Sub OpenBook1()
    LibPath = Application.LibraryPath & Application.PathSeparator
    fName = LibPath & "BOOK1.XLS"
    Set myBook = Workbooks.Open(Filename:=fName)
    MsgBox myBook.Worksheets(1).Range("A1").Value
End Sub
```

Instead of hard-coding a filename in the **Open** method, you may want to allow a user to select a file to open. The **GetOpenFilename** method displays the standard Open dialog box, but it returns a string instead of opening a file. The string contains the fully qualified path and filename. The following example demonstrates the **GetOpenFilename** method by displaying the return value in a message box and then opening the file.

```
Sub DemoGetOpenFilename()
    Do
        fName = Application.GetOpenFilename
    Loop Until fName <> False
    MsgBox "Opening " & fName
    Set myBook = Workbooks.Open(Filename:=fName)
End Sub
```

Creating and Saving Workbooks

You create a new workbook by applying the **Add** method to the **Workbooks** collection. Remember to set the return value of the **Add** method to an object variable so that you can refer to the new workbook in your code.

When you save a new workbook for the first time, use the **SaveAs** method. For subsequent saves, use the **Save** method. The **GetSaveAsFilename** method is very similar to the **GetOpenFilename** method described in the preceding section. The following code shows how to create a new workbook and then save it using the **GetSaveAsFilename** method.

```
Sub CreateAndSave()
    Set newBook = Workbooks.Add
    Do
        fName = Application.GetSaveAsFilename
    Loop Until fName <> False
    newBook.SaveAs Filename:=fName
End Sub
```

Closing Workbooks

To close a workbook, use the **Close** method of the **Workbook** object. You can close a workbook without saving changes, as shown in the following code.

```
Sub OpenChangeClose()
    Do
        fName = Application.GetOpenFilename
    Loop Until fName <> False
    Set myBook = Workbooks.Open(Filename:=fName)
    '
    ' make some changes to myBook
    '
    myBook.Close savechanges:=False
End Sub
```

This code uses the **GetOpenFilename** method to select the workbook to open, makes some changes to the workbook (indicated by the comments), and then closes the workbook without saving the changes.

When to Use the ThisWorkbook Property

Suppose that you're developing a small application using Visual Basic and that you want to save the workbook as a Microsoft Excel add-in when you finish. The macro contains a custom dialog box, Dialog1, and you display the dialog sheet using the following code.

```
Public DlgValue

Sub DisplayDialog()
    DlgValue = DialogSheets("Dialog1").Show
End Sub
```

You finish writing and debugging the application, and then you click Make Add-In on the Tools menu, creating an add-in named MYADDIN.XLA. However, when your add-in runs the DisplayDialog procedure, a run-time error occurs (error 1004, "DialogSheets method of Application class failed"). What happened?

In the DisplayDialog procedure, the **DialogSheets** method applies to the active workbook because you omitted the object qualifier. However, the active workbook isn't MYADDIN.XLA; it's whichever workbook is displayed by Microsoft Excel. You could try the following fix.

```
DlgValue = Workbooks("MYADDIN.XLA").DialogSheets("Dialog1").Show
```

This introduces the potential for more bugs, however, because the filename is hard-coded and must be in the current folder. You could use the folder management techniques described in "Opening Workbooks" earlier in this chapter, but there is a much safer and more robust way to fix this bug.

The **ThisWorkbook** property returns a **Workbook** object that refers to the workbook containing the code that's running. Therefore, you should use **ThisWorkbook** whenever you write code you intend to save as an add-in. The following example shows the robust code for the DisplayDialog procedure.

```
Public DlgValue

Sub DisplayDialog()
    DlgValue = ThisWorkbook.DialogSheets("Dialog1").Show
End Sub
```

Using the Object Browser

While writing your Visual Basic procedures, you might want to see what objects are available in the active workbook, including the names of procedures you've already written. You can look at this information using the Object Browser.

The Object Browser performs three important functions:

- It gives you a quick way to navigate in your code.
- It shows you what objects are available for your procedures, including the properties and methods of those objects.
- It gives you a way to paste code templates into a module. You can edit the pasted code to make writing procedures faster and less prone to typing errors.

▶ To display the Object Browser

- On the View menu, click Object Browser.

Object Browser button

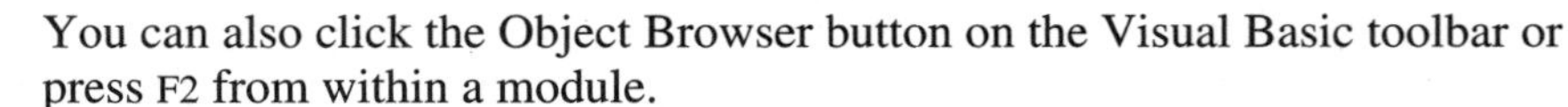

You can also click the Object Browser button on the Visual Basic toolbar or press F2 from within a module.

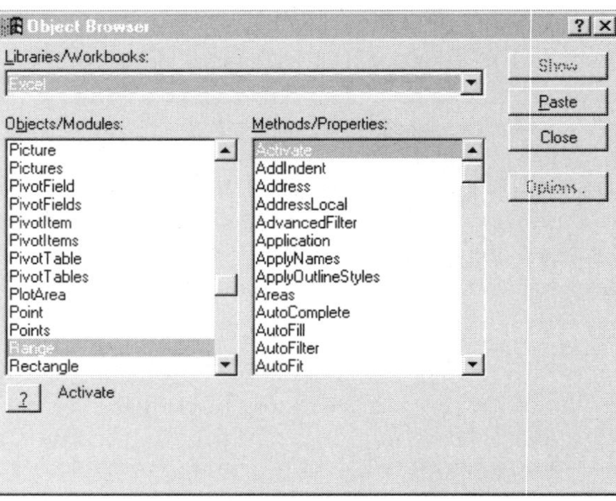

What Appears in the Object Browser

The Object Browser dialog box displays either of two sets of information:

- The names of all the objects in a library, in addition to all the properties and methods of each object
- The names of all the Visual Basic modules in a workbook, in addition to the names of all the procedures in each module

The Object Browser contains a box that lists the names of all the *object libraries* and all the workbooks referenced by the workbook that contains the module you're creating. An object library is a file or a part of an application that provides Visual Basic with information about objects. Libraries and workbooks identify the objects you can use in your procedures. For more information about references to libraries and workbooks, see "Creating a Reference to a Workbook" in Chapter 1.

The list in the Libraries/Workbooks box includes:

- Microsoft Excel, which provides a library of objects specific to Microsoft Excel
- VBA (Visual Basic for applications), which provides functions and other language features you can use in Microsoft Excel
- The open workbook, which contains your code
- Any other libraries referenced by the code in your workbook

Below the Libraries/Workbooks box is the Objects/Modules box. The contents of this box depend on whether the selection in the Libraries/Workbooks box is an object library name or a workbook name, as described in the following table.

If the Libraries/Workbooks box shows	The Objects/Modules box shows
The name of an object library	The available objects in the library, or the categories of available functions
The name of a workbook	The names of all the modules in the workbook

To the right of the Objects/Modules box is the Methods/Properties box. The contents of this box depend on whether the items listed in the Objects/Modules box are the objects in a library or the modules in a workbook, as described in the following table.

If the Objects/Modules box shows	The Methods/Properties box shows
The objects in an object library	The properties and methods of each object in the library
The modules in a workbook	The names of the procedures in each module, including property procedures

Moving Between Procedures

You can use the Object Browser to move quickly from one procedure in a workbook to another.

▶ **To move to a procedure in a workbook**

1. Switch to a Visual Basic module.
2. On the View menu, click Object Browser.
3. In the Libraries/Workbooks box, click the name of the workbook that contains the procedure you want to use.
4. In the Objects/Modules box, click the name of the module that contains the procedure you want.
5. In the Methods/Properties box, click the name of the procedure.
6. Click Show.

The Object Browser moves you to the module that contains the procedure you selected. The insertion point appears to the left of the line immediately following the procedure declaration line.

Browsing Objects

You can also use the Object Browser to see:

- The objects available in the libraries referenced by your workbook.
- The properties and methods of those objects.

▶ **To find the properties and methods of objects**

1. On the View menu, click Object Browser.
2. In the Libraries/Workbooks box, click the name of the object library you want to browse or that contains the object you want to use.
3. In the Objects/Modules box, click the name of the object for which you want to see properties and methods.

Pasting Code

When you finish using the Object Browser to find an object with a property or method you want to use, you can paste a fragment of Visual Basic code from that property or method into your procedure. You can then edit the code fragment to fit the needs of your procedure. The Object Browser pastes the code fragment at the insertion point in the active module.

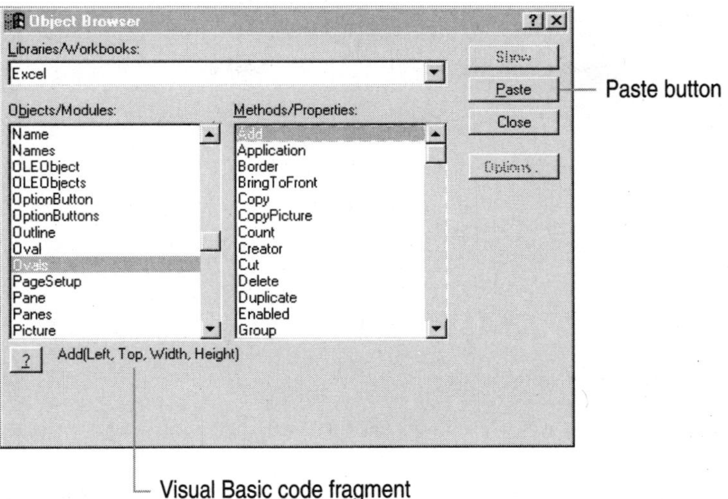

The code fragment includes syntax for named arguments when appropriate. After you paste the code fragment into your procedure, you can delete any arguments you don't need and then add the appropriate values for the arguments you want to use.

▶ To paste a code fragment into a procedure

1. In a Visual Basic module, place the insertion point at the location in the code where you want to paste the code fragment.
2. On the View menu, click Object Browser.
3. In the appropriate boxes, click the library and the object whose property or method you want to use.
4. In the Methods/Properties box, click the property or method you want to paste into the procedure.
5. Click Paste.

CHAPTER 5

Optimizing for Size and Speed

Visual Basic is an extremely flexible programming language: there are often several ways to accomplish the same task. When you first start to program, or when you write a macro that will run only once, you'll probably be satisfied with simply "getting the job done." When you write a macro that will be used many times—such as a macro that prepares a weekly report, or an Auto_Open macro that runs every time you open a workbook—or when you write a macro that will be used by other people, you'll probably want to *optimize* the macro so that it requires less time and memory to run. The techniques described in this chapter will help you write smaller, faster macros.

Contents

For information about accessing external data, see Chapter 13, "Accessing External Data."

Minimizing OLE References

Every Visual Basic method or property call requires one or more calls through the OLE IDispatch interface. These OLE calls take time. Minimizing the number of method or property calls is one of the best ways to make your macro run faster.

Using Object Variables

If you find that you're using the same object reference many times, you can set a variable for the object and subsequently use the variable in place of the object reference. This way, you'll only need to call the object accessor once, when you set the variable, instead of calling it each time you want to refer to the object. The following example calls the **Workbooks** method and the **Sheets** method twice each.

```
Workbooks(1).Sheets(1).Range("c5").Value = 10
Workbooks(1).Sheets(1).Range("d10").Value = 12
```

You can optimize this example by setting an object variable. The following example calls the **Workbooks** method and the **Sheets** method only once each.

```
Set sheet = Workbooks(1).Sheets(1)
sheet.Range("c5").Value = 10
sheet.Range("d10").Value = 12
```

Using the With Statement

You can use the **With** statement to eliminate the need for repetitive object references, without setting an explicit object variable. The example in the preceding section could be rewritten as follows, using the **With** statement. This example calls the **Workbooks** method and the **Sheets** method only once each.

```
With Workbooks(1).Sheets(1)
    .Range("c5").Value = 10
    .Range("d10").Value = 12
End With
```

Using the **With** statement eliminates the need for the intermediate variable used in the example in the preceding section; otherwise, this code is the same as in that example.

Using a For Each...Next Loop

Using a **For Each...Next** loop to iterate through a collection or array is faster than using an indexed loop. In most cases, using a **For Each...Next** loop is also more convenient and makes your macro smaller and easier to read and debug.

The following code is slow because it sets the row variable `thisRow` by calling **r.Rows(i)** each time through the loop.

```
Set r = Worksheets(1).Range("a1:a200")
For i = 1 To r.Rows.Count
    Set thisRow = r.Rows(i)
    If thisRow.Cells(1, 1).Value < 0 Then
        thisRow.Font.Color = RGB(255, 0, 0)
    End If
Next
```

The following code is faster and smaller because the **For Each...Next** loop keeps track of the row count and position.

```
For Each thisRow In Worksheets(1).Range("a1:a200").Rows
    If thisRow.Cells(1, 1).Value < 0 Then
        thisRow.Font.Color = RGB(255, 0, 0)
    End If
Next
```

For information about object variables, the **With** statement, and **For Each...Next** loops, see Chapter 3, "Controlling Program Flow," and Chapter 4, "Objects and Collections."

Keeping Properties and Methods Outside Loops

Your code can get variable values faster than it can get property values. Therefore, if your code gets the value of a property within a loop, it will run faster if you assign the property to a variable outside the loop and use the variable instead of the property inside the loop. The following example is slow because it gets the **Value** property each time through the loop.

```
For iLoop = 2 To 200
    Cells(iLoop, 1).Value = Cells(1, 1).Value
Next I
```

The following example is faster because the value of one property has been assigned to the variable `cv` before the loop begins. Visual Basic must therefore access only one property value, instead of two, each time through the loop.

```
cv = Cells(1, 1).Value
For iLoop = 2 To 200
    Cells(iLoop, 1).Value = cv
Next i
```

If you're using an object accessor inside a loop, try to move it outside the loop. The following example calls the **ActiveWorkbook** property, the **Sheets** method, and the **Cells** method each time through the loop.

```
For c = 1 To 1000
    ActiveWorkbook.Sheets(1).Cells(c, 1) = c
Next
```

Rewriting this example using the **With** statement moves the **ActiveWorkbook** property and **Sheets** method calls outside the loop. You could also move these calls outside the loop using an object variable.

```
With ActiveWorkbook.Sheets(1)
    For c = 1 To 1000
        .Cells(c, 1) = c
    Next
End With
```

Using Arrays to Specify Multiple Objects

Some of the methods that operate on objects in collections allow you to specify an array when you want to operate on a subset of objects in a collection. The following example calls the **Worksheets** method and the **Delete** method three times each.

```
Worksheets("sheet1").Delete
Worksheets("sheet2").Delete
Worksheets("sheet4").Delete
```

You can use an array to reduce this to one **Worksheets** method call and one **Delete** method call.

```
Worksheets(Array("sheet1", "sheet2", "sheet4")).Delete
```

Using Collection Index Numbers

Most object accessor methods allow you to specify an individual object in a collection either by name or by number. Using the object's index number is usually faster. If you use the object's name, Visual Basic must resolve the name to the index value; if you use the index value, you avoid this extra step.

There are, however, some significant advantages to specifying an object in a collection by name. One advantage is that using an object's name makes your code easier to read and debug. In addition, specifying an object by name is safer than specifying it by index number, because the index value for an object can change while your code is running. For example, a menu's index number represents the menu's position on the menu bar; therefore, the index number can change if menus are added to or deleted from the menu bar. This is one instance where faster isn't necessarily better. You should use this technique only when you're sure that the index value cannot change.

Minimizing Object Activation and Selection

Most of the time, your code can operate on objects without activating them. If you learned Visual Basic programming by using the macro recorder, you're probably accustomed to activating or selecting an object before you do anything to that object. The macro recorder does this because it must follow your keystrokes as you select and activate sheets and cells. However, you can usually write much simpler and faster Visual Basic code that produces the same results without activating or selecting each object before working with it. For example, filling cells C1:C20 on Sheet5 with random numbers (using the **AutoFill** method) produces the macro recorder output shown in the following example.

```
Sheets("Sheet5").Select
Range("C1").Select
ActiveCell.FormulaR1C1 = "=RAND()"
Selection.AutoFill Destination:=Range("C1:C20"), Type:=xlFillDefault
Range("C1:C20").Select
```

All of the **Select** method calls are unnecessary. You can use the **With** statement to write code that operates directly on the worksheet and range, as shown in the following example.

```
With Sheets("Sheet5")
    .Range("C1").FormulaR1C1 = "=RAND()"
    .Range("C1").AutoFill Destination:=.Range("C1:C20"), _
        Type:=xlFillDefault
End With
```

Keep in mind that the macro recorder records exactly what you do—it cannot optimize anything on its own. The recorded macro uses the **AutoFill** method because that's how the user entered the random numbers. This isn't the most efficient way to fill a range with random numbers. You can do the same thing with a single line, as shown in the following example.

```
Sheets("Sheet5").Range("C1:C20").Formula = "=RAND()"
```

When you optimize recorded code, think about what you're trying to do with the macro. Some of the operations you can perform in the user interface (such as dragging a formula from a single cell into a range) are recorded as methods (such as **AutoFill**) that can be eliminated in the optimized code because there is a faster way to perform the same operation in Visual Basic.

Removing Unnecessary Recorded Expressions

Another reason the macro recorder produces inefficient code is that it cannot tell which options you've changed in a dialog box. The recorder therefore explicitly sets all available options when you close the dialog box. For example, selecting cells B2:B14 and then changing the font style to bold using the Format Cells dialog box produces the recorded macro shown in the following example.

```
Range("B2:B14").Select
With Selection.Font
    .Name = "Arial"
    .FontStyle = "Bold"
    .Size = 10
    .Strikethrough = False
    .Superscript = False
    .Subscript = False
    .OutlineFont = False
    .Shadow = False
    .Underline = xlNone
    .ColorIndex = xlAutomatic
End With
```

Setting the cell format to bold can be done with a single line of code without selecting the range, as shown in the following example.

```
Range("B2:B14").FontStyle = "Bold"
```

Again, if you think about what you're trying to do with the macro and you look through the lists of properties and methods that apply to the **Font** object, you'll see that you could also write this macro using the **Bold** property, as shown in the following example.

```
Range("B2:B14").Font.Bold = True
```

You can also experiment with the macro recorder by recording the same operation done different ways in the user interface. For example, if you format a range using the Bold button on the Standard toolbar, the macro recorder uses the **Bold** property.

Minimizing the Use of Variant Variables

Although you may find it convenient to use **Variant** variables in your code, Visual Basic requires more time to process a value stored in a Variant variable than it needs to process a value stored in a variable declared with an explicit data type. Your code can perform mathematical computations that don't involve fractional values faster if you use **Integer** or **Long** variables rather than **Variant** variables. **Integer** or **Long** variables are also the best choice for the index variable in **For...Next** loops. The speed you gain using explicit variable types can come at the expense of flexibility. For example, when using explicit data types, you may encounter cases of overflow that **Variant** variables handle automatically.

For more information about data types, see Chapter 2, "Variables, Constants, and Data Types."

Using Specific Object Types

References to objects and their methods and properties are resolved either when your macro is compiled or when it runs. References that are resolved when the macro is compiled are faster than references that must be resolved while the macro is running.

If you declare variables and arguments as specific object types (such as **TextBox** or **Worksheet**), Visual Basic can resolve references to the properties and methods of those objects when your macro is compiled. For a list of specific object types, see the Object Browser.

If you declare variables and arguments with the generic **Object** data type, Visual Basic may have to resolve references to their properties and methods when it encounters them at run time, resulting in a significantly slower process.

For information about object types, see Chapter 4, "Objects and Collections." For more information about declaring object variables, see Chapter 2, "Variables, Constants, and Data Types."

Using Constants

Using constants in an application makes the application run faster. Constants are evaluated once and are stored when your code is compiled. Variables can change, though, so Visual Basic must get the current variable value each time the macro runs. Constants also make your macros more readable and easier to maintain. If there are strings or numbers in a macro that don't change, declare them as constants. For more information about creating constants, see "Constants" in Chapter 2.

Using Worksheet Functions

A Microsoft Excel worksheet function that operates on a range of cells is usually faster than a Visual Basic macro that accomplishes the same task. For example, the SUM worksheet function is much faster than Visual Basic code that iterates a range and adds the values in the range's cells. For example, the following code runs relatively slowly.

```
For Each c In Worksheets(1).Range("A1:A200")
    totVal = totVal + c.Value
Next
```

The following code runs faster than the preceding example.

```
totVal = Application.Sum(Worksheets(1).Range("a1:a200"))
```

Aggregating worksheet functions (such as PRODUCT, COUNT, COUNTA, and COUNTIF) are good candidates for replacing slower Visual Basic code, as are worksheet functions (such as MATCH and LOOKUP) that can take a range as an argument. For more information, see "Worksheet Functions" in Help.

Using Special-Purpose Visual Basic Methods

There are also several special-purpose Visual Basic methods that offer a concise way to perform a specific operation on a range of cells. Like worksheet functions, these specialized methods are faster than the general-purpose Visual Basic code that accomplishes the same task.

For example, the following code changes the value in each cell in a range in a relatively slow way.

```
For Each c In Worksheets(1).Range("a1:a200").Cells
    If c.Value = 4 Then c.Value = 4.5
Next
```

The code in the following example, which uses the **Replace** method, performs the same operation much faster.

```
Worksheets(1).Range("a1:a200").Replace "4", "4.5"
```

The following example shows a relatively slow way to add a blue oval to each cell in the range A1:A500 that contains the value 4.

```
For Each c In Worksheets(1).Range("a1:a500").Cells
    If c.Value = 4 Then
        With Worksheets(1).Ovals.Add(c.Left, c.Top, c.Width, c.Height)
            .Interior.Pattern = xlNone
            .Border.ColorIndex = 5
        End With
    End If
Next
```

The code in the following example, which uses the **Find** and **FindNext** methods, performs the same task much faster.

```
With Worksheets(1).Range("a1:a500")
    Set c = .Find(4)
    If Not c Is Nothing Then
        firstAddress = c.Address
        Do
            With Worksheets(1).Ovals.Add(c.Left, c.Top, _
                    c.Width, c.Height)
                .Interior.Pattern = xlNone
                .Border.ColorIndex = 5
            End With
            Set c = .FindNext(c)
        Loop While Not c Is Nothing And c.Address <> firstAddress
    End If
End With
```

For more information about special-purpose Visual Basic methods, see the topic in Help that covers object you're working with, and examine the list of that object's methods. You can also examine the list of all Visual Basic methods on the Contents tab of Help.

Turning Off Screen Updating

A macro that makes changes to the appearance of a worksheet or chart—such as a macro that changes the color of every other cell in a large range or that creates a large number of graphic objects—will run faster when screen updating is turned off. You won't be able to watch the macro run (the changes will appear all at once when you turn screen updating back on), but it will run much faster. You may want to leave screen updating turned on while you write and debug the macro, and then turn it off.

To turn off screen updating, set the **ScreenUpdating** property to **False**, as shown in the following example.

```
Application.ScreenUpdating = False
```

Microsoft Excel automatically sets the **ScreenUpdating** property back to **True** when your macro ends.

Tip You can sometimes achieve the same effect by not activating the object you're changing. For example, if you create graphic objects on a sheet without first activating the sheet, you don't need to turn screen updating off because the changes won't be visible.

CHAPTER 6

Debugging

Visual Basic provides debugging tools to help you analyze how your macros operate. These tools are particularly useful in locating the sources of errors (bugs). You can also use them to experiment with changes to your macros or to learn how macros created by others work.

This chapter shows you how to use the debugging tools included in Visual Basic.

Contents

Avoiding Bugs

The first step in avoiding or fixing bugs is understanding the three kinds of errors you can encounter:

- **Language errors** These errors, which are also called syntax errors, are the result of an incorrectly constructed statement. You may have misspelled a reserved word, omitted some necessary punctuation (especially parentheses around arguments to methods), or forgotten to balance statement blocks, such as **If** and **End If** or **For** and **Next**. Visual Basic detects these errors either when you type the statement or during compilation, before the code executes.
- **Run-time errors** These errors occur, and are detected by Visual Basic, when a statement attempts an impossible operation while the code is executing. An example of an impossible operation is division by 0 (zero). Suppose you have the following statement:

```
Speed = Miles / Hours
```

If `Hours` = 0 (zero), division is an invalid operation even though the statement itself is syntactically correct. The error is a run-time error because the code must execute before Visual Basic can detect the error. Not all run-time errors are easily anticipated or fixed. For example, a "Disk full" error that occurs when you use the **Save** method could be very difficult to fix.

- **Program logic errors** Code that contains a program logic error can be both syntactically valid and capable of performing operations that are entirely valid, but still produce incorrect results. Visual Basic cannot detect program logic errors; you must test the code and analyze the results to verify that the code is performing correctly.

Debugging tools are designed to help you analyze run-time errors and Visual Basic code in general, but they're particularly helpful in analyzing program logic errors. These errors can be far more elusive than language errors or run-time errors. For example, an incorrect result may inexplicably be produced at the end of a long series of calculations. When you're debugging, your task is to determine where something went wrong. Perhaps you chose the wrong operator, used the wrong function somewhere, or forgot to initialize a variable.

There are no magic tricks to debugging, and there is no fixed sequence of steps that works every time. Essentially, debugging involves understanding what's going on when your code executes. The better you understand how your code works, the faster you can find and fix bugs. Debugging is easier if you:

- Design your modules carefully by breaking up your code into **Sub** and **Function** procedures, with each procedure having a specific, well-defined purpose.
- Include numerous comments. As you go back and analyze your code, you'll understand it much better if you've written comments that describe the purpose of each procedure.
- Use the **Option Explicit** statement in the declarations section of each of your modules. One of the most common sources of errors is misspelling a variable name. If you have an **Option Explicit** statement in each module, Visual Basic generates an error message when it discovers a variable that hasn't been explicitly declared. This helps you quickly find misspelled variable names.
- Examine your code to try to find statements that may be causing the problem. Set breakpoints at these statements, and then restart the code. Breakpoints are described in "Entering Break Mode at a Problem Statement" later in this chapter.
- Use the Immediate pane of the Debug window (described later in this chapter) to examine variables and expressions when a breakpoint occurs.

Using Debugging Tools and Break Mode

You work with modules when you write a macro (design time) and when you run it (run time). This chapter introduces a third state for modules—when execution is suspended. This is called *break mode*. In this state, the code is running but is suspended between executing statements. In break mode, you can use the debugging tools to examine your code.

Four buttons on the Visual Basic toolbar provide shortcuts to commands you use when debugging your code. The following illustration shows this part of the toolbar.

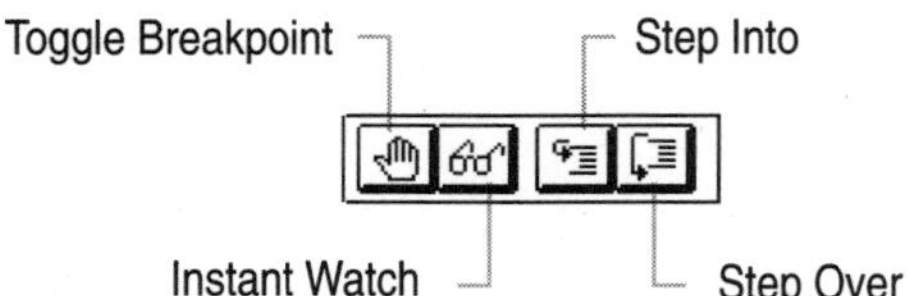

The following table briefly describes the function of each button. The following sections in this chapter explain how each of these buttons can help you debug or analyze code more efficiently.

Debugging button	Function
Toggle Breakpoint	Creates or removes a breakpoint. A breakpoint is a location in the code where Visual Basic halts execution.
Instant Watch	Displays the current value of an expression while the code is in break mode.
Step Into	Runs only the next executable line of code. If the code calls another procedure, your view into the code shifts to the called procedure until it ends.
Step Over	Runs the next executable line of code. If the code calls another procedure, runs the entire procedure without shifting your view of the code to the called procedure.

Using the Debug Window

Sometimes you can find the cause of a problem by executing portions of code. More often, however, you have to analyze what's happening to the data as well. For example, you might isolate a problem in a variable or property with an incorrect value. Then you must determine how and why that variable or property was assigned an incorrect value.

In the Debug window, you can monitor the values of expressions and variables while stepping through the statements in your code. You can also use the Debug window to change the value of variables and properties in break mode to see how different values affect your code.

You display the Debug window by doing one of the following:

- Entering break mode. The Debug window automatically appears when Visual Basic enters break mode.
- Clicking Debug Window on the View menu.

The Debug window has two halves: The upper half is either the Watch pane or the Immediate pane; the lower half is the Code pane. In the Code pane, the current execution point in the code has a rectangular outline around it. You can scroll through the Code pane to look at other parts of the code.

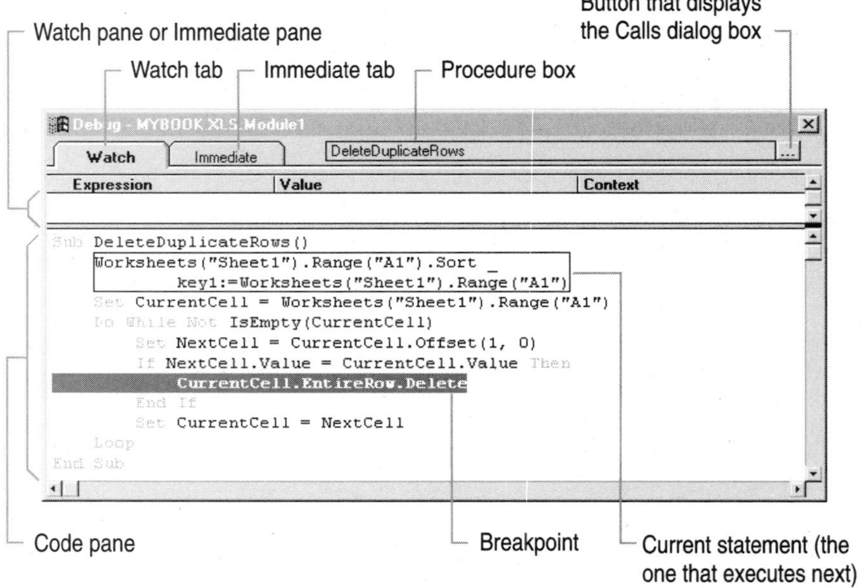

The Watch pane displays the current *watch expressions*—expressions whose values you decide to monitor as the code runs. The Immediate pane displays information that results from debugging statements in your code or information you request by typing commands directly in the pane. The first time you display the Debug window, the Immediate pane is on top; thereafter, the last pane you chose is on top.

In the Watch pane, the Context column indicates the procedure, module, and workbook in which each watch expression is evaluated. The Watch pane can display a value for a watch expression only if the current statement is in the specified context; otherwise, the Value column displays a message indicating that the statement is out of context. For example, if you set a watch expression on a statement in a procedure, the statement is out of context until you run the procedure. For more information about using watch expressions, see "Monitoring Data with Watch Expressions" later in this chapter.

Entering Break Mode at a Problem Statement

To use debugging tools, you must be in break mode. If you suspect that the problem you're debugging occurs at a certain place in the code, you'll probably want to enter break mode at that location. This is why Visual Basic enables you to use *breakpoints* and the **Stop** statement. A breakpoint is a statement at which Visual Basic automatically enters break mode.

Visual Basic enters break mode at a line if one or more of the following conditions exist:

- The line is a breakpoint.
- There is a **Stop** statement on that line.
- A statement on the line generates a run-time error. (This is true only if there is no error trapping in effect.)
- You've set a watch expression of the type Break When Value Is True, and a statement on the line causes the value of the watch expression to change and evaluate to **True**.
- You've set a watch expression of the type Break When Value Changes, and a statement on the line causes the value of the watch expression to change.

You can also enter break mode by pressing ESC or CTRL+BREAK while code is running.

Using a Breakpoint

When Visual Basic encounters a breakpoint while executing a procedure, it enters break mode just before executing the breakpoint line. You can set or remove a breakpoint when you're writing code in a module or whenever you're in break mode. When you set a breakpoint, Visual Basic highlights the breakpoint line with a dark red background. Visual Basic also displays a rectangular outline around the statement at which the procedure is suspended. This outline indicates the *current statement*, or the next statement to be executed.

To set a breakpoint

1. In the module, move the insertion point to a line of code that isn't already a breakpoint.
2. On the Run menu, click Toggle Breakpoint, or click the Toggle Breakpoint button on the Visual Basic toolbar.

Toggle Breakpoint button

To clear a breakpoint

1. In the module, move the insertion point to the line of code that's the breakpoint you want to clear.
2. On the Run menu, click Toggle Breakpoint, or click the Toggle Breakpoint button on the Visual Basic toolbar.

After a breakpoint occurs, you can examine what's happened up to that point by inspecting code and data in the Immediate pane of the Debug window and by using the Calls dialog box. For more information about the Calls dialog box, see "Using the Calls Dialog Box to Trace Nested Procedures" later in this chapter.

If the problem you're trying to solve has already occurred, you know that a previously executed line of code is causing the problem. If not, a line of code that has not executed yet is causing the problem. If the breakpoint line is the cause, the problem won't occur until you execute at least one more statement. After you enter break mode, you can step through your code line by line to find the problem, as discussed later in this chapter.

Important The problem may be something other than a line of code. A statement can be the indirect cause of the problem if it assigns an incorrect value to a variable. You can examine the values of variables while you're in break mode. For more information, see "Inspecting Code and Data in the Immediate Pane" later in this chapter.

Using a Stop Statement

As an alternative to setting a breakpoint, you can put a **Stop** statement in a procedure. Visual Basic enters break mode whenever it encounters a **Stop** statement. A **Stop** statement is very similar to a breakpoint, but it isn't set or cleared the same way a breakpoint would be.

Note There is one important difference between a **Stop** statement and a breakpoint. If you close the workbook or quit Microsoft Excel, all breakpoints are cleared. **Stop** statements are more permanent; they stay in the code until you remove them.

Fixing a Run-Time Error

Some run-time errors result from simple oversights while you're writing the code; these errors are easily fixed. Suppose, for example, that you try to customize the title bar of the main application window by setting the **Name** property, as in the following code.

```
Application.Name = "My Custom Application"
```

When you run the code, a run-time error occurs. In this case, the solution is to fix the problem statement so that it uses the correct property, the **Caption** property, as in the following example.

```
Application.Caption = "My Custom Application"
```

You can use error handling to correct run-time errors that result from conditions other than simple coding errors. Error handling is discussed in the next chapter, "Handling Run-Time Errors."

Stepping Through Code

If you know exactly which statement caused an error, the use of a single breakpoint may be sufficient. More often, however, you can only guess the general vicinity of the statement that caused the error. Setting a breakpoint helps you get to that general area; when you get there, you can step through your code and execute it line by line to see the effect of each statement.

You can also step through each line of code in a called procedure (a procedure the current procedure calls) or step over the called procedure code.

Stepping Through Statements

Stepping is the process of executing one statement at a time. Stepping through statements is sometimes referred to as *tracing*. After executing each statement, you can see how the statement affected the variables and objects in your macro.

▶ **To step through code one statement at a time**

Step Into button

- On the Run menu, click Step Into, or click the Step Into button on the Visual Basic toolbar.

When the Step Into command is carried out, Visual Basic executes the current statement and then automatically advances to the next statement and enters break mode.

A line of code can contain two or more statements separated by a colon (:). You can step from one statement to the next even if they're in the same line. However, the breakpoint is always the first statement in the line.

Stepping Over Procedures

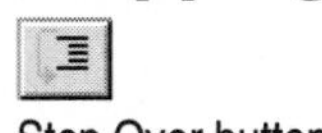
Step Over button

If you don't want to step through the lines of code in a called procedure, you can step over the entire procedure by clicking Step Over on the Run menu (or clicking the Step Over button on the Visual Basic toolbar). The Step Over command is identical to the Step Into command except when the current statement contains a call to a procedure. The Step Into command steps into the procedure that was called and lets you step through it line by line, whereas the Step Over command executes the called procedure as a unit and then steps into the next statement in the calling procedure. In the following example, the current statement calls the procedure GetQueryCriteria.

```
GetQueryCriteria Criteria
```

If you choose the Step Into command, the Debug window displays the GetQueryCriteria procedure, and the first statement in that procedure is the current statement. The Step Into command is the best choice if you want to analyze the code within GetQueryCriteria.

If you choose the Step Over command, the module continues to display the calling procedure while Visual Basic executes the GetQueryCriteria procedure. Execution then advances to the statement immediately after the call to GetQueryCriteria. Step Over is a better choice than Step Into if you want to stay at the same level of code and you don't need to analyze how GetQueryCriteria works.

You can freely alternate between the Step Into and Step Over commands. The command you choose depends on which portions of code you want to analyze at any given time.

Monitoring Data with Watch Expressions

As you debug your code, you might find that a problem occurs only when a certain variable or property assumes a particular value or range of values. Or you might learn that a calculation isn't producing the desired result. Many debugging problems aren't immediately traceable to a single statement, so you might need to observe the behavior of a variable or expression throughout a procedure.

You can monitor the value of a particular variable or expression in a *watch expression*. Visual Basic monitors watch expressions for you. In break mode, watch expressions appear in the Watch pane of the Debug window, where you can observe their values.

You can also direct a watch expression to enter break mode whenever the watched expression's value changes or becomes **True**. For example, instead of using Step Into to move through hundreds of loops, you can use a watch expression to put the code in break mode when a loop counter reaches a specific value. Or you can enter break mode each time a certain variable changes value.

Adding a Watch Expression

You can add a watch expression before running a procedure or after entering break mode. You use the Add Watch dialog box to add watch expressions.

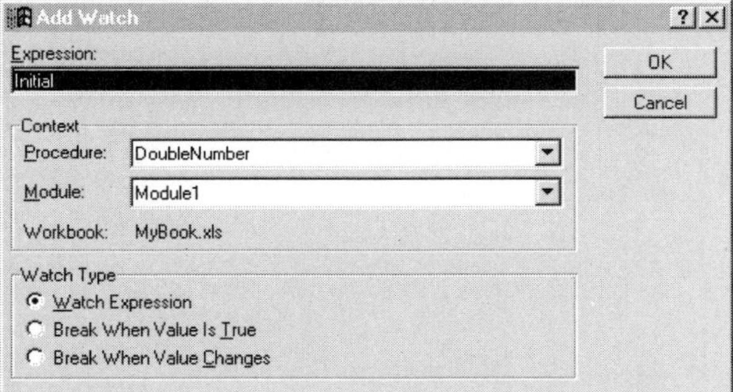

In the Expression box, enter the expression you want the watch expression to evaluate. The expression can be a variable, a property, a function call, or any other valid expression.

Under Context, click items in the list boxes to set the scope of the variables you want watched in the expression. Use these options if you have variables of the same name with different scope. You can also use these options to restrict the scope of watch variables. Visual Basic can evaluate a variable in a narrow context more quickly.

Under Watch Type, click an option button to set how you want Visual Basic to respond to the watch expression. Visual Basic can watch the expression and display its value in the Watch pane when the code enters break mode. Or you can have the code enter break mode automatically when the expression evaluates to **True** or when the value of the expression changes.

▶ **To add a watch expression**

1. On the Tools menu, click Add Watch.
2. In the Expression box, type the expression you want to evaluate.
3. To set the scope of the expression to be watched, click the procedure or module name in the appropriate box under Context.
4. To determine how you want Visual Basic to respond to the watch expression, click an option button under Watch Type.

Editing or Deleting a Watch Expression

You can edit or delete any watch expression you select in the Watch pane of the Debug window. When you click Edit Watch on the Tools menu, the Edit Watch dialog box appears. This dialog box looks just like the Add Watch dialog box with a Delete button added.

▶ **To edit a watch expression**

1. In the Watch pane of the Debug window, click the watch expression you want to edit.
2. On the Tools menu, click Edit Watch.
3. In the Edit Watch dialog box, make any changes you want to the expression, the scope for evaluating variables, or the watch type.

Tip You can also edit any watch expression displayed in the Debug window by double-clicking the watch expression in the Watch pane. Visual Basic displays the selected watch expression in the Edit Watch dialog box.

▶ **To delete a watch expression**

1. In the Watch pane of the Debug window, click the watch expression you want to delete.
2. On the Tools menu, click Edit Watch.
3. In the Edit Watch dialog box, click Delete.

Tip If your keyboard has a DEL key, you can delete a watch expression by selecting it in the Watch pane of the Debug window and then pressing DEL.

Identifying Watch Types

To the left of each watch expression in the Watch pane of the Debug window is an icon that identifies the watch type of that expression. The following illustration shows the icons for the three watch types.

Watch expression
Break when value is True
Break when value changes

Using Instant Watch

While in break mode, you can check the value of an expression for which you haven't defined a watch expression. You can check such expressions in the Instant Watch dialog box.

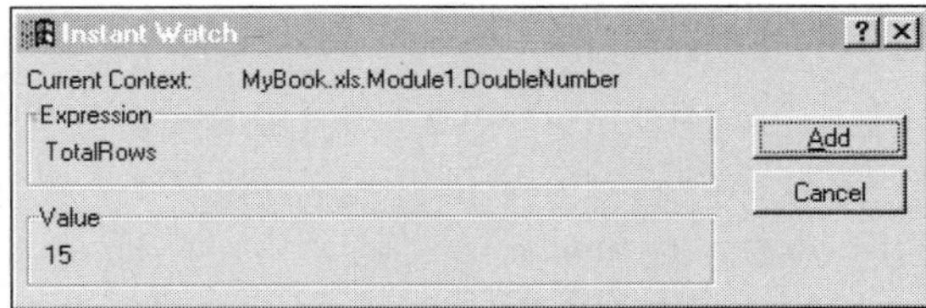

The Instant Watch dialog box displays the value of an expression you select from either of the following:

- A Visual Basic module
- The Code pane of the Debug window

To continue watching this expression, click Add. If Visual Basic cannot evaluate the current expression, an error message appears.

▶ **To add a watch expression from the Instant Watch dialog box**

1. Select the expression you want to watch.
2. On the Tools menu, click Instant Watch.

   You can also click the Instant Watch button on the Visual Basic toolbar.
3. Click Add.

Instant Watch button

Using the Calls Dialog Box to Trace Nested Procedures

The Calls dialog box displays a list of all active procedure calls. Active procedure calls are the procedures that have started but haven't finished executing. For example, you can use the Calls dialog box to trace the procedure calls in the following code.

```
Sub Demo1()
    Call Demo2
End Sub

Sub Demo2()
    Call Demo3
End Sub

Sub Demo3()
    MsgBox "Demo3 is running"
    Stop
End Sub
```

The Calls dialog box lists three active procedure calls when execution is suspended by the **Stop** statement in the Demo3 procedure.

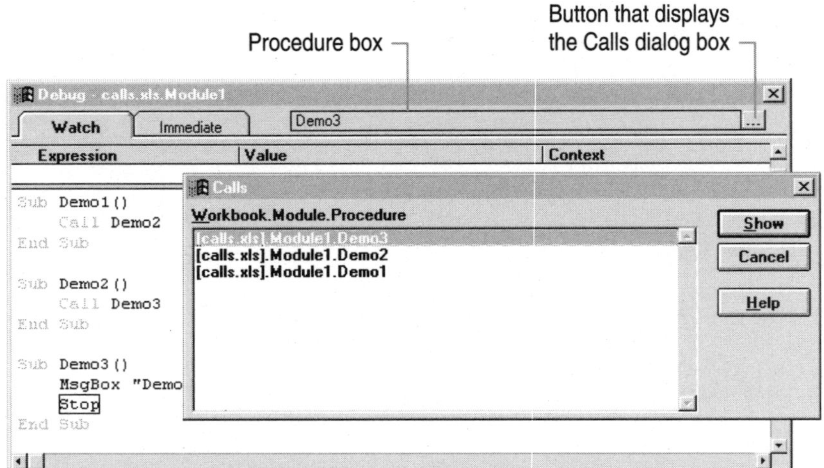

▶ To display the Calls dialog box

- In the Debug window, click the button to the right of the Procedure box (the box containing the name of the current procedure).

The Calls dialog box is especially helpful if you want to trace nested procedures. For example, a procedure can call a second procedure, which can call a third procedure—all before the procedure that started this chain has finished executing. In the preceding illustration, the Demo1 procedure called the Demo2 procedure, which called the Demo3 procedure.

The Calls dialog box lists all the active procedure calls in a series of nested procedure calls. It places the most recently started procedure call at the top of the list; earlier procedure calls appear in order below that. The information given for each procedure includes the name of the workbook and module that contains the procedure, followed by the name of the procedure.

You can click Show to display the statement that calls the next procedure listed in the Calls dialog box.

▶ **To display the statement that calls the next procedure in the Calls dialog box**

1. In the Calls dialog box, click the procedure call you want to display.
2. Click Show.

   Visual Basic displays the procedure in the module. The insertion point indicates the statement that calls the next procedure in the Calls dialog box (the procedure above the displayed procedure).

If you click the current (top) procedure in the Calls dialog box and then click Show, Visual Basic displays the current statement (the statement at which execution is suspended).

Inspecting Code and Data in the Immediate Pane

When you're creating and testing Visual Basic code, you may often want to check the results of an expression, the value of a property, and so on. You can do this in the Immediate pane of the Debug window. The Immediate pane is a kind of "scratch pad" window in which expressions are evaluated immediately.

▶ **To view the Immediate pane**

1. Enter break mode, or click Debug Window on the View menu. The Debug window appears.
2. If the Immediate pane isn't on top, click the Immediate tab.

There are several uses for the Immediate pane: checking the values of properties; evaluating expressions; printing the results of expressions; and printing the values of properties. You can also test your **Sub** and **Function** procedures by calling them from the Immediate pane. And when you're in break mode, you can use the Immediate pane to examine the values of variables and arguments in a procedure.

Testing Procedures Using the Immediate Pane

In the Immediate pane, you can evaluate any valid Visual Basic executable expression or statement, including calls to **Sub** and **Function** procedures. You can evaluate an expression or **Function** procedure by printing the value it returns in the Immediate pane. You can also test the possible effect of a **Sub** procedure with any given set of arguments by entering it as a statement in the Immediate pane just as you would in a module.

From a module, you can print a value to the Immediate pane by using the **Print** method of the **Debug** object (the **Debug** object refers to the Immediate pane). The following example prints the name of the active workbook in the Immediate pane.

```
Sub DebugExample()
    Debug.Print ActiveWorkbook.Name
End Sub
```

Note The Immediate pane doesn't open automatically when Visual Basic encounters **Debug.Print**. If you don't have the Immediate pane open, you won't see the values displayed by **Debug.Print**.

From the Immediate pane, you can use the **Print** method without the **Debug** object qualifier. You can also use a question mark (?) as shorthand for the **Print** method. When you type the following code in the Immediate pane and then press ENTER, Visual Basic displays the same result as it does when you run the preceding code example from a module.

```
? ActiveWorkbook.Name
```

You can test a **Sub** procedure by typing it and its arguments in the Immediate pane, as in the following example.

```
SizeIt 5000, 3000
```

Note You cannot use the **Print** method or a question mark in the preceding example because a **Sub** procedure doesn't return a value to display.

You can execute any built-in function or statement in the Immediate pane. However, a control structure is valid only if it can be completely expressed on one line. For example, the following **For Each...Next** loop can be executed in the Immediate pane.

```
For Each s In Sheets : Print s.Name : Next s
```

Printing to the Immediate Pane from Code

While you're testing your code, you may want to display the results of expressions in your code as it's running. You can use **Debug.Print** to display the results in the Immediate pane. For example, you could add **Debug.Print** to the DueDate function, as shown in the following code.

```
Function DueDate(ByVal AnyDate As Variant) As Variant
' This function calculates and returns the date of the first day
' of the month that follows the supplied date.

    Debug.Print "Year "; Year(AnyDate); "Month "; Month(AnyDate)
    DueDate = DateSerial(Year(AnyDate), Month(AnyDate) + 1, 1)
End Function
```

Now whenever this function is called, it will display the year and month of the passed-in value in the Immediate pane. For example, you can call the DueDate function from the Immediate pane, passing in the current date using the **Now** statement. The value of the year and month, and the function's return value, will be displayed as shown in the following illustration.

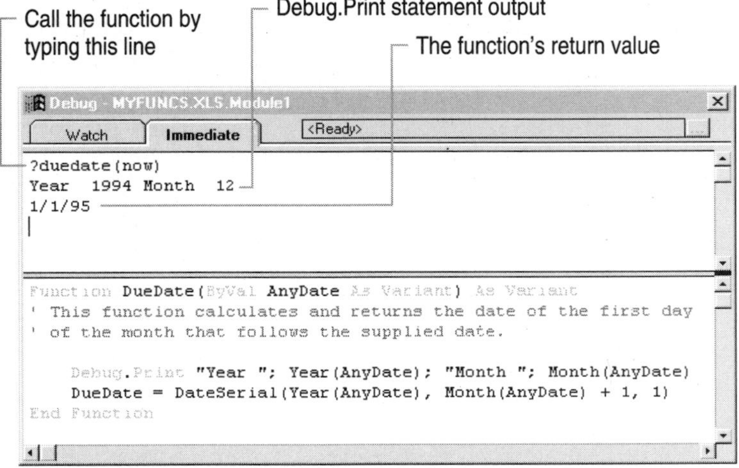

Debug.Print always sends its output to the Immediate pane. You can use the function from the preceding example in any expression in Microsoft Excel (including formulas on a worksheet), and it will always display the value of the year and month in the Immediate pane.

The advantage of printing to the Immediate pane from code is that the feedback is displayed in a separate area (the Immediate pane), so it doesn't interfere with output you want users to see.

When you're sure that your code is working correctly, you can remove the **Debug.Print** statements. Printing to the Immediate pane slows your code slightly, so you don't want to leave **Debug.Print** in your code when you don't need to use it.

Finally, you can print debugging messages to the status bar using the **StatusBar** property. The advantage of the status bar is that you don't need to display the Debug window to read the debugging messages. The text you display in the status bar remains there until you set the **StatusBar** property to another string, or until you set the **StatusBar** property to **False**, which returns control of the status bar to Microsoft Excel. If you don't set the **StatusBar** property to **False**, the text displayed there remains after the macro ends.

Using the Immediate Pane in Break Mode

In break mode, you can use the Immediate pane to examine the values of expressions and variables in the suspended procedure. As shown in the following illustration, if you place a breakpoint in the DueDate function and then call the function, the Debug window is displayed when the breakpoint occurs, and you can use the Immediate pane to examine the value of the function's argument.

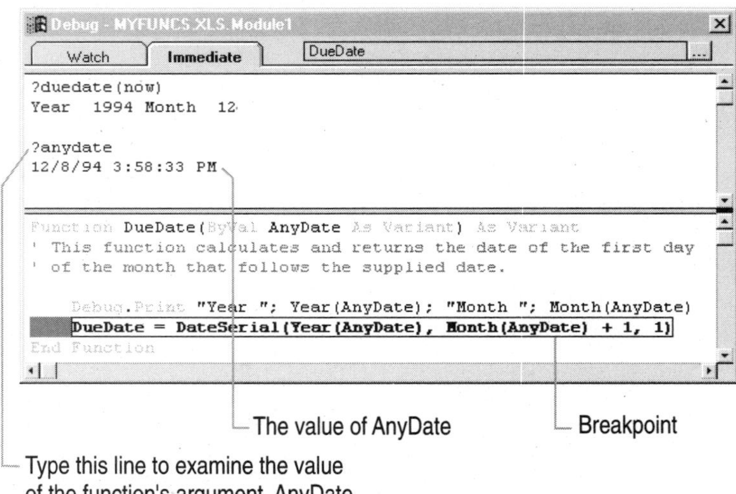

Notice that you can display a variable's value only if the variable has the appropriate scope relative to the current statement. Whenever Visual Basic enters break mode, the Debug window identifies:

- The current workbook and module (indicated in the title bar of the Debug window).
- The procedure that's currently executing (displayed in the window).
- The current statement (identified by a rectangular outline in the Code pane).

Only variables defined in the current module and the procedure that's currently executing can be displayed in the Immediate pane. For example, suppose that the Immediate pane indicates that Module1 is the current module. In this case, you can display the value of any of the module variables from Module1. You can also display local variables in the procedure that's currently executing. But you cannot use or display the variables in other modules or procedures.

You can always display the value of public variables.

Scope applies to procedure calls just as it does to variables. In the Immediate pane, you can call any procedure in the current module, and you can call any public procedure from any other module in the workbook. However, you cannot call a private procedure from another module.

Assigning Values to Properties and Variables

In addition to using the Immediate pane to examine the values of variables and expressions, you can use it to assign new values to properties and variables. This is useful when you're debugging code; as you develop hypotheses about the cause of an error, you may want to test the effects of particular values.

Tips on Using the Immediate Pane

You can use the following shortcuts in the Immediate pane:

- After you've executed a statement in the Immediate pane, you can execute it repeatedly by placing the insertion point anywhere in the statement and then pressing ENTER.
- Before pressing ENTER, you can edit the statement the insertion point is located in.
- You can use either the mouse or the arrow keys to move the insertion point in the Immediate pane. Press ENTER only if the insertion point is in a statement you want to execute.
- You can use the PAGE UP and PAGE DOWN keys to move through your code one page at a time. Pressing CTRL+PAGE DOWN always moves the insertion point to the end of the Immediate pane.
- You can use the HOME key to move the insertion point to the beginning of the current line and the END key to move the insertion point to the end of the current line.

CHAPTER 7

Handling Run-Time Errors

This chapter explains how to handle *run-time errors*—errors that occur while your code is running. A run-time error occurs when your code attempts to perform an invalid operation, such as opening a file that was deleted, using a property that doesn't exist, or setting the value of a read-only property. Although you can prevent many run-time errors by being careful and thorough when writing and checking your code, there will always be a potential for unforeseeable errors cropping up. To prevent one of these unexpected errors from stopping your code prematurely and leaving your data in an unpredictable state, you can add error-handling code to your procedures.

Contents

How to Handle Errors

If you haven't set up a mechanism to handle errors, run-time errors in your code can lead to a variety of unfortunate outcomes. Some errors may abruptly halt the execution of your code, leaving the user no way to recover data, correct the source of the error, or resume execution. Other errors might allow execution to continue but will cause your code to act unpredictably.

For example, the following FileExists function, which contains no error-handling code, returns **True** if the specified file exists or **False** if it doesn't exist.

```
Function FileExists(filename)
    FileExists = (Dir(filename) <> "")
End Function
```

The **Dir** function returns the first file that matches the specified filename; it returns a zero-length string if no matching file is found. Therefore, the code `Dir(filename) <> ""` returns **True** if **Dir** returns a filename or **False** if **Dir** returns a zero-length string.

Although this code appears to cover either of the possible outcomes of the **Dir** call, if the drive letter specified in the argument doesn't refer to a valid drive, error 68 ("Device unavailable") occurs. Also, if the specified drive is a floppy disk drive, the code will work correctly only if there is a disk in the drive and the drive door is closed. If not, Visual Basic generates error 71 ("Disk not ready") and halts execution of your code.

To avoid this situation, you can use the error-handling features in Visual Basic to intercept errors and take corrective action. (Intercepting an error is also known as *trapping* it.) For example, the disk-drive errors described in the preceding paragraph could be handled by the following code.

```
Function FileExists (filename)
On Error GoTo CheckError        ' Turn on error trapping so error handler
                                ' responds if any error is detected.
    FileExists = (Dir(filename) <> "")
    Exit Function               ' Avoid executing error handler
                                ' if no error occurs.

CheckError:                     ' Branch here if error occurs.
    ' Define constants to represent Visual Basic error code.
    Const ERR_DISKNOTREADY = 71, ERR_DEVICEUNAVAILABLE = 68
    FileExists = False
    If Err = ERR_DISKNOTREADY Then
        Msg = "Put a floppy disk in the drive and close the drive door."
        ' Display message box with an exclamation mark icon and with OK
        ' and Cancel buttons.
        If MsgBox(Msg, vbExclamation + vbOKCancel) = vbOK Then
            Resume
        Else
            Resume Next
        End If
    ElseIf Err = ERR_DEVICEUNAVAILABLE Then
        Msg = "This drive or path doesn't exist: " & filename
        MsgBox Msg, vbExclamation
        Resume Next
    Else
        Msg = "Unexpected error #" & Str(Err) & ": " & Error(Err)
        ' Display message box with Stop sign icon and OK button.
        MsgBox Msg, vbCritical
        End
    End If
End Function
```

In the preceding code, the **Err** function returns the error number associated with the run-time error that occurred. When Visual Basic generates error 71, the FileExists function displays a message that tells the user to insert a floppy disk in the floppy disk drive and allows the user to click either OK or Cancel to dismiss the message box.

If the user clicks OK, the **Resume** statement returns program control to the statement at which the error occurred—in this case, the line containing the **Dir** function—and attempts to reexecute that statement. This statement succeeds if the user has corrected the problem; otherwise, the program returns to the error-handling code.

If the user clicks Cancel, the **Resume Next** statement returns program control to the statement following the one at which the error occurred—in this case, the **Exit Function** statement.

If error 68 occurs, Visual Basic displays a message describing the problem. The **Resume Next** statement then causes the function to continue execution at the statement following the one at which the error occurred.

If an unanticipated error occurs, Visual Basic displays an alternative message and halts the code at the **End** statement.

Note In the preceding example, the error numbers that the **Err** function returns are compared with constants that you've defined. For a list of the error numbers, see "Trappable errors" in Help.

The constants that begin with the letters "vb" are built-in constants that pertain to dialog boxes displayed by the **MsgBox** function. For more information about the **MsgBox** function, see "MsgBox" in Help.

Designing an Error Handler

The example in the preceding section contains an error handler called CheckError. The code in the example includes three steps you can apply to most error handlers:

- Setting an error trap
- Writing an error handler
- Exiting an error handler

Setting an Error Trap

Visual Basic enables an error trap whenever it encounters the **On Error** statement, which specifies an *error handler* (the routine within a procedure that handles the error). The error trap remains enabled while the procedure that contains it is active—that is, until an **Exit Sub**, **Exit Function**, **End Sub**, or **End Function** statement is run in that procedure.

Although only one error trap can be enabled at any one time in any given procedure, you can create several alternative error traps and enable different ones at different times. You can also disable an error trap by using a special form of the **On Error** statement—**On Error GoTo 0**. For more information about disabling error handling, see "Turning Off Error Handling" later in this chapter.

Writing an Error Handler

A common convention is to add the error handler code at the end of the procedure, before the **End Function** or **End Sub** statement. Add an **Exit Sub** or **Exit Function** statement immediately before the error handler line label, to prevent the error handler from running when no error has occurred.

To branch within the error handler, use the **Err** function, which returns the error number, in conjunction with either the **Select Case** statement or the **If...Then...Else** statement. The following section includes an example of this technique.

Exiting an Error Handler

The FileExists function presented earlier in this chapter uses the **Resume** statement within the error handler to rerun the statement that originally caused the error, and it uses the **Resume Next** statement to run the statement following the statement at which the error occurred.

You can use one of a number of statements to exit an error handler. The statement you use on any given occasion depends on the circumstances, as explained in the following table.

Statement	Description
Resume Next	Resumes execution at the statement immediately following the one that caused the error. Use this statement to skip over the statement that caused the error.
Resume	Resumes execution at the statement that caused the error. Use this statement to repeat an operation after you've corrected the error.

Statement	Description
Resume *line*	Resumes execution at the label specified by *line*, where *line* is a nonzero line number or line label that's in the same procedure as the error handler. Because jumping to specific line numbers results in unstructured code, using this statement isn't recommended.
Error Err	Triggers the most recent run-time error again. When this statement is run within the error handler, Visual Basic searches the calls list for another error handler.

The preceding table assumes that the error occurred in the same procedure as the error handler. If this isn't the case, Visual Basic searches the procedures in the calls list for another error handler. For more information about this situation, see the following section, "Handling Unanticipated Errors."

The following illustration shows how the **Resume** and **Resume Next** statements differ.

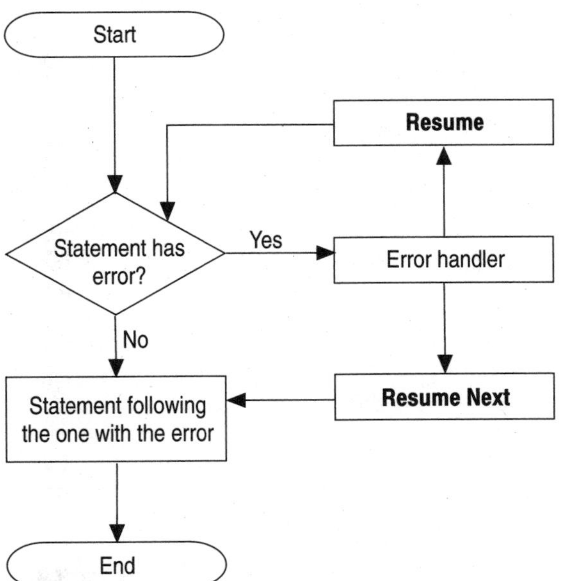

Generally, you use **Resume** whenever the user must correct the situation that caused the error before program execution can continue. Use **Resume Next** whenever a correction by the user isn't required, and you want to continue program execution without trying again to run the statement that caused the error. With **Resume Next**, you can write an error handler that never reveals run-time errors to the user.

For example, the following function uses an error handler to perform "safe" division on its arguments without revealing errors that might occur. **Null** is returned if errors do occur.

```
Function Divide(numer, denom)
Const ERR_DIV0 = 11, ERR_OVERFLOW = 6, ERR_ILLFUNC = 5
On Error GoTo MathHandler
    Divide  = numer / denom
    Exit Function
MathHandler:
    If Err = ERR_DIV0 Or Err = ERR_OVERFLOW Or Err = ERR_ILLFUNC Then
        Divide = Null           ' If error was Division by zero, Overflow,
                                ' or Illegal function call, return Null.
    Else
        MsgBox "Unanticipated error " & Err & ": " & Error, _
          vbExclamation
        Divide = Null
    End If                      ' In all cases, Resume Next continues
    Resume Next                 ' execution at the Exit Function statement.
End Function
```

Handling Unanticipated Errors

When an error occurs in a procedure that doesn't have an enabled error handler, or within an error handler that's currently running, Visual Basic searches the calls list for another enabled error handler.

For example, suppose the following sequence of calls occurs:

1. Procedure A calls Procedure B.
2. Procedure B calls Procedure C.
3. Procedure C calls Procedure D.

If an error occurs in Procedure D and this procedure doesn't have an enabled error handler, Visual Basic searches backward through the calls list—first Procedure C, then Procedure B, and then Procedure A—and executes the first enabled error handler it finds. If it doesn't encounter an enabled error handler anywhere in the calls list, it displays the appropriate run-time error message and halts your procedure.

Tip The effect of the search backward through the calls list is hard to predict, because if a **Resume** or **Resume Next** statement is encountered in the error handler, execution continues in the procedure where the error handler is found, which isn't necessarily the procedure where the error occurred. To avoid this situation, write a fail-safe error handler that all your error handlers can call as a last resort for errors they cannot handle themselves. This fail-safe procedure can both save the user's data and close your application in an orderly way.

Turning Off Error Handling

If an error trap has been enabled in a procedure, it's automatically disabled when the procedure finishes running. However, you might want to turn off an error trap earlier. To turn off an enabled error trap, use the **On Error GoTo 0** statement. You can use **On Error GoTo 0** to turn off error handling anywhere in a procedure—even within an error handler.

For example, try single stepping through the following procedure.

```
Sub ErrDemoSub()
On Error GoTo SubHandler
' Error trapping is enabled.
' Errors need to be caught and corrected here.
    Kill "OLDFILE.XYZ"
On Error GoTo 0              ' Error trapping is turned off here.
    Kill "OLDFILE.XYZ"
On Error GoTo SubHandler     ' Error trapping is enabled again.
    Kill "OLDFILE.XYZ"
Exit Sub
SubHandler:                  ' Error handler goes here.
    MsgBox "Caught error."
    Resume Next
End Sub
```

Defining Your Own Error Values

The preceding section explains how you can use run-time error values to diagnose problems in your code and respond appropriately to the problems. There may be times, however, when you want to detect and respond to situations that don't cause Visual Basic to generate errors. To do this, you need to create your own *user-defined error values* for those situations.

This type of error value is commonly used in procedures that accept several arguments and then return a value. Suppose the return value is valid only if the arguments fall within certain ranges. Your procedure can test the arguments that the user provides; if they aren't in the acceptable range, you can have the procedure return an appropriate error value.

The following sections describe how to create a user-defined error value using the **CVErr** function and how to test for an error value using the **IsError** function.

Creating Error Values

You use the **CVErr** function to create error values. For example, he following code creates two error values.

```
NoRadius = CVErr(50000)

NotANumber = 50001
InvalidArgument = CVErr(NotANumber)
```

User-defined error values are always stored in a variable of the **Error** data type, which is a subtype of the **Variant** data type. For more information about the **Error** data type, see "Storing Values in Variant Variables" in Chapter 2.

Checking for Error Values

Each error value you create must be associated with a specific error. After you've done this you can use the **IsError** function to test whether a particular error has occurred. You can test for specific user-defined error values the same way you test for specific built-in errors, using the **Select Case** statement or the **If...Then...Else** statement.

The following example uses the **CVErr** function to return an error value. The AreaOfCircle procedure asks for a radius value. The CheckData function checks the `Radius` variable and, if it isn't an acceptable number, converts it into one of two possible error values. In the AreaOfCircle procedure, the **IsError** function returns **True** if its argument is an error value.

```
Public NoRadius, NotANumber

Sub AreaOfCircle()
    Const PI = 3.14
    NoRadius = CVErr(50000)
    NotANumber = CVErr(50001)
    Radius = CheckData(InputBox("Enter the radius"))
    If IsError(Radius) Then
        Select Case Radius
            Case NoRadius
                MsgBox "Error: No radius given."
            Case NotANumber
                MsgBox "Error: Radius isn't a number."
            Case Else
                MsgBox "Unknown error."
        End Select
    Else    ' there's no error
        MsgBox "The area of the circle is " & (PI * Radius ^ 2)
    End If
End Sub
```

```
Function CheckData(TheRadius)
    If Not IsNumeric(TheRadius) Then
        CheckData = NotANumber
    ElseIf TheRadius = 0 Then
        CheckData = NoRadius
    Else
        CheckData = TheRadius
    End If
End Function
```

It's important to remember that if Visual Basic attempts to compare an error value with a number or other value in an expression, a run-time error will occur.

```
If NoRadius = 50000 Then...  'Causes an error. Cannot compare error to a
                             'number or other value.
```

The following code doesn't cause an error because you can compare an error value with another error value.

```
If NoRadius = CVErr(50000) Then...
```

For more information about **IsError** or **CVErr**, see the appropriate topic in Help.

Using Worksheet Error Values

Names and cell formulas in Microsoft Excel worksheets can contain one of seven error values: #DIV/0!, #N/A, #NAME?, #NULL!, #NUM!, #REF!, or #VALUE!. You can pass one of these error values from a worksheet to a procedure only if the passed argument is a **Variant** variable. To work with these error values, you can test the arguments using the **IsError** function and treat the error values as if they were user-defined error values (described in the preceding section).

You can also pass an error value from a user-defined function back to cells on a worksheet, as shown in the following example.

```
Function Commission(SharesSold, PricePerShare)
    If Not (IsNumeric(SharesSold) And IsNumeric(PricePerShare)) Then
        Commission = CVErr(xlErrNum)    ' xlErrNum corresponds to the
                                        ' #NUM! error value.
        Exit Function
    Else
        TotalSalePrice = SharesSold * PricePerShare
        If TotalSalePrice <= 15000 Then
            Commission = 25 + 0.03 * SharesSold
        Else
            Commission = 25 + 0.03 * (0.9 * SharesSold)
        End If
    End If
End Function
```

You work with Microsoft Excel worksheet error values the same way you work with user-defined error values. However, as you can see in the following table, Visual Basic provides two ways to refer to worksheet error values: built-in constants that represent the error numbers, and literal error values (which must be enclosed in square brackets).

Error number (constant)	Literal error value	Converted error value
xlErrDiv0	[#DIV/0!]	CVErr(xlErrDiv0)
xlErrNA	[#N/A]	CVErr(xlErrNA)
xlErrName	[#NAME?]	CVErr(xlErrName)
xlErrNull	[#NULL!]	CVErr(xlErrNull)
xlErrNum	[#NUM!]	CVErr(xlErrNum)
xlErrRef	[#REF!]	CVErr(xlErrRef)
xlErrValue	[#VALUE!]	CVErr(xlErrValue)

If you want to use the literal error value for #NUM! in the preceding example, just substitute `[#NUM!]` for `CVErr(xlErrNum)`, as shown in the following code.

```
If Not (IsNumeric(SharesSold) And IsNumeric(PricePerShare)) Then
    Commission = [#NUM!]
    Exit Function
.
.
.
```

Advanced Error-Handling Techniques

This section describes several more error-handling techniques. It also explains how your code can control what happens when a user interrupts a procedure while it's running.

Simulating Run-Time Errors

Simulating run-time errors is useful when you're testing your applications or when you want to treat a particular condition as a run-time error. For example, you might write a module that calls routines in a dynamic-link library (DLL) and want the rest of your application to handle the DLL's return values as actual Visual Basic errors—that is, to generate run-time errors in Microsoft Excel.

You can simulate any Visual Basic run-time error by supplying the error code for that error in the **Error** statement, as in the following example.

```
Error 71    ' Simulate "Disk Not Ready" error.
```

You can also use the **Error** statement to generate your own, user-defined errors by supplying an error code that doesn't correspond to a Visual Basic run-time error. Of course, this is useful only if you also write code that handles the new errors you define. For a list of built-in errors, see "Trappable errors" in Help.

Note As new errors are defined in future versions of Visual Basic, more error numbers will be assigned to built-in errors. If you want to generate and trap your own errors, begin your numbering scheme with 50,000 and work upward from there. This way, you'll avoid using the same number for your own error that a future version of Visual Basic might use for a built-in error.

Minimizing Code Size by Handling Errors in a Central Location

As you add error handlers to your applications, you'll soon discover that you're handling the same errors over and over again. You can reduce code size and save yourself time and effort by writing a few procedures that your error handlers can call to handle common error situations.

The following code is a function called FileErrors that can be called by an error handler. This function displays a message corresponding to the error that has occurred and, where possible, allows the user to choose a button to specify which action the function should take next. It then returns a code number to the procedure that called it (the calling procedure isn't shown in the example). The code number indicates which action—out of a set of actions—the program should take.

```
Public Const RESUME_STATEMENT = 0       'Resume
Public Const RESUME_NEXT = 1            'Resume Next
Public Const UNRECOVERABLE = 2          'Unrecoverable error
Public Const UNRECOGNIZED = 3           'Unrecognized error
Public Const ERR_DEVICEUNAVAILABLE = 68
Public Const ERR_BADFILENAMEORNUMBER = 52, ERR_PATHDOESNOTEXIST = 76
Public Const ERR_BADFILEMODE = 54
```

```
Function FileErrors (errVal As Integer) As Integer
Dim MsgType As Integer, Msg As String, Response As Integer
    MsgType = vbExclamation
    Select Case errVal
        Case ERR_DEVICEUNAVAILABLE                          ' Error #68
            Msg = "That device appears unavailable."
            MsgType = MsgType + vbAbortRetryIgnore
        Case ERR_BADFILENAMEORNUMBER  ' Errors #52
            Msg = "That filename is not valid."
            MsgType = MsgType + vbOKCancel
        Case ERR_PATHDOESNOTEXIST                           ' Error #76
            Msg = "That path doesn't exist."
            MsgType = MsgType + vbOKCancel
        Case ERR_BADFILEMODE                                ' Error #54
            Msg = "Can't open your file for that type of access."
            MsgType = MsgType + vbOKCancel
        Case Else
            FileErrors = UNRECOGNIZED
            Exit Function
    End Select
    Response = MsgBox(Msg, MsgType, "Disk Error")
    Select Case response
        Case vbOK, vbRetry
            FileErrors = RESUME_STATEMENT
        Case vbIgnore
            FileErrors = RESUME_NEXT
        Case vbCancel, vbAbort
            FileErrors = UNRECOVERABLE
        Case Else
            FileErrors = UNRECOGNIZED
    End Select
End Function
```

What Happens to Errors That Your Error Handler Doesn't Handle?

The function in the preceding example handles a select group of file-related and disk-related errors. If an error you encounter doesn't belong to this set of errors, the function returns the value 3. The procedure that calls this function should then either handle the error itself, call another procedure to handle it, or just let the original run-time error occur again, as shown in the following example.

```
Function FileOperationsDemo(FileName As String)
'Demo of how you would call the FileErrors Function
On Error GoTo ConfirmFileError
.
.
.
```

```
'Code that attempts some file operation
.
.
.
ConfirmFileError:
Action = FileErrors(Err)          'Call the FileErrors function
    Select Case Action
        Case RESUME_STATEMENT     'User chose OK or Retry when FileErrors
                                  'displayed its message, so try again.
            Resume
        Case RESUME_NEXT          'User chose Ignore when FileErrors
                                  'displayed its message, so ignore error
                                  'and continue.
            Resume Next
        Case UNRECOVERABLE        'User chose Cancel or Abort when
                                  'FileErrors displayed its message,
                                  'so abort procedure.
            Exit Function
        Case Else                 'Cannot handle original run-time
                                  'error, so repeat it and display
                                  'the normal System error.
            Error Err
    End Select
End Function
```

Handling Errors with Inline Code

In previous sections of this chapter, you've used the **On Error GoTo** statement to jump to an error-handling subroutine and then resume running the rest of your code. You can also handle errors without branching to a subroutine.

If you anticipate that a particular statement might cause an error, include an **On Error Resume Next** statement before the potential error-causing statement to prevent the application from being interrupted. You can then test the value of the **Err** function and proceed accordingly.

The following procedure is a revision of the FileExists procedure shown earlier in this chapter. This revised version doesn't branch to a subroutine; instead, it handles errors in-line.

```
Function FileExists(filename)
Dim Msg

Const ERR_DISKNOTREADY = 71, ERR_DEVICEUNAVAILABLE = 68

' Resets the Err code to zero; handles errors inline
On Error Resume Next

CheckOnFile:
    FileExists = (Dir(filename) <> "")
    If Err = ERR_DISKNOTREADY Then
        Msg = "Put a floppy disk in the drive and close the drive door."
        If MsgBox (Msg, vbExclamation + vbOKCancel) = vbOK Then
            GoTo CheckOnFile
        End If
        FileExists = False
    ElseIf Err = ERR_DEVICEUNAVAILABLE Then
        Msg = "This drive or path doesn't exist: " & filename
        MsgBox Msg, vbExclamation
        FileExists = False
    ' If not successful, and if not one of the above errors, handle
    ElseIf Err <> 0 Then
        Msg = "Unexpected error #" & Str(Err) & ": " & Error(Err)
        MsgBox Msg, vbCritical
        FileExists = False
    End If
End Function
```

Handling User Interrupts

When a Visual Basic procedure is running, a user can interrupt it by pressing CTRL+BREAK or ESC. Although you may need to be able to interrupt procedures when you're debugging, you might want to prevent the user from interrupting procedures in the finished application. If you do allow user interrupts in a finished application, however, you can make sure that your procedures are notified of them so that the procedures can close files, disconnect from shared resources, or restore modified variables before returning control of the application to the user.

You can trap user interrupts in your procedures by setting the **EnableCancelKey** property to **xlErrorHandler**. With this property setting in effect, all interrupts generate run-time error 18, which you can trap using an **On Error** statement. You can handle this error to halt the procedure and exit the program. However, if you use the **Resume** statement to continue running the procedure after a run-time error has been trapped, the interrupt is ignored.

The following example illustrates a procedure that requires a long time to complete. If a user interrupts the procedure while it's running, an error is trapped—first to confirm that the procedure should be stopped, and then to exit the procedure in an orderly way. Note that you can use only one interrupt handler for each procedure, and that the same handler is used for all other run-time errors encountered in that procedure.

```
Sub ProcessData
    ' Set up user interrupt trapping as a run-time error
    On Error GoTo UserInterrupt
    Application.EnableCancelKey = xlErrorHandler
    'Start a long duration task
    OpenDataFile
    For x = 1 To 1000000
        ProcessRecord x
        WriteOutRecord x
    Next x
    CloseDataFile
    Exit Sub

UserInterrupt:
    If Err = 18 Then
        If MsgBox ("Stop processing records?" , vbYesNo) = vbNo Then
            ' Continue running at the point we were interrupted
            Resume
        Else
            ' Close open files before returning
            CloseDataFile
            Exit Sub
        End If
    Else
        ' Handle other errors that occur
        MsgBox Error(Err)
        Resume Next
    End If
End Sub
```

You can also ignore user interrupts completely by setting the **EnableCancelKey** property to **xlIgnore**. With this property setting in effect, Microsoft Excel ignores all attempts by the user to interrupt the procedure that's running.

Note Use caution when disabling or ignoring user interrupts. It's possible to write code that never returns or ends. If you disable interrupts by setting the **EnableCancelKey** property to **xlIgnore**, or if you always use the **Resume** statement to return from a trapped error, your procedure won't return control to the user.

You can restore the default interrupt processing of Microsoft Excel by setting the **EnableCancelKey** property to **xlInterrupt**. To prevent a procedure from permanently turning off user interrupts, Microsoft Excel always restores the value of the **EnableCancelKey** property to **xlInterrupt** whenever code execution ends. To ensure that interrupts are handled properly, you must write your procedure so that it explicitly disables or traps interrupts each time it's run.

CHAPTER 8

Controls and Dialog Boxes

When you've gotten beyond writing simple macros for your own use and have started writing complete applications that several people use, you'll want to help your users accomplish tasks simply and conveniently. It's not enough to foresee the needs of the user and provide features that attend to those needs; you must also provide quick, convenient, and intuitive access to those features. Microsoft Excel offers several powerful user interface enhancements to help you effectively present features to the user: menus, toolbars, controls on worksheets or chart sheets, and controls in dialog boxes.

You use controls—such as buttons, check boxes, and list boxes—to create a custom user interface. This chapter discusses the use of controls and dialog boxes to manage the way the user interacts with your application, whereas Chapter 9, "Menus and Toolbars," discusses the use of menus and toolbars to achieve the same effect. Each of these enhancements has different advantages and disadvantages. As you design your user interface, you must decide which enhancement best suits the user's needs in a given situation.

In this chapter, you'll first get a brief overview of controls and dialog boxes and how they can enhance your application. Next, you'll learn to use simple, predefined dialog boxes and Microsoft Excel's built-in dialog boxes. Finally, you'll learn to create and use controls and custom dialog boxes.

Contents

Choosing the Best User Interface Enhancement

Controls (such as buttons and check boxes) can be placed on worksheets or chart sheets next to the data they access so that they're easy for the user to find and understand, and so that using them causes only minimal interruptions during a work session. In addition, because controls are always stored with the sheet they appear on, you never have to worry about losing them when you distribute the application. On the other hand, controls are tied to one sheet—and often to a particular object on that sheet—so they're not the best solution if you need a way to access commands in a variety of situations.

If you need to display a single message or ask the user for one string or number, you can use a message box or an input box. These predefined dialog boxes are easy to create and use, but they can be used only for simple input and output.

You can place controls on a dialog sheet to create a custom dialog box. Custom dialog boxes are useful when you want to manage a complex interaction between the user and the application. However, custom dialog boxes don't offer the quickest access to commands and can interrupt the flow of work.

Whereas dialog boxes are best suited to offering the user a set of complex options and returning information to the user, and controls offer the most visually obvious connection to the data they act on, menus and toolbars offer a quicker, more convenient way to expose simple options and commands to the user.

This chapter discusses using simple predefined dialog boxes and built-in dialog boxes; using controls on worksheets, chart sheets, and dialog sheets; and creating custom dialog boxes. Chapter 9, "Menus and Toolbars," describes in detail how to enhance the user interface of your application using customized menus and toolbars.

Using Built-in Dialog Boxes

Before you add custom controls to a sheet or design a custom dialog box, you should determine whether a built-in dialog box meets your needs.

Using Message and Input Dialog Boxes

The easiest way to add a dialog box to your application is to use a *predefined built-in dialog box.* Visual Basic provides two types of predefined dialog boxes: the message box and the input box. Both types are easy to use, but you have limited control over how they look and what type of information you can get from or display for the user.

The following table lists the functions and methods for adding predefined dialog boxes to your Visual Basic application.

Use this	To do this
MsgBox function	Display a message and return a value indicating the command button the user clicked.
InputBox function	Display a prompt and return the text the user typed.
InputBox method	Display a prompt and return the information the user entered. This method is similar to the **InputBox** function, but it provides additional functionality, such as requiring input to be of a specific data type.

Message Box

The **MsgBox** function creates a simple dialog box that can display a short message and a predefined set of buttons. The user can click one of the buttons to respond to the message or to cancel the message box. The simplest message box contains only a message string and an OK button, as in the following example.

```
MsgBox prompt:="Please close all files", title:="Files"
```

The **MsgBox** function performs any necessary string conversions before it displays the message string. You can use any data type for the prompt argument.

Tip You can use a message box as a simple debugging tool. Use the message box text to display an interim value in a long calculation or to display a status message in a large procedure. For more information about debugging, see Chapter 6, "Debugging."

You can also create more complex message boxes that contain different icons and buttons. The following example uses the **MsgBox** function to display a message box containing the Warning Message icon and Yes and No buttons. The No button is the default response. The value that the **MsgBox** function returns depends on the button the user clicks;when you use the return value, you must enclose the **MsgBox** function arguments in parentheses (the preceding example ignores the return value, so the parentheses aren't required).

```
Sub CreateSampleBox()
    msg = "Do you want to continue?"
    dialogStyle = vbYesNo + vbExclamation + vbDefaultButton2
    title = "Error"
    response = MsgBox(msg, dialogStyle, title)   ' Get user response.
    If response = vbYes Then                     ' Evaluate response and
        msg = "You clicked Yes."                 ' act appropriately
    Else
        msg = "You clicked No or pressed ENTER."
    End If
    MsgBox msg                                   ' Display action taken.
End Sub
```

Note The constants **vbYesNo**, **vbExclamation**, and so on are built into Visual Basic. For a list of these constants, see "MsgBox function" in Help.

Input Box

The **InputBox** function creates and displays a simple dialog box that contains a prompt, an edit box, and OK and Cancel buttons. You can use this input box to allow the user to enter data. You can change the text in the title bar, the prompt displayed to the user, and the position of the dialog box on the screen. To create a more elaborate dialog box, you must use a dialog sheet and create a custom dialog box. For more information about creating a custom dialog box, see "Using Custom Dialog Boxes" later in this chapter.

The return value from the **InputBox** function is a string containing the data in the edit box. If the edit box is empty or the user clicks Cancel, the return value is an empty string (""). The following code displays a simple input box.

```
radius = InputBox("Enter the circle's radius:", "Circle Radius")
```

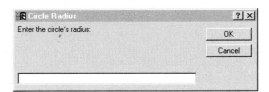

For more information about the **InputBox** function, including the complete syntax, see "InputBox function" in Help.

The **InputBox** method of the **Application** object works like the **InputBox** function, but the method also allows you to specify the desired data type for the entered data (a range or a string, for example). If the user enters data with an incorrect type, Microsoft Excel displays a message box indicating that the entry isn't valid.

If you specify a desired data type, the return value from the **InputBox** method has that data type if the user clicked OK or pressed ENTER to dismiss the dialog box. If you don't specify a data type, the return value is a string (which can be an empty string if the user clicked OK with nothing in the edit box). Whether or not you specify a data type for the entered data, the return value is **False** if the user clicked Cancel or pressed ESC to cancel the dialog box. For more information about the **InputBox** method, including the complete syntax, see "InputBox method" in Help.

Note Notice the difference between the terms *dismiss* and *cancel*. When the dialog box is dismissed, the **Show** method returns **True**, and Microsoft Excel processes the changes made to the dialog box. When the dialog box is canceled, the **Show** method returns **False**, and Microsoft Excel ignores changes made to the dialog box.

The following code uses the **InputBox** method to ask the user for a search range and a search value. The search range must be a valid **Range** reference (sheet1!a1:a20, for example), and the search value must be a number.

```
Sub CountValues()
    cellCount = 0
    Set rangeToSearch = Application.InputBox( _
        Prompt:="Enter the range to search", _
        Type:=8)     'type 8: must be a Range object
    searchValue = Application.InputBox( _
        Prompt:="Enter the search value", _
        Type:=1)     ' type 1: must be a number
    If searchValue = False Then Exit Sub     'user clicked Cancel
    For Each c In rangeToSearch
        If c.Value = searchValue Then
            cellCount = cellCount + 1
        End If
    Next c
    MsgBox cellCount
End Sub
```

Displaying Built-in Microsoft Excel Dialog Boxes

In addition to the message box and the input box, Microsoft Excel has approximately 200 built-in dialog boxes. Each dialog box allows the user to perform actions that change some feature of Microsoft Excel. For example, the built-in File Open dialog box allows the user to open a file, and the Clear dialog box allows the user to clear a range of cells.

The **Dialogs** method returns a built-in dialog box. This method takes as an argument a built-in constant that begins with "xlDialog" and that corresponds to a dialog box name. For example, the constant for the Find File dialog box is **xlDialogFindFile**.

The **Show** method displays the dialog box. You cannot replace the dialog box functionality (write your own file open code, for example) or trap the events that occur in the dialog box. The dialog box functions normally, and Microsoft Excel performs any actions the user requests.

The following example displays the built-in File Open dialog box, with the default folder set to Xlfiles.

```
Application.Dialogs(xlDialogOpen).Show("C:\XLFILES")
```

The **Show** method doesn't return to the calling procedure until the user has dismissed or canceled the dialog box and Microsoft Excel has completed any requested actions. The return value is **True** if the user clicked OK or pressed ENTER to dismiss the dialog box; the return value is **False** if the user clicked Cancel or pressed ESC to cancel the dialog box. The following example runs the **ProcessWorkbook** procedure if the user clicks a workbook in the File Open dialog box.

```
Sub NewWorkbook()
    If Application.Dialogs(xlDialogOpen).Show("c:\") And _
        ActiveWindow.Type = xlWorkbook Then ProcessWorkbook
End Sub
```

The **Show** method may fail if you try to show a dialog box in an incorrect context. For example, the method fails if you attempt to display the Format Data Labels dialog box (using the Visual Basic expression `Application.Dialogs(xlDialogDataLabel).Show)` when the active sheet isn't a chart.

You cannot copy a built-in dialog box, but you can create a custom dialog box that looks just like the built-in dialog box and write a series of procedures that duplicates the features of the built-in dialog box. You can then add and delete controls and change their behavior. For more information about creating and using custom dialog boxes, see "Using Custom Dialog Boxes" later in this chapter.

Note Visual Basic does provide some methods that allow you to use duplicates of built-in dialog boxes. For example, the **GetOpenFileName** method displays the File Open dialog box and returns the filename the user selects. The **GetSaveAsFileName** method displays the File Save As dialog box.

Using Controls

You can place controls—such as buttons, check boxes, and list boxes—on worksheets, chart sheets, or dialog sheets (you cannot place controls on a module). Placing controls on a dialog sheet creates a custom dialog box.

One advantage of placing controls on a worksheet is that you can put them close to the data they're used with. Another advantage of placing controls on a worksheet is that you can create a document that looks like a dialog box but contains cells that recalculate automatically.

By using a dialog box to group controls together, on the other hand, you can reduce the degree of complexity that confronts a user who's working with a system of worksheets and procedures you've developed. You can keep the user interface for your application uncluttered so that the user isn't overwhelmed with infrequently used options. To minimize errors on a worksheet, you can isolate the process of entering data from that of transferring the data to the worksheet. You can also create dialog boxes that apply to many worksheets or charts or to the Microsoft Excel environment as a whole.

The following sections discuss placing and using controls on worksheets, chart sheets, and dialog sheets. Most of the techniques for using controls are the same, no matter what sheet type you use. In this section, the term "sheet" refers to a worksheet, chart sheet, or dialog sheet. This discussion is followed by the "Using Custom Dialog Boxes" section, which details the specific issues involved in working with custom dialog boxes.

Using Custom Controls in Your Application

You use the Forms toolbar to choose a control and place it on the sheet. After you've placed the control, you set its initial properties, such as whether a check box appears checked or whether a button should be resized when an underlying cell on a worksheet is resized.

Next, you can assign a Visual Basic procedure to the control. When the user clicks a button, check box, or option button, or when the user edits the text in an edit box, Visual Basic runs the associated procedure.

You can also link a control directly to a cell on a worksheet, without using procedures. This way, you can simplify the user interface for a worksheet so that the user can set options using the mouse rather than by typing data in a cell. For example, you can group a series of check boxes that represent options in a feasibility study and then link each check box to a cell used elsewhere on the worksheet. If the user selects a check box, the value linked to the worksheet cell becomes **True**, and the worksheet is recalculated. For more information about linking controls to cells, see "Linking Controls to Worksheet Cells" later in this chapter.

Choosing and Placing Controls

The first step in using a control on a worksheet, chart sheet, or dialog sheet is choosing the control from the Forms toolbar and placing it on the sheet.

▶ **To place a control on a sheet**

1. On the Forms toolbar, click the button for the control you want to add.
2. Click on the sheet, and drag until the control's outline is the size and shape you want.

The following table describes the control created by each button on the Forms toolbar.

Button		Description of control
Aa	Label	Text you provide for the user, including names, instructions, and cautions.
ab|	Edit Box	A box where a user can enter text, numbers, or cell references.
xyz	Group Box	A border containing a group of option buttons or other controls.
	Create Button	A command button such as the OK or Cancel button.
x	Check Box	A box that indicates whether an option is set, regardless of the state of other options in the dialog box.
	Option Button	A button for selecting one of a group of mutually exclusive options. Place a series of option buttons in a group box to group them.
	List Box	A list of text strings, one or more of which can be selected.
	Drop-Down	An uneditable text box and an arrow, paired with a drop-down list box that appears when the user clicks the arrow.
	Combination List-Edit	An editable text box combined with a list box.
	Combination Drop-Down Edit	An empty edit box and an arrow, paired with a drop-down list box that appears when the user clicks the arrow.
	Scroll Bar	A horizontal or vertical scroll bar for changing numeric values. To create a horizontal scroll bar, size the scroll bar so that it's wider than it is high.
	Spinner	A pair of buttons for incrementing or decrementing a displayed value.

The Forms toolbar contains four additional buttons for working with controls on dialog boxes, as described in the following table.

Button		Description
	Control Properties	Used to view or change the properties belonging to the selected object; equivalent to clicking Object on the Format menu.
	Edit Code	Used to create or edit code assigned to the selected object.
	Toggle Grid	Used to align controls on a grid.
	Run Dialog	Used to display the dialog box as it appears when it's run.

You can also add a control using the **Add** method for the appropriate control collection. Arguments for the **Add** method specify the position of the upper-left corner of the control and its height and width. The following example places a new button on the worksheet named "sheet1."

```
Worksheets("sheet1").Buttons.Add 50, 25, 100, 20
```

On a worksheet or chart sheet, you specify the coordinates of the upper-left corner of the control relative to the upper-left corner of the sheet. On a dialog sheet, you specify the coordinates of the upper-left corner of the control relative to the upper-left corner of the dialog frame. For more information, see "Add method" in Help.

Selecting a Control

Selecting a control is different from *clicking* it. Typically, clicking a control on a sheet or in a dialog box has the same result as clicking a control in a built-in dialog box. For example, clicking a button on a worksheet causes the button to appear pushed down, or pressed, and clicking an empty check box causes a check to appear in the box.

Selecting a control causes a gray box to appear around it and allows you to change the control's properties, move it around on the sheet, or assign a procedure to one of the events it supports. (You select a control in Visual Basic using the **Select** method.)

▶ **To select a control on a sheet**

- While holding down CTRL, click the control.

  –Or–

- Using the right mouse button, click the control. This selects the control and displays its shortcut menu. Press ESC to dismiss the shortcut menu and leave the control selected.

Drawing Selection

You can also click the Drawing Selection button on the Drawing toolbar and then drag a rectangle around the control you want to select. If you don't see the Drawing toolbar, click Toolbars on the View menu, and then select the Drawing check box in the Toolbars box.

Note To select a group of controls on a dialog sheet, drag a rectangle that encloses the controls you want to select. You can also add controls to a group of controls that's already selected by holding down SHIFT and selecting the additional controls.

Sizing, Moving, and Deleting a Control

To change the dimensions of a control, select it and drag one of its sizing handles. To change its position, drag one of its borders. A grid constrains the control's movement on a dialog sheet to specific increments, which vary with the type of display you're using; this behavior is called *snap-to-grid.*

▶ **To turn on or turn off snap-to-grid**

Toggle Grid

- On the Forms toolbar, click the Toggle Grid button.

You can temporarily override the snap-to-grid feature by holding down ALT while dragging a handle, border, or control. Holding down ALT while dragging on a worksheet constrains vertical movement to multiples of a worksheet cell's height and constrains horizontal movement to multiples of a cell's width.

▶ **To delete a control**

1. Select the control.
2. Press DEL.

You can also click the control using the right mouse button and then click Clear on the shortcut menu, or you can point to Clear on the Edit menu and then click All.

Setting Control Properties

When you create a control, Microsoft Excel assigns it a set of default properties like those found in the built-in Microsoft Excel dialog boxes. The properties and their default values vary depending on the control. You can change these properties using the Object command on the Format menu.

▶ **To display or change a property of a control**

1. Select the control.
2. On the Format menu, click Object.
3. Click a tab, and then review or change the property.

You can also click the control using the right mouse button and then click Format Object on the shortcut menu.

Assigning Code to Controls

After you place a control on a worksheet, chart sheet, or dialog sheet and establish its initial properties, you can assign a Visual Basic procedure to the control.

Whenever an action (also called an *event*) occurs on the control, Microsoft Excel runs the procedure assigned to the control. The following table describes the events that the various types of control respond to.

Controls	Event
Command buttons, group boxes, check boxes, option buttons	The user activates the control. This event is used for controls that have no value or that have only a simple value, such as **True** or **False**.
Edit boxes, list boxes, drop-down boxes, combination list-edit boxes, combination drop-down edit boxes, scroll bars, spinners	The user changes the control. This event is used for controls that support a complex value.
Dialog frames	The dialog box appears.

For example, if you assign a procedure to an edit box, the procedure is called whenever the user enters or changes data in the edit box. When you assign a procedure to a dialog frame, the procedure runs when the dialog box is first made visible.

Note You can assign any Visual Basic procedure to a control. Functionally, there's nothing special about the procedure name; creating a procedure called "Button4_Click" doesn't automatically assign the procedure to Button4—you must use the Assign Macro dialog box or the **OnAction** property to assign the procedure to the control.

You can also assign code to drawing objects (such as ovals and rectangles). For more information, see Chapter 11, "Automatic Procedures and OnEvent Procedures."

Using the Assign Macro Dialog Box

The Assign Macro dialog box allows you to specify the procedure that runs when an event occurs.

► **To associate an existing procedure with the event belonging to a control**

1. Select the control.
2. On the Tools menu, click Assign Macro.

   You can also click the control using the right mouse button (to display the shortcut menu) and then click Assign Macro.
3. In the Macro Name/Reference box, enter the name of the procedure you want to assign to the event.

► **To create a new procedure and associate it with the event belonging to a control**

1. Select the control.

Edit Code

2. On the Forms toolbar, click the Edit Code button.

   Microsoft Excel opens a Visual Basic module scrolled to display an empty procedure.
3. Between the **Sub** and **End Sub** statements, write the procedure you want to associate with the event.

► **To edit a procedure previously associated with the event belonging to a control**

1. Select the control.

Edit Code

2. On the Forms toolbar, click the Edit Code button.

   Microsoft Excel opens a Visual Basic module scrolled to display the associated procedure. If the associated code belongs to the Microsoft Excel 4.0 macro language, Microsoft Excel switches to the macro sheet containing the associated macro.
3. Edit the code.

Using Visual Basic

The **OnAction** property sets the name of the procedure that runs whenever an event occurs. The following example causes the **StartDialog** procedure to run whenever the dialog box first starts and causes the **ButtonPressed** procedure to run whenever the user clicks a button on the first dialog sheet.

```
With DialogSheets(1)
    .DialogFrame.OnAction = "StartDialog"
    .Buttons.OnAction = "ButtonPressed"
End With
```

Tip The **ButtonPressed** procedure can use the **Caller** property to determine which button was clicked. For buttons, the **Caller** property returns the button name.

Linking Controls to Worksheet Cells

Some controls can be linked to one or more worksheet cells. If the cell value changes, the control value changes, and vice versa. For example, if you've linked an option button to a worksheet cell, the cell value is **True** as long as the option button is turned on. If you change the cell value to **False**, the option button is turned off. You can use linked cells to set initial conditions for controls and to create worksheets that respond immediately to user input.

Because changing the state of the control changes the value in the linked cell, any formulas referencing the linked cell are recalculated when you change the control. You might use this feature to implement a loan calculation worksheet for which the results depend on the interest rate. Linking a spinner to the interest rate cell would allow you to change the interest rate simply by clicking the spinner. This way, the loan payment would automatically recalculate when the interest rate changes.

Note If you have the Automatic Calculation option set, changing a linked control will cause the entire worksheet to recalculate. To turn off Automatic Calculation, click Options on the Tools menu, click the Calculation tab, and then click Manual under Calculation.

Worksheet cells can be linked to check boxes, list boxes, drop-down list boxes, option buttons, scroll bars, and spinners. The link is a property of the control, not of the linked cell.

You can link the same cell to more than one control, but the control can be linked to only one cell. You can reference the linked cell in any other cell where you want to use the linked value.

You can link a control on a dialog sheet to a worksheet cell, but the link is always active, so changing the state of the control immediately changes the value appearing in the linked cell. This means that changes appear on the worksheet even if the user clicks Cancel to close the dialog box. This behavior is usually not desired. As a rule, you'd like to have the changes appear only when the user clicks OK or presses ENTER to dismiss the dialog box. For this reason, it's usually a better idea to use a procedure to transfer information from a dialog box to the cells on a worksheet and to run that procedure only when the user clicks OK. For more information, see "Getting Information from a Dialog Box" later in this chapter.

You can link a control to a cell and assign a procedure to the same control. In this case, the link is updated before the procedure runs. For more information, see the preceding section, "Assigning Code to Controls."

You can specify the cell link reference for a control on the Control tab in the Format Object dialog box.

▶ **To link a control to a worksheet cell**

1. Select the control.
2. On the Format menu, click Object, and then click the Control tab.
3. In the Cell Link box, type the name or reference of the linked cell.

   You can also click the cell to enter its reference in the box.
4. Enter any additional information that pertains to the linked control, as described in the following sections. For example, use the Input Range box to specify the cells you want to use to fill a list box.

Note You can also establish a link by selecting the control on the worksheet or dialog sheet and then typing the cell reference in the formula bar.

The **LinkedCell** property, which corresponds to the Cell Link box in the Format Object dialog box, sets the cell link reference for a control. The following example links the check box named "Check Box 3" on the worksheet named "sheet1" to cell A5 on the same worksheet.

```
Worksheets("sheet1").CheckBoxes("Check Box 3").LinkedCell = "sheet1!a5"
```

List boxes and drop-down list boxes also use the **ListFillRange** property, which corresponds to the Input Range box in the Format Object dialog box. This property sets the worksheet range used to fill the list box. The following example fills the list box named "List Box 2" on the sheet named "sheet1" with the contents of cells A5:A10 on the same worksheet. Changes to the worksheet cells appear in the list box.

```
Worksheets("sheet1").ListBoxes("List Box 2"). _
    ListFillRange = "sheet1!a5:a10"
```

Check Boxes

For a check box, the value in the linked cell reflects the state of the check box. The check box can appear checked, unchecked, or grayed. These values correspond to the linked cell values **True**, **False**, and **#N/A**. Typing one of these values in the linked cell changes the state of the check box. Manually changing the check box changes the value in the linked cell.

Option Buttons

For grouped option buttons that are all linked to the same cell, the value in the linked cell shows the ordinal number of the option button that's turned on. For example, if an option button group contains four buttons and the third button is turned on, the value in the linked cell is 3. Changing the value in the linked cell to 1 turns on the first option button in the group. A linked cell value smaller than 1 or larger than the total number of buttons in the group (four, in this example) causes all buttons in the group to be turned off.

List Boxes

For a list box in which you can select only one item at a time (called a single-select list box), the value in the linked cell shows the ordinal number of the selected item in the list box (item one is at the top of the list box). For a multipleselection list box (a list box in which more than one item can be selected at a time), the value in the linked cell has no meaning.

You can also specify a range of cells on a worksheet that contains the list of items to appear in the list box, using the Input Range box on the Control tab in the Format Object dialog box, or using the **ListFillRange** property.

Formulas that depend on the linked cell are recalculated whenever the selected item changes;this is useful for creating what-if models in which the user can watch results change while moving the selection up and down in the list box.

Scroll Bars

For a scroll bar, the value in the linked cell specifies the position of the scroll box in the scroll bar. The Format Object dialog box allows you to specify minimum and maximum values for the scoll bar and to specify the amount by which the position value changes when the user clicks the arrows or the scroll bar. You can also specify these values using the **Min**, **Max**, **SmallChange**, and **LargeChange** properties.

Changing the value in the linked cell changes the position of the scroll box. Changing the value in the linked cell to a number smaller than the minimum value moves the scroll box to the minimum position. Likewise, setting the value in the linked cell to a number larger than the maximum value moves the scroll box to the maximum position.

Spinners

For a spinner, the value in the linked cell represents the current "value" of the spinner. Unlike a scroll bar, a spinner has no visible position indicator (such as a scroll box). However, you set a minimum and maximum value for a spinner just as you do for a scroll bar, and the spinner value is incremented when you click the up arrow and decremented when you click the down arrow. Spinners support only the **Max**, **Min**, and **SmallChange** properties.

Using Custom Dialog Boxes

When you need to manage a complex interaction between the user and your application, it's usually best to create a custom dialog box. The custom dialog box can present all the options in one location, making it easier to read and use than controls placed directly on a worksheet or chart sheet. When the user is finished choosing options from the dialog box, the dialog box can be dismissed; this way, the controls take up screen space only as long as they're needed.

Creating and managing a custom dialog box is more complex than using controls directly on a sheet, however. You must carefully consider the trade-off between the convenience to the user and the amount of work involved for you to create and manage the dialog box.

Creating a Dialog Sheet

To create a custom dialog box, you must first insert a new dialog sheet.

► **To insert a new dialog sheet**

1. On the Insert menu, point to Macro, and then click Dialog.

   Microsoft Excel inserts a new dialog sheet on top of the current sheet in the active workbook and places within it a dialog box frame containing an OK button and a Cancel button.
2. To change the name that will appear at the top of the dialog box, select the text at the top of the dialog box frame, and then type a new name.
3. To change the size of the dialog box, drag a sizing handle until the dialog box frame is the size you want.

Note Although you can change the location of a dialog box frame on its dialog sheet, you cannot set or change the position of the displayed dialog box using Visual Basic. Microsoft Excel displays the resulting dialog box with its upper-left corner in the same position as the last dialog box displayed, regardless of whether it was a built-in or custom dialog box. For more information, see "Displaying the Custom Dialog Box" later in this chapter.

After you've created a dialog sheet, you choose and place controls on the sheet using the same process you used to place controls on a worksheet or chart sheet. For more information, see "Choosing and Placing Controls" earlier in this chapter.

Testing the Custom Dialog Box

As you add controls to the dialog sheet, you'll want to test the dialog box. Unlike controls on a worksheet or chart sheet, controls on a dialog sheet aren't active—that is, they cannot be clicked. You can select, move, and resize them, and you can set their properties, but you cannot click them to activate the associated Visual Basic procedures. You must run the dialog sheet to see the working dialog box and test the controls.

Run Dialog

On the Forms toolbar, click the Run Dialog button to display the dialog box while you're creating and testing it. After you've finished creating the dialog box, you can use the **Show** method to display it from a Visual Basic procedure. For more information, see "Displaying the Custom Dialog Box" later in this chapter.

Setting Control Properties on a Dialog Sheet

You use the same process to set most properties for controls on worksheets, chart sheets, and dialog sheets. For more information, see "Setting Control Properties" and "Assigning Code to Controls" earlier in this chapter. For controls on a dialog sheet, you can also set the tab order and access key to control how the user accesses the controls. For buttons, you can set them to either dismiss or cancel the dialog box. For edit boxes, you can restrict the kind of data the user can enter.

Assigning Tab Order

There are several ways for a user to access a control in a dialog box (a process also called *setting the focus* to the control). One way is simply to click a control such as a button, edit box, or list box. Another way is to press ALT and then click the access key for the control (discussed in the next section).

You can also establish a tab order for the controls in a dialog box. When the user presses TAB, controls become active in the sequence, or *tab order*, you've established. Establishing a logical tab order is particularly useful for custom data-entry forms, because it minimizes the number of keystrokes it takes to get from one edit box to the next. You can set a tab order only for controls on a dialog sheet, not for controls on a worksheet or chart sheet.

► **To change the tab order of controls**

1. Switch to the dialog sheet.
2. On the Tools menu, click Tab Order.
3. Click the item whose place in the tab order you want to change.

   To select more than one control, hold down CTRL as you click the items.
4. Click one of the arrow buttons above or below Move.

Assigning an Access Key

An access key is the key you press in conjunction with the ALT key to access a control in Microsoft Excel. As with setting the tab order, defining access keys works only for controls on a dialog sheet. You can assign an access key to a label, command button, check box, option button, or group box. When you do this, a single character in the text associated with the control is underlined when the dialog box is displayed.

▶ **To set an access key for a control**

1. Select the control.
2. On the Format menu, click Object.
3. Click the Control tab.
4. In the Accelerator box, type the key you want to use as the access key.

Note If you want to create the effect of an access key for a control on a worksheet, you can develop a procedure associated with the **OnKey** event that runs when the user presses a certain key combination. Creating an **OnKey** procedure is discussed in Chapter 11, "Automatic Procedures and OnEvent Procedures."

Button Properties

When you create a new dialog sheet, Microsoft Excel adds an OK button and a Cancel button. When the user clicks the OK button, the default behavior is to dismiss the dialog box and cause the **Show** method to return **True**. For the Cancel button, the default behavior is to cancel the dialog box and return **False**. In addition, Visual Basic runs any procedures associated with the buttons. By default, only these two buttons dismiss and cancel the dialog box.

You can change this default behavior using either the Control tab in the Format Object dialog box or the **DismissButton** and **CancelButton** properties. You can set any number of buttons to dismiss the dialog box, but you can set only one button to cancel it. For more information, see "DismissButton property" and "CancelButton property" in Help.

Note Notice the difference between the terms *dismiss* and *cancel*. When the dialog box is dismissed, the **Show** method returns **True**, and Microsoft Excel processes the changes made to the dialog box. When the dialog box is canceled, the **Show** method returns **False**, and Microsoft Excel ignores changes made to the dialog box.

Edit Box Data Validation

By default, an edit box allows the user to enter any data type. You may want to restrict each edit box to a single data type (for example, if you want the user to enter a filename, you can specify that the entry must be a string). You can set this either by using the Control tab in the Format Object dialog box or by using the **InputType** property for the edit box. When the user dismisses the dialog box, Microsoft Excel checks the entries in any edit boxes with data validation turned on. If the contents of an edit box are invalid, Microsoft Excel displays a message and switches the focus to the edit box so that the user can supply a value of the correct data type. This process continues until every edit box contains valid data.

Displaying the Custom Dialog Box

Run Dialog

The Run Dialog button on the Forms toolbar displays the dialog box. You will usually use this toolbar button while you're testing the dialog box. You can use the **Show** method to display the custom dialog box from a procedure. When the dialog box appears, the user is free to interact with its controls—entering text in an edit box, clicking an option button, clicking an item in a list box, and so on.

Note Although you can change the position of a dialog frame on its dialog sheet, you cannot set or change the position of the displayed dialog box using Visual Basic. The dialog box appears with its upper-left corner in the same position as the last dialog box displayed.

When the user clicks a button that dismisses the dialog box (that is, a button for which the **DismissButton** property is **True** and the **CancelButton** property is **False**), the following actions occur:

- Visual Basic runs any procedure assigned to the button.
- Any edit boxes with data validation turned on are checked for valid data.

  If the contents of an edit box are invalid, Microsoft Excel displays a message and switches the focus to the edit box so that the user can supply a value of the correct data type. This process continues until every edit box contains valid data.
- The dialog box is removed, and the **Show** method returns **True**.

When the user clicks a button that cancels the dialog box (that is, a button for which the **CancelButton** property is **True**), the following actions occur:

- Visual Basic runs any procedure assigned to the button.
- The dialog box is removed, and the **Show** method returns **False**.

For example, suppose that there's a button named "Object Color" on a worksheet. To change a drawing object's color, the user clicks this button to display a dialog box.

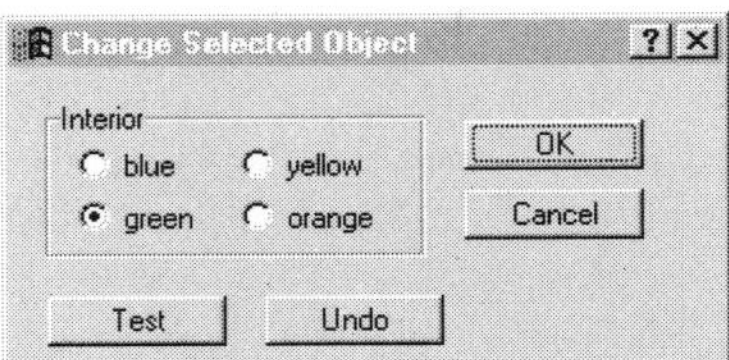

The following example shows the procedure assigned to the Object Color button.

```
Sub DoColorDialog()
    colors(1) = 5   'blue
    colors(2) = 10  'green
    colors(3) = 6   'yellow
    colors(4) = 22  'orange
    originalColor = Selection.Interior.ColorIndex
    saveInteriorColor = originalColor
    If DialogSheets("ChangeColorDialog").Show = False Then
        Selection.Interior.ColorIndex = originalColor
    End If
End Sub
```

The `colors` array must be declared at the module level so that it can be used by all procedures in the module. The colors in the array should be set in the same order as the tab order for the color option buttons.

When the user selects a graphic object and clicks the Object Color button, the procedure sets the color-index array values to the four color options, sets the saved color value and the original color value to the current selection color, and then displays the dialog box on the dialog sheet named "ChangeColorDialog."

The user can choose one of the four color options and then click Test, Undo, OK, or Cancel. The ChangeColor procedure is assigned to both the OK and Test buttons, so it runs whenever the user clicks either OK or Test. The UndoColor procedure is assigned to the Undo button. These procedures are discussed in the following sections. If the user clicks Cancel or presses ESC, the **Show** method returns **False**, and the procedure resets the object to its original color. For more information about using code with controls, see "Assigning Code to Controls" earlier in this chapter.

Getting Information from a Dialog Box

You can read and set the state of dialog box controls at any time. Typically, you set initial conditions before the dialog sheet runs or use a procedure assigned to the **DialogFrame** object to set controls when the dialog box starts. You will usually read controls when a specific event occurs in the dialog box or when the user dismisses the dialog box.

The **ChangeColor** procedure runs whenever the user clicks either Test or OK. This procedure saves the current color of the selected object and then reads the option buttons to determine the new color.

```
Sub ChangeColor()
    Dim selInterior As Interior
    With DialogSheets("ChangeColorDialog")
        Set selInterior = Selection.Interior
        saveInteriorColor = selInterior.ColorIndex
        selInterior.ColorIndex = colors(GetOptionIndex(.OptionButtons))
    End With
End Sub
```

The **GetOptionIndex** function scans the option buttons and returns the index value of the button that's turned on (the button's ordinal value in the button tab order). This index number is used to return the correct color value from the `colors` array, as in the following example.

```
Function GetOptionIndex(opBtns As OptionButtons)
    For Each ob In opBtns
        If ob.Value = xlOn Then
            GetOptionIndex = ob.Index
            Exit Function
        End If
    Next
End Function
```

The dialog box also has an Undo button that causes the **UndoColor** procedure to run. This procedure saves the current color and then resets the color to the saved value.

```
Sub UndoColor()
    With Selection.Interior
        temp = .ColorIndex
        .ColorIndex = saveInteriorColor
        saveInteriorColor = temp
    End With
End Sub
```

Modifying Controls While a Dialog Box Is Visible

You can make any dialog box you've created easier to use and understand by modifying controls while the dialog box is visible. For example, you can disable controls, change the focus, modify worksheet cell links, and change the dialog box size.

Enabling a Control

You can use the **Enabled** property of a control to prevent the user from making changes to an option unless a specified condition is met. This is often used to make a set of option buttons available only when the user selects a check box, as shown in the following code. This procedure is assigned to the check box, and it runs whenever the state of the check box changes.

```
Sub SetOptions()
    With ActiveDialog
        If .CheckBoxes(1).Value = xlOn Then
            .OptionButtons(Array(1, 2, 3, 4)).Enabled = True
        Else
            With .OptionButtons(Array(1, 2, 3, 4))
                .Enabled = False
                .Value = xlOff
            End With
        End If
    End With
End Sub
```

You could also use the **Enabled** property to create a procedure for an edit box that makes the OK button available only when the user has entered a part number that conforms to a standard pattern.

Setting the Focus to a Control

You can set the focus to a control in a dialog box by setting the **Focus** property of the dialog box (the control with the focus is acted on whenever the user presses ENTER). The following example sets the focus in the active dialog box to the button named "test."

```
Sub SetFocus()
    ActiveDialog.Focus = "test"
End Sub
```

Note You can set the focus only while the dialog box is running. For more information, see "Focus property" in Help.

Modifying Links Between a Control and a Worksheet

You can establish links between a control and a cell on a worksheet when the control is created, but you can also create, modify, and delete links between a control and a cell while a procedure is running. You use the **LinkedCell** property of the control to do this. The **LinkedCell** property belongs to the linked control and not the linked cell. The **ListFillRange** property also specifies the input range for list boxes. For more information, see "Linking Controls to Worksheet Cells" earlier in this chapter.

Changing Dialog Box Properties

You can change some of the properties of the dialog box itself (such as its size) while it's running. A common use for this is to expand a dialog box to reveal additional options when the user clicks the Options button. You can place controls below what's usually the bottom border of the dialog box. When the user clicks Options, the procedure changes the vertical size of the dialog box to reveal the hidden options.

```
Sub DisplayOptions()
    ActiveDialog.DialogFrame.Height = 91
End Sub
```

Hiding a Custom Dialog Box

To remove a dialog box from the screen, either you can wait for the user to click a button whose **DismissButton** property is **True**, or you can create an event procedure for a control, as shown in the following example.

```
Sub HideDialog()
    If MsgBox("Remove dialog box?", vbYesNo) = vbYes Then
        ActiveDialog.Hide
    End If
End Sub
```

When the user clicks the control this procedure is attached to, a message is displayed asking whether the dialog box should be removed. If the user answers yes, the dialog box is removed. If the **CancelButton** property for the control is **True**, the **Show** method returns **False**. Otherwise, the **Show** method returns **True**.

CHAPTER 9

Menus and Toolbars

An essential part of creating a useful custom application is providing a simple and consistent way for the user to interact with your application. Chapter 8, "Controls and Dialog Boxes," describes two user interface enhancements that help you achieve this goal: dialog boxes and controls. Dialog boxes are well suited to presenting the user with a set of complex options or returning information to the user, whereas controls offer the most visually obvious connection to the data they act on. However, menus and toolbars often provide quicker, more convenient, and more widely accessible ways to expose simple commands and options to the user.

In this chapter, you'll first get an overview of menus and toolbars and how each can enhance your application. Next, you'll examine menus and their components in detail. You'll see how to make design-time changes to the menu system, such as adding a new menu to a menu bar, using either the Menu Editor or Visual Basic code. Then you'll learn how to make run-time changes to the menu system, such as adding a check mark to a menu item.

In the second part of the chapter, you'll examine toolbars and toolbar buttons. You'll learn how to modify toolbars and toolbar buttons while you're designing your user interface. For example, you can create a new toolbar or add a toolbar button to the toolbar. Then you'll see how to change the properties of toolbars and toolbar buttons in response to user input while your application is running. For example, you can hide a toolbar when the user no longer needs it, or you can change a button so that it will look "pushed" after a user has clicked it.

Contents

Choosing the Best User Interface Enhancement

Menus are lists of commands from which the user can choose. Menus offer a convenient and consistent way to group commands and an easy way for users to access them. Commands for performing related tasks can be grouped on the same menu, and separator bars can be used to divide commands on a menu into logical groupings. Submenus offer additional levels of organization, and shortcut menus offer a way to group related commands that apply to the limited context of a specific task.

You can assign access keys to make commands accessible from the keyboard, and you can assign shortcut keys to provide the user even quicker access to the commands. In addition, menus take up less space than toolbars, as the items on a menu are displayed on demand and don't take up dedicated screen space. On the other hand, if you want quick, graphical access to a command, a toolbar may be a better choice.

Toolbars contain buttons that perform frequently used commands. Toolbars are ideal for presenting individual property settings (such as bold, italic, or font size), commands that are best represented visually, and commands you want to access with one click of the mouse. In addition, toolbars remain displayed while the user works, whereas menus are displayed only on demand; this makes scanning a toolbar for a particular button easier than scanning the menus on a menu bar for a particular command. However, if you need easy keyboard access to a command, if you want to display your commands hierarchically, or if you're short on screen space, a menu may be a better choice.

If you need to present a more complex set of options to the user, a dialog box may be a better choice than a toolbar or a menu. If you want to place a tool closer to the data the user is working with, the best solution may be to place a control directly on a worksheet or chart. Chapter 8, "Controls and Dialog Boxes," describes these user interface enhancements in detail.

The Menu System

The *menu system* in Microsoft Excel is composed of the entire set of available menus and the items on each menu. Each menu is either a drop-down menu, a submenu, or a shortcut menu. Each menu item is either a command, a separator bar, or a submenu caption. In this chapter, the term *component* refers generically to any menu or menu item.

A menu bar is a bar at the top of the active window that displays the captions of all the drop-down menus contained in the menu bar. Microsoft Excel changes the menu bar it displays in response to a change in the active sheet type or in response to a Visual Basic instruction. When you edit a chart, for example, Microsoft Excel automatically displays the menu bar containing a set of menus that apply to the charting environment.

A drop-down menu is a list of menu items that's displayed (drops down) when you select the appropriate menu caption on the menu bar.

A submenu (child menu) is a menu attached to the right side of a menu item (the submenu caption) on another menu (the parent menu). Each submenu caption is marked with an arrowhead pointing to the right. Submenus can be added to drop-down menus or shortcut menus. A submenu is displayed when you point to the appropriate submenu caption on the parent menu.

A shortcut menu is a floating menu that contains a group of commands pertinent to a specific task. A shortcut menu appears when the user clicks the right mouse button while the pointer is over an object. Unlike other menus, shortcut menus have no caption.

You've already worked with these components of the built-in menu system. For example, to insert a chart on a worksheet, you click the caption of the Insert drop-down menu on the worksheet menu bar, point to the Chart menu item (the caption for the Chart submenu), and then click the On This Sheet menu item. To change the chart type, you select the chart, click the right mouse button to display a shortcut menu containing commands that apply to charts, and then click the Chart Type menu item.

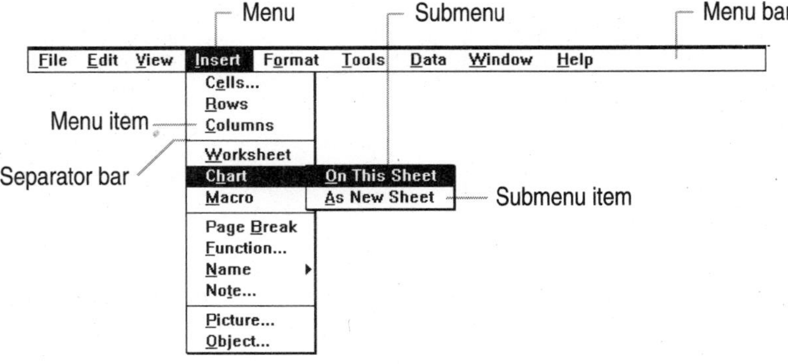

Guidelines for Customizing the Menu System

Microsoft Excel offers you a wide range of ways to modify the menu system: you can create new menu bars; add new drop-down menus to built-in or custom menu bars; create new shortcut menus; add new menu items (commands, submenus, or separator bars) to built-in or custom drop-down menus, shortcut menus, or submenus; and assign procedures to menu items. In addition, you can restore the built-in menu system to its default state at any time.

Adding Custom Components or Modifying Built-in Components

Microsoft Excel comes with a built-in menu system. You can modify components of this built-in system or create and modify custom menu components, using either the Menu Editor or Visual Basic.

Modifying a built-in menu bar, menu, or menu item is appropriate if you're adding or changing a small number of components. For example, if you just want to provide menu access to a macro, you can add a menu item to a built-in menu and then link the macro to that item.

If you need to make more extensive changes, it may be more appropriate to create a completely new component. For example, if you want to add several new drop-down menus, each containing several new menu items, it may be more appropriate to create an entirely new menu bar to contain the new menus.

Using Submenus

If your menus become crowded and difficult to scan, you can use submenus to organize them more effectively and add clarity to your application by reducing the amount of information presented to the user at any one time. For example, suppose you create a menu that presents a number of options, as shown in the following illustration.

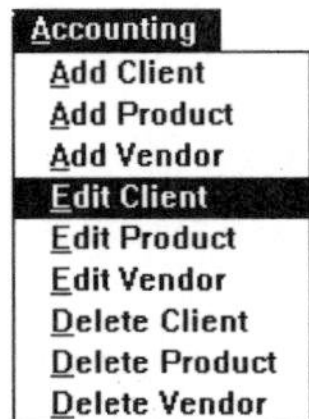

Using submenus, you can present the same items in either of the following ways.

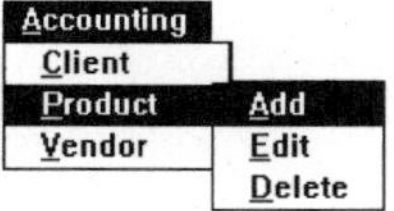

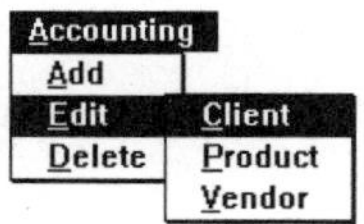

With submenus, the user can browse through commands that might otherwise be available only through a series of custom dialog boxes. However, if you need to create a complicated array of submenus to present a set of commands, a dialog box may in fact be a better solution.

Using Shortcut Menus

If you want to give the user access to a command that applies to the limited context of a selected object, you can add the command to the shortcut menu for that object.

Making Changes While the Application Is Running

In addition to making changes to the design of the menu system, you can also use Visual Basic to modify properties of menu components in response to conditions that change while the application is running. For example, you can display or hide a component, enable or disable a component, or add or remove a check mark next to a menu item.

Scope of the Changes

In Microsoft Excel, you can add, delete, and modify menu components using either the Menu Editor or Visual Basic. Although the two methods produce many of the same changes to the menu system, the scope of the changes they produce is different: Visual Basic produces changes that apply to all workbooks during a specific Microsoft Excel session, whereas the Menu Editor produces changes that apply to all Microsoft Excel sessions whenever a specific workbook is open. Defining the appropriate scope for the changes you want to make will help you decide which method to use.

Changes Made with Visual Basic

Changes you make to the menu system using Visual Basic methods and properties apply to all open workbooks until the end of the Microsoft Excel session during which the changes are made, even if you close the workbook where you've made the changes. If you want to limit the scope of changes made by Visual Basic to a specific sheet, set the sheet's **OnSheetActivate** property to the procedure that makes these changes, and set the sheet's **OnSheetDeactivate** property to the procedure that undoes these changes.

When you close Microsoft Excel, any changes you made to the menu system using Visual Basic are lost. If you want the menu changes to be available when you restart Microsoft Excel and reopen the workbook, you must use Visual Basic to reset the menus to the desired configuration when you reopen the workbook. An easy way to do this is to use an Auto_Open procedure. Because the changes you make to the menu system with Visual Basic are stored globally for the duration of a session, rather than in a particular workbook, these changes aren't shown in the Menu Editor.

Changes Made with the Menu Editor

Changes you make to the menu system using the Menu Editor—including adding or deleting menu items—are stored as a *menu editing list* in the active workbook. The changes aren't lost when you close Microsoft Excel, and they're automatically reapplied to the menu system when you reopen the workbook.

For example, suppose you've only one workbook open: You edit the menu system in the workbook using the Menu Editor, and you develop procedures that support the menus, worksheets, and other objects in your application. If you then save and close the workbook, the menu system reverts to its built-in state. When you reopen the workbook, the menu system is revised according to the menu editing list that was stored when the workbook was last saved.

Changes you make to the menu editing list for a workbook are reflected in the menu system whenever that workbook is open, but the Menu Editor shows only the changes made in the active workbook, no matter how many workbooks are open. If multiple workbooks containing menu editing lists are open, the menu system will combine and display the changes in all the workbooks, but the Menu Editor will still show only the changes made in the active workbook.

Note Because the Menu Editor doesn't show changes made with Visual Basic or changes made by the Menu Editor in other workbooks, the menu components shown in Microsoft Excel may not agree with the menu components shown in the Menu Editor.

For example, suppose you make some changes to the built-in File menu on the worksheet menu bar, where the first three menu items are New, Open, and Close. First, you open a new workbook, name it Mybook1.xls, and add an Open Special menu item to the File menu, just above the Close item. Then you close Mybook1.xls, open a second workbook, name this new workbook Mybook2.xls, and add an Open Database menu item just above the Close item on the File menu. If you then reopen Mybook1.xls (with Mybook2.xls still open), the File menu contains all the menu items: New, Open, Open Database, Open, and Close. (Because the workbook whose menu editing list contains Open Special is the most recently opened workbook, Open Special appears below Open Database on the menu.)

However, if you start the Menu Editor while Mybook1.xls is the active workbook, select the worksheet menu bar, and then open the File menu, you see only the New, Open, Open Special, and Close menu items. If you bring up the Menu Editor while Mybook2.xls is active, you see New, Open, Open Database, and Close on the File menu. The Menu Editor displays the effects of only the *active* workbook's menu editing list.

Design-Time Modifications to the Menu System

Design-time changes to the menu system are any changes you make before the application runs. This includes adding, deleting, moving, and restoring menu components, as well as setting menu component properties that won't change in response to changing conditions at run time. Depending on the scope of the modifications you want to make, you can either use Visual Basic procedures or make changes in the Menu Editor dialog box. For more information about a Visual Basic procedure, see the specific property or method in Help. For more information about the Menu Editor, see "menu editor" in Help.

▶ **To display the Menu Editor dialog box**

- While a Visual Basic module is active, click Menu Editor on the Tools menu.

Menu Editor button

You can also click the Menu Editor button on the Visual Basic toolbar while any worksheet is active.

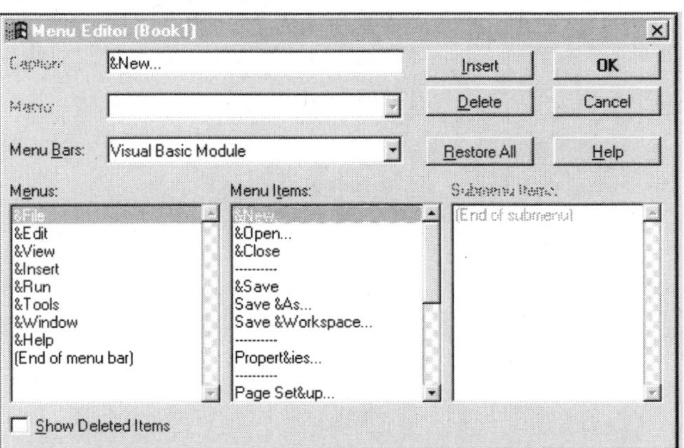

Adding a Custom Menu Bar

If you want to design a set of drop-down menus that differs significantly from what is available on the built-in menu bars, you may need to create a new menu bar. You can accomplish this using the Menu Editor or Visual Basic procedures.

Using the Menu Editor

The Menu Editor provides a convenient way to add a custom menu bar to the active workbook.

▶ **To add a menu bar to a workbook**

1. While a Visual Basic module is active, click Menu Editor on the Tools menu.
2. In the Menu Bars box, click the arrow to display the drop-down list, and then click the name of any menu bar.

   This step cancels the selection of items in the Menus, Menu Items, and Submenu Items boxes. If you omit this step, the text you type in the Caption box becomes the first menu item on the first menu that's selected in the Menus box.
3. Click Insert.
4. In the Caption box, either type a name for the new menu bar or accept the default name.

The new menu bar is added to the list in the Menu Bars box, below the final item. The default list of built-in menu bars is shown in the following table. The custom menu bars you create are listed in the order they're created. You can use up to 15 custom menu bars at one time.

Menu bar	Description
Worksheet	The menu bar that appears when a worksheet is active
Chart	The menu bar that appears when a chart is active
No Documents Open	The menu bar that appears when no workbooks are open
Visual Basic Module	The menu bar that appears when a Visual Basic module is active
Shortcut Menus 1	A group of shortcut menus that appears when the user clicks a toolbar, toolbar button, cell, column or row selection, workbook tab, window title bar, or the desktop with the right mouse button
Shortcut Menus 2	A group of shortcut menus that appears when the user clicks a drawing object, button graphic object, or text box graphic object with the right mouse button
Shortcut Menus 3	A group of shortcut menus that appears when the user clicks a chart series, text, plot area, axis, gridline, floor or arrow, legend, or the entire chart with the right mouse button

Note A shortcut menu is a type of menu, and each shortcut menu is represented by a **Menu** object in Visual Basic. Although shortcut menus are shown grouped into menu bars in the Menu Editor, a shortcut menu group isn't represented by a **MenuBar** object in Visual Basic.

Using Visual Basic

Use the **Add** method of the **MenuBars** collection to create a new menu bar; specifying the name of the new menu bar is optional.

```
MenuBars.Add "myWorksheetMenubar"
```

The **MenuBars** collection contains all the menu bars available in Microsoft Excel. The shortcut menu groups that appear in the Menu Editor cannot be accessed with the **MenuBars** method, as they aren't true menu bars. Use the **ShortcutMenus** method to access a shortcut menu, as described later in this chapter.

Activating a Menu Bar

Microsoft Excel automatically displays a built-in menu bar that's appropriate for the active sheet unless you explicitly activate a custom menu bar using a Visual Basic procedure. When you want Microsoft Excel to return to its normal menu bar behavior, you must deactivate the custom menu bar by activating the appropriate built-in menu bar.

Before you can activate a specific menu bar, you must access it using the **MenuBars** method, with the menu bar caption, index number, or built-in constant as an argument. You can use any of the constants in the following table as an argument to specify a built-in menu bar.

Constant	Associated menu bar
xlWorksheet	The menu bar displayed when a worksheet, macro sheet, or dialog sheet is active
xlChart	The menu bar displayed when a chart is active
xlModule	The menu bar displayed when when a Visual Basic module is active
xlNoDocuments	The menu bar displayed when no documents are open
xlInfo	The menu bar displayed when the Info Window is active
xlWorksheetShort	A short version of the worksheet menu bar (for compatibility with Microsoft Excel version 3.0)
xlChartShort	A short version of the chart menu bar (for compatibility with Microsoft Excel version 3.0)
xlWorksheet4	An old version of the worksheet menu bar (for compatibility with Microsoft Excel version 4.0)
xlChart4	An old version of the chart menu bar (for compatibility with Microsoft Excel version 4.0)

After you've accessed the custom or built-in menu bar you want to activate, use the **Activate** method to activate it. Microsoft Excel won't allow you to activate a built-in menu bar that isn't appropriate for the active sheet.

```
MenuBars(xlWorksheet4).Activate
```

Adding Menus

You can add a drop-down menu to any built-in or custom menu bar. Because Microsoft Excel displays different built-in menu bars when different sheet types are active (for instance, the Chart menu bar appears when you switch to a chart), you may have to add a command to more than one menu bar to make sure the user has access to the command regardless of what sheet type is active. For example, you might want to add a special Accounting menu to each menu bar so that employees in a company can run the corresponding macros from any sheet.

When you add a drop-down menu to a menu bar, you can specify an access key for the menu; the access key appears underlined when the menu is displayed. Although shortcut menus appear as "menu bar" groups in the Menu Editor, you can neither add custom shortcut menus to these menu bars nor delete built-in shortcut menus from them. You can, however, add items to or delete items from shortcut menus.

Using the Menu Editor

The Menu Editor provides a convenient way to add a drop-down menu to a built-in or custom menu bar.

▶ **To add a drop-down menu to a menu bar**

1. While a Visual Basic module is active, click Menu Editor on the Tools menu.
2. In the Menu Bars box, click the name of the menu bar to which you want to add your new menu.
3. In the Menus box, click the name of the menu to the left of which you want to insert the new menu.

   –Or–

   To add a menu to the right of the rightmost menu on the menu bar, click End Of Menu Bar.
4. Click Insert to create the new menu.
5. In the Caption box, type the name of the new menu.

   Type an ampersand (&) before the character you want to use as the access key for the menu.

Using Visual Basic

Use the **Add** method of the **Menus** collection to add a menu to the specified menu bar. The following example adds a new drop-down menu, myWorkMenu, to the left of the Help menu on the Chart menu bar.

```
Set newMenu = MenuBars(xlChart).Menus.Add( _
    Caption:="&MyWorkMenu", _
    before:="Help")
```

Note You use an ampersand (&) in the menu name in front of the character that will be used as the access key for the menu. After the menu has been added, you can specify the menu name either with or without the ampersand when you reference the menu using the **Menus** method.

Adding Commands and Separator Bars

You can add commands and separator bars to any built-in or custom menu. This section deals with adding these items to drop-down menus and shortcut menus. The following section addresses the specific issues of adding submenus and then adding menu items to those submenus.

Using the Menu Editor

The Menu Editor offers an easy method for adding items to menus.

▶ **To add a menu item to a drop-down menu or shortcut menu**

1. While a Visual Basic module is active, click Menu Editor on the Tools menu.
2. In the Menu Bars box, click the name of a menu bar or a group of shortcut menus.
3. In the Menus box, click the name of the menu to which you want to add the menu item or the object for which a shortcut menu is defined.
4. In the Menu Items box, click the name of the menu item above which you want to insert the new menu item.

   –Or–

   To add a menu item to the bottom of the menu, click End Of Menu.
5. Click Insert to create the new menu item.
6. In the Caption box, type a name for the new menu item.

   Type an ampersand (&) before the character you want to use as the access key for the new menu item. To create a separator bar, type one hyphen (-).
7. To specify that a particular procedure run whenever the user clicks the new menu item, enter the name of the procedure in the Macro box.

Using Visual Basic

Use the **Add** method of the **MenuItems** collection to add a new menu item to the specified menu. You can specify the menu item caption, its position on the menu, and the name of the procedure to run when the user clicks the menu item.

The following example adds an Open Database menu item to the File menu on the Worksheet menu bar. Microsoft Excel runs the OpenDatabaseProc Visual Basic procedure whenever the user clicks the menu item. Open Database appears directly above the Close item on the File menu.

```
Set databaseItem = MenuBars(xlWorksheet).Menus("File") _
    .MenuItems.Add(Caption:="Open &Database", _
        OnAction:="OpenDatabaseProc", _
        before:="Close")
```

To place the menu item at the end of the specified menu, omit the ***before*** argument.

To create a separator bar, specify "-" for the new menu caption, as shown in the following example.

```
MenuBars(xlWorksheet).Menus("File").MenuItems.Add _
    Caption:="-", before:="Close"
```

You cannot create a new shortcut menu, but you can modify a built-in shortcut menu by adding or deleting menu items. The following example adds a Format Special menu item at the end of the Worksheet Cell shortcut menu. Notice that although shortcut menus are displayed as groups in the Menu Editor, those menu groups don't actually belong to the **MenuBars** collection. To access shortcut menus, you must use the **ShortcutMenus** method instead of the **MenuBars** method.

```
ShortcutMenus(xlWorksheetCell).MenuItems.Add _
    Caption:="Format &Special", OnAction:="FormatSpecialProc"
```

Adding Submenus and Submenu Items

A submenu (child menu) is a menu attached to the right side of a menu item (the submenu caption) on another menu (the parent menu). Submenus can be added to both drop-down menus and shortcut menus.

Note A submenu caption is a menu item on the submenu's parent menu. Any commands, separator bars, or submenu captions on the submenu are also menu items; the submenu is their parent menu.

Just as you display the items on a drop-down menu by clicking the menu caption on the menu bar,you display items on a submenu by pointing to the submenu caption on the parent menu. Similarly, just as you first add an empty drop-down menu (containing a caption but no menu items) to a menu bar and then add individual menu items, you first add an empty submenu to a parent menu and then add menu items.

You can add submenu items to existing custom or built-in submenus, but you cannot add submenu items to built-in commands. For example, you can add a submenu item to the Record Macro submenu on the Tools menu, but not to the Macro command on the Tools menu. You can, however, delete a built-in command, add a custom submenu caption with the same name as the built-in command, and then add submenu items to the custom submenu.

Using the Menu Editor

To add a custom submenu using the Menu Editor, you start by adding the submenu caption as a new menu item on the parent menu. To do this, simply follow the instructions in the preceding section for adding a command to a menu, and add the submenu caption as a menu item. You don't need to specify a procedure in the Macro box. After you've added the submenu caption, you can add the submenu items. You can also add submenu items to an existing custom submenu or custom command (after you add a submenu item to a custom command, the command becomes a submenu caption).

▶ **To add a submenu item**

1. While a Visual Basic module is active, click Menu Editor on the Tools menu.
2. In the Menu Bars box, click the name of a menu bar or a group of shortcut menus.
3. In the Menus box, click the name of the menu to which you want to add the submenu or the object for which a shortcut menu is defined.
4. In the Menu Items box, click the name of the menu item to which you want to add the submenu item.
5. In the Submenu Items box, click the name of the submenu item above which you want to insert the new submenu item.

   –Or–

   To insert a submenu item at the bottom of the submenu, click End Of Submenu.
6. Choose Insert to create the new submenu item.

7. In the Caption box, type the name of the new submenu item.

   Type an ampersand (**&**) before the character you want to use as the access key for the new submenu item.

   To create a separator bar, type one hyphen (**-**).

8. To specify that a particular procedure run whenever the user chooses the submenu item, enter the name of the procedure in the Macro box.

Using Visual Basic

Adding a submenu to a menu using Visual Basic entails two main steps. First, you add the submenu caption to the parent menu, and then you add submenu items to the submenu.

The **AddMenu** method of the **MenuItems** collection adds a submenu caption. You cannot add submenu items to a command or separator bar created with the **Add** method. (This is different from the Menu Editor, where you use the same technique to add commands, separator bars, and submenu captions.)

The following example creates a custom menu.

```
MenuBars(xlModule).Menus.Add "myMenu"
```

The following example adds a submenu caption to a menu.

```
MenuBars(xlModule).Menus("myMenu").MenuItems.AddMenu "mySM"
```

Adding items to a submenu can be confusing because you must apply the **MenuItems** method once to access the submenu caption (a menu item on the parent menu), and then you must apply the method again to access the collection of menu items on the submenu. The following example adds a menu item to the submenu created in the preceding example.

```
MenuBars(xlModule).Menus("myMenu").MenuItems("mySM") _
    .MenuItems.Add "mySMItem"
```

The following example places a check mark next to a menu item on a submenu.

```
MenuBars(xlModule).Menus("myMenu").MenuItems("mySM") _
    .MenuItems("mySMItem").Checked = True
```

Note The **MenuItems** method returns a **MenuItem** object when the menu item is a command or a separator bar, and it returns a **Menu** object when the menu item is a submenu caption.

The following example combines the preceding four examples into one.

```
MenuBars(xlModule).Menus.Add("myMenu").MenuItems.AddMenu("mySM") _
    .MenuItems.Add("mySMItem").Checked = True
```

The following example adds a new menu to the Worksheet menu bar and then adds several new menu items and a submenu to the new menu.

```
Sub AddNewMenu()
    Set sortMenu = MenuBars(xlWorksheet).Menus.Add("&Sort By")
    With sortMenu.MenuItems
        .Add "Company Name", "SortByCompany"
        .Add "Category ID", "SortByCategory"
        .Add "Type", "SortByType"
        .Add ("-")
        .Add "Random", "SetRandomOrder"
        Set sortSubMenu = sortMenu.MenuItems _
                .AddMenu("Cost", before:="-")
            sortSubMenu.MenuItems.Add "Ascending", "SortByCostAscending"
            sortSubMenu.MenuItems.Add "Descending", _
                "SortByCostDescending"
    End With
End Sub
```

Deleting Menu Components

You can delete built-in or custom items from menus; you can delete built-in or custom menus from menu bars; and you can delete custom menu bars. Note, however, that although you can delete all the items on shortcut menus and built-in menu bars, you cannot delete the shortcut menus or built-in menu bars themselves.

Deleting built-in menu components can help you tailor your application to the needs of your user. For example, you might want to delete a built-in command from a menu and replace it with a custom version of the command that performs specialized tasks for the user. Or you might want to remove certain menu items to simplify the interface or reduce the possibility that inexperienced users will choose commands you didn't intend for them to use.

Note You can restore built-in menu bars, menus, or menu items that you've deleted. However, you cannot restore *custom* menu bars, menus, or menu items that you've deleted; you must recreate them.

Using the Menu Editor

The Menu Editor provides a quick, simple way to delete menu components. Remember that changes you make in the Menu Editor will be in effect whenever the workbook where you made the changes is open. If you want to restore built-in components that you've deleted, you must open the Menu Editor from the workbook where you originally made the deletions. For more information, see the following section.

▶ **To delete a menu system component**

1. While a Visual Basic module is active, click Menu Editor on the Tools menu.
2. In the appropriate box, click the name of the menu bar, menu, menu item, submenu item, or shortcut menu item that you want to delete.
3. Click Delete.

Using Visual Basic

Use the **Delete** method to delete a custom menu bar, a custom or built-in drop-down menu or submenu, or a custom or built-in menu item. You cannot delete a built-in menu bar or a shortcut menu.

The following example deletes the custom menu bar that has the caption myWorksheetMenubar.

```
MenuBars("myWorksheetMenubar").Delete
```

This example deletes the Edit menu from the Chart menu bar.

```
MenuBars(xlChart).Menus("Edit").Delete
```

This example deletes the Group menu item from the Drawing Object shortcut menu.

```
ShortcutMenus(xlDrawingObject).MenuItems("Group").Delete
```

You can restore built-in components that you've deleted. For more information, see the following section.

Restoring Built-in Menu Components

You can restore built-in menu bars, menus, or menu items that you've deleted. However, you cannot restore *custom* menu bars, menus, or menu items that you've deleted; you must recreate them.

Using the Menu Editor

If you want to restore built-in components that you've deleted using the Menu Editor, you must open the Menu Editor while the workbook where you originally made the deletions is active. You can restore menu components one at a time, or you can restore the entire default menu system for the active workbook at once. The Menu Editor cannot restore components deleted with Visual Basic code.

▶ **To restore a deleted menu item**

1. While a Visual Basic module is active, click Menu Editor on the Tools menu.
2. Select the Show Deleted Items check box.

   Deleted menu items appear dimmed.
3. In the appropriate box, select the deleted item that you want to restore.
4. Click Undelete.

To restore all the built-in menu bars, menus, menu items, and submenu items (that is, the entire default menu system) at once, click Restore All.

Caution Clicking Restore All not only restores deleted built-in components, but it also deletes from the active workbook every custom menu bar, menu, menu item, and submenu item that was added with the Menu Editor. Unless you're absolutely sure that there are no custom menu components you want to save, you should restore any deleted components one by one, using the foregoing procedure.

Using Visual Basic

Use the **Reset** method of the **MenuBars** collection to restore a built-in menu bar and all the menu components it contains to their default configuration.

```
MenuBars(xlWorksheet).Reset
```

Caution Be careful when you use this method; the **Reset** method not only restores any deleted built-in components of the menu bar, but it also deletes any custom components that have been added. Keep in mind that another macro may have added custom components to the menu bar in question, and resetting the menu bar will remove these as well. In addition, resetting the menu bar may cause conflicts with the menu editing lists of open workbooks. To avoid these problems, remove any menu components that your macro has added (and restore any menu components that you've deleted) one by one, without resetting the entire menu bar.

Set the ***restore*** argument of the **Add** method to **True** to restore a previously deleted built-in drop-down menu, shortcut menu, or menu item. To restore a previously deleted built-in submenu, set the ***restore*** argument of the **AddMenu** method to **True**. The following example restores the previously deleted Edit menu to the Chart menu bar.

```
MenuBars(xlChart).Menus.Add caption:="Edit", _
    before:="View", restore:=True
```

This example restores the previously deleted Open menu item to the File menu on the Worksheet menu bar.

```
MenuBars(xlWorksheet).Menus("File").MenuItems.Add _
    caption := "Open...", _
    restore := True, _
    before := "Close"
```

This example restores the previously deleted Protection submenu to the Tools menu on the Visual Basic Module menu bar.

```
MenuBars(xlModule).Menus("Tools").MenuItems.AddMenu _
    caption := "Protection", _
    restore := True, _
    before := "Add-Ins..."
```

Note If you omit the ***restore*** argument, Visual Basic adds a custom command that has the same name as the deleted built-in command but lacks its built-in functionality. If you omit the ***before*** argument, Visual Basic places the restored command at the end of the menu, rather than in its original position.

Run-Time Modifications to the Menu System

The menu system that you create at design time can be programmed to respond dynamically to changing conditions at run time. If a particular menu item is an inappropriate choice in certain contexts, you can prevent the user from selecting it by removing it or disabling it (also called *dimming* the menu item, or making it gray). If a menu item represents an option with two possible states, you can place a check mark next to it to show that the option is turned on and remove the check mark to show that it's turned off. For example, the Microsoft Excel default menu system uses a check mark on the Record Macro submenu on the Tools menu to show that the Use Relative References option is turned on.

Finally, you might want to rename a menu item in response to current conditions. For example, clicking the Freeze Panes command on the Windows menu causes it to be renamed "Unfreeze Panes."

Note that although you can make design-time changes to the menu system using either the Menu Editor or Visual Basic, you must use Visual Basic to make any run-time changes.

Displaying Menu Components Dynamically

If a menu component applies only to a particular sheet or workbook, it's best if that menu component appears only when that sheet or workbook is active; this reduces needless clutter in the interface. However, unlike changes made to the menu system with the Menu Editor, changes made using Visual Basic are stored globally, and their effects cannot be limited to a given workbook or sheet. You can, however, limit their lifetime to the period between the opening and subsequent closing of a particular workbook or the period between the activation and subsequent deactivation of a given sheet.

If you want a menu or menu item to appear only on a specific sheet, Visual Basic must add the component to the menu system every time the user activates the sheet and delete it every time the user deactivates the sheet. If you want to associate a menu bar with a sheet, Visual Basic can activate the menu bar when the user activates the sheet and then deactivate the menu bar when the user deactivates the sheet, rather than add the entire menu bar and then delete it. To do this, set the sheet's **OnSheetActivate** property to a procedure that adds or activates the component, and set the sheet's **OnSheetDeactivate** property to a procedure that removes or deactivates the component.

The following example causes the procedure AddNewMenu to run whenever the worksheet named "data108" is activated. This procedure adds a new menu to the Worksheet menu bar. The procedure RemoveNewMenu removes the menu when the worksheet is deactivated.

```
With Worksheets("data108")
    .OnSheetActivate = "AddNewMenu"
    .OnSheetDeactivate = "RemoveNewMenu"
End With
```

Use the Auto_Open and Auto_Close procedures attached to a workbook to add and remove menu components or to activate and deactivate a menu bar whenever that workbook is opened and closed. If you close the workbook without removing any new menus that you created while it was open, these menus will remain on the menu bar until you quit Microsoft Excel.

Enabling or Disabling Menu Components

If you want to prevent the user from choosing a particular menu item under certain conditions, you can disable it. A disabled command still appears on the menu, but it appears dimmed and doesn't respond to user actions. Use the **Enabled** property to enable or disable a menu item. The **Enabled** property is **True** if the menu item is enabled, and it's **False** if the menu item is disabled (you cannot set the **Enabled** property for a built-in menu item). The following example adds the Open Database menu item to the File menu on the Worksheet menu bar and then disables Open Database.

```
MenuBars(xlWorksheet).Menus("File") _
    .MenuItems.Add("Open Database").Enabled = False
```

If you want to disable all the commands on a drop-down menu, you can disable the menu itself. This effectively disables all the commands on the menu, as the user cannot access them. The following example disables the entire File menu on the Worksheet menu bar.

```
MenuBars(xlWorksheet).Menus("File").Enabled = False
```

Note You can disable all the menu items on a submenu, but you cannot disable the submenu itself.

The following example disables all the menu items on the Cost submenu that was created by the example in "Adding Submenus and Submenu Items" earlier in this chapter.

```
With MenuBars(xlWorksheet).Menus("sort by").MenuItems("cost")
    For Each mnItem In .MenuItems
        mnItem.Enabled = False
    Next
End With
```

You can enable or disable a shortcut menu by setting the **Enabled** property for menu item 0 (zero). The following example disables the Worksheet Cell shortcut menu.

```
ShortcutMenus(xlWorksheetCell).MenuItems(0).Enabled = False
```

Adding or Removing a Check Mark

If a menu item represents an option that has only two states, you can add or remove a check mark next to the menu item to indicate the current state of the option. The check mark should be alternately added or removed—and the option turned on or off, accordingly—each time the user clicks the menu item.

Use the **Checked** property to add or remove a check mark next to a menu item. The **Checked** property is **True** if the menu item is checked, and it's **False** if the menu item isn't checked. To see how this works, suppose the following procedure is assigned to the custom menu item Database on the View menu on the Worksheet menu bar. This menu item offers the user the option of viewing a worksheet either in database view or in worksheet view. Every time the user clicks the Database menu item, the procedure adds or removes a check mark next to the item and then switches views.

```
Sub DatabaseView()
    With MenuBars(xlWorksheet).Menus("View").MenuItems("Database")
    .Checked = Not .Checked
    If .Checked Then
            'Switch to database view
            .
            .
            .
        Else
            'Switch to worksheet view
            .
            .
            .
        End If
    End With
End Sub
```

Renaming a Menu Item

You can use the **Caption** property of a menu item to change the item's name in response to changing conditions in your Visual Basic code. Suppose, for example, that you've a menu command that opens a database. After the user has opened a database, you may want to replace the original command with a command that closes the database. The following example shows how you could accomplish this.

```
MenuBars("MyMenubar").Menus("File").MenuItems("Open Database") _
    .Caption = "Close &Database"
```

When you rename a menu item this way, make sure that the other procedures in your application reference the menu item by its new name (Close Database, in this example).

You can also use variables to refer to a menu item. An advantage of this technique is that variables continue to work even if the item's caption changes. For example, the following line of code sets a variable to the Open Database menu item.

```
Set myMenu = MenuBars("My Menubar").Menus _
    ("File").MenuItems("Open Database")
```

You can change the caption later using the following code.

```
myMenu.Caption = "Close &Database"
```

Toolbars and Toolbar Buttons

Microsoft Excel provides a system of toolbars containing toolbar buttons that the user can click to access frequently used commands. Each toolbar can appear as a bar docked at the top, at the bottom, or on either side of the application window, or as a floating window positioned anywhere on the workspace. Each toolbar button is a simple, graphical control that allows the user to exchange information with your application.

There are several types of controls that are classified as toolbar buttons.

The most common type of toolbar button is simply a button control containing a graphic. The graphic, called the *button image*, is a visual representation of the command or option accessed by the toolbar button. The user can click one of these toolbar buttons to execute a command (for example, clicking the New Workbook button on the Standard toolbar creates a new workbook) or to alternate between the two possible states of an option represented by a button (for example, clicking the Bold button on the Formatting toolbar alternately applies and removes bold formatting from selected text).

Another type of toolbar button is composed of a button control containing a graphic and an attached drop-down palette. The user clicks the drop-down arrow to display a palette and chooses an option from the palette. The user clicks the button control to apply the current option. For example, clicking the drop-down arrow of the Font Color button displays a palette of font colors. Clicking the button control of this toolbar button applies the color to the selected text.

A combination drop-down edit box can also be a toolbar button. The user either types text in the box or clicks the drop-down arrow and then clicks an item in the list. For example, you can set the font size of the selected text by either clicking an item in the drop-down list contained in the Font Size button or typing an entry in the edit box.

The last type of toolbar button is the TipWizard® box, which consists of a text box containing tips pertinent to the user's current task and a spinner that lets the user browse through tips.

To display any Microsoft Excel toolbar, click Toolbars on the View menu, and then click the name of the toolbar you want to display. To see additional available buttons, click Customize in the Toolbars dialog box, and browse through the items in the Categories box.

Now that you understand what toolbars and the various types of toolbar buttons are, you can study the specifics of modifying the toolbars and toolbar buttons described in the preceding paragraphs. In the following sections, you will learn how to customize toolbars, how to control the availability of the toolbar changes you've made, and how to make specific types of changes.

Guidelines for Customizing Toolbars

Microsoft Excel offers you a wide range of ways to modify the built-in toolbar system to better serve the needs of the user. You can create new toolbars; add new toolbar buttons to built-in or custom toolbars; modify the image on a toolbar button face; and assign macros, ToolTip text, and status bar text to toolbar buttons. If a toolbar button contains an edit box or a text box, you can adjust the width of the box.

Whether you modify a built-in toolbar or create a new one depends on the extent of the changes you want to make. Modifying a built-in toolbar makes sense if you're adding or changing only a few toolbar buttons; creating a new toolbar may be more convenient if you want to provide an entirely different assortment of commands than are found on any of the built-in toolbars or if you want to present a number of custom toolbar buttons as a distinct group. Regardless of how many changes you make, you can restore the built-in menu system to its default state whenever you want.

In addition to the above changes, which are usually made at *design time*, you can use Visual Basic procedures to change the properties of toolbars and toolbar buttons in response to user input while your application is running (at *run time*). For example, you can hide a toolbar when the user no longer needs it, move or resize a toolbar to keep it out of the user's way, disable a toolbar button to prevent the user from clicking it at an inappropriate time, or switch between the "pushed" appearance and the "not pushed" appearance of a toolbar button every time the user clicks it.

Scope of the Changes

Besides making changes to the system of toolbars, you can control the scope of the changes by choosing whether to store them with the workspace or with a workbook.

Storing Toolbars in a Workspace or a Workbook

Custom toolbars can be stored with the workspace or with the workbook. When you quit Microsoft Excel, the toolbars in the workspace are saved in the file *Username*.xlb (where *Username* is the Windows 95 logon name of the current user). If the user isn't logged on, the filename is Excel5.xlb. The toolbars saved in a workbook are stored in the workbook file.

Workbook-level toolbars make it easier to create a polished user interface for a custom application, such as an add-in, and to distribute custom toolbar buttons and their supporting procedures. If you're going to distribute a custom toolbar with a custom application, you should attach it to the workbook containing the application so that the toolbar is stored in the same file as the application.

▶ **To move a toolbar from the workspace to a workbook**

1. While a Visual Basic module is active, click Attach Toolbars on the Tools menu.
2. In the Custom Toolbars box, click the name of the toolbar you want to copy to the active workbook.
3. Click Copy.

   The name of the toolbar you copied appears in the Toolbars In Workbook box.

You can delete the original workspace-level toolbar by clicking Toolbars on the View menu, selecting the check box next to the name of the toolbar you want to delete, and then clicking Delete. If you don't delete the workspace version of the toolbar, you can change it without affecting the version stored in the workbook. If you make changes to the workspace version of the toolbar and would like to update the workbook version to match it, you can copy the current workspace version of the toolbar to the workbook again, replacing the previous workbook version.

After you've copied a toolbar to a workbook, the toolbar becomes available only after the user has opened that workbook. A workbook toolbar retains not only the name and contents of the toolbar, but also the assignment of code to toolbar buttons; the location, size, and shape of the toolbar; its on-screen position; and whether it's visible or hidden.

You can also delete a workbook toolbar.

▶ **To delete a workbook toolbar**

1. While a Visual Basic module is active, click Attach Toolbars on the Tools menu.
2. In the Toolbars In Workbook box, click the name of the toolbar you want to delete.
3. Click Delete.

How Workbook and Workspace Toolbars Interact

When you open a workbook that contains one or more toolbars, Microsoft Excel first determines whether a workspace toolbar with that name already exists. If not, Microsoft Excel creates a new workspace toolbar and copies the workbook toolbar into it. This way, the you get a fresh copy of the toolbar that you can alter by hiding it or by copying toolbar buttons to or from the workspace-level copy of the toolbar. When you quit Microsoft Excel, changes made to this copy of the toolbar are stored with the workspace file.

There is no way to rename the toolbar, so when the workbook or add-in is reopened, the workspace already contains a toolbar with the same name as the workbook toolbar, and Microsoft Excel uses the workspace copy rather than reloading the workbook toolbar. However, the procedures that support the toolbar buttons in the open workbook still run when the user clicks the corresponding toolbar button.

As a developer, you can design a toolbar and then attach it to an add-in workbook, as shown in the preceding section. When the user opens the add-in workbook, the custom add-in toolbar appears. The user can then edit it and move toolbar buttons from it to personal toolbars, without affecting the copy stored in the add-in workbook. The user's changed toolbars are stored with the workspace file when he or she quits Microsoft Excel. When the user starts Microsoft Excel again, the edited toolbar appears; clicking one of the developer's toolbar buttons loads the add-in workbook containing the procedure attached to that toolbar button. To generate a fresh copy of the workbook toolbar, the user can delete the edited copy.

Design-Time Modifications to Toolbars and Toolbar Buttons

The simplest way to make design-time changes to toolbars or toolbar buttons is from the user interface. To display the Customize dialog box, click Toolbars on the View menu, and then click Customize.

With the Customize dialog box open, you can create a new toolbar, add new or built-in toolbar buttons to a toolbar, delete toolbar buttons from a toolbar, adjust spacing between toolbar buttons, and change the width of a toolbar button containing an edit box. You can use the Button Image Editor to customize the image associated with a particular toolbar button; and you can use the Assign Macro dialog box to assign a procedure that runs when the user clicks that toolbar button.

Although the user interface provides the most practical way to make design-time changes to the toolbars, you can also make these changes using Visual Basic. If you want to see how Visual Basic would make a particular change, turn on the macro recorder, make the change manually, stop the recorder, and then examine the code that the macro recorder has produced. If you want more information about a specific object, property, or method that you find in the code, click anywhere in the term in question, and press F1. For more information about using the macro recorder, see "Recording and Running Macros" in Help.

Run-Time Modifications to Toolbars and Toolbar Buttons

If you want to make changes to toolbars and toolbar buttons while your application is running, you must use Visual Basic procedures to access the **Toolbar** and **ToolbarButton** objects and apply the appropriate properties or methods. For more information about using these objects, see "Toolbar Object" and "ToolbarButton Object" in Help.

Note Be careful when you use the toolbar button index number to access a member of the **ToolbarButtons** collection. The index number represents the position of the button on the toolbar, and this number can change when buttons are added to or deleted from the toolbar.

Displaying or Hiding Toolbars

A toolbar takes up screen space that could otherwise be used to display data; you can display a toolbar when necessary and hide it when the user no longer needs it. A toolbar is visible if its **Visible** property is **True**, and it isn't visible if this property is **False**. Setting this property to **True** corresponds to selecting the check box next to the name of the toolbar in the Toolbars dialog box and then clicking OK.

For example, the following procedure, assigned to the View MyToolbar menu item on the View menu, toggles the value of the **Checked** property of the menu item and the visible property of the toolbar every time the user clicks the menu item. When the toolbar is made visible, it reappears in the same position it occupied when it was made invisible.

```
Sub ViewMyAppToolbar()
    With MenuBars(xlWorksheet).Menus("View").MenuItems("View MyToolbar")
        .Checked = Not .Checked
        Toolbars("MyAppTools").Visible = .Checked
    End With
End Sub
```

When a toolbar is visible, the user can click any toolbar button on it to run that button's assigned procedure.

Moving and Resizing Toolbars

You may want to adjust the prominence of a toolbar on the screen in response to changing conditions while your application is running. To do this, you can change the size or position of the toolbar. Toolbars support several properties that you can use to resize them; to dock them at the top, bottom, left, or right edge of the workspace; or to position them elsewhere on the screen (if they're *floating* toolbars). For more information about the properties and methods you can use with **Toolbar** objects, see "Toolbar Object" in Help, and use the jumps at the top of the topic to display the lists of properties and methods.

Restoring a Built-in Toolbar

If one of the default toolbars has been modified—either by a user or by a Visual Basic procedure—you can return the toolbar to its default state by using the **Reset** method. Using this method corresponds to clicking the Toolbars command on the View menu, selecting the check box next to the name of the customized built-in toolbar in the Toolbars dialog box, and then clicking Reset.

For example, you can use the following code to reset all the toolbars to their default state and simultaneously delete all the custom toolbars.

```
For Each thisToolbar In Toolbars
    If thisToolbar.BuiltIn Then
        thisToolbar.Reset
    Else
        thisToolbar.Delete
    End If
Next
```

Caution Be careful when you use the **Reset** method; it not only restores any built-in toolbar buttons that have been deleted, but it also deletes any custom toolbar buttons that have been added. Keep in mind that another macro may have added custom toolbar buttons to the toolbar, and resetting the toolbar will remove these buttons as well. To avoid these problems, remove any toolbar buttons added by your application one by one, without resetting the entire toolbar.

Adding and Deleting Toolbar Buttons

If you want a specific toolbar button to appear on a toolbar only under certain conditions, you can add and delete the button at run time. When you add a toolbar button, you can attach a macro to it or change the ToolTip text associated with it.

The **Add** method for the **ToolbarButtons** collection adds a new toolbar button to an existing built-in or custom toolbar. The ***onAction*** argument of the **Add** method specifies the procedure that will run when the user clicks the toolbar button.

Use the **Name** property for the new toolbar buttons to set the ToolTip text (the text that appears beneath a toolbar button when the mouse pointer is directly over that button). To set the status bar text (the text that appears appears in the status bar when the mouse pointer is directly over a button), use the ***statusBar*** argument of the **Add** method.

The following example adds two toolbar buttons, separated by a gap, to the toolbar "MyAppTools."

```
With Toolbars("MyAppTools").ToolbarButtons

    ' Add a button with the clock face
    Set newButton1 = .Add( _
        Button:=213, _
        before:=1, _
        OnAction:="Module1.MyScheduler", _
        Enabled:=True, _
        Pushed:=False, _
        StatusBar:="Run custom scheduler")   ' sets status bar text
    newButton1.Name = "Scheduler"            ' sets tool tip text

    ' Add a button with the scissors face
    Set newButton2 = .Add( _
        Button:=12, _
        before:=2, _
        OnAction:="Module1.MyCutProc", _
        Enabled:=True, _
        Pushed:=False, _
        StatusBar:="Custom cut command")     ' sets status bar text
    newButton2.Name = "Custom Cut"           ' sets tool tip text

    ' Add a space between the buttons
    .Add Button:=0, before:=2
End With
```

If you don't specify a position for a new toolbar button, the button is added at the end of the toolbar. If you don't specify a procedure to run when the toolbar button is clicked and it's a built-in button, the default action occurs. If you don't specify a procedure for a custom toolbar button, nothing happens when the button is clicked.

The **Delete** method deletes a toolbar button. The following example deletes toolbar button three from the Standard toolbar.

```
Toolbars("Standard").ToolbarButtons(3).Delete
```

Enabling or Disabling Toolbar Buttons

You may want to control the availability of a toolbar button while your application is running, to prevent the user from clicking the button at inappropriate times. To do this, you can dynamically enable and disable the toolbar button. When a toolbar button is disabled, it beeps when it's clicked and doesn't run the procedure associated with it. The **Enabled** property sets or returns the state (enabled or disabled) of a toolbar button.

The following example disables button three on the Standard toolbar.

```
Toolbars("Standard").ToolbarButtons(3).Enabled = False
```

Making Custom Toolbar Buttons Look Pressed

If a toolbar button represents an option with two possible states, you can change the appearance of the toolbar button to indicate the current state of the option: When the option is turned on, the associated button looks pressed; when the option is turned off, the button looks raised. This is analagous to placing or removing a check mark next to a menu item.

The **Pushed** property for a toolbar button is **True** if the button appears pressed, and it's **False** if the button doesn't appear pressed. For example, the following procedure, assigned to a new Database View toolbar button, changes the appearance of the toolbar button before switching between special views on the worksheet.

```
Sub DatabaseView()
    With Toolbars("MyAppToolbar").ToolbarButtons(3)
        .Pushed = Not .Pushed
        If .Pushed Then
            'Switch to database view
            .
            .
            .
        Else
            'Switch to worksheet view
            .
            .
            .
        End If
    End With
End Sub
```

CHAPTER 10

Communicating with Other Applications

In addition to working with Microsoft Excel data, you may want your application to exchange data with other applications, such as Microsoft Project, Word, or PowerPoint®. There are several ways to communicate with other applications, including OLE automation, dynamic data exchange (DDE), and dynamic-link libraries (DLLs). This chapter shows you how to use these methods to communicate with other applications.

Contents

Using OLE Automation from Microsoft Excel

OLE Automation is a feature (introduced in Microsoft OLE version 2.0) that allows you to retrieve, edit, and export data by referencing another application's objects, properties, and methods. Objects that can be returned from outside the application are *OLE Automation objects*. An application that exposes its OLE Automation objects to other applications is called an *OLE server application*. An application that can access and manipulate OLE Automation objects is called an *OLE controller application*. Not all applications support OLE Automation; the applications that do support it are said to be *OLE compatible*.

To exchange data with another application by using OLE Automation while working in Microsoft Excel, you first create a reference to the application you want to communicate with (the OLE server application). Then, using the objects, properties, and methods of the other application, you add, change, or delete information. When you finish making changes, you close the OLE server application from inside the OLE controller application.

Referring to Another Application

When you refer to another application by using OLE Automation, you actually refer to one of the application's top-level objects. The task you want to accomplish determines the object you refer to. The following table shows the most common top-level objects for Microsoft Project and Word; for a more complete list of the top-level objects in Office applications, see the *Microsoft Solutions Development Kit.*

To return	From this application	Use this class name
A reference to the Microsoft Project **Application** object, which allows you to use all of Microsoft Project's objects, properties, and methods	Microsoft Project	MSProject.Application
A reference to a new **Project** object or a reference to the **Project** object specified in the **GetObject** method, which allows you to work with a specific project	Microsoft Project	MSProject.Project
A reference to the **WordBasic** object, which allows you to run WordBasic statements	Word	Word.Basic

There are two ways to refer to a top-level object using OLE Automation from Microsoft Excel. One way is to refer to the application's object library using the References dialog box.

▶ **To establish a reference to an application's object library**

1. Switch to a Visual Basic module.
2. On the Tools menu, click References.
3. Click the object library you want to refer to.

   If the object library you want doesn't appear in the Available References box, click Browse and then locate the file you want.

After you've established a reference to an object library, you can use commands from the library in your Microsoft Excel Visual Basic code. For example, after you've established a reference to the Word object library, you can use a command such as **FileOpen**. However, referring to objects this way can yield unpredictable results, because you cannot always be sure which object will be returned. The preferred way is either to use the **CreateObject** method to start the application and return a reference to a top-level object or to use the **GetObject** method to return a reference to a top-level object from an application that's already running. For more information about these methods, see the following sections.

Note An *object library* is a catalog of an application's objects, properties, and methods. Any application that registers object libraries in the Windows system registry allow other applications to use its objects, properties, and methods as if they were native to that application.

Word exposes three top-level objects: the **Application** object, the **CurValues** object, and the **WordBasic** object. The **WordBasic** object is the most commonly used of the three because you execute all WordBasic commands by first referring to this object.

The CreateObject Method

The **CreateObject** method starts a new instance of an application invisibly and returns a reference to a new top-level object. The following code loads Microsoft Project into memory and returns the Microsoft Project **Application** object.

```
Dim projapp As Object

Set projapp = CreateObject("MSProject.Application")
```

The following example returns a **Project** object instead of the **Application** object, specifying the **Project** class name in the **CreateObject** argument.

```
Dim projapp As Object

Set projapp = CreateObject("MSProject.Project")
```

The GetObject Function

The **GetObject** function returns a top-level object reference from an application that's is already running. The ***pathName*** argument can be either the complete path to an existing file or an empty string, or it can be omitted altogether. If you omit this argument, you must supply the class argument; the function will then create a new instance of the application. An error will be returned if the path you specify doesn't exist. For more information about the syntax for the **GetObject** function, see "GetObject function" in Help.

The following code returns the Microsoft Project **Application** object from an instance of Microsoft Project that's already loaded into memory. You can return a **Project** object instead by specifying the **Project** class name in the **GetObject** argument.

```
Dim projapp As Object

Set projapp = GetObject("", "MSProject.Application")
```

Retrieving Data

After you set an object variable to the top-level object of an application, you can use the application's objects, properties, and methods to retrieve data. The following code searches a Microsoft Project file for information and returns the information to a range on Sheet1 in the active Microsoft Excel workbook.

```
Dim proj as Object
Dim nameoftask As String
Dim writetime As Integer, edittime As Integer, incorptime As Integer
Dim busytime As Integer, i As Integer, mecount As Integer
Dim othercount As Integer, timespent As Integer

Set proj = GetObject("c:\winproj\MyProject.mpp", "msproject.project")
mecount = 0
othercount = 0

For i = 1 To proj.tasks.Count
    If proj.tasks(i).Resources.Count > 0 Then
    With proj.tasks(i)
        If .Resources(1).Name = "Jane Smith" Then
            timespent = .Duration
            Select Case .Name
                Case "write"
                    writetime = writetime + timespent
                Case "incorp. tech review"
                    incorptime = incorptime + timespent
                Case "edit incorp.", "review/edit merged art"
                    edittime = edittime + timespent
                Case "art to designer", "hand-off to production"
                    busytime = busytime + timespent
                Case Else
                MsgBox "Error " & .Name
            End Select
        End If
    End With
    End If
Next i
```

```
With Worksheets("sheet1")
    .Range("B1") = writetime
    .Range("B2") = incorptime
    .Range("B3") = busytime
    .Range("B4") = edittime

    .Range("A1") = "Writing"
    .Range("A2") = "Adding Changes"
    .Range("A3") = "Other"
    .Range("A4") = "Editing"
End With

proj.Application.Quit
```

Changing Object Properties

After data is inserted into a worksheet, the data belongs to Microsoft Excel. You can then convert that data to a Microsoft Excel chart and customize the chart by changing its properties. The following code charts the data retrieved from Microsoft Project and customizes the chart by adding a legend and a blue title.

```
Dim newEmbeddedChart As ChartObject

Set newEmbeddedChart = Worksheets(1).ChartObjects.Add(50, 50, 250, 250)
With newEmbeddedChart.Chart
    .ChartWizard Source:=Worksheets(1).Range("A1:B4"), _
        Gallery:=xlPie, Format:=7, PlotBy:=xlColumns, _
        CategoryLabels:=1, SeriesLabels:=0, HasLegend:=2
    .HasTitle = True
    .ChartTitle.Text = "My Schedule"
    .ChartTitle.Font.Color = RGB(0, 0, 255)
    .HasLegend = True
End With
```

Exporting Data

In addition to importing data into Microsoft Excel from another application, you may also want to export data from Microsoft Excel to another application so that you can create a presentation with it or combine it with other data.

Exporting Data to PowerPoint

You may want to present your data in an application other than Microsoft Excel. The following example charts the data from Sheet1 in the active workbook (the imported data from Microsoft Project) and places it in a PowerPoint slide for presentation. The code starts the PowerPoint application, creates a presentation, and adds one slide to it. The slide is then prepared to accept a chart, and you can chart the data from Sheet1 by using the Microsoft Excel ChartWizard.

```
Set pptApp = CreateObject("PowerPoint.Application.7")
Set pptPres = pptApp.Presentations.Add
Set pptSlide = pptPres.Slides.Add(1, 1)
Set pptSlideObj = pptSlide.Objects _
    .AddOleObject("Excel.Chart", 1000, 1000, 5000, 5000)
Set pptChart = pptSlideObj.Object
With pptChart
    .ChartWizard Source:=Worksheets("sheet1").Range("A1:B4"), _
        Gallery:=xlPie, Format:=7, PlotBy:=xlColumns, _
        CategoryLabels:=1, SeriesLabels:=0, HasLegend:=2
    .HasTitle = True
    .ChartTitle.Text = "My Schedule"
    .ChartTitle.Font.Color = RGB(0, 0, 255)
    .HasLegend = True
End With
pptPres.SaveAs "MayWork.ppt"
```

Exporting Data to Word

The customized **Chart** object that the example in the preceding section creates can be placed in a Word document by means of OLE Automation. However, the approach is different because you use WordBasic statements and functions instead of objects, properties, and methods to refer to and work with the **WordBasic** object.

The following example takes the first **Chart** object from Sheet1 in the active workbook, copies it to the Clipboard, and pastes it into the Word document called "MyDoc.doc."

```
Dim wdbasic As Object

Worksheets("sheet1").ChartObjects(1).Copy
Set wdbasic = CreateObject("word.basic")
With wdbasic
    .FileOpen "C:\msoffice\winword\MyDoc.doc"
    .EditPaste
    .FileSave
End With
```

Note The preceding example embeds the chart in the Word document. To link the chart into the Word document, use the **EditPasteSpecial** method. For more information about linking and embedding, see "Communicating with Embedded Word Objects" later in this chapter.

Using Conventional Arguments

When you use WordBasic commands as part of OLE Automation, you must use conventional arguments instead of named arguments—that is, you must specify arguments by position instead of by name. If you leave out a conventional argument, you must indicate the missing value with a comma; you can, however, omit trailing commas. The following line of WordBasic code uses named arguments to apply drop cap formatting.

```
FormatDropCap .Position = 1, .Font = "Arial", .DropHeight = "3", \
    .DistFromText = "6"
```

The following Visual Basic code does the same thing as the preceding example, but using conventional arguments. Your code must have already created the object variable `wordobj` and opened a file in Word before you run this line.

```
wordobj.FormatDropCap 1, "Arial", 3, 6
```

Note The syntax for most statement and function entries in WordBasic Help describes the correct order for conventional arguments. There are some exceptions, however. For a complete list of these exceptions and the correct order of their arguments, see the Position.txt file included on the companion disk in the *Microsoft Word Developer's Kit.*

Running a Macro from Outside Word

In addition to calling individual WordBasic commands, you can use the **ToolsMacro** command to run existing Word macros from outside Word. The following code runs a Word macro called "CreateDocandFormat." For more information about the **ToolsMacro** command and its arguments, see "ToolsMacro" in Help.

```
Dim wordobj As Object

Set wordobj = CreateObject("Word.Basic")
wordobj.toolsmacro "CreateDocandFormat", True
```

Quitting Applications

Because OLE Automation objects can use a significant amount of memory, you should *explicitly* close an object when you no longer need it. Many OLE Automation objects support a **Quit** method that closes an object and quits the OLE server application from inside the OLE controller application. The following code explicitly closes Microsoft Project.

```
proj.Application.Quit
```

Setting an object variable to "nothing" both releases the object variable and closes the OLE server application. The following code opens a document in Word and then sets the variable to "nothing," thereby closing the OLE server application.

```
Dim wdBasic As Object

Set wdBasic = CreateObject("word.basic")
wdBasic.FileOpen "C:\msoffice\winword\Speedup.doc"
Set wdBasic = Nothing
```

Communicating with Embedded Word Objects

When you embed a Word document in a Microsoft Excel worksheet, Microsoft Excel controls the object, and Word controls everything inside the object.

A *linked object* is an object that contains a reference pointer to its application. Data associated with a linked object isn't stored within the application that contains the object. If you change data in a linked application, the data will change in the original application as well.

An *embedded object* is an object that contains a "snapshot" of data existing at the time you embedded the object. Data associated with an embedded object is stored in the file in which the object is embedded. If you change data in an embedded object, the data in the original application doesn't change.

An OLE *container* application is an OLE-based application that can store embedded or linked objects provided by OLE object applications. An OLE *object* application is an application that exposes the OLE object.

Editing an Embedded Word Object

To edit a Word document embedded as an OLE object, you must activate it before you can refer to one of the top-level objects. The following example activates and edits a Word document, which is the first OLE object on Sheet1.

```
Dim wordobj As Object

Worksheets("sheet1").OLEObjects(1).Verb
Set wordobj = Worksheets("sheet1").OLEObjects(1).Object _
    .Application.WordBasic
With wordobj
    .Insert "This is the new first line."
    .InsertPara
    .LineUp 1
    .EndOfLine 1
    .Bold
    .LineDown 1
End With
```

Note Using the **Verb** method with no arguments, as demonstrated in the preceding example, is equivalent to using the **Activate** method. For information about the arguments you can use with the **Verb** method, see "Verb method" in Help.

Printing an Embedded Word Object

To print a Word document that's embedded on a Microsoft Excel sheet, first activate the embedded document, and then use the WordBasic **FilePrint** command. The following example activates, edits, and prints a Word document, which is the first OLE object on Sheet1.

```
Dim wordobj As Object

Worksheets("sheet1").OLEObjects(1).Verb
Set wordobj = Worksheets("sheet1").OLEObjects(1).Object _
    .Application.WordBasic
With wordobj
    .Insert "Dear Mrs. Jones:"
    .InsertPara
    .FilePrint
    .FileClose
End With
```

Using Dynamic-Link Libraries

A dynamic-link library (DLL) is a library of routines loaded into memory and linked to applications at run time. DLLs are usually created in a programming language such as C, MASM, Assembler, or FORTRAN, and they contain procedures you call in your application. You can call DLL functions from Visual Basic in Microsoft Excel. For more information about DLLs, see the *Microsoft Excel Developer's Kit.*

Using Dynamic Data Exchange

Dynamic data exchange (DDE) is a mechanism that permits two applications to communicate by automatically and continuously exchanging data. Many applications that don't yet support OLE Automation support DDE. To run a DDE conversation between applications, you establish a channel, select a topic, request and send data, and then close the channel when you finish exchanging data. The following table lists the tasks that Microsoft Excel performs with DDE and the method used for each task.

Task	Method
Starting DDE	**DDEInitiate**
Getting text from another application	**DDERequest**
Sending text to another application	**DDEPoke**
Carrying out a command in another application	**DDEExecute**
Ending DDE	**DDETerminate**

Note Not all applications support DDE. To find out whether an application supports DDE, see the documentation for that application.

The following procedure uses most of the DDE calls explained in the preceding table. The **DemoDDE()** procedure places the text string "I'm here" in cell A1 on Sheet1 of the active workbook.

```
Sub DemoDDE()
    Set dataCell = ActiveWorkbook.Worksheets("Sheet1").Range("A1")
    dataCell.Value = "I'm here!"
    ChannelNumber = Application.DDEInitiate("DDE", "Form1")
    Application.DDEPoke ChannelNumber, "Text1", dataCell
    Application.DDETerminate ChannelNumber
End Sub
```

Sending Keystrokes

When you're operating in the Microsoft Windows operating system, the only way to communicate with applications that don't support OLE, OLE Automation, or DDE is by sending keystrokes using the **SendKeys** method.

Note You can send keystrokes only to a Windows-based application that's running. MS-DOS–based applications and Macintosh applications don't accept keystrokes.

The **SendKeys** method is processed when your system is idle or when the **DoEvents** method is called. If the wait argument of the **SendKeys** method is **True**, Microsoft Excel waits for the keys to be processed before it returns control to the procedure; if the wait argument is **False**, the procedure continues to run without waiting for the keys to be processed. The following example sends keystrokes to the Calculator that add the numbers from 1 to 10 and then close the Calculator.

```
Sub DemoSendKeys()
    returnvalue = Shell("calc.exe", 1)
    AppActivate returnvalue
    For i = 1 To 10
        SendKeys i & "{+}", True
        Next i
        SendKeys "=", True
        SendKeys "%{F4}", True
End Sub
```

Note Keystrokes are sent to the active application. If the active application isn't the one you want to send keystrokes to, you need to activate it using the **AppActivate** statement. If the application you want to send keystrokes to isn't already running, start it using the **Shell** function. If you don't specifically activate another application, your DDE procedure will send keystrokes to itself.

To specify characters that aren't displayed when you press the key (such as ENTER or TAB), enclose the key code in braces ({ }), and enclose the braces in double straight quotation marks. To specify a key to be used in combination with SHIFT, CTRL, or ALT, precede the braces with "+", "^", or "%", respectively. The following example sends the key combination ALT+F4.

```
SendKeys "%{F4}", True
```

For a complete list of key codes, see "SendKeys method" in Help.

Note You cannot send keystrokes that generate interrupts instead of character codes; for example, you cannot send ALT+CTRL+DEL or PRINT SCREEN.

CHAPTER 11

Automatic Procedures and OnEvent Procedures

An *event* in Microsoft Excel is the occurrence of an action such as opening a workbook, switching to a sheet, using a particular key combination, or recalculating a worksheet. Some events are initiated by the user; others are initiated by Microsoft Excel or by other applications. By assigning procedures to events, you can enhance or alter the way users interact with your application.

There are three main classes of event-driven procedures, organized by the way you associate the procedure with the event:

- You can associate a procedure with the action of clicking a button or other object; you do this by using the Assign Macro command on the Tools menu, as discussed in the preceding chapters.
- You can associate a procedure with one of a specfic set of workbook-level and worksheet-level events by giving the procedure a special automatic procedure name that begins with "Auto_".
- You can associate a procedure with a defined event for an object by setting an OnEvent property of the object (such as the **OnWindow** or **OnCalculate** property) to the procedure name.

Contents

Creating Automatic Procedures

An *automatic procedure* runs automatically whenever one of a specific set of events occurs. You can associate automatic procedures with either workbook-level or worksheet-level events.

Using Workbook-Level Automatic Procedures

A workbook-level automatic procedure is stored in a workbook and runs automatically whenever an event such as opening or closing a workbook occurs. You can place automatic procedures in any Visual Basic module in the workbook.

Workbook-level automatic procedures are identified by their names as they appear in a module—Auto_Open or Auto_Close, for example. When you name the procedure in a module, the name isn't case sensitive; therefore, Auto_Open and auto_open are equivalent.

The following table lists the automatic procedure names available in Microsoft Excel and describes the event that causes each procedure to run.

Procedure name	Event that causes the procedure to run
Auto_Open	User opens the workbook that contains the procedure.
Auto_Close	User closes the workbook that contains the procedure.
Auto_Add	User installs the add-in that contains the procedure, or the **Installed** property of the add-in is set to **True**. For more information, see Chapter 12, "Creating Add-Ins."
Auto_Remove	User removes the add-in that contains the procedure, or the **Installed** property of the add-in is set to **False**. For more information, see Chapter 12, "Creating Add-Ins."

Note To give you more programming flexibility, the Auto_Open and Auto_Close procedures don't run if you open or close a workbook under program control. For example, the statement `Workbooks.Open filename:="book2.xls"` opens the workbook but doesn't run the Auto_Open procedure. To run the Auto_Open procedure under program control, use the **RunAutoMacros** method. For more information, see "RunAutoMacros method" in Help.

▶ To define an automatic procedure

1. Switch to the Visual Basic module where you want to store the automatic procedure.
2. Create a new procedure named "Auto_Open," "Auto_Close," "Auto_Add," or "Auto_Remove."
3. Write the code for the procedure.

To test an automatic procedure without having to explicitly open or close the workbook, click Macro on the Tools menu, click the name of the procedure, and then click Run.

You can use at most one Auto_Open and one Auto_Close procedure in each workbook. If more than one Auto_Open or Auto_Close procedure exists in a workbook, none of them will run when the user opens or closes the workbook.

If more than one Auto_Add or Auto_Remove procedure exists in an add-in, an error occurs when the user installs or removes the add-in.

Note You can prevent an automatic procedure from running by holding down SHIFT while opening or closing a workbook or switching to or from a worksheet. For example, you can hold down SHIFT while opening an application that's under development to avoid running any of its Auto_Open procedures.

Auto_Open Procedures

An Auto_Open procedure runs when the user opens the workbook that contains the procedure. You can use an Auto_Open procedure to set up menu bars under program control, to customize the workbook for the operating system it's running with, to display a custom startup screen, or to initiate links to other files or other applications.

For example, the following procedure automatically adds a custom menu item to the worksheet Tools menu.

```
Sub Auto_Open()
    MenuBars(xlWorksheet).Menus("Tools").MenuItems.Add _
        caption := "My Analysis", _
        onAction := ThisWorkbook.Name & "!Module2.MyAnalysisProc", _
        before := 1
End Sub
```

Auto_Close Procedures

An Auto_Close procedure runs just before the workbook containing the procedure closes. You can use this feature to restore menu bars, toolbars, and other elements of the user interface to their previous condition and to save and close the files that support an application.

You can also use an Auto_Close procedure to ensure an orderly disconnection from another application. For example, if your application uses Windows Terminal to download stock quotations from a remote information service, you probably want Terminal to log off from the service before you close the workbook, as shown in the following procedure.

```
Sub Auto_Close()
    MenuBars(xlWorksheet).Menus("Tools"). _
        MenuItems("My Analysis").Delete
    CloseLogFile         'Procedure: close transaction file.
    DisconnectService    'Procedure: disconnect info service.
End Sub
```

Using Worksheet-Level Automatic Procedures

A worksheet-level automatic procedure is associated with a specific worksheet and runs automatically when an event such as activating or deactivating a worksheet occurs. In most cases, it's better to use workbook-level automatic procedures than worksheet-level procedures. This is because when you use worksheet-level procedures, you must explicitly define procedures for each worksheet you want to support, and because these worksheet-level procedures are then not available for chart sheets and Visual Basic modules.

Worksheet-level automatic procedures are associated with defined names that begin with Auto_Open_, Auto_Close_, Auto_Activate_, or Auto_Deactivate_. These defined names aren't case sensitive; therefore, Auto_Open_ and auto_open_ are equivalent. The following table lists the automatic procedure names available in Microsoft Excel, and it describes the event that causes each procedure to run.

Beginning of procedure name	Event that causes the procedure to run
Auto_Open_	User opens the workbook that contains the worksheet.
Auto_Close_	User closes the workbook that contains the worksheet.
Auto_Activate_	User activates the worksheet.
Auto_Deactivate_	User deactivates the worksheet.

► **To create a defined-name automatic procedure**

1. Switch to the worksheet for which you want to define an automatic procedure.
2. On the Insert menu, point to Name, and then click Define.
3. In the Names In Workbook box, type a name that begins with Auto_Open_, Auto_Close_, Auto_Activate_, or Auto_Deactivate_. Precede the name with the worksheet name, followed by an exclamation point—for example, type **Sheet1!Auto_Open_First**

4. In the Refers To box, type an equal sign and the name of the procedure you want to associate with the defined name; for example, **=CheckData** would be a valid entry in the Refers To box.

   The procedure named in the Refers To box runs when the workbook that contains the worksheet is opened or closed or when the worksheet is activated or deactivated. You can use the same name you typed in the Names In Workbook box, or you can type a different name.

5. Click Add.

Note If the procedure you want to associate with the defined name is in a different workbook, you must specify the name of the workbook, followed by an exclamation point, along with the procedure name. For example, if the CheckData procedure were in another workbook named "DataBook," you would type **=DataBook!CheckData** in the Refers To box.

If the procedure you want to associate with the defined name has the same name as another procedure in the same workbook, you must specify the name of the module, followed by a period, along with the procedure name. For example, to specify the CheckData procedure in the module called "DataLib" in the workbook that contains the defined name, you would type **=DataLib.CheckData** in the Refers To box.

To specify one of several procedures with the same name in a workbook other than the one that contains the defined name, specify the workbook name and the module name in the Refers To box; for example, type **=DataBook!DataLib.CheckData**.

Defined-name automatic procedures differ from standard automatic procedures in that the name defined on the worksheet needs only to begin with the name of the type of the procedure you want to run for the event. For example, you can define the names Auto_Open_Public, Auto_Open_StartupScreen, and Auto_Open_Files on the same worksheet; when the user opens the workbook containing the worksheet, the procedures associated with all three names run.

Standard automatic procedures run before defined-name procedures. For example, suppose that you place an Auto_Open procedure in a module, and on a certain worksheet you define the name Auto_Open_ThisWorksheet as the text StartupWorksheet. When the user opens the workbook, the workbook-level Auto_Open procedure runs before the StartupWorksheet procedure. Note that you cannot set the order in which the Auto_Open procedures defined in a worksheet will run.

Note You can prevent an automatic procedure from running by holding down SHIFT while opening or closing a workbook or switching to or from a worksheet. For example, you can hold down SHIFT while opening an application that's under development to avoid running any of its Auto_Open procedures.

Creating OnEvent Procedures

Certain objects in Visual Basic have properties and methods that are associated with specific events. For example, the **Button** object has an **OnAction** property, which is associated with clicking the button; and the **Application** object has an **OnRepeat** method, which is associated with clicking Repeat on the Edit menu. These events are generated by Microsoft Excel, sometimes as the result of user input. An example of an event that isn't the result of user input is the arrival of data from another application by means of OLE (see the **OnData** property).

If you associate a procedure with one of these properties or methods, that procedure—called an *OnEvent procedure* or an *event handler*—will run whenever the event associated with the property or method occurs.

The following table lists the properties and methods you can use to trap events.

Property or method	Event that causes the associated procedure to run
OnAction	Clicking a control or graphic object, clicking a menu command, or clicking a toolbar button
OnCalculate	Recalculating a worksheet
OnData	The arrival of data from another application by way of DDE or OLE
OnDoubleClick	Double-clicking anywhere on a chart sheet, dialog sheet, module, or worksheet
OnEntry	Entering data using the formula bar or editing data in a cell
OnKey	Pressing a particular key or key combination
OnRepeat	Clicking Repeat on the Edit menu
OnSheetActivate	Activating a chart sheet, dialog sheet, module, worksheet, workbook, or Microsoft Excel itself
OnSheetDeactivate	Deactivating a chart sheet, dialog sheet, module, worksheet, workbook, or Microsoft Excel itself
OnTime	Waiting until a specific time arrives, or waiting for a specified time delay
OnUndo	Clicking Undo on the Edit menu
OnWindow	Activating a window

There are several steps involved in creating and using any type of OnEvent procedure:

- You must create the procedure (the event handler) you want to run when the specified event occurs.
- Elsewhere in your Visual Basic code, you must associate the event handler with the event you want to respond to. After the statement that associates the event with its handler is executed, the handler runs whenever the event occurs; this is called *trapping* the event.
- When you want to stop trapping this event, you must disassociate the event from the event handler.

▶ To associate an event with an OnEvent procedure

- Set the property associated with the event—or set the ***procedure*** argument of the method associated with the event—to the name of the OnEvent procedure, as shown in the following examples.

```
ActiveSheet.Buttons("MyButton").OnAction = "ButtonClickHandler"
Application.OnRepeat text:= "Paste Again", procedure:= "PasteAgain"
```

▶ To disassociate an event from an OnEvent procedure

- Set the property associated with the event—or set the ***procedure*** argument of the method associated with the event—to the empty string (""), as shown in the following examples.

```
ActiveSheet.Buttons("MyButton").OnAction = ""
Application.OnRepeat text:= "Paste Again", procedure:= ""
```

The following sections show how event trapping is done with specific types of events.

OnAction Property

An OnAction event handler runs when you act on a control or when you click a graphic object or a toolbar button. For example, if you create a custom dialog box, you can use the **OnAction** property of each control in the dialog box to associate the controls with their event handlers. Unlike other OnEvent properties and methods, the **OnAction** property of a control retains its value between sessions, so you don't have to run a procedure to set its value at the beginning of each session.

The following example causes the StartDialog procedure to run when the dialog box first starts, and it causes the ButtonPressed procedure to run whenever the user presses a button on the first dialog sheet.

```
With DialogSheets(1)
    .DialogFrame.OnAction = "StartDialog"
    .Buttons.OnAction = "ButtonPressed"
End With
```

Note that you can also set the **OnAction** property for a control by selecting the control, clicking Assign Macro on the Tools menu, and entering a procedure name in the Macro Name/Reference box.

For more information about using the **OnAction** property, see Chapter 8, "Controls and Dialog Boxes," and Chapter 9, "Menus and Toolbars," or see the appropriate topic in Help.

OnCalculate Property

An OnCalculate event handler runs immediately after a worksheet is recalculated. Use the **OnCalculate** property of the **Worksheet** object to associate a procedure with the recalculation of a single, specified worksheet. Use the **OnCalculate** property of the **Application** object to associate a procedure with the recalculation of any open worksheet.

For example, you might use an OnCalculate handler to update column widths when new data is recalculated, as shown in the following example.

```
Sub TrapCalculate()
    Application.OnCalculate = "FitColumns"
End Sub

Sub FitColumns()
    Columns("A:H").EntireColumn.AutoFit
End Sub
```

If you've assigned a procedure to the **OnCalculate** property of the **Application** object, the procedure runs for any recalculated worksheet that doesn't have its own OnCalculate handler.

Note The OnCalculate event handler doesn't run if you recalculate under program control. For example, the statement `Application.Calculate` recalculates all open workbooks, but it doesn't cause the OnCalculate event handler to run.

OnData Property

An OnData event handler runs when data arrives from an application other than Microsoft Excel. You can use the **OnData** property of either the **Worksheet** or **Application** object to associate a procedure with the arrival of data linked to one of these objects through dynamic data exchange (DDE) or OLE.

For example, the following code associates the arrival of stock price data on a worksheet with a procedure that validates each item of information..

```
Sub TrapData()                           'Set up OnData trapping
    Worksheets("StockAnalysis").OnData = "ValidateData"
End Sub

Sub ValidateData()                       'OnData handler
    For Each Cell in InputRange          'InputRange is a public variable
        CheckData                        'Run my validation procedure
    Next
End Sub
```

For more information about using DDE and OLE, see Chapter 10, "Communicating with Other Applications."

OnDoubleClick Property

An OnDoubleClick event handler runs when you double-click anywhere on a sheet. You can use the **OnDoubleClick** property of a **Chart**, **DialogSheet**, or **Worksheet** object to associate a procedure with double-clicking anywhere on the sheet. You can use the **OnDoubleClick** property of the **Application** object to associate the event handler with double-clicking on any sheet in any open workbook.

This property overrides the normal behavior of a double-click in Microsoft Excel. For example, you can double-click a cell to edit its contents in the cell instead of in the formula bar. If you set an OnDoubleClick handler, your event handler can override the in-cell editing. This may confuse users, so be careful when you use the **OnDoubleClick** property.

The following code runs the DoubleClickEvent procedure whenever you double-click a cell on Sheet1.

```
Sub TrapDoubleClick()
    Worksheets("Sheet1").OnDoubleClick = "DoubleClickEvent"
End Sub

Sub DoubleClickEvent()
    MsgBox "Something was double-clicked on Sheet1"
End Sub
```

Note The OnDoubleClick event handler doesn't run if you simulate double-clicking under program control. For example, the statement `Application.DoubleClick` simulates double-clicking the active cell, but the OnDoubleClick event handler doesn't run.

OnEntry Property

An OnEntry event handler runs when the user either enters data on a worksheet using the formula bar or edits data in a cell. You can use the **OnEntry** property of a **Worksheet** object to associate a procedure with the entry of data on any worksheet. You can use the **OnEntry** property of the **Application** object to associate the event handler with the entry of data on any worksheet in any open workbook. The event handler runs after the user enters data in a cell or in the formula bar and then either presses ENTER, selects another cell, or clicks the enter box on the formula bar.

For example, the following code associates the OnEntry event with a procedure that validates the data entered in a cell in column B on the GeneCountDB worksheet.

```
Sub TrapEntry()
    ActiveWorkbook.Worksheets("GeneCountDB").OnEntry = _
        "ValidateColB"
End Sub

Sub ValidateColB()
    With ActiveCell
        If .Column = 2 Then                'Test for second column.
            If IsNumeric(.Value) Then
                If .Value < 0 Or .Value > 255 Then
                    MsgBox "Entry must be between 0 and 255."
                    .Value = ""
                End If
            Else
                'Handle non-numeric entry
                MsgBox "Entry must be a number between 0 and 255."
                .Value = ""
            End If
        End If
    End With
End Sub
```

Note The OnEntry event handler doesn't run if you enter data in a cell by clicking either Cut, Copy, or Paste on the Edit menu, or if you change the contents of a cell under program control.

OnKey Method

An OnKey event handler runs when the user presses a specified key combination. To associate a procedure with a specified key combination, use the ***procedure*** argument to the **OnKey** method of the **Application** object. Unlike many of the other OnEvent handlers, the OnKey handler does run if you simulate sending keystrokes to Microsoft Excel under program control. You would use the **SendKeys** method to do this.

The following code runs the DoReports procedure when the user presses F12.

```
Sub TrapKeys()                              'Trap key combinations.
    Application.OnKey _
        key := "{F12}" , _
        procedure := "DoReports"
End Sub

Sub DoReports()                             'F12 OnKey handler.
    AssembleReports
    PrintReports
End Sub
```

For a complete list of special codes for key combinations, see "OnKey method" in Help.

Note The OnKey event handler doesn't run if its associated key combination is pressed while another procedure is running. Therefore, you cannot use an OnKey handler if you want to run a special procedure when the user presses ESC to stop the currently running procedure. You can, however, use the **EnableCancelKey** property to modify the behavior of the ESC key. For more information, see "EnableCancelKey property" in Help.

OnRepeat and OnUndo Methods

An OnRepeat event handler runs when the user clicks Repeat on the Edit menu. A good use for an OnRepeat event handler is to allow the user to rerun a macro that performs a series of complicated operations on a worksheet. (Usually, clicking Repeat on the Edit menu after a macro has run will repeat only the last operation in the macro.)

You can use the ***procedure*** argument to the **OnRepeat** method of the **Application** object to customize the the Repeat menu item and to associate a procedure with the action of clicking this menu item.

For example, suppose that after pasting a date into a cell, you want to increment the date by one day in each successive paste from the cell above the active cell. To do this, you might use code such as that shown in the following procedure.

```
Sub TrapRepeat()
    Application.OnRepeat _
        text:= "Paste Next Day", _
        procedure := "PasteIncrement"
End Sub

Sub PasteIncrement()                            'OnRepeat handler.
    With ActiveCell
        .Value = .Offset(-1, 0) + 1             'Add a day.
    End With
End Sub
```

Similarly, an OnUndo event handler runs when the user clicks Undo on the Edit menu. You use the ***procedure*** argument to the **OnUndo** method of the **Application** object to customize the Undo menu item and to associate a procedure with the action of clicking this menu item.

For example, in a procedure that inserts a row containing data for a new record, the last action might be to enter data in a cell; when this happens, the Undo menu item changes to Undo Entry. However, choosing this command removes the information entered in the cell, when you'd probably want to delete the entire row with a command named Undo New Record instead.

OnSheetActivate and OnSheetDeactivate Properties

An OnSheetActivate event handler runs whenever the user switches to a sheet in an open workbook. Set the **OnSheetActivate** property for the **Application** object to run a procedure whenever the user switches to any sheet in the application. Set the **OnSheetActivate** property for a **Workbook** to run a procedure whenever the user switches to any sheet in a specific workbook. Set the **OnSheetActivate** property for a **Chart**, **DialogSheet**, **Module**, or **Worksheet** object to run a procedure whenever the user switches to a specific sheet in a workbook.

You can use **OnSheetActivate** to ensure that a toolbar that belongs to the workbook is displayed whenever the user switches to that workbook. For example, the following Auto_Open procedure in a workbook initiates trapping for the OnSheetActivate event for the workbook and runs a procedure that displays an Engineering Analysis toolbar whenever the user switches to the workbook.

```
Sub Auto_Open()
    ThisWorkbook.OnSheetActivate = "WBActivateHandler"
End Sub

Sub WBActivateHandler()
    If ActiveSheet.Name = "My_Data" Then
        Toolbars("EngAnalysisToolbar").Visible = True
    Else
        Toolbars("EngAnalysisToolbar").Visible = False
    End If
End Sub
```

Another use for an OnSheetActivate procedure is to display a custom menu bar whenever the user switches to a sheet of a certain type. For example, if the user switches to a chart sheet, the built-in chart menu bar is displayed automatically. If you create a custom chart menu bar, Microsoft Excel doesn't display it unless you create a procedure that runs whenever the user switches to a chart sheet.

Similarly, an OnSheetDeactivate procedure runs whenever the user switches away from a sheet or workbook. OnSheetDeactivate procedures are useful for resetting a customized user interface—for example returning menu bars, toolbars, and view settings to their original states.

Note The OnSheetActivate and OnSheetDeactivate event handlers don't run when you activate a sheet under program control.

When you activate a workbook, the workbook becomes active before the OnSheetDeactivate procedure in the previous workbook runs. Therefore, using the **ActiveSheet** or **ActiveWorkbook** property in the OnSheetDeactivate handler may produce unpredictable results.

OnTime Method

An OnTime event handler runs at a specified time in the future—either at a specified time of day or after a specified period of time has passed. This event handler runs only if Microsoft Excel is running and the workbook containing the OnTime event handler is loaded. You can use the arguments to the **OnTime** method of the **Application** object to specify the time you want the handler to run and the name of the handler. For example, to accumulate and print a series of reports every day at noon, you might use the following code.

```
'Initialize trapping using OnTime method
Sub TrapTime()
    'Set OnTime arguments
    Application.OnTime _
        earliestTime := TimeValue("12:00:00"), _
        procedure := "DoReports"
End Sub

Sub DoReports()                'OnTime handler
    AssembleReports
    PrintReports
End Sub
```

The TrapTime procedure initializes trapping of the OnTime event; at the first noon after TrapTime runs, Microsoft Excel runs the DoReports handler. To run the procedure only once, set the ***earliestTime*** argument to a date and a time rather than using the time alone.

If another procedure is running when the event occurs, Microsoft Excel waits for an additional interval specified by the ***latestTime*** argument of the **OnTime** method. For example, the following version of the TrapTime procedure waits for half an hour for Microsoft Excel to become free, and then it stops the event.

```
Sub TrapTime()                     'Initialize OnTime trapping.
    Application.OnTime _
        earliestTime := TimeValue("12:00:00"), _
        procedure := "MyOnTimeHandler", _
        latestTime := TimeValue("12:30:00")
End Sub
```

If you don't supply the ***latestTime*** argument, the procedure runs when Microsoft Excel next becomes available. You can schedule multiple OnTime handlers to run at different times; if you schedule more than one OnTime handler for the same time, the last-scheduled procedure runs first.

Tip The initialization of an OnTime event isn't stored from session to session. To achieve the effect of its being stored, you can place in the startup folder a workbook that contains both an Auto_Open procedure and the OnTime handler itself. The Auto_Open procedure must initialize OnTime trapping for a specific time. Then, whenever Microsoft Excel is started, trapping of that event is reinitialized.

To remove a pending OnTime event, you must specify the exact time of the event and the name of its handler, and you must set the ***schedule*** argument to **False**. For example, if there are two OnTime events scheduled for noon—one handled by DoReports and the other one handled by a procedure called CleanUp—you can stop the CleanUp handler request with the following code.

```
Application.OnTime _
    earliestTime := TimeValue("12:00:00"), _
    procedure := "CleanUp", _
    schedule := False
```

Note With the **OnTime** method, the user can work until an OnTime event occurs; with the **Wait** method, the user cannot interact with Microsoft Excel until the wait is over. To suspend all activity except for printing and recalculation, use the **Wait** method as shown in the following statement.

```
'Wait 15 seconds
Application.Wait Now + TimeValue("00:00:15")
```

For more information about the **Wait** method, see "Wait method" in Help.

OnWindow Property

An OnWindow event handler runs whenever the user switches to a window. To associate a procedure with switching to any window in the Microsoft Excel application, use the **OnWindow** property of the **Application** object, as shown in the following example.

```
Application.OnWindow = "AllWindowHandler"
```

To associate a procedure with switching to any window in the Microsoft Excel application, use the **OnWindow** property of a **Window** object. To associate a procedure with switching to a specific sheet in a workbook, use an Auto_Activate procedure, as described earlier in this chapter.

For example, the following code contains a procedure that traps each instance of switching to the second window called BikeDB.xls and then forces the window to appear at a specific location on-screen.

```
Sub TrapBicycle2()
    Windows("BikeDB.XLS:2").OnWindow = "PositionWindow"
End Sub

Sub PositionWindow()
    With Windows("BikeDB.XLS:2")
        .Left = 0
        .Top = 100
        .Width = 300
        .Height = 50
    End With
End Sub
```

If a workbook, worksheet, or other sheet has an associated OnSheetActivate procedure, it runs after the procedure specified in the **OnWindow** property.

Note The OnWindow event handler doesn't run if you switch to a window under program control.

CHAPTER 12

Creating Add-Ins

This chapter shows you how to package Microsoft Excel worksheets, controls, menus, toolbars, and supporting Visual Basic modules in the form of an add-in application. You can use add-ins to assemble and distribute custom features that, from the user's point of view, act as if they're built into Microsoft Excel itself.

An add-in is a hidden, read-only workbook in which the Visual Basic code has been fully compiled from a source workbook. Because the code is already fully compiled, there is no compiler-induced delay when you run a procedure from an add-in. The add-in is hidden so that users can run procedures without having to see your code in a workbook. This also saves the system resources that would otherwise be required to display a workbook. Finally, the add-in is read-only so that users cannot make inadvertent changes to your code.

Contents

Improving Performance with Add-Ins

You can improve your code's performance by compiling a workbook to an add-in. In a workbook that isn't an add-in, Visual Basic uses incremental compilation to reduce the amount of time it takes to compile changes to code. However, when you compile an add-in, Visual Basic fully compiles the code, which may slightly improve performance.

You can further improve performance by compiling the add-in on the platform in which you want to run it. For example, you can write an add-in that runs in both the Windows and Macintosh operating systems. Although you can successfully move the compiled add-in from one platform to another, performance suffers. Instead, move the source workbook and recompile it in the other platform.

Preparing a Workbook to Compile to an Add-In

You create a source workbook for an add-in the same way you create any other workbook. However, before you compile the source workbook to an add-in, there are several unique issues associated with add-ins that you need to be aware of.

Note Because add-in applications cannot be edited, it's extremely important that you keep a copy of your original workbook so that you can update its procedures or add new procedures.

Tips for Debugging Add-ins

Before compiling a workbook to an add-in, you can hide the workbook and then run its procedures from another workbook. This will help you find reference errors and errors that occur because the workbook is hidden. If your code uses error handling, you can turn on the Break On All Errors option to disable the error handler and display error messages. The Break On All Errors option is located on the Module General tab in the Options dialog box (Tools menu).

Note After you compile the add-in, Microsoft Excel ignores the state of the Break On All Errors option. Therefore, your add-in's error handler will run, regardless of whether this option was on or off when you compiled the add-in.

After an add-in is compiled, it can be difficult to debug. The add-in's procedures don't appear in the Run dialog box, so you cannot use the debugging features such as Step Into and Step Over, nor can you see the add-in code in the Debug window. This behavior is intentional—you usually don't want users to be able to single-step through your code or to see your code in the Debug window.

You can use an error handler, line numbers, and the **Debug.Print** statement to continue debugging after you compile the add-in. Although line numbering may sound archaic, it does give you a way to indicate where an error occurred. You can number all the lines in your code, or just the lines in certain critical sections, as shown in the following example.

```
Sub AddinSub()
    Dim x, y As Integer
    On Error GoTo ErrHandler
    ' Notice the line number in the following statement
10  For x = 1 To 10
        For y = 1 To 10
            If x = 7 And y = 7 Then
                ThisWorkbook.Worksheets("Sheet" & x * y).Cells(1, 1) = 5
            End If
        Next y
    Next x
```

```
    ' Here's another line number . . .
50  ' Do some more stuff
    ' Exit sub before running error handler
Exit Sub
ErrHandler:
    ' This statement prints the error information
    Debug.Print "Error " & Err & " " & Error(Err) & _
        " in line no. " & Erl
    ' This line prints the values of two variables of interest
    Debug.Print "x ="; x; Chr(13); "y ="; y
End Sub
```

To use code in the following example, compile it to an add-in; create a new workbook, add a module to it; and then create a reference to the add-in using the References dialog box (Tools menu). In the new workbook, create a small sub that calls the AddinSub procedure:

```
Sub dbg()
    AddinSub
End Sub
```

The AddinSub procedure should fail on the line that contains the **Worksheets** method call (unless the add-in contains more than 48 worksheets), although you'll see no indication of this error. Press CTRL+G to display the Debug window; notice that the **Debug.Print** statements in AddinSub wrote error information to the Immediate pane. Notice also that the error occurred on a line that didn't have a line number. In this case, the **Erl** function returns line number 10, which is the previous line number closest to the line in which the error occurred.

Before you compile a copy of a workbook in the add-in format (assuming that you've already thoroughly tested and debugged your code), remember to remove all debugging code, such as **Stop** statements and **Debug.Print** calls.

Using the ThisWorkbook Property

The most important thing to remember when writing an add-in is the definition of the active workbook. The active workbook is the one that's on top in the Microsoft Excel window. The active workbook isn't necessarily the one that contains the running Visual Basic code. In fact, an add-in can never be the active workbook, because it's invisible.

When you're writing and debugging an add-in, the workbook that contains the code is often the active workbook. Therefore, statements that contain an implicit **ActiveWorkbook** property call—such as `DialogSheets("MyDialog").Show`—work properly. When you compile the add-in and run the same code, the implicit **ActiveWorkbook** property call returns the workbook that's on top, not the workbook that contains the dialog sheet named "MyDialog." This causes the code to fail.

Using the **ThisWorkbook** property eliminates the workbook referencing problem. In addition to using **ThisWorkbook**, you should always use complete references to objects, meaning that you should start with **ThisWorkbook** and then navigate down the object hierarchy, as shown in the following code.

Implicit **ActiveWorkbook** calls cause this code to fail when it's a compiled add-in.

```
Sub Test1()
    ' Bad code
    DialogSheets("myDialog").Show
    Worksheets("AddinSheet").Range("A1") = _
        DialogSheets("myDialog").EditBoxes(1).Text
End Sub
```

```
Sub Test2()
    ' Good code
    With ThisWorkbook
        .DialogSheets("myDialog").Show
        .Worksheets("AddinSheet").Range("A1") = _
            .DialogSheets("myDialog").EditBoxes(1).Text
    End With
End Sub
```

```
Sub Test3()
    ' Good code
    Set tw = ThisWorkbook
    Set myDialog = tw.DialogSheets("myDialog")
    Set AddinSheet = tw.Worksheets("AddinSheet")
    myDialog.Show
    AddinSheet.Range("A1") = myDialog.EditBoxes(1).Text
End Sub
```

Using **ThisWorkbook** with complete references to objects eliminates the problem.

Don't forget that objects are often used in arguments to methods; it's very easy to overlook the workbook reference issue in such cases, as shown in the following code.

There's an implicit **ActiveWorkbook.ActiveWorksheet** call here, which causes the procedure to fail when it's a compiled add-in.

```
Sub AnotherTest1()
    ' Bad code
    Set tw = ThisWorkbook
    Set AddinSheet = tw.Worksheets("Sheet1")
    AddinSheet.UsedRange.Sort key1:=Range("A1")
End Sub

Sub AnotherTest2()
    ' Good code
    Set tw = ThisWorkbook
    Set AddinSheet = tw.Worksheets("Sheet1")
    AddinSheet.UsedRange.Sort key1:=AddinSheet.Range("A1")
End Sub
```

Using the AddinSheet object variable solves the reference problem.

Updating References to Procedures in Add-Ins

When you write and debug your add-in code, the workbook that contains the code probably has the filename extension .xls. When you compile the workbook, the add-in you create has the filename extension .xla.

Note If your system isn't set up to display filename extensions, you won't be able to tell the difference between your source workbook and your add-in in the Open dialog box (File menu). To display filename extensions, open the Windows Explorer, and then click Options on the View menu. Next, clear the Hide MS-DOS File Extensions For File Types That Are Registered check box on the View tab.

Suppose you create a custom button that refers to a procedure in a workbook before it's compiled to an add-in. The button's **OnAction** property contains a reference to the original workbook filename—the one with the .xls extension. When you create an add-in from the workbook, the add-in has a different filename extension. Unless you update the button's **OnAction** property to refer to the procedure in the add-in, clicking the button will cause Microsoft Excel to open the original workbook and run the version of the procedure stored there, instead of calling the procedure in the add-in.

In most cases, you can update **OnAction** references using code similar to that shown in the following example. Remember to run this code in the workbook that contains custom buttons.

```
Sub ConvertRefs()
    For Each sh In ActiveWorkbook.Sheets
        If TypeName(sh) <> "Module" Then
            For Each b In sh.Buttons
                mystr = b.OnAction
                strpos = InStr(mystr, ".xls")
                If strpos <> 0 Then
                    l = Len(mystr)
                    b.OnAction = Left$(mystr, strpos - 1) & _
                        ".xla" & Right$(mystr, l - strpos - 3)
                End If
            Next b
        End If
    Next sh
End Sub
```

Maintaining References to Other Add-Ins

If an add-in's source workbook contains a reference to another add-in—for instance, a reference to Xlodbc.xla—make sure that when you distribute the add-ins, the referenced add-in is stored somewhere on the user's machine where the calling add-in can find it. When you compile a source workbook to an add-in, Microsoft Excel stores a hard-coded path to the referenced add-in in the calling add-in. If you move the calling add-in to another computer (when you distribute the add-in to your users, for example), and if Microsoft Excel cannot find the file in the hard-coded location, it searches in the following locations (in this order):

- The folder that contains the calling add-in
- The System folder in the Windows folder
- The Windows folder
- The path defined by the Path environment setting (to see the path, type **set** in an MS-DOS prompt window)

If you experiment with the resolution algorithm, you'll also notice that after Microsoft Excel has reestablished the reference, it will keep it even if you move the referenced add-in somewhere outside the locations described in the preceding list. When you restart Microsoft Excel, however, the reference will be unresolved again.

To be safe, always store a referenced add-in in the folder that contains the calling add-in. A less advisable but still relatively safe method is to store the referenced add-in in a folder in the path.

Writing Code That Modifies the Add-In

Although an add-in is a hidden, read-only workbook, you can programmatically modify it. For example, you can add a worksheet on which you can perform calculations and store values. However, changes to an add-in are temporary—when you close the add-in, or when the add-in is unloaded from memory when you quit Microsoft Excel, the changes are lost. If you require more persistent storage, you can use your add-in to create a new workbook, transfer data into it, and then save it.

Compiling the Add-In

After you've debugged your source workbook and addressed the referencing issues discussed in the preceding section, you're ready to compile your add-in.

▶ **To compile an add-in**

1. Switch to a Visual Basic module in the workbook you want to compile.
2. On the Tools menu, click Make Add-In.
3. Click the icon for the folder in which you want to save the file.
4. In the File Name box, enter the name you want for the compiled add-in file.
5. Click Save.

Making an Add-In's Source Code Secure

The Visual Basic source code stored in the modules of a compiled add-in isn't completely protected from being read and copied. If you need complete security for your code, you can protect the structure of the source workbook using the Protection command on the Tools menu. Be sure to use a password when protecting the workbook structure. After protecting the workbook structure, compile the add-in.

When you use this protection technique, you can no longer add the add-in to the list box in the Add-Ins dialog box (Tools menu). If you attempt to add a protected add-in, you'll see an error message telling you that the add-in isn't valid. You can still use the procedures in the add-in by opening the add-in using the Open command (File menu) or by creating a reference to it from a Visual Basic module in another workbook. For more information about these techniques, see "Using an Add-In's Procedures" later in this chapter.

If you must create a secure add-in and it must appear in the Add-Ins dialog box, create two add-ins. The first add-in is the secure one; the second add-in is unprotected and contains a reference to the first add-in—a reference you create using the References dialog box (Tools menu). You can now use the functions in the second add-in, which call the protected code in the first add-in.

Creating completely secure add-in code is a complicated process, and it may add overhead to your add-in, which could reduce performance. Also, you may forget the protection password, in which case you would be unable to add, delete, move, rename, hide, or unhide sheets in the source workbook. For these reasons, you should secure add-ins only when it's absolutely necessary.

Reducing the Size of an Add-In

While developing an add-in, you can create and delete many variables and procedures. For example, you could create many temporary variables during debugging and then later delete them, or you could create procedures that you eventually delete as your code evolves. Visual Basic might not delete the variable and procedure names from its symbol table; this could cause the add-in to use more memory than it would if the symbol table were clean.

If you suspect that a heavily edited workbook is using an unusually large amount of memory, you can reduce its size by cleaning its symbol table.

Note The following technique does more than just clean the symbol table; it also removes all the information in the Macro Options dialog box, such as the shortcut key, function category, status bar text, and so on. The information is removed for every procedure in every module. If you've used the Macro Options dialog box to add any information to the procedures, you'll have to restore it after cleaning the symbol table.

▶ **To clean an add-in's symbol table**

1. Open the original source workbook.
2. Save each module in the workbook to a separate text file.
3. Delete every module from the workbook.
4. Save the workbook.
5. Create new modules, giving them the same names as the ones you deleted.
6. On the Insert menu, click File to add the code back into the new modules. Be sure to copy the code to the correct modules.

Although cleaning the symbol table may be tedious, it can reduce the memory requirements of an extensively edited add-in. You can compare the values returned by the **MemoryUsed** property (which returns the amount of memory that's currently being used by Microsoft Excel) before and after cleaning to measure the saved memory.

Using an Add-In's Procedures

There are several ways to use the procedures in an add-in. By understanding the advantages and disadvantages of each technique, you can choose the method that's best suited to your work.

Technique	Advantages	Disadvantages
Use the Open command (File menu) or the **Open** method in Visual Basic to open the add-in.	This is the simplest way to load an add-in. Custom worksheet functions in the add-in can be typed into a worksheet, and the add-in can modify the user interface by using the Auto_Open procedure.	Visual Basic procedures in the add-in aren't available to other workbooks, even though functions in the add-in are available to worksheets in other workbooks. In addition, all add-in resources are loaded into memory, whether or not they're required.
Use the References dialog box (Tools menu) to create a reference to the add-in.	Visual Basic procedures in the add-in are available to other workbooks. Custom worksheet functions in the add-in are available to worksheets in other workbooks.	No auto procedure (for example, auto_open) runs when the reference is created. In addition, there is no reliable way to create a reference using Visual Basic code.
Use the Add-Ins dialog box (Tools menu) to install the add-in.	Microsoft Excel stores the location of the add-in in the system registry and can automatically load the add-in on startup.	Visual Basic procedures in the add-in aren't available to other workbooks, even though functions in the add-in are available to worksheets in other workbooks.

Placing the add-in the Xlstart folder (so that Microsoft Excel opens the add-in when it starts) results in the same behavior as opening the add-in any other way. Remember that Visual Basic procedures in the add-in aren't available to any other workbook unless you create a reference to the add-in using the References dialog box (Tools menu).

Demand Loading Add-Ins

To increase the speed with which Microsoft Excel starts, you can have an add-in be *demand loaded*. This means that when Microsoft Excel starts, it reads only enough information from the add-in workbook file to establish references to the custom worksheet functions in the add-in. These functions are added to the list in the Function Wizard and can be entered on a worksheet. However, the add-in isn't fully loaded until Microsoft Excel recalculates one of the custom worksheet functions.

Demand loading can significantly decrease the amount of time required to start Microsoft Excel, especially when you're working with large add-ins that contain numerous custom functions. Nothing is free of course, and the time delay eventually occurs when the add-in is fully loaded at the time of the initial function recalculation. In most cases, this is an acceptable tradeoff because the user encounters individual time delays one by one instead of encountering one long time delay at startup time.

To use demand loading for custom worksheet functions that are written in Visual Basic, you must wrap the Visual Basic function procedure in a Microsoft Excel 4.0 macro function. You must also define the name __DemandLoad (the string "DemandLoad" preceded by two underscores) in the workbook. Use the following steps to create an add-in that contains demand-loaded custom functions written in Visual Basic.

▶ **To create a demand-loaded add-in**

1. Create a source workbook.
2. Insert a Visual Basic module, and then write the custom worksheet function.
3. Insert a Microsoft Excel 4.0 macro sheet. For each argument to the Visual Basic function, create an ARGUMENT function on the macro sheet.
4. The last function on the macro sheet is the RETURN function. In the argument list for this function, type the name of the Visual Basic function, including the argument strings you defined in step 3.
5. On the Insert menu, point to Name, and then click Define to define a name for the first ARGUMENT function. This will be the name that you'll use to call the custom function (the Visual Basic function name is known only to the RETURN function on the macro sheet). Be sure to click Function under Macro.
6. On the Insert menu, point to Name, and then click Define to define the name __DemandLoad (the string "DemandLoad" preceded by two underscores) on the macro sheet. In the Refers To box, type **=TRUE**
7. Save the source workbook.

8. On the Tools menu, click Make Add-In to compile the workbook to an add-in.
9. Close the add-in.

To use the add-in, install it by using the Add-Ins dialog box (Tools menu). Click Browse to locate an add-in that's not listed in the Add-Ins Available box. After the add-in is installed, the custom function name should appear in the User Defined category in the Function Wizard. The following illustration shows an example of a demand-loaded custom function called "vb_hyp," which calculates the length of the hypotenuse of a right triangle, given the lengths of the other two sides.

Add-in workbook Hyp.xla

```
Function vb_hyp(vx, vy)
    vb_hyp = Sqr(vx ^ 2 + vy ^ 2)
End Function
```

The Visual Basic function procedure vb_hyp does the calculation. This function is visible to the macro sheet, but not to any other workbooks.

Define the custom function name to refer to the first ARGUMENT macro function.

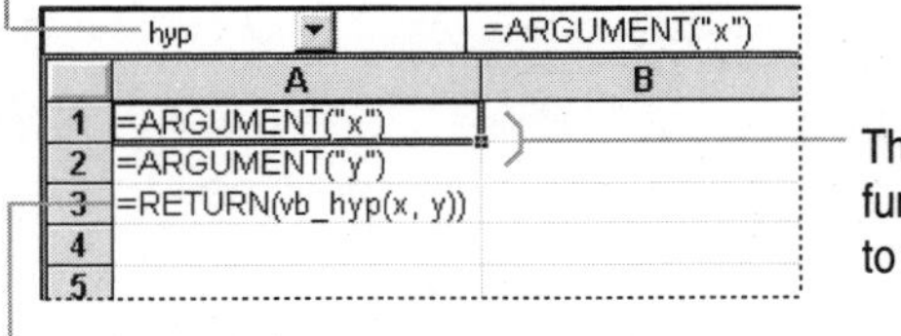

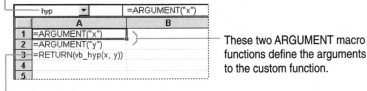

These two ARGUMENT macro functions define the arguments to the custom function.

This RETURN macro function calls vb_hyp using the passed-in argument values, and then it passes the calculated value out of the add-in.

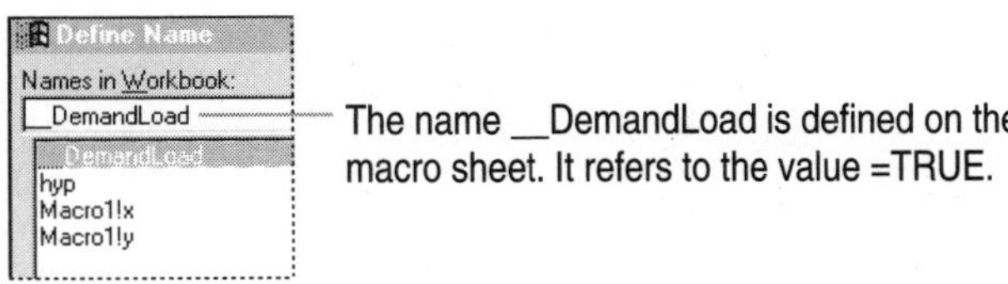

The name __DemandLoad is defined on the macro sheet. It refers to the value =TRUE.

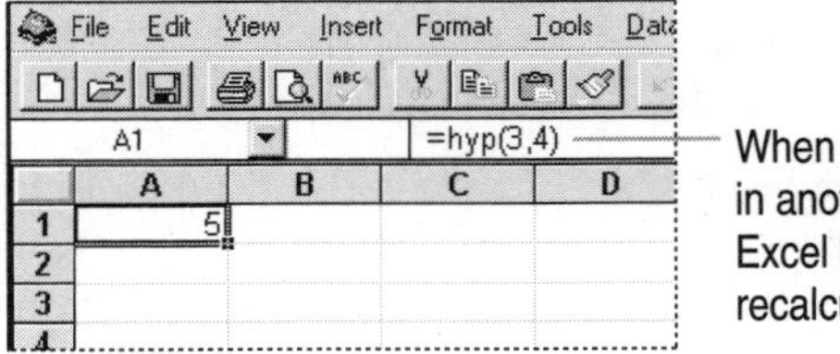

When you use the custom function in another workbook, Microsoft Excel loads the add-in only when recalculating the custom function.

When you install an add-in that contains demand-loaded custom functions, there will be an OPEN value in the Microsoft Excel key in the system registry that points to the add-in workbook, and the OPEN value will contain the /F switch to indicate demand loading. Add-ins that aren't demand loaded don't have the /F switch in the OPEN value. For more information about the system registry, see "Removing an Add-In from the List" in the following section.

Managing the Add-Ins Dialog Box

The Add-Ins dialog box provides a way for users to customize the loading of add-ins. If an add-in appears in the Add-Ins Available box, Microsoft Excel knows the location of the add-in. If the check box to the left of the add-in name is selected, the add-in is loaded when Microsoft Excel starts. Users can clear the check boxes to load fewer add-ins at startup, thus speeding up the startup process.

Adding an Add-In to the List

You can add a custom add-in to the list by clicking Browse in the Add-Ins dialog box or by using the **Add** method of the **AddIns** collections object. After the add-in appears in the list, you can use the **Installed** property to select or clear the check box. Note that whereas the **Add** method specifies an add-in by using its *path* and *filename*, the **Installed** property takes an **AddIn** object returned by the **AddIns** method, and the **AddIns** method specifies an add-in by using its *name*.

You should give the add-in a descriptive name before you compile it. This is the name you use as the argument to the **AddIns** method (it's also the name that appears in the list).

▶ **To name an add-in**

1. Open the source workbook for the add-in.
2. On the File menu, click Properties.
3. In the Title box on the Summary tab, type the name you want for the add-in.

   You can also add other information at this point, such as comments and keywords.
4. Click OK.
5. Save the source workbook, and then compile it to an add-in.

Removing an Add-In from the List

When you add an add-in to the Add-Ins Available box in the Add-Ins dialog box, Microsoft Excel stores the location of the add-in in the system registry. If you want to remove the name from the list, you use the Windows 95 Registry Editor to delete the registry value associated with the add-in. You can run the Registry Editor by typing **regedit** in the Run dialog box (Windows 95 Start menu).

If the add-in appears in the Add-Ins Available box and the check box next to it is selected (meaning that the add-in is installed), you delete the corresponding OPEN value in the Microsoft Excel key, as shown in the following illustration.

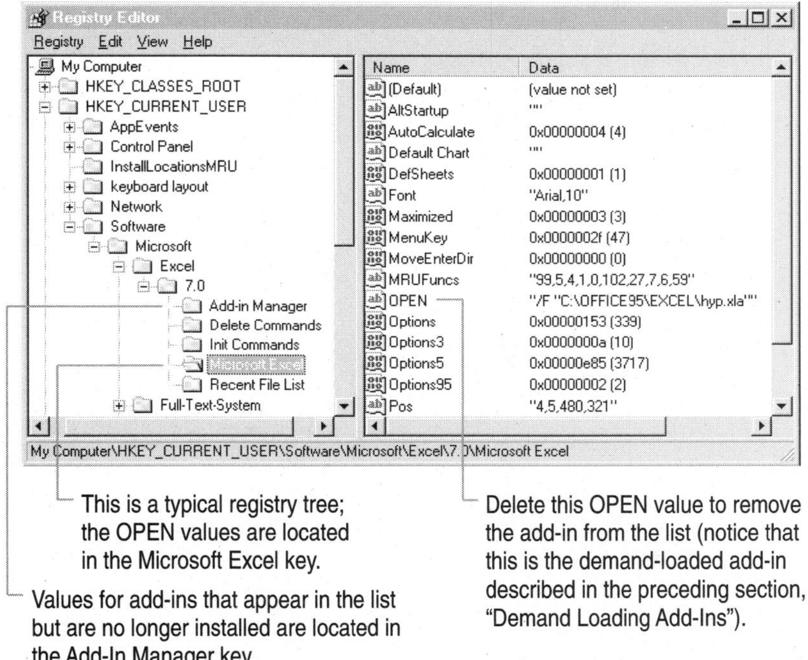

If the add-in appears in the Add-Ins Available box and the check box next to it is cleared (meaning that the add-in isn't installed), you delete the corresponding value in the Add-In Manager key instead of the OPEN value in the Microsoft Excel key.

Note Microsoft Excel updates the registry when you quit the application. Before editing the registry, be sure to quit Microsoft Excel. If the Registry Editor is already running, quit Microsoft Excel, switch to the Registry Editor, and then press F5 to refresh the display.

After you find the location of the value you want to delete, select the value name in the right-hand pane of the Registry Editor window, and then press DEL to delete the value. The add-in no longer appears in the Add-Ins dialog box list when you restart Microsoft Excel.

For more information about the Windows 95 system registry, see the *Microsoft Windows 95 Resource Kit*, which is available from Microsoft Press.

CHAPTER 13

Accessing External Data

In addition to working with Microsoft Excel data, you may want your application to access data from other sources, such as text files or databases. Microsoft Excel provides several powerful ways to access external data.

The first part of this chapter explores how to import external data as a text file. The next section discusses how to use data access objects to access the data and change the structure of a database. The final section describes how to connect to external database servers or files by using open database connectivity (ODBC).

Contents

Accessing Text Files

Microsoft Excel provides two ways to access external data that's in the form of a text file: the Text Import Wizard and the **OpenText** method.

You can import delimited or fixed-width text files into a worksheet by using the Text Import Wizard. This wizard allows you to tell Microsoft Excel what form your data is in, specify how you want to distribute the text across columns, and choose the data format for each column.

▶ **To open the Text Import Wizard**

1. On the File menu, click Open.
2. Click the name of the text file you want to import.
3. Click Open.

You can also use the **OpenText** method to load and parse a text file. This method creates a new workbook with a single worksheet containing the parsed text file data. For more information about the **OpenText** method, see "OpenText method" in Help.

Working with Data Access Objects

DAO (data access objects) is a library of objects, properties, and methods that you use to retrieve, edit, or delete data stored in a database or to change the structure of a database. Using DAO, you can insert cell values from a Microsoft Excel worksheet into records in a database; you can query a data set and bring the result set into Microsoft Excel for charting or presentation; and you can change relationships between tables.

Note that anything that you do using DAO is subject to the object permissions granted by the login user name and the login password—DAO isn't designed as a way around database security.

Important Any changes you make to the database using DAO are permanent. If you delete a record from a base table, for example, using a DAO method in your function, the record will be physically deleted from the table and cannot be recovered.

Understanding the DAO Object Model

Data Access Objects

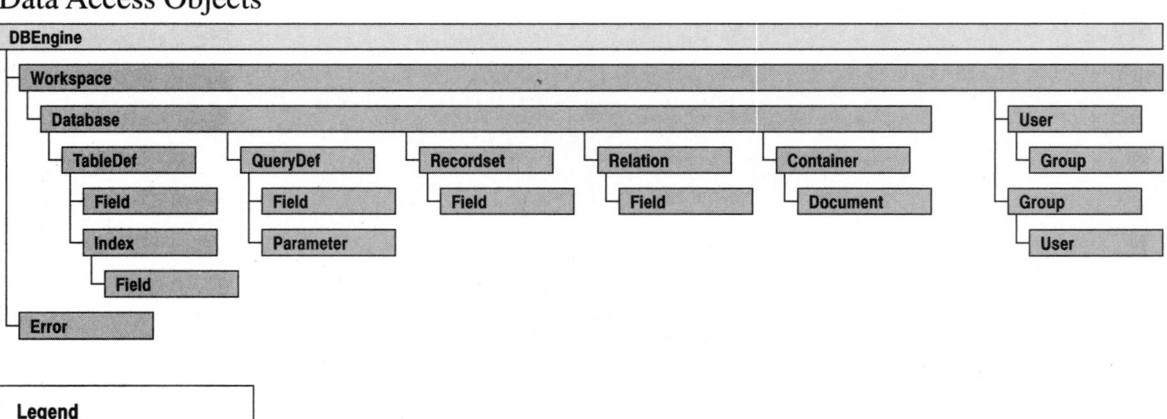

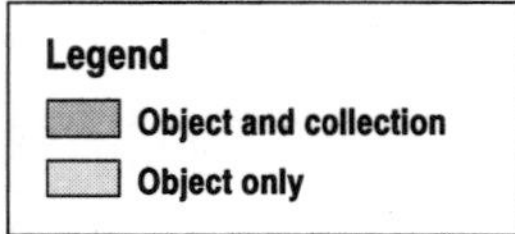

You use data access objects the same way you use objects in the Microsoft Excel object model. For example, to change a field attribute in a specific table in your application, you first need to establish a reference to the field. Beginning at the application level (using the **DBEngine** object), you define a workspace and then enter the database. From there, you navigate through the object and collection levels until you reach the object you want to change.

The DBEngine Object

The **DBEngine** object represents the Microsoft Jet database "engine," which is what powers Microsoft Access; this is the engine that Visual Basic uses to program database objects. This engine is actually a set of dynamic-link libraries (DLLs) that are linked to your application at run time. This engine is commonly referred to as "Jet," and it's the top-level object in the DAO model. It's this set of DLL files that translates the DAO code you write in your application into physical operations involving the Access .mdb file (or other database files). Also built into the DBEngine is a query processor that compiles and runs the Structured Query Language (SQL) queries you write to the database.

Note The *data file* is the file that contains the database tables. Microsoft Access data files have the extension .mdb. Microsoft FoxPro® and dBASE® databases have the .dbf extension. Other database applications have different filename extensions.

The Workspace Object

The **Workspace** object represents a workspace, which is an area in memory where you can perform a set of DAO operations. It's similar to a Microsoft Excel worksheet in that more than one workspace can be open at a time, but only one workspace can be active at a time. Depending on your system configuration, you may be able to open as many as 255 workspaces at once. Because Workspace objects are zero-based, the first workspace you open is Workspace(0).

You can define a workspace variable and open any workspace you specify. Most applications use only one workspace; therefore, it's faster to use the default workspace that's automatically assigned when you open a database.

Note It's possible to open a database without defining a workspace variable or using a **Workspace** object. To do this, define a database variable only; the variable will be assigned a default workspace when it's opened.

The Database Object

The **Database** object represents a Jet database, which is a collection of tables, indexes, fields, and links to outside sources. Whereas in Microsoft Excel you can define and set a range of cells as a database, in a Jet database the range you defined would be a single table. A Jet database is composed of a collection of tables (among other things).

The TableDef Object

The **TableDefs** collection object represents the collection of all the tables in a database. Each **TableDef** object represents a separate base table or attached table in the database.

The QueryDef Object

The **QueryDefs** collection object represents all the compiled SQL code in the database. Each **QueryDef** object represents one compiled SQL command string.

The Recordset Object

A **Recordset** object represents a set of records drawn from the database. The records can be drawn from a base table, or they can be the result of a single SQL query or a series of queries. The records that make up a **Recordset** object don't have to be stored in the same table. The **Recordset** object has three subtypes: the **Table** object, the **Dynaset** object, and the **Snapshot** object.

The Table Object

The **Table** object represents a base table, which is a logical set of records that are physically stored together. For example, a set of employee records can be stored in the same table because all the employees work for same company. The records can then be subdivided, or grouped with other records from other tables; in the base table, however, they're still a logical, physical set of records.

The Dynaset Object

The **Dynaset** object represents an updatable group of records. The group can be either a base table or a virtual table. A **Dynaset** object is updatable because the table indexes are loaded into memory, and the other fields in the record are retrieved from a buffer when they're needed.

The Snapshot Object

Like a **Dynaset** object, a **Snapshot** object can represent either a base table or a virtual table. Unlike a **Dynaset** object, a **Snapshot** object isn't updatable; all fields in a **Snapshot** object record are loaded into memory so that the set can be searched faster for matching records. The result of a SQL pass-through query is always a **Snapshot** object.

Using DAO from Microsoft Excel

You can use DAO properties, objects, and methods the same way you reference and use Microsoft Excel properties, objects, and methods. After you establish a reference to the DAO object library, you're free to open or create databases, run queries to create result sets, and bring the result sets back to Microsoft Excel.

Referencing DAO

Before you can use DAO, you must establish a reference to the DAO object library using the Microsoft Excel References dialog box.

▶ **To establish a reference to the DAO object library**

1. Switch to a Visual Basic module.
2. On the Tools menu, click References.
3. In the Available References box, click Microsoft DAO 3.0 Object Library.

If you don't see Microsoft DAO 3.0 Object Library in the Available References box, rerun Setup to install it.

▶ **To install the Microsoft DAO 3.0 Object Library**

1. Run Setup in maintenance mode, and click Custom Setup.
2. Click Add/Remove.
3. Clear the Data Access check box, and then click Change Option.
4. Under Options, select the check boxes for the data access drivers you want to install, and then click OK.
5. Click Continue, and proceed with the installation.

Opening a Database

To open an existing database using DAO, create a database variable. Then, in an open workspace, use the **OpenDatabase** method and specify the path to the existing database. The following example opens the Microsoft Access sample database Nwind.mdb.

```
Dim db As Database

Set db = OpenDatabase("e:\access\sampapps\nwind.mdb")

db.Close
End Sub
```

Running a Query and Returning a Recordset object

There are two ways to query a database using DAO: you can run a query that already exists, or you can create a new query. If you run a query that already exists, you simply refer to the name of the existing query in the **OpenRecordset** method. If you create a new query, you can choose to write it back to the database when you're finished, or you can choose to load it into memory.

To run any type of query, define a database variable and then set it to the database you want to work in.

```
Dim db As Database
Set db = OpenDatabase("e:\access\sampapps\nwind.mdb")
```

Opening an Existing Query

To open an existing query, use the **OpenRecordset** method to open the specified query and return the **Recordset** object. The first argument contains the name of the stored query you want to open, and the second argument describes the type of **Recordset** object that's returned.

```
Dim myset as Recordset
Set myset = db.OpenRecordset("Country", dbOpenDynaset)
```

If you omit the **Recordset** object type, DAO will try to return the fastest **Recordset** object type that allows you to modify the data. If you need only to read the data or append new data, see "OpenRecordset method" in Help for information about **Option** arguments that may make your application run faster.

To store a query in the database, use the **CreateQueryDef** method. The result of a **CreateQueryDef** method is compiled SQL code written back to the database as a query definition. You can store the SQL code in the database this way and then run it later using the **OpenRecordset** method to return a result set. The string you specify in the first argument is the query name that will be stored in the database, and the second argument is the SQL command string.

```
Dim qd As QueryDef

Set qd = db.CreateQueryDef("Country", "select distinctrow orders. _
    [ship country],sum(orders.[freight])as SumofFreight from  _
    orders group by orders.[ship country] order by orders.[ship _
    country];")
```

Note If you're not familiar with writing SQL code, you can examine the examples that go with a specific object, property, or method in Help, or you can construct a query in Access and view the resulting SQL code. If necessary, you can copy and paste most SQL code from the SQL view in Microsoft Access into a **CreateQueryDef** method.

Creating a New Query from a SQL Statement

To run SQL code and return a **Recordset** object that exists entirely in memory, use the **OpenRecordset** method, and specify a SQL string (instead of a stored query definition) as the first argument.

```
Dim myset As Recordset
Dim SQLString As String
```

After you set the database variable to the database you want to work in, load the SQL string into a string variable. Then use the **OpenRecordset** method, using as arguments the name of the SQL string and the **Recordset** object type.

```
SQLString = "select distinctrow orders.[ship
    country],sum(orders.[freight])as SumofFreight from orders  _
    group by orders.[ship country] order by orders.[ship country];"
Set myset = db.OpenRecordset(SQLString, dbOpenSnapshot)
```

For information about optimizing your SQL statement, see "SQL" in Help. For information about optimizing your application, see "Optimizing DAO Code" later in this chapter. If you want to run multiple queries that differ only in the records selected, you may want to use a parameter query and provide new parameters each time you open the query. For more information about parameter queries, see "Parameter object" in Help.

Filling a Range with a Result Set

You can import the contents of a result set into a Microsoft Excel worksheet either by placing the records into rows one by one or by importing the entire set at once using the **CopyFromRecordset** method. After you copy the result set to the worksheet, the record values become part of the worksheet.

Copying a Result Set Range Row by Row

If you copy the records one by one, you'll need to keep track of index variables because these dictate where the record will be placed on the worksheet. Although keeping track of index variables can be confusing if you have many fields, copying records this way gives you complete control over where your information is placed.

Copying an Entire Result Set as a Unit

You can copy an entire result set to a range on a worksheet at once by using the **CopyFromRecordset** method. This method begins to copy at the current row of the result set; when the transfer is completed, the **Recordset** object pointer is positioned just past the last row, or at EOF. Other than moving the **Recordset** object pointer, this method doesn't alter the **Recordset** object.

```
Dim db As Database
Dim rs As Recordset

Set db = OpenDatabase("e:\access\sampapps\nwind.mdb")
Set rs = db.OpenRecordset("Orders")

Worksheets("Sheet1").Range("A2").CopyFromRecordset rs

rs.Close
db.Close
```

Note In some circumstances, if you're copying either a result set containing OLE objects or pictures (such as the Categories table in Nwind.mdb), the copy operation will fail, and an exception error will be returned.

For more information about the **CopyFromRecordset** method, see "Optimizing DAO Code" later in this chapter.

Filling a List Box with a Result Set

There are two ways to fill a list box with a result set. You can specify a range of cells on a worksheet that contains a list of items you want to appear in the list box, or you can use the **Additem** method to directly fill the list box.

Filling a List Box with a Range of Cells

To fill a list box with a range of cells, use the **ListFillRange** property. The following example assumes that there's at least one dialog sheet in the active workbook, that there's at least one **ListBox** object on the first dialog sheet, and that there are values in cells A1:A10 on the worksheet named "Sheet1." The following example fills the list box with the values in cells A1:A10.

```
ActiveWorkbook.DialogSheets(1).ListBoxes(1).ListFillRange _
     = "Sheet1!A1:A10"
```

Note A cell can contain up to 255 characters; a list box can contain more than 255 characters. Therefore, if you use the **ListFillRange** property to fill a list box, be careful that the text you insert from a cell into a list box isn't truncated.

Filling a List Box with a Single Item

To fill a list box with a single item or to add selected items to a list box, use the **AddItem** method. The following example adds the second field value in the result set to the contents of the list box. The example assumes that there's at least one dialog sheet in the active workbook and that there's at least one **ListBox** object on the first dialog sheet.

```
Dim db As Database
Dim rs As Recordset
Dim x as Integer, I as Integer

Set db = OpenDatabase("d:\access\sampapps\nwind.mdb")
Set rs = db.OpenRecordset("shippers")
rs.MoveLast
x = rs.RecordCount
rs.MoveFirst

For i = 0 To x - 1
DialogSheets(1).ListBoxes(1).AddItem Text:=rs.Fields(1).Value
rs.MoveNext
Next I

rs.Close
db.Close

End Sub
```

Note Using the **AddItem** method will delete all list box entries made with the **ListFillRange** method.

Managing a Multiuser Environment

If you develop an application that allows two or more users (or applications) to refer to the same data set, you want to ensure that your application shares data effectively. This section explores strategies for managing multiuser access to data with different locking techniques, and it then discusses how to resolve locking conflicts in a multiuser environment.

Sharing Data

When one user is adding or changing data in a multiuser database, you need a way to prevent other users from changing the data until the first user is finished with it. To accomplish this, Jet provides three locking mechanisms. When a data set is locked, other users can read the records inside the data set, but only the user who initiated the lock can edit them.

By default, Jet locks an entire page of data when a record within the page is edited. A page is a block of record data that takes up approximately 2048 bytes (2 kilobytes) of memory. Depending on the size of each record, a page can contain one record or many records.

Note When Jet locks a record from an external database in Microsoft FoxPro, dBASE, Paradox®, or Btrieve® format, it locks the smallest unit of memory (that is, record, page, or file) that's lockable in the external database.

Pessimistic Locking

Pessimistic locking is the default locking scheme and is in effect when the **LockEdits** property is **True**. Jet locks the entire page containing the record you're editing as soon as you use the **Edit** method, and it releases the locked page when you either terminate a transaction or explicitly release the lock by using the **CancelEdit** method. The locked page isn't static—it moves up when you move up in the set of records, and it moves down when you move down, so it's possible to unintentionally lock a set of records.

Optimistic Locking

Optimistic locking is a locking scheme that allows you to edit a record in memory and to lock the record only when you're ready to write the changes to the database. This method attempts to lock the record when you call the **Update** method. The advantage of optimistic locking is that pages are locked only briefly. To use optimistic locking, set the **LockEdits** property to **False**.

Recordset Operations

A common practice in most applications are **Recordset** object operations: adding and editing records, or moving within a **Recordset** object. This section describes these operations.

Navigating a Recordset

One way to navigate inside a **Recordset** object is to move up or down one record at a time using the **Move** method. You can also use one of the **Find** methods (which one you use depends on your position in the **Recordset** object) and a specified criterion to locate a record in a dynaset or a snapshot. If your **Recordset** object is opened as a table, use the **Seek** method for optimal performance. For information about the syntax of the four **Find** methods and the **Seek** method, see the appropriate topic in Help.

Adding New Records

To add a new record, use the **AddNew** method to prepare the record for editing, and use the **Update** method to save the record. The **AddNew** method prepares a new, blank record and makes it the current record. The **Update** method saves the record and repositions the record pointer back to the record that was active before you used the **AddNew** method. The following code segment adds a new record to the Shippers table in Nwind.mdb.

```
Dim db As Database
Dim rs As Recordset
Set db = OpenDatabase("Nwind.mdb")
Set rs = db.OpenRecordset("Shippers", dbOpenTable)
rs.MoveFirst
rs.AddNew
    rs.Fields(0).value = "4"
    rs.Fields(2).value = "Global Parcel Service"
    rs.Fields(3).value = "(503)545-3190"
rs.Update
End If
```

Editing Records

When you edit records, you use the **Edit** method to mark the start of an editing session, and you use the **Update** method to signal the completion of the session. The **Edit** method tells Jet to buffer the changes to the specified record and write the changes to the data set when the editing tasks are completed. The **Update** method saves the record. The following code changes the job title for each sales representative in the Employees table.

```
Dim db As Database
Dim rs As Recordset
Set db = OpenDatabase("Nwind.mdb")
Set rs = db.OpenRecordset("Employees", dbOpenTable)
rs.MoveFirst
Do Until rs.EOF
If rs.Fields(3).value = "Sales Representative" Then
    rs.Edit
    rs.Fields(3).value = "Account Executive"
    rs.Update
End If
rs.MoveNext
Loop
```

Note You must use the **Edit** method before you use the **Update** method to write changes back to a record; otherwise, an error will occur.

Advanced Note If you're changing large groups of records regularly, it's faster and easier to create a SQL statement than it is to write code. For examples that could replace the code preceding these notes, see "Update method" in Help.

Managing Transactions

If your application depends on successfully adding or deleting records in one data set before proceeding to another one, you'll probably want some assurance that the first set of tasks has been completed successfully before you begin the second set. For example, if you update accounting records, you'll want records to be posted to Receivables before you delete records from Payables—otherwise, the books won't balance. When you wrap these actions into transactions, you ensure that each transaction is performed successfully before your application continues.

BeginTrans, CommitTrans, and RollBack

The **BeginTrans** method marks the beginning of a transaction. When you've completed your tasks, use the **CommitTrans** method to make the changes permanent, or use the **RollBack** method to delete the changes from memory. The most common way to implement transaction processing is within an error routine that traps errors during your procedure. If an error occurs, the routine flags the error and ignores any changes to the file; otherwise, the routine makes these changes permanent.

The following example demonstrates how transaction processing works.

```
Sub ChoiceToCommit()
On Error GoTo MyErrorHandler
Dim db As Database
Dim rs As Recordset

Set db = OpenDatabase("d:\access\sampapps\nwind.mdb")
Set rs = db.OpenRecordset("Customers")
rs.MoveFirst

BeginTrans
    MsgBox "The original record value is " & rs.Fields(0).Value
    rs.Edit
    rs.Fields(0).Value = 5000
    rs.Update
    action = MsgBox("We are changing the value to " & rs.Fields(0).Value
    & " ." & Chr(13) & " Do you want to continue? ", vbYesNo)
        If action = vbYes Then
            CommitTrans
        Else
            Rollback
        End If
```

```
rs.Close
db.Close
Exit Sub
MyErrorHandler:
MsgBox DBEngine.Errors(0)
End Sub
```

In the **BeginTrans** segment of code, `rs.Edit` marks the beginning of an editing session within the transaction; `rs.Update` marks the end of the editing session and updates the record set in memory only. The first message box displays the original value of the first field in the first record of the Customers table in Nwind.mdb. The second message box tells you that the original value is about to be changed to 5000 and asks you whether you want to continue. If you click Yes, the **CommitTrans** method is triggered, and the change becomes permanent. If you click No, the **RollBack** method is triggered, and the changes are deleted from memory, leaving the record unchanged.

Using DAO to Alter a Database

One of the more powerful features of DAO is its ability to change the structure of a database. During the development of your application, you may find that you could organize your information better by adding temporary tables to the database or adding fields to a table. You can add tables while working in an application by appending a **TableDef** object to the **TableDefs** collection; you can add fields to a table by appending a **Field** object to the **Fields** collection and then appending the **Fields** collection to the **TableDefs** collection. You can also change relationships or indexes between tables.

Mapping the Database

Before you begin modifying the objects in a database, it's helpful to get a summary of the object names and structures in the database. Getting this summary is called "mapping the database." The following example maps the Nwind.mdb database by looping through the elements in the **TableDefs** collection and transferring the structure to Sheet1 in the active workbook. This process is similar to scanning the headings of a worksheet in Microsoft Excel.

```
Dim db as Database
Dim i As Integer, j As Integer, col As Integer, rw as Integer
Dim system_Prefix as String, Current_TableName as String
Dim hidden_prefix as String
Set db = OpenDatabase("d:\access\sampapps\nwind.mdb")
With Worksheets("Sheet1")
    col = 1
    For i = 0 To db.TableDefs.Count - 1
        Current_TableName = db.TableDefs(i).Name
        ' Omit jet system tables from the list
        system_Prefix = Left(Current_TableName, 4)
        hidden_prefix = Left(Current_TableName, 1)
        If system_Prefix <> "MSys" And system_Prefix <> "USys" And
        hidden_prefix <> "~" Then
            .Cells(1, col) = db.TableDefs(i).Name
            'Display the fields inside each table
            rw = 2
            For j = 0 To db.TableDefs(i).Fields.Count - 1
                .Cells(rw, col) = db.TableDefs(i).Fields(j).Name
                .Cells(rw, col + 1) = db.TableDefs(i).Fields(j).Type
                rw = rw + 1
            Next j
        col = col + 2
        End If
    Next i
End With
```

You can set up a similar procedure to loop through the query names in the database by specifying the **QueryDefs** collection instead of the **TableDefs** collection and adjusting the index and looping variables.

Modifying the Database Structure

You can use DAO to change the structure of your database programatically. Modifying the database is similar to creating it initially. In most cases, you use the same **Create** and **Append** methods to add objects. You can add new **TableDef** objects to a database or add new **Field** and **Indexes** objects to existing tables. In addition, you can delete a **TableDef** object from a database or delete an **Index** object from a **TableDef** object.

There are some restrictions that apply to deleting field objects, however. For example, you cannot change an individual field after it's been appended to a **TableDef** object. You can delete a **Field** object only if it's not part of any **Index** or **Relation** objects. To delete an individual **Field** object, use the **Delete** method of the **TableDef** object. To change a **Field** object, you must first add a new **TableDef** object that reflects the desired changes in the structure, and then you must move the data to the new table and delete the old table. For more information about modifying the database structure, see "TableDef object" in Help.

Note To delete an indexed field, you must first delete the index. You must also delete any affected **Relation** objects before you can delete a **Field** object or a **TableDef** object that's part of a relationship.

Attaching Tables

In addition to defining your own tables, you can attach tables from any supported database to the database you're working in. When you attach an external table, the connection information is stored in your database, and the connection to the outside table is activated when you open the table. The data itself remains in the external database.

You can use attached tables the same way you use any other table in your database. You can create **Recordset** objects that include fields from attached and local tables, giving you the flexibility to perform queries with multiple databases. When you attach an external table, you must specify a **SourceTableName** string and a **Connect** string as you create the **TableDef** object.

Note Because an attached table isn't controlled by Jet, you cannot change the fields inside the table, add new fields to its structure, or delete its indexes.

Use the **CreateTableDef** method to create a new table object in your database. The name of the table in the argument is the name of the table as it will appear in your database; the table may have a different name in its native database.

```
Dim tb as TableDef

Set tb = db.CreateTableDef("Attached Customers Table")
```

Set the **SourceTableName** property to the name of the table in the source database that you want to connect to. You must specify the table name as it appears in its native database.

```
tb.SourceTableName = "Customers"
```

Set the **Connect** property by first specifying the path and filename of the source database and then appending the new table to the **Tabledefs** collection.

```
tb.Connect = ";database=e:\access\sampapps\nwind.mdb"
db.TableDefs.Append tb
```

Optimizing DAO Code

After you've gotten your application working, you can begin optimizing. There are several ways to optimize your application, many of which are described in the following paragraphs. However, the optimization you choose will depend on your computer configuration and the application you're using.

Optimizing All Queries

If your application updates data frequently or performs calculations on sections of large data sets, optimizing the queries that perform these actions will significantly improve the speed of your application. Small adjustments in the body of the query or in the SQL statement may be all you need to improve your application. For information about optimizing queries, see "Queries" in Help.

Opening Tables Directly

This method cannot be used with ODBC data sources because they cannot, by design, be opened directly as tables.

When using remote data sources, Jet provides two types of **Recordset** objects: **Dynaset** objects and **Snapshot** objects. If you don't need to update data in your result set, and if the result set contains fewer than 500 records, you can optimize your application by returning a **Snapshot** object. **Snapshot** objects are read-only optionally forward-only scrolling result sets; a **Snapshot** object is generated faster than a **Dynaset** object because it represents a picture of your data set.

Replacing the Find Method with the Seek Method

If you directly open a table that contains an index on the field you want to search, using the **Seek** method will always be the fastest way to locate a record. However, the **Seek** method can be used only on directly opened tables.

The **Find** method isn't as fast as the **Seek** method because of the overhead associated with dynasets or snapshots—specifically,copying matching records from a table and maintaining the indexes.

Using Stored Queries Instead of SQL Text

Using stored queries greatly increases processing speed—especially low-memory computers—because Jet's query compiler isn't needed. If you call a SQL text string, the query compiler is called; Jet then binds references, builds a query tree, chooses an optimization method, and then runs the query.

Using Parameter Queries Instead of SQL Text

If the values of a query aren't known before compile time, or if the application depends on user-supplied values for the query, it may not be possible to use stored static queries. In this case, using a parameter query is still faster than using a SQL text string because a parameter query is also a stored compiled query. For information about building a parameter query, see "parameter queries" in Help.

Using Transaction Processing

The **BeginTrans** method tells Jet to buffer all changes to the **Recordset** object. The changes will be written to the data set when the **EndTrans** method is applied. Without transaction processing, Jet writes changes directly to the **Recordset** object each time a change occurs, which may dramatically increase disk access. However, if the activity within the transaction is too large, changes to the **Recordset** object will be stored both in memory and in a swapfile, which increases disk access. The optimal number of records to store in a transaction depends on the computer configuration; you may need to experiment with the record numbers.

Using Bookmarks Instead of the Find Method

Using a bookmark instead of the **Find** method dramatically increases performance because a bookmark is essentially a stored primary key that Jet uses to return to the previous record location. In contrast, the **Find** method searches the entire data set for the previous record.

Using the CopyFromRecordset Method

The **CopyFromRecordset** method optimizes your application by copying large chunks of records as a unit instead of copying individual records. Variables for indexing and looping aren't needed in the result set or on the worksheet.

Using the GetRows Method

Whereas the **CopyFromRecordset** method copies and pastes an entire result set into a Microsoft Excel range, the **GetRows** method returns only a specified number of records from the result set (starting with the first record).

The following example pastes the first six records from the result set created by the **OpenRecordset** method into cells A1:B6 on Sheet1.

```
Dim db As Database, rs As Recordset
Dim data As Variant
Set db = OpenDatabase("c:\access\sampapps\Nwind.mdb")
Set rs = db.OpenRecordset("Select Customer.[City] from Customer;")
Do While Not rs.EOF
    data = rs.GetRows(6)
Loop
Sheets("Sheet1").Activate
For Each i In ActiveSheet.Range("A1:B6") _
    i.Value = data(i.Column - 1, i.Row - 1)
Next
rs.Close
db.Close
End Sub
```

Using ODBC

Open Database Connectivity (ODBC) is a standard protocol that permits applications to connect to a variety of external database servers or files. The ODBC drivers that Jet uses permit access to Microsoft SQL Server and other external databases, such as ORACLE®. An ODBC driver is a dynamic-link library (DLL) used to connect a specific ODBC data source with another (client) application. You can use the ODBC driver supplied with the application you program in, you can use a third-party driver, or you can write your own driver.

Connecting to ODBC Data

Establishing a connection to a server requires time and memory from both the client and the server. If you can limit your ODBC connection time or the number of connections to the server, you will reduce the resources your application uses and thereby optimize performance. When you connect to an ODBC data source, you supply file locations, server and user passwords, and sometimes locking information. You supply this information with the connection string, which must be verified and executed each time you access the data file. However, Jet has a built-in connection management capability that caches this information and reuses it as needed. In addition, Jet shares connections whenever possible.

You may therefore want to consider storing your ODBC tables as attached tables in an .mdb file. The only drawback to storing ODBC data this way is that if the ODBC file locations change, you must reestablish a connection to the new data file by dropping and reattaching the tables in the .mdb file.

Optimizing ODBC Performance

The fastest way to access ODBC data is first to use Microsoft Access to create linked tables in an .mdb file and then to use those linked tables in your DAO code. Although older versions of DAO permitted you to do it, one of the slowest and most inefficient ways to process server data is to open a dynaset on an attached ODBC table directly and then proceed to move through the dynaset.

Many of the same techniques used to optimize DAO code—excluding the ones previously noted—can be used to optimize ODBC performance as well. In addition to the techniques suggested in "Optimizing DAO Code" earlier in this chapter, there are several techniques that apply specifically to improving ODBC data performance.

If you don't have Microsoft Access, you can create your own linked tables in an .mdb file by using code such as that shown in the following example. You only have to do this once, after which you can reuse the .mdb file in multiple applications.

```
Dim db As Database
Dim td as Tabledef
Set db = CreateDatabase("d:\attached\CorpSQL.mdb", dbLangGeneral)
Set td = db.CreateTableDef("OrderDetail")
td.Connect = "ODBC;DSN=SSRVR1;UID=Fred;PWD=RHS;DATABASE=SQLDB;"
td.SourceTableName = "OrderDetails"
db.Tabledefs.Append td
```

For more information, see "Accessing External Databases with DAO" in Help.

Using Remote Data Caching

You can improve your application's performance by caching remote data. A cache is a space in local memory that holds the data most recently retrieved from the server. When data is requested from an ODBC source, Jet first checks the cache for the requested data, which takes less time than retrieving it from the server. If you anticipate working extensively in a small range of records (fewer than 200), you should use remote data caching. Use the **CacheStart** and **CacheSize** properties to specify the range and size you want within the result set. Use the **FillCache** method to quickly fill all or part of this range with data from the server.

```
Dim rs As Recordset
Dim db As Database

Set db = OpenDatabase("e:\attached\CorpSQL.mdb")
Set rs = db.OpenRecordset("OrderDetail", dbOpenDynaset)
rs.FindFirst "CustID = 1001"
rs.CacheStart = rs.Bookmark
rs.CacheSize = 50
rs.FillCache
```

Note This code assumes that you have an .mdb file with an OrderDetail table attached to an ODBC data source.

Using SQL Pass-Through Queries

A SQL pass-through query is a specialized type of SQL query that's designed to bypass the Jet engine and communicate directly with a SQL server. In a regular query, Jet resolves references to fields, tables, and functions when the SQL statement is compiled. In a pass-through query, Jet hands the entire query over to the server to compile and resolve references. There are several advantages to running a SQL pass-through query:

- You can take advantage of server-specific functionality that doesn't exist at the local level (such as SQL stored procedures) when you write your statement. For more information about stored procedures, see your server software manual.
- SQL pass-through queries are faster than local queries because they communicate directly with the SQL server, which can process data, compile SQL code, and return a result set faster that the Jet engine can.
- Because the entire query is processed on the server and only the **Recordset** object is returned, you have less network traffic while data is being requested and returned.

The following example creates a temporary pass-through query.

```
Dim db as Database
Dim tempqry as QueryDef

Set db = OpenDatabase("Mydb.mdb")
Set tempqry = db.CreateQueryDef("")
db.Connect = "ODBC; DSN=MySQLDBD; UIS=Guest;PWD=''
PassThrough.ReturnsRecords = True
tempqry.SQL = "UPDATE Orders Set ShipCity = 'LondonTown' WHERE _
    ShipCity = 'London'"
tmpqry.Execute
tmpqry.SQL = "UPDATE Orders Set ShipCity = 'New York City' WHERE _
    ShipCity = 'New York'"
tempqry.Execute
```

APPENDIX A

Writing Code for International Use

Using Visual Basic, it's possible to distribute Microsoft Excel applications to users in countries whose native language isn't the one you wrote your code in. This appendix offers guidelines for choosing a language to write your code in and provides tips for writing and distributing applications for international use. You'll also learn techniques to ensure that your code runs as you expect it to run—and more important, as your users expect it to run—no matter where you transport it.

In this appendix, an *application* is assumed to be a workbook or collection of workbooks that performs a specific task and that runs within Microsoft Excel. A *locale* is the country or locale selected on the Regional Settings tab in the Regional Settings Properties dialog box (Control Panel). A *language* is the country or language selected in the Language/Country box on the Module General Tab in the Options dialog box (Tools menu). Finally, an *object library* is a file that determines what words and symbols Visual Basic can understand—that is, the names of objects, properties, methods, Visual Basic statements, and so on that you type in a Visual Basic module. These words and symbols vary from language to language.

General Guidelines

Use the following guidelines to write Visual Basic code that runs effectively in other locales. These guidelines are presented as three scenarios, beginning with the scenario that provides the safest and most predictable results. If you understand these three scenarios, you can better predict how your distributed code will perform.

- Write your code in English (with English/United States selected in the Language/Country box on the Module General Tab in the Options dialog box (Tools menu)). The code will run on any computer running Microsoft Excel because Microsoft Excel registers the English object libraries as the default libraries during installation.

- Write your code in any localized language, and distribute the code with the corresponding object library files. The code will run correctly on the localized machine if the accompanying object is installed. For a complete list of languages and their corresponding object libraries, see "Names of the Object Library Files" later in this appendix.
- Write your code in any localized language, and distribute the code without object library files. The code will only run on computers that already have the proper object library files installed. For a complete list of languages and their corresponding object libraries, see "Names of the Object Library Files" later in this appendix.

Important Don't write Visual Basic code for distribution to other computers with English/(Custom) selected in the Language/Country box on the Module General Tab in the Options dialog box (Tools menu). Code you write with that option in effect won't run properly on other computers.

Writing Transportable Visual Basic Code

The following guidelines will help you write your Visual Basic code so that it runs more effectively in other locales. Understanding these guidelines is important in predicting how your code will perform. The guidelines fall into the following areas:

- Working with formulas
- Using conversion functions
- Displaying information with locale-aware functions and statements
- Working with local language text in your code
- Other considerations when writing transportable Visual Basic code

Working with Formulas

Microsoft Excel provides formulas to help you analyze data on a worksheet or to perform operations on sets of data on multiple worksheets. When you write code, you can choose to use a formula in the language of your user, or you can choose to use a formula in a language that's familiar to you and have Visual Basic convert the formula to the language of your user.

Using the Formula and FormulaLocal Properties

You can use the **Formula** property to enter a formula in a cell. If the formula you enter contains worksheet functions, Microsoft Excel converts the functions to the appropriate language. For example, suppose you use the **Formula** property to enter a formula in cell A1 on Sheet1, as shown in the following code.

```
ThisWorkBook.Worksheets("Sheet1").Range("A1"). _
    Formula = "=SUM(A2:A3)"
```

When Microsoft Excel enters the formula on the worksheet, it automatically converts it to the equivalent formula in the language that's been set for the workbook.

If, instead, you write your code so that the user enters formulas in input boxes, Visual Basic still converts worksheet functions in the provided formulas, but you must use the **FormulaLocal** property instead of the **Formula** property. The **FormulaLocal** property converts the worksheet function the user types in the input box to the equivalent formula in the language that's been set for the workbook. The following example displays an input box and then inserts the formula the user supplies into cell A1 on Sheet1.

```
FormulaText = InputBox(EnterFormulaMessage)
ThisWorkbook.Worksheets("Sheet1").Range("A1") _
    .FormulaLocal = "=" & FormulaText
```

If you subsequently open the workbook on a computer that's running the German version of Microsoft Excel, run the preceding example, and type **sum(a2:a3)** in the input box, the following formula appears in the formula bar.

```
= SUMME(A2:A3)
```

Using the NumberFormat and NumberFormatLocal Properties

The **NumberFormat** property is used to set the format code for a range on a worksheet. The format code is the string that appears in the Category box on the Number tab in the Format Cells dialog box. The following example sets the format code for cell A17 on Sheet1 to "General."

```
Worksheets("Sheet1").Range("A17").NumberFormat = "General"
```

The **NumberFormatLocal** property sets the format code for the object in the language that's been set for the workbook. The following example displays a message box showing the number format for cell A17 on Sheet1 in the language that's been set for workbook.

```
Msgbox "The number format for cell A17 is " & _
    Worksheets("Sheet1").Range("A17").NumberFormatLocal
```

Using Conversion Functions

Visual Basic provides several functions that convert data from one type to another using locale settings. However, some functions aren't locale-aware. Whenever possible, use the locale-aware functions to make your code transportable. This is especially important when you're converting strings to numbers or dates.

For example, the **Str** and **Val** functions always assume that a period is the decimal separator, but **CStr**, **CDbl**, **CSng**, **CInt**, and **CLng** use the current operating system settings to determine the decimal separator.

Special Considerations for Dates

Never type dates as strings in your code, because date formats aren't the same in every country. Even locale-aware conversion functions can process strings in ways you might not expect. For example, the following code behaves differently in different locales.

```
StartDate = "2/3/95"
NewDate = CDate(StartDate)
```

When run in an English/United States locale, NewDate contains a value equivalent to February 3, 1995; in an English/Australia locale, NewDate contains a value equivalent to March 2, 1995. This behavior is a potential source of error when you're programming, but it's very useful for processing user input from a dialog box. **CDate** converts the user's text into the date that the user intends.

However, as the programmer, you should always code dates as literals—such as **#2/3/95#**—so that Visual Basic recognizes the exact date you intend. For example, in the following code, NewDate contains a value equivalent to either February 3, 1995, or March 2, 1995, depending on the locale of the programmer, but not the locale of the user. The date is the same for all users wherever the code is run.

```
StartDate = #2/3/95#
NewDate = CDate(StartDate)
```

The date literal is interpreted in the context of the programmer's locale.

Special Considerations for Currencies

Similarly, never store a currency value as a string that includes a currency symbol, because the currency symbol varies according to locale. For example, the following code doesn't run in any locale except those where the dollar sign ($) is the currency symbol.

```
Money = "$1.22"
NewMoney = CCur(Money)
```

Instead, store a currency value as a decimal number, as shown in the following example. (This example assumes that the period is the decimal separator in the programmer's locale, but the code runs correctly no matter what the decimal separator is in the user's locale.)

```
Money = 1.22
NewMoney = CCur(Money)
```

Displaying Information with Locale-Aware Functions and Statements

As explained previously, different locales have different conventions for displaying dates, times, numbers, currency, and other information. As a programmer, you cannot know the conventions for all your users' locales, and you don't have to know them. Many Visual Basic statements use the locale settings to determine the conventions automatically at run time, but some statements are more locale-aware than others. In general, Help tells you whether a statement or function is locale-aware, and if so, in what ways.

For example, the **Print** statement provides little flexibility for different output formats; it does, however, use the operating system locale settings. Dates are printed using the correct short date format, numbers are printed with the correct decimal separator, and currencies are printed with the correct symbol.

The **Format** function can accept format codes, but format codes always produce the same type of output without regard to the user's locale. For example, the format code "mm-dd-yy" isn't appropriate for locales in which the day precedes the month.

For more flexibility, the **Format** function also provides named formats that are locale-aware, including Short Date, Long Date, Long Time, and General Number. Using named formats produces output that's based on the user's operating system locale settings.

```
MyDate = #January 27, 1994#
MyStr = Format(MyDate, "dd-mm-yy")       'Returns 01-27-94
MyStr = Format(MyDate, "Short Date")     'Returns a short date based on
                                         'the locale where the code is
                                         'running
```

Working with Local Language Text in Your Code

Visual Basic includes many features to help your code run properly in other locales, but it cannot automatically translate text from one language to another. For example, you might want your application to include menu text, dialog text, alert messages, and so on. At first, it might seem that you must type this text directly into your code, which prevents the code from becoming a truly transportable application. However, you can create a string table to replace specific quoted text with variables and references to worksheet names. The cells your worksheet names refer to can vary depending on the locale in which your code is running. In this way, you can display words and phrases that change depending on your user's locale.

For example, the following worksheet includes a string table for three languages.

	A	B	C	D
1	**Localized Strings**	**English**	**French**	**German**
2	Welcome	Welcome to West Coast Sales!	Bienvenue à la société Les Ventes de la Côte Ouest!	Willkommen bei der Nordwind GmbH.
3	CustomerName	What is your name?	Quel est votre nom ?	Wie heißen Sie?
4	AcctNumber	Enter your account number.	Entrez votre numéro de compte.	Bitte geben Sie Ihre Kundennummer ein.
5	NotValidMessage	That transaction is not valid.	Cette transaction n'est pas valide.	Dieser Vorgang kann nicht bearbeitet werden.

To use the string table, define names for cells in the Localized Strings column. You can use the **Offset** method to get the text in the other language columns. To work in English, use 0 (zero) for the ***columnOffset*** argument; to work in French, use 1 for the ***columnOffset*** argument; and to work in German, use 2 for the ***columnOffset*** argument. You can obtain the column offset value in any of the following ways:

- Use the **International** property of the **Application** object to determine the locale version of Microsoft Excel (xlCountryCode) or the current country setting of the operating system (xlCountrySetting). Make a mathematical adjustment to convert the setting to a column offset value, and then define a **Public** variable accordingly. (For more information about public scope, see Chapter 2, "Variables, Constants, and Data Types.")
- Display a dialog box asking the user for a language or country name. Then define a public variable, and assign it an offset value according to the user's input.
- Define a public constant that the user sets.

The following code determines an offset code based on the language version of Microsoft Excel you're using.

```
Public GlobalOffsetCode

Sub GetGlobalOffsetCode()
Select Case Application.International(xlCountryCode)
    Case 1:                           'US English
        GlobalOffsetCode = 1
    Case 33:                          'French
        GlobalOffsetCode = 2
    Case 49:                          'German
        GlobalOffsetCode = 3
    Case Else:                        'US English as the default language
        GlobalOffsetCode = 1
End Select
End Sub
```

The following code uses this offset code to display an appropriate message box to welcome the user.

```
WelcomeMsg = ThisWorkbook.Worksheets("LocalizationTable").Range _
    ("Welcome").Offset(0, GlobalOffsetCode).Value
MsgBox WelcomeMsg
```

You can use a similar technique to change the text, positions, and sizes of items in dialog boxes, making your code truly transportable.

Other Considerations When Writing Transportable Visual Basic Code

There are other things you need to consider when you're writing code that can vary by locale. The following are the most common of these considerations:

- Comparing strings

  The rules for comparing strings vary by locale when you're using the less-than (<), greater-than (>), equal-to (=), and **Like** operators, and the **StrComp** function. For more information, see "Option Compare," "Like," and "StrComp" in Help.

- Working with file input and output

  Locale is also a consideration for file input and output. The **Print #** statement writes to data into a file as the data is displayed on-screen in a locale-aware format. The **Input #** statement cannot read this information from the file. By comparison, the **Write #** statement puts data into a file in a fixed format, which ensures that the **Input #** statement can read it later in any user locale.

- Using the macro recorder

  The macro recorder records your actions in a module in the language specified on the Module General Tab, not in the language of the worksheet. If, for example, your language setting is English/United States and your locale setting (the setting for the worksheet) is French/France, the macro is recorded in English.

  You can use the **FormulaLocal** property to return a formula, as a string, in the same format in which it would be displayed in the formula bar (including the equal sign). For more information about the **FormulaLocal** property, see "Working with Formulas" earlier in this appendix.

Using Object Libraries to Make Your Code Transportable

During installation, Microsoft Excel registers the English object libraries as the default libraries, regardless of the language version of Microsoft Excel. However, if you install the appropriate Visual Basic object library in your Windows system folder and the corresponding Microsoft Excel object library in your Microsoft Excel program folder, you can write your Visual Basic code in a language other than English. Your code language can be different from the language of the Microsoft Excel application because the object library translates your code into statements that can run in any language version of Microsoft Excel.

Important You cannot transport code written on a system that's set up for a Far Eastern double-byte character system (DBCS) language to a system that's not similarly set up, unless the code is written in English.

Object libraries provide lexical information that Microsoft Excel uses to determine how to work with dates, times; and number separators.

With object libraries, you can write your code in a way that's familiar to you, and users in other countries can run your code in a way that's familiar to them. For example, if the decimal separator in your locale is the period, you'll want to use it when you type numbers in code. If another symbol, such as the comma, is the decimal separator in your user's locale, you'll want it to appear when your code displays numbers. And you want your code to interpret the comma correctly when a user enters a number in a cell or dialog box. Object libraries make this possible.

Choosing a Locale for your Visual Basic Code

If the appropriate object libraries are installed on your disk and registered with Visual Basic, you can choose to write your Visual Basic module code in a language other than English. You can also specify a corresponding country, thus specifying how you type dates and times and what symbols you use for the list separator, the decimal separator, and so on. The language/country combination sets the locale of your Visual Basic environment—the language in your module code can be different from the language of the Microsoft Excel application. The object library registered when you select a language translates your module code into statements that Microsoft Excel understands.

▶ **To choose a language in which to write or edit Visual Basic code**

1. On the Tools menu, click Options, and then click the Module General tab.
2. In the Language/Country box, click the language and country you want to use.

If the locale setting you want isn't listed in the Language/Country box, you must install the appropriate object libraries, as explained in "Installing and Registering Object Libraries" later in this appendix.

Current Settings and Default Settings

Under International on the Module General tab in the Options dialog box (Tools menu), you'll see the Current Settings and Default Settings option buttons. If you click Current Settings, the Language/Country and associated settings for the active workbook will be displayed. If you click Default Settings, the default settings for each new workbook you create will be displayed. For example, if you usually work in the English/United States locale and you receive a French/France application, clicking Current Settings displays locale information about the application, but the default settings for the rest of your work are still the English/United States settings.

Working in Multiple Locales

There's one locale setting stored with each workbook, so different workbooks can have different settings, even if all the workbooks are open at the same time. With this feature, you can write and call procedures written in several languages.

Visual Basic doesn't automatically translate existing code from one language into another. You must edit the code using the same locale setting that was used when the code was originally written. Using multiple locales requires using multiple workbooks and multiple object libraries. However, you can edit the code with any language version of Microsoft Excel; for example, you can edit Dutch code using Norwegian Microsoft Excel, but the code will be displayed in Dutch.

Installing and Registering Object Libraries

If you cannot find the locale you want to use listed in the Language/Country box on the Module General tab in the Options dialog box (Tools menu), you must install and register the corresponding object libraries. Visual Basic in Microsoft Excel requires two object library files for each language: the Microsoft Excel object library and the Visual Basic for applications object library.

For specific information about the names of the object library files and how you acquire the files, see the appropriate Help topics.

▶ **To install object libraries**

- For each language you want to work with, copy the Microsoft Excel object library files to your Microsoft Excel program folder, and copy the Visual Basic object library files to your Windows system folder (or your System32 folder if you're using the Windows NT™ operating system). For a complete list of object library names, see "Names of the Object Library Files" later in this appendix.

If someone gives you an application written in another language and includes the object library files, those files are registered automatically when you try to run any of the procedures in the application. However, if you write code and use the object libraries for the first time, you must register them with Microsoft Excel yourself. *Registering* files means making Microsoft Excel aware that they exist. You only have to register an object library once, unless you move or rename one or both files.

▶ **To register a new language version of the object library files**

1. Switch to a Visual Basic module.
2. On the Tools menu, click References.
3. Click Browse.
4. In the Look In box, click the name of the folder that contains the new Microsoft Excel object library file.
5. Double-click the object library filename.

   (Repeat steps 3 through 5 for the Visual Basic object library file.)
6. Click OK to close the References dialog box.

You can now click Options on the Tools menu, click the Module General tab, and select the locale you want.

If the language you want still isn't available, Microsoft Excel has already assigned a language to your workbook. You should open a new workbook and repeat the preceding steps. Remember, you can assign a language to a workbook only once, as explained in "Working in Multiple Locales" earlier in this appendix.

Distributing Object Libraries

If your Visual Basic code isn't written in English (with the English/United States option selected on the Module General tab), you must either include the appropriate language object libraries when you distribute your application or make sure that the recipients already have the appropriate object libraries installed on their computers. If your code calls procedures written in multiple languages, you should include the object libraries for each of those languages. You should also include all workbooks and other object libraries that are referenced by the application you're distributing.

Note Microsoft allows all registered owners of Microsoft Excel to distribute object libraries with their applications to other registered owners as necessary.

Object libraries are platform-specific, so if you plan to distribute your workbooks both to users of Microsoft Excel for Windows and users of Microsoft Excel for the Macintosh, you must include both the Windows and Macintosh versions of the object libraries.

Names of the Object Library Files

For Microsoft Excel for Windows, some of the object library filenames are listed in the following table.

Language	Microsoft Excel object library filename	Visual Basic for applications object library filename
English	Xl5en32.olb	Vbaen32.olb
French	Xl5fr32.olb	Vbafr32.olb
German	Xl5de32.olb	Vbade32.olb
Spanish	Xl5es32.olb	Vbaes32.olb
Italian	Xl5it32.olb	Vbait32.olb
Portuguese	Xl5ptg32.olb (Portugal)	Vbaptg32.olb
Portuguese	Xl5ptb32.olb (Brazil)	Vbaptb32.olb
Swedish	Xl5sv32.olb	Vbasv32.olb
Norwegian	Xl5mp32.olb	Vbamp32.olb
Finnish	Xl5fo32.olb	Vbafo32.olb
Dutch	Xl5nl32.olb	Vbanl32.olb
Danish	Xl5da32.olb	Vbada32.olb

Many other object libraries might become available later.

Running Your Code in Other Language Environments

The preceding sections explain how a locale setting determines how you, as a programmer, should enter Visual Basic code. However, the way you enter items such as dates, formats, and so on isn't always the same as what the user should see, depending on his or her locale.

At run time, Visual Basic functions usually behave as they should for the user. Visual Basic typically uses the locale settings of the operating system—not the locale settings of your Visual Basic editing environment—to determine how to interpret user-supplied numbers and dates, such as information the user enters in dialog boxes, values the user enters in cells, and so on. Visual Basic also uses these settings to determine how to display numbers and dates—such as the results of the **Format** function—to the user.

For example, the following two procedures are written in different languages (one in English and one in French), but they display the results in the same language when they're run on the same system. The language of the display is determined by the locale settings of the operating system. The following illustration assumes that the user has a German system with German, English, and French object libraries installed.

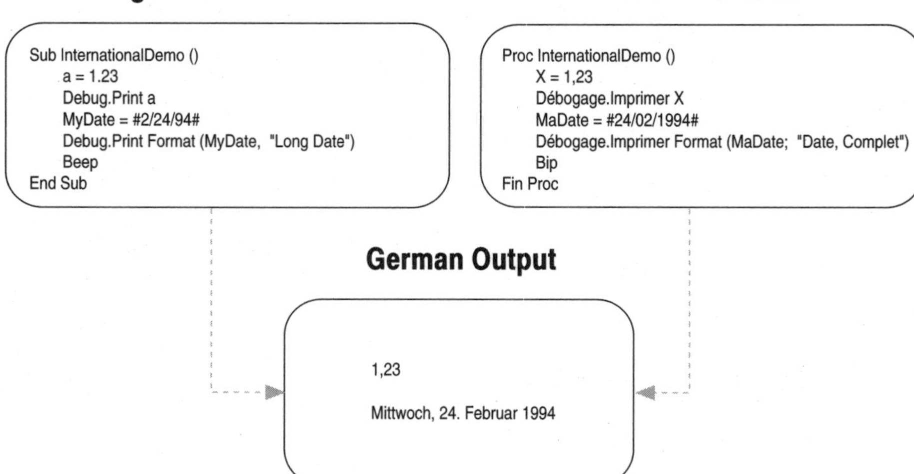

English Workbook
Sub InternationalDemo ()
a = 1.23
Debug.Print a
MyDate = #2/24/94#
Debug.Print Format (MyDate, "Long Date")
Beep
End Sub
French Workbook
Proc InternationalDemo ()
X = 1,23
Débogage.Imprimer X
MaDate = #24/02/1994#
Débogage.Imprimer Format (MaDate; "Date, Complet")
Bip
Fin Proc
German Output
1,23
Mittwoch, 24. Februar 1994

As a user, you might occasionally need to change your operating system locale settings to suit your needs. Or, as a programmer, you might want to change the settings to test applications you plan to distribute to others. Changing operating system locale settings will change the output of locale-aware functions and statements.

▶ **To change the locale (region) settings in Microsoft Windows**

1. Click Start on the taskbar, point to Settings, and then click Control Panel.
2. Double-click the Regional Settings icon.
3. On the Regional Settings tab, click a country on the map, or click the name of a language in the list box.

   The settings on the Number, Currency, Time, and Date tabs automatically change according to the language you select; however, you can also change the settings on these tabs manually.

Writing International Code That Controls Multiple Desktop Applications

If you plan to run Microsoft Excel with another desktop application that supports Visual Basic, you need the appropriate language version of the object libraries for that desktop application. For example, suppose you want to write Italian code that uses features of both Microsoft Excel and Microsoft Project. To do this, you need the following files:

- The Microsoft Excel Italian object library
- The Visual Basic for applications Italian object library
- The Microsoft Project Italian object library

For the purposes of this example, the language versions of Microsoft Excel and Microsoft Project are unimportant. Your Italian code will work with any version of Microsoft Excel and any version of Microsoft Project, provided that you include the appropriate object libraries (see the preceding list).

For more information about writing code that works with other applications, see Chapter 10, “Communicating with Other Applications.”

APPENDIX B

Switching from the Microsoft Excel 4.0 Macro Language

This appendix introduces users of the Microsoft Excel 4.0 Macro Language to programming with Visual Basic. In this appendix, you'll learn how Visual Basic differs from the Microsoft Excel 4.0 Macro Language, how you can continue using your existing Microsoft Excel 4.0 macros, and where to find more information about Visual Basic.

Visual Basic is a true programming language that features variables with scoping, an integrated editor, and enhanced dialog box tools and debugging tools. Learning Visual Basic with Microsoft Excel version 7.0 makes it easier for you to learn programming with Microsoft Access, Microsoft Project, and other Microsoft applications that use Visual Basic. You can also control these other applications easily in your Visual Basic code. You can use Microsoft Excel with Visual Basic to easily learn Visual Basic programming at your own pace, without losing any of your existing investment in Microsoft Excel 4.0 macros.

Important Most features of Microsoft Excel version 7.0 can be recorded in the Microsoft Excel Macro Language. For more information, refer to the Microsoft Answer Wizard.

Information for Users of Microsoft Excel 4.0 Macros

This section guides experienced users of Microsoft Excel 4.0 macros to information about learning and using Visual Basic. For more detailed information, see the chapters and Help topics that are cross-referenced in this section.

Recording Macros in Visual Basic

In Microsoft Excel version 7.0, you can choose the language in which to record a macro.

▶ **To choose the programming language in which to record a macro**

1. On the Tools menu, point to Record Macro, and then click Record New Macro.
2. Click Options.
3. Under Language, click an option.

In Microsoft Excel version 7.0, you can still record your macros in a workbook that opens each time you start Microsoft Excel. In Microsoft Excel version 4.0, this workbook is called Global.xlm (in Microsoft Excel for Windows) or Global Macro Sheet (in Microsoft Excel for the Macintosh). In Microsoft Excel version 7.0, this workbook is now called Personal.xls or Personal Macro Workbook, depending on the platform (Windows or the Macintosh). Your existing macros still run; new macros are simply recorded in the new workbook. Microsoft Excel version 7.0 creates your new Personal Macro Workbook when you record your first macro.

For more information about recording macros, see "Record a macro" in Help.

Acting Directly on Objects in Visual Basic

In Microsoft Excel version 4.0, macros follow the "select, then do" order of actions that pertains to all of Microsoft Excel. With Visual Basic, you don't need to select an object you want your procedure to change. You can change the object directly.

For example, to make a range of text bold in Microsoft Excel version 4.0, you have to first select the range with the SELECT function before changing the format of the text with the FORMAT.FONT function. In Visual Basic, you make a range of text bold just by setting the **Bold** property of the range to **True.** For example, type the following function in a module:

```
Sub MakeSectionBold()
    Worksheets("Sheet1").Range("C1:G5").Font.Bold = True
End sub
```

Note that you can use Visual Basic to directly change an object (in this case, the range C1:G5) without selecting it or canceling the current selection. For more information about how to change cells, sheets, charts, shapes, and other objects in Visual Basic, see Chapter 4, "Objects and Collections."

Variables: More Powerful Than Names

To store a value as a variable in Microsoft Excel version 4.0, you'd typically store the value in a name. In Visual Basic, you'd assign the value to a variable instead.

Variables are much more flexible than names. You can make variables available to all procedures, to only the procedures in a given module, or to only a single procedure. You can control the type of data that can be stored in a variable and even create variables that store a combination of your choice of data types.

In Visual Basic, you can also define constants to hold static (constant) values that you can refer to repeatedly. For more information about variables and constants in Visual Basic, see Chapter 2, "Variables, Constants, and Data Types."

Using Worksheet Functions in a Procedure

Many worksheet functions can be used directly in Visual Basic procedures; the IF function is one exception, though, as **If** is also a keyword in Visual Basic. You can use the **Application** qualifier to run a Microsoft Excel worksheet function rather than a Visual Basic function. For example, the following procedure causes a "Sub or Function not defined" error because it doesn't identify ACOS as a worksheet function.

```
Sub MissingObject()
    x = Acos(-1)
End Sub
```

The following procedure successfully uses the Microsoft Excel worksheet function ACOS because the code first refers to the **Application** object.

```
Sub ReturnArccosine()
    x = Application.Acos(-1)
End Sub
```

The only worksheet function that requires you to explicitly specify that you're referring to either the function's Microsoft Excel version or its Visual Basic version is the LOG function, because both function names are spelled the same way. The Microsoft Excel LOG function returns the logarithm of a number to the base you specify. The Visual Basic **Log** function returns the natural logarithm of a specified number.

Using Your Existing Macros in a Procedure

You can include your existing macros in new Visual Basic procedures by using the **Run** method. When you debug Microsoft Excel 4.0 macros as part of your Visual Basic procedures, the Visual Basic debugger steps into your macros as if they were written in Visual Basic. Your macros can return information to a procedure using the RETURN macro function.

For more information and an example of the **Run** method, see "Run Method" in Help.

New Tools to Make Debugging Easy

There are numerous tools in Visual Basic to help you debug your code.

- Breakpoints. A *breakpoint* defines a statement or set of conditions at which Visual Basic automatically stops your program and puts the code in break mode without running the statement containing the breakpoint. You can use breakpoints to examine your code and variables at places in your procedures where you think errors are occurring.
- Debugging buttons. The debugging buttons are included on the Visual Basic toolbar, which is displayed whenever a Visual Basic module is active. You can use these buttons to run your code one statement or procedure at a time, to control breakpoints, and to examine values of variables and expressions.
- The Debug window. You can use the Step Into command on the Run menu to display the Debug window. Using the Debug window, you can monitor the values of expressions and variables while running your code one statement at a time. You can also use this window while running your code to change the value of variables and properties to see how different values affect your code.

The Debug window contains three areas:

- The Immediate pane, which displays results from debugging statements in your code. You can also request debugging information by typing commands directly in the Immediate pane.
- The Watch pane, which displays expressions whose values you've decided to monitor as your code runs.
- The Code pane, which displays the most recently executed statement and allows you to browse surrounding pieces of code.

For more information about these tools and other aspects of debugging in Microsoft Excel, see Chapter 6, "Debugging."

Visual Basic Equivalents for Common Macro Functions

The easiest way to see the Visual Basic equivalents for common macro functions and Microsoft Excel commands is to use the macro recorder to record macros in Visual Basic. You can open two windows in your workbook: one window shows your Visual Basic module, and the other one shows the worksheet or chart you're working on while you're recording a macro. As you work, Microsoft Excel adds Visual Basic statements to your module.

No matter how you write your programs in Microsoft Excel, there are common tasks you'll want to accomplish, such as referring to ranges, controlling how macros run, accessing data in other applications, getting information about workbooks and objects, and creating procedures that run in response to certain events. The following table shows you where to look in this book for information about how to accomplish these tasks with Visual Basic.

For information about	See this chapter
Referring to cells and ranges on worksheets	Chapter 4, "Objects and Collections"
Controlling the flow of a macro	Chapter 3, "Controlling Program Flow"
Accessing data in other applications	Chapter 13, "Accessing External Data"
Getting information about objects in Microsoft Excel	Chapter 4, "Objects and Collections"
Running procedures in response to events	Chapter 11, "Automatic Procedures and OnEvent Procedures"

Microsoft Excel version 7.0 also includes example code written in both Visual Basic and the Microsoft Excel 4.0 Macro Language. To see this code, open the workbooks in the Examples folder in the folder where you installed Microsoft Excel.

Creating Custom Commands and Dialog Boxes Using Visual Basic

Microsoft Excel version 7.0 includes tools for creating custom menus, commands, and dialog boxes. For more information about creating custom commands and dialog boxes using Visual Basic, see Chapter 8, "Controls and Dialog Boxes," and Chapter 9, "Menus and Toolbars."

Creating Custom Commands

To create a custom menu or command in Microsoft Excel version 4.0, you first create a menu or command table. You then use the macro function ADD.MENU or ADD.COMMAND to place your custom menu or command on a menu bar or a menu.

To create a custom menu or command in Microsoft Excel version 7.0, you use the Menu Editor to assign custom commands and menus to menu bars. For more information about using the Menu Editor, see Chapter 9, "Menus and Toolbars."

Displaying Built-in Dialog Boxes

In Microsoft Excel version 4.0, to display built-in dialog boxes while running a macro, you use the question-mark form of the macro function corresponding to the dialog box. For example, the DEFINE.STYLE? macro function displays the dialog box used to define worksheet styles.

In Microsoft Excel version 7.0, to display built-in dialog boxes while running a procedure, you use the **Dialogs** method with the identifier of the dialog box you want displayed. For example, the following procedure displays the dialog box for the Open command (File menu).

```
Sub OpenFile()
    Application.Dialogs(xlDialogOpen).Show
End Sub
```

Creating and Displaying Custom Dialog Boxes

To create a custom dialog box in Microsoft Excel version 4.0, you use the Dialog Editor to generate a dialog box definition you place on a macro sheet. You then use the DIALOG.BOX macro function to display your dialog box.

In Microsoft Excel version 7.0, custom dialog boxes are stored on dialog sheets in your workbook. To create a custom dialog box, you use the buttons on the Forms toolbar to design and run a dialog box on a dialog sheet in a workbook. You use the **Show** method in a Visual Basic procedure to display your custom dialog box.

You can use the **DialogBox** method in your Visual Basic procedures to run a Microsoft Excel 4.0 custom dialog box. The following example uses the **DialogBox** method to display such a dialog box and then tests the result. The variable `DialogRange` refers to the range on a Microsoft Excel 4.0 macro sheet that contains the dialog-box definition table.

```
Result = DialogRange.DialogBox
If Not Result Then
    ' User canceled the dialog box
Else
    ' Result is position number of chosen control
End If
```

For more information about using dialog boxes in programming Microsoft Excel version 7.0, see Chapter 8, "Controls and Dialog Boxes."

Creating Add-in Applications

In Microsoft Excel version 4.0, all you need to do to convert a macro to an add-in macro is save the macro sheet in the add-in file format; after you do this, the macro sheet will be hidden from view. Microsoft Excel 4.0 add-in macros still run in Microsoft Excel version 7.0. (Add-in macros are called *add-in applications* in Microsoft Excel version 7.0.)

To create an add-in application in Microsoft Excel version 7.0, you use the Make Add-In command (Tools menu) while a Visual Basic module, Microsoft Excel 4.0 macro sheet, or dialog sheet is active. However, before you convert a workbook containing Visual Basic code to an add-in application, you must save your code in a workbook with a different filename if you want to continue working with the code. After you've converted a workbook to an add-in application, you cannot edit code in that workbook again. You can distribute your add-in application to other users of Microsoft Excel version 7.0, who can run your add-in application but cannot see or change your code.

For more information about add-in applications in Microsoft Excel version 7.0, see Chapter 11, "Automatic Procedures and OnEvent Procedures."

APPENDIX C

Toolbar Buttons in Microsoft Excel

Microsoft Excel provides more than 200 toolbar buttons and boxes that you can display on your toolbars. By default, most of these buttons appear on the built-in toolbars. You can add any built-in button to a built-in or custom toolbar. You can also assign a macro to a built-in or custom button on any toolbar.

Built-in Buttons

The following table lists the built-in buttons alphabetically. The face of each button is shown along with its default action, the category from which the button is selected, and its identifying number for use with Visual Basic. For more information about a built-in button, display the toolbar on which it appears, click the Help button on the Standard toolbar, and then click the toolbar button.

Button	Action	Category	Number
3-D Area Chart AutoFormat	Creates a 3-D area chart with 3-D markers.	Charting	109
3-D Bar Chart AutoFormat	Creates a bar chart with 3-D markers.	Charting	110
3-D Column Chart AutoFormat	Creates a column chart with 3-D markers.	Charting	111
3-D Line Chart AutoFormat	Creates a 3-D line or ribbon chart.	Charting	113
3-D Perspective Column Chart AutoFormat	Creates a 3-D column chart with a 3-D plot area.	Charting	112
3-D Pie Chart AutoFormat	Creates a 3-D pie chart with value labels expressed as percentages.	Charting	114
3-D Surface Chart AutoFormat	Creates a 3-D surface chart.	Charting	116
Align Left	Aligns the cell, text box, button contents, or selected text in a chart to the left.	Text Formatting	63
Align Right	Aligns the cell, text box, button contents, or selected text in a chart to the right.	Text Formatting	65

Button	Action	Category	Number
Arc	Displays a cross-hair pointer you use to draw an arc, or a segment of a circle.	Drawing	85
Area Chart AutoFormat	Creates a simple area chart.	Charting	103
Arrow	Displays a cross-hair pointer you use to draw an arrow on the active worksheet or adds an arrow to the active chart document.	Drawing	77
Attach Note	Adds a note to the current selection.	Auditing	154
AutoFilter	Displays only those rows that match the value contained in the active cell and inserts drop-down arrows next to each column label in your list.	Data	168
AutoFormat	Applies the last table format you set.	Formatting	52
AutoSum	Inserts the SUM function and a proposed sum range based on the data above or to the left of the active cell.	Utility	39
Bar Chart AutoFormat	Creates a simple bar chart.	Charting	104
Bold	Applies bold formatting to the selected cells or objects.	Text Formatting	58
Borders	Displays the Borders palette so that you can apply borders to the selection.	Formatting	198
Bottom Border	Adds or removes a border along the lower edge of cells.	Formatting	47
Bottom Double Border	Adds or removes a double border below cells.	Formatting	48
Bring To Front	Places the selected objects in front of all other objects.	Drawing	95
Calculate Now	Calculates the formulas in all the open documents or the formula in the formula bar.	Utility	126
Camera	Copies a picture of the selected range of cells. Click on the worksheet to paste the picture and link the picture to the source cells.	Utility	125
Center	Centers the cell, text box, button contents, or selected text in a chart.	Text Formatting	64
Center Across Columns	Centers the text from one cell horizontally across the selected columns.	Text Formatting	67
Chart Type	Displays the Chart Type palette so that you can change a chart's type.	Charting	234

Button		Action	Category	Number
ChartWizard		Starts the ChartWizard so that you can edit the selected chart or create an embedded chart.	Charting	121
Check Box		Creates a check box control.	Forms	140
Clear Contents		Removes only the formulas or values from the selected cells or deletes the selected objects.	Edit	15
Clear Formats		Removes only the formats from the selected cells or objects.	Edit	16
Colon		Inserts a colon in the formula bar.	Formula	35
Color		Displays the color palette you use to assign a color to the selected object.	Drawing	233
Column Chart AutoFormat		Creates a simple column chart.	Charting	105
Combination Drop-Down Edit		Creates a combination drop-down edit control.	Forms	197
Combination List-Edit		Creates a list box control linked to an edit control.	Forms	188
Comma		Inserts a comma in the formula bar.	Formula	36
Comma Style		Applies a comma style to the selected cells.	Formatting	55
Constrain Numeric		Constrains pen recognition to digits and punctuation.	Formula	42
Control Properties		Changes control properties.	Forms	238
Copy		Copies the selection to the Clipboard.	Edit	13
Create Button		Displays a cross-hair pointer you use to draw a button to which you assign a procedure or a Microsoft Excel 4.0 macro.	Drawing, Utility	80
Currency Style		Applies a currency style to the selected cells.	Formatting	53
Cut		Cuts the selection and places it on the Clipboard.	Edit	12
Cycle Font Color		Changes the color of fonts in selected objects.	Text Formatting	62
Dark Shading	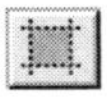	Applies dark shading to selected cells or objects.	Drawing	49
Decrease Decimal		Removes one decimal place from a number format.	Formatting	57

Button		Action	Category	Number
Decrease Font Size		Decreases the font size of the selected text to the next smaller size in the Font Size box.	Text Formatting	72
Default Chart		Creates a chart using the default chart type set on the Chart tab in the Options dialog box.	Charting	120
Delete		Removes the selected cells or objects. If you delete cells, using the Delete button shifts the surrounding cells to fill in the space.	Edit	19
Delete Column		Deletes the selected column.	Edit	21
Delete Row		Deletes the selected row.	Edit	20
Division Sign		Inserts a slash in the formula bar.	Formula	31
Dollar Sign		Inserts a dollar sign in the formula bar.	Formula	38
Double Underline		Applies double underlining to the selected cells or objects.	Text Formatting	176
Doughnut Chart AutoFormat		Creates a doughnut chart.	Charting	145
Drawing		Displays or hides the Drawing toolbar.	Drawing	240
Drawing Selection		Displays a cross-hair pointer you use to select drawing objects.	Drawing	184
Drop Shadow		Adds a shadowed rectangle around the selected cells or adds a shadow to the border of the selected objects.	Drawing	51
Drop-Down		Creates a drop-down control.	Forms	182
Edit Box		Creates an edit control.	Forms	142
Edit Code		Goes to an object macro, or creates a new macro if none exists.	Forms	244
Ellipse		Displays a cross-hair pointer you use to draw an ellipse or a circle.	Drawing	84
Equal Sign		Inserts an equal sign in the formula bar.	Formula	27
Exponentiation Sign		Inserts an exponent sign in the formula bar.	Formula	32
Fill Down		Copies the values, formulas, and formats of the cells in the top row of the selection into the cells below. To copy from the bottom row upward, hold down SHIFT and click this button.	Edit	26

Button		Action	Category	Number
Fill Right		Copies the values, formulas, and formats of the cells in the left column of the selection into the cells to the right. To copy from the right column to the left, hold down SHIFT and click this button.	Edit	25
Filled Arc		Displays a cross-hair pointer you use to draw an arc or a circle segment filled with the window background pattern and color.	Drawing	90
Filled Ellipse		Displays a cross-hair pointer you use to draw an ellipse or a circle filled with the window background pattern and color.	Drawing	89
Filled Freeform		Displays a cross-hair pointer you use to draw a polygon that's a combination of freehand and straight lines filled with the window background pattern and color.	Drawing	92
Filled Polygon		Displays a cross-hair pointer you use to draw a polygon filled with the window background pattern and color.	Drawing	91
Filled Rectangle		Displays a cross-hair pointer you use to draw a rectangle or square filled with the window background pattern and color.	Drawing	88
Find File		Displays the Find File dialog box so that you can search for files by attribute.	File	177
Font	Arial	Lists the available fonts. Select the font you want to apply to the current selection.	Text Formatting	68
Font Color		Displays a palette of colors you can use to change the font color in selected cells or the font color of selected text.	Text Formatting	236
Font Size	10	Lists the available sizes for the font shown in the Font box. Select the size you want to apply to the current selection.	Text Formatting	69
Format Painter		Copies formats from one selection to another.	Edit	185
Freeform		Displays a cross-hair pointer you use to draw a shape that's a combination of freehand and straight lines.	Drawing	87
Freehand		Displays a cross-hair pointer you use to draw a continuous freehand line.	Drawing	78
Freeze Panes		Freezes or unfreezes the split in the active window; if no split exists, splits the window above and to the left of the active cell and freezes the panes.	Utility	137

Button		Action	Category	Number
Full Screen		Toggles full-screen display.	Utility	241
Function Wizard		Displays the Function Wizard so that you can insert a function into the selected cells.	Macro, Utility	40
Group		Defines the selected detail rows or columns as a group. In a PivotTable, groups items by category to create a single item from multiple items.	Data	130
Group Box		Creates a group box control.	Forms	181
Group Objects		Joins the selected graphic objects together as a single graphic object.	Drawing	93
Help		Adds a question mark to the mouse pointer. When you choose a command or click a screen region, a Help topic on that item is displayed. Click this button again to cancel the question mark. Double-click this button to display Help Topics dialog box.	Utility	128
Hide Detail		Hides details of the selection.	Data	175
Horizontal Gridlines		Adds or deletes major gridlines for the value axis.	Charting	122
Increase Decimal		Adds one decimal place to a number format.	Formatting	56
Increase Font Size		Increases the font size of the selected text to the next larger size in the Font Size box.	Text Formatting	71
Insert		Inserts blank cells in place of the current selection.	Edit	22
Insert Chart Sheet		Inserts a new chart sheet into the active workbook.	File	8
Insert Column		Inserts entire columns in the location of the current selection.	Edit	24
Insert Dialog		Inserts a new dialog sheet to the left of the selected sheet.	File	245
Insert Module		Inserts a new module into the active workbook.	File, Macro	190
Insert MS Excel 4.0 Macro		Inserts a new Microsoft Excel 4.0 macro sheet into the active workbook.	File	6
Insert Row		Inserts entire rows in the location of the current selection.	Edit	23

Button		Action	Category	Number
Insert Worksheet		Inserts a new worksheet into the active workbook.	File	7
Instant Watch		Displays the value of the selected expression.	Macro	194
Italic		Applies italic formatting to the selected cells or objects.	Text Formatting	59
Justify Align		Increases word spacing in a text box, button, or cell with wrapped text to fill each line.	Text Formatting	66
Label		Creates a dialog label.	Forms	199
Left Border		Adds or removes a border along the left edge of the selection.	Formatting	44
Left Parenthesis		Inserts an opening parenthesis in the formula bar.	Formula	33
Legend		Adds or deletes a chart legend.	Charting	124
Light Shading		Applies light shading to selected cells or objects.	Drawing	50
Line		Displays a cross-hair pointer you use to draw a straight line.	Drawing	76
Line Chart AutoFormat		Creates a line chart with markers.	Charting	107
Line/Column Chart AutoFormat		Creates a combination chart with a column chart overlaid by a line chart.	Charting	118
List Box		Creates a list box control.	Forms	144
Lock Cell		Formats the selected cells or objects as locked so that no changes can be made to them when the document is protected.	Utility	136
Menu Editor		Displays the Menu Editor dialog box so that you can change menu bars and commands.	Macro	192
Microsoft Access		Starts Microsoft Access, or switches to it if it's already running.	Utility	216
Microsoft FoxPro		Starts Microsoft FoxPro, or switches to it if it's already running.	Utility	160
Microsoft Mail		Starts Microsoft Mail, or switches to it if it's already running.	Utility	203
Microsoft PowerPoint		Starts Microsoft PowerPoint, or switches to it if it's already running.	Utility	204
Microsoft Project		Starts Microsoft Project, or switches to it if it's already running.	Utility	205

Button		Action	Category	Number
Microsoft Schedule+		Starts Microsoft Schedule+, or switches to it if it's already running.	Utility	227
Microsoft Word		Starts Microsoft Word, or switches to it if it's already running.	Utility	202
Minus Sign		Inserts a minus sign in the formula bar.	Formula	29
Multiplication Sign		Insers an asterisk in the formula bar.	Formula	30
New Workbook		Creates a new workbook.	File	9
Object Browser		Displays procedures, objects, methods, and properties.	Macro	191
Open		Displays the Open dialog box so that you can open an existing document.	File	1
Option Button		Creates an option button control.	Forms	141
Outline Border		Adds a border around the outer edge of the selected cells.	Formatting	43
Paste		Pastes the contents of the Clipboard.	Edit	14
Paste Formats		Pastes only the formats from the copied cells into the selected cells.	Edit	17
Paste Names		Displays the Paste Names dialog box so that you can paste worksheet names into the selected cells.	Macro, Utility	41
Paste Values		Pastes only the values from the copied cells into the selected cells.	Edit	18
Pattern		Displays a palette of patterns and pattern colors you can apply to filled objects.	Drawing	232
Percent Sign		Inserts a percent sign in the formula bar.	Formula	37
Percent Syle		Applies a percent style to the selected cells.	Formatting	54
Pie Chart AutoFormat		Creates a pie chart with value labels expressed as percentages.	Charting	108
PivotTable Field		Inserts a subtotal for a row field or column field in an existing PivotTable. If you select a cell in the data area, clicking this button defines the summary functions used in the selected data field.	Data	171
PivotTable Wizard		Starts the PivotTable Wizard, which guides you through all the steps needed to create or modify a PivotTable.	Data	167
Plus Sign		Inserts a plus sign in the formula bar.	Formula	28

Button		Action	Category	Number
Polygon		Displays a cross-hair pointer you use to draw a polygon.	Drawing	86
Print		Prints the active sheet according to the current page setup and print settings.	File	3
Print Preview		Displays the active sheet in print preview.	File	4
Radar Chart AutoFormat		Creates a radar chart with markers.	Charting	117
Record Macro		Records actions to create a procedure.	Macro	98
Rectangle		Displays a cross-hair pointer you use to draw a rectangle or square.	Drawing	83
Refresh Data		Updates the data in a PivotTable after the source data is changed.	Data	170
Remove All Arrows		Removes all arrows used in auditing.	Auditing	153
Remove Dependent Arrows		Removes one level of arrows tracing dependent cells.	Auditing	147
Remove Precedent Arrows		Removes one level of arrows tracing precedent cells.	Auditing	149
Repeat		Repeats the last action or command.	Edit	11
Reshape		Changes the shape of a polygon.	Drawing	82
Resume Macro		Resumes running a paused procedure.	Macro	102
Right Border		Adds or removes a border along the right edge of the selection.	Formatting	45
Right Parenthesis	")"	Inserts a closing parenthesis in the formula bar.	Formula	34
Rotate Text Down		Rotates text sideways so that it reads from top to bottom.	Text Formatting	75
Rotate Text Up		Rotates text sideways so that it reads from bottom to top.	Text Formatting	74
Routing Slip		Adds a routing slip to the current workbook.	Workgroup	162
Run Dialog		Runs the current dialog box.	Forms	187
Run Macro		Runs the procedure you're editing, starting at the insertion point.	Macro	100
Save		Saves changes made to the active workbook.	File	2
Scenarios		Adds, displays, or edits scenarios.	Utility	166
Scroll Bar		Creates a scroll bar control.	Forms	143

Button	Action	Category	Number
Select Current Region	 Selects a rectangular range of cells around the active cell that's bounded by blank rows and columns.	Utility	133
Select Visible Cells	 Selects only the visible cells in a selection and none of the hidden rows or columns.	Utility	132
Selection	 Selects graphic objects by drawing a selection rectangle around them.	Drawing	81
Send Mail	 Sends mail using the mail system you're connected to.	Workgroup	163
Send To Back	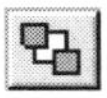 Places the selected objects behind all other objects.	Drawing	96
Set Print Area	 Sets the selected cells as the area to print.	File	5
Shape	 Displays a palette of drawing shapes.	Drawing	235
Show Detail	 Shows details of the selection.	Data	173
Show Info Window	 Displays the Info window.	Auditing	243
Show Outline Symbols	 Displays or hides the outlining symbols on a worksheet containing an outline; if no outline exists, displays a message asking whetheryou want to create one.	Utility	131
Show Pages	 Copies each page of a page field to a new worksheet in the current workbook.	Data	172
Sort Ascending	 Sorts the current list in order from the lowest value to the highest value, using the column that contains the active cell.	Data, Utility	134
Sort Descending	 Sorts the current list in order from the highest value to the lowest value, using the column that contains the active cell.	Data, Utility	135
Spelling	 Starts checking the spelling of the active document or the text in the formula bar.	Utility	127
Spinner	 Creates a spinner control.	Forms	183
Stacked Column Chart AutoFormat	 Creates a stacked column chart.	Charting	106
Step Into	 Executes the next statement by stepping into the procedure.	Macro	195
Step Macro	 Runs the procedure you're editing one statement at a time, starting at the insertion point.	Macro	101
Step Over	 Runs the next statement by stepping over the procedure.	Macro	196

Button		Action	Category	Number
Stop Macro		Stops the currently running procedure. If the macro recorder is running, clicking this button stops the macro recorder.	Macro	99
Strikethrough		Applies strikethrough formatting to the selected cells or objects.	Text Formatting	61
Style	Normal	Lists the defined cell styles. Select the style you want to apply to the current selection.	Text Formatting	70
Tab Order		Changes the tab order of controls.	Forms	186
Text Box		Displays a cross-hair pointer you use to draw a text box, in which you can type text.	Drawing, Utility	79
TipWizard		Indicates when a tip is available and displays the TipWizard toolbar.	TipWizard	179
TipWizard box	TipWizard Box	Displays the current tip. Using this box, you can scroll through a list of tips.	TipWizard	178
Toggle Breakpoint		Sets or clears breakpoints.	Macro	193
Toggle Grid		Toggles gridlines on and off.	Forms	239
Toggle Read Only		Switches between read-only and read-write status.	Workgroup	165
Top Border		Adds or removes a border along the upper edge of cells.	Formatting	46
Trace Dependents		Shows the cells that depend on the current cell.	Auditing	148
Trace Error		Shows the cell or cells that are causing the error in the current cell.	Auditing	174
Trace Precedents		Shows the cells that the current cell depends on.	Auditing	242
Underline	U	Applies underlining to the selected cells or objects.	Text Formatting	60
Undo		Undoes the last action or command.	Edit	10
Ungroup		Removes selected rows or columns from their group. In a PivotTable, separates a combined group of items, replacing each instance of the group with all the items it contained.	Data	129
Ungroup Objects		Separates grouped objects into individual objects.	Drawing	94
Update File		Updates a read-only file to the last saved version.	Workgroup	164

Button	Action	Category	Number
Vertical Gridlines	Adds or deletes major gridlines for the category axis.	Charting	123
Vertical Text	Places text characters upright, one below another, so that the text reads vertically.	Text Formatting	73
Volume/High-Low-Close Chart AutoFormat	Creates a combination chart with a column chart overlaid by a line chart containing three data series for high, low, and closing stock prices.	Charting	119
XY (Scatter) Chart AutoFormat	Creates an xy (scatter) chart with markers but no lines.	Charting	115
Zoom Control	Changes the magnification of the active worksheet.	Utility	189
Zoom In	Displays the worksheet at the next higher magnification.	Utility	138
Zoom Out	Displays the worksheet at the next lower magnification.	Utility	139

Custom Buttons

The following table describes and gives identifying numbers for the buttons available in the Custom category. None of these buttons has a built-in action. You can use these buttons with your own procedures.

Button picture	Button	Button number
	Balloon	219
	Bell	226
	Blank	231
	Calculator	237
	Camcorder	228
	Clock	213
	Club	224
	Diamond	222
	Envelope	230
	Fish	214
	Frown	212

Button picture	Button	Button number
	Hand	229
	Heart	221
	Integral	200
	Mug	218
	Note	210
	Notebook	217
	Open	206
	Palette	97
	Save	207
	Smile	211
	Solitaire	201
	Spade	223
	Speaker	209
	Tack	215
	Telephone	220
	Trash	225
	Undo	208

APPENDIX D

Microsoft Excel Object Model Graphics

Whenever you want to work with an object in Microsoft Excel, you must first build an expression that returns the object. To build the expression, you must understand where the object fits into the object hierarchy, or *object model*. This appendix contains graphical representations of the Microsoft Excel object model and the DAO (Data Access Objects) object model.

Microsoft Excel Objects

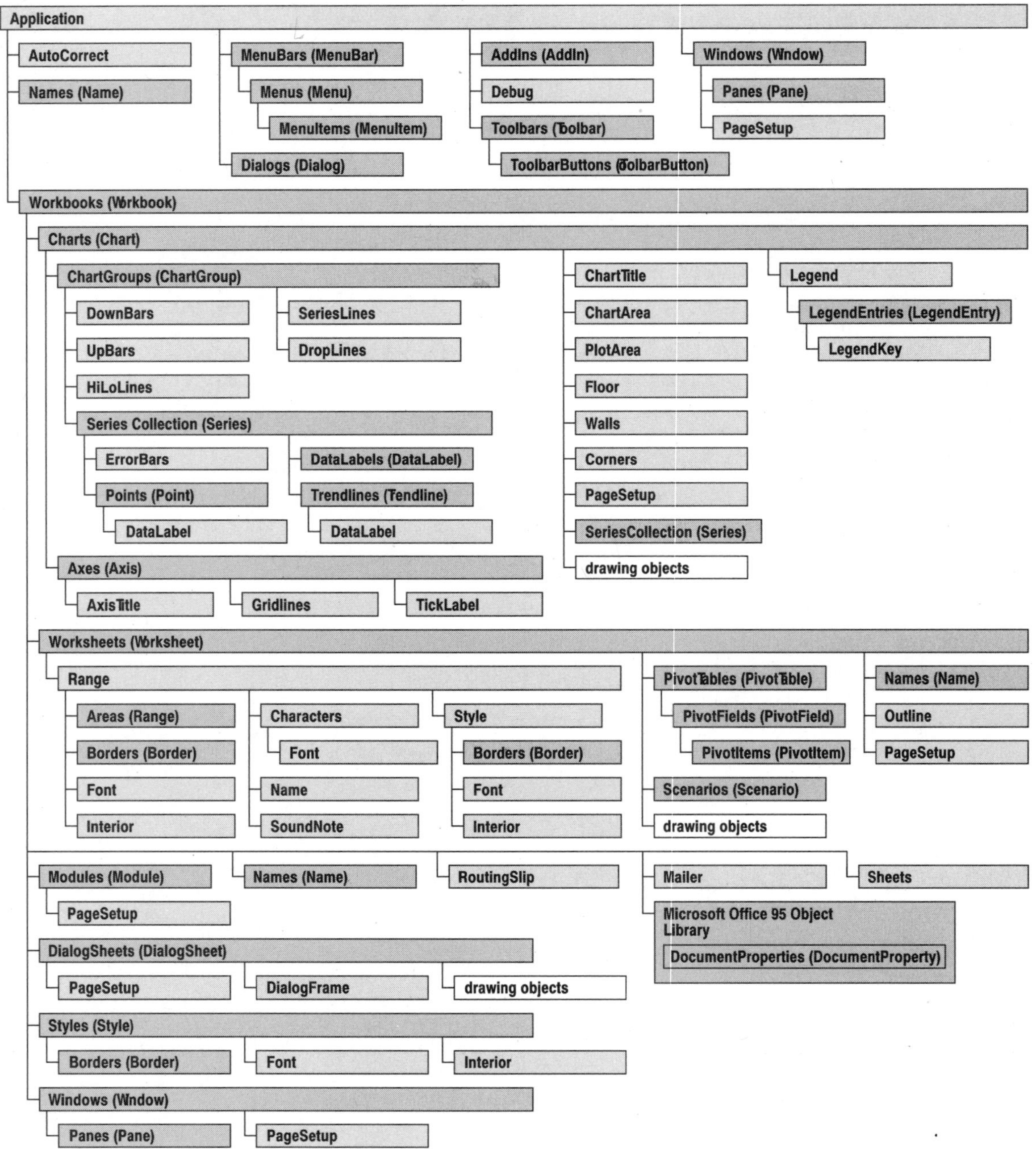

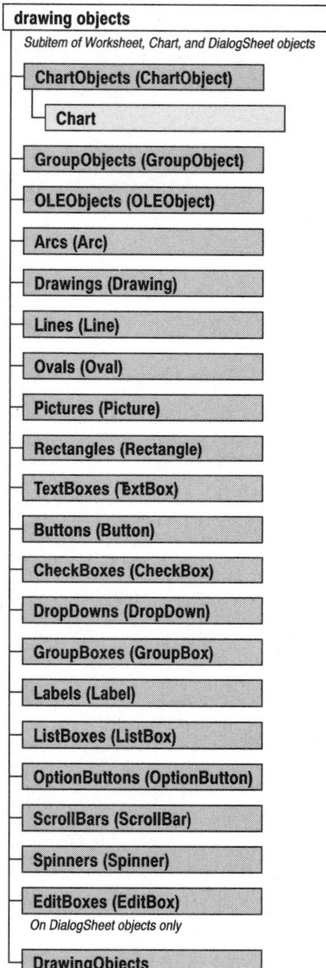
drawing objects
Subitem of Worksheet, Chart, and DialogSheet objects
ChartObjects (ChartObject)
Chart
GroupObjects (GroupObject)
OLEObjects (OLEObject)
Arcs (Arc)
Drawings (Drawing)
Lines (Line)
Ovals (Oval)
Pictures (Picture)
Rectangles (Rectangle)
TextBoxes (TextBox)
Buttons (Button)
CheckBoxes (CheckBox)
DropDowns (DropDown)
GroupBoxes (GroupBox)
Labels (Label)
ListBoxes (ListBox)
OptionButtons (OptionButton)
ScrollBars (ScrollBar)
Spinners (Spinner)
EditBoxes (EditBox)
On DialogSheet objects only
DrawingObjects

Data Access Objects

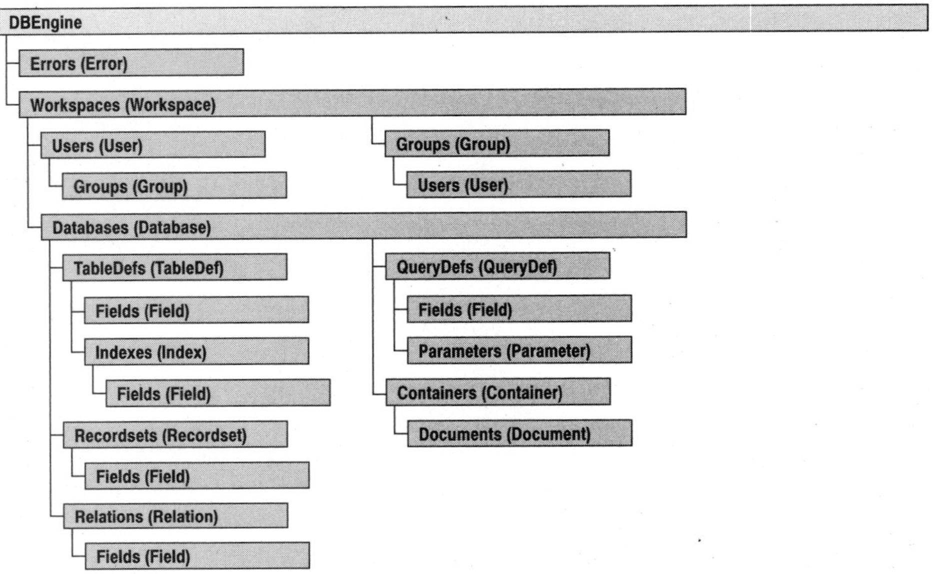

Index

B

C

D

E

G

M

N

S

T

U

V

X

Y

Z

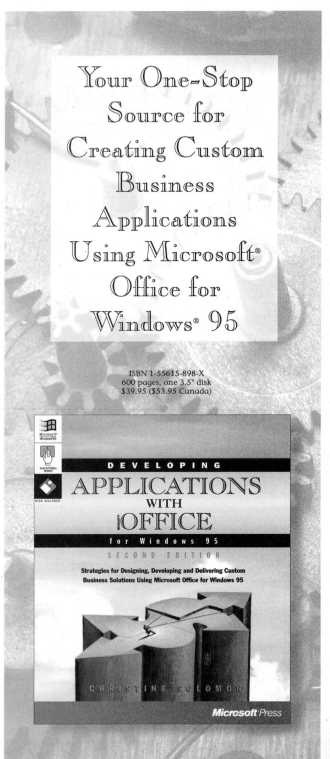

Register Today!

Return this
Microsoft® Excel/Visual Basic®
Programmer's Guide
registration card for:

- ✔ a Microsoft Press® catalog
- ✔ exclusive offers on specially priced books

U.S. and Canada addresses only. Fill in information below and mail postage-free. Please mail only the bottom half of this page.

1-55615-819-XA ***Microsoft Excel/Visual Basic Programmer's Guide*** ***Owner Registration Card***

NAME

INSTITUTION OR COMPANY NAME

ADDRESS

CITY STATE ZIP